www.wadsworth.com

www.wadsworth.com is the World Wide Web site for Wadsworth and is your direct source to dozens of online resources.

At *www.wadsworth.com* you can find out about supplements, demonstration software, and student resources. You can also send email to many of our authors and preview new publications and exciting new technologies.

www.wadsworth.com
Changing the way the world learns®

Crime and Punishment

A History of the Criminal Justice System

MITCHEL P. ROTH
Sam Houston State University

THOMSON
WADSWORTH

Australia • Canada • Mexico • Singapore • Spain
United Kingdom • United States

Acquisitions Editor: *Jay Whitney*
Assistant Editor: *Stephanie Monzon*
Editorial Assistant: *Jennifer Walsh*
Technology Project Manager: *Susan DeVanna*
Marketing Manager: *Terra Schultz*
Marketing Assistant: *Andrew Keay*
Advertising Project Manager: *Stacey Purviance*
Project Manager, Editorial Production: *Matt Ballantyne*
Art Director: *Vernon Boes*

Print/Media Buyer: *Lisa Claudeanos*
Permissions Editor: *Stephanie Lee*
Production Service: *Shepherd, Inc.*
Compositor: *Shepherd, Inc.*
Copy Editor: *Bruce Owens*
Cover Designer: *Studio B*
Cover Image:
Text and Cover Printer: *Banta*

For more information about our products, contact us at:
Thomson Learning Academic Resource Center
1-800-423-0563
For permission to use material from this text, or product,
submit a request online at:
Web: http://www.thomsonrights.com
Any additional questions about permissions can be submitted
by email to thomsonrights @ thomson.com.

Library of Congress Control Number: 2004106299

ISBN 0-534-57798-9

Thomson Wadsworth
10 Davis Drive
Belmont, CA 94002-3098
USA

Asia
Thomson Learning
5 Shenton Way #01-01
UIC Building
Singapore 068808

Australia/New Zealand
Thomson Learning
102 Dodds Street
Southbank, Victoria 3006
Australia

Canada
Nelson
1120 Birchmount Road
Toronto, Ontario M1K 5G4
Canada

Europe/Middle East/Africa
Thomson Learning
High Holborn House
50/51 Bedford Row
London WC1R 4LR
United Kingdom

Latin America
Thomson Learning
Seneca, 53
Colonia Polanco
11560 Mexico D.F.
Mexico

Spain/Portugal
Paraninfo
Calle Magallanes, 25
28015 Madrid, Spain

This book is for Ines

Contents

6   CRIMINAL JUSTICE IN ANTEBELLUM AMERICA (1817–1857)   120

9 CRIMINAL JUSTICE IN THE PROGRESSIVE ERA (1898–1928) 196

11 CRIMINAL JUSTICE AT MIDCENTURY (1941–1959) 254

13 CONTEMPORARY CRIMINAL JUSTICE (1980–1999)   306

Preface

This text is a history of the American criminal justice system. It was written with several goals in mind. It is designed as a history book that will be useful for historians, but more important it was conceived as a history text for students who thought they hated history.

What sets this book apart is a number of tools that will make the material significantly easier to digest. Each chapter begins with a time line highlighting the various events that are presented in each chapter. The "point–counterpoint" sections discuss issues important in criminal justice. For anyone confused by the difference between heresy and blasphemy or treason and sedition, a handy alphabetical glossary is included at the end of the book as well. Here students will find definitions of unfamiliar and familiar words that make up the lexicon for the history of American criminal justice. In addition, throughout the text a number of famous people make appearances, sometimes appearing several times or in some cases just making a brief cameo. In order to guide students through this crowd of individuals, some well known but many unfamiliar, the author has added a "Who's Who in Criminal Justice History" section that highlights the accomplishments and dates associated with each idividual. It is hoped that these biographical capsules will lead students to pursue the lives of these people in more detail.

Throughout this book, various vignettes and time capsules illustrate the contributions to the criminal justice system made by individuals reflecting the diversity of the American people.

Each chapter ends with a notable trial from the period covered. Many are not the traditional trials captured on Court TV. Some are political in nature (*Sacco v. Vanzetti, and the Rosenbergs*), while others were selected because they had a major effect on history (Zenger trial) or were of legal significance (*Gideon v. Wainwright*). As one criminal justice historian has noted, "Not much is known about the day-to-day work of the courtroom" prior to 1800.[1] If one wants to reveal the ordinary criminal process it would require a painstaking examination of contemporary newspaper coverage, since only the most sensational cases bothered with trial transcripts. Several sensational cases are covered as well (O. J. Simpson, and Lizzie Borden).

Chapter 1 examines the ancient roots of criminal justice. It focuses on the development of written law codes from customs that evolved before the advent of writing. Other societies developed legal codes and criminal justice–related practices. However, this book focuses on those that most inspired the development of the English and American criminal justice systems. Among the civilizations covered in this chapter are the Near Eastern Hammurabic and Mosaic codes, Greek and Roman criminal justice, and the development of church law.

Chapter 2 details the development of English criminal justice and common law. It covers the history of English criminal justice from the Anglo-Saxon period and the Viking invasions through the creation of the English Constitution and Bill of Rights. After reading this chapter, the reader will have a much better understanding of how the development of criminal justice institutions in Britain gave rise to the American criminal justice system following British colonization of America's Eastern Seaboard.

Chapter 3 follows the British colonization process as English criminal justice practices are modified in the New World.

Chapter 4 examines the evolution of American criminal justice procedures during the years surrounding the American Revolution. The ratification of the American Constitution and the Bill of Rights completes the cycle of legal development spurred on by the English Constitution a century earlier.

Chapter 5 focuses on the development of the American penitentiary and various experiments in policing ranging from city guards, Texas Rangers, and the French Surete to city marshals and high constables.

In Chapter 6, the sectional crisis takes center stage as the developing American criminal justice system is challenged on several fronts, including states' rights versus federal law, mob violence, and new sentencing procedures (good behavior and indeterminate sentencing).

Chapter 7 follows the impact of the Civil War on the nation's criminal justice institutions. The Civil War had great consequences for the southern states when half the southern population made the transition from slavery to freedom. However, a number of obstacles were created by southern criminal justice institutions that would contradict the promises of freedom contained the the Thirteenth and Fourteenth Amendments. This chapter also focuses on urban politics and corruption in New York City, attempts at prison reform, and the creation of the U.S. Secret Service.

Chapter 8 examines an era marked by political and labor dissension, new identification systems such as Bertillonage and fingerprinting, and the introduction of new methods of execution (e.g., the electric chair). It is also a period when big-city police reformers finally took on the rampant corruption and political patronage, negating the effectiveness of urban police forces.

Chapter 9 focuses attention on the reform attempts by Progressive reformers. Despite the intentions of the reformers, the Prohibition era just on the horizon would nullify many of their reforms. World War I, together with the rise of Bolshevism in Russia, intensified many of the old fears of native Americans who then lashed out at immigrants, labor agitators, and anarchists, challenging civil liberties in the process. However, this was also an era of police and prison reform that introduced college cops, motorcycle patrols, and female police and national police organizations to the front lines of crime fighting.

No years had more ramifications for the evolution of the criminal justice system than the second and third decades of the twentieth century. Chapter 10 highlights the expansion of federal criminal justice with the creation of the Bureau of Investigation and the impact of Prohibition and the Great Depression on the nation's crime problem. Other important topics include the criminalization of certain narcotics, the trend toward police professionalization, and the sensationalism of the era's crime reporting.

Chapter 11 considers the impact of the world war and anticommunism on civil liberties (e.g., Japanese internment and McCarthyism); increasing racial tensions leading to riots in Los Angeles, Detroit, Harlem, and other cities; and a new focus on organized crime in America.

Chapter 12 delves into the new challenges to the criminal justice system presented by the era's social unrest. This period was most notable for a number of Supreme Court decisions that enhanced the rights of the accused while limiting the powers of police. Rising crime rates, urban riots, and antiwar violence would lead police executives and political leaders to examine the role of police as crime fighters. These years would also be marked by an about-face in public opinion on the death penalty.

Chapter 13 covers a new, more conservative era in criminal justice policy, one markedly different from the one discussed in Chapter 12. The "get-tough" policies of the 1980s signaled a more punitive period in American criminal justice as fears of rising crime and crack wars prompted lawmakers to rewrite drug laws, shift money from schools to prisons, and lock up record numbers of people under new sentencing guidelines. Serial killers, mass murderers, FBI confrontations, domestic terrorism, police brutality, and tabloid news sensationalism also led to an increasing fear of less traditional forms of crime.

Chapter 14 examines criminal justice in the new millennium. Following the events of September 11, 2001, many Americans began to reverse course on their attitudes toward racial profiling, the death penalty, and civil liberties protection. While technological advances augured a new era in criminal investigation, this chapter demonstrates how reliant the criminal justice system remains on the time-tested traditions of the past, such as the return of horse-mounted police to city streets and shaming in the courtroom.

Nearly 175 years after the establishment of Robert Peel's London Metropolitan Police, the history of criminal justice, or at least policing, has come full circle. Today, London and New York City have roughly the same populations. However, a pedestrian is more likely to be mugged in London than in New York. Rather than borrowing from modern British police strategies as in the 1840s, a major role reversal has taken place as the mayor of London and the city's commissioner of police have taken some lessons from the policies of New York City's successful zero-tolerance approach to policing. While the court is still out on the effectiveness of this strategy in London, it offers an important historical lesson, one of many that are contained in this text.

ACKNOWLEDGEMENTS

The completion of this book could not have been accomplished without the help of several individuals. First of all I would like to thank Dean Richard Ward for his support and help with scheduling conflicts over the past several years. Thanks are also in order for Delia Frederick, my brilliant computer guru, and Janie Burwick for her assistance on a host of time consuming initiatives. Professor James Marquart prevented me from making several mistakes in my examination of death penalty issues, and Renaissance man James Olson provided stalwart advice on the development of the Puritan colonies. I also must acknowledge the advice and criticism of a number of reviewers, whose suggestions have helped make this a better manuscript. Sabra Horne and Jay Whitney shepherded the book through the editorial process, while Peggy Francomb made it a more readable manuscript. Finally, heartfelt thanks to Zoie, Maggie, Tommy, Mugsy, and Dillon, and most of all to my wife, Ines Papandrea, whose love and support inspired me to finish this book.

NOTE

1. Friedman, Lawrence M. 1993. *Crime and Punishment in American History*. New York: Basic Books, p. 236.

1

FROM CUSTOMS TO CODES

CRIMINAL JUSTICE
IN THE ANCIENT WORLD

TIME LINE

2000–1500 B.C. Great migrations through the Fertile Crescent

1700 B.C. Code of Hammurabi

1230 B.C. Traditional date for Ten Commandments

753 B.C. Founding of Rome

621 B.C. Laws of Moses accepted as being of divine origin

621 B.C. Draco's code

594 B.C. Solon appointed magistrate

509 B.C. Beginning of republican Rome

451 B.C. The Twelve Tables, first written law code of Rome

399 B.C. Trial and Death of Socrates

62 B.C. Augustus introduces organized law enforcement

A.D. 312 Constantine converts to Christianity

A.D. 325 Council of Nicaea

A.D. 518 Era of Justinian begins

A.D. 534 Publication of Code of Justinian

One of the most intriguing questions facing anthropologists, criminologists, sociologists, and other scholars is how the earliest preliterate societies managed to not only survive but also maintain peace and order without written law codes. There is little argument that the earliest laws were derived from folk customs, evolving from loose but unquestionable rules to fixed but more specific practices. Until relatively recently, many anthropologists scoffed at the notion of legal life in primitive cultures but instead saw "custom as king." Law has always existed in one form or another. Without rules to maintain order, anarchy threatens the very existence of a community.

Before the jury, the court system, and the penitentiary, early societies relied on unwritten customs that often were more rigid than written law. French Enlightenment philosophers such as Rousseau often idealized these natural societies. But free from law does not necessarily mean freedom. In reality, primitive societies are ruled by customs often as definite as any law code. Individuals in preliterate society are bound together in a web of regulations enforced by thousands of taboos. In his study of primitive law, E. Adamson Hoebel described a taboo as a "social injunction that is sanctioned by supernatural action."[1] These unwritten rules are rigid and uncompromising and in some cultures can determine when one should stand or walk, sit or rise, and sleep or eat.

The earliest societies relied on customs, magic, and religion to maintain order prior to the advent of complex systems of law. In primitive cultures, any breach of the customary code could expose an offending individual as well as his corresponding social group to the wrath of the gods. Responsibility was collective in nature, as was punishment. By violating taboos, an individual was committing a serious transgression (beginning with Mosaic code, these were equivalent to sins).[2] Hence, it was necessary for the community to punish the individual to prevent supernatural forces from taking revenge on the tribal group. When members of a society believe that consequences of a sinful act will spread to the entire group rather than just the sinner, sins become crimes.

Taboos in primitive cultures ranged from incest and witchcraft to treason and sacrilege. In eighteenth-century England, the most serious secular crime was treason, and the worst religious offense was sacrilege, both demanding the most gruesome modes of punishment. Englishmen, one and all, saw these crimes as a threat to the state much in the way primitive societies saw them as threats to the existence of their meager communities. Accordingly, it should not be unexpected that these offenses remain serious charges into the twenty-first century.

In preliterate cultures, it was understood that if members were to live together in communities comprised of a family or tribe, they must respect the rights of other members of that unit. Over time, these rights became recognized customs approved by the community. Obviously, the origins of these customs are obscure, but there is little doubt that the acceptance of certain rules of conduct enabled families and tribes to evolve into larger communities and finally into nation-states.

Courts, police, corrections, and laws are basic components of the modern criminal justice system. With the coming of personal property, which gave individuals economic authority, and the state, which defined citizenship and rights, the individual became a distinct entity. Paralleling these advances was the development of courts to levy fines and render judgments that allowed societies to make the transition from custom to law. Here, then, the broad outlines of criminal justice begin to take shape. Although formal law enforcement is nonexistent in primitive society, the development of legal procedures led to the introduction of a central authority, law codes, courts, and constables or a police presence to enforce the developing system.

Primitive cultures did not need to develop complex legal concepts until they began to congregate in communities of hundreds or thousands. It was only then that conditions necessitated the establishment of an authority to enforce sanctions, rules, and regulations. While custom emanated from the people, law was forced on the community by the decree of a master, a ruler, a monarch, or a group of elders, such as an oligarchy.

The first stage in the evolution of law was personal revenge. Without a formal apparatus to adjudicate criminal behavior, preliterate societies allowed private disputes to be settled in a personal manner. Among the Indian tribes of lower California, every man was regarded as his own policeman and was allowed to administer justice in the form of vengeance. As individuals banded together in communities, conflict was viewed as a personal affair to be arbitrated privately between the victim and the perpetrator. It became acceptable for the victim's kin to extract revenge and not the community, clan, or tribe. Because this system was accepted by both parties, it was assumed that the killing of the perpetrator would resolve the conflict. Hence, the injured party was imbued with many of the components of today's criminal justice system, acting as judge, jury, and executioner.

Revenge or vengeance is a natural component of most criminal justice systems. Nowhere is this more obvious than when it comes to capital punishment. Today, the United States remains one of the few in the industrialized world to maintain the death penalty, but in the spirit of *lex talionis* ("an eye for an eye, a tooth for a tooth"), Hammurabi, and the Bible, although there are other capital crimes, over the past half century the penalty has been used only to punish those who take a life: the most literal interpretation of accountability.

A community's reaction to antisocial behavior was governed by a simple basic drive: revenge. By killing a perpetrator, there would be no recurrence of that behavior. Victims initially determined the extent of retribution, which was usually not proportional to the original offense. In such instances, then, it was not unusual for the perpetrator to become the victim, leading to an indefinite cycle of violent revenge or a feud. Living on the bare margins of existence, primitive

communities could ill afford the continuous destruction of life and property. The negative ramifications of an unbroken cycle of revenge led preliterate communities to place limits on vengeance, which over time became the first laws and codes of the historical era.

The first constraints on blood feuds took the form of what is better known as "blood revenge." The first step toward controlling the magnitude of vengeance was to place the responsibility for punishing the perpetrator in the hands of the group rather than allowing a specific family member to gauge the measure of revenge. In this case, an injury suffered by the member of a family, clan, or tribe was regarded as an injury to the entire community, and revenge was arbitrated in like fashion by the victim's immediate community. This was a major step in the development of law because it took the mode of revenge out of the hands of a private offender and placed it into the collective hands of the community.

Over time, the consequences of this behavior could prove devastating to a community, and a system of compensation was introduced—the next major contribution to the foundations of early criminal justice. One measure of a civilization's complexity is the distance between the feuding individuals and the administration of revenge. After measures were taken to replace vengeance with compensation, this new protocol became more complex as community leaders began to maintain order and settle conflicts through a range of activities, including adjudication, mediation, and arbitration.

The transition to the legal stage of government occurs when a society recognizes certain rules and procedures, a level of development that usually requires the knowledge of writing. The use of writing allows substantive laws to pass from the oral tradition, often the preserve of certain recognized individuals, to the society at large. For example, prior to the development of writing in Iceland in the twelfth century, the "lawspeaker" was the only authority on the country's laws, and every year he was required to recite one-third of the laws to the common people. His term in office lasted three years, just long enough to recite the complete collection.

In order to understand the development of the Western legal tradition as well as the roots of the American criminal justice system, an understanding of historical developments pertaining to crime and punishment in classical antiquity is necessary. Readers will find many similarities between crime in the ancient world and the present with all forms of criminality surviving the transition from antiquity to the modern era. Treason, murder, adultery, robbery, and rape were all defined as criminal behavior in earlier eras, although the definition of some of these offenses has evolved over time.

If anything has changed, it is the individuality of punishment that existed in classical antiquity. Burning, scourging, impalement, and mutilation have fortunately been scuttled in favor of the warehousing of criminals in sterile, modern prisons and the introduction of more painless methods of capital punishment. The following is a brief survey of the earliest lawmaking advances, beginning with Hammurabi's code in the ancient Near East and ending with the relocation of the Roman capital to Constantinople following the fall of the western Roman Empire in the fifth century.

CODE OF HAMMURABI

Almost 4,000 years ago, the plains between the Tigris and Euphrates rivers, in what is today Syria and Iraq, became the setting for one of the world's first great civilizations. By 5000 B.C., this region was home to large communities of people. Population pressure gave stimulus to better ways of doing things. The concentration and energies of many people living together, along with the pooling of ideas and a larger labor force, led to advances in agriculture and animal domestication. A wider variety of food sources (lentils, grapes, and olives) and a broader range of domesticated animals soon led to a transition

from more nomadic hunter-gatherer cultures to more sedentary settlement patterns.

Over the ensuing centuries, life became more complex as people congregated in urban enclaves. A more stratified town life emerged in which potters, artisans, brick makers, weavers, and leather workers encouraged a transformation in methods of lawmaking. The convergence of several factors in this region of Mesopotamia gave rise to one of the greatest inventions in world history: writing. As life became more complicated and complex, some manner of record keeping was necessary to keep track of temple stores and the contributions of the citizens to the community (everyone was expected to give their share to the Gods; without writing, people could lie and say that they had already contributed). Without writing, the past and the future were indistinguishable, and opportunities for shirking responsibilities and for theft were rampant.

Scribes invented writing in the fourth millennium B.C. using reeds to inscribe pictographs or cuneiform on flattened clumps of clay. These earliest forms of writing allowed not only record keeping but also the promulgation of laws. The oldest extant literature of most ancient cultures is in the form of laws written by scribes. In the earliest period, laws were written codes issued at the request of a royal authority. The legislation of ancient kings became written history for future scholars who have studied how the law was amended, expanded, and handed down through the generations.

The Lawgivers

It has generally been accepted that the earliest written law codes were produced in Babylonia (part of Mesopotamia) in the ancient Near East. Hammurabi's code (ca. 1700 B.C.) is accepted as the only substantially complete pre-Mosaic code of law. Legislators frequently borrowed from the works of other cultures, such as the Romans copying from the Greeks. Although Hammurabi (ca. 1728–1686 B.C.) is often credited with conceiving the first law code, we now know that he borrowed extensively from earlier rulers. In the 1940s, archaeologists uncovered clay tablets in Iraq that pre-dated Hammurabi's by perhaps several hundred years. Both law codes share a high proportion of technical phrases, leading some legal historians to the conclusion that Hammurabi was influenced by earlier administrators. Regardless, these laws have a familiar ring to them, dealing as they do with divorce, matrimony, savage dogs, and personal injury.

Hammurabi's code, uncovered by French archaeologists in 1901–1902, consists of 4,000 lines of laws inscribed on an eight-foot-high slab of black stone. At the top of the stone, the king is depicted looking on the sun god with adulation as authority is conferred on Hammurabi. This ancient code contains both civil and criminal law, regulating virtually every aspect of his subjects' lives. More complex and comprehensive than any law code previously attempted, Hammurabi's code is considered the apogee of legal codification prior to Roman law. Much better organized and comprehensive than biblical law, the code took a very literal view of accountability and introduced the law of retaliation, as in *lex talionis*. There were no ambiguities, and it did not take into account that circumstances change with the times. The world was viewed as part of a fixed, divine order; hence, the code was rigid and reflected absolute justice. For instance, if an architect built a structure that collapsed because of poor design and killed a client, the architect could be executed. In a similar manner, surgeons were responsible for the health of their patients. If it was determined that surgery led to the death of a patient, the surgeon could have his hand amputated.

Although Hammurabi's code is credited with attempting to protect the disenfranchised from the power of the elite, no thought was given to ending slavery or granting women equal rights. Men could divorce at will, but women had to prove they lived a blameless life before being allowed to do the same. If after petitioning for divorce her neighbors denounced her, she could be drowned in a river, a common method of execution in a land of rivers.

Crime and Punishment

What is most striking about this law code is the distinction of punishments by class; punishment varied according to the social status of the victim and the perpetrator. If the daughter of a gentleman was struck and suffered a miscarriage, the fine was ten shekels. However, if the daughter of an ordinary citizen was injured, the fine would only be five shekels. In like fashion, if the ordinary citizen's daughter died, the perpetrator was liable for a fine; if it was the gentleman's daughter, the wrongdoer could face execution.

Several ingredients of Hammurabi's code bear little resemblance to contemporary law. Besides the variation of punishment according to class, this ancient code relied on trial by ordeal in cases involving irreconcilable conflict in sworn evidence. In such cases, a judge could order the accused to jump in a river. If the individual swore falsely to the gods, it was assumed that the deities would ensure that the accused drowned. In the event that the accused survived, the accuser was liable to be put to death. This caveat was meant to discourage false testimony.

The laws of Hammurabi introduced the world to the philosophy of *lex talionis,* a concept that would reappear later in the Old Testament. This code is extremely inflexible and took a very literal view of accountability. Law was absolute and in most respects a rich man's law, but to read these laws is to gain intriguing insight into the life of the ordinary people of the ancient Near East.

While we know little about the courts and procedures preceding punishments, the codes prescribe execution by drowning for crimes including adultery, incest with a daughter-in-law, and cheating customers by watering down alcoholic beverages. Impalement was sanctioned for any woman who procured the death of her husband for the sake of her lover or for one who procured her own abortion. Individuals caught looting during fires could be cast into the flames. When it came to capital punishment, Hammurabi's code was at its most merciless. The punishment of burning could also be used to punish a priestess who ceased to live in a cloister and began frequenting inns or a man who committed incest with his mother after the death of his father. Why burning for such obvious moral taboos? Perhaps this concept adheres to the notion of fire as a form of purification or is an attempt to avoid shedding tribal blood.

Mutilation was not uncommon under Hammurabi's code, with the amputation of hands prescribed for four offenses, ears for two different infractions, and even the removal of ears, breasts, and eyes for certain penalties. Babylonian punishments were severe and cruel, with death often inflicted and mutilations even more usual. For the student of history, it would be erroneous to assume that punishment could be no more cruel, as it has been only a few centuries since European executioners supervised the boiling of prisoners alive and the hanging, quartering, and disemboweling of political offenders.

Since Hammurabi codified the law some 4,000 years ago, most societies have relied on legal principles to arbitrate between conflicting parties. Without a system of equitable laws, humanity could not transcend its primitive roots and maintain social order. By codifying both criminal and civil laws and creating specific penalties for breaking these tenets, for the first time in recorded history a connection was established between crime and its retribution.

MOSAIC LAW

There are many striking parallels between the laws of Hammurabi and the Old Testament, which have been traditionally ascribed to the Jewish prophet Moses.[3] Whatever the Old Testament might have borrowed from Babylonian code, it is uncontestable that the biblical law code was something uniquely different from anything that occurred before. While this legal system does not stand in the pantheon of the great legal systems of the ancient world, its importance lies in its intrinsic connection with the national religion and its later relationship with the Christian religion. Committed to the elimination of class

distinctions, it contrasted sharply with Hammurabi's code by repudiating the notion of a rich man's law by applying a uniform moral standard applicable to all people. On the other hand, Hammurabi's legislation was much more orderly and comprehensive than biblical laws.

Mosaic law, or the "Law of the Moses," can be found in the first five books of the Bible and Old Testament (Genesis, Exodus, Leviticus, Numbers, and Deuteronomy). Known as the Torah to the Jewish people, the ancient Greeks referred to this part of the Bible as the Pentateuch, which means "five books" in Greek. The first five books of the Bible contain the Ten Commandments,[4] which are considered the foundation of law systems throughout much of the Western world.

 The Ten Commandments

1. Thou shalt have no other gods before me.
2. Thou shalt not take the name of the Lord thy God in vain.
3. Thou shalt not make unto thee any graven image, or anything that is in heaven above, or that is in the earth beneath, or that is in the water under the earth. Thou shalt not bow down thyself to them, nor serve them.
4. Remember the Sabbath day to keep it holy.
5. Honor thy father and thy mother.
6. Thou shalt not kill.
7. Thou shalt not commit adultery.
8. Thou shalt not steal.
9. Thou shalt not bear false witness against thy neighbor.
10. Thou shalt not covet thy neighbor's house, thou shalt not covet thy neighbor's wife, nor his manservant, nor his maidservant, nor his ox, nor his ass, nor anything that is thy neighbor's.

Hebrew law evolved through discourse between the learned elders. Unlike Hammurabi's code, the Hebrew law code is not accredited to one particular individual since, according to the biblical concept, law is no more than a statement of God's will. Therefore, crime became equated with sin since every criminal offense can be considered a crime against God.

Although the Mosaic code is rich in detail concerning the customs and moral obligations of the Jewish people—describing religious conventions such as feasting and fasting and health and sanitation—for the criminal justice scholar the Bible offers extraordinary insight into the punishment of criminal behavior in the ancient world. The book of Exodus proclaims, "Eye for eye, tooth for tooth, hand for hand, foot for foot." While this is sometimes misconstrued to be taken literally, a more appropriate interpretation suggests that there is a set limit for punishment—that a perpetrator can be punished up to losing an eye, a tooth, a hand, or a foot for a particular offense. This concept is one of the oldest legal concepts and can be found in various incarnations in criminal codes throughout the world. There is a remarkable similarity between the Mosaic code and that of Hammurabi in the literal interpretation of punishment. Similar to the Mosaic code, Babylonian law asserted that a "son was forfeited for son, daughter for daughter, eye for eye, limb for limb, tooth for tooth, life for life and slave for slave."

According to the Old Testament, legal procedures seemed relatively simple. Plaintiff and defendant appeared before a judge, elder, or other authority figures sitting in the open near the main "gate of the city," and a complaint was made. The courts relied on witnesses to swing decisions either way. Unlike most legal traditions, including most present ones, two witnesses were required to prove any capital crime; therefore, a defendant could not be put to death because of the testimony of only one witness.

Crime and Punishment

The Bible offers a fascinating array of criminal behavior, including the world's "first recorded murder," when Cain slew his brother Abel. God sentenced Cain not to death but to life as a "fugitive and vagabond on earth." The story of Cain and Abel would be used by generations of modern legal experts to defend alleged murderers against the death penalty during court trials. Under ancient Israeli law, murder was differentiated from manslaughter, a distinction that exists in the criminal law of the present day.

Murder conducted with malice aforethought, like contemporary first-degree murder, was met with capital punishment. Unlike murder, which mandated death, those guilty of manslaughter were permitted to take sanctuary in cities of refuge. Prohibitions against taking a life were typically lifted in incidents involving self-defense, warfare, and capital punishment. Decapitation was regarded as the quickest and cleanest form of execution and was applied in cases of murder aforethought and apostasy. Banishment was meted out only in crimes of unintentional homicide or manslaughter. In these cases, the defendant was expelled from his hometown to six specific cities of refuge.

 Offenses Punished by Death in the Old Testament

Murder: *Genesis 9:6*

Masturbation and coitus interruptus: *Genesis 38:7–10*

Working on the Sabbath: *Exodus 31:15*

Children disrespecting or cursing parents: *Leviticus 20:9*

Adultery: *Leviticus 20:10*

Incest: *Leviticus 20:11*

Sexual relations with a daughter-in-law: *Leviticus 20:14*

Homosexuality: *Leviticus 20:13*

Sexual relations with a mother-in-law: *Leviticus: 20:14*

Bestiality: *Leviticus 20:15–16*

Practicing witchcraft: *Exodus 22:18; Leviticus 20:27*

Gluttonous or drunken children: *Deuteronomy 21:18–23*

In sharp contrast to Hammurabi's code, under Mosaic law, property offenses did not constitute a capital crime; rather, such crimes were adjudicated through the payment of fines. Since human life was considered sacred and precious because humans were made in God's image, the Mosaic code was far more humane than previous law codes. While parts of the ancient Near East prescribed fierce physical punishments, such as facial mutilation, castration, and impalement, Mosaic law treated the body with respect, and physical cruelty was reduced to a minimum, with even flogging being limited to forty lashes.

The Bible enumerates thirty-six capital crimes,[5] with stoning the most frequent method of execution. Men and women received the same punishment, as did the rich and the poor. Stoning was imposed for crimes that threatened the whole nation, including sexual crimes.

Stoning is still used as a method of execution in some corners of the world where religious law predominates. The Taliban in Afghanistan (until their demise in late 2001) and Islamic courts in Nigeria have sentenced women to death by stoning for adultery in recent years.

Nigeria adopted strict Islamic law in 1999. Militant Islamists strongly influence court judgments in ten of Nigeria's twelve northern states. In a prominent 2002 case, an unmarried woman became pregnant. Initially, her lover admitted to their relationship and promised to care for the baby. But when it came to court, he denied everything. If this case had occurred prior to the introduction of Islamic law, both families could have made an arrangement with the support of the village. However, under the strict interpretation of Islamic law, the penalty for adultery is death. Adultery is considered the second most serious crime under Islamic law (the first being insulting Allah). Adultery is considered more serious than murder because "society is injured," and this act "will teach other people to do the same thing."[6] According to tradition, a stoning is carried out by digging a pit and burying the woman up to her neck before being stoned to death. Nigerian Attorney General Aliyu Abubakar Sanyinna claims that the recent decline in crime is the result of the new law code. As of March 2002, this case was under appeal.

Hailed as a victory by human rights groups, this case was dismissed in early 2004 when a panel of five judges ruled 4–1 in the defendant's favor. The judges cited procedural errors in the original decision, noting that only one judge was present during the first trial, instead of the three required under local Islamic law. If Amina Lawal had been stoned to death it would have been the first time since Nigeria's twelve northern states adopted Islamic law in 1999.

The Mosaic code was more strict in sexual matters, as were most other divinely inspired codes. Prior to Mosaic law, bestiality, adultery, and incest were not considered criminal offenses; however, under Mosaic law, all forms of irregular sex were prohibited. In cases of incest and adultery, a malefactor would be strangled, and, while in his death throes, a burning torch would be thrust into his mouth to "burn his intestines." This was seen as a more humane and dignified death since it preserved the appearance of the body for burial.

Mosaic law has been credited with introducing the foundations for the modern rule of liability. According to the "law of the goring ox," if an owner was aware that he possessed a dangerous animal before it caused damage or injury, the owner was culpable and must pay compensatory damages. If the ox killed a man, the ox and its owner could be stoned to death. Obviously, this departs somewhat from contemporary liable law, which would not demand the death penalty for negligence.

A recent high-profile dog-mauling death in San Francisco led a grand jury to charge two defendants with second-degree murder. This followed the death of a young woman in her apartment building in January 2001. Evidence suggests that massive dogs owned by the victim's neighbors fatally attacked her as she was entering her own apartment. Legal scholars assert that the conviction of the defendants will encourage prosecutors to file similar charges when defendants demonstrate a disregard for public safety. Harking back to Mosaic law, prosecutors in this case have upheld the right to punish individuals who disregard public safety when it came to owning dangerous animals. One law professor warns that this sensational case will "remind prosecutors and jurors that it might be appropriate in other cases," such as "deadly industrial accidents, product liability, and drunk-driving cases." While one prosecutor argues that "in most dog maulings you're not going to be able to prove murder or manslaughter," there is little doubt that dog owners could now face prison and civil penalties if their pets kill.[7]

While other cultures from the ancient Near East gave the world the wheel, cuneiform writing, and irrigation, the Jews gave the world monotheistic religion—the belief in one God—and in the process gave to the world a more compassionate vision of the world. Although the Mosaic code is considered less advanced than that of Hammurabi, it was much more humanitarian in spirit. Unlike Hammurabi's code, which was inspired by a king, the Mosaic code was inspired by a belief in God and is more people oriented.

The ancient Jewish law code later influenced the development of several future legal systems. For example, the Puritan communities of seventeenth-century New England based their law codes almost entirely on biblical law. Over the centuries, the precepts of the Old Testament have also influenced the development of law codes in continental Europe and in England. The impact of the Ten Commandments continues to resonate into the twenty-first century, bringing into question whether its display promotes one religion above others. According to Chief Justice William Rehnquist, it is not a matter of religion but "simply reflects the Ten Commandments' role in the development of our legal system." However, one opponent contends that "public buildings should display patriotic symbols that bring us together, not religious symbols that divide us."[8]

In February 2002, the Supreme Court, for the second time that year, refused to review a lower court's ban on displaying the Ten Commandments on government property. In this particular case, the justices declined to hear an appeal by Indiana's governor, who had been prevented from placing a seven-foot stone monument of the Ten Commandments on the statehouse lawn in Indianapolis (it would have replaced one that had been previously vandalized). It was hoped that the court would resolve this murky issue since there is little consensus on this issue. While judges in Indiana, Illinois, and Wisconsin have prohibited the display of the Ten Commandments on public property, judges in Oklahoma, New Mexico, Colorado, Kansas, Wyoming, and Utah have allowed it.

ANCIENT GREECE

Greek civilization did not invent or originate the notion of law, but the Greek law that would emerge in the seventh century B.C. differed from the earlier Mosaic and Near Eastern law codes in several respects. It was not intended to carry out the will of an omnipotent king, such as Hammurabi, or the will of God, as in the Mosaic code. Rather, the goal was to improve the lives of ordinary human beings. Earlier law codes could be modified at the will of a king or priest, but Greek law, particularly in Athens, was based on some kind of referendum of popular consent and could be changed only with the approval of the people.

Out of the dozens of Greek city-states that made up the ancient Greek civilization, most historical ruminations focus on the city-states of Athens and Sparta. But Athens looms large and has, for the most part, become synonymous for Greece in the ancient world. While the city of Athens was dedicated to politics, entrepreneurship, and the arts, Sparta could best be compared to a military enclave, with the concomitant suppression of nonconformity and individual rights. Life in Sparta was tightly regulated, and criminal procedure tended to be inquisitorial in nature. With a subjugated populace, ruled by customary law and institutions, the Spartans contributed little to the evolution of the criminal justice system. Unlike the martial law of the Spartans, Athenians reveled in their political freedom in the absence of dictatorship. Unlike the divinely influenced Mosaic law or the royally dictated Babylonian code, Greek law developed into the consensus of the people.

The Lawgivers

Prior to the introduction of writing, Athenian law and the administration of justice remained in the hands of an oligarchy, and each generation orally handed down the unwritten law codes. Over time, the underclasses demanded that the laws be recorded so that they would be known by all rather than being confined as the province of the well-born elite members of society.

The first written law code of Greek civilization is credited to the statesman Draco, who is considered the first legislator of Athens. Commissioned to write a new law code in 621 B.C. to control the masses and to eliminate blood feuds fueled by revenge, Draco attempted to suppress crime by imposing capital punishment for virtually every offense. Hence, Draco's name has become linked in perpetuity to ruthlessness, or draconian punishment. Citizens could be sentenced to death for stealing certain vegetables and fruit and for sacrilege, idleness, and homicide. Draco also supported the enslaving of debtors and even their families when they could not pay creditors. Draco's accomplishments are mixed from a modern vantage point. While citizens became better informed about legal procedures and protocol and forms of compensation were introduced to end the age-old cycle of private revenge, capital punishment was used to punish a wider range of crimes. In actuality, the Draconian code was no worse than customary law, but it was criticized by Athenians who were disappointed that there was no radical change in the legal system. Before passing judgment on this ancient Athenian legislator, one should remember that he did not invent these laws but simply collected and recorded the customary laws that had been unwritten until this time. But once they were recorded, Athenians could no longer ignore the need to reform such a harsh law code that then existed.

With the introduction of Draco's code, Greece made the transition from the preliterate era of customary law to written code. Greek legal developments made important strides during this era. The laws recorded by Draco (and later Solon) were published on pillars of wood for religious matters and on bronze for other types of laws.

Although no fragments of Draco's code have survived, information pertaining to the laws has been passed down to us from the early Greek historians. Criminal and civil law were apparently not distinct. However, Draco's code is notable for its views on homicide. Draco's most important innovation was the establishment of the Court of Areopagus for murder cases, arson, and other serious crimes. Many scholars consider this the first time a distinction was made between civil and criminal law.

Since time immemorial, any killing was followed by revenge killings. To avoid revenge killings and blood feuds under Draconian law, a murderer had three choices following the commission of a murder. He could acknowledge his complicity by immediately going into exile. The perpetrator could also submit to trial and was allowed to walk free until then, as long as he obeyed rules that excluded him from most sacred and public places. However, if he decided to ignore the trial process, he could be killed or immediately arrested on entering a public or sacred place by any Athenian, which was an early form of citizen's arrest.

Draco introduced radically different rules in dealing with homicide. There was voluntary, "impassioned" killings committed in the heat of the moment and involuntary or accidental ones. Justifiable homicides included accidental killings during athletic contests, the slaying of adulterers caught flagrante delicto, and killings committed in war. Offenders were liable for the death penalty only in cases of voluntary or premeditated homicide. All others were punished by exile. These distinctions are significant because they mandated that only the state now had the authority to kill, eliminating the traditional blood vengeance. The state also allowed the victim's family to trade the perpetrator's punishment sentence for a fine or material compensation.[9]

Following in the footsteps of Draco, Solon built on his predecessor's achievements. Like Draco, little is known about Solon. Born into a prosperous Athenian family in 638 B.C., Solon developed a reputation for honesty and equitable judgment. After several decades of Draco's code, demands increased for a new law code. Solon was appointed to a one-year term as chief magistrate in 594 B.C. and was granted the power to rewrite the law for Athenian society.

Although it is unsubstantiated, many historians accord Solon the distinction of having created the first permanent protocol for punishing crimes against the state. A zealous proponent of the rule of law, Solon saw lawlessness as the scourge of state building and insisted that only by punishing crimes such as theft or embezzlement of public funds, sedition, civil disorder, enslavement of the disenfranchised, and political conspiracies could the rule of law progress. As a legal reformer, Solon is credited with taking steps to protect the marginalized population from the upper classes. Among his most noteworthy reforms was the prohibition of selling debtors and their families into slavery for failure to pay creditors. In addition, he proclaimed that all Athenians who had been sold into slavery or had fled Athens to avoid this fate could return to their former status as Athenian citizens.

Perhaps his greatest accomplishment, Solon's abolition of Draco's penal code set the stage for a much more humane criminal law as he endeavored to make the punishment fit the crime. Contrasted with the Draco's code, Solon's law allowed for capital punishment only for treason and murder. However, his law protected a husband who killed his wife and her lover when caught in the act of adultery. In addition, he opened up jury service to average citizens. Solon's law reforms would last for the next 500 years. Although we have only a partial list of his laws,

his reforms were much discussed by chroniclers of the ancient world. Solon's democratic conception of justice influenced not only Athens but the development of Western society as well.

The importance of Solonic law rested on the presumption that law was the will of the people or the state and therefore could be amended. Additionally, Solon stipulated that anyone could prosecute an injustice. These principles became the foundation for the future greatness of Athens. By establishing popular assemblies and a comprehensive code of laws, Solon created the environment that would allow democracy to later flourish. Claiming no divine origin, Solon's law stood as a testament to the power of human reason. But there was still much to be accomplished. Without distinction between felonies and misdemeanors and little classification of crime according to severity of penalties involved, this system of criminal justice must still be regarded as fairly primitive.

Crime and Punishment

The Greeks were at their most pragmatic when it came to capital punishment. While they recognized that human nature was not deterred by fear of death, at the same time philosophers such as Plato viewed capital punishment as a form of civic purging—removing the most dangerous criminals from society in order to protect the state. Many Athenians would attest to the fact that banishment for life, not unlike life in prison, was a fate worse than death.

Death sentences were carried out in a variety of ways. At its earliest stages, stoning, or lapidation, was used as a form of community punishment, much in the manner of the ancient Israelites. This custom developed over the centuries into a more formal mode of punishment. The main principle behind stoning was that rather than a few individuals, the whole community should take part in order to remove guilt from an individual participant. Athenians did not consider stoning a legal means of execution during its historical era, but it was used in other regions of Greece. Typically, only crimes that affected the general welfare of the community were treated in this manner. These crimes included the murder of a king, sacrilege, and treason. Stoning was usually conducted outside the city so as to not injure passersby.

The ancient Greeks also developed the practice of precipitation, or throwing individuals from a high cliff to their deaths. This method seems to have religious origins, being that spiritual services were often conducted at high places where individuals were closer to the gods. According to some sources, this penalty is a form of the ordeal since there is a chance a person could survive the fall. In addition, the executioner is not directly shedding tribal blood in the tradition of a headsman or hangman. As law became more formalized in Greece, an excavation site known as the Barathron became the place of execution. This practice apparently ended by the fifth century B.C. since it is not mentioned after this date.

In addition to stoning and the Barathron, strangulation and hemlock were also used to punish capital crimes. The introduction of hemlock marked the transition to the most humane phase of capital punishment in Athens. In the ancient world, "hemlock" was known as "cicuta." The Anglo-Saxons introduced the word "hemlock" into the vocabulary of Old English in the tenth century.

Although hemlock was most famous for its use as a poison, it was also used externally as an aphrodisiac. Hemlock is a juice made from the pounding of the plant's seeds and leaves in a mortar. The poison worked only when a patient or perpetrator had a normal body temperature. Before Socrates took his fatal dose in 399 B.C., he was told to avoid becoming too agitated as he was prone to do because it would negate the effects of the poison. In the end, Socrates requested multiple doses of the potion. Death usually was accompanied by spasms and convulsions, but like lethal injection today, it was considered a civilized alternative to shedding blood.

Most death sentences in ancient Athens were carried out with haste. Some Greek philosophers complained that typically only one day transpired between sentence and execution. There were only two circumstances that could postpone an execution. Pregnant women could be granted a reprieve until a baby were delivered, and no one could be put to death until the return of the ship that the Athenians sent annually on a religious mission to Delos. And unlike Sparta, which conducted its executions at night, most were typically carried out during the day in Athens.

Patriotism was considered of supreme importance, and any crime directed against the state called for the maximum penalty. Traitors were executed, and their property was confiscated by the state. Treason came in a variety of incarnations: betrayal of a fortress, selling supplies, or passing information to the enemy all demanded the death penalty.

Next to treason, impiety was considered the next-greatest crime. Destruction of statues of the gods, robbing temples, or practicing magic were treated with utmost severity. The Athenian conception of filial duty brooked no mistreatment of parents, and the death penalty could be inflicted on children who assaulted their parents.

The ancient Greeks were notably less stern in their punishment of what we would regard as moral infractions. Adulterers caught in the act by an aggrieved husband could be killed with impunity. This tradition can be traced as far back as Draco's code, which proclaimed that "if one man kills another after catching him with his wife . . . he shall not go into exile for homicide on such account." However, the plaintiff also had the liberty to choose between personal vengeance or monetary compensation.

Athens recognized a variety of punishments, ranging from fines and the confiscation of property to public shaming and the destruction of the homes of condemned offenders. There is some evidence that suggests that Athenians utilized imprisonment to punish debtors and to hold those waiting for torture or execution, as in the case of Socrates (see "Notable Trials" later in this chapter). In Athens, there was even a prison called the *desmoterion,* or "place of chains."

One common tactic used by Israeli army forces during the recent intifada in contemporary Israel is to destroy Palestinian homes in retaliation for terrorist actions. But typically these actions are taken almost immediately after a terrorist action without any judicial proceedings.

Solon introduced the first jury courts to Athens. Not everyone could plead their case before a jury court. Only free male citizens of full Athenian parentage on both sides of the family were allowed to address the courts. Foreigners were tried before special courts, slaves could not testify at all, and women were represented by a male relative. Judicial procedure for most crimes except for homicide relied on juries ranging in size from 201 to 2,501 jurors, depending on the importance of the case. Jurors were required to be over thirty years old. This system did not use lawyers, allowing the plaintiff and the defendant to handle their own cases and to cross-examine each other but not witnesses. Following the speeches of the contestants, jurors cast their votes in the courtroom. Each juror was given two discs; perforated for conviction and solid for acquittal. Jurors reportedly would hold the discs so as to obscure them from fellow jurors. The discs were then collected and tallied by a presiding officer.

There is fragmentary evidence that indicates that Athens had a form of institutional police known as the Scythian archers. "Scythian" meaning "northern barbarian," these trouser-wearing policemen were essentially captured warriors who were kept at the status of slave until earning freedom. Billeted in tents, the Scythians served as town guards and ushers in the Assembly and carried out routine police duties on the main roads leading into Athens. Although there are sporadic mentions of this

unit in Greek historical records, little is known about their powers and protocol.

ROMAN LAW

No ancient culture could match the achievements of the Romans when it came to the development of law. Today's civil law tradition is based on Roman law and is considered the oldest legal tradition in the world. Countries as diverse as Spain, France, Germany, Brazil, Argentina, and Yugoslavia trace their legal codes to ancient Roman law code.

The history of Rome, from its founding in 753 B.C. until the sixth century B.C., is obscured by myth and fable. Early Roman law was based on unwritten customs and the will of the gods. Romans, like the Greeks before them, were superstitious, and their gods and goddesses were based on Greek deities. The Romans borrowed liberally from Greek culture in virtually every feature of their art, culture, and national life, and like the Athenians, the aristocracy abused its power over the lower classes in Rome. Aggravating class tensions between the patricians and plebeians was the absence of a written law code. Civil unrest and dissension led the Romans to follow in the steps of Solon when they realized that adopting a written law would be the only safeguard against oppression. As long as judges were the only individuals familiar with the law and penalties for crime, they could inflict injustices without detection.

The Lawgivers

While Solon was restructuring the laws of Athens (594 B.C.), Roman kings were expanding their mandate in both the commercial and the military realms. During the next century, Romans freed themselves from the clutches of absolute power and began experimenting with a republican form of government, necessitating a new law code. In 509 B.C., the age of the Roman kings had ended. During the subsequent years of the Republic, Rome was led by two magistrates, better known as consuls. It was during the period of the Republic (509 B.C.–A.D. 4) that the Roman Empire expanded throughout much of the known world.

The Twelve Tables, written in 451 B.C., are considered the first written laws of Rome. It was only when the underclasses, or plebeians, complained about the high-handed oppression of Roman officials that the law was codified. A commission of patricians was reportedly dispatched to Athens to absorb the laws of Solon and become familiar with the institutions, customs, and laws of the Greek city state. On their return to Rome, ten men, or decemvirs, were appointed to fashion a new body of law. These laws would be certain and definite and accessible to everyone. Subsequently, the Twelve Tables were drafted and inscribed on twelve wood or brass tablets that were then set on display in the Roman Forum, where anyone could become familiar with the law.[10] The Twelve Tables was primitive and inadequate by modern standards, but its impact on the Roman peoples cannot be overestimated. Not only did every young Roman schoolchild reportedly learn the laws by heart, but the laws are recognized for bringing together the plebeian and patrician classes and eliminating social distinctions that formerly cleaved Rome into two hostile camps. The Twelve Tables was credited with eventually breaking down one of the last social barriers, namely, the intermarriage between the two classes.

Unfortunately, we only have fragmentary evidence concerning the actual language of the original laws passed down to us by the classical historians. However, it is clear that they were intended to be not a comprehensive law code but rather a compilation of laws that could be abused by unethical judges if the citizens were not properly informed of the law. These laws dealt mainly with private disputes among individuals. Even such transgressions against the state as abetting an enemy of Rome or accepting bribes were considered matters to be prosecuted privately before an assembly of citizens.

The drafting of the Twelve Tables was a seminal event in the history of criminal justice procedure. During the subsequent centuries, these laws were carried into almost every nation of the ancient world by the victorious Roman legions. Roman reverence for the Twelve Tables can only be compared to the English respect for the Magna Carta. Unlike the Ten Commandments, this primitive law code was not a moral code but rather was composed of legal customs borrowed from other cultures to arbitrate disputes between Rome's various classes.

Roman law was developed through the promulgation of edicts, interpretations of the law by jurists, and the issuance of statutes. The era of the Roman Republic (500 B.C.–A.D. 4) witnessed the expansion of the Roman Empire as well as the evolution of a distinct legal profession. However, the greatest strides in the development of Roman legal culture would take place in the eastern Roman Empire under the Christian emperors. Emperor Constantine's conversion to Christianity in A.D. 312 was a turning point not only in the history of the Roman Empire but in Western civilization as well. Christians had been persecuted since the reign of Nero, but despite numerous obstacles, the religion continued to gain converts among all segments of society. With the economic decline of the empire in western Europe, Constantine built a new capital in the eastern part of the empire at Constantinople[11] (formerly Byzantium, now Istanbul, Turkey). While Rome declined in the West and was overrun by barbarian hordes in the fifth century, its greatness persisted for more than another millennium in the East. Roman civilization influenced the language, architecture, and literature of the modern world but was even more influential in its contributions to law.

Initially, church law had little impact on Roman law outside of protecting the faith. But following Constantine's conversion, virtually every emperor would be Christian as well. In A.D. 325, church leaders from throughout the Roman Empire met for the first time to resolve disputes concerning church protocol and to settle points of church discipline. By settling such disputes as whether clergy could migrate without the permission of a bishop, the Council of Nicaea created peace in the church, at least for the time being.

The development of Roman law reached its zenith under the direction of Emperor Justinian (483–565). The product of over 1,000 years of juristic experimentation, the codification of earlier Roman law and its compilation during the reign of Justinian stands as one of the benchmarks of Roman civilization. Not only did he bring simplicity and equity to Roman law, but Justinian saw the need to reduce the amount of laws and to arrange them in some manageable form.

Justinian's reign from 518 to 565 marks the transition from the ancient world to a medieval[12] one, ushering in an era that would witness the development of modern Europe. Subsequent developments of social and religious institutions as well as in literature and law were shaped by Roman antecedents. Shortly after becoming emperor, Justinian entrusted the distinguished lawyer Tribonian with supervising the compilation and revision of the Roman law codes. These included not only all the edicts of previous emperors but also previous Senate statutes. Justinian added so many statutes himself in the intervening years that the final product issued in 534 became known as the Code of Justinian. Under the supervision of Tribonian, Roman law was simplified, particularly in situations concerning property and inheritance. This was necessary in order to eliminate the impact of ancient customs and the power of the extended family in property matters.

Tribonian also was charged with condensing and revising more than three million lines of judicial decisions into a more usable form. After eliminating obsolete and contradictory laws, in 533 the *Digest* was completed, having distilled all previous judicial decisions into a mere 150,000 lines (about one and a half times the size of the Bible). Justinian's final contributions to the updating of Roman law was twofold. Besides bringing the law closer to the teachings of the Christian church, in 533 the *Institutes* were published. With its publication, all other law books, including the Twelve Tables, were now officially obsolete. As a law textbook, the *Institutes* were designed to help law students digest the changes in the legal code. Combined, the *Code, Digest,* and *Institutes* have become known as the *Corpus Juris Civilis,*[13] a singular achievement. Rather than a set of completely new laws, this revision of existing law would endure, and as Europeans moved out of the Dark Ages, they would turn to this work for guidance in creating a new legal system.

Crime and Punishment

At its zenith, ancient Rome was considered a lawless city of between 750,000 and one million people. Without a police force, public prosecutors, or sheriffs, crime went unchecked during the last century of the Roman Republic (137–134 B.C.). One Roman satirist warned that "only a fool would go out to dinner without having made his will." Robberies and house break-ins were common, and gangs of street toughs roamed the streets, giving the city the character of a town from America's Wild West era. Besides street crime, political assassinations were a common mode of replacing prominent leaders, including such legendary figures as Julius Caesar and the Gracci brothers.

The ascendance of Augustus Caesar to emperor in 27 B.C. signaled the beginning of organized law enforcement in the ancient world. In prior years, the Roman army functioned as police in the far-flung provinces. When crime was reported to a governor, soldiers from local legions were sent out to suppress the activity. Provincial policing efforts were inadequate because of insufficient manpower. With other nonpolicing duties, such as building roads and forts, protecting the outlying provinces was a challenging proposition for Rome's peacekeepers. In the Roman capital, there was little in the way of a police presence other than a small number of government-owned slaves who served in a constabulary capacity. When Augustus took the throne in 27 B.C., he made police reform his first order of business. He is credited with organizing a police system comprised of three independent agencies. The most respected agency was the elite Praetorian Guard, composed of 4,500 soldiers replete with togas and swords. Charged with keeping order and the political peace, the Guard was commanded by two police chiefs, or prefects.

To complement the peacekeepers, Augustus established a civilian Urban Cohort to patrol Rome during the daytime hours. Numbering 3,000 men and under the supervision of one prefect, this constabulary group was recruited from the military. The 7,000-man Vigiles patrolled the city at night. Composed chiefly of freed slaves, they were expected to fight fires as well as deal with street crime. In a world made of wood, firefighting became an inextricable link to policing and public order. The Augustan system of policing proved so efficient that it was adapted later in the fourth century by the Christian emperor Constantine when he built his capital of Constantinople in the eastern Roman Empire.

It is apparent from archeological excavations and historical accounts that the Romans belonged to a materialistic culture that liked to acquire property and show it off in public. Since togas had no pockets, civilians carried their valuables in a pouch or purse. Others stored precious possessions at home in strongboxes or in pagan temples where the gods could watch over them. Of sturdy construction and protected by outside guards, citizens were confident that if temples did not dissuade thieves, then the gods would ultimately punish them. Having invented the padlock and other locking devices, the Romans are credited with raising the science of locksmithing to a level surpassed only in modern times.

Although Roman law prohibited the displaying of most weapons, for self-protection Romans wore finger rings that are considered the prototypes for brass knuckles and eye gougers. Many became proficient in self-defense skills, including boxing, wrestling, kicking, and strangling. Others gravitated toward protective associations (precursors of today's neighborhood watch groups) or hired

bodyguards. The more superstitious wore amulets of the gods for protection that could range from minerals to parts of the human or animal body. A common charm worn by boys to ward off evil intentions until puberty was the phallic symbol known as the bulla. At home, individuals used dogs and geese as watch animals or mounted animal emblems over their doors to repel evil spirits. The progenitors of many self-defense strategies, the Romans came up with the idea of placing mannequins in their gardens to ward off criminals. Modern law enforcement has adopted similar schemes in crime-prone locations when staffing is shorthanded.

During the early Republic, the Twelve Tables prescribed definite penalties for certain crimes. Hanging would be visited on those who pastured animals at night in a neighbor's crop, while malefactors who deliberately set fire to a barn or a store of grain could be burned alive. For crimes that called for capital punishment, the method of execution was rarely left in doubt. Although some penalties could be adjudicated through compensation, a host of criminal acts were met with the death penalty. Perjury was punished by precipitation, as perpetrators were tossed from the Tarpein Cliff. Arsonists could expect to be burned to death, crop thieves were hanged, and others met their ends being clubbed to death or hanged. Considered one of the most heinous crimes by the Romans, parricides (children who killed a parent) were punished by being bound into a sack with a dog, a cock, a viper, and an ape and then being tossed into the water. As primitive as this sounds, this special punishment lived on into the Middle Ages. Regardless of the method, executions were a public occasion, but only when the convicted was male. Since victims were stripped for the occasion, women were executed in private to preserve their modesty.

By the end of the Roman Republic, capital punishment for most crimes had gone out of vogue. In most instances, convicts could instead accept an informal agreement to go into exile, particularly if they belonged to the elite class, but only with the caveat that if they returned to

Rome, they would be executed. Except for cases of debt, imprisonment was rarely used in early Rome. According to the Twelve Tables, debtors who could not or refused to pay their debts were held in private confinement by creditors for sixty days. Subsequently, the debtor's balance was announced in public on three consecutive market days. On the third and final day, the debtor might be sold into slavery or executed. One other form of imprisonment is chronicled in which Roman male heads of household were allowed to maintain their own domestic prison in which they could discipline members of the household. Called the *Ergastulum* (or "garbage pit"), the cell held immediate family members or slaves for any breach of family discipline. The works of later Roman historians describe other modes of imprisonment that ranged from chaining and quarry prisons to underground chambers similar to the prototypical dungeons of the Middle Ages.[14]

After Constantine's conversion, there was a trend toward increasingly severe punishments as the government became more autocratic. Under the Christian emperors, infractions that were formally regarded as private wrongs became public offenses and were often treated with inhuman rigor. In the time of Augustus, adulterers would be deported to separate islands. By the reign of Constantine and his successors, sexual immorality was severely punished, and the death penalty prescribed for adultery, incest, and homosexuality.

NOTABLE TRIALS

Socrates (399 B.C.)

The trial of the vagabond teacher and philosopher Socrates in Athens in 399 B.C. remains one of the most famous free-speech trials of all time. Charged with corrupting the youth of Athens and refusing to recognize the accepted divinities of the city by a distinguished body of Athenian democrats, Socrates went on trial for his life before the Court of the Heliasts, the court that

had jurisdiction over all public cases that did not involve homicide.

Socrates rose to prominence as a brave warrior during Athens' war with Sparta (431–404 B.C.) and then as an intellectual renowned for his insatiable curiosity. The charges brought against Socrates can be understood only in the context of ancient Athens. The charge of "corrupting" youth referred to Socrates' inclination of teaching young people to question the wisdom of their parents and the leaders of Athens, a charge tantamount to treason. Several of his former students were affiliated with the tyrannical oligarchy that ruled Athens for a short period before Athens returned to democratic rule in 403 B.C. To his opponents, it appeared that Socrates had been educating traitors. A well-known philosopher whose main mission in life seemed to question the wisdom of the popularly elected leaders of Athens, Socrates' political affiliations and his Sophist (identification as a professional philosopher) leanings earned him enemies who sought to remove him from society.

The administration of justice in the courts of Socrates' era bore little resemblance to contemporary courts. Missing from the ancient courtroom were the familiar actors of the modern courtroom. In place of judges, prosecutors, and defense attorneys was a jury composed of anywhere from 101 to more than 1,001. But there was always an odd number to eliminate a tie vote.

Any full Athenian citizen who was sane, over the age of thirty, and not impaired by any disabilities was qualified to become a member of the court. At the beginning of each judicial year, citizens volunteered for jury participation, and about 6,000 were selected for that year. Each juror was paid today's equivalent of nine cents per day. This leads to speculation that only members of the lower classes could be expected to participate for such low pay.

Athenian courts heard cases on about 300 days each year. In order to guard against bribery, each day juries were selected by lot and assigned to various courts. Traditionally, the more important the case, the larger the jury. Not all defendants were given the benefit of a jury trial. However, any Athenian citizen with full rights could make charges against an individual and have the case tried in the Court of the Heliasts.

While there are no independent contemporary accounts of the trial, we know many of the specifics through the writings of his disciples such as Plato. According to Plato and others, the jury hearing the case of Socrates had 501 jurors. Over the centuries, scholars have pieced together an account of the trial of Socrates. In an open-air court, a low barrier partitioned the public from the defendant and the jury. The prosecution presented its case first, followed by the defense. Each side spoke and was allowed to present its case for an hour, using a water clock as a timing device. Unlike the modern courtroom, there was no formal cross-examination.

The seventy-year-old philosopher conducted his own defense. Having never been to court before, Socrates was at a disadvantage. He had to face not only three prosecutors but also a clandestine group of accusers who had vilified his reputation in Athens for almost two decades. By the time the trial began, public opinion had already turned against Socrates. He became his own worst enemy as he delivered a long speech, punctuated with wit and defiance, but ultimately all it did was antagonize his prosecutors.

Unlike contemporary juries, Athenian juries voted twice. The first vote was whether to acquit or convict. Socrates barely lost this vote, 280 to 220. The second vote was to decide a penalty if the penalty was not prescribed by law. Under Athenian law, the jury was allowed to decide a penalty of its own and could choose between penalties proposed by the prosecution and the defense. Socrates could have avoided the death penalty if he had proposed banishment. The jury most probably would have accepted. Despite the urgings of his friends to take this way out, Socrates insisted that if he took exile, he would betray his beliefs and would be admitting that the prosecution had spoken the truth. He was willing to die for his convictions and thus ended up facing a death sentence and took a fatal dose of hemlock.

Socrates left no writings of his own, and had he been acquitted, he might have vanished into obscurity as a harmless Athenian eccentric. Having reached the ripe old age of seventy, Socrates went to his death in Athens, a city famous for free speech, prosecuted for a philosopher's ideas and his use of free speech.

CONCLUSIONS

An examination of early law codes suggests that in complex societies, everyone is immersed in a vast network of legal rules. In more primitive societies, individuals go about their daily lives unconscious of most of these legal rules. A variety of legal documents have survived to offer students insight into the legal institutions of ancient Mesopotamia, Israel, and Greece. However, evidence abounds related to Roman law. Unlike earlier societies, we have not only legislation but also juristic commentaries of the law, lay literature referring to the law, and documents of daily legal relationships.

Suffering from political, economic, and military exhaustion, by the end of the fifth century the western Roman Empire had capitulated to the invasion of Germanic tribes. Still flourishing in the eastern half of the empire, the Byzantine Empire would not succumb until 1453. During the subsequent Middle Ages, Roman law would be resurrected and exert a lasting influence on the development of legal institutions throughout continental Europe. Events in England, including the early organization of a national common law, later gave rise to a different legal tradition.

Point–Counterpoint
Ancient Law Codes: God v. King Inspired Law

Hammurabi's Code stands out in sharp contrast to Mosaic Code, in that it was written by a king as opposed to being inspired by God. Hammurabi was the king of Babylonia in the late eighteenth and early seventeenth century B.C. The

---

Source: *The Code of Hammurabi,* trans. by L.W. King, Jr., New York, 1915); Exodus xxii.

prologue to the code indicates that the king drafted the code by the command of the gods. It was the king's duty to proclaim and enforce the law and to make sure law enforcement was distributed equally. He was also imbued with the power to make amendments in order to make the code current with the needs of the day. Some of its provisions, including the disappearance of blood feuds and revenge, indicate a semi-advanced condition. On the other hand it still preserved vestiges of a more primitive past, such as retaliatory punishments (an eye for an eye), reliance on the ordeal (#2), and liability for accidental harm. The following are several excerpts taken from the 282 sections. Although Mosaic Law is often remembered for its elucidation of the fundamental rules of social conduct contained in the Ten Commandments, it also contained strict punishments for ordinary as well as serious offenses. The following excerpts are from the Book of Exodus.

CODE OF LAWS

2. If any one bring an accusation against a man, and the accused go to the river and leap into the river, if he sink in the river his accuser shall take possession of his house. But if the river prove that the accused is not guilty, and he escape unhurt, then he who had brought the accusation shall be put to death, while he who leaped into the river shall take possession of the house that had belonged to his accuser.

3. If any one bring an accusation of any crime before the elders, and does not prove what he has charged, he shall, if it be a capital offense charged, be put to death.

5. If a judge try a case, reach a decision, and present his judgment in writing; if later error shall appear in his decision, and it be through his own fault, then he shall pay twelve times the fine set by him in the case, and he shall be publicly removed from the judge's bench, and never again shall he sit there to render judgement.

6. If any one steal the property of a temple or of the court, he shall be put to death, and also the one who receives the stolen thing from him shall be put to death.

9. If any one lose an article, and find it in the possession of another: if the person in whose possession the thing is found say "A merchant sold it to me, I paid for it before witnesses," and if the owner of the thing say, "I will bring witnesses who know my property, "then shall the purchaser bring the merchant who sold it to him, and the witnesses

before whom he bought it, and the owner shall bring witnesses who can identify his property. The judge shall examine their testimony—both of the witnesses before whom the price was paid, and of the witnesses who identify the lost article on oath. The merchant is then proved to be a thief and shall be put to death. The owner of the lost article receives his property, and he who bought it receives the money he paid from the estate of the merchant.

10. If the purchaser does not bring the merchant and the witnesses before whom he bought the article, but its owner bring witnesses who identify it, then the buyer is the thief and shall be put to death, and the owner receives the lost article.

11. If the owner do not bring witnesses to identify the lost article, he is an evil-doer, he has traduced, and shall be put to death.

12. If the witnesses be not at hand, then shall the judge set a limit, at the expiration of six months. If his witnesses have not appeared within the six months, he is an evil-doer, and shall bear the fine of the pending case.

[editor's note: there is no 13th law in the code, 13 being considered and unlucky and evil number]

14. If any one steal the minor son of another, he shall be put to death.

15. If any one take a male or female slave of the court, or a male or female slave of a freed man, outside the city gates, he shall be put to death.

16. If any one receive into his house a runaway male or female slave of the court, or of a freedman, and does not bring it out at the public proclamation of the major domus, the master of the house shall be put to death.

21. If any one break a hole into a house (break in to steal), he shall be put to death before that hole and be buried.

22. If any one is committing a robbery and is caught, then he shall be put to death.

23. If the robber is not caught, then shall he who was robbed claim under oath the amount of his loss; then shall the community, and . . . on whose ground and territory and in whose domain it was compensate him for the goods stolen.

108. If a tavern-keeper (feminine) does not accept corn according to gross weight in payment of drink, but takes money, and the price of the drink is less than that of the corn, she shall be convicted and thrown into the water.

109. If conspirators meet in the house of a tavern-keeper, and these conspirators are not captured and

delivered to the court, the tavern-keeper shall be put to death.

110. If a "sister of a god" open a tavern, or enter a tavern to drink, then shall this woman be burned to death.

195. If a son strike his father, his hands shall be hewn off.

196. If a man put out the eye of another man, his eye shall be put out. [An eye for an eye]

197. If he break another man's bone, his bone shall be broken.

198. If he put out the eye of a freed man, or break the bone of a freed man, he shall pay one gold mina.

199. If he put out the eye of a man's slave, or break the bone of a man's slave, he shall pay one-half of its value.

200. If a man knock out the teeth of his equal, his teeth shall be knocked out. [A tooth for a tooth]

201. If he knock out the teeth of a freed man, he shall pay one-third of a gold mina.

202. If any one strike the body of a man higher in rank than he, he shall receive sixty blows with an ox-whip in public.

203. If a free-born man strike the body of another free-born man or equal rank, he shall pay one gold mina.

204. If a freed man strike the body of another freed man, he shall pay ten shekels in money.

205. If the slave of a freed man strike the body of a freed man, his ear shall be cut off.

206. If during a quarrel one man strike another and wound him, then he shall swear, "I did not injure him wittingly," and pay the physicians.

207. If the man die of his wound, he shall swear similarly, and if he (the deceased) was a free-born man, he shall pay half a mina in money.

208. If he was a freed man, he shall pay one-third of a mina.

209. If a man strike a free-born woman so that she lose her unborn child, he shall pay ten shekels for her loss.

210. If the woman die, his daughter shall be put to death.

211. If a woman of the free class lose her child by a blow, he shall pay five shekels in money.

212. If this woman die, he shall pay half a mina.

213. If he strike the maid-servant of a man, and she lose her child, he shall pay two shekels in money.

214. If this maid-servant die, he shall pay one-third of a mina.

215. If a physician make a large incision with an operating knife and cure it, or if he open a tumor (over the eye) with an operating knife, and saves the eye, he shall receive ten shekels in money.

216. If the patient be a freed man, he receives five shekels.

217. If he be the slave of some one, his owner shall give the physician two shekels.

218. If a physician make a large incision with the operating knife, and kill him, or open a tumor with the operating knife, and cut out the eye, his hands shall be cut off.

219. If a physician make a large incision in the slave of a freed man, and kill him, he shall replace the slave with another slave.

220. If he had opened a tumor with the operating knife, and put out his eye, he shall pay half his value.

221. If a physician heal the broken bone or diseased soft part of a man, the patient shall pay the physician five shekels in money.

222. If he were a freed man he shall pay three shekels.

223. If he were a slave his owner shall pay the physician two shekels.

Exodus xxii:

"12. He that smiteth a man, so that he die, shall be surely put to death.

"13. And if a man lie not in wait, but God deliver him into his hand; then I will appoint thee a place wither he shall flee.

"14. But if a man come presumptiously upon his neighbor, to slay him with guile; thou shalt take him from mine altar, that he may die.

"15. And he that smiteth his father, or his mother, shall be surely put to death.

"16. And he that stealeth a man and selleth him, or if he be found in his hand, he shall surely be put to death.

"17. And he that curseth his father, or mother, shall surely be put to death.

"18. And if men strive together, and one smite another with a stone, or with his fist, and he die not, but keepeth his bed;

"19. If he rise again, and walk abroad upon his staff, then shall he that smote him be quit; only he shall pay for the loss of his time, and shall cause him to be thoroughly healed.

"20. And if a man smite his servant, or his maid, with a rod, and he die under his hand; he shall be surely punished.

"21. Notwithstanding, if he continue (to live) a day or two, he shall not be punished; for he is his money.

"22. If men strive, and hurt a woman with child, so that her fruit depart from her, and yet no mischief follow; he shall be surely punished, according as the woman's husband will lay upon him; and he shall pay as the judges determine.

"23. And if any mischief follow, then thou shalt give life for life

"24. Eye for eye, tooth for tooth, hand for hand, foot for foot

"25. Burning for burning, wound for wound, stripe for stripe.

"26. And if a man smite the eye of his servant, or the eye of his maid that it perish; he shall let him go free for his eye's sake.

"27. And if he smite out his man servant's tooth, or his maid servant's tooth, he shall let him go free for his tooth's sake."

SOURCES

Archer, Gleason L. 1928. *History of the Law.* Boston: Suffolk Law School Press.

Bauman, Richard A. 1996. *Crime and Punishment in Ancient Rome.* London: Routledge.

Berman, Harold J. 1983. *Law and Revolution: The Formation of the Western Legal Tradition.* Cambridge, Mass.: Harvard University Press.

Crook, J. A. 1967. *Law and Life of Rome, 90 B.C.–A.D. 212.* Ithaca, N.Y.: Cornell University Press.

Davies, A. Powell. 1956. *The Ten Commandments.* New York: Signet Key Books.

Diamond, A. S. 1971. *Primitive Law, Past and Present.* London: Methuen.

Dowden, Richard. 2002. "Death by Stoning." *New York Times Magazine,* January 27, pp. 28–31.

Drapkin, Israel. 1989. *Crime and Punishment in the Ancient World.* Lexington, Mass.: Lexington Books.

Driver, G. R., and J. C. Miles. 1952, 1955. *The Babylonian Laws.* 2 vols. Oxford: Clarendon Press.

Freeman, Charles. 1999. *The Greek Achievement: The Foundation of the Western World.* New York: Viking.

Freeman, Kathleen. 1946. *The Murder of Herodes and Other Trials from the Athenian Law Courts.* London: McDonald.

Gagarin, Michael. 1986. *Early Greek Law.* Berkeley: University of California Press.

Grant, Michael. 1977. *Jesus: An Historian's Review of the Gospels.* New York: Charles Scribner's Sons.

Harries, Jill. 1999. *Law and Empire in Late Antiquity.* Cambridge: Cambridge University Press.

Hoebel, E. Adamson. 1954. *The Law of Primitive Man.* Cambridge, Mass.: Harvard University Press.

Jacoby, Susan. 1983. *Wild Justice: The Evolution of Revenge.* New York: Harper & Row.

Kelly, Martin. 1988. "Citizen Survival in Ancient Rome." *Police Studies* 11 (winter): 195–201.

Kolbert, C. F., trans. 1979. *Justinian: The Digest of Roman Law.* London: Penguin Books.

MacDowell, Douglas M. 1966. *Athenian Homicide Law in the Age of the Orators.* Manchester: Manchester University Press.

Menninger, Karl. 1973. *Whatever Became of Sin?* New York: Hawthorn Books.

Morris, Norval, and David Rothman, eds. 1995. *The Oxford History of the Prison.* New York: Oxford University Press.

Peters, Edward M. 1995. "Prison before the Prison." In *The Oxford History of the Prison,* ed. Norval Morris and David Rothman, pp. 17–21. New York: Oxford University Press.

Pound, Roscoe. 1953. *The Lawyer from Antiquity to Modern Times.* St. Paul: West Publishing.

Reinert, Patty. 2002. "Commandments Case Rejected." *Houston Chronicle,* February 26, p. A5.

Reith, Charles. 1952. *The Blind Eye of History: A Study of the Origins of the Present Police Era.* London: Faber and Faber.

Robinson, O. F. 1995. *The Criminal Law of Ancient Rome.* London: Duckworth.

Saggs, H. W. F. 1962. *The Greatness That Was Babylon.* New York: Hawthorn Books.

Stone, I. F. 1988. *The Trial of Socrates.* Boston: Little, Brown and Company.

Squatriglia, Chuck, and Kevin Fagan 2002. "Many Dog Owners Worry That Case Will Restrict Liberties." *San Francisco Chronicle,* March 22. p. A1.

Watson, Alan. 1985. *The Evolution of Law.* Baltimore: Johns Hopkins University Press.

White, Edward J. 1935. *The Law in the Scriptures.* St. Louis, Mo.: Thomas Law Book Company.

Wolff, Hans Julius. 1951. *Roman Law: An Historical Introduction.* Norman: University of Oklahoma Press.

CRITICAL THINKING QUESTIONS

1. If you were charged with committing a serious crime in the ancient world (e.g., Israel, Babylonia, Athens, or Rome), which system of law would you rather be judged under and why? Cite the negative and positive attributes of this system. Discuss in terms of one of the following types of crime: sexual offenses, homicide, or theft.

2. All ancient cultures used the death penalty in one form or another. Discuss methods of execution in the ancient world (from Hammurabi through the Roman Empire).

3. Discuss the development of law enforcement in the Roman Empire.

4. Compare and contrast court procedures in the ancient world.

5. What differences and similarities can you identify between the modern criminal justice systems and ancient criminal justice–related developments.

6. How do preliterate cultures maintain law and order without the written word? How did the invention of writing influence the development of early legal codes?

CRIMINAL JUSTICE HISTORY
ON THE INTERNET

A helpful site dedicated to the study of history is located at www.historyguide.org/guide/guide.html. History instructors often jump directly into class material without first considering larger questions, such as the following: Why study history? What is history? and How do you write a research essay? These questions and many more are answered at "A Student's Guide to the Study of History," an excellent tool for introducing students of criminal justice to this related discipline.

There are numerous Internet sites for the history of ancient law. The Avalon Project at the Yale Law School offers access to many ancient legal documents, including Hammurabi's code, at www.yale.edu/lawweb/avalon/hamcode.htm, and *Ancient Law* by Henry Maine (1861) at www.yale.edu/lawweb/avalon/econ/mainea01.htm. One of the best sites on the ancient world is the Internet Ancient History Sourcebook, which includes full texts of legal documents. Virtually every legal document referred to in this chapter can be found at www.fordham.edu/halsall/ancient/asbook-law.html (e.g., the Twelve Tables at www.fordham.edu/halsall/ancient/12tables.html). Also useful at this site is a guide to ancient history in the movies, listing films that can be used to document criminal justice practices in the ancient world. The Ten Commandments is on line at the Law Museum Archives collection at www.duhaime.org/tencomm.htm.

LEARN MORE

Ancient city of Athens: www.indiana.edu/~kglowack/athens

Ancient Greek world: www.museum.upenn.edu/Greek_World/Intro.html

Greek law readings: www.law.pitt.edu/hibbitts/greek.htm

Other ancient law sites: www.law.pitt.edu/hibbitts/connect.htm#Ancient

Crime and punishment at Olympia and Delphi: www.perseus.tufts.edu/cl135/Students/Rachael_Samberg

Historical map Web sites: www.lib.utexas.edu/maps/map_sites/hist_sites.html

Interactive general map of the ancient Near East: mercator.ens.fr/home/letourne/serveur/map-orient.html.en

Socrates: www.historyguide.org/ancient/socrates.html

The law of Islam: www.fordham.edu/halsall/med/schacht.html

Roman law sources: www.iuscivile.com

Legal status of women in the Greek world: www.uky.edu/ArtsSciences/Classics/wlgr/wlgr-greeklegal.html

Legal status of women in the Roman world: www.uky.edu/ArtsSciences/Classics/wlgr/wlgr-romanlegal.html

NOTES

1. Hoebel (1954).

2. Menninger (1973, p. 50).

3. Hammurabi reigned at least 400 years before Moses. The Bible, however, did not connect the name of Moses with the writing of the Torah until almost ten centuries later. Although tradition has it that Moses authored the first five books of the Bible, how could Moses then have written an account of his own death? By implication, the Torah was written several centuries after the death of Moses in the thirteenth century B.C.

4. While the first four commandments are religious in nature, the remaining six are more secularly significant, including prohibitions against killing, adultery, stealing, and perjury.

5. Of the thirty-six capital offenses, eighteen were moral offenses, twelve were religious, and three were specifically for parents to control their children.

6. Dowden (2002, p. 31).

7. Squatriglia and Fagan (2002).

8. Reinert (2002, p. A5).

9. Drapkin (1989, pp. 181–87).

10. According to most historical accounts, the original tablets were destroyed by Germanic invaders during the sack of Rome in 390 B.C.

11. This strategic location on the Bosporus was formerly an ancient Greek colony called Byzantium. Constantine enlarged the site and named it for himself.

12. According to Berman (1983), the term *medieval* (or Middle Ages) came into use in the sixteenth century as a way to designate the era between early Christianity and the Protestant Reformation as well as the period between classical antiquity and the Renaissance.

13. During the Middle Ages, experts on Roman law were often called "civilians."

14. Peters (1995, pp. 17–21).

2

ENGLISH CRIMINAL JUSTICE ANTECEDENTS (570–1725)

TIME LINE

570	Laws of Aethelbert of Kent	1351	Passage of Statute of Laborers
860s	Viking invasion of British Isles	1361	Justice of the peace becomes cornerstone of British law and order
1066	Norman invasion of England		
1166	Assize of Clarendon	1477	First use of printing press in London
1176	Assize of Northampton		
1180	Henry II centralizes law and justice in England	1530s	Protestant Reformation
		1556	The first house of correction opened at Bridewell Palace
1194	Birth of coroner's office		
1215	King John signs the Magna Carta	1606	Guy Fawkes trial
1215	Fourth Lateran Council abolishes trial by ordeal	1689	English Constitution and Bill of Rights
1285	Statute of Winchester institutes system of watch and ward	1718	Thief taking elevated to a capital offense
1349	Black Death decimates England	1725	Execution of Jonathan Wild

When the Romans invaded the British Isles in 55 B.C., they found a primitive island inhabited by Celtic tribes who had immigrated there from what today is southern Germany. There was no unity among these cultures, and the term *England* had not yet been coined. The Romans unsuccessfully attempted to put the stamp of its legal traditions on the people they came into contact with, but by the time Roman troops were withdrawn 400 years later, except for Roman roads, walls, and town sites, little had changed on the island. When the legions were removed in the early fifth century, the romanized Britons proved ill equipped to defend their borders against marauding invaders from northern Europe. Among the Germanic and Scandinavian invaders were Saxons, Angles, and Jutes.[1] Their prolonged conquest of the island swept away any vestige of Celtic or Roman legal traditions and gave the island its Teutonic name England, or "Land of the Angles." Out of this welter of cultures emerged the tribal foundation that would give birth to English common law. The three tribes that were to become known as the English would go on to conquer and prosper in most parts of England.

ANGLO-SAXON ENGLAND

The Saxon tribal units that migrated to England in the wake of the Roman retreat had originally lived in what is now northern Germany. These tribes fashioned iron-age weapons and tools, herded cattle, and had an extensive agricultural system. At the same time, they were warlike with a loose military organization. The most important component of their social relationship was the blood ties of the kinship group, a form of extended family. In many respects, the tribe functioned as a group of kinsmen.

Between the fifth and seventh centuries A.D., a succession of Saxon invasions brought these tribal kinship groups to England. Subsequently, the tribal chief would give way to a king who would function as military leader and landlord. The king was elected by the major landlords of the community, an assembly that became known as the witan, which is considered an early precursor to Parliament. In time, the witan was empowered to declare law, elect kings, and dole out lands to lords and clergy. Each kingdom was subdivided into shires, composed of smaller territorial subdivisions known as hundreds.[2] British policing can be traced to the tribal customs of these invading Germanic peoples. Each hundred was composed of 100 families and was ruled by a hundredman, or king's *reeve,* who held court every thirty days. The shire reeve was the forerunner of what became known as the sheriff. Responsible for maintaining the peace, enforcing and proclaiming laws, and collecting taxes, the shire reeve was analogous to American sheriffs who policed frontier counties in the nineteenth century.

Hundreds were divided into *tithings,* each composed of ten men, all responsible for the behavior of one another. In the event one of the tithing members committed a crime, the other members were responsible for sounding the hue and cry and apprehending the offender. This early peacekeeping system was based on an objective of mutual and collective responsibility in which the community was liable for keeping the peace and delivering lawbreakers to the hundred and shire courts.

The Lawgivers

The earliest written laws, or dooms, of the Anglo-Saxons can be traced back to the Laws of Aethelbert of Kent (570).[3] These laws were based on local customs and are considered one of the earliest legal documents in English history. Far from comprehensive, they enumerate the punishment of various crimes, ranging from homicide to fornication. Each crime specified punishment and compensation. In this complex society of noblemen, commoners, freedmen, and slaves, individuals had values placed on their lives by class. Hence, in the event that a commoner was killed, his life was valued at 200 shillings, while a nobleman was worth perhaps six times that. Penalties and fines varied by class, not unlike the stark punishments of Hammurabi's code.

During the Anglo-Saxon era, there was no distinction between felonies or misdemeanors. Although it is uncertain when the concept of felony[4] originated, it has been suggested that it developed at the time of the Norman Conquest as a category for more serious crimes. One of the earliest mentions of felony can be found in the *Assize*[5] *of Northampton* (1176), which mentions "murder and other felony."

In the sixth century, the notion of the state had not yet evolved, and the kinship groups or family remained the chief social institution in Britain. Therefore, a crime against an individual was a crime against the family, typically resulting in a blood feud. Kinship members were expected to seek revenge from the perpetrators. Naturally, if the murder occurred between kinship group members, there was no bloodletting, and the perpetrator was banished.

Over time, systems of compensation were established in lieu of blood feuds. Some sources suggest that this softening of retaliation was in response to the growth of Christianity and the feudal system. Inspired by the need for collective responsibility, the wergild replaced the blood feud among Germanic tribes. Since the tribe was responsible for transgressions by clan members, a collective effort was made by the group to collect the blood money and compensate the victim's family.

During the ninth century, the British Isles endured its first recorded attacks by the Danish Vikings. Finally, in 878, King Alfred of Wessex defeated the Danish forces in battle and made peace after granting land concessions in an area that became known as the Danelaw. One only has to look at today's map of England to discover the widespread impact of the Scandinavian peoples on the British Isles. There are more than 700 towns that end in the suffix *-by*, which was the Scandinavian term for village or town, hence *bylaw,* meaning "town law."

The word *law* was introduced by the Danes in a region known as Danelaw, an area controlled by the Danes that stretched approximately from the Thames River to Liverpool. For almost half a century beginning in 886, the Danelaw was regarded as a separate political entity comprising almost half of England. Here Scandinavian settlers blended in with Anglo-Saxon neighbors, borrowing agricultural methods while contributing their own variation of legal codes and institutions.

The Danes convened local assemblies called *Things,* where farmers met under the supervision of a lawman to make decisions concerning the community. According to Danish legal code, the compensation to be paid for taking the life of a man, or *wergild,* was determined by the status of the victim. This contrasts with the Anglo-Saxon tradition, which was determined by the status of the victim's master. The Danes are also credited with devising a precursor to the English jury system. At local courts held at the Things, twelve freeholders were required to swear that they would not accuse an innocent man or shield a guilty one.

Anglo-Saxon Legal Tradition

More important to the development of criminal justice customs in England were the influences brought in by waves of Germanic invaders. Saxon tribal customs were preserved in oral traditions and were accepted and enforced by the entire society. Early Anglo-Saxon society was based on bonds of kinship and the extended family. A primitive form of social organization to be sure, the collective nature of this society diminished the importance of the individual, although each individual was responsible for the actions of his kinsmen. Whenever an individual killed or injured an individual, he brought the enmity of the victim's kin on his own family, ensuring a feud. By law, families were allowed to exact vengeance on the perpetrator's kin. Over time, attempts were made to downplay the vengeance in return for "blood money" in the form of a *wergild,* which was determined by an individual's status in society. When a defendant was charged with a crime, the only methods for determining guilt or innocence were the ordeal or compurgation. Considered another major precursor to the jury trial system, compurgation required both the defendant and the accuser to provide oath helpers to swear to the truthfulness of each party. Oath helpers were initially kinsmen and later on members of the tithing group. The number of required oath helpers depended on rank and the seriousness of the offense. Typically, an accused defendant would supply twelve relatives or close neighbors who swore to the veracity of his case.

Trial by ordeal can be found in cultures throughout the world and in many time periods. As practiced in England, it was typically conducted by fire or water and was administered with the help of a priest. Considered God's judgment, the ordeal was compulsory for individuals who were caught in the act, who were formerly guilty of perjury, or who were unable to provide the appropriate number of compurgators. Built on ancient methods of determining guilt or innocence, trial by ordeal was based on the notion that the gods would protect the innocent. In Christian Britain, no less faith was placed in this method. Trial by ordeal was actually the court of last resort since it was hoped individuals would repent or confess before undergoing the ritual. There were also opportunities to stack the odds in favor of the accused for a price by corrupting officials or bribing clerics to cool off the instruments prior to the ordeal.

Trial by fire often involved the accused walking blindfolded over hot coals or plowshares or placing an arm into scalding water. If the wounds did not heal within three days, the defendant was judged guilty and faced the consequences. There were other forms of ordeal that could be adjudicated without waiting three days. Without a neutral waiting period, crowds and bystanders could have their curiosity sated by immersing heretics in cold water to see if they would float or sink. Naturally, if they sank, they were innocent. It would seem that the immediate ordeal was preferable from the community point of view. The 400 years before the Fourth Lateran Council (1215) is considered the heyday of trial by ordeal. Virtually every law code in the world in this era makes some type of reference to this procedure. Crimes ranging from murder, forgery, and witchcraft to heresy prescribed ordeals of hot iron and cold water. However, the method of ordeal was not the first resort. Since it coexisted with other methods of giving proof, it was not used until other ways for determining the truth had been exhausted.

Anglo-Saxon Crime and Punishment

Introduced in the ninth century, outlawry, or the placing of an offender outside the protection of the law, was used to punish individuals who refused to appear at court, failed to pay the *wergild,* or attempted to evade the machinery of justice by fleeing. Individuals who were outlawed also forfeited their property and lost all civil rights. According to the procedure of the day, if an individual accused of a crime failed to appear at county court four consecutive times, he was pronounced an outlaw, in essence branding him an animal to be hunted down. If he was not killed while resisting capture, he could then face the hangman on proof of his sentence of outlawry. By the time of Edward III, only the sheriff had the power to kill fugitives, unless it occurred in the process of capture.

Beginning with the Laws of Aethelbert, fugitives could be accorded sanctuary at a church or other consecrated place under certain circumstances. However, a specific protocol had to be followed in which a fugitive confessed his crime to a priest, gave up any weapons, paid a fee to the church, and recounted the particulars of the offense. The perpetrator could be given sanctuary for only forty days, after which he had to appear before the coroner and promise on oath to leave the realm. Sanctuary continued through the Norman era until its abolition in 1623 under James I.

After confessing to the coroner and taking an oath to leave the country, fugitives were promised safe conduct and directed to the nearest seaport to leave the country. As an alternative to outlawry, the process of abjuration (the process whereby a fugitive left the country) allowed the abjurer, dressed in a simple white robe and carrying a wooden cross, to safely avoid the consequences of many crimes. Prohibited from staying for more than two nights at any stop along the way, fugitives were expected to leave quickly to avoid confrontation with the victim's families. By the sixteenth century, Henry VIII insisted on the branding of abjurers so that they could be easily recognized if they returned to England without being pardoned.

NORMAN ENGLAND

The Norman Conquest of England by forces under William, Duke of Normandy, in 1066 is considered one of the most pivotal events in English history. Following the wishes of Edward the Confessor, who died childless in 1066, his brother-in-law Harold was appointed as his successor. However, William claimed that he had been promised the Crown earlier by Edward and, with the support of the papacy, invaded England. After his victory at the Battle of Hastings and the death of Harold in battle on Christmas Day 1066, William was crowned king of England at the newly completed Westminster Cathedral.

The Normans of northern France were descended from northern tribes (Vikings or Northmen), not unlike the Anglo-Saxons and the Danes. But during their 150 years in France, they had developed their own unique identity and a continental style of feudalism. This system was a military structure, strictly enforced through a structure of mutual obligation. The social classes of Norman England were divided into three general groups, with feudal lords, knights, and barons at the top. In the middle were the ordinary citizens, usually skilled workers. At the bottom were the serfs and peasants of the estates, perhaps two-thirds of the population. Barons, who were the highest level of Norman lords, maintained huge landholdings, or manors, on which lived vassals or serfs who toiled the land. In return for an oath of faithfulness and certain well-understood obligations, the lords of these estates would protect the vassals. Likewise, the peasants would heed the call to arms when the lord's interests were threatened.

A serf was tied to the land and had no right to leave his lord's estate. They could be punished for idleness, disorderly behavior, and poor workmanship. In return for working so many days a week for the lord, delivering a certain amount of lumber, or loaning his lord's horses, serfs could expect the lords to build them a new house if theirs burned down or to care for their children if they were orphaned.

In the years following the Norman Conquest, as Normans and Saxons lived more peacefully together, the authority of the sheriff was taken over by the local lord of the manor. Subsequently, the work of the hundred court was replaced by a manor court. This court chose manor officers each year, including an ale taster, bread weigher, swine ringer, and, most important, a constable. Responsible for helping keep the king's peace on the estate, the unpaid constable had a multitude of duties, including reporting behavior problems to the court, arresting malefactors and guarding them until trial, and calling out the hue and cry and raising posse comitatus (meaning "power of the county"), a posse of locals, to capture a criminal.

Under English common law, all male persons over the age of fifteen were required to assist in law enforcement when summoned by the sheriff through the hue and cry. The term posse has a lasting resonance that most Americans identify with the nineteenth-century West, when county sheriffs enlisted the aid of all able-bodied men when encountering forces beyond their control. In late twentieth-century Kingston, Jamaica, gangs were so enamored with Hollywood Western movies that they adopted "posse" as the name for their organized crime gangs.

We know little about the Norman law codes, but we do know that William did not speak

English, nor did he initially understand the laws of his new subjects. In order to win the allegiance of his new subjects, he compiled the laws of Edward the Confessor while at the same time introducing familiar Norman customs. Adhering to the Middle Ages custom of allowing conquered peoples to keep their legal systems, William adopted most of the Anglo-Saxon criminal justice ideas while introducing a number of customs from the European continent. Another explanation for William's reverence for the Anglo-Saxon laws was that they were evidence of a more highly developed body of jurisprudence than the unwritten customs of Normandy. William adopted the existing law-keeping systems, including the tithing system, the use of the hue and cry, the hundred courts, and the shire courts. The Normans introduced a feudal system, a system of baronial courts, as well as separate ecclesiastical or church courts. Building on existing English customs, the Norman era would give rise to the common-law legal tradition. The Normans introduced the framework of a strong centralized government that would eventually lead to the development of national unity and a national system of law. Following the Norman Conquest, for the first time all land was owned either directly or indirectly by the Crown.

The late eleventh century witnessed a recrudescence of Roman law on the European continent. The fall of the Roman Empire saw Justinian's *Corpus Juris Civilis* fall into disuse as less sophisticated versions of the Roman civil law were applied by Germanic invaders to the peoples of the Italian peninsula. The invaders introduced Germanic legal customs as well. During the Renaissance, which followed the so-called Dark Ages, an intellectual and scholarly interest in law emerged, beginning in Bologna, Italy. This city was home to Europe's first modern university, where law was a featured object of study. The jurists of the day recognized the high intellectual quality of Roman law in stark contrast to the "barbarized compilations" of the Germanic invaders. Subsequently, the universities of northern Italy became the center for the study of the civil legal tradition, drawing scholars and students from all over Europe. Those who studied in Bologna returned to their home nations imbued with the superiority of Justinian's civil law (including England during the reign of Henry II). Roman civil law would soon influence the development of common law, featuring a common body of law, a common legal vernacular, and a common method of instruction and scholarship.[6]

The Lawgivers

With the transition to the feudal system, each lord held a special court for his tenants. The Normans adopted Saxon procedures for determining guilt and innocence: the compurgatory oath and trial by ordeal. The Normans introduced another procedure, closely related to the ordeal: trial by battle. A precursor to the adversarial legal system, trial by battle involved a physical contest between a defendant and a complainant. These would be fought either by the individuals directly involved in the complaint or through proxy champions. Women, children, priests, and the elderly or infirm were allowed to appoint champions to fight on their behalf. Initially, champions could be used only in disputes over land. In the case of murders, the defendant had to appear in person. These judicial duels were conducted with much formality. Knights met in battle with the accoutrements of warfare, while commoners often fought using lethal agricultural implements. The two parties then fought to a stalemate. If the loser was not killed in the battle, he was hanged. Similar to and as ancient as trial by ordeal, credence was given the notion that God gave the judgment and would not have permitted an innocent man to be defeated. Most individuals attempted to avoid this form of arbitration, fearful of the outcome. Despite its unpopularity, trial by battle remained common into the thirteenth and fourteenth centuries.

England had been Christianized for 400 years by the time William introduced separate church courts in 1066. The creation of these courts led to the separation of ecclesiastical and secular law as the church withdrew from the adjudication of secular disputes. In return, church courts controlled spiritual matters without secular interference. Initially, church, or canon, law superseded the national law of England, with the pope regarded as the supreme legislator. Ecclesiastical courts decided spiritual affairs, including clerical matters and decisions of marriage, legitimation, and status. The church also dealt with such offenses of morality, ranging from incest and adultery to perjury, blasphemy, usury, and heresy. Under this new system, all clergymen were tried by church courts, as were commoners who breached ecclesiastical law.

The church was particularly intrusive when it came to marriage. Ecclesiastical courts could annul a marriage if either party could not procreate children or was related by blood or matrimony. Possessing the exclusive right of annulment gave the church a heightened influence in medieval society. There were also legal consequences resulting from marriage. When a man and woman married, the woman was considered to have merged her identity with her husband. This apparently gave rise to the long-standing common-law rule that one party in a marriage could not testify against the other.

Occasionally, the two systems of secular and church law overlapped. Until the twelfth century, for instance, the king insisted that sins were secular offenses. Under church rules, the harshest penalty an ecclesiastical court could pass was excommunication. Other punishments included serving penance and degradation of clerical status. In order to take advantage of the less severe penalties arbitrated by the church courts, crafty laymen claimed to be members of the cloth in order to win benefit of clergy. This should not be surprising in an era when secular defendants routinely faced beheading, hanging, strangulation, impalement, boiling to death, or being broken on the wheel.

Benefit of clergy surfaced at a time when clerics were subject to both secular and ecclesiastical law. The clergy were eventually given an exemption from secular rulings and would be punished only by the church. During the Middle Ages, clerics were the only members of society likely to be able to read and write. In order to separate the thief from the cleric, a sight-reading test was devised. This would be proven by the ability to read Psalm 51, or "neck verse," which, if the defendant did successfully, saved him from the gallows. But as more people learned to read, the test became obsolete. The more astute criminals often learned the psalm by heart and could recite it word for word with a book in front of them, even though they could not actually read a word.

An individual could take advantage of benefit of clergy only one time. In order to prevent a person from pleading a second time, the fatty part of the thumb was branded for future identification. By the fourteenth century, benefit of clergy was given to literate individuals outside the clergy.[7] This literacy test was not abolished until 1706.

Norman Crime and Punishment

One of the more notable changes implemented by William was a movement away from capital punishment in favor of mutilation. No criminal was hanged for the next forty years. This did not mean that no one died from criminal sanctions. Indeed, scores of the convicted succumbed to mutilations after having eyes put out and testicles cut off.

With the support of the witan, or king's assembly, William became not only the Duke of Normandy but also the King of England, beginning a new line of succession. Building on the Anglo-Saxon criminal justice apparatus, the Normans introduced a variety of new law enforcement positions in order to remove some of the power from the rapacious sheriffs. In 1194, the coroner was introduced. Selected at the county level, the coroner was expected to conduct inquiries in cases of suspicious deaths and house break-ins.

 Originating in twelfth-century England, the coroner is a familiar feature of the criminal justice system in most of the United States. Today the coroner performs specific duties in investigating cases of death where there are questionable circumstances or where there was no attending physician at the time of death. While some states have replaced the coroner with the medical examiner, most counties have one elected coroner.

By the time of the Norman invasion, the position of constable had become a position of high prestige under the French kings. Derived from the Latin *comes stabuli,* which means "head of the stables," ancient Roman constables, really just glorified servants, were given this moniker because they had demonstrated honesty while protecting the royal stables. The constable became more identifiable in a peacekeeping capacity following the conquest of England. Over time, their tasks included collecting taxes, arresting malefactors, transporting prisoners, and serving legal papers. Most first-time offenders usually became familiar with the local constable. It was the constable that was expected to make the arrest once the hue and cry was raised and then hand over the quarry to the sheriff on apprehension. However, by the fifteenth century, life was becoming increasingly complex, and inhabitants were less willing to participate in the traditional hue-and-cry process.

William I introduced the curfew procedure to England to "protect against the risks of fire." In a world of wood, this was a natural concern to control the spread of fire. With homes heated by open fires, usually in the middle of the floor and directly under the roof, the hazards were very real. However, the curfew can be interpreted as a clever bit of subterfuge since in reality it was probably designed to keep subversive Anglo-Saxons from meeting during the hours of darkness. When the curfew bell tolled at eight o'clock each evening, inhabitants were expected to extinguish their fires and retire for the night or face harsh consequences. Within a few decades of the Norman Conquest, the curfew was relaxed to allow fires to burn after the curfew bell.

Curfews have been around for hundreds of years. The word's origins can be traced back to its Latin and French roots. Curfews were traditionally created by the upper-class members of society who wanted to limit the movements of the lower class. Originally, curfews operated under the presumption that an entire class of people was guilty. In the United States, curfews were originally implemented to control African Americans in the South. During the early 1900s, curfews became popular for controlling juveniles. The ringing of the curfew bell alerted teenagers and children it was time to go home. In recent years, cities and towns across the country have expanded the use of youth curfews to address the growing concern about juvenile crime and violence, treating in like fashion an entire demographic group as if it is guilty. Curfews remain a controversial crime control strategy. There is little empirical evidence that they actually work, and according to civil libertarians curfews violate constitutional protections.

The Domesday Book

In a time when land equaled wealth, the Domesday[8] survey was a comprehensive inquest of the English land tenure system that redistributed the land from the Saxon upper class to the Norman nobles. Although the survey was incomplete, it is still considered the high-water mark of administrative achievement for the Middle Ages for the speed and precision with which it was conducted. Twenty years after the Norman Conquest, in order to determine the extent of his landholdings and fiscal rights, William initiated a complete survey of the number of individuals who belonged to each class, including serfs, knights, barons, and so forth. In effect, this inquest reduced all social relationships to a land tenure system. The survey also enumerated the amount of arable land, water mills, meadows and pastures, and forests and fisheries and the value of the estates. The survey was conducted under mounting popular resentment, as the Saxons saw it as an attempt to strengthen the power of the invaders.

Prior to the Norman Conquest, sheriffs were drawn from the ranks of landowners and functioned as royal agents in the shires. Within five years of the conquest, Saxon sheriffs were replaced by Normans. As their duties were expanded over time, they became more oppressive as well. The stereotype of the oppressive sheriff figures prominently in the Robin Hood ballads. The Domesday survey records a number of high-handed actions in which sheriffs enriched their own coffers.

Compiled between 1085 and 1086, the Domesday Book offers an interesting picture of eleventh-century England. With a population estimated at more than 1.5 million, only 290,000 names are recorded. Of these, 9,000 settled there following the Norman Conquest. This group controlled 80 percent of the land. What becomes clear is that following the Norman invasion, a social revolution had occurred that essentially placed a feudal Norman aristocracy between the king and the Saxon farmers, creating a national feudal system that would last for centuries. Over the next century, the Normans and Saxons coalesced into one people: the English people.

The Reforms of Henry II

The reign of Henry II, which lasted from 1154 to 1189, signaled a turning point in the history of the English legal system. Henry and his ministers would shape many legal and administrative procedures that would determine the direction that the developing English criminal justice system would take. At the time Henry took the throne, England was well supplied with numerous courts reflecting the feudal system of twelfth-century England. Hundred courts handled petty crimes committed by the lower classes, while the shire courts were concerned with the judicial aspects of more serious offenses. Complementing the judicial arrangements of the day were courts of the manor (landlord's private estate), borough courts, honorial courts (concerned with pleas of land), and ecclesiastical courts. Despite the suggested distinctions of the various courts, the system was confusing. What actually determined to which court an individual took his plea was his status in the complicated nature of his tenure under the feudal system. The competing and overlapping jurisdictions of the old customary law (Anglo-Norman) became a source of serious trouble during the 1100s.

Under Henry II's administration, the power of the Crown increased at the expense of the clergy and the feudal barons. A chain of events led to a transition from the old tribal–feudal system of law to royal courts and to the practice of common law throughout England. During this era, the oppressive power of the sheriff diminished as it became more subordinate to the Crown. Subsequently, the sheriff would become a minor official.

In 1166, England was beset by a growing crime problem. In response, during this centennial year of the Norman Conquest, Henry II issued the Assize of Clarendon, which established trial by grand jury. Juries consisted of twelve men in each hundred with four from each township. Together they submitted the names of all reputed criminals in the district for trial by ordeal (similar to today's grand juries, which review the facts of a case and issue either a true bill or a no bill). When traveling judges paid a visit to a district, communities were given an efficient means for stemming the crime wave. Ten years later, the Assize of Northampton divided the country into six circuits, and justices in Eyre were made responsible for traveling to shires and hundreds throughout the realm. These judges superseded the local courts and were considered a means of controlling the conduct of sheriffs, bailiffs, and coroners in the Middle Ages. Henry encouraged all freemen to furnish themselves with arms and armor according to their means through the 1181 Assize of Arms, trusting his subjects to heed the call to arms in event of an emergency. According to Henry's proclamation, "Whoever possesses one knight's fee shall have a shirt of mail, a helmet, a shield, and a lance." Some homicide scholars have suggested that with each man armed day and night, murder rates soon rose as well.

The introduction of itinerant judges was considered one of Henry's greatest legal innovations since their regular visits would eventually lead to a common law throughout the realm. What stifled the progress of the itinerant judges was the basic problem of how to delegate royal authority without at the same time putting too much discretionary power into the hands of the judges. This problem was resolved with the publication of *The Treatise on the Laws and Customs of England* toward the end of Henry's reign. Commonly known by its shortened title *Glanvill,* its author is unknown. According to this lawbook, there was officially a court that traveled with the king, a "chief court" that resided at Westminster, and a royal court that was periodically carried throughout the country by a group of royal justices who traversed a certain circuit of the shires.

Historian James Buchanan Given has made an extensive examination of the reports by the king's justices. The Eyre rolls offer insight into the procedure for investigating homicide in the thirteenth century. Apparently, when someone died under suspicious circumstances, the coroner was summoned to conduct an inquest. Once he arrived, he summoned an inquest jury made up of men from the vicinity where the body was found. He then examined the body and ascertained whether the homicide occurred at the scene or elsewhere. If someone was suspected of the crime, he was arrested by the coroner, who then, with the help of the jury, estimated the value of the perpetrator's property. All this was recorded on loose leaves of parchment paper. The work of Givens suggests that compared to the low homicide rates of present-day Europe, medieval England was the scene of unremitting violence.

According to one of Henry II's biographers, H. L. Warren, during his tenure as king, "criminal law did not show the same progress toward the development of rational processes" in the administration of punishment as in other areas of criminal justice reform.[9] Beginning in 1166, in the midst of a growing crime problem, criminal punishment was designed as a deterrent. After the Assize of Clarendon, anyone who failed the ordeal was sentenced to be hanged or to have a foot amputated and then be banished from the realm for forty days. The Assize of Northhampton, ten years later, introduced even more serious punishments. Mutilation, following conviction by ordeal, was extended to include the right hand and foot.

The early years of Henry II's reign witnessed great conflict between the church and the state over the jurisdiction of church law. Separate ecclesiastical courts were responsible for arbitrating cases involving church clergy. Since the shedding of blood was not allowed in church courts, the worst penalty a murderer in church court could expect was excommunication. By demanding "benefit of clergy," monks, priests, students, sextons, and others could win the right to be tried in church courts to escape severe sentences. The royal courts had no jurisdiction in these cases. Henry was troubled by the fact that almost any person with a scintilla of education or any connection with the church could take advantage of this legal loophole and wanted to end the immunity of the church from secular jurisdiction and bring it under the control of the royal courts.

Matters came to a head in 1161, when Henry II appointed Thomas Becket as the Archbishop of Canterbury. The assumption that Becket would continue to cooperate with the Crown would lead to one of the most famous murder cases of the Middle Ages and once again bring into question the relationship between church and state. The son of a London merchant, Becket lived a life of luxury after Henry appointed him chancellor in 1154. After the death of the current archbishop in 1161, Henry appointed Becket as the successor, confident he would remain a friend and loyal servant of the king and the state. However, things did not quite work out that way, with Becket adopting a more ascetic lifestyle. Realizing that he could not serve two masters, Becket resigned his chancellor's post under the king and was now resolute in becoming the champion of the church.

In 1164, Henry stated that he wanted to return to the customs of Henry I, which included a clause stating that if clergymen were accused in a royal court and then tried in an ecclesiastical court, found guilty, and unfrocked, they should then be sent back to the royal court for sentencing and punishment. Henry's new rules extended the jurisdiction of the royal courts in several directions. Becket retaliated by refusing to put the archbishop's seal on any documents containing the king's proposals. The conflict between the two men intensified, leading Becket to flee to Rome and subsequently excommunicate the king and his ministers. In response, Henry confiscated Canterbury's revenues.

After Becket returned to England, relations soon worsened, leading Henry to brand Becket a "turbulent priest" as he launched into a tirade of invective that convinced several of Henry's retainers to kill Becket. Becket's martyrdom at Canterbury Cathedral at the hands of four knights forced Henry to accept an agreement with the pope by which benefit of clergy would persist. This resulted in an increase in papal authority and a check on Henry's power by the church. Over the next century, scores of monasteries would be erected in England, signifying the expanding power of the church. To Henry's credit, he was able to make peace with the church and, through a spectacular act of public contrition, was able to retain the loyalty of the middle classes.

One of the greatest English lawmakers, Henry combined Norman–French legal concepts with the ancient common law, completing the work begun by William the Conqueror. No less a source than F. W. Maitland noted that Henry II's reign was "a critical moment in English legal history,"[10] coinciding with an era in which customary law was no longer adequate for the needs of a rapidly changing society. With the revival of the study of Roman civil law, Henry perhaps saw the possibilities of adapting rational jurisprudence to meet the needs of an evolving criminal justice system. At his death, he could look back on numerous achievements, having made the Crown the source of all justice at the expense of the baronial courts.

The Jury

The origins of jury trial are still a subject of much debate. While some authorities credit its introduction in England to Danish settlements, most evidence suggests that it was inaugurated by the Normans. A variety of prototypes for the English jury system had been suggested. As an alternative to compurgation and trial by battle or ordeal, a new form of trial was inaugurated called inquisition. According to this method, a judge who was selected to hear a case between two parties would order a number of men familiar with the particulars of the case, usually twelve, to investigate the case and give a sworn verdict as to who should win the dispute. These selected men became known as jurors because they had to swear to tell the truth and were required to decide in favor of one of the parties in the case. Thus we see the beginning of trial by jury, in which jurors are peers of the defendant.

One explanation as to why the Normans extended the alternative of the jury trial was that trial by battle too often favored the omnipotent warlike leaders over the poor and often defenseless lower classes. Unlike present-day juries, which are supposed to be unfamiliar with the case, the early Norman juries were composed of those most likely to be familiar with the proceedings.

The Fourth Lateran Council

The year 1215 was a pivotal one for the history of common law. That year, not only was the Magna Carta signed, but the Fourth Lateran Council convened and withdrew church support for trial by ordeal. The Fourth Lateran Council, held in Rome, was the largest assembly of its kind in the history of the Christian church. The church apparently withdrew its support for this ancient method of gathering proof because it was felt that the clergy should not be involved in taking the lives of fellow Christians. Since these trials could not be conducted without the presence of priests, trial by ordeal diminished. The abolition of the ordeal left few alternatives for determining guilt or innocence besides compurgation, jury trials, and trial by battle. Family men typically did not prefer trial by jury since, on conviction, their property would be confiscated and forfeited to the king's treasury. In certain cases, in order to force an accused to enter a plea at arraignment, defendants were forced to undergo *peine forte et dure*,[11] in which weighty rocks were stacked on their chests until they either agreed to a jury trial or died. Under English common law, no accused could be tried unless the accused formally entered a plea. Therefore, under the practice of *peine forte et dure*, the accused either entered a plea or died under the weights. In modern practice, if an accused stands mute at arraignment, the presiding judge will automatically enter a plea of not guilty on behalf of the accused.

Since news traveled slowly in the Middle Ages, the ruling from the Fourth Lateran Council took time to reach England and other Catholic countries from Rome. But in 1219, trial by ordeal was abolished in England. Without trial by ordeal, other methods had to become more developed for reaching resolutions in more difficult criminal cases. The demise of the ordeal led to several major developments in the quest for proof, including an increasing reliance on torture as a replacement for the ordeal procedure. But, like the ordeal, it was also meant to be the procedure of last resort. England, however, diverged from the European continental tradition at this juncture, as it made swift progress toward the trial jury, resulting in a legal tradition that became increasingly different from Roman civil legal conventions.

As England moved more toward an adversarial system characterized by a jury, continental countries went through a different evolution in criminal justice procedure. Not to be confused with the Spanish Inquisition of the fifteenth century, the European inquisitorial process placed the judges at center in the fact-gathering process (not torture). By the sixteenth century, the inquisitorial method was standardized. While the adversarial process that we are so familiar with assumes that the truth will come out after a free and open competition by two lawyers over who had the correct facts, the inquisitorial trial is more like a continuing investigation, as the judges and not the attorneys call and examine the witnesses.

Prior to the Norman Conquest, there was no legal profession in England. William introduced lawyers to Britain in the form of his "servants of the king at law." Many of the first judges were selected from their ranks. By the fourteenth century, guilds of lawyers known as Inns of Court could be found in London. Four of the original fourteen Inns still exist. At London's Inns of Court, the legal profession trained apprentices in the common law. Here, legal education included lectures, oral disputation, and attendance at court. Over time, the Inns made the transition from apprentice training to law school and for several centuries were more popular law schools than those at Oxford and Cambridge.

The Magna Carta

The Magna Carta is probably the best-known document in English history. Translated from Latin, it meant "Great Charter."

Signed by King John at Runnymede on June 15, 1215, the Magna Carta established the fundamental principles of human rights. John ruled England from 1199 to 1216 and is considered among the least capable of the nation's kings. Violent, capricious, and vengeful, he succeeded in alienating virtually every faction of his realm. Commoners, clergy, and lords were united in their hatred for the monarch. His unpopularity was not confined to the British Isles, for in 1208 he was excommunicated by Pope Innocent III. The barons met several times prior to 1215 and decided that before taking up arms, they would try and compel the king to sign a charter of rights. With the support of the citizens of London, John capitulated to the demands and on June 15, 1215, signed the Magna Carta at Runnymede.

Almost 300 years before the invention of the printing press, twenty to twenty-five copies of the Magna Carta were painstakingly written out by clerks for distribution around the country. Of these, only four survive. Copies were sent to various towns and read aloud so that everyone was privy to the king's concessions. In an era of almost universal illiteracy, the documents were sent to cathedrals, where the literate clergy could read the Magna Carta publicly.

Containing the basic principles that would be incorporated in the American Constitution 500 years later, the Magna Carta had great impact on subsequent developments in constitutional law and political freedom. One of the most important developments was the notion of due process found in chapter 39 of the Magna Carta: "No free man shall be taken, imprisoned, outlawed, banished, or in any way destroyed, nor will We proceed against or prosecute him, except by the lawful judgment of his equals and by the law of the land." By the seventeenth century, due process of law and habeas corpus would be united and contribute to significant constitutional developments.

Regarded as one of the foundations of modern democracy, the Magna Carta guaranteed legal tax collection (with permission of Parliament), justice to all men without fear or favor, and no imprisonment without trial. A turning point in legal history, the document set up a permanent judicial center at Westminster as well as annual assizes held by circuit judges throughout the country. Westminster became the repository for legal records and the site of the Court of Common Pleas, where suits between private individuals were held. It is during this era that one can discern the evolution of an expanded legislature comprising upper and lower houses of delegates. What would become the House of Lords was based on the hereditary right passed from father to son, while the House of Commons was filled with representatives from the commoners. This parliament sat at Westminster.

The faint origins of Parliament can be found not in law but in custom. The development of this body was spurred by the king's increasing need for revenue, which forced him to negotiate with the assorted classes of thirteenth-century England. By the early 1250s, the word *parliamentum* came into use to designate a meeting of the shire knights to consider new taxes. Although the first official Parliament convened in 1265, it would be another thirty years before Parliament was reorganized under the reign of Edward I[12] on the basis that it occupies today. By 1295, the representative nature

of Parliament had been established. Often referred to as the "English Justinian," Edward became one of England's greatest lawgivers.

With the growth of towns and expanding urban areas, the prevalence of nighttime crime was increasing at an alarming rate. In order to counter the rising crime wave, King Edward I issued the Statute of Winchester in 1285. One of the most important pieces of criminal justice legislation to come out of the Middle Ages, this proclamation ordered all freemen between the ages of fifteen and sixty to own armor and weapons according to their social status in order to defend the peace. These accoutrements would be inspected twice a year by constables elected from each hundred. But more important, this statute ordained that every walled town should establish a system of watch and ward, a form of day and night watch to maintain security. According to this statute, all large walled towns were ordered to shut their gates from sunset to sunrise. The watch was ordered to arrest any suspicious strangers and lock them up until morning. Other proactive measures included widening highways leading to market towns and eliminating potential hiding spots along the roads for thieves and highwaymen. The night watch and day ward would be the main police presence in English town life for almost 600 years.

The Black Death

In 1348, a trading ship reached England with an unwanted cargo of flea-ridden rats carrying the devastating bubonic plague pestilence from its origins in central Asia. The plague was usually fatal, and with no cure, perhaps 25 to 50 percent of the population perished. The impact was felt everywhere. The demographic crisis saw the clergy pared by 40 percent. According to estate records, perhaps two-thirds of the workforce perished, leading to a huge reduction in the labor force. In turn, serfs no longer felt their traditional obligations to their lords and barons and began to leave the manorial estates to take wage-paying jobs in towns. The labor shortage resulting from the Black Death made it inevitable that workers would demand rights and advantages that had been previously confined to the upper classes. However, as feudal restrictions seemed less persuasive, the state stepped in to preserve order. With the Statute of Laborers (1351), state control of the labor force supplanted the power of the feudal lords, leaving peasants and artisans in a stronger bargaining position with their lords and masters, with Parliament serving as an intermediary. By stepping in when it did, the English government was able to ensure a continuing adequate supply of agricultural workers at rates that existed prior to the pandemic while leading to a dramatic increase in wages. Ultimately, Parliament became a more formidable presence in English society by prohibiting idleness and preventing the free movement of the menial classes under the threat of imprisonment and branding.

Medieval Crime and Punishment

Late medieval England was known throughout Europe for its high crime rate. In the fourteenth century, most people lived on the bare margins of existence, as nine out of ten people still lived in the countryside. As violence escalated, English common law reacted by zealously punishing the crime of homicide. Individuals caught in a deadly encounter were cautioned that they had "a duty to retreat" in order to avoid possible bloodshed. With an increasingly centralized government, the Crown sought to maintain a monopoly on conflict resolution. It was expected that individuals would settle acrimonious disputes either amicably or in court. In the event that your adversary threatened you, you were expected to leave the scene immediately and retreat until your back was literally against the wall. At this point, it was permissible to stand and fight in self-defense. In this way, the state attempted to reduce the homicide rate by shifting the battle scene from the streets to the courts.

In response to the rise in felonies and with the escalation of organized criminal activities, trailbaston commissions were inaugurated beginning in

1304. Because of a combination of rural unemployment, demobilized soldiers, and social unrest, several judicial innovations were introduced. The trailbaston was a special judicial commission of judges empowered to travel to crime-ridden villages and set up grand juries to help wipe out local gangs. Historians have compared the activities of this commission to twentieth-century crime commissions led by Thomas Dewey (1930s) and Rudolph Giuliani (1980s) that successfully went after organized crime in New York City. These medieval justices, like their modern-day counterparts, made headway through the use of informants who were convinced to turn state's evidence and testify against their former colleagues in return for a lighter sentence. Known as approvers in the Middle Ages, once a gang member was convicted, he could accuse the former gang members. But in order to prove his accusation, he was forced to vanquish each one through the ancient trial by battle. On defeating each defendant, he was pardoned. Conversely, if he was not victorious or was not killed in battle, he was executed.

Beginning in 1361, the justice of the peace (JP) became the cornerstone of British law and order. This peacekeeping position can be traced back to the 1260s, when it was known as the "keeper of the peace." Considered another self-help approach to maintaining rural law and order, each shire had three or four JPs who were charged with restraining the ever-present rioting. Imbued with the power to pursue and punish malefactors, they were allowed to try less serious offenders without the presence of the king's judges. In order to alleviate the caseloads of the various courts, JPs were authorized to confront most types of misdemeanors, including poaching, petty thievery, and drunken fighting. Occasionally, they were also allowed to try felony cases. In effect, London was authorizing the landed gentry to maintain law and order in their districts to reduce the pressure on the criminal justice apparatus in London. Although this was an unpaid position, wealthy landowning families saw it as a position that could lead to a better marriage or a seat in Parliament. As the powers of the JPs increased, so too did the authority of the once-mighty sheriffs erode. The JP system would persist into the late nineteenth century.

One of the oldest criminal justice positions in the United States, contemporary justices of the peace (JPs) are state magistrates whose duties include administering justice for minor offenses and committing cases to trial at higher courts. They are usually elected within a minor civil division, but their jurisdiction usually extends throughout a county. In most states, they are compensated from fees. Most JPs have had little formal legal training, and in some states they are allowed to conduct hearings and fix bail for future court appearance. But clearly, the position of JP has lost much of its former luster.

By the fourteenth century, the constable was still an unpaid position, recognizable only by his official staff. Over time, his duties had multiplied. While he still had to capture wrongdoers, he now had to apply unpleasant punishments as well. The constables became increasingly unpopular as they whipped vagrants and ducked scolds in the village pond. They also had to make regular reports of public complaints to the courts. While all adult males were responsible for serving stints as constables, those who could afford to would pay replacements. Such an odious job, then, was usually performed by the indigent, the elderly, and whoever else was in dire enough straits to accept the payoff. In William Shakespeare's time, the constable usually offered comic respite in his plays, not unlike the Keystone Kops of the silent-film era.

Introduced in the fifteenth century, the Court of Star Chamber[13] was created to punish wealthy supporters of organized crime activity. As organized crime declined, it was used to quell riots and other social disturbances and to punish the instigators. Procedure was rather simple. With no jury present, a defendant was ordered to stop some sort of antisocial behavior or to refrain from committing a particular offense, or else face punishment. Although the court was prohibited from imposing capital punishment, mutilation, shaming, and short imprisonment could be levied on defendants. The court remained popular through the sixteenth century. Its decline and disappearance in the seventeenth century resulted from its harsh and arbitrary sentencing and its association with the king's unpopular policies of the 1630s. Particularly glaring was its suppression of the large Puritan minority for indiscretions, real or imagined. Among the more questionable judgments of the court was the punishment in 1637 of barrister William Prynne, who had his ears cut off and was then pilloried and imprisoned for writing a book that allegedly insulted the queen. In 1642, a statute was passed in Parliament that not only abolished the court but also prohibited the procedure of making a defendant testify against himself (similar to the Fifth Amendment protection in the American Constitution).

The Court of Star Chamber retained its sinister menace for the 1983 film *The Star Chamber*. Similar to the original court, formed in the fourteenth century to try criminals without the benefit of a jury, in this film nine angry judges convene privately to decide the fate of criminals who have escaped retribution because of legal technicalities. Judge Hardin, played by Michael Douglas, is sick of criminals getting off because of the Fourth Amendment, which requires him to prohibit evidence obtained by unlawful search and seizures. In the tradition of the vigilante genre, this film suggests that the rule of law allows dangerous criminals back on the streets and that sometimes it is tempting for individuals to take the law into their own hands. In the case of this 1983 Star Chamber, if it votes guilty, hired killers kill the criminals. The film is ultimately a fantasy, produced at a time when America was experiencing rising crime rates (like England in 1347).

Under William the Conqueror's watch, the Normans introduced the murder fine, or murdrum.[14] Since there was significant resentment against the Normans, often resulting in the killing of local leaders and their servants, William instituted the murdrum. According to the law, if a Norman was found dead under suspicious circumstances, the district was required to arrest the perpetrator or pay a murder fine. However, in the event that the evidence proved the victim was not Norman, the fine was excused. By the Assize of Clarendon in 1166, there was little differentiation between Normans and Englishmen, and deliberate killings became known as murders. It is clear that by the end of the fourteenth century, the Crown had taken a harder line toward murders, especially those committed from ambush or with "malice aforethought." In the early sixteenth century, the crime of manslaughter became distinct from murder, the difference being the presence or absence of premeditation, and in 1531 Henry VIII removed murder from benefit of clergy. From that time on, murder became synonymous with killings involving malice aforethought.

Between the fourteenth and fifteenth centuries, punishment had become somewhat less cruel, with many mutilations being abolished. But to stall recidivism, barbaric penalties were still meted out to rapists who were castrated or blinded and thieves who could be scalded to death or have an eye gouged out. Although individuals were still buried and burned alive, disemboweled, hanged, and beheaded, a movement was afoot to introduce more lenient exhibitory punishments, such as stocks and pillories, to shame individuals into reforming their criminal ways.

The popular image of the pillory shows the defendant spending an inexorable amount of time attached to this device, when in reality an individual might spend three hours in it every three months, often with a whetstone around his neck. However, this punishment was not altogether benign, particularly when prolonged exposure could lead to death. In the early Middle Ages, individuals were mutilated while ensconced in the pillory. Conveniently incapacitated, the law enforcer might be called on to slit a nose or cut off an upper lip or even both ears. Recidivist felons were often pinned by their ears to the pillory, and the only way to secure freedom was to

pull away from the nail until the ear came off. Stocks and pillories were used to punish offenders who engaged in deceitful business practices, forgery, begging under false pretenses, and even masquerading as a king's officer. One baker appeared at court so often that he was nicknamed "pillory" for his penchant for the shaming device.

Perhaps the most glaring form of exhibitory punishment was branding, a punishment that could be traced back to the ancient Babylonians. During the Middle Ages, individuals were branded on either the face or the body with a mark that would be instantly identifiable with the crime committed. The letter B stood for blasphemer, R for robber, SL for seditious libel, and so forth. In the mid-sixteenth century, Edward VI signed a law allowing for vagrants and vagabonds to be defaced with the letter V. This law would not be repealed for almost a century. In an era before fingerprinting and the Bertillon system, branding was one of the few identification systems recognizable to all. One of the drawbacks for society was that, like prison tattoos today, society tended to stigmatize these individuals who were left virtually unemployable for life and therefore had no choice but a life of crime. While branding fell out of popularity by the fourteenth century, it was not outlawed in Britain until 1779.

Until the nineteenth century, virtually all felonies were punishable by death. Beginning in 1768, judges were given the prerogative of sending certain felons to the American or Australian colonies. Surely, there were plenty of felons to go around. In the case of theft, distinctions were based on the value of the stolen object. Early in the Norman era, if a felon stole an object worth twelve pence, it was considered grand larceny, a capital offense. If it was under twelve pence, it was petty larceny, which carried much less severe punishment. By the nineteenth century, juries often assigned fictitious values to stolen goods to downgrade a capital offense to petty larceny and spare the defendant from the gallows. By the late 1820s, England's bloody code was on the wane.

Henry VIII and the Protestant Reformation

Succeeding to the throne in 1509, the eighteen-year-old monarch who would author the song "Greensleeves," the lover of sports and music, gave no hint of the controversy and cruelty that would characterize his reign. The story of Henry's quest for a male heir that led him through six wives and into conflict with the Catholic Church is well known. For our purposes, we will concentrate on the constitutional crisis that followed Henry's establishment of the Church of England, placing himself as the supreme head of the church. Henry's determination to have a male heir led to his breach with Rome and the Act of Treason and Supremacy in 1534, which officially made him the supreme head of the Church of England. Anyone who questioned his authority, whether in public or in private, could expect a date with the headsman.

Henry was always cognizant of the fact that he ruled with the consent of Parliament. Summoning Parliament in 1529, he initiated a great social and ideological revolution that would go far toward establishing Crown and Parliament together as the foundation for the new England. He kept Parliament in session for seven years, allowing him to pass successive measures that changed the structure of the Church of England, including having the clergy accept him as head of that church. After passing a law that prohibited the clergy from convocation without his consent, Sir Thomas More, chancellor and author of *Utopia,* resigned. More would sign his death warrant by differing with the king over the legitimacy of his matrimonial life. He would not be alone. According to one estimate, 72,000 people were executed during Henry's reign.

When Henry VIII broke with the Church of Rome and declared himself supreme head of the Church of England, the resulting Reformation brought harsh punishments to anyone who stood in its way. One of the most prominent monarchs of the Renaissance era, Henry VIII was well known for his propensity for cruelty, which included the passage of an act authorizing boiling to death anyone convicted of poisoning. It would be left to his only son, Edward VI, to finally abolish this sadistic penalty.

The invention of the printing press in the fifteenth century heralded a new era in the history of humankind. Prior to this time, manuscripts were expensive and slow to produce, and few copies of any work existed. It should not be surprising that few were literate and that education was restricted to the clergy. In 1477, the first book was printed in England. With the ability to print the Bible in English, Henry set the stage for the growth of Protestantism. At the time Henry was distancing England from the papacy, a recrudescence of Roman law was occurring across the European continent. Without Henry's break with the Vatican, Roman law might have crossed the English Channel and altered the course of criminal justice history.

Bridewells

Poverty and lawlessness were rampant in sixteenth-century England. With the influx of destitute beggars from the rural environs to the city, upscale inhabitants feared the threat to public order, concerned that social unrest could result. In the 1550s, Edward VI, son of Henry VIII, established the first house of correction, or Bridewell. Named after Bridewell Palace, a former royal mansion, its substantial space made the transition from a palace for foreign dignitaries to a place for the relief of the poor. Initially used as a poorhouse, by the seventeenth century the Bridewell was transformed into a house of correction.

The Bridewell became an institution in which individuals had to work for their room and board. Among the more mind-numbing tasks were making nails, beating hemp, cleaning sewers, and working the treadmills. Like the modern prison, these houses of correction were designed to be self-financing while at the same time forging better citizens. In 1576, Bridewells were mandated by law throughout England.

Eventually, 300 would be in operation. These institutions would survive into the nineteenth century.

The English Bill of Rights

The Levellers were among the most outspoken reformers of the seventeenth century. While there is still debate over their long-term influence, some historians have accorded them the distinction of having anticipated some of the tenets found in the American Constitution as well as the birth of modern democracy. The Levellers originated among London's artisans and claimed that all Englishmen had the right to suffrage.

Although the Levellers' demands went unheeded in their era, much of their platform would come to fruition in America in the next century. The Levellers' prescience included the prohibition of debt imprisonment, a written constitution and bill of rights, the abolition of aristocratic titles, and a parliament elected by and for the people. Furthermore, they argued that the legal system should be simplified by purging it of Latin and French phraseology, allowing the common people to conduct their own legal affairs without the impediment of expensive legal representation. However, dissension within the Leveller ranks, together with lack of political clout, sealed their ultimate demise.

One of the most valuable legacies of the development of law in England was the writ of habeas corpus.[15] Originally found in article 39 of the Magna Carta, over time it had been often overlooked by those in power. But the Habeas Corpus Amendment Act of 1679 made it impossible to secretly confine anyone. As a result of this legislation, a writ could be issued requiring that an individual accused of a crime be present in court at the time of trial and could not be convicted in absentia.

On the death of King Charles II in 1685, with no legitimate heir in sight, the Crown was passed to his Roman Catholic brother James II. Over the next three years, he retracted the denial of political and civil rights to the Roman Catholic minority. The Glorious Revolution that followed signaled the beginning of a new era in English criminal justice history. As the landed classes rose as one against the monarchy, James fled the country, leaving his Protestant daughter Mary and her husband William the throne.

In 1689, before the Parliament offered the Crown to William III and Mary II, it required their support for a bill of rights. For the first time in English history, Parliament decided who should succeed to the throne. Its impact would reach to the American colonies in the next century. Following this bloodless revolution, the power of absolute monarchy diminished in favor of a constitutional monarchy in which Parliament played an important role. In this new constitutional system, the judiciary was independent of the executive and legislative branches. The rights of all subjects would be protected regardless of one's status. Henceforth, it was illegal for the Crown to levy taxes without the consent of Parliament or to raise or keep a standing army in peacetime without the consent of Parliament. According to the English Bill of Rights, individuals had the right to a speedy trial, the right of freedom from arbitrary arrest, the right to a jury trial, and the right of petition. And almost exactly 100 years later, the American Bill of Rights repeated word for word from its British forerunner that "excessive bail ought not to be required, nor excessive fines imposed, nor cruel and unusual punishments inflicted."

Thief Taking

In 1692, the profession of thief taking (bounty hunting) was inaugurated by the Act for Encouraging the Apprehending of Highwaymen.[16] Without a public police force and suffering a tremendous outlaw problem, the English government began offering a forty-pound reward for the arrest and successful prosecution of any highwayman. In addition, thief takers were entitled to the highwayman's horse, harness, arms, and other possessions, unless they proved to be stolen. Initially, thief takers were bandits who turned in accomplices for the promised blood money (reward). However, despite the best intentions of the Highwayman Act, highway robbery continued unabated. Closer to medieval-style policing, thief taking was completely ineffective in tracking down criminals beyond parish boundaries. It was more effective on the local level.

In 1715, underworld boss Jonathan Wild elevated thief taking to a science and over the next ten years was credited with sending over 100 criminals to the London gallows. His exploits earned him the title "thief-taker general," even though he eventually followed his colleagues to the gallows himself in 1725. Most police historians consider thief taking a precursor to the 1740s Bow Street Runners of Sir Henry Fielding (see chapter 3). According to one historian, "Nature intended Jonathan Wild for a sleuth, and had he been born two centuries later it is probable that he would have won a responsible position at Scotland Yard."[17]

As the leading criminal of London in the first half of the eighteenth century, Jonathan Wild (1682–1725) dominated the London underworld from 1715 until his death in 1725. During the 1720s, London suffered one of its worst crime waves. Since most powerful criminals were protected from prosecution through bribes and graft, the only response the government could muster was to begin paying rewards for the capture of robbers and prescribe the death penalty for most offenses. After a criminal apprenticeship to the London city marshal, who taught him the trade of receiving stolen goods, Wild set up an office near the Old Bailey, where he acted as agent between thief and victim.

A master at self-promotion, Wild called himself thief-taker general by 1718. Wild exploited the law to the fullest, and his posse of thief catchers is considered by many a precursor to police departments. For ten years, he was considered the most efficient gang breaker in England. Wild improved an ingenious system for receiving stolen goods developed by Moll Cutpurse[18] in the previous century that involved getting higher prices for stolen goods by selling them back to the original owners who were willing to pay more. Wild improved on the system by posing first as a private thief taker who went after offenders to subsequently collect a reward once the objects were returned. He then organized bands of thieves whom he directed in his various schemes. Any thieves who attempted to compete with him he would set up for arrest and execution. Therefore, by aiding the law in his capacity as thief taker, Wild used the law to fatten his own coffers. Highwaymen gave London a wide berth between 1723 and 1725, as evidenced by the fact none were hanged at Tyburn during this time span.

In 1718, anti–thief taker legislation was passed, elevating thief taking to a felony—a capital offense. Over the next seven years, Wild enjoyed the protection of influential patrons, survived an assassination attempt, and had acquired extensive real estate holdings. Despite supporters who argued that he helped control the gang problem, Wild was hanged in 1725.

NOTABLE TRIALS

Guy Fawkes (1606)

During the early seventeenth century, Protestantism was firmly entrenched as the state church in England. Under James I, both Catholics and Puritans felt the sting of oppression. When the Anglican clergy noted that their congregations were dwindling, James ordered Catholic priests to leave the country. Naturally incensed, Catholics hatched the desperate Gunpowder Plot, hoping to reclaim the Crown and country. The Gunpowder Plot, which was probably hatched in 1604, was the brainchild of Robert Catesby, who suggested to several others that Catholics could seize power in one fell swoop by blowing up Parliament when it met on November 5, 1605. On that day, King James I and members of the House of Commons and the House of Lords would be assembled, and in the resulting chaos the plotters hoped to establish a Catholic government.

One of the plotters traveled to the Continent to recruit aid from British Catholics in exile.

Among those who jumped at the chance to restore Catholicism was a dashing, young man named Guy Fawkes (ca. 1570–1606). Having assembled their cast of conspirators, the plotters next rented a house next to Parliament and continued with their plan to detonate the building with gunpowder. In October 1605, a letter was delivered to the king warning him not to attend the forthcoming session of Parliament. The conspirators soon fled, leaving only Fawkes behind to complete the plan. He either had been assigned or had volunteered to ignite the explosion minutes before making his own escape. On November 4, Fawkes was arrested before the plan could take effect. Three days later, four conspirators were killed and several arrested, tried, and executed.

The trial of Guy Fawkes and seven others began on January 27, 1606. The conspirators stood waiting in Star Chamber waiting for the arrival of the judges. After the indictment was read out, the eight pleaded not guilty. The first lawyer to speak for the Crown noted that the matter before the court was one of treason, "but of such horror, and monstrous nature." In the subsequent proceedings, every attempt was made to tarnish the Catholic Church by implicating it in the plot. All the conspirators eventually confessed to treason after lengthy torture and questioning in the Tower of London. According to protocol in treason trials in this era, it was customary for the defense not to offer any testimony. The defendants were then asked if they had anything to say as to why the sentence of death should not be pronounced against him. Several asked for mercy. In a day of quick justice and little time for appeals, on January 29, 1606, just two days after the trial, four of the men were dragged lying on their backs to the scaffold at St. Paul's churchyard for the traditional punishment for treason: being hanged, drawn and quartered. If an individual committed murder, he was usually hanged, unless it was an aristocrat, in which case he was beheaded. The only offense considered worse than murder was high treason, which was considered the equivalent of murdering one's

country, by killing or plotting to kill the nation's sovereign lord, the king. The following day, Guy Fawkes was among the last four executed.

Until the eighteenth century, convicted traitors in many parts of western Europe were hanged, drawn, and quartered. The prisoner was typically drawn to the place of execution on a hurdle. Then he was hanged until almost dead. He was then cut down, and the real terror began. The victim, still alive and conscious in most cases, was next disemboweled. Occasionally, this was preceded by castration in order to symbolize that the traitor would be unable to sire future traitors. The bowels and entrails were then burned, and the victim was beheaded and quartered into four parts. At the conclusion of the public spectacle, the body parts were mounted on the city gates as a warning to future traitors. The head would be parboiled before being exhibited on London Bridge for deterrence value.

There is a certain mystery as to why Fawkes became a legendary figure. Perhaps it was because he did not flee with the others or had volunteered for the most dangerous task. Although the plot was never carried out, the Gunpowder Plot revived the old fear of Catholics and of papist conspiracy. Fawkes's display of courage under painful torture and his position as an almost legendary malefactor is celebrated each November 5 in Great Britain with fireworks displays and bonfires.

CONCLUSIONS

Placed in historical perspective, the signing of the Magna Carta in 1215 was preceded by Germanic invasions and followed by the Renaissance. It signaled an era that would witness the erection of the great European cathedrals and an age of faith marked by the Crusades. The growth of an urban economy gave rise to towns, commerce, markets, and fairs as European civilization expanded in all directions. The thirteenth century witnessed the birth of Parliament and rising crime rates in England. Universities flourished in Oxford, Paris, and

Salerno. In a society dominated by the church and theology, craft and merchant guilds prospered; windmills, mechanical clocks, and eyeglasses soon became commonplace; and hard liquor was distilled in Salerno.

Although the Tudor era saw great strides in the development of criminal justice institutions, torture and confinement still characterized the treatment of defendants. British subjects had acquired certain basic rights, but much was ill defined and arbitrary. The Norman era introduced many of the prototypes that would become familiar components of the American criminal justice system, ranging from constables, coroners, bailiffs, and justices of the peace to the sheriff and the marshal. Meanwhile, Parliament saw a steady development from the innovations of Edward I to the Stuart Restoration in 1660, when the House of Lords and Commons began to organize as separate branches of Parliament. At this point, the power of the Commoners increased quickly as the social distinction between lords and commoners diminished. Helping bring the classes closer together was the evolution of the English language, which integrated the French of the Normans with the German of the Anglo-Saxons.

The position of bailiff as an officer of the court developed out of the Statute of Winchester of 1285, in which King Edward endeavored to create a uniform law enforcement system. Initially responsible for tracking transient strangers in medieval towns after dark, today's bailiff is responsible mainly for keeping order in the court and protecting the security of jury members during deliberations.

Point–Counterpoint
Trial by Ordeal and the Fourth Lateran Council: Determining guilt or Innocence (1215)

Prior to the 13th century there were few methods for determining the guilt or innocence of suspected criminals. In the years leading up to the Fourth Lateran Council, most communities relied on the time tested methods of trial by ordeal or battle or the compurgation oath. Such "judgements of God" were accepted by most members of the community,

since there was little if any protocol that could be confused with trial by jury.

In 1215 church leaders convening for the Fourth Lateran Council forbade clergy members from taking part in the ordeal. Although the curtailment of such practices in most of Europe was gradual, the ordeals were almost immediately ended in England. The decline of the ordeal was a turning point in the history of adjudication procedure. Subsequently, the English common law system would adopt the adversarial jury trial, while continental Europe leaned toward an inquisitorial system. The first passage describes the variety of ordeals popular since before the Norman Conquest of 1066. The second passage illustrates the persistence of trial by battle and oath helpers as a method of determining guilt or innocence. Notice that the "normal" number of oath helpers was twelve, a harbinger of the future jury system.

The ordeal was more extensively employed in the procedure of the pre-Norman period than in the later. It was the typical mode of trial among the English, contrasting English procedure with the procedure of their Norman conquerors. With them it was, until the Conquest, the only *Judicium Dei* so far as existing monuments bear witness.

This mode of trial finally received a fatal blow from the well-known decree of the Lateran Council of the year 1215, at which it was ordered that the ordeal should be discontinued throughout Christendom.

There were four forms of ordeal, to wit, by cold water, by hot water, by hot iron and by morsel or "corsnaed." The first two were in the time of Glanvill for the poor and partly unfree classes, the "rustics"; the third was for the lay freemen; whilst the last, as we have seen, was for the clergy. The accused, however, appears to have had an election at one time between the modes by fire and by water. Whether this was true in the twelfth century is doubtful.

Each was undergone after the most solemn religious ceremonial. In the case of the cold water ordeal, a fast of three days duration was first submitted to in the presence of a priest; then the accused was brought into the church, where a mass was chanted,

Source: Roscoe Pound, *Readings on the History and System of Common Law*, Boston: Boston Book Company, 1913, pp. 105–107; Sir Frederick Pollock and Frederic William Maitland, *The History of English Law Before the Time of Edward I*, London, 1898, 2nd edition, pp. 599–601.

followed by the communion. Before communion, however, the accused was adjured by the Father, Son and Holy Ghost, by the Christian Religion which he professed, by the only begotten Son, by the Holy Trinity, by the Holy Gospels, and by the Holy Relics, not to partake of the communion if he was guilty. Communion having been partaken, *adjuratio aquae* is made by the priest in which the water is asked to cast forth the accused if guilty, and to receive him into its depths if innocent. After these ceremonies, the accused is stripped, kisses the book and the cross, is sprinkled with holy water, and then cast into the depths. If he sank he was adjudged not guilty; if he swam he was pronounced guilty.

Similar religious ceremonies were performed in the other forms of ordeal. If the accuser elected for the accused the trial by hot water, the water was placed in a vessel and heated to the highest degree. Then if the party were accused of an inferior crime, he plunged his arm into the water as far as the wrist and brought forth a stone suspended by a cord; if he were accused of a great crime, the stone was suspended deeper, so as to require him to plunge his arm as far as his elbow. The hand of the accused was then bandaged and at the end of three days the bandage was removed. If it now appeared that the wound was healed, the accused was deemed innocent, but if it had festered he was held guilty.

If trial by hot iron was elected, a piece of iron weighing either one or three pounds, according to the nature of the crime charged, was heated under the direction of men standing by, whose duty it was to see that a proper heat was obtained, and kept until the time for the test had arrived. During the final ceremonies the fire was left and the iron allowed to remain in the embers. It was raised and with an invocation to the Deity, given into the naked hand of the accused, who carried it the distance of nine feet when it was dropped, and the hand bandaged as in the case of the hot water ordeal to abide by the same test.

The ordeal of the morsel, accompanied by similar ceremonials, was undergone by the accused undertaking to swallow a piece of barley bread or a piece of cheese of the weight of an ounce; if he succeeded without serious difficulty, he was deemed innocent, but if he choked and grew black in the face he was deemed guilty.

Then came a sudden change. The Lateran Council of 1215 forbad the clergy to take part in the ceremony. Some wise churchmen had long protested against it; but perhaps the conflict with flagrant heresy and the consequent exacerbation of ecclesiastical law had something to do with the suppression of this old test. In England this decree found a prompt obedience such as it hardly found elsewhere; the ordeal was abolished at once and for ever. Flourishing in the last records of John's reign, we can not find it in any later rolls. Our criminal procedure was deprived of its handiest weapon; but to this catastrophe we must return hereafter.

The judicial combat is an ordeal, a bilateral ordeal. The church had shown less favour to it than to the unilateral ordeals, perhaps because it had involved pagan ceremonies. Therefore we hear nothing of it until the Normans bring it hither. In later days English ecclesiastics had no deep dislike for it. It was a sacral process. What triumphed was not brute force but truth. The combatant who was worsted was a convicted perjurer.

The ordeal involves or is preceded by an oath; but even when the proof is to consist merely of oaths, a supernatural element is present. The swearer satisfies human justice by taking the oath. If he has sworn falsely, he is exposed to the wrath of God and in some subsequent proceeding may perhaps be convicted of perjury; but in the meantime he has performed the task that the law set him; he has given the requisite proof. In some rare cases a defendant was allowed to swear away a charge by his own oath; usually what was required of him was an oath supported by the oaths of oath-helpers. There are good reasons for believing that in the earliest period he had to find kinsmen as oath-helpers. When he was denying an accusation which, if not disproved, would have been cause for a blood-feud, his kinsmen had a lively interest in the suit, and naturally they were called upon to assist him in freeing himself and them from the consequences of the imputed crime. The plaintiff, if he thought that there had been perjury, would have the satisfaction of knowing that some twelve of his enemies were devoted to divine vengeance. In course of time the law no longer required kinsmen, and we see a rationalistic tendency which would convert the oath-helpers into impartial 'witnesses to character.' Sometimes the chief swearer must choose them from among a number of men designated by the court or by his opponent; sometimes they must be his neighbours. Then again, instead of swearing positively that his oath is true, they may swear that it is true to the best of their knowledge. In some cases few, in others many helpers are demanded. A normal number is 12; but this may be reduced to 6 or 3, or raised to 24, 36, 72.

SOURCES

Bartlett, Robert. 1986. *Trial by Fire and Water: The Medieval Judicial Ordeal*. Oxford: Clarendon Press.

Bellamy, John. 1973. *Crime and Public Order in England in the Later Middle Ages*. London: Routledge and Kegan Paul.

———. 1979. *The Tudor Law of Treason: An Introduction*. London: Routledge and Kegan Paul.

Blackstone, William. 1962. *Commentaries on the Laws of England*. Boston: Beacon Press.

Bleackley, Horace. 1929. *The Hangmen of England*. London: Chapman and Hall.

Brown, Richard Maxwell. 1991. *No Duty to Retreat: Violence and Values in American History and Society*. Norman: University of Oklahoma Press.

Cantor, Norman. 1997. *Imagining the Law: Common Law and the Foundations of the American Legal System*. New York: HarperCollins.

Cockburn, J. S., ed. 1977. *Crime in England, 1550–1800*. Princeton, N.J.: Princeton University Press.

Given, James Buchanan. 1977. *Society and Homicide in Thirteenth-Century England*. Stanford, Calif.: Stanford University Press.

Gladwin, Irene. 1974. *The Sheriff: The Man and His Office*. London: Victor Gollancz.

Goebel, Julius, Jr. 1976. *Felony and Misdemeanor: A Study in the History of Criminal Law*. Philadelphia: University of Pennsylvania Press.

Hamil, Frederick C. 1936. "The King's Approvers: A Chapter in the History of English Criminal Law." *Speculum* 11(April): 238–58.

———. 1937. "Presentment of Englishry and the Murder Fine." *Speculum* 12(July): 285–98.

Hamilton, Bernard. 1981. *The Medieval Inquisition*. New York: Holmes and Meier Publishers.

Hamilton, Dick. 1979. *Foul Bills and Dagger Money: 800 Years of Lawyers and Lawbreakers*. London: Cassell.

Haynes, Alan. 1994. *The Gunpowder Plot*. London: Sutton Publishing.

Hibbert, Christopher. 1957. *The Road to Tyburn: The Story of Jack Sheppard and the Eighteenth Century London Underworld*. Cleveland: World Publishing Company.

Howson, Gerald. 1971. *Thief-Taker General: The Rise and Fall of Jonathan Wild*. New York: St. Martin's Press.

Kaye, J. M. 1967. "The Early History of Murder and Manslaughter." *Law Quarterly Review* 83: 365–95.

Keeton, George W. 1966. *The Norman Conquest and the Common Law*. London: Ernest Benn.

Maitland, F. W. 1965. (H. A. L. Fisher, ed.), *The Constitutional History of England*. Cambridge: Cambridge University Press.

McCall, Andrew. 1979. *The Medieval Underworld*. London: Hamish Hamilton.

McMullen, John L. 1984. *The Canting Crew: London's Criminal Underworld, 1550–1700*. New Brunswick, N.J.: Rutgers University Press.

Merryman, John Henry. 1969. *The Civil Law Tradition*. Stanford, Calif.: Stanford University Press.

Pike, Luke Owen. 1968. *A History of Crime in England*. 2 vols. Montclair, N.J.: Patterson Smith.

Pollock, Frederick, and Frederic William Maitland. 1978. *The History of English Law: Before the Time of Edward I*. Cambridge: Cambridge University Press.

Poole, A. L. 1986. *Domesday Book to Magna Carta, 1087–1216*. 2nd ed. Oxford: Clarendon Press.

Pringle, Patrick. 1958. *The Thief-Takers*. London: Museum Press.

Sharpe, J. A. 1984. *Crime in Early Modern England*. London: Longman.

Tobias, J. J. 1979. *Crime and Police in England, 1700–1900*. New York: St. Martin's Press.

Warren, W. L. 1973. *Henry II*. Berkeley: University of California Press.

CRITICAL THINKING QUESTIONS

1. Discuss the development of law enforcement in England during the Anglo-Saxon and Norman periods. How did the Norman invasion impact the evolution of English peacekeeping?

2. Which culture had the most impact on the development of English criminal justice institutions? Discuss in terms of German, French, and Danish influence.

3. What was the role of the church in the English criminal justice system? What were some of the differences between canon and secular law?

4. Trace the evolution of the legal system in England between the Norman Conquest (1066) and the English Bill of Rights (1689).

5. Why is the reign of King Henry II considered a turning point in the history of the English legal system?

6. Discuss patterns of criminal activity and violence in England between the Norman period and the emergence of the thief takers in the seventeenth century.

7. Choose several English legal documents and discuss their impact on English criminal justice (Statute of Winchester, Magna Carta, English Bill of Rights, and so on).

8. Why are the thief takers considered progenitors of modern policing?

CRIMINAL JUSTICE HISTORY
ON THE INTERNET

A plethora of links on British legal history are accessible at www.lgu.ac.uk/lawlinks/history.htm. A vast collection of English legal history materials is located at vi.uh.edu/pages/bob/elhone/elhmat.html. Anything a student wants to know about the British monarchy through the ages can be found at www.royal.gov.uk/history/index.htm.

The history of the coroner's office is at www.users.imaginet.fr/~jebrana/students/dinh.html. For Danelaw and Scandinavian impact on Great Britain, see www.wmich.edu/medieval/rawl/keynes1/biblioh.htm. The story of early English policing is covered in detail at www.drsoft.com/allsaints/pnotes.htm. The Internet Medieval Sourcebook is a great resource for Medieval legal history at www.fordham.edu/halsall/sbook-law.html.

The Medieval Sourcebook has many links covering early English justice issues. The 1170 Inquest of Sheriffs is at www.fordham.edu/halsall/source/isheriffs.html, and the laws of William the Conqueror are at www.fordham.edu/halsall/source/will1-lawsb.html.

LEARN MORE

Assize of Clarendon:
www.yale.edu/lawweb/avalon/assizecl.htm

Constitutions of Clarendon:
www.yale.edu/lawweb/avalon/constcl.htm

The Domesday Book: www.socserv2.socsci.mcmaster.ca/~econ/ugcm/3113/maitland/domesday

Fourth Lateran Council:
www.newadvent.org/cathen/09018a.htm

Magna Carta:
vi.uh.edu/pages/bob/elhone/Magna.html

Magna Carta and its American legacy:
www.nara.gov/exhall/charters/magnacarta/magintrp.html

Map of Anglo-Saxon England:
www.georgetown.edu/cball/oe/oe-map.html

Links to law museums:
www.duhaime.org.museum.htm

Dictionary of medieval terms:
orb.rhodes/Medieval_Terms.html

Origin of Lady of Justice:
www.commonlaw.com/Justice.html

Secrets of the Norman invasion:
www.cablenet/pages/book/index.htm

Time line of British history:
britannia.com/history/time1.html

Torture and death penalty instruments:
www.cecut.org.mx/galeria/tortura/torture.htm

Women and the law:
vi.uh.edu/pages/bob/elhone/rules.html

NOTES

1. The Angles came from southern Denmark, the Saxons from continental Germany, and the Jutes from Jutland.

2. The most convincing explanation for the origin of the term *hundred* was that this unit comprised 100 households or perhaps was responsible for furnishing 100 men for the national defense.

3. Only the laws of Kent and Wessex from this era have survived.

4. The word *felony* is probably derived either from the Latin *fel,* meaning "one filled with venom," or from *fee*

(property held under feudal tenure) and *lon* (price), suggesting that there is a price or loss of property if one commits a crime.

5. The *assize,* which literally means "a sitting" in Norman French, was a twice-yearly royal court held in each county, normally at the county town. This procedure is credited with establishing the practice of local citizens forming grand juries to present the accused for trial by the traveling justices.

6. Merryman (1969, pp. 10–11).

7. In the time of Edward III, benefit of clergy was not available for highway robbers, and in 1531 it was prohibited in cases of robbery and murder. Benefit of clergy was finally abolished for all crimes in 1841.

8. There are several explanations for the title of this survey. One contemporary writer implied that the inquiry was so all-encompassing and inquisitive that it reminded people of the day of judgment, hence "Domesday." Others speculate that the hundreds convened for inquests on the Domesdays, or lawdays.

9. Warren (1973, p. 354).

10. Pollock and Maitland (1978, 2:673).

11. This phrase was misconstrued from the phrase *prison forte et dure.* According to tradition, the accused was tortured until entering a plea at arraignment. Although the last fatal use of this torture occurred in 1658, the practice was not discontinued until 1772, when it was replaced by a simple plea of guilty.

12. A warrior as well as a lawmaker, Edward's legacy in popular culture seems to be his brutal execution of William Wallace of Hollywood's *Braveheart* fame.

13. It got its name because of its interior design, which included a painted wooden ceiling replete with painted stars.

14. *Murdrum* is derived from *morth,* which means "secret killing."

15. Meaning "you have the body," the writ of habeas corpus was designed to aid those wrongfully imprisoned. The writ ordered any official who is holding another in confinement to bring "the body" into court to establish whether the confinement is legal.

16. English highwaymen operated on horseback and usually wore masks during their robberies committed on the roads leading into London. Most sources suggest that highwaymen killed fewer victims than their horseless counterparts because of their ability to escape quickly. Although they occasionally engaged in gun battles with their victims or soldiers, treacherous accomplices and informers represented a far greater danger.

17. Bleackley (1929, p. 47).

18. Born Mary Frith in 1584, from a young age she dressed like a man, carried a sword, and smoked a pipe as she made the rounds of local taverns. She became so adept at a ruse by which she cut the strings on leather purses that were used in the sixteenth century to carry valuables that she was accorded the sobriquet "Moll Cutpurse." Despite a life of crime in which she was branded four times on the hands as a thief, she lived until 1659, well into her seventies.

3

CRIMINAL JUSTICE IN EARLY AMERICA (1597–1740)

TIME LINE

1597	Transportation to America authorized	1620	Mayflower Compact and settlement of Plymouth by Pilgrims
1603	James I condemns witchcraft and enchantment	1630	Massachusetts Bay Company and settlement of Boston by Puritans
1607	Settlement of Jamestown by Anglicans	1631	First night watch established in Boston
1611	Virginia introduces *Lawes Divine, Moral, and Martiall*	1640	Origin of the Dutch *schout*
1615	James I introduces transportation by decree	1641	Massachusetts *Body of Liberties* adopted
1619	House of Burgesses first convenes	1648	*Body of Liberties* revised and renamed *Laws and Liberties*
1619	First African slaves brought to Virginia	1648	Dutch experiment with paid night watch in New York City

1661	Barbadian slave code provides model for southern colonies
1676	Bacon's Rebellion
1682	Penn's *Frame of Government,* or "Great Law"
1692	Salem witchcraft trials
1704	First slave patrol established in the South
1705	Virginia Slave Code passed
1718	Quaker Code repealed and replaced by harsh English laws
1718–1776	Under the Transportation Act, 30,000 British convicts transported to American colonies
1727	Virginia creates its first slave patrols
1735	Trial of John Peter Zenger
1740	South Carolina introduces basic slave laws of the South

The history of American criminal justice begins with the transplanting of European institutions to the New World. While several Spanish communities existed in parts of what is now the United States decades prior to the first permanent English settlements in Jamestown and Plymouth, they did not contribute much to the development of American criminal justice institutions. Initially, the history of colonial criminal justice is the story of thirteen separate colonies prior to the American Revolution and independence in 1776. The criminal codes, law enforcement systems, courts, and punishments resembled those of England, Holland, Spain, and France, depending on the colony. The development of American criminal justice is the story of the modification of this heritage. In order to understand the history of the American criminal justice system, it is necessary to appreciate the remarkable diversity of colonial America.

The first steps toward English colonization of North America were taken not by the Crown but by private enterprise. Because of the high costs associated with establishing a colony, the English monarchy could not afford to colonize on its own. Instead, the Crown was content to sit back as a passive partner in the endeavor, a role that would later come back to haunt the English in the subsequent American Revolution. Except for granting charters, contracts, trade rights, and permitting migration, English officialdom let merchant entrepreneurs, Anglicans, Puritans, Catholics, and Quakers lay the foundations of early America.

An examination of the development of criminal justice in each of the thirteen colonies is beyond the scope and aim of this chapter. Instead, the focus will be on an important colony representing each of three colonial regions—regions that were culturally, politically, and socioeconomically similar. Virginia represents the southern colonies. Pennsylvania exemplifies many of the characteristics of the middle colonies, and Massachusetts personifies the complexities of life in colonial New England. Those drawn to Virginia had economic ambitions, while mainly religious idealism motivated those who came to early New England and Pennsylvania. Each immigrant group required discipline and order to realize its goals. Since the colonists were recruited in different ways and lived in divergent conditions of climate and soil, it should not be surprising then that the laws and customs of the colonies were quite diverse.

During the 1600s, England was awash in political and religious upheaval, both of which would influence the structure of the English colonies as well as their developing criminal justice systems. Religious persecution in England proved a particularly powerful motivating force for colonization in the early years of the American colonies. Roman Catholics found a haven in Maryland, while Quakers sought refuge in Pennsylvania, southern New Jersey, and Rhode Island. Nearly 30,000 English Puritans, technically part of the official Church of England, immigrated to New England. Other religious minorities migrated from continental Europe seeking sanctuary from oppression as well.

Not all newcomers to America came of their own accord. In 1615, King James I introduced transportation, or banishment, as one way to rid England of its hordes of convicts and "sturdy beggars." Offenders were not shipped to places unknown or to freedom but were sent to English colonies to perform profitable service. Between 1718 and 1776, close to 30,000 British convicts were transported to the American colonies. Mostly male and in their twenties, not unlike their twentieth-century incarcerated counterparts, the majority were destined for the Chesapeake plantations of Maryland and Virginia. At only a third of the price of an African slave, white indentured servants were affordable to the smaller planters, much to the dismay of the large plantation owners who protested the system. An alternative to branding, hanging, mutilation, and execution at home, transportation marked an important transition in penal practice and provided a much-needed labor source to the developing colonies.

Indentured servants arrived in America after signing a contract in which they agreed to work anywhere from four to seven years without wages in exchange for transportation to America. A servant's contract could be bought and sold without his consent, and he could be beaten for disobedience or running away. In the early years, on completion of their terms of indenture, servants received fifty acres of land and, later cash, clothing, and food. Beginning with the first African slaves in the early 1600s, the institution of racial slavery evolved slowly in the seventeenth-century

colonies. By the 1680s, there was a shortage of white indentured servants, leading to dependence on African slavery. By the 1680s, it would be the preferred form of labor on the plantations.

The English colonists who ventured to America in the early seventeenth century were used to a rigid social system and determined to maintain order among themselves at any cost. The structure of each colony would later influence not only what crimes would be punished but also how punishment would be meted out. Early colonial communities were tiny villages, worlds to themselves where everyone knew each other's business. Many authorities suggest that you could fit the entire European population of 1650s America inside a modern sports complex. No scandal was too small to incur the wrath of the community.

Despite a number of experiments with religious laws and political compacts, the only source of government that was regarded as legitimate was one that recognized the Crown as the source of all legitimate authority. Thus, colonial institutions mirrored the government in England. Each colony had a governor, usually appointed (several were elected) by the king and in a sense corresponding to the monarch, as well as a governor's council, or upper house of the legislature, that was appointed by the monarch and corresponded to the hereditary House of Lords. And each had an elected lower house of the legislature, selected by voters who had to meet various property, race, gender, and age qualifications. The variety and complexion of the colonial courts was so complicated that they almost defy description.

VIRGINIA AND THE SOUTHERN COLONIES

In 1606, King James I granted the Virginia Company a charter to establish a colony in the New World. According to the document, the inhabitants of the colony would enjoy "all liberties, franchises, and immunities . . . as if they had been abiding and borne within this realme of

Englande." On May 13, 1607, English common law dropped anchor on the banks of the James River in Virginia in the form of 104 English colonists. No one could have then imagined the degree to which the common law would be altered in the new land. The transmutation of legal codes and procedures were in part due to the new environment and harsh living conditions. Indians, disease, lack of discipline, and distance from the motherland, in time, gave birth to criminal justice procedures significantly different from those that landed on American shores with the first English colonists.

The founding of Jamestown was a venture financed as a short-term joint stock company, each investor sharing the costs, risks, and profits that Virginia might yield. Members of the early Virginia Company were an assortment of gentlemen, servants, and vagrants. They settled in the New World hoping to make a profit for the company and for the Crown and to improve their own prospects at the same time. After agreeing to work for the company for seven years to pay for their passage over, the servants were free to seek their own fortunes.

The Virginia colonists found neither gold nor silver as the Spanish had previously. Unprepared, ill supplied, and sickly from the confines of ship travel, survivors of the passage over continued to perish in the hostile climate. Tropical disease, poor nutrition, and outright starvation ensured that since debarking, about four in five, regardless of rank or race, died within the first year. Rations were in such short supply that one of the first recorded executions in the colonies resulted from one man's murdering of his wife and unborn child for the purposes of cannibalism.

Instead of precious metals, Virginians' wealth would come from the cultivation of tobacco. With the introduction of this moneymaking crop, settlers refused to grow anything else. A "boomtown" mentality took root in which the single men of the colony, at least the few who were healthy enough, lay about the streets in a raucous display of drinking and gambling. Before resorting to slavery in the late seventeenth century, a large labor force of white indentured male servants was required to harvest the tobacco crops, resulting in a ratio of from four to six men for every one woman. These conditions contrasted sharply with New England's settlement by families. The contrasts would also be reflected in criminal justice developments in the first colonies of each region: Virginia in the South and Massachusetts in New England.

The Lawgivers

Initially, Virginia was supposed to be governed by a royal council appointed by the king. Few could have predicted that the small band of settlers would fashion their own government. By the eighteenth century, all colonies, except for one, had bicameral legislatures like the English Parliament. The upper house, or council as it was known, consisted of between twelve and eighteen members appointed by the Crown or other high-ranking officials, such as the colony's governor. Usually members of the landed gentry and the elite, they were the dominant group of the colony. The lower house was an elected body, selected from the smaller, propertied class. Voting privileges were initially restricted to free white Englishmen who were heads of households. This left a large portion of inhabitants and dependents, including tenant farmers, indentured servants, laborers, blacks, artisans, and women disenfranchised with little voice in political life.

The first representative assembly held in America was convened at Jamestown's House of Burgesses in 1619. Each of Virginia's eleven settlements sent two representatives who sat with the governor and his Council. A miniature Parliament, the initial convocation introduced "Blue Laws" prohibiting drunkenness, gambling, idleness, "excess in apparel," absence from church, and sundry misdemeanors. During the six-day meeting of the first assembly, the Church of England was proclaimed the established church, and the Virginia Company was solicited for financial assistance to establish a college. In short order, Virginia made the transition from martial law (1611–1616) to a self-governing community, laying the foundation for genuine democracy. However, it would prove a false start by 1624, when the Crown revoked the Virginia Company Charter and took over Virginia as a royal colony.

Within two decades of their arrival, Virginia colonists had adapted English criminal justice practices to the New World. Although most procedures dealing with indictment, arrest, bail, trial, judgment, and execution of sentence were familiar to any Englishman, alterations were made to these traditional processes. For example, during the early years of Virginia, the court system changed. While the county courts tried minor criminal cases, felony cases were heard at the General Court, which convened in Jamestown. But traveling to Jamestown could be a hardship for slave owners from the more far-flung reaches of the colony. A specialized type of court, called Oyer and Terminer, was created to handle serious criminal complaints involving slaves. These special courts were held specifically to try slaves accused of capital offenses in county courts. Here we see an example of how the institution of slavery and the widely dispersed population contributed to the modification of criminal justice procedures in America.

The status of blacks in colonial Virginia was incredibly complicated. Initially, some were indentured servants who were allowed to own property and marry and testify against whites in court once free of their indentures. In rare instances, free blacks even purchased white indentured servants. A very few arrived free, one even owning a slave himself. But most were permanently unfree. Virginia passed the first statute revealing the central position of slavery in the colonies in 1660. In a rather simple statement, the law identified a class of blacks as servants for life. Any white servant who attempted to escape with one of these servants for life was expected to serve the same amount of time as his accomplice after being captured, in essence creating a few white slaves. The subsequent passage of the Virginia Slave Code of 1705 was one of the first

slave codes in the South and established slavery as essentially race based and an integral part of the plantation economy. This Slave Code also contained provisions concerning the murder and torture of slaves, the legal status of children born to enslaved women, restrictions for interactions with nonslaves, and penalties for failing to obey commands. In perhaps the most draconian section of the code, escaped slaves could be dismembered if returned home alive.

According to Michael Stephen Hindus, although blacks were "accorded few procedural rights in the courts," a "formal system of trying slaves shows that despite plantation justice, formal law and authority reached the plantation to a considerable extent."[1] As evidence, Hindus cites the basic slave law of South Carolina. Established in 1740, it continued as the basic penal code for blacks until the end of the Civil War in the 1860s. The South Carolina code typified southern law for this era. Prohibited from offering sworn testimony, blacks were also not permitted to initiate prosecutions, unless it was done by a free third party. While all white laws applied to blacks, there were many others that only applied to blacks. Crimes such as assault with intent to rape, wounding a white man, burning crops, attempted poisoning, and insurrection were all capital crimes for black slaves. Punishment for white offenders who committed similar crimes was usually less punitive.

Blacks received some protections under the 1740 law code. Brutal treatment was prohibited, and any person who killed a slave was fined 700 pounds. By the 1820s, when the killing of slaves became more common, it became a capital offense, leading a court justice to submit that this action "elevated slaves from chattels personal to human beings."[2]

By the 1660s and 1670s, servants and slaves became more clearly defined within the legal code. Black slaves were barred from interracial marriage and sexual relations and prohibited from traveling or owning weapons without written permits. Slaves were even forbidden to learn to read or write. If a slave was caught learning to write, the slave would have a finger amputated. In 1669, Virginia won the distinction as the first colony to allow the killing of "rambunctious" slaves without fear of criminal sanctions. At that same time, slave masters were forbidden to free slaves unless they left the colony when freed. Any white person who married a nonwhite individual was banished from the colony. As the components of racial slavery became more rigid, white servants were enjoying more privileges. In contrast to their former black counterparts in bondage, white servants could no longer be stripped and publicly whipped.

Crime and Punishment

The early years of the Virginia colony were lean ones, rife with poor health, starvation, discord, Indian conflict, and mutinous conditions. Circumstances dictated law codes more severe than common law, and from its earliest days colonial authorities relied on brutal corporal punishments and hangings. When Sir Thomas Dale succeeded Captain John Smith (ca. 1580–1631) as leader of the colony in 1611, he instituted martial discipline and the law code titled *Lawes, Divine, Morall and Martiall*, known as "Dale's Laws." The harshness of the law code has led some commentators to draw parallels with Draco's code of ancient Athens. Not only were the colonists expected to attend daily church services under penalty of six months' service in the galleys of Virginia company ships, but repeated absence from Sunday services could elicit the death penalty. On one occasion, a Virginia colonist was severely punished for making false charges against another colonist. As punishment, the offender was sentenced to be "disarmed and have his arms broken and his tongue bored through with an awl" and was then forced to walk through a gauntlet of forty men and battered by each one. Finally, the unfortunate individual was kicked out of the fort and banished from the vicinity.[3]

Under Dale's Laws, capital punishment was mandated for almost two dozen offenses, including repeated blasphemy, unlicensed trading with the Indian tribes, stealing boats, embezzlement,

the unlicensed killing of cattle, and the destruction of crops. Punishments for even minor violations were barbaric under the military courts, with accounts of individuals being burned at the stake, broken on the wheel, and bound to a tree with a bodkin thrust through the tongue and left to starve to death.

In 1618, a more moderate law code was introduced, but before the Enlightenment of the eighteenth century and the creation of the penitentiary system, there were few alternatives to the tradition of harsh corporal punishment and hanging. Public shaming, or exhibitory punishment, was often effective in curbing petty crime. Criminals that placed a burden on society, such as drunkards, vagrants, and other ne'er-do-wells, were treated as a serious threat to the community. Malefactors were forced to sit in the stocks or stand in pillories or offer public penance in church for violating conventional moral standards. As in the medieval past, women were often punished using local water sources. The ducking stool astride a prominent riverbank saw frequent use when women acted outside their traditional gender roles. The most frequent offenses committed by women included "bad speeches" or verbal abuse. The aegis of guilt fell more readily on women in cases of fornication and adultery since pregnancy outside the confines of marriage was sure witness to the act. Women who committed bastardy, or childbirth outside marriage, were also harshly punished in the Chesapeake colonies. If the recent mother could not afford to pay a fine, she was liable to be publicly whipped while naked to the waist. Adultery was a serious crime, but only for women because it was defined in terms of the woman's status. If she was married, illicit sex was considered adultery; if she was unmarried, it was fornication even if her partner was married. Infanticide and witchcraft were also mainly the domain of females. However, no woman was ever executed for witchcraft in Virginia and the southern colonies.

One way to contrast the punishment of sexual offenses in New England and Virginia is to examine the punishment for adultery. In Massachusetts, both parties received equal punishment, while in the Chesapeake, women were punished more severely. In some cases, women were either flogged or dragged in the water behind a boat until almost drowned. In this case, adultery was less a threat to marriage than to bloodlines, which were important in colonial Virginia.

When it came to capital punishment, the harshest sanctions were also found in the southern colonies. In order to control a large labor force of indentured servants and slaves, the entrepreneurial planters of Virginia and other southern colonies fostered codes designed to frighten rebellious slaves and forestall any uprisings. The first twenty Africans reached Virginia in 1619, signaling more than three centuries of hardship for the black South. Slave owners were initially given free rein to punish their slaves just as they were with indentured servants. Since slaves were always a valuable commodity, punishments were designed not to incapacitate but to teach a lesson. Mutilation, whippings, and other corporal punishments were administered quickly and visibly to set an example and not interfere with agricultural work.

By the 1700s, the African slave population was soaring, and white colonists feared insurrection, real or imagined. Slave laws proscribed execution for slaves who attacked their masters. Punishments revolving around rumors of slave rebellions were always harsh and public and like their English counterparts were designed to demonstrate the power of the state.

Unlike the more religiously oriented colonies founded just a few years later, the sting of punishment fell disproportionately on the lower classes in the southern colonies. The wealthier felons were often branded with a cold iron so as not to dishonor their reputations. While the poor and the illiterate went to the gallows, their landed and more literate neighbors could plead "benefit of clergy" by reciting the age-old neck verse from the Bible and get off with a stiff reprimand and a brand on the thumb.

In the Chesapeake South, the county court played an integral part in the developing criminal justice system. Here the landed gentry presided at court much like their forefathers at their manor courts. Here accusations were leveled at defendants in front of juries composed of a cross section of the inhabitants. Run-of-the-mill offenses monopolized the court docket—fighting, swearing, failing to attend church, and slander kept the grand juries most busy. In most cases, the defendant would eventually plead guilty, and the court would arrange for two people to put up a bond of surety to guarantee against recidivism.

MASSACHUSETTS AND THE NEW ENGLAND COLONIES

A religious movement known as Puritanism emerged in sixteenth-century England. The Puritans' main goal was to purify or purge the Church of England of its Roman Catholic tendencies. In 1609, another group, later known as the Pilgrims, who refused to conform to the Church of England, which they felt was corrupt, actually separated from the official church. Fearing persecution, they fled to Holland, a country known for its religious toleration. After more than a decade, some of the separatist families, fearing that their children were becoming too assimilated to Dutch ways, decided to migrate to America. They were able to secure permission to settle in Virginia. Following a series of storms and misadventures, the Pilgrims aboard the *Mayflower* were blown off course and ended up founding the Plymouth colony in November 1620, the first permanent European settlement in Massachusetts. They had not disembarked blindly, having been provided with a map by the explorer and Virginia pioneer John Smith, who not only named the region "New England" but had already christened the protected harbor "Plimouth."

In order to unify the factionalized community and since they were in lands that did not have any recognized political authority (being outside the domain of the Virginia Company as well as the government of England), the Pilgrims drew up the Mayflower Compact, which is considered the first charter of liberties ever framed by English common people. Unlike the earlier laws of Jamestown, which were enacted under the direction of a royally appointed governor and his councilors, the Pilgrims were acting only under the authority of the 102 members of their party (many of whom were non-Pilgrims, or Strangers).

The Mayflower Compact was not actually a law code but rather a covenant signed by forty-one male company members that bound them together in a political union with the full powers of a sovereign state. Their contract established the concept that "for our better ordering and preservation . . . and by virtue hereof to enact, constitute, and frame such just and equal laws . . . as shall be thought most meet and convenient for the general good of the Colony."[4] Without the aid of Crown lawyers, the signatories of this document set forth their ideal of government by the consent of the governed in a written document that anticipated the fundamental concepts of American constitutionalism. For the next seventy-one years, the Mayflower Compact was the formal mechanism for the political order of the colony. In the meantime, the governments of Connecticut, Providence, and New Haven would establish similar compacts. However, none of these would be permanent, and none was recognized under English law. Once Plymouth was absorbed by the Massachusetts Bay Colony in 1686, it came under the domain of traditional English law.

Following the establishment of Plymouth, King Charles granted another charter to the Massachusetts Bay Company in 1629. The charter authorized the company to establish laws for its settlement "not contrary to the laws of our realm of England" and to inflict "lawful correction" on the spot to violators. The following year saw the establishment of the Massachusetts Bay Colony under the watchful eye of Governor John Winthrop and his Puritan colleagues. Both the Plymouth and the Massachusetts colonies would independently establish their own criminal justice statutes and procedures, reflected in the current state of Massachusetts.

During the Great Migration between 1629 and 1640, almost 80,000 English inhabitants left their Old World homes in search of religious freedom. This coincided with the era when the ill-fated Charles I ruled England without calling Parliament into session. Even more significant was the oppression faced by Puritan members of the Anglican church. Other factors for the momentous migration included widespread pestilence and economic depression. Of these immigrants, more than a quarter of them would settle in Massachusetts.

The Puritans differed from other immigrant groups in that they migrated with the highest number of family units, they had a relatively equal ratio of men to women, and their members were older than most other immigrants. The majority of them were from the middling classes, counting among their numbers artisans and craftsmen, merchants, traders, and farmers. While perhaps three-quarters of the Virginia colonists were indentured servants, less than 25 percent of the Massachusetts settlers were in this subservient position. Highly skilled and literate (for they believed that each person must know the scriptures as opposed to a priest interpreting for them) and often traveling in village or family units to the New World, this emigrant group would clearly distinguish itself from the more secular societies to the south.

Village life in Massachusetts was dominated by the family, from which much governance emanated. Consequently, in some provinces it was illegal for single persons to live alone. In 1668, one Massachusetts court scrutinized its communities for any single people and then placed them into existing families. Failure to comply could result in a term in the local house of correction.

The Lawgivers

Initially, judicial operations in early New England settlements were connected to other business of the government. Therefore, justice was administered by various executive and legislative bodies rather than by a separate judicial arm of government. Judicial power was often relegated by charter provisions. According to the Massachusetts Charter, all government power was vested in an executive council known as the assistant's court and the General Court, which was the highest regulating body in the colony. By the 1640s, most judicial functions of the General Court were turned over to other courts established by the General Court.

Typical justice procedure involved an assistant, also known as a magistrate, who filled a role similar to the English justice of the peace. Malefactors were brought before the assistant, who had the power to try minor cases without a jury. After the arraignment of the individual and hearing the evidence, the assistant could decide whether to press further with the case. However, before any corporal punishment could be meted out, another assistant was required to determine whether the judgment was appropriate.

The assistant's court, similar to a state supreme court, included the governor, deputy governor, and twelve assistants (magistrates) and tried cases that were punishable by banishment, dismemberment, or capital punishment. If there was disagreement between the assistants or between the assistants and the jury, the case could be appealed to the General Court. In the 1640s, Massachusetts established county governments and seven county courts. Each court was assigned five judges, and three needed to be present for there to be quorum. In the following decade, a four-tiered pyramid structure of judicial administration developed in Massachusetts. At the bottom were town courts, which conducted trials. Any appeals would go to the next level, the county courts, which also held trials but also heard appeals. County court appeals would be filed at the assistant's court, which heard trials and appeals, and at the top was the General Court, the highest court of appeal. In 1671, the General Court transferred its power to the Court of Assistants, which made it the highest trial and appellate court in the colony. While there was some variance in the judicial systems

of other early New England colonies, such as Connecticut, Rhode Island, and New Haven, they were very similar in the hierarchical nature of the appeals process.

In 1685, the trial functions of the assistant's court was given over to the newly created county courts. Over time, the county courts became the most prominent ingredient in the criminal justice process. Convening as a court of common pleas, county courts heard civil suits and misdemeanors but were restricted from hearing felony cases, which were punishable by death or dismemberment.

The administration of the early Massachusetts Bay Colony criminal justice system was influenced by the teachings of the Bible. Indeed, biblical law codes superseded the English common law. Technically, there was no separation of church and state; as such, church elders tended to hold the reins of civic authority.[5] Motivated by the Old Testament, one of the early religious leaders proposed a law code based on the Mosaic code. Known as *Moses His Judicials,* it was subsequently rejected in favor of the more formal *Body of Liberties.* The most substantial criminal code of the early Massachusetts colony, the *Body of Liberties* of 1641, subscribed to many of the notions contained in the rejected document. More important, it verified that everyone is entitled to specific rights or "liberties," including the right to plead or petition in the local courts. The *Body of Liberties* was composed of ninety-eight civil and criminal laws. Although inspired by the Mosaic code, these laws were still considerably less severe than the ruthless laws of England. While *The Body of Liberties* recognized some property and personal rights, it perpetuated a tradition in which the colony was governed by a select few: an oligarchy of elite church members. Revised and renamed the *Laws and Liberties* in 1648, the new document is considered a turning point in colonial criminal justice. A fusion of biblical injunctions against immorality, the *Laws and Liberties* of 1648 also included more secular concepts, such as due process and the right to a jury trial, and enumerated specific crimes and sanctions.

Colonial historian Peter C. Hoffer suggests that *Laws and Liberties* is written "in language reminiscent of the 'Great Charter (Magna Carta)' of English liberties."[6] According to the document, "No mans life shall be taken away, no mans honour or good name shall be stained, no mans person shall be arrested, restrayned . . . no mans goods or estate shall be taken away from him . . . unless it be of vertue or equitie of some xpresse law of the Country warranting the same, established by a general court and sufficiently published. . . . Every person within this jurisdiction, whether inhabitant or forreiner shall enjoy the same justice and law."[7]

Although the Puritans are associated with freedom of religion, it did not mean that every religion would be tolerated in the colony; they were seeking to practice their version of Christianity. While Puritan law was equitably dispensed in the Puritan community, non-Puritans were not protected under the same laws. Deviation from the values and culture of the dominant group had a price. Particular animosity was reserved for the Quakers, in part because they loudly and publicly criticized the established churches and did not believe that ministers, or the symbol of church authority, were necessary. In 1658, the Massachusetts General Court passed several measures that included banishing practicing Quakers from the colony under the threat of capital punishment. The following year, in order to test the new law, several Quakers returned to Boston with twenty followers in tow. They were promptly thrown in jail, and three were selected to be executed. Prior to sentencing, one official lamented that "neither whipping nor imprisonment, nor cutting off ears, nor banishment upon pain of death, will keep you from among us . . . I desire not your deaths."[8] Two of the men were executed, with drummers drowning out their last words, while the third, a woman, was reprieved at the last moment, although she would hang in Boston for testing the authorities once again in 1660. These events did little to quiet the Quaker voice in Massachusetts, even when followed by months of suppression.

A familiar fixture in urban England, lawyers were not always available let alone wanted, so ministers often were consulted. In Puritan New England, the Bible supplied the law codes; hence, magistrates and lawyers were unnecessary for most litigation. Judges need not be schooled in the secular law, and few ordinances outside the scriptures were necessary. It was not until 1712 that an actual lawyer served as chief justice of Massachusetts. By the end of the seventeenth century, lawyers were in such disrepute in Connecticut that they were categorized along with those guilty of public drunkenness and keepers of disorderly houses.

In 1691, Great Britain granted a new charter to Massachusetts that united the colonies of Maine, Massachusetts Bay, and Plymouth into the province of Massachusetts Bay. In this new structure, the governor, with the consent and advice of his council, appointed sheriffs, marshals, justices of the peace, and the judiciary. The Puritan theocracy had governed the colony for six decades, and now, with the new charter, religious freedom was granted to all Protestant denominations. This signaled a new era that allowed a transition to the common law as the colony was weaned from Mosaic law.

Crime and Punishment

Within the first few years of the colony, church attendance was made compulsory under threat of fine and prison. The literal acceptance of the Bible led to oppressive legal measures that some saw as no better than the laws they left behind in England. No case illustrated this more than the Salem witch trials in 1692 (see "Notable Trials"). In another instance, an apparently mentally deficient denizen of the colony was whipped, had his ears cropped, and was banished from the colony for speaking critically of the local theocracy. No critic would be tolerated by the colonial elders.

Conforming to the biblical law codes, the Puritans were least tolerant when it came to non-procreative forms of sex. Multiple convictions for masturbation was a capital offense in the

New Haven colony. Considered the most sinister perversion, however, bestiality was punishable by a death sentence with little room for compromise. Although a capital sentence could not be passed without the testimony of two witnesses, magistrates often created loopholes in order to ensure that justice was done. In one case, a servant with one eye and a tarnished past was believed to have committed numerous depravities. When a one-eyed pig was born in the vicinity, he was accused of siring it. The magistrates exerted considerable pressure on the suspect until he confessed and recanted twice. The magistrates ruled then that the deformed pig could be considered one witness and the withdrawn confession of the suspect would serve as another. Subsequently, the one-eyed servant was hanged.

Adultery and fornication were particularly targeted by the law. Extramarital sex was not only a sin; if it involved a married woman it also was considered a capital offense. Records for the seventeenth-century Puritan colonies indicate that at least three people were executed for this crime. However, for a capital punishment to be levied, it was required that there be two eyewitnesses to the actual offense. On occasions when there was only one witness, other sanctions were employed. Historian David Hackett Fischer cites a case where a man was whipped, fined, and sentenced to the house of correction while the straying wife also spent a stint in the same institution and then was instructed to wear a sign indicating her unwholesome behavior at a town meeting. According to Puritan law, fornication between an unmarried woman and a man, unmarried or married, sanctioned the man to be imprisoned, whipped, disenfranchised, and then forced to marry his partner if single.[9] The degree to which sexual immorality was suppressed in Massachusetts was probably responsible for its having the lowest rate of premarital pregnancy in the seventeenth-century Western world. It is just as likely that many individuals charged with fornication were forced into marriage.

Obedience within the family was considered sacrosanct. The laws of 1648 mandated the death penalty for rebellious sons over sixteen years of age. Failure to obey one's parents or any verbal or physical assault against them could lead to capital sanctions, although there is little evidence that this law was ever literally enforced. In lieu of the death penalty, several examples suggest that fines and whippings were the normal modes of punishment for such transgressions.

Infanticide has been an underreported crime throughout history since birth usually occurs in private with little fanfare. Midwives were typically present at birth to ensure a safe birth and to testify if the baby was stillborn. One of the earliest cases of infanticide was reported in Boston in 1646. Reaching back to the dark days of the Middle Ages, officials ordered the accused to undergo a form of ordeal known as "ordeal of touch." This was similar to the Germanic bier-right, in which a suspect is made to touch an alleged victim, and if the corpse bled or frothed at the mouth, the suspect was adjudged guilty. According to this relic of medieval judicial procedure, the birth mother was made to touch the face of her purported dead infant in front of a jury. When blood flushed the child's cheeks, the mother confessed. She was then hanged. Other cases of this judgment are recorded, the last apparently in 1769.

One of the main goals of Puritan punishment was to have a church member repent and return to the congregation. Although law was draconian, in reality it was rarely as punitive as the law allowed. Recent scholarship notes that Massachusetts colonists were rarely punished for Old Testament infractions and that "even those prosecuted very rarely suffered the prescribed penalty."[10] According to colonial historian Peter C. Hoffer, laws based on the Old Testament "were not meant to function in a literal way"; rather, it was hoped that they would function as a "solemn public warning to those at the edges of the Puritan community against violation of the deeper social mores that held the Puritan towns in the wilderness together."[11]

Besides punishment, another response to crime was the admonition, in which magistrates or clergymen lectured offenders privately in order to elicit a promise of reform. According to the procedures of the day, penitent reformers appeared in open court for a formal admonition by the magistrate. After a public confession of wrongdoing, there was a pronouncement of sentence, which was typically a suspended one. The admonition as it developed in Massachusetts had no precise analogue in English criminal justice practice. Its adoption followed the Puritan theology, which emphasized a "gentle correction" to impede sin, at least with the first offense.

The colonists of Massachusetts brought from England sumptuary laws that restricted certain fashions in favor of the more dour and drab. This tendency reflected the elite's efforts to exercise restraint in personal matters and to maintain social order in a society that witnessed significantly more social mobility. Nowhere were these laws more strict than in Massachusetts, where men and women were prohibited by law in the 1630s from displaying "new fashions, or long hair, or anything like the nature." Fashionable beaver hats were regarded as "superfluous and unnecessary" under threat of a fine.[12]

Not only were numerous other fashion statements strictly prohibited, but the mere manufacture or sale of such products was banned by statute. Over the following decades, the sumptuary laws would reflect the growing hierarchical nature of the colony. By 1651, individuals were allowed to flaunt their rank through various statements of sartorial elegance. Despite the loosening of the sumptuary prohibitions, early Puritan women continued to refrain from cosmetics, bright colors, and even false teeth.

Setting aside the periodic devastation of the Indian population, there was little in the way of violent crime in New England. Low crime rates have persisted in this region for more than 300 years. Fewer people are executed or murdered in this region than anywhere else in modern America.

According to Massachusetts court records, property crimes were more common than personal crimes. Crimes against the hierarchical social order were the most common offenses, including Sabbath violations, sexual offenses, idleness, drunkenness, and domestic disorder, all of which were apparently common.[13] Regardless of the punishment in New England, the interval between sentencing and punishment was set by law at four days.

The most prevalent form of sanctions involved fines, which was the punishment of choice for a variety of petty offenses and misdemeanors. Other public sanctions exposed offenders to an array of corporal punishments, including whippings, the stocks, and pillories. These exhibitory chastisements were administered publicly before the assembled community, usually on a market, lecture, or military training day. While public punishment and shaming was a standard response to many property and moral offenses, most of these minor offenses would have probably been tolerated back in England with perhaps a warning.

The Puritans were especially pragmatic when it came to methods of public punishment. In some instances, individuals accused of premarital sex were required to stand silently, attired in white sheets, in front of their congregation and recount their sins. Habitual drinkers wore the shame letter *D,* for "drunkard," for an entire year. An unscrupulous baker sometimes stood in the stocks supporting a lump of dough on his head. Chronic property offenders were branded on the cheek or forehead or mutilated, leaving a "mark of infamy" to warn the community of their criminal disposition.

One penalty reserved for the most serious crimes included "warning out," or banishment, which was used in New England until the eighteenth century to get rid of undesirables. Banishment was often the last resort available to long-time residents faced with patterns of criminality. In colonial Massachusetts, where labor was relatively scarce, it was impractical to run out the disorderly, though it was used in cases of heresy and political misconduct.

Particular disdain was reserved for betting, games of chance, and gambling. The General Court banned games, ranging from shuffle board to cards and dice. What most provoked the Puritan was the waste of time associated with these types of activities. In this society, a work ethic, or the notion that constant work was beneficial materially as well as spiritually because it kept one out of trouble, was revered. Time wasting, or idleness, therefore became a criminal offense in Massachusetts, punishable by fines.

Massachusetts colonists were surely familiar with England's predilection for capital punishment. In the home country, people were executed for crimes great and small, for routine theft and burglary as well as murder. However, only a fraction of the condemned were actually executed thanks to safety valves such as royal pardons, benefit of clergy, and the intercession of a jury. Among the most heinous forms of execution were burning at the stake and hanging. While hanging was the most common form of capital punishment, there are records of servants being burned at the stake for committing petty treason, defined as the killing of a master by a servant. Of the two known cases, both involved women of African descent.

Like the wearing of shame letters, which sent a message to the community, specific forms of maiming also sent a warning to potential miscreants. Among the more grotesque punishments administered by the Puritans were the amputation of ears, slitting of nostrils, and branding of faces and hands. Unlike shame letters sewn into a garment, these were permanent reminders to both offender and community. Particular ferocity was reserved for the Quakers, who were often the target of facial brandings of the letter *H,* for "heresy."

PENNSYLVANIA AND THE MID-ATLANTIC COLONIES

Dutch and Swedish colonists had established settlements along the Delaware River decades before William Penn was granted his proprietary charter by King Charles II in 1681. The founder of Pennsylvania and a lifelong crusader for

religious and civil liberty, Penn was expelled from Oxford University in his youth for his controversial and nonconforming religious views. Hoping to rid his son of his Puritan convictions, his father, an admiral in the British navy, sent him on a tour of Europe. However, this ploy backfired when, in 1667, Penn converted to Quakerism, an equally nonconformist sect, leading to a short prison sentence in England's infamous Tower of London.

What set the Quakers apart from the Puritans was their rejection of the Calvinist belief in predestination and their emphasis on the inner spirit. As a consequence of these beliefs, ministers were no longer necessary, leading Puritans to view these meetings of "Friends" as anarchy. The Quakers were a radical sect that emerged in England in the 1640s and 1650s as the Society of Friends. In their earlier days, they developed a reputation for defiance—refusing to swear oaths or remove their hats in front of magistrates and even going as far as denouncing Anglican ministers in church. Presaging their participation in nineteenth-century women's rights and anti-slavery reform movements, from the start the Quakers were vehemently opposed to war and contended that women had the right to speak at public meetings.

On his father's death, Penn not only inherited the family fortune but also became the proprietor of Pennsylvania. This land had been given to Penn's father by the king as repayment for an outstanding loan to Charles II. Persecuted at home, the young Penn set about creating his vision of an ideal Christian commonwealth on the banks of the Delaware River.

The Lawgivers

In December 1682, the colony's first assembly, dominated by Quakers, adopted Penn's *Frame of Government,* also known as "The Great Law or Body of Laws," the first criminal code of Pennsylvania, providing the blueprint for the colony. It laid out a political structure that was composed of a governor, council, and assembly elected by freeholders. It also laid the groundwork for trial by jury, free elections, and religious liberty. Penn came as close as anyone to allowing religious freedom in the colonies, although he excluded atheists and nonbelievers from his colony and barred non-Christians from holding office. From the start, Penn was imbued with a strong sense of English liberties. Within the first five years of his arrival, he ordered the entire text of the Magna Carta to be reprinted in Philadelphia.

The Quakers embraced an austere and ascetic mode of life once they settled in the New World. Prior to the eighteenth century, the Quakers were considerably more humane in the punishment of crime than either England or New England. Nowhere was this more true than in the use of the death penalty. At a time when Massachusetts inflicted capital punishment for offenses including adultery, man stealing, bestiality, blasphemy, burglary, cursing or smiting a parent, bearing false witness, arson, poisoning, and rape, Pennsylvania demanded death only for traitors and murderers. When Pennsylvania became a royal colony in 1718, and with Anglicans now dominating the legislature, a more severe penal code was introduced in order to bring the laws into conformity with England's bloody code.

Quaker punishments for deviant behavior did not range widely and were inclined to favor forfeiture of property, fines, imprisonment, and shaming over other methods. Their use of a variety of prison sentences no doubt demonstrates the influence of Enlightenment philosophy and foreshadows the birth of the penitentiary in the Quaker colony. For indiscretions such as incest and sodomy, individuals forfeited a large percentage of their estate and spent six months to one year of imprisonment at hard labor. A second offense could earn the culprit life in prison. Gambling, swearing, cursing, and drunkenness could earn malefactors a five-shilling fine or five days of imprisonment at hard labor on a bread-and-water diet. Prostitution, bigamy, and adultery were treated more seriously, but much less severely than in Massachusetts. Sanctions included public whippings

and up to a year of imprisonment at hard labor and, for repeated offenses, life imprisonment.

Crime and Punishment

Crime trends in Pennsylvania offer numerous contrasts with other British colonies. In New England, property crimes outnumbered personal crimes, and in Virginia the reverse was true. But in Pennsylvania, these crimes tended to be distributed rather evenly among the classes. Prior to the mid-1750s, most crimes in the Quaker colony were crimes against authority, such as confronting peace officers on duty. Individuals arrested for civic disorder or physical violence were punished severely, particularly in rape cases. One individual, facing the shame and pain of a public whipping for rape, slit his own throat before the sentence could be carried out.

Paralleling the waning power of the Quakers in the Pennsylvania legislature in the eighteenth century was the increase in the number of capital crimes under more secular rule. But Pennsylvania's number of capital crimes always remained small in comparison to the other colonies. The Quaker codes were changed and became more harsh by the English influence beginning in 1718. Whipping remained in fashion in Pennsylvania throughout the eighteenth century. Neighboring Delaware, heavily influenced by early Quaker code, even had a name for its permutation of this device known as "Red Hannah." An anachronism, Delaware authorities continued to whip prisoners into the 1940s.[14]

The development of prison reform in America can be traced back to William Penn's code. Penn and his Quaker contemporaries were adamantly opposed to the severe physical penalties exacted in England and considered imprisonment the best alternative. As previously mentioned, except for murder and treason, imprisonment at hard labor was often prescribed for crimes that typically demanded bloody retribution in the other colonies. Penn's system was the first in the colonies to put inmates to hard labor to compensate for a crime as well as to rehabilitate. Penn added other measures in an attempt to reform lawbreakers, including making all prisoners eligible for bail and allowing the wrongfully imprisoned to sue for damages. Instead of jails funded by jailers charging prisoners room and board, inmates in Pennsylvania were given free food and boarding.

Penn, a proponent of the Enlightenment philosophy that the punishment should fit the crime, enacted measures for penal reform that were considered the most humane in colonial America. In contrast to British jails, which consisted of dungeons or were often run by venal private contractors, Penn's prisons were adequately built and provided for by the government. However, like the other reforms introduced in the Quaker colony, they would endure only as long as the Quakers were in the majority. It was not long before the more tolerant Quakers were outnumbered by Anglican settlers who introduced more harsh measures based on English procedures. Penn's efforts established a tradition of institutional reform that would be reintroduced following the American Revolution.

COLONIAL LAW ENFORCEMENT

Like its precursors in Europe, early American law enforcement was the bailiwick of unskilled amateurs. There was little innovation in the early colonies, with most preferring what they were familiar with: some incarnation of the English parish constable and the county sheriff. Between 1608 and the end of the revolution, most American sheriffs and constables were appointed by colonial governors and performed the same tasks as their English counterparts. In Maryland's Chesapeake settlements, the sheriff was expected not only to maintain order but also to collect taxes and fees, of which he was entitled to 10 percent.

In small-town New England, local church elders and settlement laws filled the void in law enforcement by regulating the behavior of new arrivals, townspeople, and land dealings of the citizenry. There was no clear demarcation between amateur and professional law enforcement in the colonial world. The system hinged on laypeople and on traditional institutions, including the hue and cry, sheriff, constable, night watch, magistrate, and coroner.

In New England, as need arose for peacekeepers outside the church setting, village constables were selected locally to serve processes and warrants, make arrests, collect taxes, and be on the lookout for unsavory new arrivals lurking in the community. Never wavering from the Puritan ethos, the constable was also required to visit each household in the township at least four times a year to remind the inhabitants of the Sabbath laws. When more serious situations arose, the constable could depend on his neighbors to come to his aid, harking back to the centuries-old hue and cry. According to the evidence, the system worked well in seventeenth-century Massachusetts, where the murder rate was less than half that of Maryland and Virginia, known as the Chesapeake colonies.

While the town constables were the most popular peace officers in New England, in Virginia, which was more sparsely populated, the sheriff played a more significant role. According to early custom, sheriffs were expected to reside in the county they served in and were to be members of the landowning gentry. Sheriffs were expected to fulfill a wide assortment of services, ranging from organizing courts and calling elections to running the jail and keeping county records. But they could not possibly meet their obligations without the assistance of a coterie of undersheriffs, deputies, jailers, county clerks, and whippers. Ever the most odious duties, hangmen and mutilators were often selected from the ranks of the criminal element.

In contrast to the gentry-controlled sheriff of the South and the theocratically appointed constables of New England, Pennsylvanians used a more complex method for selecting county sheriffs. Counties were required to conduct an election with multiple candidates. The names of the two men receiving the most votes would be forwarded to the governor, who would then pick one as sheriff. Sheriffs in Pennsylvania served one-year stints and were limited to three consecutive terms.

In the more urban reaches of Boston, New York, and Philadelphia, the British night-watch system was adopted to complement the duties of the constable. During the 1630s, the dim outlines of American policing were beginning to take shape in Massachusetts. The towns were policed by the familiar English amateurs: the constable and the night watchman. In 1631, a night watch was established in Boston, the first in America. The Boston night watch was composed of six men and an officer and would form at sunset in preparation for the tasks ahead. Their duties included walking rounds crying the time of night and the state of the weather "in a moderate tone." In 1634, Joshua Pratt was appointed constable of Plymouth. His duties included serving as jailer, executing punishments, sealer of weights and measures, and surveyor of lands. One problem that would remain consistent into the nineteenth century was watchmen "cooping" (or sleeping on duty) and drinking on the job.

The Dutch colonists of New Amsterdam became familiar with the *schout* and rattle watch in the 1650s.[15] When the English took over the colony and renamed New Amsterdam the more familiar New York, they introduced a new system composed of watchmen supervised by constables elected from wards and headed by a high constable.

In 1700, the Philadelphia provincial council appointed a watchman, and a system was established by which all citizens, typically the heads of households, were obligated to take turns in the duty of watch and ward. By the early eighteenth century, this institution was established in most existing towns and cities.

For the next 200 years, little would change in American policing, in part because American citizens saw a standing police force as a reminder of the oppression and exploitation that they had left behind in Europe. The Dutch in New York City (1648) and the English in Boston (1663) experimented with a paid watch system but found it too expensive and abandoned it in favor of the amateur approach.

The evolution of the southern slave patrols in the early 1700s marked the first real advances in American policing. Slave patrolling originated not in the American colonies but in the Caribbean, where French, Spanish, Portuguese, and English slaveholders faced the same challenges as slave-owning American colonists as early as the sixteenth century. According to historian Sally E. Hadden, "The Barbadian slave code of 1661 provided the model for several other English slave-holding colonies."[16] Many Barbadian planters would bring this code with them to South Carolina in the 1670s, where they exerted a major influence in designing the first laws governing slave law enforcement in America.

The ancient system of hue and cry was poorly suited for sparsely populated parts of Virginia. With black slavery coming to dominate southern society, the southern colonies introduced slave codes beginning with South Carolina's in 1712. The slave codes provided for the creation of brutal slave patrols, charged with protecting the plantations and punishing those responsible for serious crimes. Virginia introduced a slave patrol in 1727 in the wake of a 1721 slave revolt. Slave patrols were implemented as a proactive response to the insurrectionists. Rather than allowing bands of slaves to plot when they gathered during holidays, patrollers were ordered to break up the meetings and disperse the slaves.

While they varied in structure, many slave patrols consisted of three to five armed men on horseback who covered a prescribed beat of almost fifteen square miles. However, in South Carolina, regulations prohibited a beat from being larger than a few square miles. While making their rounds, the slave patrols were responsible for maintaining discipline, apprehending runaway slaves, and preventing slave uprisings. Routinely invading slave quarters at night and whipping and terrorizing those caught without passes after curfew, over time slave patrols became a feared presence among the black population.

Slave patrols were authorized to enforce laws against black literacy, trade, and gambling. Until recently, most historians have accepted the notion that while all white males were expected to participate in patrol service, most planters paid for substitutes, who were typically landless poor whites. However, recent research by Sally E. Hadden suggests that in the first decades of the eighteenth century, slave patrols "frequently included men of superior social status, not just poor slaveless whites." One explanation for this was that wealthy whites lobbied for slave patrols in order to avoid serving in the militia.[17] In 1721, this practice was abolished. Despite friction between the white underclass and the owners of large plantations who controlled the best lands, the slaves became the target of the slave patrols. In response, slave communities resisted by setting up warning systems and sometimes ambushing the riders.

One of the most important American criminal justice modifications in the colonies was the "district attorney." There was no such analogue in England, where people were expected to prosecute criminals at their own expense, making it cost prohibitive for most farmers and small merchants. The district attorney, or county attorney, evolved as a public prosecutor in charge of prosecution in the colonies, an official paid by the government to prosecute crimes on behalf of the citizenry.

COLONIAL CORRECTIONS

The Massachusetts Bay Colony built its first prison in Boston in 1636, the only one the colony would have for eighteen years. More jails were constructed as the population expanded into the wilderness. By the mid-1770s, the era of the American Revolution, Massachusetts was divided into twelve counties, with each required to maintain its own jail. Early jails functioned as holding facilities for debtors and others delinquent in paying taxes and fines. Initially, jails were considered a method of coercion to make someone pay rather than as a criminal sanction. Jails served as holding facilities for a variety of prisoners, including Indians and soldiers (both British and French) and Quaker, Jesuit, and Loyalist political prisoners. Serving mostly in a custodial capacity, jails were also used for presentence detention for those awaiting trial or punishment. Although jails were considered a last resort, in some cases they performed penal functions in the late colonial period. Incarceration was an expensive investment and a loss of industrious labor, so it rarely exceeded twenty-four hours. Forgers convicted after 1692 faced the loss of an ear and imprisonment without bail for one year. Prior to 1750, incarceration by statute was rare, with mutilation and other punishments more common.

Other New England colonies developed various versions of the pre-Enlightenment prison. Connecticut confined prisoners in a copper mine named Newgate Prison, while Maine relied on small earth pits that barely measured nine and a half by four and a half by ten feet deep. Incarceration did not become an important criminal sanction until the Enlightenment of the eighteenth century.

CAPITAL PUNISHMENT

It has been several generations since the last person was executed in New England, and at this writing only Connecticut has prisoners actually sitting on death row. Recent attempts by Massachusetts to return the death penalty were narrowly defeated. However, for close to 400 years, capital punishment has been a transcendent feature of American criminal justice.

According to the *Body of Liberties,* capital punishment was the sanction for idolatry, witchcraft, blasphemy, murder, manslaughter, poisoning, bestiality, sodomy, adultery, kidnapping, and treason but not for property crimes. Contrary to English criminal practice, blasphemy, adultery, and other moral offenses became capital crimes in order to conform with Mosaic law. By the eighteenth century, less moral offenses were capital crimes, as the tendency was to less vigorously enforce the death penalty. In reality, a shortage of population and other exigencies created a system in which the statutes were rarely enforced to the letter of the law. By English standards, the colonies were far from bloody. However, there were cases in which colonial law was more severe. Adultery did not demand death in England but was considered a capital crime in Massachusetts, though it was rarely carried out. After the mid-seventeenth century, no one was executed for adultery.

In contrast to Puritan New England, executions were a common occurrence in Virginia, where hundreds of crimes demanded the death penalty by the mid-1700s. According to one survey of the 164 people convicted of capital crimes between 1737 and 1772, 125 were executed without benefit of clergy. Like most English colonies, hanging was the standard method of execution. The gallows were often constructed at the scene of the crime, and the condemned individual was brought to the site in a cart. Usually surrounded by a huge crowd, the only formality was to allow the convicted to say his last words and then go to his death. Standing in the back of a cart, a noose was placed around his neck. To complete the ghastly scene, the cart was driven forward, leaving the individual to grotesquely twist in the wind as he strangled to death. It was not uncommon for bystanders to grab the legs of the culprit to facilitate an end to the macabre ceremony. As a denouement to this chain of events, the body was often given to physicians for dissection and research or was left in a public place as a warning to others. Finally, at least in the colony of Virginia, the felon's property was forfeited to the Crown.

Today the death penalty is most often used in the South; the same was true in the colonial era, when the burden was carried mostly by African slaves and indentured servants. Between 1706 and 1784, some 555 slaves, more than any northern colony, were sentenced to death in Virginia. Since the death penalty was reinstated in 1976, Virginia is second only to Texas in the number of executions carried out in America.

COLONIAL VIOLENCE

In the 1960s, the black militant activist H. Rap Brown proclaimed that "violence is as American as apple pie." He had learned his history lessons well, for since America's earliest days the land was locked in intermittent conflicts between white colonists and indigenous cultures, between blacks and whites, and between the various religious denominations. No colony had a monopoly on violence in the colonial era. Slave insurrections and accompanying mass executions occurred both north and south. In fact, the first mass execution of blacks occurred in New York in 1712 after a group of African slaves set buildings on fire and killed from ambush nine white colonists who responded to the conflagration. As a result, fourteen slaves went to the gallows, and five others were executed using more grisly methods. Twenty-nine years later, almost three dozen men, black and white, were charged with conspiring to torch the city. Subsequent trials led to the immolation of thirteen African Americans at the stake and the hanging of two white men and two white women. Dozens more were banished from the city for their unruly behavior.

Beginning in the eighteenth century, rioting plagued the burgeoning cities of the Eastern Seaboard. Political unrest shaped American institutions and eventually stimulated the creation of modern policing. No day occasioned unrest more than election days in Philadelphia, Boston, Baltimore and wherever antagonistic constituents were in great numbers. Before the silent ballot and the private voting box, opposing factions in a political contest used violence to prevent the other side from voting.

Another cause for rioting was impressment, the traditional method for keeping the British navy well stocked with young men. "Press gangs" were used to force citizens into service. Boston rioting broke out over impressment as sympathetic townsfolk violently resisted in 1747. Although the citizens resisted successfully this time, impressment continued to be an issue until after the War of 1812. In the decade leading up to the American Revolution, riots became more common. According to historian Richard Maxwell Brown, between 1641 and 1759 there were at least forty-one riots, including riots over land disputes, anticustoms riots, jailbreak riots, food riots, and even fish-dam riots. Between 1645 and 1769, there were eighteen insurgent movements by white colonists aimed at overthrowing colonial governments, the best known being Bacon's Rebellion (1676).

During the first decades of colonial America, there was little violent crime between the white colonists. What violence that did take place usually occurred in local taverns or along desolate trails. Most homicides took place between whites and the indigenous cultures. Any Indian accused of killing a white was expected to face a white court. However, if the circumstances were reversed, the whites occasionally paid compensation but were never turned over to the Indian justice system. Though subject to British law, Indians were rarely accorded the rights of white British citizens.

While hanging enjoyed popularity in America from the colonial era to the nineteenth century, colonial punishments were less severe than penal punishment in England. As previously noted, when Pennsylvania was ruled by the Quakers, most capital punishment was prohibited. Although the colonial era is best remembered by criminal justicians for the Salem witchcraft trials, this was an anomaly. Compared to England, which executed perhaps 30,000 for witchcraft and France 75,000, less than forty were hanged for the offense in colonial America.

NOTABLE TRIALS

Salem Witchcraft Trials (1692)

The Salem (derived from the Hebrew word *Shalom,* meaning "peace") witchcraft trials in Massachusetts were probably the most famous trials of colonial America. They have inspired books and plays such as Arthur Miller's *The Crucible,* and many parallels have been drawn with the McCarthy hearings of the 1950s [see chapter 11]. But accusations of witchcraft were hardly unique. They were much more common in Europe, where thousands were condemned to death. In New England, in the fifty years leading up to the Salem trials, dozens of people were executed for witchcraft. And after the Salem incident, trials continued to crop up. According to one source, a mob killed a suspected witch outside Philadelphia's Independence Hall as late as 1787 as the U.S. Constitution was being haggled over inside. The victims of witchcraft prosecutions were almost exclusively women, many of them old and destitute, and were perceived as a drain on the community.

Over 90 percent of witchcraft accusations and more than 90 percent of executions occurred in New England colonies where the Puritans dominated.[18] The events surrounding the outbreak of witchcraft in Salem are probably the best-documented witch trials in American history. Most accounts of the Salem hysteria begin with the Reverend Samuel Parris's West Indian slave Tituba. Well versed in the superstitions of the Caribbean by the time she arrived in Salem, Tituba regaled young girls during the cloistered winter months with her knowledge of the occult. Tutoring the girls in the finer arts of palmistry, fortune-telling, necromancy, magic, and spiritualism, everything seemed rather innocent at first. Partly out of boredom, the students began to show off to neighbors. In macabre displays, they lurched into spasmodic convulsions, gesturing incoherently, and unleashed unintelligible sounds. It was not long before their sideshows came to the attention of the local arbiters of morality, of which there was a ready supply.

The diagnosis of a village doctor was that they were bewitched, and it was not long before the entire community was alarmed. The young girls continued to draw attention by interrupting church services with incongruous statements that lent credence to the charge of witchcraft; however, they were not punished but rather became objects of pity and compassion. With the assistance of local citizens, authorities embarked on a witch hunt to find the source of the bewitchment. It was not long before the young girls succumbed to pressure to name names, and warrants were served on Tituba, Sarah Good, and Sarah Osborne.[19] What ensued was a spiraling series of accusations against hundreds of persons that culminated in the hanging of nineteen individuals and the imprisonment of hundreds more.

None of the accused women was provided legal representation, and the line of questioning indicates that they were presumed guilty. Even before trial, the three accused women had attracted the community's scrutiny. Tituba, an Indian slave raised in the West Indies and schooled in the healing arts, quickly admitted her guilt and implicated the two Sarahs. The pipe-smoking Good had been deserted by her husband, which caused overwhelming and burdensome poverty. Osborne was earlier censured by her neighbors for buying out the balance of an indentured servant's contract, hiring him, and then marrying him. A subject of envy as a propertied widow, then marrying beneath her station, Osborne was soon bedridden and missed church services regularly—a scandalous situation but one that envious neighbors were happy to point out. Before the year was out, nineteen people would be executed and hundreds imprisoned.

What made the Salem witch trials so unique was the sheer number of people accused and convicted. The court in this case allowed disputed "spectral evidence" (in which witnesses claimed visions of their tormentors) and torture and encouraged the accused to confess, repent, and name names in order to gain freedom. Traditionally, a higher degree of proof was required, and the majority were eventually exonerated.

There is another, more sinister explanation for what happened at Salem that hinges on complicated social relations in a community in flux. As the community made the transition to a prosperous port town, earlier rivalries between the wealthier merchant class at the center of town and the struggling farmers on the periphery cre-

ated an atmosphere of tension. The rural faction won a petition to form a new church. However, the faction was not sanctioned by a town charter. This unique but uncertain status, combined with old socioeconomic rivalries, ensured that all the ingredients were in place for a massive outbreak of witchcraft accusations. In the end, what was most unusual about this episode was that most accusers were from the disadvantaged rural faction, which felt left behind in the movement toward a more commercial economy, and that the majority of victims were the more prosperous members of the community.[20]

In 2001, descendants of five of the accused and executed Salem witches petitioned the Massachusetts legislature to declare them innocent. This is just the most recent attempt to clear the names of victims of the "largest witch hunt in American history." The first exonerations occurred as early as 1711, when colonial authorities absolved twenty-one of the twenty-seven (not all had been hanged) who had been convicted after family members presented petitions on their behalf. The other six, who had been hanged, had no survivors in the colony to plead for them, so their convictions stood until 1957, when all were cleared, but only one of them was cleared by name. In the pending measure, the other five women would be mentioned by name and added to the 1957 resolution.

John Peter Zenger (1735)

Zenger, a German immigrant, arrived in the New York colony in the early 1700s as an indentured servant. Apprenticed to a printer, there was little to suggest that in a matter of years he would be embroiled in one of the most important free-speech cases of his era. In 1731, Zenger was working for the *New York Weekly Gazette*. He came to public attention while covering the scandals that followed the election of William Cosby as governor of the New York colony. Zenger sought to capture readership with reports that dozens of Quakers had been illegally disqualified from voting because of their religious beliefs and that Cosby's supporters intimidated voters and had tried to stuff ballot boxes. Apprenticed to a Cosby supporter who refused to print his stories about the governor, Zenger was soon fired. Subsequently, a rival of the governor saw the chance to inflict revenge and set about financing a rival newspaper, hiring Zenger as publisher. The new paper grew in popularity as it chronicled the scandalous behavior of Governor Cosby. Cosby, in turn, ordered four issues of the paper to be condemned and publicly burned by the hangman. It was not long before Zenger himself was arrested and charged with seditious libel. Unable to raise the excessive bail, Zenger languished in jail before obtaining the services of one of the colony's leading lawyers.

The Zenger case filled the New York City courtroom to capacity as the trial got started on August 4, 1735. His attorney argued that for his client to be adjudged guilty, his words must be "false, scandalous, and seditious." The prosecutor responded that it made no difference if the libel was true because "the government is a sacred body and it was a crime to libel it." After several more skirmishes between the attorneys, the jury left the court. Ignoring instructions by Governor Cosby's handpicked judges, the jury came back with a verdict of not guilty on the charge of "publishing seditious libel." An important moment in colonial justice, the Zenger ruling did not immediately establish freedom of the press in the American colonies. No new law was promulgated in respect to seditious libel, but in the aftermath of the case, "prosecutions for seditious libel began to falter with increasing consistency."[21] According to legal scholars, legal precedents change the law, and since these come from judicial opinions that interpret the law, the outcome of the Zenger trial was not the result of a judicial opinion. However, the acquittal indicated that the public was opposed to such prosecutions. Subsequently, the threat of jury nullification would discourage similar prosecutions.

The Zenger acquittal resulted from the independent decision of the jury to ignore the instructions of the judge. Modern legal scholars view the verdict as an example of jury nullification; in other words, the jury refused to enforce the law because they thought the prosecution was unfair. Thus, while the Zenger case did not immediately change the law, it did set an important political precedent for a free press, the right of the people to criticize the government, and the right of a jury to ignore the technical requirements of the law in order to protect a defendant from an overbearing government. Legal scholar Paul Finkelman argues that the "case inspired patriots during the Revolution, supporters of a Bill of Rights during the struggle for ratification of the Constitution, and opponents of the Sedition Act of 1798" and "laid the groundwork for the evolution of the ideology of freedom of the press."[22]

During the proceedings, Zenger was never called as a witness or said a single word, but the judgment spoke volumes. Having spent ten months in jail, the case also illustrated the threat and nature of excessive bail. The Zenger case was not the first in colonial America involving jury independence, but the acquittal went a long way toward establishing a basic right that would be reaffirmed a half century later by the Constitution. One of the main contributors to the drafting of the Constitution, Governor Morris wrote, "The trial of Zenger in 1735 was the germ of American freedom, the morning star of that liberty which subsequently revolutionized America."[23]

CONCLUSIONS

The modification of English criminal justice procedures in the New World was the result of numerous abortive attempts to introduce Old World practices to America. By the mid-eighteenth century, the early religious laws of Pennsylvania and New England had been replaced by English legal precedents. Paving the road to revolutionary America, according to the historian David Rothman, "the mother country had stifled the colonists' benevolent instincts, compelling them to emulate the crude customs of the old world. The result was the predominance of archaic and punitive laws that only served to perpetuate crime."[24]

Although colonial criminal law was influenced by English criminal law, it was rarely as severe. Prior to the outbreak of the American Revolution, a distinctly American approach to criminal justice had emerged. American criminal justice was becoming more democratic than the English system and moving toward more humane and rational punishments as the number of capital crimes was reduced and defendants were provided legal rights.

Southern criminal codes more closely followed English antecedents than the northern colonies. In the South, "concern for status of offender and victim more closely paralleled the mother country's."[25]

The Puritans played a critical role in the shaping of American values. Although they have frequently been lambasted for their religious zeal and caricatured as dour prudes, recent research suggests that almost the opposite was true. Although they harshly punished fornicators and adulterers, it was because so much value was placed on the institution of marriage and the family. Perhaps this explains their low rates of premarital pregnancy compared to those of the more secularized southern colonies. Because the Puritans frowned on public drunkenness does not mean that they abstained from alcohol themselves. The Puritans left a legacy of their work ethic and moral sensibility that became the foundation of America's sense of mission. Rejecting the idea of church courts, the Puritans were committed to the separation of church and state.

At the beginning of the eighteenth century, colonial criminal law began to more closely resemble English criminal law. Concerns about labor scarcity compelled earlier lawmakers to refrain from more punitive punishments since the contributions of each settler were needed in the New World. With plenty of labor by the 1700s, there was more need for order than

leniency. Legal scholars view this period as "an end of an era of leniency in punishment of crimes against property."[26]

By the 1750s, colonial cities were already teeming with gangs of thieves, robbers, and cutpurses. Ordinary crimes against property flourished. Without a professional police force, concern for crime was on the rise. For almost 150 years, the night watchman and constables were the sole protection in urban areas. While crime was much higher in London than in Philadelphia, it was only because of higher population density. Jails existed, but the concept of the penitentiary was still on the horizon. While punishment was less punitive in the New World, people still hanged for crimes ranging from murder, piracy, and arson to repeated acts of robbery. Execution day became a spectacle as crowds gathered around the gallows to listen to a felon's final words and a minister's sermon.

Point–Counterpoint
Salem Witchcraft Trials (1692)

With few methods to ascertain guilt or innocence the Puritans of the Massachusetts Colony relied on time tested procedures not far removed from the ordeals of the Middle Ages. In the following passages Increase Mather (1639-1723), a prominent Puritan minister and leader supports certain grounds for convicting individuals of witchcraft. Arguing against the tests for witchcraft is Thomas Brattle (1658-1713). An opponent of the Puritan theocracy, Brattle was born into a wealthy Boston family, graduated from Harvard and won distinction as a mathematician and astronomer.

As to the method which the Salem justices do take in their examinations, it is truly this. A warrant being issued out to apprehend the persons that are charged and complained of by the afflicted children, . . . said persons are brought before the justices (the afflicted being present). The justices ask the apprehended why

Source: Increase Mather, *Cases of Conscience Concerning Evil Spirits Personating Men* in Cotton Mather, *The Wonders of the Invisible World* (London, 1862), pp. 277-284; Thomas Brattle, "Letter, 1692," in G.L. Burr, ed., *Narratives of the Witchcraft Cases 1648-1706*, New York, 1914., 170-190.

they afflict those poor children; to which the apprehended answer, they do not afflict them. The justices order the apprehended to look upon the said children, which accordingly they do; and at the time of that look. . . the afflicted are cast into a fit. The apprehended are then blinded, and ordered to touch the afflicted; and at that touch, . . . the afflicted ordinarily do come out of their fits. The afflicted persons then declare and affirm, that the apprehended have afflicted them. Upon which the apprehended persons, though of never so good repute, are forthwith committed to prison, on suspicion for witchcraft. . . .

I cannot but condemn this method of the justices, of making this touch of the hand a rule to discover witchcraft; because I am fully persuaded that it is sorcery, and a superstitious method, and that which we have no role for, either from reason or religion. . . . I would fain know of these Salem gentlemen, but as yet could never know, how it comes about, that if these apprehended persons are witches, and, by a look of the eye, do cast the afflicted into their fits by poisoning them, how it comes about I say, that, by a look of their eye, they do not cast others into fits, and poison others by their looks; and in particular, tender, fearful women, who often are beheld by them, and as likely as any in the whole world to receive an ill impression from them. This Salem philosophy, some men may call the new philosophy; but I think it rather deserves the name of Salem superstition and sorcery, and it is not fit to be named in the land of such light as New England is. . . .

But furthermore, I would fain know. . . what can the jury or judges desire more, to convict any man of witchcraft, than a plain demonstration, that the said man is a witch? Now if this look and touch, circumstanced as before, be a plain demonstration, (as their philosophy teaches), what need they seek for further evidences, when, after all, it can be but a demonstration?. . . Yet certain is it, that the reasonable part of the world, when acquainted herewith, will laugh at the demonstration, and conclude that the said Salem gentlemen are actually possessed, at least, with ignorance and folly. . ..

Secondly, with respect to. . .such as confess themselves to be witches,. . . there are now about fifty of them in prison; many of which I have again and again seen and heard; and I cannot but tell you, that my faith is strong concerning them, that they are deluded, imposed upon, and under the influence of some evil spirit; and therefore unfit to be evidences either against themselves, or anyone else. . . .

These confessors. . .do very often contradict themselves, as inconsistently as is usual for any crazed, distempered person to do. . . . Even the judges themselves have, at some times, taken these confessors in flat lies, or contradictions, even in the courts; by reason of which, one would have thought, that the judges would have frowned upon the said confessors, discarded them, and not minded one tittle of any thing that they said. But instead. . . the judges vindicate these confessors, and salve their contradictions, by proclaiming, that the Devil takes away their memory, and imposes on their brain. . . .

In the next place, I proceed to the form of their indictments, and the trials thereupon.

The indictment runs for sorcery and witchcraft, acted upon the body of such an one. . .at such a particular time. . . . Now for the proof of the said sorcery and witchcraft, the prisoner at the bar pleading not guilty.

1. The afflicted persons are brought into court; and after much patience and pains taken with them, do take their oaths, that the prisoner at the bar did afflict them. . ..Often, when the afflicted do mean and intend only the appearance and shape of such an one, (say Goodwife Proctor) yet they positively swear that Goodwife Proctor did afflict them; and they have been allowed so to do, as though there was no real difference between Goodwife Proctor and the shape of Goodwife Proctor. This. . .may readily prove a stumbling block to the jury, lead them into a very fundamental error. . . .

2. The confessors do declare what they know of the said prisoner; and some of the confessors are allowed to give their oaths; a thing which I believe was never heard of in this world; that such as confess themselves to be witches, to have renounced God and Christ, and all that is sacred, should yet be allowed and ordered to swear by the name of the great God!. . .

3. Whoever can be an evidence against the prisoner at the bar is ordered to come into court. And here it scarce ever fails but that evidences, of one nature and another, are brought in, though, I think, all of them altogether alien to the matter of indictment; for they none of them do respect witchcraft upon the bodies of the afflicted, which is the lone matter of charge in the indictment.

4. They [the accused] are searched by a jury; and as to some of them, the jury brought in, that [on] such or such a place there was a preternatural excrescence. And I wonder what person there is, whether man or woman, of whom it cannot be said but that, in some part of their body or other, there is a preternatural excrescence. The term is a very general and inclusive term. . . .

In short, the prisoner at the bar is indicted for sorcery and witchcraft acted upon the bodies of the afflicted. Now, for the proof of this, I reckon that the only pertinent evidences brought in are the evidences of the said afflicted.

It is true, that over and above the evidences of the afflicted persons, there are many evidences brought in, against the prisoner at the bar: either that he was at a witch meeting, or that he performed things which could not be done by an ordinary natural power; or that she sold butter to a sailor, which proving bad at sea, and the seamen exclaiming against her, she appeared, and soon after there was a storm, or the like. But what if there were ten thousand evidences of this nature; how do they prove the matter of indictment! And if they do not reach the matter of indictment, then I think it is clear, that the prisoner at the bar is brought in guilty, and condemned, merely from the evidences of the afflicted persons. . . .

As to the late executions, I shall only tell you, that in the opinion of many unprejudiced, considerate and considerable spectators, some of the condemned went out of the world not only with as great protestations, but also with as good shows of innocency, as men could do.

They protested their innocency as in the presence of the great God, whom forthwith they were to appear before. They wished, and declared their wish, that their blood might be the last innocent blood shed upon that account. With great affection they entreated Mr. C[otton] M[ather] to pray with them. They prayed that God would discover what witchcrafts were among us; they forgave their accusers; they spoke without reflection on jury and judges, for bringing them in guilty, and condemning them. They prayed earnestly for pardon for all other sins, and for an interest in the precious blood of our dear Redeemer; and seemed to be very sincere, upright, and sensible of their circumstances on all accounts. . . .

I cannot but admire that the justices, whom I think to be well-meaning men, should so far give ear to the Devil, as merely upon his authority to issue out their warrants, and apprehend people. Liberty was evermore accounted the great privilege of an Englishman; but certainly, if the Devil will be heard against us, and his testimony taken, to the seizing and apprehending of us, our liberty vanishes, and we are fools if we boast of our liberty. Now, that the justices have thus far given ear to the Devil I think may be mathematically demonstrated to any man of common sense: And for the demonstration and proof hereof, I desire, only, that these two things may be duly considered, viz.

1. That several persons have been apprehended purely upon the complaints of these afflicted, to whom the afflicted were perfect strangers, and had not the least knowledge of imaginable, before they were apprehended.

2. That the afflicted do own and assert, and the justices do grant, that the Devil does inform and tell the afflicted the names of those persons that are thus unknown unto them. Now these two things being duly considered, I think it will appear evident to anyone, that the Devil's information is the fundamental testimony that is gone upon in the apprehending of the aforesaid people.

If I believe such or such an assertion as comes immediately from the minister of God in the pulpit, because it is the word of the everliving God, I build my faith on God's testimony: and if I practice upon it, this my practice is properly built on the word of God. Even so in the case before us, if I believe the afflicted persons as informed by the Devil, and act thereupon, this my act may properly be said to be grounded upon the testimony or information of the Devil. And now, if things are thus, I think it ought to be for a lamentation to you and me, and all such as would be accounted good Christians. . . .

The chief judge is very zealous in these proceedings, and says, he is very clear as to all that hath as yet been acted by this court, and, as far as ever I could perceive, is very impatient in hearing anything that looks another way. I very highly honor and reverence the wisdom and integrity of the said judge, and hope that this matter shall not diminish my veneration for his honor; however, I cannot but say, my great fear is, that wisdom and counsel are withheld from his honor as to this matter, which yet I look upon not so much as a judgment to his honor as to this poor land.

But although the chief judge, and some of the other judges, be very zealous in these proceedings, yet this you may take for a truth, that there are several about the Bay, men for understanding, judgment, and piety, inferior to few, (if any), in New England that do utterly condemn the said proceedings, and do freely deliver their judgment in the case to be. . . that these methods will utterly rain and undo poor New England. . . . Several of the late justices, viz. Thomas Graves, Esq., N. Byfield, Esq., Francis Foxcroft, Esq., are much dissatisfied; also several of the present justices; and in particular, some of the Boston justices, were resolved rather to throw up their commissions than be active in disturbing the liberty of Their Majesties' subjects, merely on the accusations of these afflicted, possessed children.

Finally; the principal gentlemen in Boston, and thereabout, are generally agreed that irregular and dangerous methods have been taken as to these matters. . . . Nineteen persons have now been executed, and one pressed to death for a mute: seven more are condemned; two of which are reprieved, because they pretend their being with child; one, viz. Mrs. Bradbury of Salisbury, from the intercession of some friends; and two or three more, because they are confessors.

The court is adjourned to the first Tuesday in November, then to be kept at Salem; between this and then will be [the] great assembly [the General Court], and this matter will be a peculiar matter of their agitation. I think it is matter of earnest supplication and prayer to Almighty God, that He would afford His Gracious Presence to the said assembly, and direct them aright in this weighty matter. . . . I am very sensible, that it is irksome and disagreeable to go back, when a man's doing so is an implication that he has been walking in a wrong path. However, nothing is more honorable than, upon due conviction, to retract and undo, so far as may be, what has been amiss and irregular. . . .

Many of these afflicted persons. . . do say. . . that they can see specters when their eyes are shut, as well as when they are open. This one thing I evermore accounted as very observable, and that which might serve as a good key to unlock the nature of these mysterious troubles, if duly improved by us. Can they see specters when their eyes are shut? I am sure they lie, at least speak falsely, if they say so; for the thing, in nature, is an utter impossibility. It is true, they may strongly fancy, or have things represented to their imagination, when their eyes are shut; and I think this is all which ought to be allowed to these blind, nonsensical girls. And if our officers

and courts have apprehended, imprisoned, condemned, and executed our guiltless neighbors, certainly our error is great, and we shall rue it in the conclusion.

There are two or three other things that I have observed in and by these afflicted persons, which make me strongly suspect that the Devil imposes upon their brains, and deludes their fancy and imagination; and that the Devil's book (which they say has been offered them) is a mere fancy of theirs, and no reality; that the witches' meeting, the Devil's baptism, and mock sacraments, which they oft speak of, are nothing else but the effect of their fancy, depraved and deluded by the Devil, and not a reality to be regarded or minded by any wise man. And whereas the confessors have owned and asserted the said meetings, the said baptism, and mock sacrament,. . .I am very apt to think, that, did you know the circumstances of the said confessors, you would not be swayed thereby, any otherwise than to be confirmed, that all is perfect devilism, and an hellish design to ruin and destroy this poor land. For whereas there are of the said confessors fifty-five in number, some of them are known to be distracted, crazed women;. . . . Others of them denied their guilt, and maintained their innocency for above eighteen hours, after most violent, distracting and dragooning methods had been used with them, to make them confess. Such methods they were, that more than one of the said confessors did since tell many, with tears in their eyes, that they thought their very lives would have gone out of their bodies; and wished that they might have been cast into the lowest dungeon, rather than be tortured with such repeated buzzings and chuckings and unreasonable urgings as they were treated withal. They soon recanted their confessions, acknowledging, with sorrow and grief, that it was an hour of great temptation with them. . . .

But, finally, as to about thirty of these fifty-five confessors, they are possessed (I reckon) with the Devil, and afflicted as the children are, and therefore not fit to be regarded as to anything they say of themselves or others. . . .

What will be the issue of these troubles, God only knows; I am afraid that his own children, to afflict and humble them, for some sin they have been guilty of before Him. . . .

This then I declare and testify, that to take away the life of anyone, merely because a specter or devil, in a bewitched or possessed person does accuse them, will bring the guilt of innocent blood on the

land. . . . What does such an evidence amount
unto more than this: Either such an one did afflict
such an one, or the Devil in his likeness, or his eyes
were bewitched. . . .

. . . . But then the inquiry is, what is sufficient
proof? . . .

A free and voluntary confession of the crime made
by the person suspected and accused after examination,
is a sufficient ground of conviction. Indeed, if persons
are distracted, or under the power of phrenetic
melancholy, that alters the case; but the jurors that
examine them, and their neighbors that know them,
may easily determine that case; or if confession be
extorted, the evidence is not so clear and convictive;
but if any persons out of remorse of conscience, or
from a touch of God in their spirits, confess and show
their deeds . . . nothing can be more clear. . . .

If two credible persons shall affirm upon oath that
they have seen the party accused speaking such
words, or doing things which none but such as have
familiarity with the Devil ever did or can do, that's a
sufficient ground for conviction. . . . The Devil
never assists men to do supernatural things undesired.
When therefore such like things shall be testified
against the accused party not by specters which are
devils in the shape of persons . . . but by real men or
women . . ., it is proof enough that such an one has
that conversation and correspondence with the Devil,
as that he or she, whoever they be, ought to be
exterminated from amongst men. This
notwithstanding I will add. It were better that ten
suspected witches should escape, than that one
innocent person should be condemned. . . . I had
rather judge a witch to be an honest woman, than
judge an honest woman as a witch.

SOURCES

Beckman, Gail McKnight, comp. 1976. *The Statutes at Large of Pennsylvania in the Time of William Penn: 1680–1700.* Vol. 1. New York: Vantage Press.

Billias, George Athan, ed. 1965. *Law and Authority in Colonial America.* Barre, Mass.: Barre Publishers.

Blumenthal, Walter Hart. 1962. *Brides from Bridewell: Female Felons Sent to Colonial America.* Rutland, Vt.: Charles E. Tuttle.

Caldwell, Robert Graham. 1947. *Red Hannah: Delaware's Whipping Post.* Philadelphia: University of Pennsylvania Press.

Christianson, Scott. 1998. *With Liberty for Some: 500 Years of Imprisonment in America.* Boston: Northeastern University Press.

Conrad, Clay. 1998. *Jury Nullification: The Evolution of a Doctrine.* Durham, N.C.: Carolina Academic Press.

Dow, George Francis. 1988. *Everyday Life in the Massachusetts Bay Colony.* New York: Dover Publications.

Erikson, Kai T. 1966. *Wayward Puritans: A Study in the Sociology of Deviance.* New York: John Wiley & Sons.

Finkelman, Paul, ed. 1997. *A Brief Narrative of the Case and Tryal of John Peter Zenger, Printer of the New York Weekly Journal.* St. James, N.Y.: Brandywine Press.

Fisher, David Hackett. 1989. *Albion's Seed: Four British Folkways in America.* New York: Oxford University Press.

"Free the Salem Five!" *American Heritage,* December 2001, p. 15.

Friedman, Lawrence M. 1973. *A History of American Law.* New York: Simon and Schuster.

———. 1993. *Crime and Punishment in American History.* New York: Basic Books.

Greenberg, Douglas. 1982. "Crime, Law Enforcement and Social Control in Colonial America." *American Journal of Legal History* 26 (October): 293–325.

Hadden, Sally E. 2001. *Slave Patrols: Law and Violence in Virginia and the Carolinas.* Cambridge, Mass.: Harvard University Press.

Hall, Kermit L. 1989. *The Magic Mirror: Law in American History.* New York: Oxford University Press.

Hindus, Michael Stephen. 1980. *Prison and Plantation: Crime, Justice, and Authority in Massachusetts and South Carolina, 1767–1878.* Chapel Hill: University of North Carolina Press.

Hoffer, Peter Charles. 1992. *Law and People in Colonial America.* Baltimore: Johns Hopkins Press.

Konig, David Thomas. 1979. *Law and Society in Puritan Massachusetts: Essex County, 1629–1692,* Chapel Hill: University of North Carolina Press.

McManus, Edgar J. 1993. *Law and Liberty in Early New England: Criminal Justice and Due Process, 1620–1692.* Amherst: University of Massachusetts Press.

Miller, Helen Hill. 1965. *The Case for Liberty.* Chapel Hill: University of North Carolina Press.

Perry, Richard L., ed. 1964. *Sources of Our Liberties: English and American Documents from Magna Carta to the Bill of Rights.* New York: McGraw-Hill.

Powers, Edwin. 1966. *Crime and Punishment in Early Massachusetts, 1620–1692: A Documentary History.* Boston: Beacon Press.

Reis, Elizabeth. 1997. *Damned Women: Sinners and Witches in Puritan New England.* Ithaca, N.Y.: Cornell University Press.

Rothman, David. 1971. *The Discovery of the Asylum: Social Order and Disorder in the New Republic.* Boston: Little, Brown.

Semmes, Raphael. 1938. *Crime and Punishment in Early Maryland.* Baltimore: Johns Hopkins University Press.

CRITICAL THINKING QUESTIONS

1. Compare and contrast the development of criminal justice procedures in the Pennsylvania, Virginia, and Massachusetts colonies.

2. What influence did religion have on the development of colonial law?

3. How did the emergence of slavery influence criminal justice procedures? Which colonies were most influenced?

4. What impact did the acquittal of John Peter Zenger have on American freedoms?

5. Discuss variations of crime and punishment in the different colonies.

6. Why did colonial punishment become more punitive after 1700? Why was it more relaxed in the earlier period?

7. Describe the various characteristics of America's developing criminal justice system in the colonial period (i.e., police, courts, and corrections).

CRIMINAL JUSTICE HISTORY
ON THE INTERNET

An excellent source for colonial trials can be found at Professor Douglas Linder's Famous American Trials Web site at wysiwyg://13/http:// jurist.law .pitt.edu/trials20.htm. Students can find a full discussion and narrative of the Zenger trial. An issue of Zenger's newspaper is located at http:// gi/dynamic/offsite.htm?site=http//earlyamerica .com//earlyamerica/bookmarks/zenger/index .html. Documents and links related to the Salem witch trials abound at http://earlyamerica.com/ cgi-bin/search/search.pl. For more on the Salem trials, see www.salemweb.com/guide/witches.htm, www.nationalgeographic.com/features/97/salem/ splashx.html, and especially www.law.umkc.edu/ faculty/projects/ftrials/salem/salem.htm. For examination of Arthur Miller's play and movie version of *The Crucible,* based on the Salem episode, see http://movieweb.com/movie/the crucible/index.html and www.law.umkc.edu/ faculty/projects/ftrials/salem/SAL_CRU.HTM.

For the history of the early courts of Virginia, including the Supreme Court of Virginia, see www.courts.state.va.us/scov/cover.htm. Links to legal history Web sites are located at http://mailer.fsu.edu/~shadden/Legal18links.htm. A bounty of seventeenth- and eighteenth-century legal documents are linked to Yale Law School's Avalon Project at www.yale.edu/lawweb/ avalon/pre18.htm. Colonial charters, grants, and related documents are available at www.yale.edu/lawweb/avalon/states/statech.htm.

An excellent article on forfeiture in England and colonial America is at www.fsu.edu/~crimdo/ forfeiture.html. Links to the Mayflower Compact, first Virginia charters, and the Fundamental Orders of Connecticut can be accessed through www.law.ou.edu/hist.

For links to Quaker history, see the Religious Society of Friends at www.quaker.org and, for early Quaker history, http://thorn.pair.com/ earlyq.htm. On William Penn and his first *Frame of Government,* see www.quaker.org/wmpenn.html.

The text of the Massachusetts *Body of Liberties* can be located at http://history.hanover.edu/ texts/masslib.htm or at www.winthropsociety.org/liberty.htm.

Virginia's early martial law, known as *Lawes Divine, Morall, and Martiall,* is examined at www.leaderu.com/orgs/cdf/ff/chap10.html.

NOTES

1. Hindus (1980, p. 130).
2. Quoted in Hindus (1980, p. 132).
3. Quoted in Christianson (1998, p. 7).
4. Perry (1964, p. 60).

5. The one exception to this was the minister, who was not allowed to hold office, appointed or elected, because of the Puritan belief that politics would taint, or corrupt, the minister's soul.

6. Hoffer (1992, p. 18).

7. Quoted in Hoffer (1992, p. 18).

8. Quoted in Erikson (1966, p. 120).

9. According to David Hackett Fisher, men were treated more harshly in New England, while the reverse was true in the Chesapeake region.

10. Hoffer (1992, p. 19).

11. Hoffer (1992, p. 20).

12. Quoted in Fisher (1989, pp. 141–42).

13. Fisher (1989).

14. Caldwell (1947, pp. 69–82).

15. The *schout* watched for infractions of the law, and the rattle watch carried rattles to warn of their approach and functioned as night watchmen.

16. For more on Caribbean slave patrols, see Hadden (2001, pp. 10–14).

17. Hadden (2001, p. 21).

18. Fisher (1981, p. 127).

19. More than half of all girls in the Massachusetts Bay Colony were named either Mary, Elizabeth, or Sarah. These names were selected from the Bible because of their moral connotations.

20. "Free the Salem Five!" (2001).

21. Conrad (1998, p. 38).

22. Finkelman (1997, pp. 10–11).

23. Quoted by Douglas Linder, "Famous American Trials: The Trial of John Peter Zenger," wysiwyg://13/http://jurist.law.pitt.edu/trials20.htm, p. 8.

24. Rothman (1971, p. 59).

25. Hoffer (1992, p. 82).

26. Hoffer (1992, p. 83).

4

CRIMINAL JUSTICE IN
REVOLUTIONARY TIMES
(1718–1797)

TIME LINE

1718	English government reinstates Sanguinary Laws in Pennsylvania	1788	U.S. Constitution is ratified
		1789	Creation of the office of U.S. marshal
1749	Publication of Henry Fielding's *An Enquiry into the Causes of the Latest Increase in Robberies*	1789	Judiciary Act
		1790	Federal Crimes Act
1764	Publication of Cesare Beccaria's *Essay on Crimes and Punishment*	1790	Birth of the penitentiary at Philadelphia's Walnut Street Jail
1767	Creation of South Carolina Regulators	1791	Bill of Rights added to Constitution
1770	Boston Massacre and trial	1794	Whiskey Rebellion, first test of the American Constitution
1786	Shays' Rebellion	1794	First law enforcement officer killed following birth of Republic
1787	Publication of Benjamin Rush's "Enquiry into the Effects of Public Punishments upon Criminals and upon Society"	1797	Newgate Prison opens doors in New York

Following the French and Indian War, Britain left troops in its American colonies to maintain peace between the Americans and the Indians. From the start, American citizens were hostile toward attempted peacekeeping measures by the British military because troops were not stationed along the frontiers but instead were left in important coastal cities, particularly in Boston. As the American colonies approached the revolutionary era, criminal justice procedures were still rooted in seventeenth-century British common law. Trained peace officers and the penitentiary system as we now know it did not yet exist. If there was a serious emergency in major cities such as Boston or Philadelphia, civilian authorities relied on militia who met annually and elected their own officers. But drawn from the community, they could not be counted on to repress political unrest and mob actions by such "treasonous" groups as the Sons of Liberty. Therefore, the only real alternative for peacekeeping were the soldiers of the British army stationed in important coastal cities. Sentries who perhaps challenged passers-by too exuberantly sometimes faced criminal charges for assault against the peace. As the army became more visible, it tended to provoke civilians more than maintain order. Boston resistance to the presence of British soldiers would culminate in the Boston Massacre and other seminal events leading to the American Revolution.

Various historians have speculated on what might have occurred had an effective police apparatus existed at the time of the American Revolution. The breakdown of the parish constable police system was most apparent in Boston in the 1760s, as mobs of Patriots who undoubtedly included local constables ran roughshod through the cobblestone streets. According to police historian Charles Reith, if there had been an alternative to the parish constable system, "Samuel Adams would be unknown to history. There would have been no Boston mobs worthy of historical mention. Without him and his mobs there would have been no war in the American colonies."[1] There is some doubt whether the Revolution could have proceeded as smoothly had there been an effective police system in place.

The American Revolution took on many of the characteristics of a civil war, with British troops firing on British Americans and neighbor sometimes fighting neighbor. After the meeting of the first Continental Congress in September 1774, steps were taken for a planned boycott of British goods. Every county, city, and town appointed local committees called Committees of Safety to scrutinize the conduct of citizens and to publish the names of those who violated terms of the boycott. Individuals reluctant to participate in the boycott were often physically intimidated. With many citizens still loyal to the Crown, active and organized groups rapidly separated the colonies into two camps, Tories, or Loyalists, whose sympathies lay with England, and Patriots, who favored armed resistance.

THE LAWGIVERS

Since the 1660s, English Parliament attempted to regulate overseas trade with its colonial empire through a series of Navigation Acts. New England merchants resisted these restraints through an ingenious campaign of coastal smuggling or bribing customs agents. If smugglers were caught, they were tried in nonjuried admiralty courts, but for the most part these illicit activities were ignored by British officials, rendering it a period of "salutary (healthy) neglect." This period of neglect ended abruptly at the conclusion of the French and Indian War (also known as the Seven Years' War) in 1763. Parliament introduced new legislation to refill British coffers and give officials better control over trade. However, colonists continued smuggling, and English officials responded with oppressive measures known as writs of assistance. These writs allowed royal officials to use search warrants issued by courts as devices to hunt down violators of the customs laws. The writs were viewed as unwarranted infringements on individual privacy and freedom by the colonists who took seriously the adage "An Englishman's house is his castle." The violation of this fundamental principle of the common law by customs officials, who were authorized to enter any house on suspicion, contributed to the alienation of the colonists from England.

In 1765, protests and social unrest broke out throughout the American colonies in response to the passage of the Stamp Act, the first direct, or internal, tax that Parliament had ever imposed on the Americans. Previous to this, only colonial legislatures had directly taxed their citizens. Colonial leaders such as Benjamin Franklin and Patrick Henry recognized that if this act were permitted, it would usurp the taxation functions of individual colonial legislatures, rights that Parliament had tacitly relinquished in the past. According to the new law, Americans had to purchase specially stamped paper for newspapers, pamphlets, college degrees, playing cards, liquor licenses, dice, and most legal forms, including marriage licenses, death certificates, and court documents. While the purpose of the Stamp Act was to help pay the cost for British military forces left in America for the protection of the colonists from Indian attacks, practically all colonists opposed it and resented the presence of troops in their cities, far from the Indian frontier. Attempts to circumvent the Stamp Act led to trials in vice-admiralty courts. These courts were set up in 1696 in each colony and did not use juries, so it was only natural that colonists feared that these special courts threatened the right to trial by jury.

A special Stamp Act Congress was convened and led to a systematic plan of opposition to the tax, while at the same time it still professed its subordination to the Crown. The Congress maintained that to remain a free people, no taxes could be imposed on them without their consent. This Congress was created outside the British constitutional system and functioned as an extralegal governing body, working toward a peaceful resolution of the colonists' complaints. Patrick Henry expressed this same thought in a speech delivered to Virginia's House of Burgesses

in which he proclaimed, "No taxation without representation." On the local level, common people in Boston and other towns formed an organization known as the "Sons of Liberty." That summer, a Boston crowd targeted the house of city stamp collector Andrew Oliver, which they destroyed in one fell swoop. This episode led to the resignation of stamp collectors throughout the colonies and exposed the inability of current criminal justice practices to enforce the peace. Although Parliament repealed the act in 1766, most historians cite the Stamp Act riots as the beginning of the colonial struggle for independence from England.

In the years leading up to the American Revolution, the court and legal systems were rooted in British common law. Those arrested in political actions such as the Stamp Act riots faced a court system based on English common law, and little changed until the 1770s. At the time of the Declaration of Independence, the colonies were still using a variety of court systems established a half century earlier; Maryland, Massachusetts, and New York had created their courts as early as the 1690s.

The American legal profession was in its infancy, with few lawyers plying their trade in the early colonies. Some colonial legislatures even prohibited the practicing of law for fees without a special license from the local courts. Most colonies were hostile to the legal profession, with New York recording only forty-one lawyers between 1695 and 1769, and these were appointed by the governor. If one wished to study law in this era, it would have to be in England, where more than 100 sons of wealthy American families studied between 1760 and 1776. By the time of the Revolution, South Carolina and Pennsylvania could claim the greatest number of lawyers trained at the Inns of Court in England.

Prior to the American Revolution, the colonial world was moving away from its homogeneous roots. The mainly middle- and working-class English colonies would undergo a demographic transformation between 1700 and 1775, with the influx of Scots-Irish, German refugees, debtors and convicts from England, and African slaves. This feature became the new nation's greatest strength as well as a major source for social and political discord.

The U.S. Constitution and Bill of Rights

Barely 100 years elapsed between the English Bill of Rights (1689) and the American Bill of Rights. Both evolved from the insistence of the citizens on a recognition by the government of what they termed their "natural" rights. This idea of a contract between those governing and those governed can be traced back to the writings of John Locke and Montesquieu, political theorists who asserted that individuals possessed certain natural rights above and beyond the law of the state. Some of these rights were considered "inalienable" and could not be surrendered. A bill of rights was included in the new nation's Constitution, and it specifically enumerated the inalienable rights of the people on which the state was forbidden to infringe.

Prior to the War of Independence, in some of the colonies Americans enjoyed more liberties than their English counterparts. In one important study of colonial criminal justice, historian Bradley Chapin listed sixteen procedural guarantees found in colonial codes:

1. No search and seizure without warrant
2. Right to reasonable bail
3. Confessions out of court invalid
4. Right to have cause determined with reasonable speed
5. Grand jury indictment in capital cases
6. Right to know the charges
7. Straightforward pleading with double jeopardy barred
8. Right to challenge jurors
9. Process to compel witnesses for the defense
10. Right to confront accusers
11. Trial by jury
12. Limitation of punishment to the convict: no corruption of blood or forfeiture
13. No cruel or unusual punishment
14. Equal protection of the law: dependent classes—women, children, and servants—have access to the courts
15. Equal execution of the law: no capricious mitigation or application of penalties
16. [Limited] right of appeal[2]

The U.S. Constitution that was ratified in 1788 included several checks and balances to guarantee that the central government could not become omnipotent. Except for guaranteeing such rights as trial by jury and the privilege of habeas corpus, the Constitution did not specifically address individual rights. Many of the framers of the document were unhappy with the finished product, which did not offer enough protection of individual liberties, including most of those in the previous list. To remedy this deficiency, ten amendments, known as the Bill of Rights, were adopted in 1791.

It may seem surprising that these amendments identifying personal liberties were left out of the original document. However, some of the men who composed the Constitution were hoping to restrict the rights of common citizens, thus reducing the power of the ordinary American. But Americans, many of them veterans of the conflict, had anticipated these rights since the Declaration of Independence. Others at the Constitutional Convention represented this perspective and agreed to ratification of the new government only on the condition that a bill of rights be added later. Those additions are the first ten amendments to the U.S. Constitution and are known as the Bill of Rights.

Several of the amendments of the Bill of Rights have important ramifications for the study of federal criminal justice. Although the Bill of Rights applied only to the citizens' federal rights and federal law until the mid-twentieth century (see chapter 11), the states adopted bills of rights modeled on the federal bill. As legal historians have made clear, since the Bill of Rights applied to the federal government and not the states, the amendments did not "create a national standard."[3] Criminal justice remained the bailiwick of the states until the 1950s. It would be more than a 150 years before a system was devised "for coordinating the work of the states."[4] But, according to one authority, the mere existence of these standards at this time period "marked a subtle but important shift in priorities, away from the emphasis on community order and toward a preference for individual liberty."[5]

The First Amendment affirmed the basic rights of freedom of religion, speech, and press and the right to assemble peacefully and to petition the government for a redress of grievances. This amendment provides perhaps the most important protections of the American democratic system. As previous chapters have demonstrated, there are few, if any, precedents for religious freedom without the interference of the state.

The Second Amendment, commonly known as "the right to bear arms," which protects the right of states to form militias, is today at the center of the debate over gun control. Stating that "a well-regulated militia being necessary to the security of a free state," the amendment allows for the existence of a citizen's militia. However, critics of gun control argue that it extends to every citizen the right to have arms for one's personal defense. Unlike the English right to bear arms, which limited ownership with various specifications, in America gun ownership became ingrained as both a collective duty (militia) and a personal right (protection).

The Fourth Amendment, prohibiting arbitrary search and seizure, is derived almost directly from an English court decision in 1765. The Fifth Amendment's prohibition against self-incrimination can be traced back to the 1642 abolition of the Star Chamber.

Several amendments would figure in future constitutional challenges to the death penalty. The Fifth Amendment has been cited for its guarantee that no person shall be compelled to testify against himself and for its assurance of due process of law in a capital case. The Sixth Amendment has been summoned for its promise of an impartial jury in all criminal prosecutions. And the Eighth Amendment has been used to argue against cruel and unusual punishments (particularly in cases involving the electric chair).

Following the revolutionary era's hostilities with Great Britain and the Constitutional Conventions, the foundation for the federal criminal justice system was now in place. Along with the Bill of Rights and the U.S. Constitution, the federal Crimes Act of 1790 formed its nucleus. The act changed several punishments that had been popular in British common law but were prohibited by the new U.S. Constitution. It defined seventeen crimes, ranging from obstruction of process to treason. Death by hanging was prescribed for six crimes, including treason, murder, piracy, forgery, and helping individuals convicted of capital crimes escape from prison. Some aspects of the Crimes Act were rather unusual. It allowed the body of a person hanged for murder, at the discretion of the court, to be transferred to a surgeon for dissection. It was left to the marshal to carry out the postmortem part of the sentence. If an individual was apprehended while trying to rescue the body beforehand, he could be fined and imprisoned. It also permitted benefit of clergy only after a convicted defendant was branded on his right thumb. This brand denoted that the individual had made use of benefit of clergy already and guarded against repeated attempts.

The Judiciary Act of 1789

The Judiciary Act of 1789 created the federal courts that exist almost unchanged to this day, including the Supreme Court. During its first 100 years, justices of the Supreme Court complained about their heavy workloads, particularly the requirement that they "ride circuit." Without the assistance of separate federal judges for the federal circuit courts, the early Supreme Court justices listened to all federal cases, whether before the U.S. Supreme Court or circuit courts. This tradition played an important role in establishing the concept of a national government and a federal judiciary. Justices were expected to travel long distances on rough roads and put up with poor accommodations, often under hazardous conditions, to sit with district court judges at circuit courts. In 1792 alone, the six justices were required to sit at a total of twenty-seven circuit courts as well as at two sessions of the Supreme Court.

The Judiciary Act of 1789 also created what became known as the "U.S. attorneys." The president was authorized to appoint "a person learned in the law" in each judicial district to act as attorney for the United States in all criminal and civil cases in which the United States had an interest. These attorneys were appointed with the consent of Congress to four-year terms (just like the marshal). The act did not give a title to this position but merely appointed an attorney in each district. Henceforth, whenever this position was mentioned in statutes or court decisions, it was referred to as either "district attorney," "attorney," or "United States attorney." Sometimes an individual would be referred to by all three terms in a single statute or legal decision. In 1870, this position became more commonly known as "United States attorney."

The position of attorney general was also introduced by the Judiciary Act. The attorney general was created to handle all lawsuits in which the United States was embroiled as well as to advise the president on questions of law. For the next eighty years (until the creation of the Department of Justice in 1870), the attorney general was assisted by only a small staff that worked together with U.S. attorneys in the states.

LAW ENFORCEMENT

Law enforcement, for the most part, followed the same patterns from the earliest English colony in 1607 until the end of the American Revolution in 1781. However, the Enlightenment and more democratic principles underlying the American Revolution gave rise to many of the basic ideas that influenced modern policing. It was in the

eighteenth century that the dim outlines of American policing began to take shape. In the more rural areas, sheriffs and constables were selected from the ranks of the great landholders and performed the same functions as their counterparts across the ocean. As in medieval England, the colonial sheriff was expected to perform both police and financial duties. As chief financial officer of the county, he was entitled to 10 percent of the tax revenue he collected. From the beginning, the colonies committed themselves to this style of local peacekeeping rather than a centralized system of law enforcement. Today's decentralized police system in America, with more than 20,000 police forces and lacking a national force, is a testament to this earlier tradition.

In the eighteenth century, the theory of crime prevention was discussed by several prescient police officials in Great Britain, but little would come of it until the nineteenth century. By the late 1700s, it had become rather obvious that the traditional peacekeepers of London, such as the constable and night watch, were no match for the social and economic transformation of England. England's population doubled between 1700 and 1800, aggravating social tensions. Most English cities increased the number of constables and watchmen while at the same time making the transition from voluntary policing to a paid watch. With an ever-rising crime rate, little thought was given to innovation until the Fielding brothers came on the scene.

The Fieldings

Perhaps the most accomplished police reformers of the eighteenth century, the Fielding brothers of London laid the groundwork for the subsequent development of modern policing in nineteenth-century England and America. An impressive physical presence at over six feet tall, Henry Fielding (1707–1754) is best remembered as a novelist and playwright and as author of the novel *Tom Jones*. Because of censorship restrictions in the literary world, he left his writing career behind to become magistrate in the criminal justice system in 1748. During his six-year tenure at this post, he implemented several policies that led to increased safety on the streets of London. Fielding introduced the Bow Street Runners, initially called "Mr. Fielding's people," a specially formed group of constables who were expected to run to the aid of crime victims and in the pursuit of criminals. Henry Fielding demonstrated his foresight in police matters in 1749 with the publication of his essay *An Enquiry into the Causes of the Latest Increase of Robberies,* which called for the establishment of a professional full-time police force. Despite the reluctance of the public to accept a professional police force, Fielding persisted in his attempts to win the support of the government for this endeavor.

Following his death, he was succeeded by his brother John (1721–1780). Blind since birth, John served as magistrate for several years and in tribute to his brother kept the Bow Street Runners alive. His 1755 pamphlet *Plan for Preventing Robberies within Twenty Miles of London* explained his strategy for breaking up organized gangs of robbers that plagued the periphery of England's capital city. An astonishing detective in his own right, blind or sighted, Fielding was sometimes referred to as the "Blind Beak" and reportedly could identify thousands of criminals by voice alone. During his tenure as head of the Bow Street Runners, he made Bow Street the official police headquarters, where two horses were always posted at the ready to apprehend highwaymen. A police reformer like his brother Henry, he was perspicacious in his attempts to implement preventive police strategies. But it would be almost half a century before the ideas of the Fieldings became fully integrated into the London model of policing.

Patrick Colquhoun

Beginning with his appointment as London magistrate in 1792, Patrick Colquhoun (1745–1820) would focus on law enforcement reform for the next twenty-five years. He was recognized for his police acumen after the publication of several lengthy treatises on police reform. He endorsed the notion that the government should be responsible for regulating the conduct of the citizenry instead of neighborhood watch groups. This was a heretical idea at a time when local communities relied on neighborhood watchmen and local constables.

Colquhoun became interested in police reform through the work of the Fieldings, leading to the publication of his book *Treatise on the Police of the Metropolis* in 1797. Among the most important police concepts introduced in this work was the notion of crime prevention, a radical departure for the traditionally reactive police establishment. Following in the footsteps of the Fieldings, Colquhoun suggested that the police should gather information on the criminal element, keep a register of known offenders, and publish a police gazette to assist communication and apprehension of wrongdoers. To justify these reforms, he reportedly conducted research that estimated that more than 10,000 criminals resided in London.

Colquhoun was credited with the creation of the Thames River Police in 1789. His writings led to improved police professionalism and the first systematic examination of crime costs and origins. An advocate of paid professional policing and recruitment and management under a central authority free of political interference, he spurred police reform and introduced new solutions for maintaining public order in an era of urbanization and industrialization.

Police Efforts in the Colonies

Various explanations have been given for the rise in crime in the years preceding the American Revolution. Rising poverty, declining religious zeal, and urban growth all contributed to a climate of fear where robberies and burglaries became common and law-abiding citizens yearned for better law and order. Some of the earliest strides in countering the urban crime problem in the American colonies were taken in Philadelphia. Prior to 1750, the only street lighting consisted of oil lamps carried by safety-conscious citizens. In 1749, a Quaker-led citizen group initiated a street-lighting campaign that included raising funds to pay someone to install and light the lamps. The following year, these efforts spurred the assembly to chip in to pay for the initiative. Over the next decade, most major colonial cities adopted this strategy.[6] Street lighting was an important first step toward crime control.

During the revolutionary era, British troops occupied America's leading cities, which were usually important seaports. Throughout most of the war, the British occupied New York City, where they were also responsible for police protection. Dissatisfied by the British attempts at law enforcement, New York City residents harkened to the past and banded together and formed a civilian watch. In 1773, "Centinel Boxes" were placed around the city for the use of the watchmen. By the following year, sixteen regular watchmen were on duty every night. In extraordinary situations, the watch was augmented using different strategies. On a notoriously raucous evening, New Year's Eve, the city militia or a military garrison could be called on. The introduction of a paid night watch in the 1770s represented a great improvement over the citizen's watch but did little to stem New York City's growing crime problem. The growth of the population brought increased stratification, leading to the concomitant development of a dangerous criminal element. The night watch could not keep up with the increasing complexity of urban life. Required to be on constant vigil in the event of fire or social disorder while the city slept, the night watch was no match for the changing conditions. Without the resources or authority to maintain order, the night watch was outmatched by their criminal counterparts not only in New York City but also in most other eighteenth-century cities around the world.

Following the Revolutionary War and the evacuation of the British army from New York, the city's police problem was amplified by the diminished presence of many upper-class Loyalists who had previously provided an element of stability to the city's social structure. War historians have long noted how the ends of wars were often followed by a breakdown in morality, particularly after armies of occupation vacated sections of town that, in the case of New York, became districts notorious for vice and crime. The American army served a brief interlude as peacekeeper until the city could resume its civil authority and traditional judicial processes. Surprisingly, with few innovations in law enforcement and a burgeoning population, New York City was recognized as a peaceful law-abiding community on the cusp of the next century. But new waves of immigration would auger important changes for the criminal justice apparatus of America's cities in the next century.

Following the defeat of Britain and its German mercenaries, America's colonists were no more eager for a national police force than they had been before the outbreak of hostilities. City fathers were unable to overcome the reluctance of their citizens to support regular police through taxes. Ever-vigilant against a standing army and despotism, citizens resisted any efforts in the direction of uniformed police officers. Some state constitutions even limited the number of night watchmen. The resilient night watch had clearly outlasted its initial mandate and was usually under fire for sleeping and drinking on duty while doing nothing concerning crime prevention.

The Birth of Federal Law Enforcement

After ratifying the new Constitution, in 1789 the U.S. Congress created the nation's first federal law enforcement officer late in that year. The Judiciary Act established the federal judiciary as well as the office of United States marshal.[7] The marshal was transplanted to America and was readily identifiable in most colonies. Following the Judiciary Act, U.S. marshals and their deputies were required to make arrests while enforcing rulings by the federal courts. Early marshals were unsalaried but were paid on the basis of the work they completed. According to most accounts, the first law enforcement officer killed in America following the birth of the Republic was U.S. Marshal Robert Forsyth, who was shot down in 1794 while trying to serve court papers in Georgia.

The decades following the American Revolution were a time of social upheaval and transformation as the political system made the transition from one based on British colonialism to an American republic. The laws set forth by the U.S. Constitution received their first test in the fall of 1794, when farmers, distillers, and artisans in southwestern Pennsylvania protested a federal excise tax on whiskey through armed demonstrations. Marshals took early action, quelling the whiskey rebels in 1794. At issue was the federal government's early attempts to raise money by imposing an excise tax on all distilled liquors. With a depleted treasury, the government embarked on an aggressive effort to pay off the nation's staggering debt. But the tax brought the new government into conflict with western Pennsylvania farmers. Unable to afford to get their grain to market, these Scotch-Irish farmers distilled the grain into whiskey, a much easier commodity to transport. Living on the bleak margins of existence, the farmers, many of whom were Revolutionary War veterans, were reluctant to cooperate with the emerging but powerful new government. Tax collectors and supporters of the tax found themselves the target of angry farmers who would rather tar and feather the government representatives than pay their taxes. Several U.S. marshals were selected to issue summons to seventy-five distillers to appear in a Philadelphia district court, but they were no match for the 500 whiskey rebels who showed up. As a result, President Washington took steps to send in the militia. Ultimately, negotiations headed off conflict, and the militia arrested eighteen rebel leaders.

Law enforcement and criminal justice figured little in the discussion of the founding fathers over which direction the new nation would take. The only mention of law enforcement in the U.S. Constitution is the power of the president during times of national emergencies. Historian David R. Johnson suggested that "there was no debate . . . as to whether the new nation should have a national police force, because such an idea did not occur to them."[8] This would have important ramifications for future developments in American policing as it became increasingly decentralized over the next 200 years.

CORRECTIONS

By the time of the American Revolution, three major categories of confinement existed in Great Britain, including debtors' prisons, jails, and houses of correction (in England better known as bridewells). According to the customs of the day, debtors and their families were often confined together until debts were absolved by creditors or Parliament. However, prisoner categories often overlapped to such an extent that jails housed together debtors, felons, children, and the insane. Complicated and confusing, penology still resembled that of the Dark Ages. While similar establishments evolved in America during the eighteenth century, new theories of incapacitation would herald the development of improved methods of confinement.

Prior to the American Revolution, prison reform experiments were already under way in Pennsylvania. Following William Penn's death in 1718, his penal reform measures were quickly replaced by England's "Sanguinary Laws," which remained in effect until the Revolution. Under Penn's more lenient Quaker leadership, few crimes were considered capital offenses. However, once the colony came under secular leadership, new capital crimes were added, including burglary, rape, sodomy, buggery, malicious maiming, certain cases of manslaughter, arson, and witchcraft.

By the late eighteenth century, men, women, and children were still mixed together in many American jails. Before the birth of the modern penitentiary at Walnut Street (Philadelphia) in 1790, prisoners endured unimaginable squalor. In smaller facilities, inmates were tethered by chains to the floors and walls. Prisoners had to rely on charity for their most basic provisions, and seldom were beds or bedding provided.

In nascent American communities, the position of jailer was a lucrative endeavor since they derived their income from charging the inmates for most services, including removal of chains, release from jail, and the furnishing of food and bedding or even a private cell. Jailers supplemented their income by selling liquor to their charges. Eighteenth-century prison life was a raucous affair. The wealthier prisoners could afford to live in relative comfort and even leave the prison sporadically. Others might have their families with them or an occasional prostitute. In the years following the American Revolution, England's jails were bulging with criminals who could no longer be transported to America. In response, prisoners were confined in prison hulks (ships), which were frequently ravaged by "gaol fever."

In prerevolutionary America, there was no real criminal class in the colonies because their labor was too valuable and colonists were reluctant to spend precious time and money building jails. But throughout the eighteenth century, debtors were often jailed until they could pay their creditors, a tradition dating back to ancient times. In some colonies, the creditor was made responsible for paying for a debtor's keep, and if he did not pay the debtor, he was freed. In some cases, debtors were allowed to leave their cells during the day to work or beg on the streets and then return to jail to spend the evening hours. It was in this way that the indigent sought relief and release from debt in the days prior to the modern welfare state. By the 1760s, special "debtors' prisons" were common. In 1767, Mt. Holly, New Jersey, was the site of what was reportedly the first fireproof stone structure in the country. This edifice was comprised of small cells for debtors as well as a common room where they could commiserate together during the day. In 1786, an enterprising Virginian was selected by county officials to build a log cabin especially for debtors.

The fact remained that until the nineteenth century the jail functioned as a holding facility where convicted persons waited for corporal or capital punishment or were held until trial. Considered one of America's earliest jails for felons, Connecticut officials opened the Simsbury underground prison in an abandoned copper mine in 1773, and in 1790 it was designated as the state prison. Little more than a mine shaft, this vestige of a more primitive era was the scene of riots and mayhem from its earliest years. The prison was hampered by severe overcrowding, so authorities secured prisoners with iron fetters around their ankles so that they could be easily guarded as they worked inside the prison.

At the local level, early county jails were more often the residence of the pauper, the ill and insane, the aged and infirm, the habitual drunkard, or deserted wives and orphans rather than of the felons we expect today. Larger cities might have poorhouses or almshouses for the relief of the poor or maybe even workhouses where vagrants could be imbued with a work ethic. However, when neither of these edifices was available, the local jail would suffice.

John Howard

It was not until the late eighteenth century that prison reformer John Howard (1726–1790) brought home to the English public the sad state of affairs in the country's prisons. Prior to the modern penitentiary, prisoners were housed in fetid convict hulks and jails. Initiated as a temporary measure in the late 1700s because of prison overcrowding, the British utilized broken-down war vessels and abandoned transport ships to hold inmates. These "floating hells" or "hell holds" were anchored in the rivers and bays of Britain as the prisoners died by the score from disease, malnutrition, floggings, and unsanitary conditions that were worse than the era's prisons and workhouses. After visiting some of these facilities, Howard devoted himself to prison reform to improve sanitation and to diminish abuses.

Howard would embark on an examination of continental prisons and later publicize what he saw in a series of lectures. His findings led to the removal of the insane from British prisons and separating women and children from the men.

During his travels in Europe, Howard was probably most impressed by the Hospice (Asylum) of San Michele in Rome. Constructed in 1704, it contained individual cells and a system of silence. San Michele was used exclusively for delinquent boys under the age of twenty and is considered one of the first institutions in the world to exclusively house juvenile offenders. As a result of his studies, in 1777 Howard's *State of the Prisons* was published, revealing the abuses of Europe's prisons and suggestions for reforms. His campaign paid off two years later when Parliament passed the Penitentiary Act, which initiated four major reforms: provisions for a reformatory regime, secure and sanitary structures, abolition of fees for basic services, and regular inspections. In 1785, England constructed Wymondham Prison, England's first penitentiary. The prison incorporated many of Howard's reforms. Cells were furnished for separate types of offenders, and inmates worked and slept in separate cells. Solitary confinement was deemed more effective than whipping, and initially the prison was considered an overwhelming success, so much so that the Quakers would adopt many of its reforms in the construction of the Walnut Street Jail in 1790. The philosophy of separate confinement at hard labor as a mode of discipline became the model for the Pennsylvania system of prison discipline in the nineteenth century. Howard, a towering figure in prison reform, the reformer who introduced the word *penitentiary* and the philosophy of penitence for one's crimes, perished from "jail fever," or typhus, in 1790 while visiting Russia. Today his legacy lives on in so-called John Howard societies, which commemorate his name and reform agenda as they continue to press for prison reform throughout the world.

Benjamin Rush

The Revolutionary War had just ended four years earlier when a small group of citizens met in 1787 at Benjamin Franklin's Philadelphia home to discuss the current state of public punishment in Pennsylvania. Among those present was thirty-one-year-old Dr. Benjamin Rush. The youngest Pennsylvania signer of the Declaration of Independence, Rush was born near Philadelphia and became the most famous physician of his era. At this gathering, Rush presented a paper outlining a new program for treating criminals. His 1787 work "Enquiry into the Effects of Public Punishments upon Criminals and upon Society" criticized Pennsylvania's practice of inflicting humiliating public punishment on malefactors. Rush was a firm believer that "crimes should be punished in private or not punished at all." Among Rush's other propositions were provisions for classifying prisoners for housing, a rational system of prison labor that would lead to each prison becoming self-supporting, plans for gardens for producing food, and outdoor exercise for prisoners. In addition, he proposed indeterminate periods of punishment and individualized treatment for convicts according to the nature of their crimes. Not long after this meeting, Philadelphia Quakers founded the Philadelphia Society for Alleviating the Miseries of Public Prisons, America's first prison reform organization. In 1790, the Pennsylvania assembly passed legislation that laid the groundwork for the beginning of modern prison administration in America.

Walnut Street Jail

Considered the birthplace of the American penitentiary, Philadelphia's Walnut Street Jail opened in 1790. Originally used as a workhouse and debtor's prison, the Walnut Street facility contrasted sharply with the workhouses, prisons, and jails that already existed. Thanks to Quaker reformers, one wing of the jail was designated to handle all convicted felons except those sentenced to death. Unlike its predecessors, the Walnut Street Jail was used almost exclusively for the "correction" and rehabilitation of convicted felons. In time, this system of discipline became known as the "Pennsylvania system" and was heavily influenced by the efforts of reformers such as Benjamin Rush.

Contrary to existing penal protocol, Rush envisioned a prison system in which convicts were housed in a large building equipped with single cells to segregate the more dangerous and disruptive prisoners. All others were lodged in apartments. According to Rush, gardens could be provided for prisoner exercise and to grow food. One of his most prescient notions was that prison industries should provide marketable products to outsiders in order to financially support the prison system. Building on the writings of Enlightenment thinkers, Rush saw the purpose of prison punishment as a path to reformation, the prevention of future crimes, and the removal of the antisocial from society.

His influence on the design of the Walnut Street Jail is readily discernible. A precursor to the Pennsylvania system, the facility called for solitary confinement without work. It was thought that if prisoners had nothing to do but reflect on their crimes, they would reform more quickly. However, this approach proved to be ineffective and was eventually amended. After prisoners began to suffer the debilitating physical and psychological effects of solitary confinement, work was introduced along with moral and religious instruction.

The offenders housed at Walnut Street were divided into several classifications that were not necessarily related to the seriousness of the offense. More dangerous inmates were confined to six-by-eight-foot solitary cells, and separate compartments were provided for women and debtors, perhaps the greatest advance instituted by the new facility. In earlier years, all the prison inhabitants were kept in crowded common rooms. Promiscuous behavior was rampant, and the rooms became schools for crime as career criminals taught the neophytes the secrets of their criminal trades.

Initially, the Walnut Street Jail met with almost universal praise. Having introduced prison industries, health care, educational opportunities, and religious services to the prison environment, Walnut Street was widely lauded. But as more and more prisoners were accepted into the prison, it became overcrowded, leading to the now familiar riots and uprisings that continue to plague overtaxed and poorly run modern prisons.

Thomas Eddy and Newgate Prison

Thomas Eddy, a Quaker and former Loyalist during the American Revolution, became one of the major architects of New York State's penal code in the 1790s. A visit to the Walnut Street jail influenced Eddy's plans for a new prison system in which death was abolished for all crimes except treason, murder, and stealing from the church. Whipping was eliminated as punishment, and judges were given broad powers to determine lengths of imprisonment. According to Eddy's plan, outside visitors and corporal punishment were prohibited, and prisoners were provided food and clothing at no cost. The design of the jail eschewed solitary confinement in favor of congregate housing. The institution held felons but not debtors and incorporated a chapel. Like Walnut Street, it separated men and women and young and older offenders. An admirer of John Howard, Eddy soon developed a reputation as "the Howard of America" and the "Father of New York State Prison." Located on the banks of the Hudson River, Newgate Prison, the first prison modeled on the Pennsylvania model, received its first inmates in late 1797. Eddy went on to become the leading advocate of humane disciplinary methods and was the first American to call for separate cells for all prisoners.[9]

In order to develop successful prison industry, Eddy encouraged convicts to improve their conduct and productivity through a system of incentives. Records were kept of each inmate's production and behavior, and on discharge inmates were given a share of the profits they helped generate if they reached specific production and behavioral goals. During its early years, Newgate achieved a creditable record. But in 1802, a bloody riot and mass escape led Eddy to question his prison model. He concluded that his design was a mistake and that he should have opted for a single-cell system for nighttime confinement combined with a congregate work room during the day administered in strict silence. He soon began a campaign to build a second state prison at Auburn.

CRIME AND PUNISHMENT

The eighteenth century is often referred to as the Age of Reason, or the Enlightenment. During this era, great thinkers, such as Beccaria, Bentham, Howard, and Penn, had a great impact on the treatment of criminals. Their efforts resulted in a transition from corporal punishment to correction and laid the groundwork for the modern penitentiary. While this rationalistic movement began in England, the most effective work in the field of criminal justice reform came from the European continent.

Some of the most convincing ideas aimed at the reform of criminal jurisprudence flowed from the pen of the Italian nobleman Cesare de Beccaria. Unburdened by the limited perspective of a lawyer or jurist, Beccaria was free to draw his own conclusions as an informed outsider. According to Beccaria, punishment should be certain but equal for all men regardless of their station in life. He asserted that punishment "must be essentially public, prompt, necessary, the least possible in the given circumstances, proportionate to the crimes, dictated by the laws."[10]

Beccaria is considered one of the first modern writers to publicly oppose capital punishment. His celebrated treatise *On Crimes and Punishments,* published in 1764, was not only an incisive indictment of the excesses of the Italian criminal justice system; it recommended reform measures as well. His work was couched in language that indicted criminal justice in the world at large. He harshly condemned the use of torture in punishment and interrogation, the corruption of state officials, and disproportionately severe penalties for minor offenses. He reserved some of his harshest comments for the penal system, which, he argued, should exist solely to maintain law and order rather than to degrade prisoners. During the Enlightenment, his theories laid the groundwork for the subsequent reform movement of the European criminal justice system.

Beccaria argued forcefully for a humane legal system and proposed that trials be prompt and that punishments be fair and impartial and commensurate to the crime. His ideas caught the attention of numerous jurists and would have a direct influence on the penal reforms of Pennsylvania in the late eighteenth century. More than 200 hundred years ago, Beccaria wrote,

> Capital punishment cannot be useful because of the example of barbarity it presents. If human passions or the necessities of war have taught men to shed one another's blood, the laws, which are intended to moderate human conduct, ought not to extend the savage example, which in the case of a legal execution is all the more baneful in that it is carried out with studied formalities. To me it seems an absurdity that the laws, which are the expression of the public will, which abhor and which punish murder, should themselves commit one; and that, to deter citizens from private assassination, they should themselves order a public murder.[11]

These words carry weight to this day, as capital punishment in America is once again a hotly debated issue. Beccaria's ideas proved popular with some of the most prominent voices of colonial America. Thomas Jefferson cited Beccaria's influence in his composition of a "Bill for Proportioning Crimes and Punishments in Cases heretofore Capital" (1778), and Pennsylvania's Dr. Benjamin Rush claimed that Beccaria inspired his essay *Consideration of the Injustice and Impolicy of Punishing Murder by Death* (1792). Although Jefferson's bill was initially rejected, it was approved later in 1796. However, it did not eliminate the death penalty in Virginia but rather limited it to the crimes of murder and treason.

By the 1790s, hanging was considered the only legal method of execution for federal crimes. Following the lead of Enlightenment thinkers such as Beccaria, some of the leading voices of the day, including Benjamin Rush, argued for the elimination of the death penalty altogether. But Rush remained in the minority. Nevertheless, the federal government, in sharp contrast to Great Britain, retained only four capital offenses: murder, treason, rape, and arson. According to historian Roger Lane, executions decreased from almost thirty-five per 100,000 annually to less than five.[12] Although no state abolished the death penalty altogether, Pennsylvania came the closest in 1794 by eliminating the death penalty for all crimes except first-degree murder.

AMERICAN VIOLENCE

Historian Richard Maxwell Brown has suggested that "violence has accompanied virtually every stage and aspect of our national existence."[13] America was created by violence, and violence has remained part of the nation's legacy to this day. In the years leading up to the American Revolution, violence was a frequent visitor to colonial America. Relations between the colonists were often more antagonistic than their relations with Great Britain. Conflicts broke out over colonial boundaries, and tensions sometimes escalated between westerners and easterners over concerns such as representation, taxation, Indian policy, and the delayed establishment of government institutions in frontier areas. In 1764, a group of Scotch-Irish frontier settlers from western Pennsylvania known as the Paxton Boys descended on Philadelphia, threatening to overthrow the government. The Quaker-dominated provincial assembly capitulated to their demands for better protection against Indian raids for their homes in Paxton and greater representation in the provincial assembly.

A tradition developed in the South that tended to punish property crimes more severely than crimes of personal violence. The treatment of backcountry violence varied according to region. For example, during the eighteenth century, Virginia courts sentenced individuals to death for hog stealing and collected a one-shilling fine for the rape of an eleven-year-old girl. According to historian Edward Ayers, these values persisted into the nineteenth century, when the county courts "treated property offenders much more harshly than those accused of violence" (see chapter 6 for more discussion on southern violence).[14]

Rioting and mob violence were common throughout the revolutionary era. Between 1750 and 1800, every one of the original thirteen states except for Virginia experienced large-scale social violence. Although most of these activities took place in a rural environment, the cities also experienced lethal violence during the revolutionary era. Without a modern police department, citizens formed bands of regulators and vigilante organizations in futile attempts to suppress disorder. On other occasions, sheriff's posses or the militia could be called in to enforce the law.

No city saw more mob violence in this era than Boston, the scene of seminal mob actions that culminated in the Stamp Act riots of 1765, the Boston Massacre, and the Boston Tea Party of the 1770s. Revolutionary violence came in many forms. Beginning with mob violence in seaport towns, American Patriots then resorted to violence to intimidate Tory sympathizers, often utilizing the brutal method of tar and feathering, in which individuals were stripped naked and smeared with a coat of hot tar and then rolled in feathers.

Finally, large-scale bloodshed broke out with skirmishes between militia members and British regulars at Lexington and Concord, Massachusetts. Next to the American Civil War (1861–1865), the American Revolution had the second-highest ratio of casualties to population of any American military conflict. During the ensuing hostilities, bands of loosely organized Tories (Loyalists) and Whigs (Revolutionaries) fought savage guerrilla campaigns in the backcountry. The Carolinas proved a singularly bloody theater of conflict with atrocities committed by both sides. Some historians have argued the backcountry warfare between Tories and Patriots in South Carolina introduced a subculture of violence into the region that persists to this day.[15] Several British officers earned sordid reputations for violence during the conflict. For example, Sir James Beard ordered that rum privileges be revoked for every soldier who took a live prisoner, leading to the murder of captured rebels. Similarly, in 1780,

Colonel Banaster Tarleton captured a Virginia regiment and showed them no quarter. "Tarleton's Quarter," as this killing of prisoners became known, served only to ignite patriotic passions in backcountry South Carolina and led to similar outrages by the Americans.

There is little debate that the violence of the American Revolution furnished ample justification for the use of violence against enemies for the public good. Vigilantism, lynching, and other methods of violence would sporadically appear in American history whenever formal mechanisms of law enforcement were absent. According to Revolution historian Gordon S. Wood, the "long tradition of extra-legislative action by the people, action that more often than not had taken the form of mob violence and crowd disturbance,"[16] ingrained in Americans a propensity to utilize extralegal devices to ensure the sovereignty of the people.

One of the earliest examples of an extralegal device, though rare in America before the Revolution, was formal dueling. The first recorded duel took place in Plymouth, Massachusetts, in 1621. In this incident, two gentlemen had their servants serve as their stand-ins and duel with swords and daggers to a standstill. The first fatal duel was reported in Boston a little more than a century later. While cases of dueling can be found in every colony, it did not become widely accepted until the revolutionary era, when officers of the Continental armies borrowed the practice from their French allies.

American Vigilantism

With a virtual absence of law enforcement and local government on the colonial frontier, settlers sometimes organized themselves into vigilante groups to maintain order. In the rural South, sheriffs and slave patrols were the main exemplars of law enforcement. However, citizens occasionally resorted to taking the law into their own hands, beginning with the "Regulators,"[17] America's first vigilante organization, which appeared in South Carolina in 1767.

During the 1760s, organized bands of outlaws plagued the scattered settlements of the South Carolina backcountry. After a campaign of terror by the bandit gangs, which included acts of rape, theft, torture, kidnapping, and murder, the local gentry responded by organizing the Regulators to destroy the outlaw villages that shielded them on the frontier. The Regulators were organized after the governor of South Carolina pardoned five of six criminals convicted for robbery and horse stealing. This group of vigilantes tried, convicted, and punished the offenders, totally disregarding the established criminal justice system of South Carolina.

During a two-year campaign, bandit activity was eliminated, and the gangs were broken up. The Regulators, however, did not disband immediately but became the moral arbiters of the colony, waging a law-and-order crusade against the marginalized members of the colony. In the end, they disbanded when the colony agreed to establish district courts and sheriffs to maintain peace in the county backwaters. A phenomenon peculiar to America, historian Richard Maxwell Brown has documented 326 vigilante operations in the United States between 1767 and 1904.[18]

The vigilante movements of the revolutionary era were confined to the southern backcountry. In Virginia, vigilantism was legitimated by what became known as "Lynch's law." There is some debate as to the origins of the term since its source has been attributed to two individuals bearing the name. William L. Lynch (1724–1820) led a 1780 vigilante movement to purge Pittsylvania County, Virginia, of lawbreakers. The members of this group signed a written charter, but the document did not specifically mention hanging as the punishment, although hanging was typically the punishment for a capital offense. Virginian Charles Lynch (1736–1796) served as justice of the peace in the 1760s but is best remembered in law enforcement circles for his participation with other leading citizens in local vigilante activities. Along with other justices of the peace and militia officers, Charles Lynch arrested suspects and, following informal trials, punished anyone who threatened to upset the traditional social order. A society often on the edge of anarchy, Loyalists, slaves, Indians, and English officials were all viewed with distrust and at one time or another might find themselves tethered to the whipping post, where Lynch law was administered. Although both Lynches have been cited as the possible inspiration for the term *lynching,* the term's origins are still inconclusive.[19]

There was a darker side to American vigilante movements that essentially operated outside the boundaries of the legal system. In the case of the South Carolina Regulators, heady from their success at stifling the outlaw bands, they were not content to cease and desist once the menace was erased. Subsequently, the vigilantes aimed their "police functions" at the lower classes, whom they chastised for not living up to the Regulators' moral standards and work ethic. According to their new "Plan for Regulation," Regulators embarked on a crusade against the vagrants, idlers, and dissolute women of the backcountry, employing such violent mechanisms of social control as flogging, ducking, and various corporal punishments. In opposition, the settlers formed the "Moderators" to counter the Regulators. By 1769, peace was restored to South Carolina after Charleston's governor and assembly acquiesced to the Regulators' requests to establish circuit courts.

By the 1760s and 1770s, a distinctive American identity emerged, one that reflected an increasingly "republican" society that emphasized personal independence and public virtue and that scorned the notion of concentrated power in the hands of the few. At the same time, many (though not all) Americans rejected the governing attributes of Great Britain, which hinged on its landed aristocracy, political corruption, patronage, and bureaucracy. The beginning of the imperial struggle between the colonies and Great Britain and the subsequent Declaration of Independence were the by-product of a series of British abuses of power. Initially, American leaders were not outspoken in their opposition to

the new Navigation Acts. They defended the British constitution and assumed that their grievance would be resolved. By 1776, however, it was too late. When Parliament began to directly tax Americans, regulate their intercolonial trade, station troops in their cities, and prohibit settlers from moving westward, Americans saw these as efforts to deprive them of their property and freedom.

NOTABLE TRIALS

Boston Massacre Trial (1770)

Resentment against oppressive English tax measures had declined in most colonies but was reinvigorated after the so-called Boston Massacre. In the late 1760s, British warships disembarked infantry and cannon for police duty in Boston in order to "rescue the Government from the hands of a trained mob." The British "lobsterbacks" (so named for their bright red uniforms) were intended as part police force and part army of occupation. Off duty, the soldiers often supplemented their pay with daily dock work, causing deep resentment from patriotic day laborers. Deep antagonism developed between the soldiers and the local inhabitants, leading to the pivotal events of that cold March night in 1770.

Local Patriot leaders were determined to rid the city of the British army of occupation. Crowds often convened in front of the Customs House, the symbol of British oppression. It is unknown whether the crowd that showed up to taunt the solitary sentry on that March night assembled by deliberate design, but the day before there had been trouble at the docks between off-duty soldiers and local longshoremen. Alarmed, the lone sentry called for help, and Captain Preston and seven soldiers responded. In the subsequent confusion, the soldiers, apparently without any orders, fired into the crowd, killing five and wounding more than a dozen others. The Massachusetts governor called for calm, promising the outraged citizens that justice would be done. Soon the captain and eight men stood trial for murder. The ensuing trial offers a conspicuous example of Anglo-American justice in action.

No experienced lawyer would agree to defend the eight British soldiers until Patriots Josiah Quincy and John Adams, the cousin of Patriot leader Samuel Adams, offered to do so. Many Boston Patriots charged that they lacked patriotism. There was little for the lawyers to gain. Compensation for the emotionally charged case amounted to about one week's wages for a working man.

It was decided that Captain Preston would be tried separately from his men. Despite requests by the soldiers for a joint trial, they were denied without explanation. Apparently, the soldiers felt that if Preston were tried first and denied giving orders to fire, then the subsequent defense of the eight soldiers would be compromised.

The trial was apparently transcribed in shorthand, but no copy survives. Preston's testimony has been determined by the existing deposition that he gave before the trial. As part of the defense, thirty-four-year-old Boston attorney John Adams quoted from Beccaria's recently translated *On Crimes and Punishments,* proclaiming, "If I can but be the instrument of preserving one life, his blessing and tears of transport shall be sufficient consolation to me for the contempt of all mankind." Adams is credited with creating some doubts of Preston's culpability among the jurors. The twelve jurors, who had been sequestered on a very meager diet of "biscett and cheese and syder," deliberated quickly and two hours later returned with an acquittal on all charges.

The transcripts for the trial of the soldiers, or the *Rex v. Weems* case, has survived and offers a thorough account of the proceedings. Forty witnesses would eventually testify. After deliberating three hours, the jury came back with an acquittal for six of the eight soldiers. The other two were convicted of manslaughter. Pleading "benefit of clergy," the soldiers escaped imprisonment and were instead branded on their right thumbs.

Contemporary records indicate that the behavior of certain segments of the crowd were as responsible for the tragedy as the soldiers. No matter, for the incident was grossly exaggerated for propaganda purposes. Hundreds of colonial Americans pinned on their walls copies of master silversmith Paul Revere's rendering of the "massacre" as a constant reminder of British transgressions. Imbued with the traditional rights of Englishmen who cherished the privileges and immunities of the freeborn, the citizens of Massachusetts and elsewhere could not be assumed to relinquish their expectations. Immensely proud of his actions in the courtroom, John Adams would look back on his stellar career that would eventually take him to president and note that his involvement in the defense was "one of the most gallant, generous, manly, and disinterested Actions of my whole Life, and one of the best Pieces of service I have ever rendered my country. Judgement of Death against those soldiers would have been as foul a Stain upon this Country as the Executions of the Quakers or Witches." According to Boston Massacre historian Hiller B. Zobel, this incident can be remembered as "The Birth of American Justice" or perhaps "Even the Guilty Deserve a Fair Trial."[20]

CONCLUSIONS

Criminal justice historian Samuel Walker noted that "the American Revolution had a major impact on criminal justice, speeding up the process of reform and accentuating the differences between American and English law."[21] According to one scholar, the era of the American Revolution saw the development of three different criminal justice systems—for whites, blacks, and Indians.[22] By the end of the eighteenth century, the influx of Europeans with non-English backgrounds found a confusing and unfamiliar criminal justice system.

While the emergence of the American criminal justice system was still years away, by the end of the revolutionary era a once-beleaguered legal profession was flourishing: twenty-five of the fifty-six signers of the Declaration of Independence and thirty-one of the fifty-six members of the Constitutional Convention were practicing lawyers.

By the late eighteenth century, Pennsylvania had abolished the barbaric "bloody code" of Great Britain, which imposed capital and corporal punishment for a broad array of offenses. Other states followed suit so that by 1800 most states authorized capital punishment only for murder and treason. During the same period, fines and imprisonment were substituted for the punitive measures of mutilation and exhibitory forms of punishment. Between 1794 and 1814, most states had been inspired by the Walnut Street experiment to build their own model penitentiaries, launching a new era in the treatment of criminals.

The Declaration of Independence, the Articles of Confederation, and the United States Constitution signify three successive stages in the development of America and a government of laws where "law was king" and not of hereditary monarchy. The decade of the 1790s was a formative era in the nation's history. It saw the inauguration of the first periodic national census in history, the country's first federal criminal statute (which defined which crimes were subject to federal prosecution), and the construction of the first modern penitentiary. Also established in the 1790s by the First Congress was the position of attorney general. Prior to the creation of the Department of Justice, the first attorney general maintained his own legal practice while acting as a legal adviser to the president. Until the Department of Justice was created in 1870, to the detriment of federal criminal justice the attorney general was assisted by a relatively small coterie of clerks and messengers.

At the turn of the nineteenth century, America was still overwhelmingly rural, with only Philadelphia and New York possessing populations of more than 25,000. With most Americans still living along the Atlantic seaboard, the country's population was only a quarter of England's and one-sixth of France's. But from 1750 to 1800, the population would explode from 1.17 million to 5 million, creating new problems for the developing criminal justice system. The era of the American Revolution furnished the foundation for the subsequent development of more modern criminal justice institutions during the first half of the nineteenth century. But first, more effective police agencies, courts, and prisons would have to be established.

Point–Counterpoint
Interpreting the Second Amendment

Few constitutional issues have been more hotly debated than the "right to bear arms" clause in the Second Amendment: "A well regulated Militia, being necessary to the security of a free State, the right of the people to keep and bear Arms, shall not be infringed." The debate over the wording of this amendment has resulted in several popular interpretations. On one hand, gun control advocates have stressed the clause related to militias, asserting that the purpose of the amendment was to protect the formation of militias in the face of government intrusions. Opponents of gun control have focused on a "militia-of the whole" made up of all healthy white males. They were expected to perform their duties with privately owned weapons. Rather than viewing the clause as a qualifying clause, many advocates cite it as more an amplification or mandate of the need for a "well-regulated militia." There is little doubt this controversy will ever be put to rest.

In the following passage a Tennessee resident named William Aymette appealed his conviction for carrying a concealed Bowie knife in violation of state law. In 1840 the Supreme Court of Tennessee rejected Aymette's contention that the right to bear arms was not specific, and that he had understood it to mean the right to carry any weapon. The Court made an important distinction here: that there is a difference between weapons useful for the common defense and those that are not (the civilized-warfare test).

AYMETTE vs. THE STATE.

1. The act of 1837-8, ch. 137, sec. 2, which prohibits any person from wearing any bowie knife, or Arkansas tooth-pick, or other knife or weapon in form, shape or size resembling a bowie knife or

Source: *Aymette vs. The State* 21 Tenn. (1840), reprinted in Robert J. Cottrol, ed. *Gun Control and the Constitution: Sources and Explorations on the Second Amendment,* New York: Garland Publishing, 1994, pp. 154–162.

Arkansas tooth-pick under his clothes, or concealed about his person, does not conflict with the 26th section of the first article of the bill of rights, securing to the free white citizens the right to keep and bear arms for their common defence.

2. The arms, the right to keep and bear which is secured by the constitution, are such as are usually employed in civilized warfare, and constitute the ordinary military equipment; the legislature have the power to prohibit the keeping or wearing weapons dangerous to the peace and safety of the citizens, and which are not usual in civilized warfare.

3. The right to keep and bear arms for the common defence, is a great political right. It respects the citizens on the one hand, and the rulers on the other; and although this right must be inviolably preserved, it does not follow that the legislature is prohibited from passing laws regulating the manner in which these arms may be employed.

At the January term, 1840, of the circuit court of Giles county, Judge Dillahunty presiding, an indictment was filed against William Aymette. This indictment charged: 1st. That Aymette on the 26th day of June, 1839, in the county of Giles, "did wear a certain bowie knife under his clothes, and keep the same concealed about his person, contrary to the form of the statute," &c. 2d. "That on the same day, &c., the said Aymette did wear a certain other knife and weapon, in form, shape and size resembling a bowie knife, and under the clothes of him the said Aymette, and concealed about the person of him," &c.

The defendant pleaded not guilty, and the case was submitted to a jury at the October term, 1840, Judge Dillahunty presiding.

It appeared that Aymette, during the sitting of the circuit court in June, 1839, at Pulaski, Giles county, had fallen out with one Hamilton, and that about 10 o'clock, P.M. he went in search of him to a hotel, swearing he would have his heart's blood. He had a bowie knife concealed under his vest and suspended to the waistband of his breeches, which he took out occasionally and brandished in his hand. He was put out of the hotel and proceeded from place to place in search of Hamilton, and occasionally exhibited his knife.

The jury, under the charge of the court, returned a verdict of guilty.

The defendant moved the court in arrest of judgment, but the motion was overruled and the defendant sentenced to three months imprisonment

in the common jail of Giles county, and to pay a fine of two hundred dollars to the State. From this judgment defendant appealed in error.

To bear arms in defence of the State, is to employ them in war, as arms are usually employed by civilized nations. The arms, consisting of swords, muskets, rifles, &c., must necessarily be borne openly; so that a prohibition to bear them openly, would be a denial of the right altogether. And as in their constitution, the right to bear arms in defence of themselves, is coupled with the right to bear them in defence of the State, we must understand the expressions as meaning the same thing, and as relating to public, and not private; to the common, and not the individual defence.

But a prohibition to wear a spear concealed in a cane, would in no degree circumscribe the right to bear arms in defence of the State; for this weapon could in no degree contribute to its defence, and would be worse than useless in an army. And, if, as is above suggested, the wearing arms in defence of the citizens, is taken to mean, the common defence, the same observations apply.

We think, therefore, that upon either of the grounds assumed in this opinion, the legislature had the right to pass the law under which the plaintiff in error was convicted. Let the judgment be affirmed.

SOURCES

Ayers, Edward L. 1984. *Vengeance and Justice: Crime and Punishment in the Nineteenth-Century American South.* New York: Oxford University Press.

Barnes, Harry Elmer. 1968. *The Evolution of Penology in Pennsylvania: A Study in American Social History.* Montclair, N.J.: Patterson Smith.

Beccaria, Cesare. 1963. *On Crimes and Punishment.* Translated with an introduction by Henry Paolucci. Indianapolis: Bobbs-Merrill.

Bodenhamer, David J. 1992. *Fair Trial: Rights of the Accused in American History.* New York: Oxford University Press.

Brown, Richard Maxwell. 1963. *The South Carolina Regulators.* Cambridge, Mass.: Belknap Press of Harvard University Press.

———. 1975. *Strain of Violence: Historical Studies of American Violence and Vigilantism.* New York: Oxford University Press.

Butterfield, Fox. 1995. *All God's Children: The Bosket Family and the American Tradition of Violence.* New York: Alfred A. Knopf.

Chapin, Bradley. 1983. *Criminal Justice in Colonial America, 1606–1660.* Athens: University of Georgia Press.

Ferguson, Robert A. 1994. *The American Enlightenment, 1750–1820.* Cambridge, Mass.: Harvard University Press.

Friedman, Lawrence M. 1993. *Crime and Punishment in American History.* New York: Basic Books.

Howard, D. L. 1958. *John Howard, Prison Reformer.* New York: Archer House.

Johnson, David R. 1981. *American Law Enforcement: A History.* Wheeling, Ill.: Forum Press.

Lane, Roger. 1997. *Murder in America: A History.* Columbus: Ohio State University Press.

———. 1999. "Capital Punishment." In *Violence in America.* Vol. 1, pp. 198–203. New York: Charles Scribner's Sons.

Maestro, Marcello. 1973. *Cesare Beccaria and the Origins of Penal Reform.* Philadelphia: Temple University Press.

Masur, Louis P. 1989. *Rites of Execution: Capital Punishment and the Transformation of American Culture, 1776–1865.* New York: Oxford University Press.

Miller, Helen Hill. 1965. *The Case for Liberty.* Chapel Hill: University of North Carolina Press.

Reith, Charles. 1952. *The Blind Eye of History: A Study of Police Origins to the Present Police Era.* London: Faber and Faber.

Scott, Kenneth. 1957. *Counterfeiting in Colonial America.* New York: Oxford University Press.

Walker, Samuel. 1998. *Popular Justice: A History of American Criminal Justice.* New York: Oxford University Press.

Wood, Gordon S. 1975. *The Creation of the American Republic, 1776–1787.* Chapel Hill: University of North Carolina Press.

Zobel, Hiller B. 1770. *The Boston Massacre.* New York: W. W. Norton.

CRITICAL THINKING QUESTIONS

1. How did the Judiciary Act of 1789 influence criminal justice developments in the postcolonial era?

2. Discuss the impact of the Bill of Rights on personal freedoms and criminal justice procedure.

3. What lessons about American criminal justice can be found in the events related to the Boston Massacre trial?

4. Describe the historical events surrounding the birth of the penitentiary.

5. Compare and contrast law enforcement developments in Great Britain and America during the revolutionary era.

CRIMINAL JUSTICE HISTORY ON THE INTERNET

One of the most comprehensive legal history sites can be found at Documents for American Legal History at http://vi.uh.edu/pages/alh.html. Students will find important court cases from the Marshall and Taney courts and documents such as the Bill of Rights chronicling the revolutionary period.

Students can read about crime and criminals up to the year 1800 at http://crime.about.com/library/blfiles/blearly.htm?pid=2826&cob=home. Particularly instructive is Peter Zenger and Freedom of the Press at http://gi/dynamic/offsite.htm?site=http//earlyamerica.com/earlyamerica/bookmarks/zenger/index.html.

A Century of Lawmaking for a New Nation houses U.S. congressional documents and debates (1774–1873) at http://lcweb2.loc.gov:8081/ammem/amlaw/lawhome.html.

Almost 200 sites on the Salem witchcraft trials can be accessed through http://earlyamerica.com/cgi-bin/search/search.pl?/lang=en&q=salem. The Alien and Sedition Acts can be found at fifty-six sites from http://earlyamerica.com/cgi-bin/search/search.pl. For other sites related to colonial America such as the Boston Massacre, Jamestown, Plymouth, and the Whiskey Rebellion, see http://earlyamerica.com/towncrier.

The history of Eastern State Penitentiary is available at www.libertynet.org80/~e-state. For information on Cesare Beccaria, his life, his stance on the death penalty, and his publications, see www.utm.edu/research/iep/b/beccaria.htm.

Resources on Jeremy Bentham are available at www.epistemelinks.com/Main/Philosophers .asp?PhilCode=Bent.

See the sites Making Sense of English Law Enforcement in the 18th Century at www.best.com/%7Eddfr/Academic/England_ 18thc.html; History of the Supreme Court of Virginia at www.courts.state.va.us/ scov/cover.htm; Documentary History of the American Constitution at www.yale.edu/ lawweb/avalon/constpap.htm; Lewis Wetzell, Frontier Hero or Serial Killer? at earlyamerica.com/review/ spring97/wetzel.html; History of the Federal Judiciary at air.fjc.gov/history; and History of Forfeiture in England and Colonial America at www.fsu.edu/~crimdo/forfeiture.html.

NOTES

1. Reith (1952, p. 81).

2. Chapin (1983, p. 3; quoted in Bodenhamer 1992, p. 19).

3. Friedman (1993, p. 297).

4. Friedman (1993, p. 72).

5. Walker (1998, p. 38).

6. At this time, lamps were fueled with whale oil.

7. The word *marshal* is a derivation of the Old High German words for "horse": *marah* and *calc,* which means "servant." Combined, these words mean "horsekeeper." Formerly servants, marshals rose to the rank of knight and commanded cavalry units under the Frankish kings. Over subsequent generations, they were given more duties, including the maintenance of law and order, and were permitted to hire deputies.

8. Johnson (1981, p. 9).

9. Barnes (1968).

10. Beccaria (1963).

11. Beccaria (1963).

12. Lane (1991).

13. Brown (1975, p. 3).

14. Ayers (1984, p. 111).

15. For an examination of the subculture of violence in Edgefield, South Carolina, from the 1760s to the twentieth century, see Butterfield (1995).

16. Wood (1975, pp. 319–21).

17. The term *regulator* was used generically until replaced with *vigilante* in the nineteenth century.

18. Brown (1975).

19. The phrase "lynch law" did not enter American and English dictionaries until the 1850s.

20. Zobel (1770, p. 3).

21. Walker (1998, p. 37).

22. Lane (1997).

5

CRIMINAL JUSTICE
IN THE NEW NATION
(1777–1834)

TIME LINE

1777	Vermont abolishes slavery	1807	Aaron Burr treason trial
1789	Judiciary Act of 1789	1809	New Orleans City Guard
1790	First national census	1811	Vidocq takes command of the French Surete
1790	Opening of the Walnut Street Jail	1812–1814	War of 1812
1790	First session of U.S. Supreme Court	1815	Prison stripes first introduced in New York
1790	Pennsylvania begins movement to prohibit flogging	1817	Opening of Auburn Prison
1798–1800	Alien and Sedition Acts	1823	Birth of the Texas Rangers
1801	New York City creates position of high constable	1823	Boston adopts office of marshal of the city
1803	*Marbury v. Madison*	1826	First report of Boston's Prison Discipline Society

1827	New York abolishes slavery	1831	Nat Turner's rebellion
1829	Creation of the London Metropolitan Police	1834	First private execution in the United States held behind prison walls in Pennsylvania
1829	Completion of Eastern State Penitentiary		

In the four decades following the American Revolution, experimental steps were taken toward organizing American criminal justice procedures and institutions. Postrevolutionary American criminal justice made the transition to the nineteenth century with groundwork for an organized correctional system. Meanwhile, the state of law enforcement lagged far behind, still firmly rooted in the community-oriented volunteer policing of the previous centuries. But developments in Great Britain and France would soon find voice in the emergence of organized twenty-four hour police forces in several major American cities in the first half of the new century.

One of the most important criminal justice measures enacted by the First Congress in 1789 was the approval of the Judiciary Act of 1789, which established the Supreme Court, divided the country into districts, and established the parallel structure of federal and state courts. Each district had a court that was given jurisdiction over crimes that were "cognizable under the authority of the United States." Most penalties ran the gamut from small fines and short terms of imprisonment to whipping and longer prison terms.

The Judiciary Act also established the positions of U.S. marshal and U.S. district attorney for each district. The ratification of the Bill of Rights two years later completed the construction of the early federal criminal justice system. Although a department of justice was not initially created, the position of attorney general was initiated as legal adviser to the president.[1]

Despite the American Revolution's promise of natural rights and equality, there still existed widespread opposition to the emancipation of slaves in the aftermath of the war. Warfare had also interrupted the cooperative antislavery efforts of American and British Quakers. In 1777, Vermont's constitution became the first to specifically abolish slavery. Judicial decisions in Massachusetts (1783), Connecticut (1784), and Rhode Island (1784) would follow Vermont's example. However, other states were more reluctant, with gradual emancipation accepted in New York (1799) and New Jersey (1804). New York would finally abolish slavery in 1827.

According to the first census in 1790, the nation was still rural in character, with the majority of Americans living near the Atlantic coast. Although the center of population was clustered around the Chesapeake Bay, the West was becoming the most rapidly growing part of the nation. Between 1790 and 1800, American society made incredible economic advances, measured in the growth of banks, corporations, and transportation companies. With the construction of the country's first mechanized factories, American industry was soon producing a cornucopia of items, ranging from nails and hats to firearms.

Between 1790 and 1820, at least 250,000 immigrants arrived in America, contributing to increasing social tensions in urban areas as well as mob violence. Beginning in the colonial era and continuing to this day, immigrant minorities have been victimized by those that preceded them, with established groups showing little tolerance for diversity. Recent immigrants were expected to shed their foreign traditions and quickly assimilate if they wished to prosper. In the years surrounding the American Revolution, the largest non-English immigrant groups were Irish-Catholics and Germans, immigrants who would often be targeted as scapegoats for social problems. The Protestant majority in the New World restricted their economic and political opportunities. Some colonial laws prohibited Catholics from voting or holding government offices. The years from 1790 to 1830 witnessed the economic, social, and political transformation of America. As the nation's population became more diverse and cities more populated, the developing criminal justice structures were faced with the task of coming to terms with new tensions exacerbated by the turmoil.

When the War of 1812 halted the commercial trade between America and Great Britain, a factory system began to flourish in New England, joining the American economy to the Industrial Revolution. After the War of 1812, crime increased as soldiers returned home to unemployment. A growing population and rising industrialization led to a new form of class struggle that would take its place next to the growing sectional conflict.

THE LAWGIVERS

Following the Revolution, there was an increasing willingness among Americans to disregard British precedents of criminal law. This in part was stimulated by the fact that in many new cases there were no legal precedents to rely on. After the defeat of Great Britain, America became the first modern nation to design a system of government based on certain basic philosophical principles. Most of the states designed new constitutions based on republican goals and ideals to specifically curb the abuses that provoked the Revolution. Each state constitution included provisions to curb executive power and included a bill of rights guaranteeing certain freedoms, including freedom of the press, freedom of religion, and the right to a jury trial.

With the fear that the new federal system might give too much power to one government body, each state constitution reflected the sovereignty of the people.

Criminal Courts

After the War of Independence, the former colonies agreed to relinquish a measure of their newly won independence to a central government. But these powers were limited and clearly defined. The acceptance of the Constitution ensured that powers not specifically conferred to the federal government would remain with the states. In due course, each state created its own criminal justice system to be enforced by their own courts. For example, a New York citizen accused of keeping a disorderly house would be tried in county or local courts under the domain of New York State. However, if the charge were federal postal robbery, a federal offense, the case would come before a federal judge. As criminal justice procedures became increasingly complex during the nineteenth and twentieth centuries, criminals often found themselves wanted by both federal and state authorities, creating complicated jurisdictional issues.

Although they are now abolished in England, grand juries adopted by the new states offered an additional safeguard to accused persons. A federal grand jury was composed of between sixteen and twenty-three members, at least twelve of whom must agree that there is a prima facie case against an accused person before an indictment can be issued and a trial held before a petit jury.

The Supreme Court

In 1790, the Supreme Court held its first two sessions in New York City's Royal Exchange Building.[2] Elegantly attired in black and scarlet robes, the justices were little appreciated by constituents who had recently won independence from England. During its first ten years, the Court handled few matters of significance and was little considered during the construction of the new Capitol building in Washington. The low standing of the nascent Court was symbolically demonstrated by the construction of the new Capitol without any chamber reserved for the Supreme Court. When the seat of government made the transition to the banks of the Potomac River, the Supreme Court was assigned to an undignified room in the basement under the Senate Chamber. According to one visitor, "A stranger might traverse the dark avenues of the Capitol for a week, without finding the remote corner in which Justice is administered to the American Republic." With the ascendance of John Marshall to chief justice in 1801, all this would change.

John Marshall

Born into the Virginia plantocracy in 1755, despite little formal education (tutored at home by parents), Marshall was appointed chief justice of the Supreme Court by President John Adams in 1801. Over the next thirty-five years, his decisions would lay the groundwork for American constitutional law. During his term as chief justice, Marshall was credited with writing 519 of the 1,106 decisions issued by the highest court of the land. Among his most important cases was *Marbury v. Madison* (1803), which established the principle that the Supreme Court has the final word over whether an act of Congress or a state legislature violated the U.S. Constitution. This opinion laid down the doctrine of judicial review, which to this day remains the cornerstone of constitutional law.

Marshall's imprint on constitutional law cannot be underrated. If not for his powerful intellect and direction, a lesser chief justice may have employed a more uncompromising construction of the language of the Constitution. Well versed in the legal implications of the Constitution for the solidification of the new republic, Marshall interpreted the document in the broadest national sense. Ever the proponent of a strong central government, his decisions on the court left a legacy demonstrating his support of the Constitution.

The Alien and Sedition Acts

In 1797–1798, America witnessed one of its first international scandals when it was revealed in the American press that agents of the French government had attempted to extort money from American ambassadors instead of publicly negotiating a treaty with them. The XYZ affair (which alluded to three French agents known only as X, Y, and Z) resulted in a backlash of anti-French sentiment against America's former ally.

More important, this cause célèbre led to the passage of the Alien and Sedition Acts, measures that provided an early test for the Bill of Rights. A series of legislative acts passed in 1798, the Alien and Sedition Acts included the Naturalization Act, the Alien Act, the Alien Enemies Act, and the Sedition Act—legislation that targeted immigrant populations and prescribed new procedures for attaining citizenship. It also established an element that would run throughout American history: the creation of a category of aliens, outsiders who were measured or impugned for their otherness.

The Alien and Sedition Acts were promulgated in an era during which the boundaries of the new country were still being determined; thus, national security was an issue of paramount importance. Of the four laws, the most controversial was the Sedition Act, which clearly impinged on accepted civil liberties. The Alien and Sedition Acts proved an early test of the First Amendment's protection of free speech and free press. The Sedition Act was so controversial because it barred individuals from speaking or printing "any false, scandalous and malicious writing" about the president or Congress. Despite intense criticism by Thomas Jefferson and his supporters, the Sedition Act was not immediately abolished. However, what the debate over the act brought about was a wide-ranging examination of the "issues of free speech and free press in a republican society." According to legal historian John E. Semonche, "Lessons were learned, and more than a century would pass before Congress would again inhibit free political discussion."[3]

During the administration of President John Adams, this legislation targeted unpatriotic speech and brought into question the boundaries of freedom of the press and freedom of speech. According to the act, "any person [who] shall write, print, utter, or publish, or shall cause or procure to be written, printed, uttered or published . . . any false, scandalous and, malicious writing or writing against" the government could be accused of sedition. In order to regulate criticism of the presidential regime, the office was given broad powers to squelch criticism of presidential policy or the office itself. From 1798 to 1800, close to twenty-five individuals were charged with seditious offenses, and ten were convicted.

Besides official sanctions, many individuals were targeted through an informal campaign of violence and harassment as mobs of young Federalists (Anglophile supporters of the president and a strong central government) roamed the streets attacking supposed enemies of the state who often included emigrant political writers, Francophiles, and Radical Republicans (who supported the republican politics of Thomas Jefferson and were thus perceived as anti-British, hence "un-American"). Following the election of Thomas Jefferson over John Adams in 1800, the acts were allowed to essentially languish unused as Jefferson pardoned convicted defendants in an attempt to end political partisanship. His proclamation that "we are all federalists; we are all republicans," laid to rest for the time being this threat to individual liberties. However, some of the Alien and Sedition Acts would be revived sporadically under future wartime conditions.

LAW ENFORCEMENT

The early development of police forces in Europe was stimulated by their affiliation with the state. France introduced the office of lieutenant of police as early as 1667. Charged with suppressing crime, this office became a political office of considerable importance in the Napoleonic era (1799–1815) under Joseph Fouche.

The birth of modern policing in the nineteenth century came after centuries of static and unsuccessful attempts at law enforcement. The end of the American Revolution coincided with the gradual curtailment of patronage in favor of the popular election of constables and sheriffs. By the late eighteenth century, American communities were still largely reliant on self-policing strategies. In the first decades of the nineteenth century, several cities began to incorporate a day watch to supplement the traditional night watch.

In a time before large cities, property and personal crime rates were not considered much of a problem. But by the turn of the nineteenth century, social change augured by increasing urbanization necessitated a reevaluation of the existing law enforcement systems. Prior to the American Revolution, most sheriffs and high constables were appointed by the Crown. Following the war, these positions were filled by supporters of local political leaders. Rooted in the concept of popular sovereignty, early officials of the Republic were elected by their neighbors. The history of early American policing was the history of distinctly different forces in different cities. By the early nineteenth century, American policing was still firmly rooted in the English system of part-time magistrates, sheriffs, constables, and the occasional paid watchman.

The federal government provided no direction for the construction of police forces. In rural America, it was left to elected sheriffs and their deputies to maintain peace and to arrest malefactors. As the country moved farther west, the task of policing increasingly fell under the domain of the army, federal marshals, or anyone carrying a gun.

As the nation struggled with the forces of urbanization and industrialization during the first decades of the nineteenth century, communities created civil police forces, making the transition from amateur unpaid watchmen to more formal arrangements. Port cities such as Boston, New York, and Philadelphia endured growing pains in the late eighteenth century, and the old reliance on the community consensus broke down. In the first years of the new century, Boston became the first city to require by statute the maintenance of a permanent night watch with pay fixed at fifty cents per night. In 1807, Boston established its first police districts, and by 1823, the city had selected a Harvard graduate as its first marshal.

While the United States continued to make headway in the realms of communications and transportation, American law enforcement continued to rely on outdated seventeenth-century police methods. The nineteenth century saw the dawning of a more complicated urban environment, but city fathers persisted in responding to growing crime problems by adding more watchmen.

The French Police System

The development of the French police was given early stimulus in 1817, when the French convict Eugene Vidocq (1775–1857) was given the job of setting up a brigade of detectives known as the Surete. Former criminals like Vidocq, these early detectives saw spectacular results, credited with more than 750 arrests in their first year of operation.

Following a stint in the military, Vidocq fell in with some unsavory characters before winning acclaim as an escape artist after escaping from prison three times. Released from prison, he was placed in command of a group of ex-convicts who became the nucleus of the Surete (now the Police Judiciare). Considered the world's first private detective, Vidocq employed numerous police detection techniques considered standard procedures today, including disguises, decoys, informants, autopsies, blood tests, ballistics, criminal files, and handwriting analysis. He directed the Surete until his retirement in 1827.

Considered the father of police intelligence operations, Joseph Fouche served as minister of police during most of Napoleon Bonaparte's tenure as emperor. An early proponent of preventive policing, Fouche is credited with establishing a centralized police force that was responsible to the national government. The French police system was considered superior to anything the British had to offer in the way of peacekeeping during the early nineteenth century. According to police historian Philip Stead, "Paris was safer for the individual than was London in the eighteenth century,"[4] noting the contrasts between London's watchmen and parish constables and Paris' centralized police system manned by armed and professional officers.

The London Metropolitan Police

During the early nineteenth century, London policing gradually came to grips with the growing crime problem. With the defeat of Napoleonic France in 1815, thousands of soldiers returned home to England looking for jobs and places to live. Like most wars, the Napoleonic Wars were followed by a period of unemployment. With the added transition to a factory-based economy that favored machine over man, the unemployment situation further escalated. As London grappled with the growing pains occasioned by the Industrial Revolution, pressure mounted for more professional law enforcement. To combat the rising social unrest and riots, the army was often called on to handle the situation, leading to bloody incidents such as the Peterloo Massacre (1819), in which government troops fired into a crowd, killing eleven and wounding 400 (including 100 women).

Although there was a growing constituency in favor of a police force, most British opposed the idea. With a tradition that ran counter to the centralized police system in vogue in continental Europe, British reformers envisioned a preventive police system rather than one in the oppressive punitive tradition of the Napoleonic police. One of the toughest barriers in creating a London police force was convincing the inhabitants that a police force would not be used as spies and persecutors as it was in France. It would prove a daunting mission to convince Londoners that the police could help protect the public and keep order without spilling innocent blood.

By 1828, steps had been taken toward creating a professional police force. In that year, Home

Secretary and future prime minister Robert Peel controlled almost 450 policemen, including officers of the Thames River Police, the Bow Street foot and horse patrols, and nine police offices. A rather insignificant force for a city of one and a half million people (one officer per 3,000 citizens), this number paled in comparison to Augustan standards of ancient Rome. The London police were supplemented by 4,500 ineffective Charlies, a remnant of the seventeenth century.

Building on the innovations of the Fielding brothers, Patrick Colquhoun, and others, in 1829 Home Secretary Robert Peel led the passage of a bill through Parliament that created the Metropolitan Police to replace the outdated watch system. A firm proponent of the adage that it was better to prevent crime than to punish and investigate in the aftermath of the crime, Peel was cautious in implementing his reforms lest he arouse the fears of his electorate.

Peel had originally hoped to create a nationwide police force, but to his constituency this suggested oppression and totalitarianism. Peel realized that he would have to focus his ambitions on a more concentrated area. So he selected London, which at that time was awash in crime. After seven years of opposition from the public and Parliament, Peel finally got his wish with the creation of the London Metropolitan Police. A preventive rather than reactive force, it replaced the ages-old night watch with professional, paid, full-time officers. The London "bobbies," or peelers (in deference to Robert Peel), patrolled regular beats, wore uniforms, and were paramilitary in structure and discipline.

According to the military requirements of the new force, prospective officers had to be under thirty-five years of age and at least five feet seven inches tall. Many former army officers would make the transition from the battlefield to the streets of London, including Waterloo veteran Colonel Charles Rowan, who would serve as the first police commissioner along with barrister Richard Mayne. Under the direction of Commissioners Rowan and Mayne, the force was able to overcome the trepidation of the public about a strong police force by improving community relations and reinforcing its image as a civilian police force.

Attired in uniforms designed to look as civilian as possible, every policeman was expected to begin service as a constable and work his way through the ranks for promotion. Headquartered at 4 Whitehall Place in Westminster, the back door of the new police quarters faced Scotland Yard. Since this door was used mostly by constables, the headquarters became known by the moniker Scotland Yard. The police were initially regarded with disdain. However, their suppression of a riot at Cold-Bath Fields in 1833 won the public over when they were able to do it without seriously injuring anyone in the crowd despite losing one of their own to mortal injury. Within the decade, the London Metropolitan Police became the model for modern policing. Although London had made the transition, the rest of Great Britain still lagged far behind in police reform.

New York City

The dawning of modern policing in America would take place in the largest cities. By the end of the American Revolution, New York City was well on its way to becoming the country's most populated city. Between 1790 and 1820, the city's population almost quadrupled, from 33,000 to 123,000, surprisingly with little increase in crime. Historian James Richardson suggested that perhaps this was due to the homogeneous nature of its population. In the decades before tumultuous immigration, life and property remained well protected. In the early 1820s, one English visitor reported that regarding crime, "New York compared favorably with that of any English city."[5] However, this was not necessarily a compliment considering the changing environs of industrial-age London. New York City was undergoing rapid changes by the 1820s but was still reliant on late eighteenth-century police strategies.

In 1801, the position of high constable was created in New York City. Subservient to the mayor, this position was charged with enforcing state laws and maintaining public order. Jacob Hays would carve out an enviable reputation during his half-century stint as New York City's first high constable. By 1800, New York City was policed by sixteen constables serving one-year terms. As the chief police officer of the city, the mayor also appointed marshals (forty served in 1800 alone) who served terms at his discretion. In 1811, the legislature passed an ordinance limiting the number of city marshals to sixty. Constables and marshals alike were expected to protect courts, serve process, and fulfill the accepted duties of police officers, such as making arrests, maintaining order, and apprehending criminal suspects.

Early New York City marshals and constables did not wear uniforms or carry identification of their position. Instead of a salary, they depended on fees for services rendered. In 1827, night watchmen, known as "leatherheads" for their leather hats, were carrying thirty-three-inch clubs to dispatch the more violent elements of New York society. A figure of derision, watchmen were notorious for sleeping on duty, or "cooping." Widely regarded as incompetent if not corrupt, most night watchmen held day jobs, ranging from masons to cartmen. Until the 1840s, New York City policing remained fundamentally an amateur business of volunteer or poorly paid watchmen and constables. Marshals and other functionaries complemented the law enforcement apparatus, but the only true professionals in criminal justice remained the criminals themselves.

With the phenomenal growth of the city in the 1840s, the old system of constables and night watchmen was soon overwhelmed by the problems accompanying the new economic and social order. Mass immigration in the 1830s and 1840s contributed to the growing juxtaposition between the well-to-do and the poor. As the nation's population exploded and settlers moved west thanks to improvements in transportation, new markets for manufactured goods were opened.

Business entrepreneurs soon enlarged labor forces and introduced a division of labor to mass-produce goods. But while the manufacturers reaped a profit, many laborers found their status and job security on the decline. Recent immigrants were often targeted as the scapegoat for the changing environment. Much of the urban violence was directed at recent Irish-Catholic immigrants. Mobs attacked Irish communities in many northeastern cities from Philadelphia to Charlestown, Massachusetts. In fact, this mayhem was so prevalent that the nascent insurance companies would refuse to issue the Irish policies. Rioting and an increasing crime and vice problem led, by 1844, to growing sentiment for a police force in New York City based on the London model.

Southern Policing

In the antebellum years, white southerners struggled with the problem of runaway slaves and potential slave insurrections. Most southern states established surveillance systems to curb slave mobility. According to one scholar, whites "exploited slave folk beliefs, planting rumors so that blacks would assume the 'paterollers' (patrols) possessed more power than they actually did."[6] Night riding and terror became a legitimate means for southerners to maintain their domination of slave society.

Recent research suggests that some of the earliest law enforcement reforms occurred in the South.[7] Charleston, South Carolina, could boast a paramilitary municipal police force by the beginning of the 1780s that grew to a guard of 100 men by 1822. To one visitor in 1842, Charleston had "the best organized system of police that has ever been devised."[8] Some scholars reject the notion that the early southern city guards constituted actual police forces, comparing them more to their slave patrol predecessors. While it is true that they walked a beat, wore uniforms, and carried weapons, the forces operated more as military slave patrols with little regard for republican society or values. Established to control the large slave population, Savannah, New Orleans, and Mobile soon followed with similar forces. Unlike the nonuni-formed constables and night watchmen of the northern cities, the city guards of the southern cities, similar to the militia, wore uniforms and carried muskets or swords. Regarded as city employees decades before the northern cities had uniformed forces, the city guards were usu-ally on duty at night, while a reserve force was available for daytime emergencies. In addition, they were salaried rather than dependent on fees.

One of the most notable police experiments of the early Republic took place in New Orleans when a city guard emerged in 1809. The very ethnic diversity of New Orleans that gave birth to the guard also had sown the seeds of its demise by the 1830s. Wearing uniforms and car-rying pikes and sabers, most of the members were French speakers, and by the end of the War of 1812, few could speak English. The influx of German and Irish immigrants in the 1820s and 1830s, ever wary of armed military-style polic-ing, would lead to friction with the native French-speaking population, and the guard dis-solved in 1836.

The Texas Rangers and the Mounted Police Tradition

While it is unknown when horses were first used in a police action, most historians can trace the utilization of mounted forces in peacekeeping operations to King Charles's *Articles of War* (1629). By 1758, the London Bow Street Run-ners police were established as the mounted branch of the London Metropolitan Police. In the early 1800s, the Bow Street Horse Patrol was charged with patrolling the main roads leading into London. Like most later personifications of the mounted police, officers came from the mili-tary, typically the cavalry. Mounted police forces in the British tradition appeared throughout the British Empire over the next 150 years.

In the United States, the Texas Rangers exemplified the ranging tradition and are credited as America's first statewide law enforcement agency. Created by Stephen Austin in 1823, they did not appear in official legislation as the "Texas Rangers" until 1874. The first incarnation of state policing in American history, during the nineteenth century the Rangers would have an off-and-on existence. A formally organized force of Texas Rangers did not appear until the out-break of the Texas Revolution in 1835, when they were formed as an auxiliary military body. With the main goal of eliminating the bandit and Indian threat, the Rangers originally con-sisted of ten volunteers whose duties were to "range" over the seemingly endless Texas land-scape. It was from this "ranging" activity that the Rangers derived their name. With wages of fif-teen dollars a month, payable in land, these men were in a constant state of preparedness. During the fifty years between the creation of Stephen Austin's colony in Texas and the establishment of a permanent force, the functions of the Texas Rangers continued to evolve.

CORRECTIONS

In the aftermath of the American Revolution, the former colonies attempted to come to terms with rising crime rates. Philadelphia had initially implemented hard labor as a substitute for more draconian punishments. However, it was less than a rousing success. The sight of prisoners with shaved heads and in primitive garments working on public roads proved more exhibitory specta-cle than reformative in nature. After Thomas Jefferson inaugurated a plan for hard labor in lieu of punishment in Virginia, he learned of the Philadelphia experiment and backtracked. Capi-talizing on Jefferson's notions combining work and punishment in 1796, Virginia authorized the construction of a penitentiary in Richmond. Opening in 1800, architect Benjamin Henry Latrobe's vision so impressed Jefferson that he selected him to design the U.S. Capitol building and to oversee its construction.

The city of Philadelphia proved a source of disappointment for European visitors in the late eighteenth century. Philadelphia was the home of Benjamin Franklin and the American capital city (between 1790 and 1800), and visitors such as the Englishman Isaac Weld found the city tedious and blandly constructed with "heavy tasteless piles of red brick."[9] Of all the red-hued buildings, none surpassed the Walnut Street Jail as an exemplar of criminal justice experimentation in the postrevolutionary era. Intended to reform rather than to punish, few could have imagined how this facility would stimulate the development of the penitentiary in America over the next three decades. A product of Quaker benevolence and the humanitarian concerns of Cesare Beccaria, Montesquieu, Bentham, Howard, and other Enlightenment thinkers, the nineteenth-century penitentiary shunned torture and public humiliation in favor of imprisonment.

In 1790, the Pennsylvania legislature commanded the erection of a cell house in the yard of the Walnut Street Jail for the solitary confinement of convicted felons in order to separate the more dangerous offenders from witnesses, suspects, and more benign misdemeanants. In this solitary complex, each of the twenty-four cells contained "one small window, placed high up and out of reach; the window well secured by a double iron grating, so that, provided an effort to get to it was successful, the person could perceive neither heaven nor earth, on account of the thickness of the wall. The criminal, while confined here, is permitted no convenience of bench, table, or even bed, or anything else but what is barely necessary to support life."[10]

It was not long before this jail became the destination for prison innovators from around the world. During its short history, Walnut Street Jail was the setting for numerous correctional innovations. In 1791, better conditions for debtors were implemented, and by the following year, prison keepers were subsisting on an actual salary rather than collecting fees from prisoners. By the end of the decade, Pennsylvania witnessed the abolition of the death penalty for all crimes except premeditated murder as well as the complete revision of its penal code.

Officials soon became cognizant of one of the inherent contradictions of a prison that housed inmates in any congregate setting—that this created an environment akin to a "school for crime." In making the transition from a county jail to a state penal establishment, Walnut Street Jail was soon faced with problems of overcrowding and inadequate financing, which in turn led to riots, mass escapes, and assaults on guards.

Despite an untimely retreat from the initial attempt providing separate confinement, Quaker-inspired organizations such as the Pennsylvania Prison Society and the Philadelphia Society for Alleviating the Miseries of Public Prisons embarked on a new attempt at a separate system. Two new prisons were built in Pennsylvania following this concept. Pittsburgh's Western Penitentiary, built according to Jeremy Bentham's Panopticon, was completed in 1818 but was slightly regarded. However, the completion in 1829 of the Cherry Hill Prison, better known as Eastern State Penitentiary, would become the showplace for prison reform in America.

According to the noted French traveler Alexis de Tocqueville, by the 1830s Philadelphia was still "infatuated with the prison system." This would be an oversimplification. The Quaker reform impulse was indeed still strong in Philadelphia by the 1830s as civic idealism merged with new architectural professionalism. New penal, medical, and philanthropic institutions dotted the city's landscape. Large in scale and progressive for their time, the Orphan Asylum, the House of Refuge, the Alms House, and Moyamensing Prison would all pale in comparison to Eastern State Penitentiary, America's largest building in 1829.

While Great Britain could point to the Penitentiary Houses Act in 1799 as a universal attempt to reform the English prison system, no such umbrella of legislation came to fruition in America. The republican system of government remained a formidable obstacle to any comprehensive prison legislation and would leave it to the various states to confront the enduring problem of the American prison system.

One goal shared by the state prison building movement in the 1820s and 1830s was to make the new institutions self-sufficient. State legislators demanded that penitentiaries pay their own way, although they would be consistently at loggerheads with private businesses that worried that prison industries would flourish because of unfair business competition. The most outstanding feature of the separate system worked against the very profitability it sought since the rigid segregation of prisoners worked against the viability of prison industries. Legislators looked for a compromise in Virginia by refraining from keeping prisoners continuously in stir as in the Pennsylvania model, allowing them to work for a time in congregate conditions while spending a good part of the day in unemployed solitude. However, when they did have the chance to work, borrowing a page from the Auburn model, they worked in silence in prison shops.

In 1826, the First Report of the Prison Discipline Society of Boston, organized under the zealous leadership of the Reverend Louis Dwight was published. According to this work, there were approximately 3,500 prisoners in state penitentiaries, with 60 percent of them housed in New York, Pennsylvania, and Massachusetts. Although prison stripes were introduced in New York in 1815, prison uniforms would vary from state to state. Since different colors were used for first-time offenders and recidivists, the purpose of the different-colored stripes was to reveal at a glance the prisoner's classification in the case of an escape. The states were never consistent in the training and equipping of jail keepers. For example, prison guards in New York were initially unarmed, while early Massachusetts keepers were provided a gun and bayonet.

Having originally trained for the ministry, Louis Dwight was kept from fulfilling his ambition after a chemical laboratory accident injured his lungs so that he could not preach. By 1824, he was traversing Massachusetts dispensing Bibles to prisoners. After discovering the abuses of the new penal institutions, he devoted his life to improving prison conditions. In 1825, he organized the Prison Discipline Society of Boston, an organization he would lead until his death in 1854. A champion of the Auburn system, Dwight led the opposition against the Pennsylvania model.

Newgate and Auburn Prisons

The early success of Walnut Street Jail led other states to implement the penitentiary idea (New York, 1796, 1816; Virginia, 1800; Massachusetts, 1804; Vermont, 1808; Maryland, 1811; and New Hampshire, 1812). Heavily influenced by the Pennsylvania model, most of the new prisons contained solitary cells for dangerous felons, common night rooms for less serious offenders, and large rooms for congregate labor.

At the dawn of the nineteenth century, New York State was grappling with its own penal obstacles. Its foremost prison at the time was Newgate Jail located in Greenwich Village. New York advocates for prison reform had visited Philadelphia in 1796 and returned to New York with plans to build a new edifice that took the shape of Newgate Prison in 1797. Implementing many of the ideals of the Pennsylvania system, Thomas Eddy (1758–1827), a Quaker and New York businessman, earned a philanthropic reputation that led to his sobriquet "the John Howard of America." An advocate for humanitarian disciplinary methods, Eddy has been credited as the first American to call for separate cells for all prisoners as he helped design Newgate.

During its first five years, Newgate earned an enviable record for subsistence, with prison industries paying nearly all the prison's expenses. Eddy was credited with establishing a prison hospital and pharmacy and hiring the first full-time prison physician. A firm believer in rehabilitation, Newgate emphasized schooling and strict religious instruction for inmates while prohibiting corporal punishment. A proponent of individualized punishment, prisoners were classified into four categories that included juveniles under the age of eighteen, men and women, those capable of improvement, and hardened offenders.[11] But despite showing a small profit and eliminating corporal punishment in 1803, the following year Eddy resigned as conditions in the prison deteriorated. Eddy then left Newgate to dedicate himself to building a better prison that would soon take shape at Auburn.

With the support of the state legislature, Auburn was selected as the site for a new prison facility, and in 1816 construction began under the direction of architect-builder John Cray. Patterned after other early American prisons with a sprinkling of solitary cells and larger night rooms, in 1823 a new plan was adopted in which all prisoners would be locked in separate cells at night but ate and worked in a congregate environment in absolute silence under threat of corporal punishment.

Unlike its Pennsylvania progenitor, which relied on solitary confinement, Auburn Prison would take off in another direction. Construction would hinge on providing double cells and apartments to house inmates and congregate rooms for inmates to work together during the day. In 1819, the solitary arrangements of Philadelphia influenced New York officials to construct an additional wing of the prison that provided single cells for the more uncontrollable prisoners. In 1821, a new cell block was erected, composed of two rows of cells built on five floors. Placed back to back, the cells were much smaller than those in Pennsylvania, measuring three and a half feet wide, seven feet long, and seven feet high. However, the inauguration of solitary confinement at Auburn proved disastrous. In solitary confinement and faced with the restriction of absolute silence, five of the original eighty-three inmates died the first year.

Later in 1821, Captain Elam Lynds took over control of the prison and was credited with establishing the Auburn silent system. Under the new scheme, men were allowed to work in strictly supervised congregate shops during the day but were locked in individual cells at night. The Auburn design of prison, with five-tiered cell blocks containing narrow single cells for nighttime separation, would become the most influential design of American prison in the early nineteenth century. The strict code of silence was maintained under threat of flogging in an attempt to thwart the contamination of criminal behavior and put an end to the "schools for crime."

Lynds has been given credit as "inventor of the Auburn system." However, this distinction was tarnished by his darker side, which led many critics to brand him a borderline sadist. Following service in the local militia and the federal infantry, Lynds was selected principal keeper of Auburn Prison, where he rapidly gained a reputation for military discipline. He enforced lockstep marching and rigid silence with the zeal of a martinet. Any motion at the dining table that violated the prescribed protocol would elicit harsh punishment that could include solitary confinement in the "hole" or a whipping. An advocate of whipping, when Lynds was questioned by the Frenchmen Gustave de Beaumont and Alexis de Tocqueville in the 1830s as to whether he believed "that bodily chastisement might be dispensed with," Lynds responded, "I am convinced of the contrary. I consider the chastisement by the whip, the most efficient, and, at the same time, the humane which exists; it never injures health, and obliges the prisoners to lead a life essentially healthy. . . . I consider it impossible to govern a large prison without a whip."[12] With his penchant for corporal punishment, Lynds maintained order in Auburn until 1825, when he was authorized to take 100 inmates to the Hudson River town of Ossining to build what would become known as Sing Sing Prison. On his return to Auburn, his methods were finally brought into question, and in 1838 he was fired for his cruelty. Ever the disciplinarian, his acumen would soon be required at Sing Sing.

The Auburn system would flourish in the first half of the nineteenth century with thirty state prisons following this pattern, including the infamous Sing Sing Prison in 1825. New York prisons following the Auburn plan are also credited with introducing prison uniforms in 1815 using different-colored stripes to distinguish the various categories of inmates. This was particularly helpful in the event of a prison escape where a prisoner's classification could be noted by colored stripes (striped uniforms were out of fashion by the 1950s).

Eastern State Penitentiary

In 1829, Pennsylvania responded to the Auburn model with the opening of Eastern State Penitentiary, admitting its first prisoner on October 25. Often referred to simply as "Cherry Hill" because it was built on the site of a cherry orchard, it was the largest building project in America up to that time. Prisoners were housed in extra-large cells, each with a walled garden-exercise yard, and were expected to live and work in the cell without contact with any other prisoners. Having replaced the Walnut Jail, which was not permanently closed until 1835, the new facility was considered the nation's greatest testament to the penitentiary concept.

Architecturally, Eastern State Penitentiary resembled a medieval castle with towering thirty-foot walls surrounding seven cell blocks that branched out from a central rotunda like the spokes of a wheel. Long corridors extended through each cell block and contained at least thirty solitary cells. Here prisoners often spent years ensconced in solitary confinement. The most expensive prison of its kind, each cell had its own private exercise yard, running water, and heat. With little provided for reading besides the Bible, it was hoped that prisoners would seek solace in the holy book and spend their lonely hours reflecting on their misspent lives. Despite the noble goals of the system's creators, many convicts became insane from the monotony of solitary confinement. After a visit to the prison in 1842, the novelist Charles Dickens lamented that "the system here is rigid, strict, and hopeless solitary confinement. I believe it, in its effects, to be cruel and wrong" and that the "slow and daily tampering with the mysteries of the brain" was "immeasurably worse than any torture to the body."[13]

CRIME AND PUNISHMENT

The creation of the federal criminal justice system in the 1790s not only created courts but also authorized punishments such as imprisonment, corporal penalties, and, in capital cases, execution. However, while English law still recognized 240 capital offenses in 1780 (although 94 percent were commuted to transportation),[14] the penal codes of the American states were far less punitive. Capital punishment was rarely meted out to whites for crimes other than murder. During the late eighteenth century, traditional punishments were clearly ineffective. With population growth, increasing mobility, and migration, the emergence of a distinct poor population made sanctions such as fines, whippings, and the pillory less effective than in the past.

While the use of capital punishment had diminished, corporal punishment was another matter, with many criminal offenses still being punished with the public infliction of pain and suffering. Most towns in New England boasted whipping posts and stocks near the commons or meetinghouse. As late as 1805, the penalty in Massachusetts for counterfeiting was the amputation of an ear after sitting in a pillory for an hour. The penalty for manslaughter consisted of having one's forehead branded in public, and many communities flogged perpetrators of petty theft. But by the 1830s, public corporal punishment began to disappear from statute books as prison became a more accepted sanction for most crimes. In 1790, Pennsylvania began the movement to prohibit flogging, and in 1805, Massachusetts followed suit. The movement to abolish corporal punishment was haphazard at best, with Connecticut constables continuing to whip petty criminals until 1828 and Delaware officials flogging black and white prisoners well into the twentieth century.

Capital Punishment

Following the American Revolution and the Enlightenment, the movement to abolish the death penalty was inextricably linked with the developing penitentiary movement. But despite an emphasis on milder punishments, executions still occurred in the first part of the nineteenth century. With a rise in public disorder in the 1820s and 1830s, some states began to steer away from the inflammatory spectacle of public executions. Pennsylvania once again led the way in criminal justice reform as the first state to hold private executions behind prison walls beginning in 1834. During the 1830s, New York and Massachusetts would join Pennsylvania in ending public executions as sheriffs made the transition to carrying out death sentences behind prison walls.

Following the American Revolution, a new, more humanitarian age was ushered in by the protections granted by the Bill of Rights, which eliminated "cruel and unusual punishments." Hanging would predominate as the only sanctioned form of capital punishment in America for the next 100 years. Although Benjamin Rush and others were in favor of the abolition of the death penalty, they were clearly in the minority. But in sharp contrast with England's "bloody code," the few capital offenses in America consisted of murder, treason, arson, and rape. The rate of executions clearly fell after the colonial era, from a high of almost thirty-five per 100,000 to only three or four per 100,000 in the postrevolutionary years.[15] As the 1820s got under way, northern states abolished outdated traditions such as "benefit of clergy" as penitentiaries and reformatories became accepted alternatives to more punitive methods of punishment.

Until executions were hidden from the public behind prison walls, spectators would drive many miles to witness public hangings. Entertainers, vendors, and peddlers lent an air of festivity—a carnival atmosphere to what should have been a somber event. Although the gallows was the typical mode of hanging east of the Mississippi River, there are accounts during the years before the Civil War of prisoners walking up a ladder to a noose on a tree limb and then having the ladder withdrawn. The influence of the new industrial age would lead to the development of new hanging machines that were considered more humanitarian.

Juvenile Delinquency

As America grew more urban during the early nineteenth century, a new class of servants, orphans, and indigents for whom no one felt responsibility began to dot the municipal landscape. As early as 1766, one of New York City's leading citizens was lamenting that "children nightly trampouze the streets with lanthorns upon poles and halloing . . . the magistry either approve of it, or do not dare suppress it."[16] More an irritant than a public crime hazard, youth gangs would gradually evolve into an urban menace by the early 1800s.

By the 1790s, the rise in wage labor and the increasing prosperity of slavery led master artisans to move away from the old system, which required apprentices. With few outlets for subsistence, once young boys left their homes, they often found themselves on the streets, stealing food and sleeping in alleys. In earlier days, the moral arbiters of the village would council the youths, but with society becoming increasingly complex, city fathers were powerless to police every street corner, with more pressing matters of public health and order taking precedence.

Groups of young homeless boys were soon congregating on the fringes of crowded cities where they could survive by robbing travelers or doing odd jobs. By the early 1820s, the Five Points district (derived from the intersection of five streets) of New York was a breeding ground for every kind of criminal element. It is generally conceded that some of America's earliest organized criminal gangs were born out of this locale, where thieves, cutthroats, and pickpockets found refuge from a society intent on bringing order to the chaos that was urban America. Chief among the first Five Points gangs were the Forty Thieves, whose organization can be traced back to 1826.

Alcoholic Republic

Virtually every American community had a village church and local tavern in the late eighteenth century. Diametrically opposed to one another in spirit, the tavern was the most accessible local institution for the male world of the early nineteenth century. Even the former Puritan communities of New England could boast more licensed taverns than meetinghouses. Like their British counterparts in the medieval world, the taverns were scenes of gambling, heavy smoking, hard drinking, and even harder fighting. The winter months proved a boon to local tavern keepers with little competition for the entertainment dollars of men in the fallow months of an agricultural-based society.

When not preoccupied by drinking, the men of the early Republic could find solace in gambling and games of chance such as dice and cards. Gambling united the classes as few other endeavors did. When weather permitted, they wagered on horse racing, cockfights, and wrestling matches. Mostly indifferent to the suffering of animals, the blood sports of dogfighting, bull and bear baiting, and cock matches were especially popular in both the North and the South.

Regardless of the social activity, alcoholic beverages were never far away, being as common as traditional victuals. The problem was not the act of drinking but the enormous quantity consumed. One estimate suggests that during the revolutionary era, each person consumed the equivalent of three and a half gallons of pure, 200-proof alcohol. By the end of the 1790s, perhaps because of anxieties generated by rapid social and economic change, men were drinking even more, with consumption rising to an all-time high of four gallons per capita by the late 1820s.

Over the next twenty years, liquor consumption began to decline in some regions of the country. A product of temperance crusades by mostly New England clergymen, the campaign against drinking found a voice in the creation of the American Temperance Society in 1826. A highly charged crusade against "demon rum" and its accompanying social disorder was supplemented by pamphlets from medical doctors such as Benjamin Rush advising Americans of the potentially poisonous effects of alcohol. By 1840, alcohol consumption had declined from four gallons per person each year to less than one and a half gallons. And in less than a century, temperance societies would become victorious with the passage of the Volstead Act in 1920.

AMERICAN VIOLENCE

As America became more diverse as it moved from its colonial roots, so too did the relationships of its myriad citizens become more complex, often degenerating into violence. The early

Republic years saw casual violence become part of the daily fabric of American life. Recreational bare-knuckle boxing and wrestling offered more acceptable outlets for male violence. For slaves, violence was part and parcel of the peculiar institution. Violence was rarely absent from any aspect of the social arena. Harsh corporal punishment was common within the family and at school. Servants, slaves, student, and children were often the target of brutal corporal and public punishments.

During the American Revolution, the southern colonies witnessed not only traditional warfare but also what has been called an "uncivil war" where vigilantes, Tories, and bands of bandits waged war against each other and the civilian populace. Following the war, the southern region's association with violence became more pronounced. During the early Republic, while northern states outlawed dueling and abandoned the institution of slavery, white southerners continued to glorify the virtues of honor, violence, and masculinity. The persistence of southern slavery guaranteed that violence would continue to be identified with southern culture. Flogging and branding and the threat of violence were emphasized for maintaining social control at a time when northern cities experimented with policing and prisons.

The Slave Revolts

During the 1790s, the legal status of slavery became increasingly complicated. In 1791, the former Haitian slave Pierre-Dominique Toussaint Louverture led the first large-scale slave uprising in the Americas. His forces defeated troops from Spain, Britain, as well as mulatto-French forces. American slaveholders restlessly followed the subsequent events in Haiti with great interest, fearing similar uprisings in the South. Increasingly paranoid, the southern slavocracy closed ranks and suppressed even the slightest hint of insurrection. According to historian Scott Christianson, "Reported American slave revolts during the 1790s grew by 150 percent over the previous decade."[17]

In 1800, Virginia planters had reason to fear insurrection when Gabriel Prosser (owned by

Thomas Prosser) was accused of conspiring with insurgent slaves to attack Richmond, seize the arsenal, and kill white residents. Despite the twenty-eight-year-old Gabriel's contention that he was motivated by the ideals contained in the Declaration of Independence, thirty of the accused conspirators were executed before they could put any plot into action. According to most sources, the plan came very close to succeeding if not for an informer.

With the slave states still dependent on slave patrols, militia, and informal methods of law enforcement, Prosser's rebellion led to the organization of a public guard in Virginia. Wary of future uprisings, General Assembly of Virginia authorized the creation of a "paid militia with its barracks in Richmond." For the next six decades, the Public Guard would patrol Richmond's penitentiary, armory, Capitol Square, and other important public places. Keepers for the new Richmond penitentiary would be selected from the ranks of the Guard as well.

Eleven years later, the largest slave insurrection in American history flared up in two isolated Louisiana parishes, but federal troops were able to suppress it before it could spread any farther. Among the more notorious near conspiracies was the Denmark Vesey plot in Charleston, South Carolina, led by a free black who reportedly was intent on ridding the state of its draconian slave system. Despite South Carolina's black majority, Vesey and his coconspirators were executed. In retaliation for the near calamity, South Carolina's planters introduced even harsher laws prohibiting contact between freed blacks and slaves.

It was not until the 1831 Nat Turner revolt that a slave insurrection was allowed to come to fruition. By the end of the Virginia rebellion, Turner and his followers killed more than sixty whites. Virginia authorities took six weeks to suppress the rebellion and bring Turner and his followers to "justice." This event marked a turning point in the history of slavery in the South. Prior slave rebellions had existed in plot only. The outbreak of the Turner rebellion led southern authorities to become more aggressive in their defense of slavery and in their control of the slave population. Following the rebellions, southerners turned increasingly to slave patrols and local militia to control the slave population.

Native Americans

The American Revolution was a turning point in Anglo-Indian relations. Violence was formerly restrained between the indigenous peoples and Europeans because of various alliances with the French and English. Prior to the war, the British attempted to block the settlement of the western lands by American colonists while granting Indians protection of their hunting lands. But having made the irrevocable decision to side with the British late in the war, the Indians lost their protectors as the colonists rapidly invaded the Indian sanctuaries. Within several generations, military campaigns and Indian removal would reduce the Indian population east of the Mississippi River to a fraction of its prewar population.

Former Patriots saw nothing wrong with retaliating against the Indian cultures. While not all sided with the British, for the most part the Americans branded all cultures as traitorous. Among the more lamentable examples of using broad brushstrokes to paint the diverse Indian cultures was the scandalous treatment accorded the Stockbridge Indians of Massachusetts who had so valiantly aided the Patriots but were forced from their homelands to New York.

Dueling

Prior to the American Revolution, dueling had not yet made its mark on the American consciousness. While southern gentlemen might resort to wrestling or their fists to settle matters of honor, dueling was rare before the conflict, when French and British officers introduced the tradition to American officers who helped assimilate the practice into civilian culture. Never very popular in the northern states, it soon became a fixture in the southern subculture of violence. After Aaron Burr killed his political adversary Alexander Hamilton in a duel in 1804, dueling was prohibited in the North but would flourish in the South among those who valued competitive self-assertion and skill with weapons as a means of maintaining personal honor. Southern towns such as New Orleans and St. Louis maintained secluded dueling grounds on the outskirts of the city as legislatures and courts turned a blind eye toward the practice. Duels were conducted under a strict protocol that found expression in books such as John L. Wilson's *The Code of Honor* (1838). While movements against dueling were sporadically organized in the South, once and future politicians, such as Andrew Jackson, Judah P. Benjamin, Thomas Hart Benton, and Sam Houston, would endear themselves to their constituents because of their participation in violent encounters at some time in their adult lives. Historian Bertram Wyatt-Brown suggested that besides confirming the worthiness of the upper classes, dueling also "enabled lesser men" to advance into the higher echelons of society.[18]

NOTABLE TRIALS

Aaron Burr Treason Trial (1807)

On March 30, 1807, former vice president of the United States Aaron Burr was delivered to Richmond, Virginia, to stand trial for treason. In almost every civilization, treason has been viewed as the most serious secular crime, and a capital crime at that. The charges leveled at Burr included plotting to divide the Union and attempting to make himself emperor of a new nation that would encompass Mexico and most of the American territories west of the Allegheny Mountains. The Burr case is one of the most famous treason trials in American history, and the adjudication of the case would play a part in the larger drama of a young nation attempting to define itself.

No stranger to controversy, Burr today is probably best remembered for his deadly duel with Alexander Hamilton in 1804 that would not only deprive America of a great statesman and sully the reputation of another but also make

dueling illegal in the northern states. Treason was the one crime defined by the U.S. Constitution. According to article III, section 3, "Treason against the United States shall consist only in levying War against them, or in adhering to their enemies, Giving them Aid and Comfort. No Person shall be convicted of Treason unless on the Testimony of two Witnesses to the same overt Act, or on Confession in open Court." The charge of treason has long been used as a tool of destruction against political opposition, and the Constitution defined the limits of legal opposition to the federal government.

During the trial, Burr did not deny committing many of the acts he was accused of committing, but he denied that they were treasonable offenses. Following his indictment on murder charges for killing Hamilton in the duel in 1804, Burr's political career had effectively ended. But his controversial life had one more chapter yet to come. In the spring of 1805, Burr reportedly concocted a scheme with James Wilkinson, the military governor of Louisiana, the actual nature of which is still unclear. According to some accounts, Burr told the British minister that he would separate the states and territories west of the Appalachians from the Union and create an empire with himself as leader if the British would offer $500,000 and naval support.

As Burr and his sixty coconspirators traversed the Ohio River destined for New Orleans, his accomplice Wilkinson betrayed Burr to President Thomas Jefferson. Burr was captured and tried for treason with Chief Justice John Marshall presiding. Using the Constitution's definition of treason, it would take two witnesses to convict an individual on that charge. Unable to meet this standard, Burr was exonerated. There are still lingering questions concerning Burr's guilt or innocence, but to his dying day, Burr denied the charges. Despite having the charges against him dismissed by two grand juries, he never regained the respect of his fellow Americans, never able to escape the label of traitor.

The trial of Aaron Burr is considered the most often cited source for understanding the basic federal criminal procedure prior to the 1840s. For most of America's history, circuit courts created by the Judiciary Act of 1789 were the primary trial courts in the federal judicial system. These courts had jurisdiction over federal criminal offenses and disputes between citizens from different states that involved $500 or more. For most of the nineteenth century, except for affidavits certifying the opinion between the two judges holding the circuit court, there was no judicial review. As a result, court opinions, decisions, and especially transcripts are rare for this period.

CONCLUSIONS

There was little discussion of a crime problem before the American Revolution. However, independence from Great Britain would lead to a dramatic transformation of the country and the dawning of a crime problem that would haunt American culture for more than two centuries. By the early 1800s, various communities and cities could identify particular areas considered unsafe to the public at large. New York City, Boston, Baltimore, and Philadelphia became hotbeds for sectarian strife. The more rural parts of America were not left untouched by the growing crime problem. During the late eighteenth and early nineteenth centuries, the Natchez Trace between Nashville and Natchez was one of the most dangerous regions in the country. Among the most prolific killers of this era were brothers Micajah and Wiley Harpe, who were estimated to have killed dozens of innocent victims, making them probably the earliest recorded multiple murderers in American history.

During the first four decades of the American Republic, the country had grown to a manufacturing power as cities teemed with new immigrants. Peace officers in the 1820s were concerned more with issues of public health and municipal regulations than enforcing criminal laws or preventing crimes. American cities began a transformation that would not be completed

until the 1840s and 1850s. Although larger cities, such as New York and Boston, contended with increasing crime and riots, only limited steps were taken toward adopting the 1829 London Metropolitan model of policing. Recent historians have concluded that "in neither Boston, New York nor any other American city was the establishment of uniformed preventive police as rapid and as dramatic as in London in 1829."[19]

Meanwhile, states struggled with the adoption of various prison designs, mainly having to decide whether to keep prisoners confined in a "solitary" environment or in a "silent" one. It was hoped the solitary system, inaugurated in Philadelphia, would give prisoners time to reflect on their crimes and become better citizens. Advocates of the silent system saw the Pennsylvania solitary system as inhumane and allowed prisoners to work with others in a congregate setting, albeit in a rigidly enforced silence. The silent system ultimately triumphed. But the main reason for the success of the Auburn model over the Pennsylvania one was the economic difference since most states would adopt the plan that saw the greatest profit. Slave states, meanwhile, had little need for large penitentiaries, reliant as they were on the punishments that accompanied slavery. Between 1790 and 1817, Pennsylvania, New York, New Jersey, Kentucky, Virginia, Massachusetts, Vermont, Maryland, New Hampshire, Ohio, and Georgia all constructed their first penitentiaries. The reform impulse remained strong in America between 1790 and 1830.

Point–Counterpoint
Creating the Penitentiary (1835)

During their tours of America in the 1830s European visitors rarely failed to be impressed by the nation's new penitentiary buildings at Eastern State Penitentiary and Auburn Prison. The differences between these two systems were glaring. The Pennsylvania system, exemplified at

Source: William Crawford, *Report of William Crawford, Esq., on the Penitentiaries of the United States,* London: Home Department, 1835, pp. 6, 25–26.

Eastern State, was a solitary system that often led prisoners to go insane and sometimes attempt suicide. No less foreboding, the silent Auburn system, with its reliance on military discipline, became the more popular of the two systems, keeping discipline with the threat of a flogging for the slightest infraction.

The following passages are taken from William Crawford's 1835 report on American prisons. In 1831 Crawford (1788–1847), a London wine seller and philanthropist, was selected by the British Home Office to embark on an investigation of American prisons and to determine which system was most superior (he selected Pennsylvania regimen). He would eventually visit 14 state penitentiaries and a number of local jails. The twin evils of solitary confinement and its accompanying mental health problems are chronicled in the passage on Eastern, while the issue of flogging is addressed in the Auburn selection.

The tendency of the system to produce mental disease is a subject of such vast importance that I felt it my duty to make every enquiry into the cases of the individuals who had been thus afflicted, in order to ascertain if their lamentable condition could in any degree be ascribed to the peculiar nature of their imprisonment. The information on this point contained in the following letter, addressed to me by the warden of the penitentiary, is so very satisfactory, and was so fully corroborated by other enquiries which I instituted, that no doubt whatever remains on my mind that the parties in question had suffered mental derangement before their committal to this penitentiary. It is proper to observe, that there is no state lunatic asylum in Pennsylvania, and that offenders who are afflicted with disorders of the mind, and who are considered too dangerous to be at large, are consequently sent to the penitentiary for security.

"Philadelphia, first month 20th, 1834." In reference to the subject mentioned yesterday, of the cause of the insanity of four and the idiotcy of one of our prisoners, I must refer to the several reports made annually to the Legislature. In addition to what is contained in them I may add that No. 10 appeared very strange on his admission, and told the inspectors, physician, and myself, remarkable tales of his being concerned in killing men, women, and children, in Charleston (South Carolina), who were salted up and sold for pork, and of being concerned with gangs of counterfeiters; that General Jackson was the prime

mover of all this, and such a mass of nonsense that we all came to one conclusion that he was either insane, or wished us to think he was so. A two years' residence here induced us to believe that the former was the case. He was sometimes more excited than at others, but went away apparently in very much the same state of mind to that in which he came in. As he talked in the same manner on the day of his admission as on that of his discharge, no one for a moment believed that separate confinement had been the cause of his insanity, *if he was insane*. We knew nothing of him before his reception, and have never heard of him since he left the doors of the penitentiary."

"There was something odd and singular in No. 48 when he arrived here, but this was attributed more to a want of education and an unbroken irritable temper than to insanity. We were told that he had ascended a chimney in the county prison at Lancaster (where he was convicted), and that he remained there three days without food, until it was supposed that he had made his escape. This feat was considered as an attempt to escape, and not attributed to insanity. He was received here Nov. 29th, 1830. On the 7th of Dec. he was set to work as a cabinet maker, at which trade he said he had served two years. We found, however, that he knew but little. On the 11th he refused to do any work, and said that he had been ordered otherwise by a higher authority than any one here. During this night the watchman found him at prayers. About eight o'clock on the morning of the 12th my attention was called to him. He was sitting with his lamp burning and a bible before him. I directed him to put out the light: this he would not do. Thomas Bradford and S. W. Crawford saw him this day, and believed him to be under the influence of religious excitement. On the contrary I thought that he was feigning insanity. He became better, but again worse, and continued so until discharged by pardon.

In the workshops the convicts are arranged in such a way as not to face each other, and to labour separately as much as possible. In each shop prisoners are selected as attendants, whose business it is to distribute the materials, hand out and grind the tools, and clean the shops, under the direction of the

Source: William Crawford, *Report of William Crawford, Esq., on the Penitentiaries of the United States*, London: Home Department, 1835, pp. 6, 35–26.

assistant-keeper. All this, however, is done principally by signs, so that the attention of the other convicts is not distracted. Privies are placed in the corners of the shops. Each workshop has a supply of water to which a prisoner can help himself at pleasure. In every mechanical or trade department there is at least one assistant-keeper who attends to the instruction of learners. The assistant-keeper directs the appropriation of all raw materials, keeps a daily account of the work performed by each convict, and regulates his daily task. He also superintends the removal of his men to and from their cells. A prisoner who wilfully or negligently injures his work, tools, wearing apparel, or bedding, is immediately flogged by the assistant-keeper. The prisoners are not allowed to speak to each other on any pretence, except by special direction of the officers. They are not at any time to leave their places without permission. They are never to speak to any person who does not belong to the prison, and must not look off from their work at spectators. They are not to speak even to an officer, except when absolutely necessary relative to their business. For a violation of any of these rules they are immediately flogged. A convict's word is never taken even against another convict, and much less against an officer.

The prisoners are not allowed to write nor receive any letters, or intelligence from or concerning their friends, or on any subject out of the prison. No relative, or friend, is allowed to visit or speak to a convict, except in some extraordinary case which may require a personal interview, and which can only take place in the presence of the keeper or his deputy.

The assistant-keepers are twenty in number. They are required to enforce strictly the general observance of the regulations. They are not to hold any conversation with the convicts, nor even allow them to speak on any subject except on necessary business. Each assistant-keeper must keep a list of the names of the prisoners under his charge, with the respective numbers of the cells occupied by them, and the description of work at which they are employed. If an assistant-keeper punishes a convict for misconduct, he is required within a reasonable time to make a report in writing to the keeper, or his deputy, stating the prisoner's name and offence, and the nature and extent of the punishment inflicted. The assistant-keepers are to correct convicts for every breach of discipline by stripes which are to be inflicted with a raw-hide whip, and applied to the back in such a manner as not to expose the head, face, eyes, or in any way to put the convict's health or limbs in danger. In aggravated cases, a "cat," made of six lashes of small twine, may be applied to the bare back, under the direction of the keeper or deputy. The prisoner is compelled to strip immediately on the commission of an offence, and is flogged before the other prisoners. No superior officer is required to be present on these occasions.

SOURCES

Attorney General's Survey of Release Procedures (1940). 1973. "State Prisons in America—1787–1937." In *Penology: The Evolution of Corrections in America,* ed. George G. Killinger et al., pp. 23–73. St. Paul, Minn.: West Publishing

Ayers, Edward L. 1984. *Vengeance and Justice: Crime and Punishment in the 19th-Century South.* New York: Oxford University Press.

Barnes, Harry Elmer. 1968. *The Evolution of Penology in Pennsylvania: A Study in American Social History.* Montclair, N. J.: Patterson Smith.

Beaumont, Gustave de, and Alexis de Tocqueville. 1979. *On the Penitentiary System in the United States and Its Application in France.* Carbondale: Southern Illinois University Press.

Christianson, Scott. 1998. *With Liberty for Some: 500 Years of Imprisonment in America.* Boston: Northeastern University Press.

Dickens, Charles. 1985. *American Notes: A Journey.* New York: Fromm International Publishing.

Emsley, Clive. 1984. *Policing and Its Context, 1750–1870.* New York: Schocken Books.

Finkel, Kenneth. 1994. "Philadelphia in the 1820s: A New Civic Consciousness." In *Eastern State Penitentiary: Crucible of Good Intentions,* ed. Norman Johnston, pp. 9–19. Foner, Philip S. 1975. *History of Black Americans: From Africa to the Emergence of the Cotton Kingdom.* Westport, Conn.: Greenwood Press.

Howard, D. L. 1960. *The English Prisons.* London: Methuen.

Johnson, David R. 1979. *Policing the Urban Underworld: The Impact of Crime on the Development of the American Police, 1800–1887.* Philadelphia: Temple University Press, 1979.

Johnston, Norman. 1994. *Eastern State Penitentiary: Crucible of Good Intentions*. Philadelphia: Philadelphia Museum of Art.

Lane, Roger. 1967. *Policing the City: Boston, 1822–1885*. Cambridge.: Harvard University Press.

———. 1999. "Capital Punishment." In *Violence in America*. Vol. 1. New York: Charles Scribners, pp. 198–203.

Masur, Louis P. 1989. *Rites of Execution: Capital Punishment and the Transformation of American Culture, 1776–1865*. New York: Oxford University Press.

McKelvey, Blake. 1977. *American Prisons: A History of Good Intentions*. Montclair, N. J.: Patterson Smith.

Miller, John C. 1951. *Crisis in Freedom: The Alien and Sedition Acts*. Boston: Little, Brown.

Mintz, Steven. 1995. *Moralists and Modernizers: America's Pre-Civil War Reformers*. Baltimore: Johns Hopkins University Press.

Monkkonen, Eric. 1981. *Police in Urban America 1860–1920*. New York: Cambridge University Press.

Reed, V. B., and J. D. Williams, eds. 1960. *The Case of Aaron Burr*. Boston: Houghton Mifflin.

Richardson, James. 1970. *The New York Police: Colonial Times to 1901*. New York: Oxford University Press.

Rorabaugh, William J. 1979. *The Alcoholic Republic: An American Tradition*. New York: Oxford University Press.

Rothman, David J. 1971. *The Discovery of the Asylum: Social Order and Disorder in the New Republic*. Boston: Little, Brown.

Rousey, Dennis C. 1996. *Policing the Southern City: New Orleans, 1805–1889*. Baton Rouge: Louisiana State University Press.

Semonche, John E. 1998. *Keeping the Faith: A Cultural History of the U.S. Supreme Court*. Lanham, Md.: Rowman & Littlefield.

Stead, Philip J. 1957. *The Police of Paris*. London: Staples.

Stokes, I. N. 1915. *The Iconography of Manhattan Island*. Vol. 5. New York: Robert H. Dodd.

Sullivan, Larry. 1990. *The Prison Reform Movement: Forlorn Hope*. Boston: Twayne Publishing.

Teeters, Negley, and John D. Shearer. 1957. *The Prison at Philadelphia, Cherry Hill: The Separate System of Penal Discipline, 1829–1913*. New York: Columbia University Press.

Turner, Patricia A. 1993. *I Heard It through the Grapevine: Rumor in African-American Culture*. Berkeley: University of California Press.

Walters, Ronald G. 1978. *American Reformers, 1815–1860*. New York: Hill and Wang.

Wright, Donald R. 1993. *African Americans in the Early Republic, 1789–1831*. Arlington Heights, Ill.: Harlan Davidson.

Wyatt-Brown, Bertram. 1986. *Honor and Violence in the Old South*. New York: Oxford University Press.

CRITICAL THINKING QUESTIONS

1. What impact did the development of modern police forces in Europe have on American law enforcement?

2. How did the ideas of the Enlightenment change Americans' thinking about the causes of crime? How do these ideas compare with mainstream thought about crime and punishment today?

3. What did Auburn Prison hope to achieve with its silent system of prison discipline? How does the silent system compare to today's use of boot camp prisons?

4. Did Eastern State's use of solitary confinement with labor solve the crime problem or improve prison administration? Can you make any comparisons with today's supermax or control unit prisons?

5. Discuss the trial of Aaron Burr, the Judiciary Act of 1789, and the Alien and Sedition Acts in terms of the development of federal criminal justice.

CRIMINAL JUSTICE HISTORY ON THE INTERNET

There are a number of Web sites covering the history of the U.S. Supreme Court. At the Supreme Court archives, famous cases are reproduced verbatim. A menu and links are located at www.bowdoin.edu/~sbodurt2/court/index.html. *Marbury v. Madison* is chronicled at www/bowdoin.edu/~sbodurt2/court/cases/

marbury.html. A complete home page is devoted to the background and the explanation of the *Marbury v. Madison* case at www.jmu.edu/ madison/marbury/ background.htm.

The Judiciary Act of 1789 can be found at http://civnet.org/resources/teach/basic/8.htm and http://lawbooksusa.com/documents/ judiciaryact1789.htm.

The Yale Law School Avalon Project grants extensive coverage to the Alien and Sedition Acts at www.yale.edu/lawweb/avalon/alsedact.htm. More on these acts can be found at the Electric Library at www.encyclopedia.com/articlesnew/ 00344.htm and at www.earlyamerica.com/ earlyamerica/milestones/sedition.

There are a number of sites dealing with the early American penitentiary. An excellent teacher's guide on American prisons prior to 1900 can be found at www.forgedimages.com/esptg.html. The Walnut Street Jail is featured at www.ushistory.org/birch/plates/plate24.htm, www.notfrisco.com/prisonhistory/origins/ origins04c.html, and www.pbs.org/wgbh/ aia/part3/3h89.html.

The Correctional Photo Archives offers a variety of pictures of Auburn at www.cpa.eku.edu/ auburn.htm, the evolution of the New York prison system at www.correctionhistory.org/ html/chronicl/state/html/nyprisons.html, the history of Auburn Prison at www.geocities.com/ MotorCity/Downs/3548/facility/auburn.html.

Eastern State Penitentiary (Cherry Hill) gets its due at www.libertynet.org/~e-state, a photo exhibit can be accessed at http://northstargallery.com/ pages/eastern/easternstategallery01.htm, and the Quaker experiment with "black hoods and iron gags" is chronicled at www.missioncreep.com/ mw/estate.html.

Policing gets its due at a number of sites. The London Metropolitan Police and Scotland Yard are given ample coverage at http://members.aol.com/ _ht_a/tychocat/web/police.html and http://ndad.ulcc.ac.uk/datasets/AH/1.htm.

The relationship between early British police and the prisons is covered at

http://dspace.dial.pipex.com/town/terrace/ adw03/peel/police.htm. A time line for Sir Robert Peel is provided at http://65.107.211.206/ victorian/history/peel.html.

The French detective Eugene François Vidocq, founder of the Surete, is profiled at www.vidocq.org/vidocq.html, www.crimelibrary.com/classics2/vidocq/4.htm, and www.mtholyoke.edu/courses/rschwart/ hist255/popcorn/vidocq.html.

Early American police forces are accessible at www.ppdonline.org/ppd_history.htm (Philadelphia), www.ci.baltimore.md.us/ government/police/history.html (Baltimore), and www.nyhistory.org/previous/police/ ptimeline.html and www.ci.nycny.us/html/ nypd/html/3100/retro.html (New York City).

NOTES

1. The Department of Justice would not be created until 1870. Until that time, its future activities and responsibilities were handled by State and Treasury Departments.

2. New York City was then the nation's capital.

3. Semonche (1998, pp. 54–55).

4. Stead (1957, pp. 45–48).

5. Richardson (1970, p. 15).

6. Turner (1993, p. 38).

7. See Rousey (1996).

8. Ayers (1984, p. 83).

9. Finkel (1994, p. 9).

10. Howard (1960, p. 61).

11. Sullivan (1990, p. 18).

12. Beaumont and Tocqueville (1979, pp. 162–163).

13. Dickens (1985, p. 99).

14. McKelvey (1977, p. 2).

15. See Lane (1999).

16. Quoted in Stokes (1915, p. 760).

17. Christianson (1998, p. 92); Foner (1975, p. 451).

18. Wyatt-Brown (1986, p. 142).

19. Emsley (1984, p. 109). See also Lane (1967) and Monkkonen (1981).

6

CRIMINAL JUSTICE
IN ANTEBELLUM AMERICA
(1817–1857)

TIME LINE

1847	The Colt .45 revolver enters American gun culture	1851	Boston creates nation's first police detection division
1847	Michigan abolishes the death penalty	1851	San Francisco Committee of Vigilance organized
1849	Astor Place riot leads to improved methods of riot control	1853	New York City Police adopt complete uniforms
1850	Fugitive Slave Act	1855	Allan Pinkerton founds his private detective agency
1850	Formation of nativist Know-Nothing Party	1857	*Dred Scott* decision
1851	Christiana riot		

The ascendance of Andrew Jackson to the presidency in 1828 inaugurated the "Age of the Common Man." Jackson's two terms in office would coincide with the dramatic transformation of American society and social institutions as he presided over a country entering the maelstrom of sectional politics, unprecedented immigration, and a criminal justice system still undergoing transition from its colonial roots.

A self-made man, Jackson was the first president born west of the Appalachian Mountains and the first born in a log cabin. Espousing a platform that favored the common people, he harbored a lasting animosity against the well born and the gentry as he worked to remove the obstacles that kept ordinary white citizens from climbing the social ladder to economic prosperity. Jackson introduced an important component to urban politics by embracing a spoils system that opened public offices to partisan supporters. Although Jackson claimed that his goal was to prevent the development of a class of corrupt civil servants, the results of his efforts would prove otherwise.

The Jacksonian period in America coincided with the years 1820–1850, a period when

Americans first perceived crime as a threat to the order and security of the Republic. In response, various constituencies turned to the developing police forces of urban America, others to the developing prison systems. Since colonial Americans felt little threatened by problems of crime, many Americans suggested that the new environment was the result of the declining authority of the church and family. With Americans on the move to the western frontier or to the new urban centers, it seemed to many that a lack of community pressure had left a void in the moral center.

By the late 1820s, Irish immigration had begun to make an impact on eastern seaport cities. These towns witnessed a concomitant growth of slums as the Irish exodus continued to America over the next thirty years. The flood of immigrants into cities such as New York impacted every segment of society, particularly the development of the criminal justice system. In a time without building codes, sanitation and health services, and even professional policing, lower Manhattan reached a population density unmatched in the world. By 1855, New York was crammed with 290,000 people per square mile compared to London's 175,816.[1] Among the most vociferous opponents to the Irish immigrants were Protestant workers who surmised that the Irish Catholic workers represented a threat to their wages since the immigrants would work for less money. According to Protestants, the Catholic Church represented despotism and subservience to Rome; thus, nativist writers would infer that the Catholics represented a papist threat to American democratic institutions, presaging the conspirational xenophobia of the Know-Nothing Party in the 1850s.

The Irish immigration of the antebellum years was the first large-scale immigration to America of non–Anglo-Saxon Protestants. Most were unskilled laborers, and by 1850 they represented more than one-third of New York City's population. Restricted from upward mobility by the Protestant upper classes, they congregated in close-knit enclaves where they found that joining the Democratic Party could lead to social and economic advancement. The prevailing nativism of the period led to an early affinity between urban immigrants and the developing political machines of New York and Chicago.

By the 1830s, the nation was becoming increasingly factionalized over the issue of slavery. During the previous decade, slavery had spread west into Alabama, Mississippi, Texas (still part of Mexico), and Louisiana. Racial unrest was viewed as a continuous threat in both the North and the South. Although racial warfare was an omnipresent threat in the South with the large population of slaves, northern cities saw white mobs repeatedly attack African American neighborhoods from the 1830s into the 1850s.

One alternative to slavery and revolt that gained increasing currency in the 1830s was the abolition movement. By the late 1830s, there were 1,300 antislavery societies in the North comprised of tens of thousands of members. Foremost among the abolitionists was William Lloyd Garrison (1805–1879) of Massachusetts. Unlike British abolitionists who supported the gradual emancipation of the slaves, Garrison was of a more radical mind, insisting on immediate and unconditional emancipation. Garrison became the most reviled man in

the South, and in 1831, Georgia was offering a reward of $5,000 to anyone who would transport him to Georgia for trial. Abolitionist groups drew an increasingly diverse constituency as they distributed their literature to a more receptive audience in the 1840s.

Abolitionists were often targeted by mobs in both sections of the country. Antiabolitionist mobs were usually led by prominent members of the community, including bankers, judges, merchants, and physicians. Mobs singled out the homes and businesses of abolitionists and particularly their printing presses.

THE LAWGIVERS

The Democratic era ushered in by the Jacksonian presidency swept away many of the barriers that had reserved the legal professional as the preserve of the more respected members of society. Massachusetts was among the states leading the way in 1836, when it proclaimed that "any citizen of this Commonwealth of the age of twenty-one years, and of good moral character, who shall have devoted three years to the study of law, in the office of some attorney within this State, shall on application to the Supreme Court or Court of Common Pleas, be admitted to practice as an attorney in any court of this Commonwealth."[2] Within a few years, not even a high school education would be required for admission to the state bar. Over the next several years, the same "democratic" movement swept the country, and requirements to practice the law would become so lax that Abraham Lincoln was admitted to the Illinois bar in 1837 with less than a grammar school training in school credits.

Voting Qualifications

One of the most profound political developments of the early nineteenth century was the gradual elimination of property qualifications for voting and holding political office. Having initially followed the English precedent during the colonial era of expecting voters to own a stake in the community by owning a certain minimum amount of land as a voting qualification, prospective officeholders were required to meet even higher property qualifications. By the 1830s, many states had discarded voting qualifications for white men. This transition from voting qualifications to universal white male suffrage was made with little dissension. One of the more notorious episodes of violence occurred in Rhode Island, where suffrage was still limited to landowners and oldest sons in the 1830s. Without a charter granting a bill of rights, in 1841 less than half the adult white males were qualified to vote. That same year, Harvard-educated attorney Thomas W. Dorr organized a campaign to draft a new state constitution that would abolish voting restrictions. Subsequently, the state militia was called out to arrest Dorr and his followers for insurrection. After an unsuccessful attempt to seize the state arsenal, Dorr was arrested and sentenced to life in prison for high treason. This turn of events unleashed a wave of popular resentment, leading the governor to pardon Dorr and Rhode Island to adopt a new constitution.

States' Rights and Federal Law

During the Jacksonian era, states' rights came into conflict with federal law, setting the stage for numerous precedent-setting events. During the decades leading up to the Civil War, most Americans felt that they had the right to govern themselves without interference by the federal government. No real demarcation between state and federal rights had been established. No small part of the responsibility for resolving this controversy lay with the Supreme Court, which had not sufficiently settled these issues at the termination of John Marshall's career on the court. Leaders in both the North and the South, particularly those who took firm stands in favor of the rights of individual states, were left with the impression that they could leave the Union over certain grievances. While other states did not

recognize the right of secession, they maintained that they had the right to nullify state laws that they found unacceptable.

In one of the best-known test cases, South Carolina's John Calhoun proclaimed the right of his state to nullify any federal legislation that it disapproved of. In 1833, he was given an opportunity to test the murky waters of states' rights during the presidency of Andrew Jackson. Almost thirty years before the outbreak of the Civil War, South Carolina's resolve was tested when it attempted to nullify the "tariff of abominations," which southern states felt ruined its interests for the benefit of the North. Calhoun claimed that the tariff made southerners "the serfs of the system—out of whose labor is raised, not only the money paid into the Treasury, but the funds out of which are drawn the rich rewards of the manufacturer and his associates in interest."

With South Carolina threatening to secede, Jackson, determined to uphold national authority over his leanings for the slave system, prepared for military action. The president asserted that American nationhood existed before state sovereignty and that nullification was "incompatible with the existence of the Union." Jackson denounced nullification as treason but eventually convinced Congress to pass a compromise tariff, but not before South Carolina backed down from its threat to leave the Union. In the process, this southern state learned an important lesson, namely, that successful resistance to northern "tyranny" would require the cooperation of other southern slave states.

The Taney Court

Succeeding John Marshall as chief justice of the Supreme Court in 1836, Roger Taney (1777–1864) and other justices appointed by Andrew Jackson reflected the transition to a new era in which the focus of the court shifted from federal to state power. A product of a different era, Taney was the first chief justice to wear trousers rather than traditional knee breeches. Under Taney's direction, the Supreme Court would reflect Jackson's emphasis on public power in contrast to the Marshall Court's constitutional protection of property rights. During his three decades at the helm, Taney increased the power of the states and limited the reach of the national government.

The Fugitive Slave Act

Since the introduction of slavery in the seventeenth century, slaves had fled from the repressive restraints of bondage. During the colonial era, most legislatures enacted laws prohibiting slaves from running away and sanctioning specific punishments for recaptured slaves. Various strategies were employed to capture runaway bondsmen, ranging from using native Indians as slave catchers to utilizing reward systems.

In the early nineteenth century, several northern states initiated programs to emancipate slaves, and abolitionists became more vocal and numerous. By the 1820s, New York, Massachusetts, and Pennsylvania had passed laws that required jury trials to convene before a master could take an alleged fugitive slave out of the state. Southerners were outraged by these "personal liberty laws" and argued that the laws violated the Constitution, which protected individual property. In 1842, the Supreme Court ruled in *Prigg v. Pennsylvania* that Pennsylvania's personal liberty laws violated the Constitution's fugitive slave clause.

In response, many northern states adopted more stringent policies for preventing the return of fugitive slaves to the South. Southerners demanded a tougher fugitive slave law, arguing that it had become virtually impossible to retrieve runaway slaves in the North. The passage of the pivotal Compromise of 1850 was accompanied by the passage of a much more uncompromising fugitive slave law.

According to the Fugitive Slave Act of 1850, alleged runaways were prohibited from testifying in court, and decision making was taken out of the hands of local officials and placed within the purview of federal officials. Most inflammatory was the use of the army and federal marshals as security forces to protect slave masters and federal officials from the violent attempts at slave rescue by abolitionists. Opposition to the law took a variety of forms, including riots, rescue attempts, and attacks on courthouses and jails.

The arrest of the slave Thomas M. Sims in 1851 demonstrates the subterfuge that was used by law enforcement to enforce the law. Reputedly a runaway from Virginia, he was arrested on a false charge of theft in Boston. Following an arraignment at the courthouse, the police commissioner overruled constitutional objections to the Fugitive Slave Act, and, in the quiet of early morning, Sims was clandestinely spirited from his cell to a ship that would carry him south to slavery. This case, as did many others, served only to rouse the antislavery factions into more ardent opposition, and in 1854 a U.S. marshal was killed during a failed rescue attempt. Many Civil War historians credit the Fugitive Slave Act with escalating sectional tensions, leading to the Civil War.

The Temperance Movement

The transformation of American society in the first half of the nineteenth century was accompanied by growing clamor for a temperance movement and the growth of nativism. Nativism found political expression in 1843 with the formation of the American Republic Party in New York. Subsequently, the party attracted a national following as the Know-Nothing Party in 1850. Anti-Catholic and antislavery, the moral prejudices of the party found a voice in the antebellum temperance campaign of the 1840s and 1850s. Among the more vociferous temperance groups was the Sons of Temperance, which could claim 250,000 dues-paying members by 1850. Whether religious or secular in nature, reform groups soon resorted to political action to accomplish their objectives. In 1833, a resolution was introduced by an abolitionist, declaring "the traffic in ardent spirits" morally wrong.[3] The author of the resolution followed up by asking that communities be allowed to pass laws prohibiting the traffic in liquor within their jurisdictions. In

1838, temperance advocates won their first major victory when Massachusetts banned the sale of liquor in amounts under fifteen gallons. This attempt to keep distilled liquor from taverns and the poor was repealed in 1840, but not before fomenting episodes of civil disobedience.

In the mid-1840s, abolitionists joined the crusade for temperance in Maine, and in 1846, a law was passed prohibiting the sale of intoxicating beverages in less than twenty-eight-gallon increments. Enforcement of the law was added to the duties of town selectmen, who typically looked the other way when infractions occurred. Prohibitionists received their greatest victory with the passage of the Maine Law of 1851, which prohibited the sale and manufacture of all intoxicating beverages within the state. By 1855, thirteen states had passed similar laws, and New England, New York, and parts of the Midwest were considered dry. As a consequence, the per capita consumption of alcohol between 1830 and 1850 plummeted. Although most of the prohibition laws were repealed by the late 1850s, from the antebellum era on, the temperance crusade played an instrumental role in American politics and would offer many challenges to law enforcement on both the local and the state level.

Reforms

Pennsylvania introduced a statute differentiating the two degrees of murder in 1794, with only murder in the first degree a capital offense. Other states soon changed their laws to reflect the degrees of culpability in deciding on the death penalty for murder. According to Pennsylvania law, first degree included the use of poison, any premeditated murder, or murder perpetrated during the commission of an arson, a robbery, or a burglary. Other murders were classified as second degree. Virginia was the first to borrow this definition and was soon followed by Ohio (1824), New York (1827), and Missouri (1835).[4] This innovation reflected a growing movement against the death penalty during the antebellum years that saw the amount of capital crimes reduced

significantly. South Carolina saw capital offenses plunge from 165 in 1813 to 22 by 1850.

LAW ENFORCEMENT

As American cities grappled with the problems of industrialization, urbanization, and immigration in the 1830s and 1840s, numerous experiments in policing were attempted. Southern cities such as New Orleans and Charleston tried uniformed city guards with sporadic successes. With the financial support of a wealthy local philanthropist, Philadelphia established day and night police forces in the 1830s, one of the first American cities to do so. The experiment proved only temporary, disbanding in a short time.

Boston made hesitant first steps toward police reform following incessant ethnic rioting in the 1830s. After calling on the militia to suppress a riot between Irish mourners and local firemen, Marshal Francis Tukey was hired to build a proficient police force. But with a rising index of efficiency measured by the capture of several hundred criminals, the public's antagonism turned instead against the force. In 1851, Boston created the country's first police department detective division and four years later would establish a force along Robert Peel's London model.

The New York City Police

In 1844, New York City's traditional night watch was legislated out of existence and replaced with a new system comprised of separate day and night police forces, becoming the first city to merge the day and night forces into a uniformed police department model after Peel's English bobbies. Initially, the state authorized the hiring of 800 men to man the new force, but the city council demurred, hiring only a quarter of that number. The force quickly demonstrated its inadequacy, but the following year the state legislature adopted the original plan for 800 uniformed municipal police officers with the passage of

New York City Municipal Police Act. According to police historian Wilbur R. Miller, this act "created the first police force modeled on London's precedent outside of the British Empire."[5]

With a long-established antipathy for uniforms of any kind, many of the original officers objected to wearing specially designed uniforms, preferring to choose their own outfits. Like many Londoners in the years before the acceptance of the uniformed bobbies, there was a strong resistance to the British innovation of uniformed policing. Worried that uniforms were an infringement on American freedoms and represented the dangers of a standing army to democratic institutions, opponents compared uniformed officers to "liveried lackeys." Thus, a compromise was reached in which police officers wore eight-point, star-shaped copper badges over their left breasts instead of a complete uniform, hence their identification as the "star police," "coppers," or just plain "cops."[6]

The year 1845 saw the introduction of New York City's first patrol guide, which emphasized Peel's objectives of the prevention of crime, noting that "the prevention of crime being the most important object . . . the absence of crime will be considered the best proof of the efficiency of the police." Responding to a fire at the Bowery Theater in 1845, wearing uniforms dignified by gleaming brass buttons, crowds of street toughs laughed at the them, accusing the new police of mimicking the London bobbies. And so the experiment with uniforms ended, and it was not revived until eight years later in 1853, when the New York City police finally adopted full uniforms.

The development of modern policing after 1845 was hampered by a lack of consensus about wearing uniforms, whether police should be armed, and the use of force. The lack of a uniform hindered the goal of policing, which was to be visible. Those against uniforms argued that it would offer criminals an advantage by immediately identifying the police. New York City was the first city to surmount the controversy by mandating that when the current officers' four-year terms of duty ended in 1853, the police

commissioners would fire whoever refused to don a uniform. Boston and Chicago followed suited in a few years, and as the Civil War years approached, American men felt less insecure about wearing uniforms. In a major departure from the London model, there was little argument that American police should be armed, although it did not occur immediately.

One of the early turning points for the new force took place in 1849, when a riot developed out of a rivalry between supporters of two leading actors at the Astor Place Theater. When a mob attempted to prevent one of the performers from taking the stage, a wild melee ensued, with the mob throwing rocks at a small, outmatched police detachment. The local militia was called to the scene and opened fire on the crowd, killing twenty-two and wounding forty. A public uproar led the police force to implement riot control training and military drills for police officers, probably the first riot training in American police history.

From 1845 to 1853, New York City policemen were appointed by aldermen. Beginning in 1853, a board of police commissioners, made up of the mayor, the city recorder, and the city judge, took over the appointment of policemen. The new protocol ensured that a system of graft would determine the selection of police rather than any specific requirements. In the early years of the force, it cost a $40 bribe to the precinct captain to become a patrolman and at least another $150 to a political champion. The most sought-after position was the $1,000 per year captain's position, which cost a minimum of $200 for appointment.

Federal Law Enforcement

For at least the first half of the nineteenth century, federal policing was mainly within the domain of the U.S. Marshals Service. Created by the Judiciary Act of 1789, marshals were originally restricted to four-year appointments by the president. During the first year of their existence, the marshals were hamstrung by a lack of direction and power. With an absence of an immediate supervisor and the political nature of their appointment, their capacity as criminal justice professionals was severely limited. Particularly vexing was their poor renumeration due to their dependence on a fee list that had been used by county sheriffs until the 1850s. But as late as 1842, legislators capped a marshal's salary at $6,000, with any additional income required to be turned over to the Treasury Department. In 1853, the outmoded fee system was discarded in favor of a more equitable pay scale.

In the years leading up to the Civil War, U.S. marshals would face the widespread counterfeiting of the skilled "coneymen," so named because of the wide diversity of currency issued in the years before a modern banking system. According to most estimates, one-third of the currency in circulation between 1815 and 1860 was counterfeit. With individual banks issuing various bank notes in a bewildering array of denominations, together with U.S. Treasury notes and postal currency, opportunities were many for those skilled in duplicating currencies. Although the marshals were the first line of defense, the Treasury Department occasionally hired detectives to crack the counterfeiting rings. In 1865, Congress finally recognized the need for special measures to suppress counterfeiting by creating the Secret Service under the secretary of the treasury.

During the 1840s and following the conflict with Mexico (1846–1848), the United States increased its boundaries, adding sparsely populated territories to its domain. In these unorganized territories, the U.S. marshals provided the only formal law enforcement. According to federal law, when a population of a federal territory reached 5,000 free white males, a bicameral legislature could be elected and territorial laws promulgated. After reaching 60,000 free white males, the territory could be nominated for statehood, and the nomination would then be forwarded to Congress for final approval.

On several occasions, marshals required the army to assist them in their law enforcement

functions in the vast West, and in 1854 a presidential proclamation authorized marshals to call on the army as posse comitatus. During the period before a territory became a state, any crime was considered a federal violation; hence, marshals saw continuous action as the only lawmen. As territories made the transition to statehood, marshals gave up much of their authority to territorial lawmen, such as sheriffs. As the only federal law enforcement officers prior to the Civil War, federal marshals were continually tested as America teetered on the brink of sectional conflict.

One form of federal law enforcement that has not received its proper due is the Postal Service inspectors. In 1836, Congress reorganized the Post Office and authorized it to hire full-time special agents with broad authority to investigate any aspect of the Postal Service. Imbued with arrest powers, police historian David Johnson credits the postal inspectors as "the first formal police force within the executive branch of the federal government."[7]

Private Police and San Francisco Vigilantes

During the 1850s, law enforcement was often absent from the developing communities west of the Mississippi River. In 1855, Allan J. Pinkerton (1819–1884) founded what would become Pinkerton's National Detective Agency, which initially handled cases in communities with limited law enforcement expertise. The private detective has a rich tradition dating back to the eighteenth-century thief takers of England and the exploits of Eugene François Vidocq in France. The arrival of the Pinkertons on the national stage in the 1850s heralded new developments in policing strategies and investigative techniques in America as the nation moved toward sectional conflict.

Born in Glasgow, Scotland, Pinkerton found his life's calling after playing an instrumental role in the capture of a gang of counterfeiters soon after migrating to America in 1842. Pinkerton entered law enforcement in 1846 as a deputy sheriff in Illinois. In

1850, he became the first detective hired by the Chicago Police Department and on several occasions was called on by the U.S. Treasury Department to battle counterfeiters. After opening his own detective agency in 1855, he adopted numerous investigative techniques and, according to some sources, introduced the first rogues gallery, which displayed the characteristics and idiosyncrasies of known criminals. During America's railroad expansion of the 1850s, Pinkerton was hired to create a spying system to keep railroad conductors from stealing fares. Soon after, he created an all-seeing eye as the symbol for the company, hence its motto "The Eye That Never Sleeps."

With an absence of effective law enforcement, many western communities relied on the traditional American methods of vigilantism.[8] Beginning in the 1760s, South Carolina "Regulators" resorted to the extralegal tactics of taking the law into their own hands in the absence of formal law enforcement. During the 1850s, San Francisco, in the wake of the 1849 California gold rush, became the center of vigilante activity in America. According to historian Frank Richard Prassel, "The term regulator fell into disuse after much publicity accorded the San Francisco vigilance committees of 1851 and 1856."[9]

Miner's courts dispensed justice in the gold camps of California, where formal law enforcement was almost nonexistent. According to one miner, "The marvel of marvels is, the mob-law and failure of justice were so infrequent, that society was so well and swiftly organized."[10] Forced to contend with a rapidly growing criminal element, the San Francisco Committee of Vigilance was organized in June 1851. Led by a former Mormon elder, this vigilance organization differed from other incarnations of this activity by offering those charged with crimes formal and reasonably fair trials before they were hanged. Within several months, this committee was disbanded as lawbreaking diminished.

From the Constitution of the Committee of Vigilance (1851)

"Whereas it has become apparent to the citizens of San Francisco, that there is no security for life and property, either under the regulations of society as it at present exists, or under the law as now administered; *Therefore* the citizens, whose names are hereunto attached, do unite themselves into an association for the maintenance of the peace and good order of society, and the preservation of the lives and property of the citizens of San Francisco, and do bind ourselves, each unto the other, to do and perform every lawful act for the maintenance of law and order, and to sustain the laws when faithfully and properly administered; but we are determined that no thief, burglar, incendiary or assassin, shall escape punishment, either by the quibbles of the law, the insecurity of the prisons, the carelessness or corruption of the police, or a laxity of those who pretend to administer justice."

With crime once more on the rise in 1855, a new vigilance committee was created. Under the direction of some of the town's leading citizens, hangings were soon drawing crowds by the thousands. Apologists for the vigilantes suggest that the second coming was given impetus by the collusion between corrupt city politicians and local outlaw bands. Boasting over 5,000 members, the 1856 San Francisco Vigilance Committee was perhaps the largest manifestation of the vigilante phenomenon in American history. With the return of the city to acceptable, honest officials, the group disbanded.

CORRECTIONS

By the antebellum era, prisons had become an established part of the American criminal justice tapestry as each year new institutions were constructed in various states. By the 1840s, many prison methods had become fixed with little room for experimentation as champions heralded the benefits of either the Pennsylvania or the Auburn system. The years 1787–1820 witnessed the initial stage of prison reform in America, which was followed by the construction of Eastern State Penitentiary and Auburn Prison between 1820 and 1830. The third wave of prison reform between 1830 and 1840 built on the foundations laid by the introduction of new prison designs. It was during this time that Auburn continued to reduce its state maintenance expenses as other New York prisons began to turn profits. Supporters of the Auburn system saw this as confirmation that the silent rigid system of discipline and security was the solution to the age-old problem of housing prisoners, while at the same time backers of the Pennsylvania system found solace in the fact that the solitary system had prevented the criminogenic contamination of prisoners through physical association.

In its 1850 report, the Boston Prison Discipline Society recorded 4,060 prisoners housed in nineteen different prisons (figures for six other prisons were not reported in the survey). Of these, only five state prisons had more than 200 prisoners (New York, Massachusetts, Pennsylvania, Ohio, and Maryland), a figure that would not rise until after the Civil War. During the industrial phase of prison administration, the Auburn system prevailed over the Pennsylvania system because it produced better industrial returns and was easier to maintain.

Reform

During the 1840s, numerous states established prison reform societies. In 1844, the Prison Association of New York was inaugurated and the following year saw the founding of the Massachusetts Society in Aid of Discharged Convicts and the Pennsylvania Society for the Alleviation of the Miseries of Public Prisons. Clearly, strides were being taken to counter the pervasive corruption and brutality of the contemporary prison. At the same time, a European prison congress was convened in Germany to discuss the debatable merits of the Auburn and the Pennsylvania systems.

The first critics of the Auburn system came from the ranks of the "mechanics" who saw prison industries as unfair business competition. Others pointed to the physical discipline that accompanied the silent system. Reformers maintained that the only way to maintain a system of

absolute silence was by the threat of severe corporal punishments, such as flogging.

Pennsylvania prisons also came under attack since those built under the solitary guidelines were the most costly to construct and maintain. In addition, the profits of a single individual working alone in a cell paled in comparison to New York's congregate system. In marked contrast, Eastern State Penitentiary suffered from a higher incidence of mortality, disease, and insanity. By the 1840s, many of the early efforts toward creating a functioning penitentiary had fallen on hard times, and the belief had become widespread in America that the prisons had failed to live up to earlier expectations. Reformers such as Dorothea Dix visited prisons in the early 1840s and found them in deplorable condition. She saved much of her energy for leading a reform movement to champion the rights of mentally ill prisoners.

Born in 1802, Dix worked as a schoolteacher until 1841. She found her calling while conducting a Sunday school lesson at a local jail in Massachusetts. On discovering the primitive and inhumane treatment of prisoners suffering from mental illness in the prison, Dix launched a one-woman humanitarian crusade that would reach across America and Europe during the antebellum years. Between 1841 and 1852, she was credited with modernizing and expanding facilities for the insane as well as helping pass reform legislation in many states and Canada. Although she persuaded the U.S. Congress to pass a bill raising $12 million for the care of the insane, President Franklin Pierce vetoed the legislation in 1854. Over the next four years, Dix took her crusade to Europe, procuring reform legislation for the insane in several European countries. She continued to lobby on behalf of the insane and prison inmates until 1881. She died six years later in Trenton Hospital, an institution she had helped establish.

Some of the most glaring examples of the divergent conditions between state prisons and local facilities was in the arena of punishment. State prisons in Massachusetts and Connecticut rarely resorted to corporal punishment, while in

1843 alone Sing Sing Prison in New York distributed 36,000 lashes of the whip. Although records indicate that the larger the prison, the more rigorous the punishment, a clear trend toward diminished corporal punishment typified the 1840s.

European visitors to American prisons, ranging from Charles Dickens to Alexis de Tocqueville, commented on the solemnity and silence that characterized most prisons. However, if the same observers were to have visited in subsequent decades, they would have found a cacophony of sounds emanating from overcrowded prison cells. From the 1820s through the 1850s, corporal punishment and zealous discipline ensured obedience in prisons. Added to this was the legislative willingness to supply funds to build more prisons when cells were needed, and the overcrowding problem would be put off for several decades.

One other integral hallmark of antebellum prisons was the enforced regular labor of inmates. Prison routine required prisoners to work from eight to ten hours each day under the threat of physical punishment. Intended to impart discipline as well as a satisfactory financial windfall, those prisons that showed a profit earned the most praise from the public. Hence, the Auburn system flourished over the Pennsylvania one because it paid better returns.

By the 1840s, American prison reformers initiated paramilitary discipline to augment the already elaborate regimentation. New York prisons introduced daily routines including lockstep marching, which required inmates to move in close order and single file, moving in unison, each head inclined to the right, with each man looking over the shoulder of the man in front. In this way, guards could ensure that conversations were eliminated and prisoners could not dally from place to place. Also augmenting the increased emphasis on regimentation was the introduction of striped uniforms. Another ramification of this innovation was the adoption of prison uniforms by guards as well. It was not a huge step to designing prisons that looked like medieval fortresses, promoting security and isolation while making prisoners feel more diminutive and regulated.

Juvenile Institutions

In 1817, the Society for the Prevention of Pauperism of New York became the first group in America to call attention to neglected children between the ages of ten and eighteen. Eight years later, the House of Refuge opened its doors in New York City and became the earliest child-saving institution in the country. Its charges included both the destitute and the neglected and children sentenced to incarceration for criminal activity. This would be one of the first institutions to jail children and adults separately. However, discipline was anything but benign, with punishment ranging from whipping and solitary confinement to reduction in food supply. Predicting the industrial prisons of the future, the House of Refuge kept the boys busy making goods to be sold. This could occasionally lead to apprenticeships with master artisans outside the walls as long as they followed the rules. Houses of refuge were subsequently constructed in Philadelphia and Boston, where corporal punishment was banned. Although black children were initially prohibited, in 1834 New York's made plans for a "colored section."

Despite attempts to separate the children from adult prisons, many children remained behind bars in adult jails. In the late 1820s, the Boston Prison Discipline Society reported that many of these children were under the age of twelve. As late as 1845, almost 100 children aged six to sixteen resided in the Massachusetts House of Corrections. During the 1850s, a rise in female juvenile offenders became a new concern, and reform schools were established under different guidelines from the boys. It was hoped that by offering a strong mothering environment and teaching morals, these young girls could grow up to become good mothers. In 1856, the first girl's reformatory was opened as the Massachusetts State Industrial School for Girls. Departing from the traditional dormitory-style construction, it separated children into smaller housing groups according to their offenses and backgrounds.

During the late 1850s, similar institutions were opened in Illinois and Ohio. Most avoided an urban setting in favor of a rural one. According to the theory of the day, it was presumed that city living was the root of evil and social problems and offered too many temptations to unsupervised children.

Alexander Maconochie and Indeterminate Sentencing

While the threat of physical punishment was omnipresent in the antebellum prison, alternative experiments to punishment were tried in several states. The main contribution of the reformatory era to American prisons was the introduction of the indeterminate sentence and parole laws. Considered the "father of parole" in the late 1830s and 1840s, Captain Alexander Maconochie of Great Britain began to conceive a new scheme for the punishment of convicts while assigned to England's prison colony at Van Diemen's Land (now Tasmania). Shortly after arriving on the island, he hatched an idea by which the convicts would be sentenced not to a specific period of time but rather to a certain amount of labor that was measured by a system of marks. According to his plan, convicts could earn marks for good conduct and work or lose them for bad behavior. Maconochie's reforms were in part spurred by the persistence of traditional methods of corporal punishment and physical intimidation. He had hoped that by allowing prisoners to work and associate with other convicts and with the lingering threat of punishment for all, if only one convict offended, his system would encourage mutual trust and a sense of responsibility among the prisoners.

Over the next several years, Maconochie created a more elaborate system of indeterminate sentencing that would also be applicable to prisons and not just the prison colonies in Australia.

Maconochie was given the opportunity to test his experimental program on Norfolk Island. Putting his mark system to work, he attempted to inject a certain degree of civility into what he considered a den of iniquity. He removed the bars from windows and opened prison doors, offering prisoners books and musical instruments. He tried to educate the prisoners about civilization by encouraging the planting of gardens and constructing religious sanctuaries. While he rated his experiment a success, it was not long before the colonists came into conflict with Maconochie and his charges, and after a four-year experiment the island was returned to its former state. Although Maconochie was unsuccessful in his attempt to reform England's penal system, Walter Crofton would build on his ideas in Ireland and eventually see many of Maconochie's ideas come to fruition.

In 1817, New York's legislature passed but never applied a good-time law by which prison sentences were reduced for good work and behavior. Beginning in 1836, Tennessee became the first state to actually implement a good-time reduction of prison sentences. However, this innovation would not gain wider popularity until the late 1850s and 1860s, when twenty-three states would follow suit.

CRIME AND PUNISHMENT

By the 1830s, America's largest cities began to experience a rising fear of crime. New York City became home to burgeoning legions of gangs, including the Irish-Catholic Dead Rabbits and the nativist American Bowery Boys. The developing slums of American cities paralleled the growing disparity between the living conditions of the native-born and the marginalized denizens of urban America. On his tour of America in the early 1840s, English novelist Charles Dickens noted the "leprous houses" in the Five Points section of New York City and surmised that "in respect of filth and wretchedness," it would give the most debauched environs of London a run for the money.

The rising popularity of the penny presses during the 1830s and 1840s was spurred in part by coverage of lurid, sensational crimes, such as the Mary Rogers murder case. The precursor to today's tabloids and mass media, the penny press hinged on selling papers, and nothing sold them like crimes of passion.

Crime stories marketed for popular consumption were not a new phenomenon. Beginning in the colonial era, crime literature was marketed in pamphlet form, usually accompanied by some religious lesson or moral warning. By the 1820s, a more secular society became increasingly acceptable of sensationalist literature without the heady dose of moralism so reminiscent of a Puritan-dominated society. By the 1820s, crime news began to steadily seep into journalism.

The Mary Rogers Murder Case

The inept investigation of the murder of Mary Cecilia Rogers in 1841 is considered by many scholars of policing to be a clarion call for police reform in New York City. A beautiful woman who clerked in a New York City tobacco shop, she reportedly had no shortage of admirers. She could count as customers leading literary figures, such as James Fenimore Cooper, Washington Irving, and Edgar Allan Poe. By most accounts, her murder inspired Poe to write America's first detective story, *The Mystery of Marie Roget* (1842).

The real Mary was found murdered in July 1841. Numerous theories emerged concerning her last evening. The subsequent coroner's autopsy and the inadequate police investigation that followed demonstrated to the public the limits of contemporary policing. Since the body was found just over the New Jersey border, New York City police were reluctant to investigate. Police officers traditionally did not work a homicide unless a substantial reward was offered. Since their incomes were derived from rewards and fees, police officers spent more time recovering stolen property.

In the years prior to a twenty-four-hour force, untrained and poorly paid night watchmen came under press scrutiny as newspaper editors pressed for an investigation into the murder of the famous beauty. Even New York Governor William Seward used the case to call for stronger policing. Newspapers vilified law enforcement for its zeal in pursuing robbers and thieves in order to claim reward money or worthwhile stolen property and for avoiding murders, which offered fewer financial prospects. Although the case was never solved, the murder gave impetus to a reform campaign that led to more effective policing, and within five years the New York City police had been reorganized and made great strides toward professionalism.

Crime

The antebellum era introduced new forms of criminal enterprise to America, forcing the criminal justice system to consistently play catch-up. The first bank robbery in American history was recorded in 1831. Although it was technically a burglary since no threat of violence was used, in this case an English thief utilized duplicate keys to enter a Wall Street bank in New York City and abscond with $245,000. However, his penchant for free spending and generous tipping, together with the help of informers, led the police to his door and the remaining $185,000. The thief was sentenced to five years at hard labor in Sing Sing Prison. According to one authority, he was treated more leniently than future bank thieves because "his crime was unique and the authorities were not prepared to deal with it." In the years following the Civil War, bank robberies would become much more common.

In some arenas, fresh investigative techniques heralded a new era in policing. One of the most famous murder cases of the antebellum period was the trial of Harvard professor John W. Webster for the murder of Doctor George Parkman in 1849. A cause célèbre, this crime attracted national attention. Webster apparently struck Parkman a fatal blow while arguing in Webster's laboratory over financial matters. A professor of chemistry, Webster decided to dispose of the body by dismembering it and burning it in the furnace. However, his misdeed was suspected by a college janitor who pursued his own amateur investigation and found parts of a human body. A subsequent investigation turned up a set of false teeth in the ashes. Webster's fate was sealed after Parkman's dentist identified them as belonging to the deceased, an early example of dental evidence. Webster ultimately confessed and went to the gallows.

Capital Punishment

The 1850s marked the climax of the antebellum crusade to abolish execution as a criminal sanction. Michigan (1847), Rhode Island (1850s), and Wisconsin (1850s) abolished the death penalty, but opposition was barely existent in other states, although some states replaced public hangings with private executions. Once a fixture of American society, public executions on the public square were designed for maximum deterrence value. Thousands, sometimes tens of thousands, would flock to these events, In an era with little entertainment, it was not uncommon for individuals to travel great distances to attend the spectacle. While the last public execution in America took place as late as 1936, there was clearly a movement to end this medieval practice in the antebellum period. The English ended public executions in 1868 after generations of the bloody code.

Pennsylvania passed a law in 1834 requiring private executions behind prison walls. During the 1830s, Massachusetts, New Hampshire, New Jersey, New York, and Connecticut also enacted laws prohibiting public executions. The thirty years before the Civil War are considered the height of America's abolitionist movement in the nineteenth century. However, the carnage of the Civil War stopped the abolitionist movement cold.

Sectional Variations

During the antebellum years, patterns of crime and punishment became more recognizable along sectional lines. In a study of South Carolina and Massachusetts, historian Michael Stephen Hindus

contrasted the patterns of authority and criminal law in rural slaveholding South Carolina with an industrial urbanizing Massachusetts. Hindus discerned numerous conflicting patterns of crime, prosecution, and punishment in the two states of his study, patterns that reflected the difference in the two societies representing the North and the South.

The most common crimes in Massachusetts tended to be "against property and propriety." On the other hand, violent crimes among whites were the most frequent offenses in South Carolina, while crimes against property were associated with slaves. Reflecting two diametrically opposed societies, Massachusetts, particularly as it joined the industrial era, placed a high priority on order and insisted on punishment to ensure the social order. Here conviction rates were twice as high as in South Carolina, where white crime was explained away as the result of heated passions and elicited little in the way of communitarian concern. However, when it came to property crimes committed by slaves, conviction rates were much higher, and punishment was much more severe.

AMERICAN VIOLENCE

According to violence historian Richard Maxwell Brown, the dawning of the 1830s introduced America to "what may have been the era of the greatest urban violence that [the nation] has ever experienced."[11] The years following the war with Mexico would see violence become even more prevalent. Perhaps the preponderance of reports glamorizing the carnage in Mexico inured the younger generation to violence, a generation that would make up much of the fodder in the coming sectional conflict. Others might suggest the proliferation of handguns contributed to the growing mayhem.

Most of the interracial violence between blacks and whites in the years leading up to the Civil War was disproportionately directed toward slaves and free blacks. Rarely was it the other way around. However, in 1851 the African American community of Lancaster County, Pennsylvania, took up arms against forces attempting to enforce the Fugitive Slave Law of 1850 in the town of Christiana. In the subsequent violence, black rioters killed a Maryland farmer who was attempting to reclaim several slaves. In response to this action, federal prosecutors charged thirty-eight men with taking up arms against the government, making this, according to historian Thomas P. Slaughter, "the largest mass indictment for treason in the history of our nation."[12]

Handguns and American Culture

Challenging the traditional presumption that gun ownership was widespread in America between 1765 and 1850, historian Michael Bellesiles suggests that guns played a "marginal role in American life prior to the Civil War."[13] Citing a study of 685 nineteenth-century murders prior to 1846, Bellesiles found that knives were the preferred weapon, with guns used in only less than 20 percent of the incidents. Others suggest that Bellesiles has overinterpreted his evidence, which is based on various data including a ten-year study of probate records and wills. While the debate continues, there is little argument that guns would be used increasingly in murders as America reached midcentury, with gun homicides almost doubling between 1846 and 1860. The years following the Civil War would demonstrate the centrality of the gun to American murder rates as soldiers returned home with their weapons in tow.

Although Samuel Colt's introduction of his 1832 revolver did not initially capture the imagination of the gun-buying public, by the 1840s other gun companies were inspired to offer similar revolvers. Improvements in revolver construction would be reflected by a growing number of gun deaths in urban settings.

While gun ownership is common in most of rural America, the South has been most traditionally represented as a gun-owning culture. Although rifles have predominated, since the antebellum era handguns have become an increasing presence in the South. By the late 1970s,

research indicated that 40 percent of all southerners owned handguns compared to 24 percent in nonsouthern and mountain regions. In the nineteenth-century South, anecdotal evidence indicates that an emphasis on honor and gun ownership exacerbated the homicide rate. According to 1850 mortality reports, the South had a murder rate of 2.28 per 100,000, more than seven times the murder rates of the North.[14]

In his study on crime and punishment in the nineteenth-century American South, historian Edward L. Ayers found that slavery and the culture that propagated the institution provided an environment that allowed notions of honor to thrive. According to Ayers, honor flourished in rural societies with many opportunities for personal contacts and the existence of a "hierarchical society where one is defined by who is above or below him. Honor grows well in a society where the rationalizing power of the state is weak" and where honor takes precedence over state laws when settling personal grudges.

Gunplay was not the exclusive preserve of adults, as witnessed by an 1857 newspaper account of a young boy accidentally shooting himself in the abdomen. In a perspicacious editorial, the editor warned that "young America" should "take warning by accidents of this kind, and mentions having noticed several boys in the streets lately popping about with pistols." The editor closed his screed with a rhetorical flourish asking, "Is there no town ordinance forbidding the dangerous practice of shooting in the streets?"[15]

Mob Rioting

America had experienced few outbreaks of mob violence prior to the 1830s. In the ensuing decade, the nation witnessed an increase in this increasingly destructive behavior. According to one estimate, there were 147 riots in 1835 alone, most related to the growing sectional rancor between abolitionists and proslavers. Another study found that almost three-quarters of America's cities with populations exceeding 20,000 experienced some type of "major disorder" between 1830 and 1865.[16]

However, the slavery issue was not the lone precipitator of this violence. Among the many explanations for the rising tide of violence was unprecedented urbanization and industrialization in a society rooted in institutions still based on rural community ideals of an earlier America. Add to this the catalyzing issues of race, abolitionism, the rise of party politics, and ethnic divisions, and American cities would be the setting for urban rioting for the three decades preceding the Civil War. Compounding the tensions and divisions of the era was the commercial depression of 1837 that put a squeeze on the job market at a time of increasing immigration. Between 1840 and 1860, almost three million Irish and half that many Germans immigrated to America, outnumbering all other immigrant groups.

Election riots were not uncommon in the days before private voting booths. Known as one of the most violent cities of the antebellum era, Baltimore, Maryland, had earned the moniker "Mob Town" during an 1812 anti-Federalist riot. Between 1834 and 1862, the city experienced fifteen major riots.[17] While violence often radiated from political, economic, ethnic, labor, and sectional issues, election day often led to similar strife. Baltimore was the scene of election day rioting throughout much of the 1850s, as Irish-Catholics supporting urban Democrats clashed with the nativist Protestant supporters of the Know-Nothing Party.

Ethnic and racial violence often pitted poor Irish and German immigrants against even poorer blacks and native-born Americans in a bid for unskilled jobs. In other cases, divisions were often along religious lines pitting Protestant native Americans against recent Catholic immigrants. Unlike other immigrant groups, the Irish preferred to live in the urban centers of the industrial Northeast. During the 1840s, poor Irish enclaves appeared in Boston, New York, Philadelphia, and Baltimore, leading to a wave of antagonism against Irish-Catholics that often ended in violence and discrimination. The first major anti-Catholic riot erupted in 1834 in Charlestown, Massachusetts, when lower-class Protestants objected to the convent school operated by the Ursuline sisters in their neighborhood. The subsequent burning of the convent provoked anti-Catholic violence throughout the country.

The 1844 nativist riots in Philadelphia were among the most violent incidents of the antebellum era. In his book *The Turbulent Era,* historian Michael Feldberg chronicled the cultural and religious conflict between Philadelphia's nativist Protestants and Irish-Catholic immigrants. The riots were the outcome of not simply religious intolerance but reflected the weakness of contemporary law enforcement and the social and political disorganization of the era.

Mob violence was not exclusive to the eastern states. Meanwhile, a similar epidemic of discrimination faced the Chinese immigrants who were lured to California and the West following the discovery of gold in 1848. Thousands made the journey across the Pacific seeking their fortunes. But unlike their European counterparts, the ethnic distinctiveness and competition for wages of the Chinese singled them out for racial discrimination in the 1850s.

Most of the rioting against abolitionists occurred in the antebellum North. In some cases, early New York City gangs precipitated the violence in order to use the disorder as a cover for looting. While most assaults on abolitionists were not intended to kill, the murder of abolitionist Elijah P. Lovejoy in 1837 demonstrated the heated passions of the slavery debate. After calling for the formation of a local branch of the American Anti-Slavery Society in southern Illinois, an angry mob stormed his shop and killed him as he defended it with sixty armed abolitionists.

NOTABLE TRIALS

Dred Scott v. Sandford (1857)[18]

There was little to suggest in Scott's early life the mark his name would make on the brewing sectional crisis. He was born to slave parents in Virginia in the 1790s and taken to St. Louis,

Missouri, by his master in 1827. After his owner's death, he was left to a series of owners, one of whom was an army surgeon who took him to the free territories of Illinois and Wisconsin before returning to St. Louis five years later. On his master's death, the surgeon's wife inherited all her husband's property, including Scott. However, the wife moved to New York and left Scott behind, and he eventually came under the care of a Missouri businessman and zealous abolitionist. With the support of the owner's widow in 1846, he initiated a suit in the Missouri courts to declare Scott free. While the wife of his former owner could have signed papers giving Scott his freedom, it was decided to fashion a deliberate test case in the fight against slavery designed to prove that a slave's bondage terminated when he was taken into free territory.

The end of the war with Mexico brought new lands into the American system and heightened the sectional conflict between pro- and antislavery supporters over whether the new lands would be free or slave states, and the issues raised by the *Dred Scott* case steadily gained importance. The case reached the Supreme Court finally in 1856 and was soon the focus of national attention as it became linked to more complicated questions, such as whether Congress had the power to prohibit slavery in a territory and whether a slave could sue in federal court.

In 1857, Chief Justice Roger B. Taney issued his stunning judgment ruling that Scott had no right to sue in federal court because neither slaves nor free blacks were citizens according to the U.S. Constitution. Taney rejected Scott's argument that he had become a free man by virtue of his residence in the free territory of Wisconsin because "the act of Congress which prohibited a citizen from holding and owning property of this kind in the territory of the United States north of the line therein mentioned, is not warranted by the Constitution, and is therefore void." In one fell swoop, the Supreme Court denied citizenship to blacks and barred Congress from interfering with slaveholding in the territories. Therefore, as a national

institution slavery could not be abolished without a constitutional amendment.

Taney's decision also delivered a substantive reading to the due process clause for the first time, maintaining that the due process clause limited the power of Congress to confiscate property rights no matter what procedure was set forth. Taney ruled, "Thus the rights of property are united with the rights of person, and placed on the same ground as the Fifth Amendment to the Constitution, which provides that no person shall be deprived of life, liberty, and property, without due process of law."

The *Dred Scott* decision by the Supreme Court undermined any chances for future compromise on the issue of the expansion of slavery, as it strengthened southern resolve and heightened the sense of southern superiority over its plantation economy. Rather than quelling sectional strife, the *Dred Scott* decision turned into a catalyst that helped propel the nation into the Civil War. At the same time, the Supreme Court lost considerable standing and would subsequently play a very weak role during the Civil War. Somehow, Dred Scott the man was lost in the controversial decision. In any case, he was freed by his owners several weeks after the decision and worked as a hotel porter in St. Louis until he succumbed to tuberculosis in 1858.

CONCLUSIONS

While America had established a penal system by the mid-1830s, it did little to mitigate the growing crime rates in the antebellum years. Beginning in the 1830s, urban America endured outbreaks of mob violence over a variety of issues. Although ineffectual law enforcement has been used as the scapegoat for some of the violence, the development of professional police forces in the 1840s and 1850s does not fully explain the diminution of mob rioting in America's cities. According to Feldberg, by the 1850s "municipal politics had absorbed much of the energies that nativist and immigrants had been investing in street violence," and local politics became an alternate but less deadly battleground.[19] Other explanations for the downturn in violence after the mid-1840s were the economic improvement following the panic of 1837 and the war with Mexico (1846–1848), which absorbed the energy of young combatants from the cities in a united war against Mexico.

During the antebellum years, the groundwork for modern policing, prisons, parole and probation, and indeterminate sentencing were established. By the 1850s, small and large cities were legislating the night watch out of existence in favor of organized police forces. While their establishment did not solve all the social problems of antebellum America, urban policing began to play an integral role in maintaining order, preventing crime, and regulating public morality.

Measured by its financial successes, the Auburn system of silent confinement clearly triumphed over the solitary Pennsylvania system. One of the more important developments of the antebellum era was that an increasing number of prison inmates came from the new immigrant classes, especially the Irish. This pattern would continue from the 1830s through the 1870s.

As urban rioting continued to wreak havoc on northeastern cities, sectional violence proceeded to spread farther west following the war with Mexico and the crisis over the Kansas–Nebraska territory. It was not long before guerrilla warfare broke out in this region and the nation was preparing for war. With the Civil War on the horizon, the great strides in criminal justice experimentation and reform would suddenly become a lower priority until the reconstruction of the Union after 1865.

Point–Counterpoint

Keeping the Peace: Vigilantes and Police Officers (1844, 1851)

The creation of the London Metropolitan Police Department in 1829 was a major step in the transition from medieval to modern law enforcement. It would be decades before this experiment would bear much fruit in America. The best laboratories for this experiment were the crowded eastern cities beset by urbanization and immigration. It is no

wonder then that New York City passed a police bill in 1844 that would lead to the creation of the New York City Police Department the following year. That same year there was barely a handful of Anglo setters in San Francisco (then called Yerba Buena). The discovery of gold in 1848 and the subsequent avalanche of gold seekers led to rampant lawlessness in San Francisco and its environs. San Francisco would not have the time to make the transition from town to city since it became an urban center virtually overnight. The problem that was experienced in San Francisco was typical for regions where people settled in advance of police, courts, and other formal institutions of social control. In 1851 the San Francisco Vigilance was convened to restore order. It was composed of city merchants and other prosperous types that had the most to lose. The following passages include a document detailing the composition of the prospective 24-hour police force and then the Constitution of the San Francisco Vigilance Committee.

§ 1. The Mayor of the City of New York is, and shall continue to be, the Chief Magistrate and head of all the Police of the said City, with all the powers conferred on him and now exercised by law.

§ 2. In each of the Wards of the City of New-York there shall be appointed, by the Mayor of the said City, the following number of persons to be Policemen, that is to say: 988.

§ 3. To entitle any person to be appointed such Policeman, he shall, previous to his appointed, have been a house-keeper and resident of the ward for which he shall be appointed, at least one year; shall be a person of approved discretion, integrity, courage and moral character.

§ 9. The said Captains, Sub-Captains and Policemen shall dress in respectable citizen's dress in the day-time, and in the night with the usual watchman's cap, and the only weapon which they shall use when required shall be the usual watchman's club; they shall be known in the day-time by some proper badge, to be designated for that purpose.

§ 10. The said Captains and Assistant Captains shall, within their districts, do all the duties, as well by day as by night, that are now done by the Captains and Assistant Captains of the Watch in the night time, and the duties done by Foremen of engines and Engineers; shall vigilantly see that the duties of the

Source: New York City Common Council, *Report of the Special Committee of the New York City Board of Alderman on the New York City Police Department*. Document No. 53, 1844, pp. 805–810; "Papers of the San Francisco Vigilance Committee of 1851," *Publications of Pacific Coast History*, Berkeley, 1919, Vol. 4, pp. 1–3, 634–37.

subordinate Policemen are well performed, and in addition shall do all the duties hereinafter mentioned.

§ 13. The duties of the said Sectionmen shall be both night and day, similar to the duties which are now performed by the Roundsmen and Patrolmen of the Watch at night; they shall, while on duty, be constantly patroling their section, and see that good order is observed, and the laws enforced; and shall perform such other duties as shall be prescribed by the rules and regulations to be established by the Board of Police.

§ 17. The two-thirds of the force not on duty shall be the reserve, from which, from time to time, and in due and proportionate succession, shall be detailed, by the Captain of the Ward, a sufficient number to act as Firemen, to proceed with the Engines and Hook and Ladders to the fires, on which occasion they shall wear a fire cap and suit of fire clothes; and another sufficient number shall be detailed to attend at all public landings, theatres, and such other duties as the said Captains, Superintendent or the Mayor may direct; and when any of such reserve force shall not be required to be on any duty, they may abide and remain at their places of residence till their presence shall be required.

§ 18. In case of sickness or accident to any Policeman, by which he shall be rendered unable to attend to his duties, the Captain of the Ward to which he may be attached, may, if he deem it necessary, employ a substitute in his place, during his inability to do duty; such inability to be certified daily by a licensed Physician; and in case of any falsehood or fraud, in making or procuring such certificate, all parties concerned therein shall be deemed guilty of a misdemeanor.

§ 19. In all cases when a portion of the force shall be required to proceed to a fire, or to repress a riot, at least one Captain or one Sub-captain, a proper number of Sectionmen, and the required number of Policemen shall proceed to the scene of action; and, if occasion requires, additional force shall be added, and if needful, all the reserved force, and a part, or all of the force on duty, may be employed.

§ 20.There shall be a regular and systematic arrangement of signals for fires and riots, by which the whole Police force may be promptly apprised of the place of fire or riot, and what portion of the force is required; it shall be the duty of the Policemen detailed for that purpose, from time to time, to ring the bells and give such other signals as may be agreed on.

§ 21. It shall also be the duty of such of the Policemen as shall be detailed for the purpose, from time to time, to keep the Engines, Hose Cart and Hooks and Ladders, and apparatus attached thereto, in good order.

§ 22. The horses, or any of them, provided for the Engines or Hook and Ladder Trucks may, when not on actual duty, in proceeding to the fire, be employed on general patrol, or other duty to which they can usefully be employed for the benefit of the Police.

THE SAN FRANCISCO VIGILANCE COMMITTEE, 1851

Constitution of the San Francisco Vigilance Committee
Instituted the Eighth of June 1851

Whereas it has become apparent to the citizens of San Francisco that there is no security for life and property, either under the regulations of society as it at present exists or under the laws as now administered, therefore the citizens whose names are hereunto attached do unite themselves into an association for the maintenance of the peace and good order of society and the preservation of the lives and property of the citizens of San Francisco and do bind themselves each unto the other to do and perform every lawful act for the maintenance of law and order and to sustain the laws when faithfully and properly administered but we are determined that no thief, burglar, incendiary assassin, professed gambler, and other disturbers of the peace shall escape punishment either by the quibbles of the law, the insecurity of prisons, the carelessness or corruption of the police, or a laxity of those who pretend to administer justice.

And to secure the objects of this association we do hereby agree:

First, that the name and style of the association shall be the "Committee of Vigilance for the protection of the lives and property of the citizens and residents of the City of San Francisco.

Secondly, that there shall be a room selected for the meeting and deliberations of the Committee at which there shall be some one or more members of the Committee appointed for that purpose in constant attendance at all hours of the day and night to receive the report of any member of the association or of any other person or persons whatsoever of any act of violence done to the person or property of any citizen of San Francisco and if in the judgement of the member or members of the Committee present it be such an act as justifies the interference of this Committee either in aiding in the execution of the laws or the prompt and summary punishment of the offender the Committee shall be at once assembled for the purpose of taking such action as a majority of the Committee when assembled shall determine upon.

Thirdly, that it shall be the duty of any member or members of the Committee on duty at the Committee room whenever a general assemblage of the Committee is deemed necessary to cause a call to be made by two strokes upon a bell.

Fourthly, that when the Committee have assembled for action the decision of a majority present shall be binding upon the whole Committee and that those members of the Committee pledge their honor and hereby bind themselves to defend and sustain each other in carrying out the determined action of this Committee at the hazard of their lives and their fortunes.

Fifthly, that there shall be chosen monthly a President, Secretary, and Treasurer and it shall be the duty of the Secretary to detail the members required to be in daily attendance at the Committee room. A Sergeant-at-Arms shall be appointed whose duty it shall be to notify such members of their detail for duty. The Sergeant-at-Arms shall reside at and be in constant attendance at the Committee room.

Originally entitled "Papers of the San Francisco Vigilance Committee of 1851." In *Publications of Pacific Coast History* (Berkeley, 1919), vol. 4, pp. 1–3, 634–37, 825–27.

SOURCES

Archer, Gleason L. 1928. *History of the Law.* Boston: Suffolk Law School Press.

Ayers, Edward L. 1984. *Vengeance and Justice: Crime and Punishment in the 19th-Century American South.* New York: Oxford University Press.

Barry, J. V. 1958. *Alexander Maconochie of Norfolk Island: A Study of a Pioneer in Penal Reform.* Melbourne: Oxford University Press.

Bellesiles, Michael A. 1996. "The Origins of Gun Culture in the United States, 1760–1865." *Journal of American History* 83, no. 2 (September): 425–55.

———. 2000. *Arming America: The Origins of a National Gun Culture.* New York: Albert A. Knopf.

Brown, Richard Maxwell. 1970. *American Violence.* Englewood Cliffs, NJ.: Prentice Hall.

Brown, Richard Maxwell. 1979. "Historical Patterns of American Violence," *Violence in America: Historical and Comparative Perspectives,* edited by Hugh Davis Graham and Ted R. Gurr. Beverly Hills: Sage Publications, pp. 19–48.

Bruce, Dickson D, Jr. 1979. *Violence and Culture in the Antebellum South.* Austin: University of Texas Press.

Campbell, Stanley. 1968. *The Slave Catchers: Enforcement of the Fugitive Slave Law, 1850–1860.* Chapel Hill: University of North Carolina Press.

Courtwright, David T. 1996. *Violent Land: Single Men and Social Disorder from the Frontier to the Inner City.* Cambridge, Mass.: Harvard University Press.

Feldberg, Michael 1980. *The Turbulent Era: Riot and Disorder in Jacksonian America.* New York: Oxford University Press.

Finkelman, Paul, ed. 1988. *Fugitive Slaves and American Courts.* 4 vols. New York: Garland.

Friedman, Lawrence M. 1974. *A History of American Law.* New York: Simon and Schuster.

Grimsted, David. 1998. *American Mobbing, 1828–1861: Toward Civil War.* New York: Oxford University Press.

Hindus, Michael Stephen 1980. *Prison and Plantation: Crime, Justice and Authority in Massachusetts and South Carolina, 1767–1878.* Chapel Hill: University of North Carolina Press.

Johnson, David R. 1981. *American Law Enforcement: A History.* Wheeling, Ill.: Forum Press.

Jordan, Philip D. 1970. "The Wearing of Weapons in the Western Country." In *Frontier Law and Order: Ten Essays,* pp. 1–22. Lincoln: University of Nebraska Press.

Lewis, Orlando F. 1922. *The Development of American Prisons and Prison Customs, 1776–1845.* New York: Prison Association of New York, 1922.

Marshall, H. E. 1937. *Forgotten Samaritan.* Chapel Hill: University of North Carolina Press.

Miller, Wilbur R. 1973. *Cops and Bobbies: Police Authority in New York and London, 1830–1870.* Chicago: University of Chicago Press.

Moody, Richard. 1958. *The Astor Place Riot.* Bloomington: Indiana University Press.

Morn, Frank. 1982. *"The Eye That Never Sleeps": A History of the Pinkerton National Detective Agency.* Bloomington: Indiana University Press.

Paul, Raymond. 1971. *Who Murdered Mary Rogers?* Englewood Cliffs, N.J.: Prentice Hall.

Prassel, Frank R. 1981. *The Western Peace Officer: A Legacy of Law and Order.* Norman: University of Oklahoma Press.

Sanders, Wiley B., ed. 1970. *Juvenile Offenders for a Thousand Years: Selected Readings from Anglo-Saxon Times to 1900.* Chapel Hill: University of North Carolina Press.

Senkewicz, Robert M. 1985. *Vigilantes in Gold Rush San Francisco.* Stanford, Calif.: Stanford University Press.

Slaughter, Thomas P. 1991. *Bloody Dawn: The Christiana Riot and Racial Violence in the Antebellum North.* New York: Oxford University Press.

Tucher, Andie. 1994. *Froth and Scum: Truth, Beauty, Goodness, and the Ax Murderer in America's First Mass Medium.* Chapel Hill: University of North Carolina Press.

Walters, Ronald. 1978. *American Reformers, 1815-1860.* New York: Hill and Wang.

Williams, Jack Kenny. 1959. *Vogues in Villainy: Crime and Retribution in Ante-Bellum South Carolina,* Columbia: University of South Carolina Press.

CRITICAL THINKING QUESTIONS

1. What controversies brought the question of states' rights to center stage in the antebellum period?

2. What conditions led to the development of urban police forces in America? What role did private police and vigilantes play as peacekeepers? Why was it necessary?

3. Discuss prison reform and reformers during the antebellum era.

4. What were the goals of indeterminate sentencing?

5. Discuss the impact of the Mary Rogers murder case on American policing and popular culture.

6. What conditions led to rioting in the 1830s and 1840s?

7. What impact did the sectional crisis and the abolitionist and temperance movements have on American criminal justice? How did the *Dred Scott* decision impact the growing sectional crisis?

CRIMINAL JUSTICE HISTORY ON THE INTERNET

Most major police departments offer historical sites, although they are noncritical in nature. For Chicago, see www.chipubib.org/004chicago/timeline/policedept.html. The history of the Pinkertons and the early Secret Service is covered at www.crimelibrary.com/gangsters2/pinkerton. Pinkerton history and photographs are at www.spartacus.schoolnet.co.uk/USApinkerton.html and www.americaslibrary.gov/pages/jb_0825_pinkerto_1.html. For the history of the U.S. Postal Service, see www.usps.com/history/hisl.htm.

References for the San Francisco Vigilance Committees of the 1850s can be found at http://elane.stanford.edu/wilson/Text//11a.html, www.maritimeheritage.org/vips/vigilance.html, and www.berkeley.edu/news/berkeleyan/1994/1109/immigrant.html.

There is a wealth of observations on antebellum America by the French writer Alexis de Tocqueville at http://xroads.virginia.edu/~HYPER/DETOC/home.html.

Nativism and the Know-Nothing Party is available at http://history.sandiego.edu/gen/civilwar/04/nativism.html, www.geocities.com/CollegePark/Quad/6460/dir/850amer.html, and http://dig.lib.niv.edu/message/nativism.html.

A guide to the Records of the New York House of Refuge History can be found at www.sara.nysed.gov/holding/aids/school/content.htm. For a brief history of the New York House of Refuge, see www.archives.nysed.gov/holding/aids/school/history.htm.

A number of Web sites are devoted to antebellum rioting. Philadelphia's anti-Catholic riots of 1844 are covered at http://vassun.vassar.edu/ ~sttaylor/FAMINE/Master/PhiladelphiaRiots.html. The Chicago riots of 1855 are discussed at www.chipublib.org/004chicago/disasters/lagerber_riots.html; the Charlestown, Massachusetts, riots of 1834 at www.library.georgetown.edu/dept/speccoll/mi/mi%7D186.htm; and the Bible riots of 1844 in Philadelphia at www.billofrightsinstitute.org/pdf/equality_bible_riots.pdf.

The Astor Place riot is well chronicled at www.cofc.edu/~Kattwins/Amer19thcpages/AstorPlaceint.htm. The identification of the fatalities that day make for interesting reading at www.mcny.org/astorriot.htm; a period engraving of the riot is available at www.mcny.org/astorriot.htm.

National newspaper reaction to the Christiana riot is at http://muweb.millersville.edu/~ugrr/christiana/National.html and links to riots and fugitive slaves at http://home.epix.net/~chrlib/parfitt/pathfinder.html. An excellent account of the *Dred Scott* case can be accessed at www.nps.gov/jeff/ocv-dscottd.htm. Eighty-five of the original documents related to this case can be viewed at http://library.wustl.edu/vlib/dredscott/toc.html.

The murder of abolitionist Elijah Lovejoy and links to abolitionism, which includes eleven letters written by Lovejoy on the subject, are at www.state.il.us/hpa/lovejoy/letthome.htm. A contemporary speech on the murder is at www.federalobserver.com/speeches.php?speech=1180. A biography of Lovejoy is at www.altonweb.com/history/hisl.htm.

Important issues dealing with the conflict between federal and state governments include the Indian Removal Act at www.stanford.edu/~paherman/Indian_removal.htm; the full text of this act is at www.synaptic.bc.ca/ejournal/jackson.htm. The Nullification Controversy is examined at www.kusd.edu/schools/lance/platinum/banaszynski/civil_war_2000/union_links_2000/the_north_stars.html. Antebellum America was the setting for the creation of the mental asylum. For more on reformer Dorothea Dix and mental hospitals, see www.mfh.org/specialprojects/shulp/site/honorees/dix.html and www.webster.edu/~woolfm/dorotheadix.html.

For coverage of America's first bank robbery, see www.ushistory.org/carpentershall/history/robbery.htm. The important Mary Rogers murder case is available through a number of sites and links. For female sexuality and murder in nineteenth-century America, see www.brown.edu/Facilities/ University_Library/exhibits/RLCexhibit/shes/she_is_morems.html. This case inspired Edgar Allan Poe to write the first detective story. For more on this, see www.trussel.com/detfic/hungary.htm and www.skgaze.com/content/mysteries/EdgarAllanPoe.shtml. Crucial to understanding this case is an examination of its impact on policing the pre–Civil War city at www.gliah.uh.edu/historyonline/policing.cfm.

NOTES

1. Astor (1971, p. 18).

2. Archer (1928, p. 407).

3. Walters (1978, p. 135).

4. Friedman (1974, p. 249).

5. Miller (1973, p. 3).

6. There is some disagreement here as to the actual origins of the term *copper*. Its earliest application as a synonym for police officer appeared in George Matsell's 1859 work "A Hundred Stretches Hence." Some sources trace the shortened version *cop* to 1846 and to the books of Horatio Alger in the 1860s. Outside of Augustine Costello's *Our Police Protectors* (1885), there is little or no substantiation that the word *cop* was used earlier than the 1850s.

7. Johnson (1981, p. 78).

8. Apparently, the term *vigilante* was adapted from the Spanish word for "watchman" and would eventually fine wider currency as an expression of frontier justice in the West.

9. Prassel (1981, p. 84).

10. Quoted in Bellesiles (2000, p. 365).

11. Brown (1969, p. 36).

12. Slaughter (1991, p. x).

13. Bellesiles (1996).

14. Bruce (1979, p. 242).

15. Sanders (1970, p. 339).

16. Quoted in Feldberg (1980, p. 5).

17. Brown (1970, p. 42).

18. Beginning in 1847, the case was known as *Scott (a man of color) v. Emerson,* after the family that owned the slave. In 1853, the case was taken up once more after a series of court decisions, but at this point Scott's ownership was passed to John Sandford (or Sanford), Emerson's brother-in-law.

19. Feldberg (1980, p. 121).

7

CRIMINAL JUSTICE IN THE CIVIL WAR ERA (1856–1876)

TIME LINE

1856	John Brown terrorizes proslavers in Kansas
1859	Hanging of John Brown following raid on Harper's Ferry
1861	Civil War begins
1862	Largest mass hanging in American history
1863	New York City draft riots
1865	Assassination of Abraham Lincoln
1865	Founding of the Massachusetts "state police"
1865	Creation of U.S. Secret Service
1865	Civil War ends
1865	First passage of black codes
1866	Ku Klux Klan founded in Tennessee
1866	First train robbery
1867	Allan Pinkerton publishes manual on private policing
1868	Fourteenth Amendment ratified by the states
1868	The impeachment trial of President Andrew Johnson
1868	Fourteenth Amendment
1870	Department of Justice organized
1870	First meeting of National Prison Congress

1870	**Fifteenth Amendment**	**1872**	**Credit Mobilier scandal**
1870s	**Convict leasing system established**	**1873**	**Congress enacts Comstock Law**
1871	**Exposure of Tweed Ring**	**1876**	**Elmira opens its doors**
1871	**First National Police Convention is held in St. Louis**		

The years leading up to the Civil War brought numerous critical issues dividing the nation into sharp focus, including slavery versus free labor, popular sovereignty, and the legal and political status of African Americans. The decade of the 1850s witnessed unparalleled urbanization, heralding an era from 1860 to 1900 when city dwellers would increase from six million to thirty million. Whether the interior cities of St. Louis, Cleveland, Chicago, and Milwaukee or eastern urban centers such as New York City and Philadelphia, all shared the rapid growth and wealth of the Industrial Revolution. But they would also share an equally dark side, one that was characterized by racial and ethnic tensions, poverty, and an outmanned and outdated criminal justice system still playing catch-up. As sectional matters came to the fore in the 1850s, temperance reform leaders turned their attention to the impending sectional conflict. Popular interest in the crusade against "demon rum" waned as the *Dred Scott* case, "Bleeding Kansas," and John Brown's raid on Harper's Ferry dominated the day's concerns.

The Civil War years witnessed the greatest carnage in American history and ended with probably the most famous murder of the nineteenth century: the assassination of President Abraham Lincoln at Ford's Theater less than two weeks after the conclusion of the war. At the time of his murder, Lincoln was far from the respected figure that recent historians have proclaimed as the country's greatest president. Lincoln's unpopularity in the South was well known, but the loathing reserved for the president in the North has been given less coverage in history texts. Indeed, throughout the war years, his policies came under attack from all directions. Growing opposition to the war led Lincoln to suspend the constitutionally guaranteed writ of habeas corpus and authorize the arrest of hundreds of individuals for antiwar activities. His implementation by executive order of a conscription bill over the objections of Congress in 1862 helped precipitate riots in many cities, including the New York City draft riot of 1863, the bloodiest in American history.

As Lincoln's first term came to a close, he had infuriated Congress and was thought to have violated the Constitution by issuing executive orders creating provisional courts in conquered southern states and by installing military governors in Arkansas, Louisiana, and Tennessee without apparent constitutional authority or the approval of Congress. By the end of 1864, Lincoln's support had dwindled, as antagonists opposing emancipation, resistance to the draft, and strong criticism against the manner the war was being waged began to take its toll on his administration. This would become the historical context that would lead John Wilkes Booth to take the life of perhaps America's greatest leader in 1865.

Historian James G. Randall described the Civil War as an "eccentric period" in American history, "a period when specious arguments and legal fictions were put forth to excuse extraordinary measures. It was a period during which the line was blurred between executive, legislative, and judicial functions; between state and federal powers; and between military and civil procedures."[1] Until this era, the American judicial system had never faced a precedent for such a crisis as the Civil War.

While the developing cities earned a reputation for criminality and tested the developing criminal justice system, the defeated South also presented considerable obstacles in a region that had lagged far behind the rest of the nation in modernizing its criminal justice mechanisms. As Congress attempted to reconstruct the eleven former Confederate states, white supremacists swept through the night, terrorizing black communities and anyone who favored the transition to the post-slaveholding era.

THE LAWGIVERS

One of the most important criminal justice issues to come up during the Civil War years was whether a state of war suspended the liberties guaranteed by the U.S. Constitution. Following the opening shots of the Civil War at Fort Sumter, Lincoln and his cabinet made the preservation of what was left of the Union its highest priority. Cognizant of the fact that support for the Union cause was far from unanimous in the North, the Lincoln administration set up a strategy for dealing with opposition to the war. With members of Congress, the courts, and even the army and the government suspected of sympathizing with the South, it became paramount to maintain loyalties to the Union cause.

The Civil War era would see a sustained attack on constitutional liberties of freedom of speech and freedom of the press. In perhaps the greatest attack on individual liberties in American history, President Lincoln suspended the writ of habeas corpus from areas where secession seemed imminent in 1861 to the entire country.

To justify his actions Lincoln, cited article 1, section 9, of the Constitution, which said, "The privilege of the Writ of Habeas Corpus shall not be suspended, unless when in Cases of Rebellion or Invasion the public safety may require it." Maryland, a border state with a large secessionist population, was the first state to feel the wrath of the new policy in May 1861, when several prominent state officials were "arbitrarily" arrested and imprisoned by military authorities. It was not long before a leading southern agitator who had been arrested provided the first test case for Lincoln's strategy. The last important case heard by the eighty-four-year-old Supreme Court judge Roger Taney involved a wealthy Baltimore citizen named John Merryman. In *Ex parte Merryman*, Taney ruled that only the legislative branch had the power to suspend the writ of habeas corpus and that "if the President of the United States may suspend the writ then the Constitution has conferred upon him more regal and absolute power over the liberty of the citizen than the people of England have thought its safe to entrust to the Crown," alluding to the fact that only Parliament had similar power.

While Taney had his defenders and may have been correct in his interpretation of the law, many saw him as taking sides with traitors. As the situation in Maryland abated, Merryman was eventually released. Many subsequent cases would follow a similar pattern. Individuals would be arrested on little pretext for threatening national security. After a period of time when the threat seemed to pass, the prisoners were released.

Several days after the promulgation of the Emancipation Proclamation in September 1862, Lincoln proclaimed, "During the existing insurrection . . . all rebels and insurgents, their aiders and abettors, within the United States, and all persons discouraging voluntary enlistments, resisting military drafts, or guilty of disloyal practices . . . shall be subject to martial law and liable to trials and punishments by courts martial or military commission." In addition, "the writ of habeas corpus" was suspended "in respect to all persons arrested" by military authority. On September 15, 1863, Lincoln suspended the writ for the duration of the war.

Throughout the Civil War, thousands of individuals were arrested by the military authorities at the direction of Secretary of State Seward and Secretary of War Stanton. But Lincoln historian David Herbert Donald suggests that "only a few were truly political prisoners," until more teeth were put into the proclamations in 1863.[2] Until then, the majority of those arrested were spies, smugglers, foreign nationals, and blockade runners. While researching arrests for this period in National Archive records, historian Mark E. Neely Jr. found many more arrests than earlier researchers but also discovered that most had "less significance in the history of civil liberties than anyone ever imagined."[3]

Although Taney would not live to see it, his position on the habeas corpus issue was upheld in 1866 in the *Ex Parte Milligan* decision, which vindicated his interpretation of the Constitution. According to the *Milligan* decision, Congress had no authority to establish military commissions and ruled that the Constitution could not "be suspended during any of the great exigencies of government. Such a doctrine leads directly to anarchy and despotism." Commenting on the case in the next century, Chief Justice Earl Warren noted that the case "established firmly the principle that when civil courts are open and operating resort to military tribunals for the prosecution of civilians is impermissible." As the only president to suspend the writ of habeas corpus, Lincoln has drawn fire from Civil War scholars. However, recent research suggests that his actions were well-intentioned attempts to deal with an unprecedented crisis and to conduct the war more efficiently. Although the system of military justice was deeply flawed and abuses of power did take place, Lincoln's actions must be viewed in the context of the time.

Black Codes

Following the Civil War, white legislators in the southern states instituted "black codes" to replace the old slave codes, and slave patrols returned to police the rural countryside. To the informed, the new freedom looked suspiciously like the old slavery. Unable to hold office, vote, or speak to whites, former slaves were required to be employed by whites and could not change jobs without permission, were prohibited from intermarrying with whites, and were barred from carrying weapons even for self-protection. Unemployed blacks and orphaned children could be arrested for vagrancy and then assigned to work without pay. Black codes, which attempted to uphold the old racial order in the South, radicalized Congress and led congressional Republicans to try to seize control of Reconstruction policies from President Andrew Johnson.

There had been a long tradition of "hiring out" free blacks who did not pay taxes or failed to pay fines. The practice of temporary enslavement of free blacks existed years before the Civil War. During the 1830s, any black unable or unwilling to pay a fine in Florida could be offered for public sale by the sheriff. North Carolina extended the maximum time for hiring out to more than one year simply for siring a son outside wedlock. Several slave states had prewar laws that provided that if a free black was hired but left before the expiration of the contract with the employer "without reasonable cause," he could be charged with a misdemeanor.

One historian has suggested that post–Civil War black codes were not imposed as an attempt to at reinstate slavery but rather were the result of southern officials trying "trying to erect a legal structure that would permit the economic exploitation" of blacks by granting "them technical freedom."[4] However, any reading of individual state black codes suggest an attempt to return to the pre–Civil War status quo.

 The Mississippi Black Code (1865)

Section 3. Be it further enacted. . . . That it shall not be lawful for any freedman, free Negro, or mulatto to intermarry with any white person; nor for any white person to intermarry with any freedman, free Negro, or mulatto; any person who shall intermarry shall be

deemed guilty of felony and, on conviction thereof, shall be confined in the state penitentiary for life. . . .

Section 7. Be it further enacted, That every civil officer shall, and every person may, arrest and carry back to his or her legal employer any freedman, free Negro, or mulatto who shall have quit the service of his or her employer before the expiration of his or her term of service without good cause, and said officer and person shall be entitled to receive for arresting and carrying back every deserting employee aforesaid, the sum of five dollars, and ten cents per mile from the place of arrest to the place of delivery, and the same shall be paid by the employer, and held as a set-off for so much against the wages of said deserting employee.

Section 8. Be it further enacted, That upon affidavit made by the employer of any freedman, free Negro, or mulatto, or other credible person, before any justice of the peace or member of the board of police, that any freedman, free Negro, or mulatto, legally employed by said employer, has illegally deserted said employment, such justice of the peace or member of the board of police shall issue his warrant or warrants, returnable before himself, or other such officer, directed to any sheriff, constable, or special deputy, commanding him to arrest said deserter and return him or her to said employer, and the like proceedings shall be had as provided in the preceding section.[5]

Civil Rights Legislation and Due Process

The passage of the Thirteenth Amendment abolishing slavery in 1865 and then the Fourteenth Amendment in 1868 providing blacks with citizenship and equal protection under the law represented great strides in the nationalization of civil rights. According to the Fourteenth Amendment, no person may be deprived of life, liberty, or property without "due process of law," and all persons are to have equal protection of the laws.

In an attempt to disenfranchise the new citizens, white supremacist organizations such as the Ku Klux Klan waged a campaign of terror against blacks trying to exercise their rights, and southern states enacted black codes in an attempt to impose second-class citizenship on former

slaves. Congress responded with various measures intended to protect the black population. Foremost among these was the Fifteenth Amendment, which specifically proclaimed that the right to vote should not be denied by reason of race, color, or previous condition of servitude. However, constitutional amendments did not apply to women; therefore, female former slaves were not covered by the Fifteenth Amendment.

Other civil rights acts followed, including the Act to Enforce the Fourteenth Amendment, better known as the Ku Klux Klan Act of 1871. This legislation outlawed conspiracies to deprive citizens of their voting rights. That same year, President Ulysses Grant declared martial law in parts of South Carolina, where the Klan was waging a terror campaign. The Supreme Court would strike down various sections of the civil rights legislation, but following the suppression of the Klan, federal protection of civil rights gradually diminished. The passage of the 1875 Civil Rights Act would prohibit discrimination by hotels, railroads, and other public facilities. But this law proved a last hurrah for civil rights protection. It too would be repudiated when in 1883 the Supreme Court ruled it unconstitutional, signaling a new era of disenfranchisement for African Americans.

Birth of Drug Legislation

While social reformers concentrated on alcohol abuse in the nineteenth century, the United States had been plagued by a "drug problem" for decades. Drug historian H. Wayne Morgan suggests that the "public remained uninformed about it" until the communication advances of the late 1860s.[6] Indeed, the public paid little attention to drug addiction as long as it took place among the more marginalized segment of the population. When changing patterns of addiction in the 1870s introduced narcotics to the mainstream population, social and health reformers weighed in with dire predictions and warnings.

The nineteenth century saw the onset of a drug addiction problem in America beginning in the late 1840s with Chinese immigrants who popularized the smoking of opium in the mining towns of gold rush California and then with the wide availability of morphine products in the 1850s. The introduction of the hypodermic needle in 1856 offered a way of injecting morphine directly into the bloodstream.[7] The use of morphine rose dramatically during the Civil War period, when it was used intravenously to treat battlefield casualties. Following the war, many ex-soldiers brought the "army disease" of morphine addiction back home with them. Other factors for the growing morphine addiction problem resulted from the mass marketing of patent medicines that contained narcotics as well as the psychological trauma of the Civil War.

During the Reconstruction years, morphine was cheaper than alcohol and was widely available. Prior to the acknowledgment of the disease of addiction, doctors prescribed cheap morphine for many common complaints, leading to a substantial population of addicts. While there is no way to ascertain the number of drug addicts in Reconstruction-era America, a researcher in 1868 estimated that 80,000 to 100,000 Americans were addicted to opium.[8]

After the California gold mines were played out and the transcontinental railroad was completed, many Chinese immigrants clustered in the cities and Chinatowns along the Pacific coast. The commencement of an economic depression in California in 1875 indirectly led to one of America's earliest drug prohibition laws. The high unemployment and deterioration of living standards among the working classes brought the weight of bad times disproportionately onto the Chinese. As Chinese immigrants continued to come to California, they became the target of white frustration and despair over declining economic prospects. Into the 1870s, Anglo-Californians saw the close-knit, insular Chinese as hopelessly different and unassimilative. Sensational reports of Chinese prostitution and opium use fed the anti-Chinese sentiments of the era.

In 1875, San Francisco passed the first antidrug law in the United States when it pro-hibited the continued operation of opium dens, which were linked to vice and the mingling of white and Chinese users, a combination linked to moral degradation. Similar conditions in other parts of the West would lead to comparable anti-Chinese legislation and outright violence over the next two decades.

The Judicial System

As the country moved west beyond the Mississippi River, settlers were faced with not only meager law enforcement but also an uneven judicial system. Corruption and local politics often let guilty parties walk free, and a lack of jails made it almost impossible to hold prisoners for any length of time. Well-organized outlaw gangs often seemed to have the upper hand when it came to the justice system with their abilities to bribe officials and pack juries. By the 1860s, judges, juries, and police officials were pressured by criminal intimidation and the complaints of settlers who saw a system that favored the accused over the interests of society, a refrain that would resonate throughout American history.

The end of the Civil War saw the end of reform campaigns for abolition of slavery and diminished opposition against the death penalty and liquor consumption. However, there were always reform movements in the wings waiting to take center stage. Congressional passage of the Comstock Law in 1873 was the culmination of a crusade by Connecticut dry-goods salesman Anthony Comstock (1844–1915) against obscenity. According to this piece of legislation, transmission of obscene materials through the mail became illegal. In order to enforce the legislation, Comstock took a nonpaying job as postal inspector in New York City.

In support of the law targeting obscene books and abortion, Comstock personally led raids against illegal abortionist offices and pornography shops in a campaign to rid New York City of anything immoral, a battle still raging into the twenty-first century. Like-minded activists have touched off an unending debate in America over the definition of obscenity and censorship as well as the interpretation of the First Amendment guaranteeing free expression. Comstock's campaign would lead several states to pass obscenity statutes and limit access to contraceptive and abortion information by the end of the century (see chapter 8 for more on Comstock).

LAW ENFORCEMENT

Between 1845 and 1865, major American cities established more proficient police forces that emphasized prevention over detection. As early as the 1850s, cities such as New York could boast uniformed police on the London model, while in other regions fears of a standing army led to informal vigilante groups, particularly in the trans-Mississippi West after 1850. While there is little disagreement that a breakdown in social order caused by immigration and urbanization contributed to the development of policing in urban America, historians such as Eric Monkkonnen maintained that the creation of urban police forces was an attempt by municipal authorities to first control the "dangerous classes" and then to more efficiently manage their cities. He cites similar reform goals in the improvement of fire and sanitation departments in the same era.[9] Refuting the notion that modern police forces developed in response to rioting and rising crime rates, Monkkonnen argued that if this were the case, then those cities that experienced neither problem would not have established such forces.

The development of modern urban police was a slow process, one that occurred gradually in most American cities. Initially, the new police force used a syncretic approach that assimilated part of the old watch system before making the transition to totally new strategies. By 1855, Chicago had adopted a police system similar to New York City, followed by New Orleans and Cincinnati (1852), Philadelphia (1855), St. Louis (1856), Newark and Baltimore (1857), Detroit (1865), and Buffalo (1866).[10]

With few cities having established uniformed police forces by 1860, the traditional militia was still relied on by urban areas without professional police. While many police carried firearms informally, it would be decades before it was sanctioned by law in most cities.

In order to prevent the police from becoming separate and remote from the citizens they served, efforts were made in some cities to ensure that the early police were members of the community by implementing residency requirements. As immigration politics became inextricably linked with policing in cities such as New York and Boston, Irish and Irish Americans became the most common ethnocultural group in mid-nineteenth-century police forces. Cities as diverse as New York and New Orleans could claim to have a disproportionate number of Irish police on their forces. This can be best explained by the Irish predilection for partisan politics and the spoils system that went along with it. Although large numbers of German immigrants lived in the same cities, being better capitalized and educated than the Irish they did not develop the same political organization at the ward level and remained underrepresented on the police forces.

While the London model of policing inspired many American police forces, it was seldom imitated because of the inherent differences in the two societies. In England, police officers were recruited from the military and laborers on the fringe of London. After joining the force, officers accepted the restriction of many personal liberties. Married officers were not allowed in certain parts of town, while bachelors were assigned to barracks. Barred from voting, London bobbies were ultimately responsible to Parliament rather than their local constituents. On the other hand, the exigencies of the American system would never permit such restrictions of individual liberties, for, as the police historian Roger Lane concluded, "it was impossible in the United States to adopt the London personnel polices."[11]

Police reform was slowed in many regions by the Civil War and Reconstruction. No region of the country was more impacted by the war in terms of police reform than the South. In 1861, when New Orleans was captured by Union forces, the civil government was disbanded and replaced by martial law. With the military taking on police duties, police experimentation, which had become a hallmark of southern police reform, had ended. Although steps had been taken toward creating a professional police force in New Orleans prior to the Civil War, it would take until 1898 for the establishment of such a force.

In the West, law enforcement was inadequate for much of the nineteenth century. To contend with rising crime rates, some western states and territories authorized anti–horse thief associations, detecting societies, and vigilante groups. However, the real locus of policing was typically near the county seat, town, or township. Underfinanced communities could ill afford to support constables, policemen, and sheriffs in the distant pursuit of outlaws. The additional expenditures required for capturing, trying, jailing, and sentencing could bankrupt the prototypical frontier community. Although the advent of the railroad helped transport desperadoes back to justice, law enforcement was hampered by the fixed routes of the train lines and were forced once more on horseback to navigate the patchwork of barely recognizable trails back to "civilization."

One of the more unexpected consequences of the Civil War was the decline of the U.S. militia. First used for federal peacekeeping in 1794, this ancient English tradition was transplanted to America in an era when citizen soldiers were needed to maintain order in the days before a standing army. At the outbreak of the American Revolution, the volunteer militia was initially the only military force at the disposal of the colonists. However, "a dozen years after the Civil War the United States militia had reached its nadir."[12] Explanations for the decline of the militia vary. According to historian Robert Reinders, the decline in urban riots after the Civil War and an increasingly more professional police apparatus best explain the phenomenon. Others have suggested that the war had bred an "antimilitaristic

attitude" that discouraged volunteer military service.[13] While the changing nature of urban criminal violence may have indeed led to the decline of the militia, industrial disorder and strikes beginning in the late 1870s would stimulate the return of the militia.

While few records indicate the presence of black police officers in America between 1850 and the 1870s, historians have uncovered black police officers in northern cities beginning in the 1870s and more notably in midwestern cities such as Chicago and Cincinnati. During the Reconstruction era, three out of five police commissioners were black, and one-third of the police in New Orleans were African American. But this would turn out to be an ephemeral development in the postwar South.

Urban Policing

While the New York City police had copied many of London's police model, including the adoption of uniforms, there were still important differences between the two forces. Not only were London police officers more inclined to military discipline, but they policed a more orderly society. However, the New York City police faced many more obstacles, in part because of the dearth of police officers. In 1856, the New York City police had one officer for every 812 and one-half citizens compared to London's one for every 351 and one-half.[14]

One of the recurring problems of nineteenth-century American policing was the influence of partisanship, which essentially allowed the police to control the election machinery. Nowhere was this better exemplified than in the debate over city versus state control of the New York City police between 1857 and 1870. According to Roger Lane, one of the spheres in which American policing sought to imitate its British counterpart was by "transferring the direction of the police from city to state, especially in a period of rising tensions."[15] In 1857, the New York Metropolitan Police Law transferred control of the New York City police to state officials, citing the reluctance of Mayor Fernando Wood to suppress the vice problem and his unwillingness to enforce the 1855 Prohibition law. However, Wood defied state officials by having the city council adopt an ordinance creating a municipal police force based on the London model. Thus, for a short time New York residents were confounded by the presence of two police forces. Tension escalated between the rival forces, culminating in a riot between the two in 1857 in which the metropolitans (supported by the state) were routed by the municipals. When the state court of appeals ruled in favor of the new police law, Wood disbanded the municipal force. New York police control was finally returned to the city in 1870.

Following New York's example, other urban police forces came under state control for various time periods in the nineteenth century, including those in Baltimore, St. Louis, Kansas City, Chicago, Detroit, New Orleans, Cleveland, Cincinnati, Indianapolis, Omaha, San Francisco, and Boston. According to police historian James Richardson, this phenomenon typically occurred where there was "significant social and political differences between the cities and their states." These cities were more likely "to be more cosmopolitan and pluralistic" and more predisposed to prostitution, gambling, and liquor. Moreover, these cities were typically dominated by a different political party than the state legislature.[16]

Federal Law Enforcement

During the Civil War, U.S. marshals were concerned mainly with arresting suspected traitors and Confederate sympathizers. Their role in supporting Lincoln's suspension of the writ of habeas corpus made the marshals a subject of scorn in many quarters. The passage of confiscation acts in 1861 and 1862 enlarged the marshals' powers to include confiscating the personal property of those accused of supporting the South. The government power to confiscate would not be taken away until 1868.

Following the war, marshals were confronted with protecting recently freed slaves and helping reimpose authority in the South. Ku Klux Klan groups and other white supremacists spread their campaign of terror across much of the South in defiance of the Civil Rights Act of 1866. During the early 1870s, southerners directed their efforts at regaining political control of their states. Marshals found themselves in the center of the struggle, as they were charged with supervising polling places and protecting politically active blacks from white violence. Supported by federal troops, marshals arrested almost 7,000 southerners for violating civil rights laws by 1877.

Perhaps the greatest development in federal law enforcement, the formation of the U.S. Secret Service in 1865, was a last-gasp attempt to deal with the long-standing counterfeiting problem. On April 14, 1865, the very day of his assassination, Abraham Lincoln gave his approval for the formation of what would become the U.S. Secret Service. Beginning in 1863, the federal government began issuing its own currency. Prior to this time, more than 1,600 American banks printed and designed their own currency as part of a money system in which each state released its own bank notes through private banks. Indeed, this system created a counterfeiter's paradise since merchants and businessmen were oblivious to differences between legitimate and counterfeit currency. At the behest of the secretary of the treasury, Lincoln approved the Secret Service as a division of his department.

It has been estimated that anywhere between one-third to one-half of the country's paper money was illegal during the Civil War years. Chosen to lead the new federal law enforcement organization was William P. Wood, a veteran of the war with Mexico.

 Born in 1819, William P. Wood served as superintendent of Washington's Old Capitol Prison in 1862 and was suspected of participating in all manner of intrigue and espionage during the war years. In 1864, he focused on the counterfeiting problem, taking advantage of his prison contacts in the federal prison population. However, the Secret Service was not authorized by Congress like the Customs

Service, postal inspectors, and Internal Revenue Service. In a more clandestine departure to protocol, Wood was sworn in by executive decision on July 5, 1865, in a private ceremony.

During its first year of operation, the Secret Service established field offices in eleven different cities and arrested more than 200 counterfeiters. The new branch of federal law enforcement has been credited with establishing a measure of monetary stability in the decade following the war. However, it would take two more presidential assassinations (Garfield in 1881 and McKinley in 1901) before the Secret Service was officially responsible for presidential protection in 1901.

Other federal law enforcement efforts for this era included the congressional creation of the Office of Internal Revenue, which was authorized on July 1, 1862. Its main function was the enforcement of the federal taxation of distilled spirits. The origins of the Internal Revenue Service and the Bureau of Alcohol, Tobacco, and Firearms can be traced back to this office.

State Policing

Throughout most of the nineteenth century, there was little support for state policing. Americans favored decentralization of policing in an era that placed considerable value on a republican ideology that favored local control of policing. Massachusetts was the only state besides Texas to experiment with state policing in the nineteenth century. Beginning in 1865, Massachusetts embarked on a series of state police experiments that did not lead to a permanent force until the following century. In 1865, the state legislature passed a statute that created a state police organization comprised of close to twenty officers. According to the law, the governor was given the power to select a chief constable who would direct a force composed of all state constables and their deputies. The nascent "state police" was mandated to maintain peace and order and prevent crime by controlling vice establishments, such as brothels, taverns, and gambling establishments. The force was given police powers throughout the state.

The "state police" was reorganized several times over the next fifteen years. In 1875, it was transformed into a "state detective force" of thirty men under the direction of a chief detective chosen by the governor. Within five years, the "state detectives" were transformed into the "district police," again under the supervision of a chief appointed by the governor. Throughout the various incarnations of the force, its powers and duties remained fairly consistent and focused most of its attention on enforcing liquor laws. Following World War I, the Massachusetts State Police would be reorganized as a modern state police force.[17]

Private Detectives

In 1846, the Boston Police Department created the first municipal detective division. New York followed with a similar division in 1857 and Philadelphia two years later. Subsequent scandals would reveal that like Britain's early thief takers, these detectives did little more than collect payoffs from amicable criminals and arrest those who failed to pay tribute. By the 1860s, municipal crime detection had been placed in the hands of private detectives, many of whom had former investigative experience.

The foremost detective agency of the nineteenth century was the Pinkertons, brainchild of Scottish immigrant Allan Pinkerton. Initially involved in railroad security, Pinkerton came to the attention of railroad lawyer Abraham Lincoln in the 1850s. Their chance meeting perhaps allowed Lincoln to survive to repeat the presidential oath in 1861. Pinkerton apparently stumbled on a plot to kill Lincoln as he passed through Maryland on his way to take office in the nation's capital. Interceding on the president-elect's behalf, Pinkerton convinced Lincoln not to leave the train in Baltimore. In 1861, Pinkerton was selected by the commanding Union general McClellan to lead the intelligence branch at the start of the Civil War.

Despite the reservations of former government detective Lafayette C. Baker, who noted that a detective bureau was "contrary to the spirit of . . . Republican institutions in time of peace," Pinkerton saw the lawlessness that punctuated the postwar years as an opportunity for earning new accolades. During the two decades following hostilities, the Pinkertons pursued (not always successfully) a virtual who's who of outlaw gangs, ranging from the Reno brothers in 1865–1866 to the James–Younger gang in the 1870s.

In the unorganized western territories, which had not yet made the transition to statehood, only federal law applied, leaving U.S. marshals as virtually the only law enforcement presence. In territories ranging from Wyoming to Arizona and New Mexico, all the governors, judges, and other officials were appointed by the president. When a territory reached 5,000 free white males, a bicameral legislature could be elected and laws promulgated. When the territory reached 60,000, it could be nominated for statehood (and then had to be approved by Congress). The position of U.S. marshal reflected the role of the federal courts. Since all criminal activities were viewed as a breech in federal law, marshals pursued a wide array of malefactors. But as the territory made the transition to statehood, the marshals saw other territorial lawmen take over their duties. As the territory came closer to statehood, federal marshals concentrated specifically on federal laws, while territorial laws were enforced by territorial county sheriffs.

CORRECTIONS

According to the federal census of 1860, the national prison population stood at 19,086. However, this figure increased by 72 percent to 32,901 in 1870, reflecting the social discord and disorganization that typically followed a war. By the late 1860s, prison overcrowding was an increasing concern. The sudden increase of the prison population after the war and a growing opposition to prison industries brought prison conditions to the attention of the public. In response, new institutions were built, and stimulus was given to the "reformatory" movement, an experiment in prison reform that emphasized education, trade training, a mark system, indeterminate sentencing, and parole. Building on the achievements of Captain Alexander Maconochie in Australia and Walter Crofton in Ireland, American reformatories attempted to make the transition from punitive programs to programs more reformative in nature.

According to prison historian Mark T. Carleton, the end of the Civil War was the "most decisive event in the history of southern penology."[18] With the end of hostilities, half the southern population made the transition from slavery to freedom in a region of the country where many jails and penitentiaries had been destroyed in the war.

Prior to the war, slaves who broke the law were punished on the plantation, but after 1865 new arrangements had to be made. The southern infrastructure had been destroyed during the war, and outside of prison units in several states, what little was available in the way of prison space was primitive in nature since the war had wiped out the beginnings of the penitentiary system in most states. Unprepared to handle the formidable expenses of social control by utilization of the penitentiary, southern legislatures were attracted by a cheaper alternative: convict leasing.

Convict Leasing

Unable to pay and care for the burgeoning number of prisoners following the Civil War, southern states experimented with a system of convict leasing that allowed prison contractors to utilize cheap prisoner labor for an assortment of projects, including levee and railroad construction as well as agricultural work. During the 1870s and 1880s, the convict leasing system would dominate southern penology. Two different types of leasing evolved. Under the terms of the contract system, prisoners worked behind prison walls and were fed, clothed, and guarded by prison authorities. Therefore, the lessor was only hiring the labor of the convicts behind prison walls. This system flourished in South Carolina, Texas, and Virginia by the 1880s. Other southern states and several outside the region used the lease system, in which prisoner labor was hired to work outside the confines of the prison structure.

American Prison Congress

Few Americans voiced concerns for prison conditions in 1865. The end of the Civil War and the onset of Reconstruction consumed the interest of most citizens, who had witnessed the bloodiest decade in American history. Public indifference to prison conditions was demolished in 1865 after prison reformers Enoch Wines (1806–1879) and Theodore Dwight publicized the deplorable state of several penitentiaries and reformatories they visited in the Northeast. Their tour of the prisons was chronicled and then published in seventy volumes as the *Report on the Prisons and Reformatories of the United States and Canada* in 1867.

Their conclusions offered several revealing statistics about the impact of the Civil War on the prison population. They noted that the number of male prisoners declined in state prisons anywhere from 10 to 50 percent. One explanation for this was that criminals often found refuge in the army during the war and that prison sentences were shorter in wartime. According to Wines and Dwight, the war also saw an increase in the imprisonment of women and minors. However, the years following the war saw a rapid increase in male prisoners and a general decline in female commitments.

Among their most fervent recommendations was the adoption of Sir Walter Crofton's "Irish system." This system was comprised of a series of graded prison stages. In the first phase, the convict spent two years in solitary confinement, followed by a period of congregate labor that would determine the prisoner's date of release and that would eventually earn a "ticket of release" during which the individual's progress on the outside would be monitored.

Wines soon envisioned the creation of a world organization in which all nations would come together to establish an ideal prison system. As a first step in this mission, Wines played a crucial role in convening the meeting of the National Prison Congress in America. In 1870, 130 delegates from twenty-four states, Canada, and South America met in Cincinnati. Among the most prestigious attendees were none other than Sir Walter Crofton and Enoch Wines. Both were among the forty delegates who delivered papers at the Congress. Following the delivery of various presentations, which ranged from jails and prison hygiene to executive pardon and indeterminate sentencing, the Congress joined ranks and adopted the Declaration of Principles, which is regarded as one of the most progressive documents of prison reform. The National Prison Association would eventually provide the nucleus for what would become the American Correctional Association.

Elmira Reformatory

The Elmira Reformatory in New York laid the groundwork for the development of the reformatory movement that would characterize the last three decades of the 1800s. Elmira was set up for youths aged sixteen to thirty years of age who were serving their first prison terms. Reflecting the heritage of the Auburn design, Elmira's architecture consisted of interior cell blocks for nighttime solitary confinement with congregate workshops for daily routine. The main difference between the prison and the reformatory was Elmira's greater emphasis on trade training and academic education.

Two noteworthy features of the reformatory that differentiated it from state prisons were an emphasis on indeterminate sentencing and the mark system. According to the Elmira system, all sentences had a maximum, but prisoners could earn parole through hard work and good behavior. Prisoners were graded into three classes according to accomplishments and deportment. New prisoners were entered in the second grade

for six months and could then be either
demoted to the third grade for bad conduct or
promoted to the first grade when they earned
the required "marks." Once promoted to the first
grade, prisoners could then be considered for
parole. During the heyday of the reformatory
movement, which lasted between 1877 and
1901, twelve states created similar institutions.

CRIME AND PUNISHMENT

Americans of the Civil War era were beset by all
manner of criminal activities, some new, others
harkening back to the past. Whether living in
crowded cities or living on a remote frontier
landscape, Americans had become accustomed to
violence following the massive bloodletting of
the Civil War. During the late 1870s, the cities
became a crucible for criminal activity. New
York City reported 80,000 crimes in 1868 and,
according to historian Alexander Callow, by the
early 1870s boasted 30,000 professional thieves
and 2,000 gambling dens.[19]

According to David R. Johnson in his study
of the development of the American police, the
"ingenuity and boldness" of professional criminals made them "technically superior" to the
police.[20] This was especially true in the emerging
wave of bank burglaries in the 1860s.

Birth of Organized Criminal Activity

The Civil War era created a variety of opportunities for organized crime activity. Abraham
Lincoln's conscription law with its loophole for
paying replacements presented enterprising individuals such as Chicago's Michael McDonald
with an opportunity to reap a financial whirlwind
from the sectional conflict cleaving America's
heartland. McDonald recruited numerous sordid
denizens of the underworld to work in his organized scheme by which individuals would collect
bounties ranging from $100 to $1,000 to enlist in
the Union army and then would promptly desert.
McDonald was given a commission for each case
of "bounty jumping" as he transported them to

different regions to repeat the scheme. According
to one estimate, perhaps half of the 268,000 cases
of desertion during the war were the result of
bounty jumping. While this cannot be substantiated, it is clear that McDonald profited enough
from this business to set up several gambling dens
after the cessation of hostilities.

Even New York City policemen got caught
up in the bounty racket. In 1865, Lafayette
Baker, the chief of the National Detective Police,
under the War Department, uncovered a system
in which police as well as other city officials colluded in a thriving business to earn fraudulent
bounties. According to local newspapers, after
the war an increase in robberies and burglaries
was linked to many criminals who no longer had
access to the bounty racket.[21]

Chicago would prove an inviting environment for underworld figures beginning in
the 1830s as burglars, gamblers, prostitutes, counterfeiters, and gunmen were drawn to the city
that would become synonymous with organized
crime in the next century. There was little here
in the way of law enforcement until the mid-
1850s. By the Civil War, crime lords, such as
Englishman Roger Plant, were operating enterprises offering gambling and prostitution. Gear-
ing activities toward soldiers at nearby military
outposts, Plant's operation provided a warning-
and-escape system that protected customers from
military patrols. Other gambling establishments
operated without serious interference from the
authorities, setting a pattern in Chicago that
would become all too familiar in the 1920s and
1930s. By the 1860s, gambling syndicates had
become a familiar presence on the urban landscape in Chicago and elsewhere.

Capital Punishment

Abolitionist agitation against the death penalty
peaked in the 1840s. According to one authority,
once executions in New York state were moved
indoors and other states made the transition to
private hangings, reformers began to direct their
energies elsewhere. Others suggest that the
bloodshed of the Civil War ended the move-

ment. While antigallows societies persisted into the 1850s, the outbreak of the war made it difficult for Union supporters who advocated war to end slavery to support the end of individual cases of capital punishment. Indeed, according to historian David Brion Davis, in the aftermath of the Civil War, which claimed 600,000 soldiers, "men's finer sensibilities, which had once been revolted by the execution of a fellow human being, seemed hardened and blunted."[22]

During the Civil War, soldiers were routinely executed for desertion and other crimes. According to one historian, 267 Union soldiers were executed between 1861 and 1867, more than the total of all other military executions in America's other wars.[23] This same researcher suggests that there was a certain bias toward ethnicity (Irish), race (African American), and religion (Catholic) in selecting cases of military criminals for executions. Despite Lincoln's commutation of death sentences for desertion in February 1864, the hangings and shootings apparently persisted to the end of hostilities.

The Post–Civil War West

One would be hard pressed to find a region of the country with more crime than America's large urban areas. However, the cessation of Civil War hostilities led to more complex patterns of crime and punishment in the West. While shootouts, cattle rustling, and robberies dominate popular mythology, criminal activity was more often confined to less violent crimes, such as embezzlement, petty theft and larceny, gambling, prostitution, drunkenness, and disorderly conduct.

Corruption

The 1850s and 1860s witnessed the rise of what one urban historian has described as "an American original,"[24] the city boss. No one exemplified the corruption and excesses of urban America more than William Marcy Tweed. At the zenith of his power in the late 1860s, he controlled New York City's government, courts, and police as well as the state legislature.

Best known by the sobriquet "Boss," Tweed rose to power in 1850s New York. Elected to the New York Board of Alderman in 1851 and then to an undistinguished term in the U.S. Congress, he returned home and in 1857 was elected to the Board of Supervisors, a position that audited city expenditures, appointed election inspectors, and supervised public improvements that more often than not turned into "pork barrel" spending. Over the next thirteen years, Tweed was elected president of the board four times, each time gaining more power and more access to fraud and graft. As deputy street commissioner in 1863, he had control over thousands of jobs that could be dispensed to his supporters.

While Tweed was cementing his ties to a hardy core of constituents, he also made sure to consolidate his power with the local Democratic Party organization at Tammany Hall. Following the Civil War, Tweed emerged as the leader of the Democratic Party. Considered the nation's first political boss, Tweed wielded tremendous power by using patronage powers to keep his supporters employed. The Tweed Ring began its reign in 1866, and over the next five years Tweed colluded with city leaders to create a dynasty of graft unprecedented in American history up to that time. Accepting kickbacks from contractors and embellishing building costs for his own profit, Tweed was soon targeted by reformers such as *Harper's Weekly* cartoonist and social commentator Thomas Nast.

One of the most powerful urban political machines in American history, Tammany Hall was founded in 1789. Created by a Revolutionary War veteran, it was originally an organization named the Society of Saint Tammany after a legendary Indian chief. In its early years, it was a fraternal society rather than a political party. In the early 1800s, Tammany Hall's nationwide membership declined and centered only in New York City, where it would evolve into an organizational engine, or "machine," driving the Democratic Party. From 1855 to the early 1930s, Tammany Hall's political machine would dominate New York City. Often scorned for its corruption and graft, following the arrest and conviction of Boss Tweed in 1871, Tammany made a comeback just three years later and regained control of the city government.

A campaign against Tweed came to a head in 1871 when the *New York Times* obtained reports of fraud and extravagance from a disgruntled former confidant of Tweed's. Following the publication of these charges, Tweed was soon arrested for defrauding the city treasury of at least $6 million. After two trials, Tweed was sentenced to twelve years, a sentence that was subsequently reduced to one year. Rearrested after his release, he escaped from prison and fled first to Cuba and then to Spain. He was soon recognized and extradited back to the United States and died in jail in 1878.

A sign of changing times on the horizon, the year 1872 saw America's first great "robber baron" plot during the Credit Mobilier scandal. One of the greatest congressional scandals of the nineteenth century, a financial unit known as Credit Mobilier was created to finance the construction of the Union Pacific Railroad. In order to get the best possible terms on land grants and rights-of-way, representatives of the unit sold company stocks at a huge discount to congressmen that would "do the most good." In 1872, just one year after the Tweed Ring scandal hit the newspapers, the *New York Sun* broke the story, resulting in a congressional investigation that implicated the current vice president, Schuyler Colfax, and former Speaker of the House as well as representative and future president James A. Garfield. In the end, economic historians have estimated Credit Mobilier profits to have ranged from $13 million to $23 million.

VIOLENCE

The 1850s saw a resurgence in sectional violence over the slavery issue. Nowhere was the strife more intense than in Kansas, where rival land claims, town sites, railroad routes, and the question of slavery led to violent confrontations. Also contributing to the rising tide of violence in the 1850s was the growth in American gun production. With the increased availability of firearms, American cities for the first time thrived with gun shops offering guns and their accoutrements to a "large minority of Americans [who] found confidence their guns and longed to demonstrate their proficiency."[25]

Sectional Violence

Heralding the bloodshed that was yet to come, during the 1850s many parts of the country witnessed the intimidation of civilians whose sectional leanings conflicted with their own. The region of Kansas, Nebraska, and Missouri was blighted by a guerrilla warfare pitting "Jayhawkers" and "Red Legs" against those they viewed as Confederate sympathizers. In reality, these gangs of bushwhackers used wartime hatreds as a cover for a campaign of horse stealing, looting, and terror. In areas such as southern Iowa, Illinois and Indiana, southern supporters called "Copperheads" or "Butternuts" wreaked havoc against Unionists in like fashion. The weight of secession fell even harder on Unionists living in southern strongholds that dotted Kentucky, Tennessee, and Virginia.

In May 1856, proslavery forces sacked the free-soil town of Lawrence, Kansas. For John Brown, a failed merchant and businessman, this event marked a turning point in his life. Furious at the attack, he summoned volunteers for a "secret mission."

Reviled as a terrorist fanatic and revered as a fervent abolitionist, John Brown was one of the most controversial individuals of the Civil War era. Recent scholarship traces the birth of domestic terrorism to his May 1856 attack on the proslavery hamlet along Pottawatomie Creek, Kansas. A puritanical Congregationalist, Brown believed that God had chosen him for a special purpose. In 1855, Brown followed five of his sons to Kansas to help defend antislavery settlers from proslavery "border ruffians" from Missouri. On May 23, 1856, Brown led seven men (including four of his sons) in an attack against proslavery settlers along Pottawatomie Creek, further igniting sectional tensions.

Convinced that only brutal action directed against slave owners would win the undeclared war over slavery, Brown ordered his followers to slash to death five settlers with broadswords. Brown's actions on behalf of abolitionism culminated in his ill-fated attack on the federal arsenal at Harper's Ferry in 1859. Hoping to provoke a slave uprising in the South, Brown and eighteen of his acolytes captured the armory and rifle factory and waited for escaped slaves to flock to his banner. But none came, and after two days of battle, Brown was captured.

During his subsequent trial, his lawyers tried to persuade him to plead insanity, but he would have none of it, and on December 2, 1859, Brown was elevated to martyrdom by abolitionists as he mounted the gallows to his death. Prior to his death, he handed a note to his jailer that read, "I John Brown am now quite certain that the crimes of this guilty land: will never be purged away; but with Blood." Never in American history, it seemed, were so many people willing to die for their beliefs. To this day, Brown remains a complex man, and opinions are split over his legacy. But at least one writer ascribes his behavior as an example of "conscious political terrorism." If this is true, then his deeds continue to resonate in the misdirected terrorist campaigns of modern-day zealots, such as the John Brown Brigade (which was embroiled in violent conflict with the North Carolina Ku Klux Klan), Ted Kaczynski (the Unabomber), and Timothy McVeigh (the Oklahoma City bomber).

The New York City Draft Riots

The 1863 New York City antidraft riot was probably America's greatest urban riot. Lasting from July 13 to July 16, 1863, until recently historians have accepted the number of fatalities as close to 1,000. However, research by historians Iver Bernstein and Adrian Cook suggests that the figure was perhaps one-tenth of previous estimates, which would still make it the bloodiest in American history.

The draft riots stemmed in part from President Lincoln's conscription laws, which antagonized Irish immigrants and fueled racial hatreds. Finding themselves on the lowest rungs of the social ladder, Irish immigrants resented the fact that they should fight a war to free the blacks and worried that freedom would bring black migration north to compete for jobs. Irish gangs, on the other hand, saw an opportunity to take advantage of the situation in order to loot and pillage unimpeded. Exacerbating class tensions of the era was the fact that better-capitalized draftees could pay substitutes to take their place in the ranks, while the impoverished had no other legal alternative. According to Iver Bernstein, the riot was precipitated by a variety of factors, including Confederate sympathy, resentment toward the conscription act, and ethnic hatred. However, contrary to the traditional explanations for the bloodletting, the riot should be viewed within "the context of an ongoing process of urban change beginning in the early 1850s" as well as a "a new complex of social, cultural, and political relations."[26]

The New York draft riots were driven by a variety of circumstances. Poor citizens saw it as an opportunity to protest squalid living conditions and the substitute system. Northern Democrats inflamed the racist sentiments of the Irish by telling draftees that they were being sent to free southern blacks who would thank them by coming north and taking away jobs.

Much of the racial violence was directed at New York City's sizable free black population as well as the fledgling police force. In the 1860s, the police were still poorly equipped to handle riots of this magnitude. Another problem was that while the 1850s police force was regarded as community based, the 1863 force was viewed as instruments of the state government. With little besides batons and handguns and occasional military drills, their only response against the riots consisted of violent retribution. During the New York draft riots, as policemen found themselves targeted along with any blacks, one police commissioner ordered his men to "take no prisoners," and another wrote in his memoirs that he told his men to "kill every man who has a club."[27]

The Ku Klux Klan

The birth of the Ku Klux Klan introduced a new source of American violence in the aftermath of the Civil War. Regarded as a response to the social, cultural, and economic changes that many white southerners found so disturbing during the onset of Reconstruction, the Klan has undergone a variety of personifications over the past 140 years.

Created as a club in Pulaski, Tennessee, in 1866 by six former Confederate soldiers, few could have imagined the direction the Klan would take in its various incarnations over the next century. Well-educated members from upstanding families, the six men were inspired by Greek-letter fraternities in college to borrow the Greek word *kuklos,* meaning "circle of friends," to name their small fraternity the Ku-Klux, adding "Klan" only to give it an alliterative intensity. It was not long before the name would inspire its more sinister connotations.

As the six initial members sought new members, they masked themselves in anonymity through the use of white masks with eyes cut out for the nose and eyes. This was soon complemented by a long robe. In the years of Reconstruction, it was not difficult to attract new members, especially after adopting a goal of maintaining white supremacy. Over the next decade, white terrorist groups waged an often bloody campaign to undermine the social, economic, and political reforms of the radical Republic agenda.

The main target of Klan night riders and similarly motivated standard bearers for racial supremacy were the recently freed African Americans. Lacking a formal organizational structure, individual vigilante groups attempted to violently enforce the racial codes that were threatened by the end of slavery. Striking usually at night to achieve the maximum threat, specifically targeted were blacks who defied white authority. In an attempt to restrict the free movement of blacks on local roads, open season was declared on those who attempted to move about freely. Historian James W. Clarke compared the Klan to "a uniformed, paramilitary extension of the earlier practice of slave patrols that had roamed the countryside looking for runaways."[28]

Reconstruction Violence

Simmering animosities between supporters of both sides of the war often escalated into bloodshed during the Reconstruction years from 1866 to 1877. In perhaps a warning of what could be expected in the postslavery years, on July 30, 1866, Union sympathizers and freedmen met at Mechanics' Hall in New Orleans to demand a more humiliating response to the former Confederates. It was not long before a large crowd of armed whites descended on the revelers and fired into their midst. What started as a celebration of the passage of recent civil rights legislation quickly turned into a massacre. By the time federal troops arrived, thirty-four black and three white Unionists had been murdered and dozens wounded. This incident would be repeated in other southern cities with the onset of the Reconstruction and the military occupation of the South.

Recent research indicates that continuing rivalries between Union and Confederate boosters led to the notorious Hatfield–McCoy feud, which lasted from 1873 to 1883 in the mountains of West Virginia, a region that also included the mountain communities of western Virginia and Kentucky. Mountain feuds persisted because of an absence of regular law enforcement and a tradition of people's taking law into their own hands. East Texas was perhaps the most violent region of the country during the post–Civil War era, with feuds such as the Sutton–Taylor feud of 1869–1877 rivaling the Hatfield–McCoy feud in its vitriol. The southwestern states also witnessed a host of violent conflicts in this period stemming from wartime dislocation, Reconstruction animosities, the rapid growth of the cattle industry, and the instability produced by Indian wars with the Comanches and the Kiowas.

Interracial Violence

Despite the end of slavery in the South, some planters refused to recognize emancipation, and on occasion freedmen were beaten, killed, or mutilated to prevent them from leaving the plantation. Local law enforcement often supported planters by authorizing more punitive punishment for blacks than for whites. This could include public whippings, pillories, and chain gangs, clearly an attempt to send a message to the new freemen. According to Reconstruction historian George C. Rable, with little chance of a fair hearing in local courts, the Freedmen's Bureau and the army were their last resort but were rarely able to help.[29] Justice continued to be color conscious for blacks. Officials rarely heard complaints by black litigants against white defendants, nor were great attempts made to apprehend whites who killed freedmen. According to Union General Philip Sheridan, "My own opinion is that the trial of a white man for the murder of a freedman in Texas would be a farce."[30] With little protection from local courts and law enforcement, the army was seen as the only source of protection.

The death penalty capital of the industrialized world, Texas, had until the 1990s never executed a white man for the execution of an African American.

The years following the Civil War witnessed the majority of the Indian–white confrontations in the West as settlers flocked beyond the Mississippi River to take advantage of the Homestead Act passed by congressional Republicans in 1862. That same year saw one of the worst Indian uprisings in American history when the Sioux of Minnesota revolted against inhumane treatment by government Indian agents. Following the killing of between 500 and 800 white settlers, federal troops and state militia defeated the Indians and restored order. In the end, thirty-eight Indians were hanged

at one time from the same gallows, the largest mass hanging in American history. According to one nineteenth-century source, "they were placed upon a platform facing inwards, and dropped by the cutting of rope all at one time."[31]

NOTABLE TRIALS

Trial of the Lincoln Conspirators (1865)

The trial of seven coconspirators charged with assassinating President Lincoln opened on May 9, 1865, less than a month after the assassination. The proceedings would be marked by controversy and rancor from the start. Among the most celebrated of the conspirators were Mrs. Mary Surratt and Dr. Samuel Mudd, the latter charged with helping attend the injured John Wilkes Booth on his flight from Washington, D.C., to sanctuary in the South.

The seven prisoners were given one to three days to prepare their cases and obtain counsel. The first day of the trial was held in a secret court session, reminiscent of the Star Chamber of Tudor England. Public demand soon opened up the proceedings to the press and the public. The court was almost immediately challenged on the grounds that it was a military tribunal. The main justification for this sort of trial was that the United States was at war and that the deceased president had been the commander in chief of the armed forces.

The defendants argued that a military court did not have jurisdiction since the accused were not members of the armed forces, but their pleas were overruled. The defendants then asked to be tried separately, and this too was denied. By most standards, the trial was extraordinary. The defendants at this time did not have the right to testify on their own behalf. To prevent the defendants from taking their own lives, great steps were taken to guard against suicide. The prisoners were kept in solitary confinement before their court appearances, and their faces were covered by canvas hoods with openings at the mouth for eating and breathing.

During the seven-week trial, the prosecution paraded a slew of witnesses, and after several more days of rebuttal and final presentations, the case went to military judges who then deliberated for two days. Conducted amid the clamor of postwar hysteria, the defendants were connected to every misdeed associated with the Confederacy, including the Andersonville military prison and the plot to burn New York City. Numerous witnesses who could have helped the defense were not called to testify, and little evidence connected Mary Surratt to the conspiracy outside of owning the rooming house where the plot was hatched.

At the end of June 1865, the commission reached a separate verdict for each defendant. Of the eventual eight defendants, four were sentenced to be hanged, including the only woman, Mary Surratt. An execution date was set for July 7, only twelve weeks after Lincoln's death. The public was not informed of the date until two days prior to the execution. Despite a plea for clemency on behalf of Surratt, the four mounted the gallows on a hot July day while a crowd of spectators watched. To the end, most believed that Surratt would be spared. But when all hope was lost, conspirator Lewis Paine told the executioner, "If I had two lives to give, I'd give one gladly to save Mrs. Surratt." All four were then executed at the same moment.

CONCLUSIONS

The Civil War generated extraordinary problems for the American criminal justice system. By its conclusion in 1865, many of the system's components had been altered and modified. The abolition of slavery and the return of traumatized war veterans to every region of the country would lead to a rise in crime and a strain on the courts, policing, and prisons.

The end of the Civil War tested America's developing criminal justice system and introduced new forms of criminality while stimulating the development of new crime-fighting strategies and institutions. Ku Klux Klan night riders, organized gambling, counterfeiters, train robbers, and bank robbery would test the ingenuity of law enforcement on both the federal and the local level.

Although there was a perceptible shift in public opinion over the death penalty between the eighteenth century and the Civil War, only Michigan, Rhode Island, and Wisconsin abolished capital punishment. The Civil War years sapped the abolitionist movement of much of its vigor as opponents to capital punishment found an array of issues and crusades that had more impact on everyday life to pour their energies into. As executions were removed from public spectacle to behind prison walls, there was less opportunity to incite activists and other opponents. Gauging the public reaction to these developments was the response to the public hanging of the Lincoln conspirators, which few disapproved of.

Slavery officially ended by constitutional action with the passage of the Thirteenth Amendment in December 1865. The end of the Civil War was followed by a period of Reconstruction lasting from 1865 to 1877, during which mob violence abated in northern cities as vigilantism seemed to grow in intensity west of the Mississippi River.

By the 1860s, urban policing had finally left its colonial roots behind, as uniformed officers patrolled beats in many major cities. Auguring a century of tremendous advances in investigation techniques, as early as the 1850s precincts were linked to central headquarters by telegraph wires. New York City was credited with introducing a "Rogues Portrait Gallery" in the 1850s, displaying photos of hundreds of known criminals. The next decade would see the introduction of the first telegraph police boxes, by which a police officer could turn a key in a box and have his location and number be automatically recorded at headquarters. By the late 1860s, retirement pensions were available for New York police veterans, and an insurance fund was established for the families of policemen killed or disabled on duty. In 1871, 112 police officials gathered to discuss the late increase in crime, setting into motion a series of meetings that would lead to the creation of the National Chiefs of Police Union (1893), the forerunner of the International Chiefs of Police (1902).

By the 1850s, the era of correctional reform had almost ground to a halt, as focus was diverted to the prison industry. During the war years, prisons were major manufacturers of clothing, shoes, furniture, and uniforms. Following the Civil War, southern prisons were increasingly populated by black convicts. But elsewhere, prison reform would be reinvigorated in the years prior to the meeting of the National Prison Congress in 1870, and during the next decade, opposition by trade unions led to restrictions on the interstate commerce of prison goods. As the 1870s saw the arrival of the "Gilded Age," northern prisons, modeled on factories and replete with shops and contractors, stood in sharp contrast to southern prisons, which for the most part remained an anachronism. Michael Stephen Hindus's portrait of the South Carolina penitentiary, which was "almost entirely black, with its chain gangs, field hands, work songs, and white overseers, [and] resembled the plantation,"[32] remains an indelible reminder of the divergent societies in the North and the South.

The end of the Civil War was followed by one of the most dramatic events in American constitutional history when President Andrew Johnson survived impeachment by one vote in 1868. Unlike Great Britain, where impeachment is part of the political process, impeachment American style was a legal instrument since the law stated that a president may be removed from office only for "treason, bribery, or other high Crimes and misdemeanors" and only after a trial in the Senate presided over by the chief justice. Johnson's impeachment was the result of a bitter feud between the president and Congress over Reconstruction policy and over Johnson's supposedly "unconstitutional" attempt to remove Secretary of War Edwin Stanton from office against the wishes of the Senate. Following his trial, which lasted from March to April, Johnson

narrowly kept his office but preserved the right to presidential independence.

Lincoln's assassination, the impeachment of Johnson, and the turmoil accompanying Reconstruction were larger-than-life episodes that captivated the nation and taxed every segment of the criminal justice system at all levels—federal, state, and local. The end of the Civil War would set the stage for the nation's greatest outbreak of outlawry in the West as the eastern cities came to grips with the complexities of the "Gilded Age" and the rise of the "robber barons."

Point–Counterpoint

Ex Parte Milligan: The Suspension of Habeas Corpus (1861/66)

On March 3, 1863, Congress authorized President Abraham Lincoln to suspend the writ of habeas corpus (although Lincoln evolved his own constitutional interpretation by which he suspended the writ in 1861 without Congressional approval). On September 15, 1863 the writ was suspended in cases where officers held individuals for offenses against the military. This was considered one of Lincoln's most controversial decisions as president. Resistance to this decision resonates today in the aftermath of September 11, 2001. In the first selection Lincoln defends his suspension of Habeas Corpus in 1861. The second passage is from the landmark Court decision Ex Parte Milligan. In this the Supreme Court denounced military tribunals in areas where the civil courts were open.

Soon after the first call for militia it was considered a duty to authorize the Commanding General in proper cases, according to his discretion, to suspend the privilege of the writ of *habeas corpus,* or, in other words, to arrest and detain without resort to the ordinary processes and forms of law such individuals as he might deem dangerous to the public safety. This authority has purposely been exercised but very sparingly. Nevertheless, the legality and propriety of what has been done under it are questioned, and the attention of the country has been called to the proposition that one who is sworn to "take care that

Source: Richardson, ed., *Messages and Papers of the Presidents,* VI., pp. 24–25, 1913; *Ex Parte Milligan,* 4 Wallace 2 (1866).

the laws be faithfully executed" should not himself violate them. Of course some consideration was given to the questions of power and propriety before this matter was acted upon. The whole of the laws which were required to be faithfully executed were being resisted and failing of execution in nearly one-third of the States. Must they be allowed to finally fail of execution, even had it been perfectly clear that by the use of the means necessary to their execution some single law, made in such extreme tenderness of the citizen's liberty that practically it relieves more of the guilty than of the innocent, should to a very limited extent be violated? To state the question more directly, Are all the laws *but one* to go unexecuted, and the Government itself go to pieces lest that one be violated? Even in such a case, would not the official oath be broken if the Government should be overthrown when it was believed that disregarding the single law would tend to preserve it? But it was not believed that this question was presented. It was not believed that any law was violated. The provision of the Constitution that "the privilege of the writ of *habeas corpus* shall not be suspended unless when, in cases of rebellion or invasion, the public safety may require it" is equivalent to a provision—is a provision—that such privilege may be suspended when, in cases of rebellion or invasion, the public safety *does* require it. It was decided that we have a case of rebellion and that the public safety does require the qualified suspension of the privilege of the writ which was authorized to be made. Now it is insisted that Congress, and not the Executive, is vested with this power; but the Constitution itself is silent as to which or who is to exercise the power; and as the provision was plainly made for a dangerous emergency, it can not be believed the framers of the instrument intended that in every case the danger should run its course until Congress could be called together, the very assembling of which might be prevented, as was intended in this case, by the rebellion.

No more extended argument is now offered, as an opinion at some length will probably be presented by the Attorney-General. Whether there shall be any legislation upon the subject, and, if any, what, is submitted entirely to the better judgment of Congress.

DAVIS J.: . . . The controlling question in the case is this: Upon the *facts* stated in Milligan's petition, and the exhibits filed, had the military commission mentioned in its *jurisdiction,* legally, to try and sentence him? Milligan, not a resident of one of the rebellious states, or a prisoner of war, but a citizen of Indiana for twenty years past, and never in the military or naval service, is, while at his home, arrested by the military power of the United States, imprisoned, and, on certain criminal charges preferred against him, tried, convicted, and sentenced to be hanged by a military commission, organized under the direction of the military commander of the military district of Indiana. Had this tribunal the *legal* power and authority to try and punish this man? . . .

The Constitution of the United States is a law for rulers and people, equally in war and in peace, and covers with the shield of its protection all classes of men, at all times, and under all circumstances. No doctrine, involving more pernicious consequences, was ever invented by the wit of man than that any of its provisions can be suspended during any of the great exigencies of government. Such a doctrine leads directly to anarchy or despotism, but the theory of necessity on which it is based is false; for the government, within the Constitution, has all the powers granted to it which are necessary to preserve its existence; as has been happily proved by the result of the great effort to throw off its just authority.

Have any of the rights guaranteed by the Constitution been violated in the case of Milligan? and if so, what are they?

Every trial involves the exercise of judicial power; and from what source did the military commission that tried him derive their authority? Certainly no part of the judicial power of the country was conferred on them; because the Constitution expressly vests it "in one Supreme Court and such inferior courts as the Congress may from time to time ordain and establish," and it is not pretended that the commission was a court ordained and established by Congress. They cannot justify on the mandate of the President, because he is controlled by law, and has his appropriate sphere of duty, which is to execute, not to make, the laws; and there is "no unwritten criminal code to which resort can be had as a source of jurisdiction."

But it is said that the jurisdiction is complete under the "laws and usages of war."

It can serve no useful purpose to inquire what those laws and usages are, whence they originated, where found, and on whom they operate; they can never be applied to citizens in states which have upheld the authority of the government, and where the courts are open and their process unobstructed. This Court has judicial knowledge that in Indiana the federal authority was always unopposed, and its courts always open to hear criminal accusations and redress grievances; and no usage of war would sanction a military trial there for any offense whatever of a citizen in civil life, in nowise connected with the military service. Congress could grant no such power; and to the honor of our national legislature be it said, it has never been provoked by the state of the country even to attempt its exercise. One of the plainest constitutional provisions was, therefore, infringed when Milligan was tried by a court not ordained and established by Congress, and not composed of judges appointed during good behavior.

Why was he not delivered to the circuit court of Indiana to be proceeded against according to law? . . . If it was dangerous, in the distracted condition of affairs, to leave Milligan unrestrained of his liberty, because he "conspired against the government, afforded aid and comfort to rebels, and incited the people to insurrection," the *law* said, arrest him, confine him closely, render him powerless to do further mischief; and then present his case to the grand jury of the district, with proofs of his guilt, and, if indicted, try him according to the course of the common law. If this had been done, the Constitution would have been vindicated, the law of 1863 enforced, and the securities for personal liberty preserved and defended.

Another guarantee of freedom was broken when Milligan was denied a trial by jury. . . .

It is claimed that martial law covers with its broad mantle the proceedings of this military commission. The proposition is this: that in a time of war the commander of an armed force (if, in his opinion, the exigencies of the country demand it, and of which he is to judge) has the power, within the lines of his military district, to suspend all civil rights and their remedies, and subject citizens as well as soldiers to the rule of *his will;* and in the exercise of his lawful authority cannot be restrained, except by his superior officer or the President of the United States. . . .

The statement of this proposition shows its importance; for, if true, republican government is a failure, and there is an end of liberty regulated by law. Martial law, established on such a basis, destroys every guarantee of the Constitution, and effectually renders the "military independent of, and superior to, the civil power,"— the attempt to do which by the king

of Great Britain was deemed by our fathers such an offense, that they assigned it to the world as one of the causes which impelled them to declare their independence. Civil liberty and this kind of martial law cannot endure together; the antagonism is irreconcilable; and, in the conflict, one or the other must perish. . . .

The necessities of the service, during the late rebellion, required that the loyal states should be placed within the limits of certain military districts and commanders appointed in them; and, it is urged, that this, in a military sense, constituted them the theatre of military operations; and, as in this case, Indiana had been and was again threatened with invasion by the enemy, the occasion was furnished to establish martial law. The conclusion does not follow from the premises. If armies were collected in Indiana, they were to be employed in another locality, where the laws were obstructed and the national authority disputed. On *her* soil there was no hostile foot; if once invaded, that invasion was at an end, and with it all pretext for martial law. Martial law cannot arise from a *threatened* invasion. The necessity must be actual and present; the invasion real, such as effectually closes the courts and deposes the civil administration. . . .

Martial rule can never exist where the courts are open, and in the proper and unobstructed exercise of their jurisdiction. It is also confined to the locality of actual war. Because, during the late rebellion it could have been enforced in Virginia, where the national authority was overturned and the courts driven out, it does not follow that it should obtain in Indiana, where that authority was never disputed, and justice was always administered. And so in the case of a foreign invasion, martial rule may become a necessity in one state, when, in another, it would be "mere lawless violence." . . .

SOURCES

Allen, Oliver E. 1993. *The Tiger: The Rise and Fall of Tammany Hall.* New York: Addison-Wesley.

Alotta, Robert L. 1989. *Civil War Justice: Union Army Executions Under Lincoln.* Shippensburg, PA.: White Mane Publishing.

Bechtel, H. Kenneth. 1995. *State Police in the United States: A Socio-Historical Analysis.* Westport, Conn.: Greenwood Press.

Bellesiles, Michael A. 2000. *Arming America: Origins of a National Gun Culture.* New York: Alfred A. Knopf.

Bernstein, Iver. 1990. *The New York City Draft Riots: Their Significance for American Society and Politics in the Age of the Civil War.* New York: Oxford University Press.

Bessler, John D. 1997. *Death in the Dark: Midnight Executions in America.* Boston: Northeastern University Press.

Brown, Richard Maxwell. 1970. *American Violence.* Englewood Cliffs, NJ.: Prentice Hall.

Callow, Alexander B., Jr. 1966. *The Tweed Ring.* New York: Oxford University Press.

———. 1970. *The City Boss in America: An Interpretive Reader.* New York: Oxford University Press.

Carleton, Mark T. 1971. *Politics and Punishment: The History of the Louisiana State Penal System.* Baton Rouge: Louisiana State University Press.

Chalmers, David. 1987. *Hooded Americanism: The History of the Ku Klux Klan.* 3rd ed. Durham, N.C.: Duke University Press.

Chowder, Ken. 2000. "The Father of American Terrorism." *American Heritage,* February/March, pp. 81–91.

Clarke, James W. 1998. *The Lineaments of Wrath: Race, Violent Crime, and American Culture.* New Brunswick, N.J.: Transaction Publishers.

Cook, Adrian. 1974. *The Armies of the Streets: The New York City Draft Riots of 1863.* Lexington, Ky.: University Press of Kentucky.

Donald, David Herbert. 1995. *Lincoln.* New York: Simon and Schuster.

Harring, Sidney L. 1983. *Policing a Class Society: The Experience of American Cities, 1865–1915.* New Brunswick: New Jersey: Rutgers University Press.

Hindus, Michael S. 1980. *Prison and Plantation: Crime, Justice, and Authority in Massachusetts and South Carolina, 1767–1878.* Chapel Hill: University of North Carolina Press.

Johnson, David R. 1979. *Policing the Urban Underworld: The Impact of Crime on the Development of the American Police, 1800–1887.* Philadelphia: Temple University Press.

———. 1995. *Illegal Tender: Counterfeiting and the Secret Service in Nineteenth-Century America.* Washington, D.C.: Smithsonian Institution Press.

Lane, Roger. 1967. *Policing the City: Boston, 1822–1885.* Cambridge, Mass.: Harvard University Press.

McPherson, James M. 1991. *Abraham Lincoln and the Second American Revolution.* New York: Oxford University Press.

Mississippi, *Laws of the State* [1865]. 1896. Jackson, Miss., pp. 82–86.

Monkkonen, Eric. 1981. *Police in Urban America, 1860–1920.* New York: Cambridge University Press.

Morgan, H. Wayne. 1974. *Yesterday's Addicts: American Society and Drug Abuse, 1865–1920.* Norman: University of Oklahoma Press.

Neely, Mark E. 1991. *The Fate of Liberty: Abraham Lincoln and Civil Liberties.* New York: Oxford University Press.

Oates, Stephen B. 1970. *To Purge This Land with Blood.* New York: Harper & Row.

Rable, George C. 1984. *But There Was No Peace: The Role of Violence in the Politics of Reconstruction.* Athens: University of Georgia Press.

Randall, James G. 1964. *Constitutional Problems under Lincoln.* Urbana: University of Illinois Press.

Reinders, Robert. 1977. "Militia and Public Order in Nineteenth-Century America." *American Studies* 11, no. 2 (81–101).

Richardson, James. 1970. *The New York Police: Colonial Times to 1901.* New York: Oxford University Press.

Steinberg, Allen. 1984. "From Private Prosecution to Plea Bargaining: Criminal Prosecution, the District Attorney, and American Legal History." *Crime & Delinquency* 30, no. 4 (October): 568–92.

Wade, Wyn Craig. 1987. *The Fiery Cross: The Ku Klux Klan in America.* New York: Simon and Schuster.

Wilson, Theodore B. 1965. *The Black Codes of the South.* Tuscaloosa: University of Alabama Press.

CRITICAL THINKING QUESTIONS

1. What impact did the Civil War have on corrections in the United States? Compare and contrast developments in different regions of the country.

2. Compare the development of modern policing in various regions of America between the 1850s and 1870s. Discuss the evolution of federal and state policing in the late nineteenth century.

3. What conditions necessitated the creation of private police forces such as the Pinkertons?

4. How did pre–Civil War violence differ from postwar bloodletting? Discuss the impact of race and region on violence patterns during this period.

5. Did civil rights legislation following the war have any impact on the criminal justice system? If so, at which level—state, federal, or local?

CRIMINAL JUSTICE HISTORY ON THE INTERNET

For more on the assassination of President Abraham Lincoln, see http://members.aol.com/RVSNorton/Lincoln.html. At this site, students will find links to the conspiracy trial, photographs of conspirators and their execution, an eyewitness account to the killing of John Wilkes Booth, and the Abraham Lincoln Research Site. A brief history of counterfeiting can be found at www.servicemart.com/money/histr1.htm. Ford's Theater, site of Lincoln's assassination, has its own Web page at www.nps.gov/foth/index2.htm. The history of convict leasing and prison labor is well documented at www.prisonactivist.org/crisis/labor-of-doing-time.html. The saga of the Pinkertons, including a number of links, is located at www.pinkertons.com/companyinfo/history/pinkerton/index.asp.

A discussion of the Comstock Law and associated links are available at http://womenshistory.about.com/library/ency/blwh_comstock.htm. A photograph and biographical sketch of Anthony Comstock is at www.historynet.com/picture/0205.htm. A discussion of the black codes following the Civil War can be found at www.bchm.org/wrr/recon/p10.html. Teaching Online offers a substantial number of links related to the black codes and early civil rights legislation at www.spartacus.schoolnet.co.uk/USASblackcodes.htm. Discussion of the black codes in the former Confederate states is at www.civilwarhome.com/blackcodes.htm.

There is a wealth of sites devoted to Boss Tweed, Tammany Hall, and corruption, including http://hubcap.clemson.edu/~ewgrego/ThNast and www.albany.edu/~dkw42/tweed.html.

A number of links to the post–Civil War era (1865–1880), including discussion of President Andrew Johnson's impeachment trial, the Reconstruction amendments, various court cases, Credit Mobilier, the *Slaughterhouse* cases, and *Bradwell v. Illinois,* are at www.ukans.edu/history/VL/USA/ERAS/reconstruction.html.

A first-person account of the New York City draft riots can be found at www.historynet.com/AmericasCivilWar/articles/2000/0500_text.htm. Other resources on the riots are at www.nyhistory.org/draftriots.html.

NOTES

1. Randall (1964, p. 521).
2. Donald (1995, p. 304).
3. Neely (1991, p. 234).
4. Wilson (1965, p. 138).
5. *Mississippi, Laws of the State* (1896, pp. 82–86).
6. Morgan (1974, p. 3).
7. According to Morgan (1974, p. 7), the "first proven case of morphine addiction resulting from hypodermic medication" was reported in 1864.
8. Morgan (1974, p. 9).
9. Monkkonen (1981, pp. 55–57).
10. Harring (1983, p. 31).
11. Lane (1967, p. 119).
12. Reinders (1977, p. 91).
13. Reinders (1977, p. 92).
14. Richardson (1970, p. 90).
15. Lane (1967, p. 119).
16. Richardson (1970, p. 123).
17. For the best analysis on state policing, see Bechtel (1995).
18. Carleton (1971, p. 13).
19. Callow (1970, p. 144).
20. Johnson (1979, p. 57).
21. Richardson (1970, p. 126).
22. Quoted in Bessler (1997, p. 46).
23. Alotta (1989, p. x).
24. Callow (1970, p. 3).
25. Bellesiles (2000, p. 387).
26. Bernstein (1990, p. 6).
27. Quoted in Richardson (1970, p. 143).
28. Clarke (1998, p. 84).
29. Rable (1984, p. 21).
30. Quoted in Rable (1984, p. 21).
31. Quoted in Brown (1970, p. 58).
32. Hindus (1980, p. 253).

8

CRIMINAL JUSTICE
IN VICTORIAN AMERICA
(1870–1901)

TIME LINE

1870	National Prison Congress adopts "Declaration of Principles"
1873	*Slaughterhouse* case Supreme Court decision
1873	*Bradwell v. Illinois*
1873	Passage of Comstock Law
1876	Publication of Lombroso's *Criminal Man*
1877	End of Reconstruction as final federal troops are removed from the South
1877	Ten Molly Maguires hanged on "Black Thursday"
1878	First matrons hired by police departments
1878	Massachusetts hires first paid probation officer
1879	Supreme Court upholds execution by firing squad as constitutional
1881	Assassination of President James A. Garfield by Charles Guiteau
1882	Paris police adopt Bertillon system of identification
1886	Publication of Thomas Byrnes's *Professional Criminals of America*
1886	Haymarket bombing
1890	Massacre of Sioux at Wounded Knee

1890	First execution by electric chair
1892	Homestead strike
1892	Publication of Sir Francis Galton's *Fingerprints*
1893	First meeting of National Chiefs of Police Union
1893	Trial of Lizzie Borden
1893	Publication of Hans Gross's *Criminal Investigation*
1894	Lexow hearings on police corruption in New York City
1895	Theodore Roosevelt appointed New York City police commissioner
1896	Argentina becomes first country to adopt fingerprinting as its main identification system
1896	*Plessy v. Ferguson* Supreme Court decision
1899	Passage of Juvenile Court Act by Illinois
1901	Assassination of President William McKinley
1901	Theodore Roosevelt makes Secret Service responsible for presidential protection

Prior to the Civil War, there was little support for centralization in a society that so revered the virtues of republicanism. However, the nation that emerged from the war was a much different society, and decentralization began to give way to organization in the arenas of politics and industry. Soon reformers in the area of criminal justice engaged the public conscience over poverty, insanity, crime, corruption, and vice, leading several states to create central authorities responsible for the inspection and control of prisons. The publication of the Wines and Dwight's *Report on the Prisons and Reformatories of the United States and Canada* in 1867 jump-started the movement for the central control of state prisons.

The end of the Civil War would provide the impetus for a gradual transformation of southern criminal justice. By 1865, the South was simply too impoverished to make any advances in the realm of prisons, insane asylums, and public schools. Formerly predicated on the rules and regulations of the plantation system of slavery, states and the federal government assumed control of the freed population from their former owners. According to historian Edward L. Ayers, the end of the Civil War saw the Ku Klux Klan and the Freedman's Bureau[1] attempt to "impose their vision of order upon the South."[2] Both sides faltered in their attempts but would leave the theoretical foundation for another century of conflict and tension between the races in the South.

As the nineteenth century moved to conclusion, a crusade was under way to create separate prison facilities for women. This movement, led by women on behalf of women, began in earnest in midcentury, when a handful of states hired matrons to oversee female inmates. By the late 1860s, Dwight and Wines, two of the leading authorities on prison reform, conceded that "carefully selected matrons . . . could provide role models" and that "matrons who exhibited characteristics of middle-class homemakers might inspire female criminals to become respectable women."[3] The campaign for separate prisons for women came to fruition in the 1870s.

Meanwhile, in the rest of the nation, the late nineteenth-century economy underwent a cycle of boom and bust, leading to a heavily contested debate over the role and rights of the industrial worker in the new economy. As liberal and progressive ideals found a national stage and a voice in organized labor, so too did big business and the so-called robber barons turn to private police agencies, such as the Pinkertons, to support their interests, often ending in violent confrontations.

Mirroring the growth taking place elsewhere, the federal government also began to play a more prominent role in daily life as federal courts and political parties became more influential. As citizens gained more rights thanks to the Civil Rights Act of 1866 and the Thirteenth, Fourteenth, and Fifteenth Amendments, the government took on more responsibility for protecting these rights.

In the aftermath of the Civil War, citizens were more frequently impaneled as jurors and witnesses during criminal trials. Prior to the war, the only federal criminal statutes dealt with counterfeiting, mail robbery, smuggling, embezzling federal funds, and resisting or impersonating a federal officer. With the end of hostilities in 1865, more federal crimes were added to the list. Among the new groups targeted by various criminal justice agencies were the Ku Klux Klan, Mormon settlers who practiced polygamy, and Appalachian moonshiners.

While the police became increasingly sophisticated in the late nineteenth century, professionalization and training lagged behind. Beginning in the 1850s, many forces adopted the sidearm as part of the standard equipment, but despite the improvement in revolver design, "police marksmanship proved abysmal."[4] A lack of training in safety or marksmanship characterized the use of deadly force, leading, according to one study of southern policing, to numerous accidental shootings of civilians and fellow officers.

The last half of the nineteenth century saw numerous advances in police investigation as the social sciences of anthropology, ethnology, and sociology all gained serious acceptance and photography was often used to augment studies in these disciplines. Beginning in the 1850s with the introduction of daguerreotype and the telegraph and continuing with the use of telephones in the 1880s and the Bertillon system by the 1890s, major cities in the North and the South were adopting new police technology to take the forces into the next century.

During the so-called Victorian era of the nineteenth century (which paralleled the reign of England's Queen Victoria in roughly the last half of the nineteenth century), a double standard existed in which certain moral offenses were tolerated as long they did "not threaten the general fabric of society."[5] According to this "Victorian compromise," gambling, prostitution, and other related forms of vice and crime were tolerated under the assumption that there was little that could be officially done to eradicate them. Historian Lawrence Friedman describes this compromise as "a muddled but powerful theory of social control"[6] in which private sins could be tolerated in the "dark corners and back alleys" as long as public order was not compromised.

In earlier years, only married people could legally have sexual relations. Sexual violations were criminal acts and were equated with sin. Infractions ranged from fornication, incest, adultery, and bestiality to prostitution and homosexuality. However, in the eighteenth and early nineteenth centuries, the criminal justice system devoted less time to pursuing these behaviors. Recognizing the impossibility of purging immorality from the urban landscape, law enforcement focused on more deviant behavior while coexisting with certain "acceptable" forms of vice, such as prostitution and gambling, but with specific limits.

THE LAWGIVERS

Following the Civil War, the Supreme Court was faced with numerous due process challenges to state policies predicated on the Fourteenth Amendment. Ratified in 1868, this amendment had a tremendous impact on the long-term development of the law of personal status as well as the nature of the federal system. Among its most far-reaching sections was its establishment of national citizenship, declaring that all persons were guaranteed equal protection of the laws, privileges and immunities, and due process of law.

Moreover, the post–Civil war era saw a substantial number of cases dealing with criminal due process and constitutional protections of the Bill of Rights coinciding with the expansion of federal criminal law. Among the most famous of these cases were two 1873 court decisions. In *Bradwell v. Illinois,* considered the "first decision under the Fourteenth Amendment,"[7] law student Myra Bradwell brought suit when she was denied admission to the Illinois bar even though the court admitted she was amply qualified. The case came before the Supreme Court, which affirmed the initial court decision that the Fourteenth Amendment did not restrict state power to limit the practice of law to males. But according to the legal concept of equality of 1870s America, as expressed by Justice Joseph P. Bradley, "the civil law, as well as nature herself, has always recognized a wide difference in the respective spheres and destinies of man and woman. . . . The natural and proper timidity and delicacy which belongs to the female sex evidently unfits it for many of the occupations of civil life."[8] In *Bradwell,* it became clear, at least for the moment, that the equal protection clause of the Fourteenth Amendment protected only men. Because of the efforts of Bradwell, Illinois passed a law in 1882 allowing women to practice any profession. However, it would be decades before women would be well represented in the legal profession. As late as 1920, only 3 percent of the nation's lawyers were women.[9]

The 1873 *Slaughterhouse* cases grew out of an 1869 decision by the Louisiana legislature to give a twenty-five-year monopoly to a specific New Orleans slaughterhouse to conduct its business in this city. In response, a consortium of different butchers sought an injunction against the monopoly on the grounds that it deprived them of the "privileges and immunities" guaranteed by the Fourteenth Amendment to all citizens.

After losing the case in the state supreme court, they appealed the judgment to the U.S. Supreme Court, where they were again denied by a narrow vote of five to four. According to the Supreme Court's interpretation, the amendment had been designed exclusively to grant African Americans federal protection against discriminatory state laws (such as state laws forbidding blacks to serve on juries) but was not applicable in regard to the "privileges and immunities" of other citizens. By this ruling, states had the power then to regulate all other civil rights (including property rights and rights of contract). Although the intent of the law was actually to protect due process, the decision of the Court ignored this fact, setting a precedent that would last until the twentieth century. According to legal historian David J. Bodenhamer, in the 1870s "the justices demonstrated a reluctance to apply any of the Bill of Rights to the states, especially in criminal matters."[10]

The South

In an attempt to return to familiar antebellum social control measures, southern lawmakers framed new legal codes to regulate the former slave population. These new laws did not blatantly mention race but instead resorted to enhancing the discretionary powers of local judges and juries. For example, the range of punishments meted out for crimes considered "peculiarly 'black,' " such as vagrancy, rape, arson, and burglary,[11] were widened in the decade following the war. In 1866 in Savannah, Georgia, one of the most important cities in the South, "freedmens' courts" were sometimes influenced by local officials to sentence blacks to chain gangs or resorted to exhibitory punishments by which convicted offenders would be forced to wear a barrel with armholes and a banner announcing "I am a thief."[12] Similar punishments were rarely accorded to white convicts.

Plessy v. Ferguson

White supremacy stood triumphant in the South by the 1890s, with segregation and disenfranchisement accepted features of society south of the Mason–Dixon line. Between 1877 and the 1890s, blacks continued to vote and hold public office. But the 1890s saw the implementation of grandfather clauses, literacy tests, poll taxes, and even terror to discourage black participation in the political system. Further polarization occurred with the acceptance of current "scientific" notions of racism and criminality.

In 1892, Louisiana resident Homer Plessy was riding a train out of New Orleans but was ejected from a car for whites and directed toward a car reserved for nonwhites. Light skinned and one-eighth black, Plessy claimed that a Louisiana statute that provided for separate railway carriages for whites and blacks was contrary to the Fourteenth Amendment's requirement of equal protection of the laws. Plessy took his case to court, reaching as high as the Supreme Court in 1896. In one fell swoop, the Court put the seal of approval on segregation by rejecting Plessy's contention and holding that segregation alone was not a constitutional violation. By a majority ruling, the Court approved a "separate but equal" doctrine that for more than fifty years all but nullified the Constitution's equal protection clause as an instrument of racial equality. Until 1954, *Plessy v. Ferguson,* which ruled that state-mandated segregated facilities did not violate the equal protection clause of the Fourteenth Amendment as long as facilities provided for blacks and whites were approximately equal, would serve as the constitutional cornerstone of racial discrimination in the United States.

The Comstock Laws

Cheap newspapers, known collectively as the "penny press," were filled with every manner of advertisement. Urban newspapers found abortion-related advertisements "a lucrative source of income" beginning in the 1840s and 1850s. This phenomenon accompanied the commercialization of the drug industry and reflected the desire of well-to-do women to limit their birthrate.[13] The growing abortion trade soon inspired sensationalist stories in the mass-circulation newspapers, leading to negative rhetoric and imagery that brought the entire practice of abortion into question.

During the 1870s, the Victorian compromise "began to crumble."[14] In 1873, Congress passed the Comstock Law, which prohibited the mailing of art, literature, and other materials considered obscene by the U.S. postal agent Anthony Comstock, who crusaded to make birth control and abortion illegal in the United States. The law also banned from the mails any drug, medicine, or article for abortion or contraceptive purposes (including condoms). The new legislation enjoyed widespread support. Many native-born Americans saw contraception and abortion as a form of "race suicide," particularly in the face of mounting foreign immigration. To others, these practices "violated nature's laws, bred immorality," and "damaged health."[15]

In 1873, Comstock was instrumental in establishing the New York Society for the Suppression of Vice, the first organization of its kind in America. Comstock would devote the last forty-two years of his life to this society as its secretary. Later that year, a group of New England ministers organized the New England Society for the Suppression of Vice, which would become better known as the New England Watch and Ward Society. Other antivice societies were launched in major cities, including St. Louis, Chicago, Louisville, Cincinnati, and San Francisco. All the founders of the antivice societies were stalwart members of the native-born community. Comstock's campaign against birth control and abortion led to a deadly underground abortion business that was estimated to have taken the lives of thousands of women between the 1870s and the 1970s.[16]

Anthony Comstock (1844–1915) moved to New York in the late 1860s after serving in the Union army in the Civil War. It was not long before he was campaigning against obscenity on behalf of the YMCA.

His growing influence inspired Congress in 1871 to pass what became known as the Comstock Law, which prohibited the transmission of obscene materials through the mail. In order to enforce the legislation, Comstock accepted a nonpaying position as a postal inspector. The zealous defender of morality rose to prominence by personally taking part in raids against pornography shops and abortionist offices in New York City. In one of his most controversial forays into censorship, in 1913 his crusade against artist Paul Chabas's nude painting *September Morn* led to rancorous debate over the definition of obscenity (and to its future success after it was rejected as too racy for a barbershop calendar). For his defenders, his name became a byword for morality, while his detractors regarded him as a threat to freedom of expression and the First Amendment.

Under the sway of Comstock's extremist convictions, obscenity was vaguely defined, leading to thousands of arrests. According to the *American College Dictionary, Comstockery* became a byword for "overzealous censorship of the fine arts and literature."[17] Margaret Sanger's books on birth control were banned, while poet Walt Whitman was fired from his job with the Department of the Interior for penning *Leaves of Grass*. Publishers removed any explicit language from their publications; for example, *pregnant* became *enceinte*.

LAW ENFORCEMENT

Between 1870 and 1900, most large American cities had established professional police forces. However, for the less populated areas, a vacuum in authority led to the creation of vigilante groups, lynchings, and deadly feuds. While the Ku Klux Klan attempted to preserve the antebellum status quo, others took the law into their own hands to protect their newfound freedoms.

One of the unforeseen developments of the postwar era was the diminished role of the militia at a time when urban criminal violence was on the rise. Militia historian Robert Reinders suggested that the strikes of 1877 "provided a

new stimulus and role for the militia," one that demonstrated their impracticality for the industrial era.[18] In many cases, militia members sympathized with strikers, contributing to the growing disorder. In 1877, national armed forces demonstrated their superiority to the militia in quelling civil disturbances. Better trained and disciplined, the army was more disposed to quelling riots than their militia counterparts.

Police forces saw reform efforts from local politicians, state legislatures, and chiefs of police. The New York City police chief George W. Walling, after having served forty years on the force, argued that police officers should work to improve their relations with the public, going beyond their mandate as keepers of the peace. In the same era, Cincinnati's George M. Roe boasted that his department had created a "gymnasium" and a "School of Instruction" for his officers in the late 1880s. According to Roe's memoir published in 1890, Cincinnati policemen were expected to "be a perfect specimen of physical manhood" and "must have a knowledge of the English language sufficient to make written reports intelligible," as well as be "versed in criminal and municipal laws to avoid making any mistakes" that could haunt them later during criminal proceedings.[19]

While police work remained a male domain well into the twentieth century, steps were taken to include women in a secondary role beginning in 1878, when some forces placed matrons in charge of female prisoners. By 1890, as a result of a campaign by several women's groups, thirty-six city police departments hired police matrons.

As the turn of the century approached, Irish Americans dominated the ranks of many urban police forces, with cities as diverse as Chicago, Cleveland, and San Francisco counting a disproportionate number of Irish among their ranks. Not all observers were favorable to this development, including one who wrote a diatribe in 1894 titled "The Irish Conquest of Our Cities," in which he lamented the number of Irish police chiefs in America.[20]

Police work remained a rather solitary profession in the closing decades of the nineteenth century, with most officers working either alone or in small groups. Attempts at police discipline and supervision fell short because of the limited power of police officials to enforce the rules. Outside of on-the-street supervision, there were few ways to closely supervise police on patrol. Some police commissioners sent out plainclothes patrolmen to check on colleagues. Theodore Roosevelt (the future president), New York City's police commissioner, made the rounds at night, stopping in saloons and the like. If an officer was spotted while on duty, he could expect to appear at headquarters the next morning. Some forces compiled massive rules books that included protocols for patrolling and making reports. Most violations were punished with fines. According to one police historian, "Some departments administrators punished policemen more often for violation of the rules than they did for crimes like assault and blackmail."[21]

Federal Law Enforcement

The South and the West continued to lag behind the North when it came to economic development. Both regions had little political clout in Washington (with smaller populations, they had less representation). Following the war, the belief that criminal law was a state and not a federal matter still persisted in the South. Congress in turn passed certain federal laws that disproportionately targeted the South and the West; hence, federal law enforcement was more inextricably tied to these regions.

According to historian Stephen Cresswell's study of federal law enforcement, for the years 1871–1890, the North had only fourteen federal criminal cases per 10,000 for this time period compared to fifty-four per 10,000 in the South and seventy-two per 10,000 in the West.[22] Cresswell suggested that "certain elements in southern and western society made the violation of federal laws more common than in the North." Among the elements he cites are the get-rich mentality of the West and the prevalent dislike of the federal government in the defeated South.[23]

During Reconstruction, large areas of the former Confederacy were indeed relatively peaceful and could boast efficient law enforcement. With a large portion of white citizens loath to publicly denounce acts of violence against the former slaves in the 1870s, southern blacks and former Unionists often turned to the U.S. army as their only source of protection. However, the army was usually unwilling or unable to respond to such requests.

Federal law enforcement in the American West during the last half of the 1800s was the preserve of U.S. marshals. Between 1840 and 1900, marshals were elected to cover states and territories. Their main job was to uphold federal laws, which included arresting individuals for robbing the mails, deserting from the armed forces, stealing government stock, or killing Indians. Each marshal had an office deputy who was responsible for maintaining paperwork and could pass on orders to field deputies. Until 1896, only the office deputies were paid a salary, while the other federal deputies were paid through a fee system (about two dollars per day) and mileage (six to ten cents per mile). Although the marshal received no salary, the position itself was considered a stepping-stone to better things.

The New York City Police Department

After the return of the New York City Police Department to city control in 1870, within a few years the force would be reorganized and a new set of standards implemented, including the requirements that police candidates be U.S. citizens and residents of the state for at least one year and not have a criminal record. In 1874, the force was rewarded with the sobriquet "The Finest." Other innovations followed: telephone links replaced the outdated telegraph system in 1880, a central office was created for the Bureau of Detectives, and four women joined the force as precinct matrons in 1888.

However, a darker, more sinister side of the police force was revealed in 1894, when a state senate committee was appointed to investigate alleged abuses of authority by police. In 1894, the Lexow Committee discovered a menu of bribes for rising through the ranks of the New York Police Department (e.g., $300 just to be appointed to the force) and an established system for shaking down illegitimate businesses. Although numerous officers were dismissed and the Tammany machine was replaced by reform-minded politicians, there were no enduring achievements, and just four years later Tammany was back in the hands of the bosses, and the police department had reverted back to its former corrupt excesses.

In an era of corrupt cops, none was more unscrupulous than Alexander "Clubber" Williams (1839–1910). Joining the New York Police Department in 1866, the physically imposing Williams earned the nickname "Clubber" for his dexterity with a nightstick. On one occasion, he bragged, "There is more law at the end of a policeman's nightstick than in any ruling of the Supreme Court." In 1871, he was promoted to captain and was later rewarded with a transfer to the Tenderloin district, leading the colorful cop to exclaim, "I've had nothing but chuck steak for a long-time and now I'm going to get a little tenderloin." During his eleven years as captain in the area, he was accused and exonerated of eighteen brutality complaints. When the Lexow Committee investigated him in 1894, it found that on an annual salary of $3,500, he had amassed more than $1 million in assets. His explanation for such wealth was that he made savvy real estate investments in Japan. Williams was forced to resign from the force.

In 1895, future president Theodore Roosevelt (1858–1919) was appointed as one of four newly installed police commissioners. Over the next two years, he played an instrumental role in exposing departmental corruption and rooting out unscrupulous police officials such as Alexander "Clubber" Williams. Roosevelt is credited with introducing numerous reforms, including a promotion system based on merit rather than patronage, more stringent physical and mental

qualifications, and more progressive recruitment. He hired the first female civilian secretary and lobbied for Jewish officers to join the mostly Irish–Catholic rank and file. Roosevelt's term as commissioner led to better police training, a bicycle squad charged with traffic control, and more efficient call boxes, and the .32-caliber revolver became the standard on-duty sidearm.

In the late nineteenth century, police officers in major urban centers were responsible for a number of chores unrelated to law enforcement. Officers were tasked with supervising the cleaning of streets and providing shelter at the precinct houses. An old tradition and the bane of urban reformers in New York City was the continued use of precinct house basements to accommodate the homeless and the indigent. While the police referred to the basement shelters as "lodging houses," the homeless referred to them as "green-light hotels," alluding to the green lights at the entrances to the precinct houses.[24] Without bathroom facilities or beds, they were characterized by overcrowding and poor hygiene, leading Peter Conlin, New York City police chief, to characterize them as refuges for the "lazy, dissipated, filthy, vermin-covered, disease breeding and disease-scattering scum of the city's population."[25]

Social reformer Jacob Riis (1849–1914) publicized these conditions as he accompanied Roosevelt on midnight excursions to the seedier police precincts with the hope of exposing police corruption and dereliction of duty. A Danish immigrant who had arrived in America only in 1877, Riis chronicled the plight of the underclasses in *The Children of the Poor* (1892) and *How the Other Half Lives* (1890). However, with few alternatives besides the city streets to seek refuge and no other social service institutions available, there were few alternatives for the homeless besides the precinct basements, where they would at least be sheltered from the elements and street crime.

Department morale improved during Roosevelt's short tenure as president of the Board of Police Commissioners from 1895 through 1897.

During this period, precinct house accommodations for transients were replaced with separate lodging houses, and a system for recognizing meritorious police service was inaugurated. By 1897, New York State Republicans had apparently wearied of Roosevelt's reform campaign and, in order to get him out of office, reportedly arranged to have him appointed assistant secretary of the navy.

The civil service reform taking place in New York City in the 1880s was part of a national movement led by middle- and upper-middle-class men during the era. Targeting the spoils system and political patronage, these reformers did their best to break the ties between politicians and police appointments. Some departments introduced procedures for appointments and promotions. However, politicians just as quickly found ways to sidestep medical, physical, and writing tests. Since writing tests were of the essay variety, examiners had a wide latitude in grading. In New York City, there were cases of candidates astonishingly adding inches to reach minimum height. On one occasion, a prospective candidate was rejected twice for syphilis, only to be accepted on his third try.[26]

The Pinkertons and Private Policing

During the nineteenth century, the history of private policing is closely tied to the development of the Pinkerton National Detective Agency. The Pinkertons came to national prominence during the Civil War, when they protected Lincoln from an assassination plot, and then were employed as counterespionage agents by the Union army. Following the war, Alan Pinkerton returned home to Chicago and to new challenges, ranging from pursuing train robbers to violent labor strikes.

By the 1870s, the Pinkertons claimed to have assembled the largest collection of criminal mug shots in the world as well as having created a criminal database for their agents. As the American economy struggled with the industrial upheaval of the late nineteenth century, the Pinkertons found themselves increasingly employed by corporations as strikebreakers, often leading to bloody conflict with organized labor. The most famous incident occurred in 1892 at the Carnegie Steelworks in Homestead, Pennsylvania. The veteran of more than fifty confrontations with labor by 1892, the Homestead strike, in which workers protested poor wages and other concerns, would prove the Pinkertons' most severe test.

When negotiations with labor leaders broke down at the Carnegie plant in June 1892, the company hired the Pinkertons to protect its factory. The Pinkertons sent 300 men by barges up the Monongahela River to the plant in July after prolabor elements took control of the land routes from Pittsburgh. Waiting at the Homestead docks were between 3,000 and 10,000 workers. Testimony suggests that the strikers were unsure who was approaching, mistaking the approaching detective force for an army of strikebreaking scabs. It is unknown who fired first, but as the barges approached land, gunfire was exchanged by both groups, leaving three Pinkertons and ten workers dead. The Pinkertons were soon captured, and the strikers took over the factory until the Pennsylvania National Guard arrived several days later.

This incident was a major turning point in Pinkerton's policy for dealing with strikebreakers. Henceforth, the agency avoided taking the offensive in labor face-offs, instead opting to defend only factories. A subsequent investigation into the Homestead affair awakened Americans to the growth of the private police industry and tarnished the image of the Pinkertons. The antidetective mood that resulted from the carnage led to the passage of several anti-Pinkerton laws in the 1890s.[27]

Criminal Identification

While fingerprinting, DNA, and serology are standard methods of police identification in the twenty-first century, before the 1880s there was no effective system of classification or reference of criminals. Large photo collections were amassed of convicted criminals at various police headquarters, but the very size of these collections defeated their purposes. The first police forces to make use of photographic rogues' galleries included New York (1858), Danzig (1864), Moscow (1867), London (1870), and Paris (1874). According to crime historian Luc Sante, the use of crime scene photography was first reported in Switzerland in 1860.[28]

Chief of the New York Detective Bureau in the 1880s, Inspector Thomas Byrnes was the architect of the New York rogues' gallery, popularized with the publication of *Professional Criminals of America* in 1886. By disseminating his collection of 204 tintypes of celebrated criminals to the public, Byrnes hoped he could not only advertise the exploits and cunning of the New York Police Department but also help the general public in the prevention and detection of crime. Each photograph was complemented by biographical information and criminal records detailing the methods used by specific bank robbers, forgers, confidence men, shoplifters, and other crime specialists of the era.

First used by the police of Paris in 1882, by the following year the Bertillon system had been used to identify forty-nine criminals. Named after its creator, Alphonse Bertillon (1835–1914), the system required the measurement of the width and length of the head; the length of the left, middle, and little fingers; the length of the left foot, forearm, and right ear; the height of the individual; and the measurement of the person while seated from the bench to the top of the head. Other identifying characteristics included scars, birthmarks, eye and hair color, and a description of the nose. Bertillonage would be well regarded until the 1890s, when fingerprinting replaced it, to the relief of peace officers burdened by the laborious identification procedures it required. Bertillon's system did much to raise the standard of the inefficient and corrupt police methods of the nineteenth century.

Born into a middle-class family, the son of a physician with a keen interest in anthropology and statistics, Alphonse Bertillon was drawn to the science at an early age. In 1878, he found employment as a records clerk for the Paris police, leading to a lifelong interest in identifications systems that would earn him the sobriquet the "Father of Modern Detection." Over the next seven years, Bertillon developed a methodology to identify recidivist offenders. Through the use of anthropometry, he created a system that became known as "bertillonage," based on human body measurements, prior to the introduction of a fingerprinting system. Subsequently, he would add photographic methods to other identification techniques and become an expert in using photography to identify forged documents.

Prior to the twentieth century, there was no reliable way to distinguish between the guilty and the innocent.[29] Perhaps the best-known system of identification, fingerprinting took decades for law enforcement to realize its value for crime investigation. With the recognition that no two fingerprints are alike in the late nineteenth century, fingerprinting became the identification method of choice in tracking an increasingly mobile population of criminals.[30]

As early as the 1820s, an anatomy professor named Johann Purkinje noted that every person's fingerprints were unique. However, without any type of classification system, this method of identification was useless. By the 1850s, fingerprints were being used by British magistrate William Herschel to prevent the wrong people from fraudulently collecting money on the dole. In 1880, Henry Faulds, a Scottish physician working in Tokyo, exonerated a suspected thief by comparing fingerprints left at the crime scene with those of the suspect.

In the late 1880s, Sir Francis Galton attempted to create a classification system and wrote the book *Fingerprints* (1892). However, it would be left to Sir Edward Richard Henry, inspector general of the Nepal police, to grapple with the problem, and in 1896 he created an identification system on fingerprinting. That same year, Argentina became the first country to base its identification system on fingerprinting. The adoption of fingerprinting finally gave crime investigators the first reliable proof of an individual's presence at a crime scene.

The early 1900s saw criminal identification receive increased attention as the Bertillon system proved too cumbersome and unreliable. New incentive was given to criminal identification when New York City police adopted the fingerprint system used by Scotland Yard in 1902. Although the Bertillon system was widely accepted in the United States in the 1890s, it faced its greatest challenge in 1903, when a man named Will West was arrested and sentenced to prison at Fort Leavenworth, Kansas. Despite his claims that he had never been arrested before, his photograph seemed to match that of a convicted criminal, and apparently so did his Bertillon measurements. It turned out that there was another man named Will West incarcerated in the same prison, with the same measurements, and bearing an uncanny resemblance to the other Will West. The only evidence that distinguished the two men was their fingerprints. Subsequently, fingerprinting, together with photographs, would supersede the discredited Bertillon system.

Professionalism

In 1893, twenty years after the first meeting of police chiefs in St. Louis, Chicago hosted the next national meeting of police chiefs. Of the more than fifty who attended, most were from smaller communities near Chicago, although representatives from Boston, Pittsburgh, and Atlanta were among the attendees. Among the topics discussed were civil service rules for police, the adoption of police telegraphic code, and a uniform identification system. The Chicago police chief could boast having set up the first Bertillon bureau in America. The National Chiefs of Police laid the groundwork for what would become the International Association of Chiefs of Police. One of the more important resolutions approved at the meeting was an agreement for jurisdictional cooperation between different cities and states.

Southern Policing

With few historical studies of southern police forces during the post–Civil War era, Dennis Rousey's examination of the New Orleans police is particularly valuable for making any judgments

about post-Reconstruction southern policing. The end of Reconstruction in 1877 saw the Democratic governments of the South take back control of their government, political, and social institutions. But between 1868 and 1877, the percentage of African Americans on the New Orleans police force ranged from 65 to 28 percent by 1870, almost equal to its percentage of the black population. During the heyday of Reconstruction, New Orleans had the "largest integrated force in the urban South" and with its 182 black policemen "the largest contingent of black policemen."[31] Although other southern cities also were well represented with blacks during this period, this was clearly not the rule throughout the former Confederacy. For example, Charleston, South Carolina, and Petersburg, Virginia, had well-integrated forces, while Savannah and Richmond had all-white forces.

The end of Reconstruction also put an end to well-integrated policing in the South for the rest of the nineteenth century. New Orleans would see few appointments during the new era, and in 1880 its percentage of black officers had fallen to 6.6 percent. Policing in general would suffer in the South, as it reverted to antebellum conditions that favored decentralization and smaller police budgets. In New Orleans, municipal allocations fell from $325,000 in 1877 to $171,000 in 1888. A reduction in police pay was accompanied by manpower shortages contributing to a recurring crime problem in many southern cities. According to the 1870 and 1880 censuses, out of eighteen major southern cities, fifteen saw major reductions in police manpower. With the weakest police force of America's major cities, New Orleans was well on its way to becoming one of the most inefficient forces in the land, a reputation that has marked the force into the 1990s.

Compared to New York City and other northern cities in the 1880s making major strides in the direction of professionalism, "New Orleans in most ways set an example for other cities not to follow."[32] Here a patronage system continued to determine the selection of police officers, resulting in the ascendance of politically connected individuals to the higher ranks of the police organization. But New Orleans was not alone in its aversion to civil service reform. It would not be until 1895 in Chicago and 1905 in St. Louis that major steps toward nonpartisan government service reform were taken.

The West

During the 1870s, cattle towns popped up near the intersections of Texas cattle drives and railroad lines in Kansas. More primitive in most respects to urban counterparts in the Northeast, these towns soon developed similar criminal justice problems. Towns such as Dodge City, Abilene, Wichita, and Ellsworth offered liquor, prostitution, and gambling in an attempt to lure cowboy dollars at the end of the drives. Concomitant with the financial rewards were the ever-present violence and disorder that resulted. As the towns became increasingly complex and diversified, they developed police forces, usually consisting of a marshal, assistant marshal, and varying number of police officers. The town marshal's jurisdiction ended at the town limits. Harking back to Anglo-Saxon England, the county peace officer was the sheriff. Both the county sheriff and the town marshal were responsible for civil crimes, leaving federal crimes to the U.S. marshal.

During the nineteenth century, four types of law enforcement would predominate in the West, including vigilance committees (particularly in mining areas); legal citizens police, who were citizens serving brief stints as deputies with county sheriffs or town marshals; formal police; and parapolice, such as the Pinkertons, who pursued the James–Younger gang.

CORRECTIONS

According to prison historian Blake McKelvey, prison populations in the North decreased during the Civil War because of a combination of factors, explaining that "the army had absorbed the potential criminals, afforded a refuge for fugitives, or supplied a convenient commutation of sentence."[33] During this period, there were few complaints of prison overcrowding or poor accommodations.

Meanwhile in the South, the convict lease system continued to predominate because of a dearth in prison construction. The railroad, timber, and mining industries benefited from an agreement that often let them rent out gangs of prisoners to toil where no free man would even contemplate doing so, resulting in death rates that ran as high as 40 percent per year.

The end of the Civil War and Reconstruction witnessed a sudden increase in America's state prison populations, leading to a plethora of penal problems. Massachusetts State Prison, for example, reported that 171 of the 247 convicts entering prison in 1866 were veterans of the Civil War.[34] Between 1870 and 1904, the population of state prisons increased almost 62 percent. Shortly before the outbreak of the war, the prison population stood at almost 19,000, rising to 33,000 in 1870, 45,000 in 1890, and 57,000 in 1900. With many model prisons deteriorating badly, including those at Auburn and Eastern State, states resorted to modifying existing structures and building new ones in order to house the legions of new inmates.

The Reformatory Era

An increased emphasis on reform was a product of the times, which saw the introduction of a more therapeutic understanding of criminal behavior. Lasting roughly from 1870 to 1910, the reformatory movement in America saw numerous institutions adopt indeterminate sentencing, parole, and attempts at positive reform through education. Building on the efforts of reformers Maconochie, Crofton, and Wines, by 1869 twenty-three states had adopted "good-time" laws, which reduced prison sentences for good work and deportment.

One of the most important prison reformers of his era, Zebulon Brockway (1827–1920) captured the attention of his fellow reformers in

1870 at the National Prison Congress. The scion of a venerable New England family, Brockway began his career in corrections as head of a New York almshouse and then of a penitentiary in Rochester. He came to prominence following the presentation of his paper "The Ideal of a True Prison System for a State" at the 1870 National Prison Congress. His suggestions for reform would resonate for decades. Although a zealous proponent of indeterminate sentencing and the classification of prisoners according to age, sex, and offense, Brockway would not shy away from life sentences for career criminals. The subsequent adoption of a "Declaration of Principles" is testimony to the impact of Brockway's predilection for religion, education, industrious work habits, and the supervision of convicts following release.

The "Declaration of Principles" adopted at the National Prison Congress represented an extraordinary step in the direction of progressive prison reform. Among the improvements advocated by the meeting were better sanitary conditions, the abolition of political appointment of prison administrators, the progressive classification of prisoners based on the mark system, rewards for good conduct and work, and more stress on education.

 ## Declaration of Principles Adopted at the National Prison Congress

1. Reformation, not vindictive suffering, as the purpose of penal treatment of prisoners

2. Classifications made on the basis of a mark system, patterned after the Irish system

3. Rewards for good conduct

4. Prisoners recognizing that their destiny remained in their own hands

5. Acknowledgment of obstacles to prison reform, including the political appointment of prison officials

6. Job training for prison officials

7. Indeterminate sentencing replacing fixed sentences

8. The removal of gross disparities and inequities in prison sentences

9. Heightened emphasis on religion and education as part of reformation process

10. More focus on industrial training

11. Abolition of contract labor in prisons

12. More specialized institutions for different types of offenders

13. Revision of laws pertaining to the sentencing of insane criminals

14. More judicious use of pardoning power

15. Creation of a system for the collection of uniform penal statistics

16. More adequate prison architecture, providing prison hospitals, schoolrooms, and so on as well as offering more sunlight and better air ventilation

17. Centralizing prison management in each state

18. Facilitating the socialization process of prisoners through proper associations and eradicating the regimen of silence

19. Recognizing that society is in part responsible for creating crime conditions

Brockway was given a chance to put his proposals into action in 1877, when he was appointed superintendent of the newly created Elmira Reformatory. His tenure would allow him to incorporate his many ideas, chief among them the indeterminate sentence. With overcrowding the most prominent problem plaguing prison officials in the late 1860s, new institutions were built following the reformatory model. Opening in 1876, the Elmira Reformatory initially set the standard. Formerly a Union prison camp, the state legislature consigned its notorious wartime reputation to the past and reconstructed the site as a model reformatory. Here, first-time offenders between the ages of sixteen and thirty were sentenced to a facility that placed more emphasis on education and trades training and offered early release through the mark system, which offered merits and demerits for progress and behavior.

Influenced by the current pseudosciences of anthropometry and heredity, by the 1880s Brockway was ascribing the criminal tendencies of many prisoners to heredity. He also took note of the increasing population of European immigrants behind the walls, noting that they "are to a considerable extent the product of our civilization and also of emigration to our shore from the degenerated populations of crowded European marts."[35]

Prison architecture between 1870 and 1900 continued to follow the Auburn pattern with few modifications. Improvements included the introduction of ventilating systems and steel cells that offered plumbing and running water. However, the bucket system of human waste disposal would persist in dozens of prisons into the 1930s.

Increasing resistance to prison industries by organized labor began to impact convict labor systems, causing many penal administrators to take note. Responding to claims that prison labor represented unfair competition to free labor, many states passed laws in the late 1880s prohibiting productive prison labor.

An integral part of the foundation of Elmira was its emphasis on industrial labor. Brockway found a loophole in the recent prohibitions by entering a state-supply relationship with New York that would allow his inmates to continue to produce goods, but only products that could be sold to their state facilities or departments.

Despite overcoming numerous obstacles and his noble intentions, by 1893 the Elmira Reformatory was overcrowded, and Brockway's propensity for blaming criminality on low intelligence and "physical degeneracy" lost him much of his former support. An investigation the following year exposed Elmira's dirty little secret, that the worst whippings and physical punishment were administered to boys suffering from mental and physical disabilities. Brockway's experiment never regained its luster, and in 1900 he resigned his post.

Wayward Sisters

If there was one area that the National Prison Congress failed to address, it was the incarceration of female offenders, who until the 1870s were often housed in the same prisons as men. While it endorsed the creation of treatment-oriented prisons for women, it would take until 1874 for Indiana to open the first female-run prison in America.

During the early nineteenth century, women were incarcerated in the same prisons as men. There were few women convicts in this era, and in order to prevent sexual dalliance, women were isolated. Most women were arrested for minor crimes and were usually held in county jails or houses of correction rather than state prisons, where more serious offenders were housed. During the first half of the nineteenth century, most female arrests involved prostitution, public inebriation, and petty larceny. For example, Massachusetts did not record any women in its state prison, although local jails reported that women made up almost 20 percent of their populations.[36] In 1875, Massachusetts built the Reformatory Prison for women, the second institution of its kind in America.

According to one reformer in the 1830s, there were less than 100 women in prisons of the seven most populous states. Ten years later, Dorothea Dix counted 167.[37] With typically less than a dozen women in any prison, there were too few to devote an entire wing to them, so they were usually housed in large congregate rooms either above the guardhouse or mess hall.[38] With so much attention lavished on the more numerous men, the female prisoners were often neglected.

In 1839, New York's Sing Sing Prison became the first to establish a separate prison wing for women but would be the only one until the 1870s. Women penal reformers were influential in the founding of the American Prison Association (1870). Many supported the notion of "social feminism," arguing that women had unique needs requiring prisons that could respond to their special needs. As a result, more than twenty women's reformatories were built between 1870 and 1935.

New York established the Mount Pleasant Female Prison in 1835. "Administratively dependent" on Sing Sing Prison, it welcomed its first women prisoners in 1839. According to historian

Lawrence M. Friedman, its significance lies in the fact that it was run exclusively by female prison matrons for women.[39] During its first decade, prisoners labored under a tedious routine of "sewing, button making, and hat-trimming." Except for a brief flurry of reform in the mid-1840s, when prison matron Eliza Farnham abolished the rule of silence and initiated a less punitive regime, conditions deteriorated because of overcrowding. However, by 1846, a list of punishments suggests that Farnham still relied on corporal punishment, which included solitary confinement, the cropping of hair, and utilization of gags and straightjackets. By 1865, Mount Pleasant was burdened with twice its capacity.[40] In 1874, the Female Prison and Reformatory Institution for Girls and Women, the first separate prison completely devoted to women, was inaugurated in Indianapolis, Indiana.

The opening of the Indiana Reformatory Institution in 1874 was the end result of a crusade by social feminists who campaigned for institutions suited to the specific needs of female prisoners. One of the main pressures for incarcerating women in reformatories rather than prisons was the result of the changing conceptions of female criminality in the 1870s. In the past, women prisoners were often portrayed as depraved if not uncontrollable. But this image began to undergo a transition as they became increasingly viewed as "wayward girls" "who had been led astray and could, therefore, be led back to the paths of 'proper' behavior: 'childlike, domestic, and asexual.' "[41] In order to adhere to this changing interpretation, most reformatories selected first-time offenders over hardened career female criminals.

One of the most prominent female prison reformers of the era was Katherine Bement Davis (1860–1935). The Vassar-educated penologist and social worker earned a PhD in 1900 and the following year was selected as superintendent of the Reformatory for Women at Bedford Hills, New York, where she earned a reputation as an innovator in female penology. Over the next dozen years, Davis experimented with a medical model of incarceration and was instrumental in establishing a diagnostic laboratory of social hygiene that allowed sociologists, psychologists, and psychiatrists to study prisoners. An early example of the Progressive reformer (see chapter 9), Davis emphasized the role of professionals in treating social problems, so after the classification of offenders, those who were considered incurable were given life sentences, while others entered treatment programs.

Probation

The origins of probation, or the use of a suspended sentence, can be traced back to the English "benefit of clergy," by which a member of the ordained clergy could escape the harsh penalties of the day.[42] Over time, this suspension of sentence was extended to anyone who could read Psalm 21, which acknowledged sin and promised reform.

Modern American probation has more in common with the informal practices that developed in Boston in the 1840s. Considered the oldest form of noninstitutional corrections in the United States, the development of probation has generally been credited to John Augustus (1785–1859), a Boston cobbler. Augustus had an epiphany in 1841, when he observed a man being sentenced in a Boston courtroom for public drunkenness. Surmising that the man was of good character, Augustus posted bail and promised the judge he would look after the man until his hearing. Having abstained from drinking for the next three weeks, when he appeared before the judge for sentencing, the now sober citizen was given a fine in lieu of more punitive treatment. Augustus went on to spend many days in the local courts and personally arrange bail and custody for similar misdemeanants. During a fourteen-year period, he bailed out close to 2,000 individuals, putting up almost $250,000 of his own money as bail. His efforts would lead the Massachusetts legislature to enact the first Probation Act in 1878. By the twentieth century, every state had passed similar probation acts. Contemporary probation officers continue to follow in the footsteps of their nineteenth-century counterparts, using similar methods of investigation, screening, interviewing, and supervision.

Probation has remained popular for more than a century, mainly because it is a cheap alternative to incarceration. Some observers maintain that probation tends to "subvert the concept of fair justice."[43] There has tended to be an inherent class bias to this punishment alternative, mainly because the criminal justice system considers offenders who do not have a criminal record or who appear better socialized are better risks for probation than hardened offenders. What often tips the scales in favor of one class or another is whether someone can afford to make bail, criminal record, and physical appearance at time of decision.

The Child Savers and the Birth of the Juvenile Court System

Building on the Elmira Reformatory experiment, Massachusetts (1874) and Rhode Island (1892) passed laws authorizing separate trials for children. Except for several other hesitant steps taken elsewhere, until 1899 children in most states could be arrested, detained, tried, and sentenced to adult prisons. The establishment of the first true juvenile court in 1899 gave the criminal justice system jurisdiction over neglected and dependent children and those determined to be delinquent, the so-called dangerous classes.

Until 1899, the treatment of juveniles corresponded with that of adults. Outside of several "reform schools" and children's aid societies, juveniles were arrested, detained, tried, and imprisoned like their adult counterparts. While some states provided institutions for juveniles, it would take the "child-saving" movement at the turn of the century to use the power of the state to save children from a life of crime.

The child-saving movement was mainly the purview of a group of well-educated, politically active women from the middle and upper classes. They were instrumental in providing the impetus for the creation of a separate juvenile court system. In 1899, Illinois approved the passage of the Juvenile Court Act, establishing the first comprehensive system of juvenile justice (for children under age sixteen) and giving momentum to the development to the modern juvenile justice system.

The predominance of middle-class women in the child-saving movement coincided with an era when middle-class women were becoming better educated and enjoyed more leisure time, but because of the social circumstances of the late nineteenth century, there were few career avenues to follow. By the turn of the century, middle-class women "experienced a complex and far-reaching status revolution"[44] as they championed the interests of children, the poor, and immigrants—social outsiders whom many regarded as a threat to the new industrial order.

The child-saving movement was not without its critics. Recent scholarship suggests that these reformers were tools of the "ruling class," applying the concept of parens patriae[45] for their own interests, which included the control of the political system, the continuance of the child labor system, and the advancement of upper-class values.

CRIME AND PUNISHMENT

The urbanization of America during the last forty years of the nineteenth century created new problems for urban police forces. As the ethnic makeup of cities became more diverse, police work became more complicated as well. Following the Civil War, most of the Italian, Jewish, Chinese, and African American newcomers moved into slums formerly dominated by the Irish and now policed by Irish American officers. But despite a cornucopia of endemic obstacles to keeping the peace in the 1890s, including immigration, poverty, corruption, and overcrowding, murder rates in cities such as New York were declining.

The most prominent criminals of the nineteenth century were the mythologized badmen of the West. According to recent research, these individuals were indeed men but were probably not much worse than others less well known. While poems, plays, movies, and novels have made Wyatt Earp, Billy the Kid, John Wesley Hardin, and the James Gang popular culture mainstays, the most wanted fugitives of the post-war era included Molly Maguire's assassin Thomas Hurley (according to the Pinkertons) and Mormon leader John Taylor.

As train robbery, cattle rustling, and bank robbery captured the attention of the public, the late nineteenth century introduced the nation to America's version of Jack the Ripper, except this time he had a face and a name, Herman Webster Mudgett (a.k.a. H. H. Holmes). As historian Roger Lane has noted in his magisterial study *Murder in America,* there were few known cases of multiple-sex murders (today better known as serial killings) in the nineteenth century. The thirty-four-year-old Holmes seemed a pillar of respectability during his years in Chicago. How-ever, following a trail of missing bodies and fraudulent insurance claims, Holmes was arrested for kidnapping and murdering three children. He ultimately confessed to twenty-seven murders before being hanged in 1896.

Despite the sensational qualities of many post–Civil War crimes and murders, homicide rates declined as the country approached the 1900s.[46] This was in part a reflection of the role played by better policing, temperance groups, and public schools that led the vanguard in the battle for reform and order.

Criminalistics

The physician Cesare Lombroso (1835–1909) took his first steps toward the development of a highly controversial theory that would have pro-found influence throughout the world of crimi-nal justice while still in the Italian army when he noticed a characteristic that distinguished the honest soldier from his more vicious counter-part: "the extent to which the latter was tattooed and the indecency of the designs that covered his body." Considered the founder of the positivist school of criminology and the "father of modern criminology," Lombroso's theories owe much to Charles Darwin's *The Origin of Species* (1859) and

The Descent of Man (1871), which suggested that some men are closer to their primitive ancestors than others. Earlier speculations on degeneracy can be traced back to research conducted in France as early as the 1820s.

Lombroso was consumed with resolving "the problem of the nature of the criminal." While performing a postmortem on a noted Italian brigand, Lombroso reached an epiphany that led him to build on the work of earlier writers who suggested that there was a relationship between the physical characteristics of a criminal and his behavior. Lombroso went on to collect a mass of evidence based on the close examination of a number of criminals to support his theory that the criminal can be distinguished from the non-criminal by a variety of physical anomalies that were of an atavistic or a degenerative origin. Arguing that some individuals were born crimi-nals, his conclusions would fly in the face of penal reformers who argued that prisoners could be reformed in the appropriate environment. In 1876, Lombroso's *L'Uomo delinquente* (Criminal Man) was published. Going beyond the theoreti-cal, Lombroso searched for practical applications for his research. A proponent of postmortem examination of criminal brains, he is credited with providing the impetus for the study of clin-ical criminology and the basis for the methodol-ogy of cadaver identification later employed in the field of legal medicine.

Much of the work by the early criminologists served as grist for the rise of racism in the nine-teenth century as pseudoscience was used to explain the inequality between the races. Although Lombroso's work was not published in the United States until 1911, criminologists throughout the world had become familiar with his theories soon after their initial publication in Italy.

There exists much debate regarding what exactly Lombroso contributed to the field of criminology. No less an authority than Edwin Sutherland suggested in 1962 that "Lombroso's impact had the disastrous effect of leading crimi-nology up a blind alley for forty years." The con-tention that there is a criminal type, demonstrable by certain physical dimensions—that the criminal was identifiable on the basis of certain cranial, facial, and bodily measurements—may have seemed like a great advance in the late nineteenth century. However, a growing number of dissenters began to view crime as the product of certain social factors.

Lombroso was a visionary who shifted the focus of criminology toward the scientific study of the criminal and the conditions under which a crime is committed. His greatest contribution to the emerging discipline was his recognition "that it is the criminal and not the crime we should study and consider; that it is the criminal and not the crime we ought to penalize."[47]

Capital Punishment

Efforts to abolish the death penalty came to an abrupt halt in the 1850s as reformers diverted their attention toward slavery, the Civil War, and Reconstruction issues. Between 1865 and 1900, only Iowa, Maine, and Colorado abolished the death penalty, but all three would reinstate it within several years, and only Maine would once more don the abolitionist cloak for good beginning in 1887. During the Progressive era in the first two decades of the new century, abolition would once more gain momentum.

The electrocution of William Kemmler in 1890 via the electric chair signaled a new phase in the continuing search for a more effective and humane means of execution. Convicted of an ax murder in Buffalo, New York (which ironically prided itself as the "electric city of the future"), his execution followed a decade-long debate over America's electric future involving Thomas A. Edison and George Westinghouse. During the 1880s, both men championed two forms of electricity that they hoped would dominate homes and businesses. Edison favored direct current (DC), which was cheaper to install, and Westinghouse preferred alternating current (AC), citing the danger of DC current. With Edison on the verge of winning the marketing war, the New York legislature made New York the first state to approve electrocution as its method of capital punishment; the chair replaced the gallows. Unfortunately for Edison, it also demonstrated the killing power of DC, and his rival's AC current was adopted.

Similar to the adoption of lethal injection in the 1970s and 1980s, a trend began following Kemmler's execution that saw other states adopt electrocution over the next twenty-five years, including Ohio (1897), Massachusetts (1901), Kentucky and New Jersey (1907), Virginia (1908), Tennessee (1909), North Carolina (1910), South Carolina (1912), Arkansas (1913), and Pennsylvania (1915). By the end of the 1920s, over half the states using the death penalty were utilizing the electric chair.

One development that helped in the implementation of the electric chair was a movement toward the "delocalization" of executions.[48] This, along with greater discretion in death sentencing, occurred after the Civil War, when states began to require that executions be performed under state authority at one specific location. Between 1865 and 1900, twenty states made the transition from mandatory to discretionary capital punishment, permitting the jury to decide between death and alternative punishments. The movement toward state-mandated centralized execution began in 1864 in Vermont and Maine. By the 1950s, however, there were still states that continued to conduct executions under local authority (Delaware and Montana).

Few constitutional challenges were directed at the death penalty during the late nineteenth century. In *Wilkerson v. Utah* (1879), a defendant claimed that execution by firing squad violated his protection against cruel and unusual punishment. The Supreme Court upheld the death sentence, citing the fact that this method had been used for premeditated murder for years and was therefore not unconstitutional. Ax murderer William Kemmler also had his day in court (1890), citing the same grounds under the Eighth Amendment. But again the Supreme Court ruled against the defendant. In this instance, the Court noted that "we think that the evidence is clearly in favor of the conclusion that it is within easy reach of electrical science at this day to so generate and apply to the person of the convict a current of electricity . . . to produce instantaneous, and therefore painless, death."[49] As a postscript, the current had to be applied two different times before Kemmler was pronounced dead.

VIOLENCE

According to historian Michael A. Bellesiles, "The cost of firearms continued to fall after the Civil War," reaching the point where most people could "afford the so-called 'suicide special' of the 1890s."[50] Inexpensive guns were commonly used in the commission of most murders and suicides during this era and had become so ubiquitous that one religious magazine was even offering a pistol with the purchase of a subscription.[51] In marked contrast to the stereotype of the handgun-carrying South of the twentieth century, it was illegal to carry a pistol in one's pocket in Louisiana between 1856 and 1885.[52] While many citizens carried hidden weapons for personal defense, New Orleans policemen were prohibited by law from carrying concealed guns into the 1890s. However, there were no laws barring policemen and civilians from bearing arms openly. In 1932, in the first scholarly study to examine homicide from a national perspective, H. C. Brearley asserted that the South was "that part of the United States lying below the Smith and Wesson line," an assessment that holds true for the region's past and present.

Prior to the Civil War, few states had statutes regulating the carrying of concealed handguns. By the 1920s and 1930s, some states had adopted the Uniform Act to Regulate the Sale and Possession of Firearms, a model law that prohibited unlicensed carrying of concealed weapons. Most states affirmed provisions that allowed sheriffs, judges, and police chiefs to issue concealed-handgun permits to individuals who demonstrated a legitimate need for this protection. Today, nearly one-third of the states have adopted laws permitting citizens to carry concealed firearms for protection.

Continuing a legacy of violence, the South and the West continued to have the highest homicide rates in the nation in the years between 1865 and 1915. A study of homicide in the Cumberland Mountains for this period found a rate of 130 per 100,000, more than ten times the homicide rate of the 1990s.[53] As early as 1880, journalist Horace Redfield (1845–1881)[54] noted the disproportionate number of homicides in the South compared to other regions of the country. While most studies of southern violence attribute it to the enduring notions of honor and a subculture of violence, more recent studies link this preference for violence to the fact that "much of the South was a lawless, frontier region settled by people whose economy was originally based on herding." The authors conclude that most herding societies are "characterized by having 'cultures of honor' in which a threat to property or reputation is dealt with by violence."[55] According to homicide historian Roger Lane, perhaps a more convincing explanation for the high murder rates was poverty combined with "a tradition of weak government and law enforcement."[56]

Historians continue to quarrel over the levels of violence in the post–Civil War West. Scholars have long argued that violence was not common in the late nineteenth-century West. Beginning with Robert Dykstra's *Cattle Towns* (1968), which was one of the first scholarly studies to proclaim that the American West was not violent, most examinations on this theme have been based on anecdotal evidence and newspaper accounts, with little statistical sophistication.[57] A recent study by historian Clare V. McKanna Jr. challenges earlier studies that suggest that homicide was not common in the American West. By using quantitative methods and seldom-used sources such as coroner's inquests, criminal registers, and census data,

McKanna argues that lethal violence was indeed common in the American West. Not just the bailiwick of the mythical gunfighter, he found that contrary to the prevailing belief that western violence was usually episodic, it occurred on a daily basis among "ranchers, farmers, cowboys, coal and copper miners, bartenders, cooks, butchers, gamblers, pimps, police officers, sheriff's deputies, town marshals, Baldwin–Felts detectives, coal mine guards, roisterous drunks, teenagers, old men—and occasional housewives and mothers."[58]

Southern Reconstruction was accompanied by violence on both a grand and a small scale. In some southern states, racially mixed militias banded together to protect freedmen, while whites retaliated with quasi-military organizations such as the Ku Klux Klan. White supremacist–oriented organizations fomented race riots in many parts of the South between 1868 and 1876. The end of radical Reconstruction in 1877 saw the withdrawal of Union troops from the occupied South and the dissolution of the mixed militias.

Lynching

The term *lynching* evolved from its colonial-era meaning, which was associated with punishment (typically not fatal) not sanctioned by law, to its more sinister connotations reflecting unlawful sentences of death by the 1890s. During the antebellum era, lynching was most often used against local whites who deviated from acceptable behaviors, such as those who beat their wives and children or subscribed to unorthodox beliefs or lifestyles. After the Civil War, a shift occurred in which the majority of lynching victims were people of color—Asians, Native Americans, Chicanos, and occasionally whites.

According to the research conducted in the 1890s by black newspaper owner Ida B. Wells, the overwhelming majority of cases involved the hanging of blacks in the South. A leading voice in the campaign against lynchings in the last decade of the nineteenth century, Wells was drawn to the

cause when three of her friends in Memphis, Tennessee, were murdered by a lynch mob. As Wells made the transition to investigative journalist and reformer, she began to make the connection between this utilization of ritualized violence and intimidation and its goal of impeding the progress of African Americans in their efforts to participate more fully in the social, political, and economic life of the nation. Violence authority Roger Lane explains that the onus of Reconstruction fell so heavily on the black population following the withdrawal of federal troops in 1877 because "the place of African-American men and women had not been fully settled."[59] Wells began writing editorials condemning the terror of lynching and according to her biographer was responsible for a "significant migration of thousands of African Americans to the West."[60]

According to her subsequent research, Wells studied white newspaper reports of lynchings and found that during the 1890s, there was an average of 188 lynchings per year, a number exceeding legal executions by two to one. In a time period when a charge of rape supplied the pretext for a lynching, she found this charge was present in only about 20 percent of the cases. A gradual decline in southern lynchings would not begin until the 1920s, when a group of white southern moderates organized the Commission on Interracial Cooperation and used their influence to improve race relations in the South.

In stark contrast to the prototypical lynching, the worst mass lynching of the century targeted Italian immigrants in New Orleans following the assassination of the city's police chief, David Hennessey, in 1890. In an era that found a wide audience for the theories of Lombroso, the "Italian" was assumed to display a tendency to criminal behavior. It was widely believed at the time that Hennessey had been murdered by a Mafia faction of a group of immigrant Italian dockworkers whom he had provoked for some unknown reason.

In 1890, the country was witnessing one of its periodic bouts with xenophobia that seemed to coincide with heavy immigration. Between 1870 and 1890, the Italian community grew from

3.2 to 10.5 percent of New Orleans' foreign population. Following the shooting, scores of Italian suspects were rounded up. Nineteen were indicted. In the trials that followed, suspects were acquitted, only further antagonizing local leaders. Before all the men could be freed, some more respectable members of the community organized a mob of perhaps 10,000. Reaching the jail, they unleashed their fury on the eleven Italians in custody (including three who had been acquitted). Foreign opinion cited the incident as the latest proof of American barbarism. The Italian government formerly protested the slaying of three of the men who were Italian citizens and even demanded compensation for their families. The offer to pay indemnities to the families by President Benjamin Harrison in 1891 ultimately cooled the antagonism between the two governments.

Labor Violence

Prior to the Civil War, most labor violence occurred along ethnic and racial lines. For example, Irish canal workers rioted in response to mistreatment at the hand of contractors. In other cases, Irish workers came into conflict with free blacks competing for unskilled jobs. After the war, the pattern of labor violence changed. More urban and industrialized by the 1870s, industrial conflict pitted organized labor against employers. The 1870s saw workingmen attempting to organize for collective action, igniting more than a half century of violent conflict with industrialists, their private armies, and unemployed laborers used as strikebreakers.

In the coal fields of northeastern Pennsylvania, the secret organization known as the Molly Maguires[61] rose to prominence in the 1860s and 1870s as it waged a campaign of terror against their employers. Predominantly Irish-Catholic, the so-called Mollies found themselves at odds with their Protestant bosses and neighbors over their perceived mistreatment. Unable to sustain a union organization after a labor strike was broken in 1875, the Mollies resorted to guns and dynamite and were eventually charged with killing sixteen men. Subsequently, a Pinkerton operative named James McParlan infiltrated the group. Thanks to his testimony, forty Mollies were arrested and charged with various criminal acts. All were found guilty, and twenty were hanged, half of whom were executed on June 21, 1877, a date that became known in the region as Black Thursday. The prosecution of the Irish miners is shrouded in controversy because the defendants were arrested by private policemen and convicted on the questionable testimony of informers and McParlan, who was labeled an "agent provocateur" by the defense.[62] Conducted in the most hostile of atmospheres, the prosecuting attorneys were affiliated with railroad and mining companies.

The year 1877 was a particularly violent one in American history. Following on the heels of four years of depression, the mood of the nation was volatile as labor sought to unite against the monopolistic corporations, violence and lawlessness erupted in the nation's cities, and race riots, lynchings, and government corruption made headline news. During the ongoing economic depression, unorganized railroad workers, protesting wage cuts, the use of scab labor, and the probable loss of their jobs, engaged in a series of destructive riots that hit Baltimore and Pittsburgh with particular ferocity. On the other side of the country, San Francisco workingmen rioted in sympathy with railroad strikers and engaged in hand-to-hand battles with the police and Chinese immigrants. Violence would continue to punctuate the 1880s and 1890s, culminating in the Haymarket Square bombing (1886) and the Homestead strike at the Carnegie steel plant (1892). In 1894, a Pullman strike led President Grover Cleveland to call in federal troops over the protest of the Illinois governor. Perhaps overstating the explosive confluence of troubles, historian Robert V. Bruce suggested that "the upheaval was perhaps our closest brush with class revolution in America."

In the social unrest that accompanied the labor turmoil of the late nineteenth century, the police often found themselves targeted for defending the interests of big business and the "robber barons." Events in 1885 would precipitate one of the most notorious acts of antipolice violence in American history. That year, the Knights of Labor began a series of strikes aimed at achieving an eight-hour workday at the McCormick Harvester Works. Almost one-third of the Chicago Police Department were stationed at the picket lines trying to protect strikebreakers. At a large gathering of strikers at Chicago's Haymarket Square, an unknown anarchist tossed a bomb into the crowd, killing seven police officers and injuring seventy others. In an era of growing radical politics, the incident struck a chord with the public, who rallied to the police department. In the weeks following the tragedy, tens of thousands of dollars poured into a contribution fund for the victims. One authority has suggested that the hysteria over Haymarket "gave the signal for the law and order forces throughout the country to act."[63]

NOTABLE TRIALS

Lizzie Borden Trial (1893)

In one of the most famous murder cases in American history, thirty-two-year-old Lizzie Borden was indicted for murdering her father and stepmother with an ax in Fall River, Massachusetts. Her father was one of the wealthiest and most influential members of the community, president of the bank, and a stalwart member of the business sector. At the time of the murder, Lizzie still lived at home with her parents, her older sister, and a servant girl. Although there were no witnesses to the brutal ax slaying, attention focused almost immediately on Lizzie because of her cold and unemotional response to the incident. At the time of the killing, only Lizzie and the servant were at home, with Lizzie contending that she was in the barn at the time. Despite the conflicting evidence,

the presiding judge decided that there was sufficient cause to hold Lizzie.

Lizzie was fortunate that she was rich enough to hire a substantial defense that would eventually include the Pinkerton Agency and a three-member defense team led by the state's former governor. The defense team interviewed almost 110 panelists before settling on twelve jurors: all farmers, all male, and none from the town of Fall River.

According to the prosecution, there were a number of factors that would prove their case against Lizzie, including that she did not get along with her stepmother; that she had tried to purchase a deadly poison from a drugstore the day before the murders but was rebuffed because she lacked a prescription; that there was no sign of a struggle or any property taken, so the assailant must not have seemed like a threat; that Lizzie apparently burned an ax handle and concealed the ax blade from the probable murder weapon; and that the servant was in her third-floor room and Lizzie was downstairs alone with her father and not in the barn. Without even other inconsistencies, it seemed that the prosecution had an airtight case.

The defense demonstrated how a man might have hidden in the house. The jury was taken on a walk-through of the house to become familiar with the layout of the property. In the subsequent trial, the defense was able to refute most of the evidence presented by the prosecution. During the seventh day of the trial, medical witnesses explained how Mrs. Borden was murdered at least an hour before her husband. Noting Lizzie's aloof disposition, her lawyers decided against having her testify. In their conclusions, they noted the lack of direct and circumstantial evidence— no blood, no murder weapon, no motive, and no exclusive opportunity since the prosecution could not prove that Lizzie was not in the barn as she claimed. The defense also explained that Lizzie was active in many religious and charitable groups, loved her father very much, and was not one to openly express her feelings in public.

In the end, after the thirteen-day trial, the jury deliberated for one hour and ten minutes and returned with a verdict of not guilty. Lizzie and her sister inherited the father's considerable estate and attempted to live as normal a life as possible despite an almost constant hounding by the press. Lizzie died in 1927 at the age of sixty-six.

This "crime of the century" continues to pique the interest of true crime and mystery writers. Some have offered alternative solutions, including the logical question, Why not the servant girl? And why the enduring interest in the murder? It had all the familiar hallmarks of a classic murder: there was no solution; the participants were wealthy, educated, and of a high standing in the community; the sadistic manner of the attack in an upper-class home in small-town New England that contrasted sharply with the lower-class urban murder patterns of the day; and the fact that it was a woman accused of such a deed.

In one examination of how gender, history, and law entered into the arguments of the trial, Janice Schuetz noted that the era of the Borden trial was a "critical period in the definition of the role of women."[64] With even the prosecutor telling the jury that it was hard to conceive that a woman could be guilty of such a crime, Lizzie Borden owed her life to contemporary perceptions about "true womanhood."[65] Not unlike today, patricide by an ax-wielding woman sold newspapers. From a criminal justice perspective, the Lizzie Borden case has several implications. The case demonstrated that an individual has the right not to testify and that this cannot be used against the defendant. It also constitutes a case of "trial by newspaper." However, unlike other murder cases that castigated the defendant, such as in the Bruno Hauptmann, Sam Shepard, and Charles Manson cases, most of the papers presented a favorable impression of Lizzie Borden.

CONCLUSIONS

Late nineteenth-century America was characterized by unprecedented social strife. Between 1861 and 1900, America was racked by the Civil War, severe economic depressions, massive immigration, and unforeseen advances in communication, trans-

portation, and communication. Extraordinary urbanization and industrialization transformed the country, leading to profound challenges to the ever-evolving criminal justice system. As testimony to the progress of police reformers of the late nineteenth century, American cities had become much more orderly places than the antebellum period as "daily life became more predictable and controlled."[66] Others attributed the growing order of urban life to the socialization skills provided by of public schools and industrialization.

Penal reformers during this era saw the implementation of indeterminate sentencing and education at a time when the old methods of prison discipline at Auburn and Eastern State were breaking down. While both developments met with varying degrees of success, they helped pave the way for new reforms by modifying the thinking and the recognized objectives of the Auburn system enough to make its punitive methods of discipline more tolerable.

While penal and police reformers grappled with the new realities of late nineteenth-century criminal justice, criminologists and scientists attempted to adapt scientific methods to the study of criminality. Rejecting many of the legal definitions of crime, adherents of Lombroso and others focused their attentions on the criminal act as a psychological entity, emphasized determinism, and believed that punishment should be replaced by a scientific treatment of criminals in order to protect society.

Point–Counterpoint
Police Corruption on the New York City Police Department (1894)

In late 1894, a committee was created to investigate corruption in the New York City Police Department. What would become known as the Lexow Commission, after chairman Clarence Lexow (1852–1910), would discover a pattern of bribery and corruption that extended throughout the

Source: New York State Committee, *Report and Proceedings of the Senate Committee Appointed to Investigate the Police Department of the City of New York*, Vol. V, Albany, 1895, pp. 5532–5536; Bureau of Municipal Research, *A Report on the Homes and Family Budgets of 100 Patrolmen*, March 31, 1913, pp. 4491–4494.

department. The most prominent target of the investigation was Captain Alexander "Clubber" Williams (1839–1910). The following testimony is taken from the hearings as investigators try to figure out how he amassed more than $1 million in assets on an annual salary of $3,500.

The second excerpt is taken from a 1913 investigation into the family budgets of 100 patrolmen published in 1913. The report makes clear in its summary of findings why graft and bribery might be so enticing to the underpaid police officers. What is unclear is why some officers were more susceptible to graft than others. This summary of findings suggests that the environment conducive for corruption had not measurably changed.

Alexander S. Williams, recalled and further examined, testified as follows:

Q. Inspector, how much money have you in United States bonds? A. Not a dollar.

Q. Did you ever have? A. Yes, sir.

Q. How much? A. Five hundred.

Q. How much has your wife invested in United States bonds? A. None.

Q. Five hundred what; you said five hundred? A. Five hundred dollars.

Q. You are worth $500,000 altogether? A. No, sir.

Q. How near are you? A. A long ways off.

Q. How much is your place up in Cos Cob worth, Inspector? A. It is assessed; the property up there—

Q. Never mind; I am not asking what the assessment is; we know there are millions of dollars in property not properly assessed? A. It is assessed $13,000.

Q. That is no standard; we know in New York too much about assessments to take the assessment of property as an estimate of the value; what is your place worth—all your houses; how much money have you spent on that place up there? A. I could not tell you.

Q. One hundred thousand dollars? A. No, sir.

Q. Will you swear you have not spent a $100,000? A. Yes, sir.

Q. How much did the construction of the dock cost? A. That I would not tell you.

Q. Forty thousand dollars, was it not? A. No, sir.

Q. How near it? A. About $39,000 off; possibly more.

Q. How long have you been building it?

Q. How many houses have you upon your domain anyway? A. Three.

Q. Well, you have built a new house there, Queen Anne-style? A. I don't know as to Queen Anne; I don't exactly know what style it is.

Q. That is what the architect calls it; 15 rooms in the house? A. I think it contains 17.

Q. One hundred and thirty-five feet front? A. The house?

Q. Yes. A. No, sir

Q. What are the dimensions? A. Thirty-six feet front.

Q. What is the depth? A. Forty-two feet.

Q. Is that counting all the houses connected with it? A. Yes, sir.

Q. Then you have your coachman's house, near by? A. No, sir.

Q. Haven't you a coachman's house on the grounds? A. No, sir.

Q. Have you got a coachman there? A. No, sir.

Q. How long is it since you had one? A. Never had one.

Q. How are the houses occupied? A. Which?

Q. The houses on your place; you have got three houses? A. No, sir; I have not; three dwelling-houses.

Q. Those are three houses? A. Yes, sir.

Q. How are they occupied and by whom? A. The small one I gave $1,160 for, is let for $200 a year; the one I gave $3,600 for is let for $480 a year.

Q. You had dredging there, a good deal of dredging before you could build your sea wall? A. No, sir.

Q. Did you have any dredging done? A. No, sir.

Q. You had dredging done? A. Not for that sea wall.

Q. To build what? A. To make a channel.

Q. To allow your yacht to get up there? A. No, sir.

Q. What is the channel there for? A. To allow a row boat to come up.

Q. Did your yacht ever go up the channel? A. No, sir.

Q. How long have you owned that sloop-yacht, Elenor? A. One thousand eight hundred and seventy-eight, I think.

Q. Where was she built? A. Greenpoint.

Q. Have you had any craft built in Machias, Maine? A. No, sir.

Q. Directly, have you any interest there? A. No, sir.

Q. Directly or indirectly? A. Indirectly.

Q. Was there any craft built there for you? A. No, sir.

Q. What was the indirect interest you had? A. I gave a vessel a set of flags.

Q. Is that all the interest you had? A. No, sir.

Q. What other interest? A. Two thousand dollars interest in it.

Q. In what shape? A. That much ownership.

Q. In a ship or in a vessel? A. She is a brigantine.

Q. Is that the only interest you have there? A. That is all.

Q. How much did your yacht cost? A. The contract price was $4,000.

Q. How much did your yacht cost, I asked you; I did not ask you the contract price? A. It cost me something to run her since.

Q. How much did your yacht cost when she was built? A. That was the contract price.

Q. I ask the price? A. That was the cost.

Q. Who built the yacht? A. John Parmley.

Q. Over in Greenpoint? A. Yes, sir.

Q. How many did your crew consist of? A. Three.

Q. You have had her in commission ever since? A. No, sir.

Q. Every year? A. Once in a while.

Q. Every year? A, Yes, sir; I have a commission for once in a while.

Q. And you have your guests, frequently officers of the department, on your cruises? A. No, sir.

Q. Never have any? A. No, sir.

Q. Has Captain Devery never been on your yacht? A. I do not recollect that he was.

Q. You had an income of from $7,000 to $8,000 a year from the Tenderloin while you were there? A. No, sir.

Q. No income from it? A. No, sir.

Q. Of course you are prepared to swear that you never touched a dollar? A. I am prepared to swear to the truth.

Q. You are prepared to swear you never touched a dollar? A. I am prepared to swear to the truth.

Q. Are you prepared to swear you never received a dollar outside of your salary while you were captain of the Tenderloin? A. I received money, but not from the Tenderloin, as you call it.

Q. What money did you receive? A. Five or $6,000 down town.

Q. What from? A. Stocks.

Q. From whom? A. The firm of Freece & Hoey, brokers.

Q. Freece & Hoey? A. Yes, sir.

Q. Where? A. Forty-seven Broadway.

Q. What stocks? A. I could not tell you.

Q. How much did you pay to get that $6,000? A. I didn't pay anything.

Q. Received it as a present? A. Yes, sir.

SUMMARY OF FINDINGS

1. The policemen during the first two years of service are underpaid.

The investigators' visit to the homes of the policemen who were in their first two years of service, revealed conditions, of the most convincing character in support of the contention that they are underpaid. The attached exhibits show that the average family budget for first and second year patrolmen is, for family purposes, —$871.46, and for police purposes,—$218.12, a total budget of $1,089.58; that the average patrolman's apartment consists of four rooms; that thirty-three families are without baths; that the average number of children to a family is two, and that the first year patrolman contributes $16.85 to benefit societies and $28.83 for insurance, the second year man contributing $20.07 and $27.24 respectively for benefit societies and insurance.

Attached to this report are also statements made by policemen upon certain phases of police work, such as fines, extra duties, etc.

2. Of the $800 given the patrolman for his first year's service, the minimum amount he is compelled to expend for uniform, equipment, station house charges, and contribution to the pension fund is $169.64, leaving him a balance of $630.36. From this amount again, must be subtracted approximately $73.72 which he is required to spend for meals away from home. In this connection it must be remembered that the policeman is unable to carry his luncheon with him as does the ordinary civil employee, and therefore must, buy at least one meal a day away from home. Assuming that the policeman during his first year does not become a member of any benefit or life insurance society, loses no time through sickness, and suffers no fines, he has at his disposal out of his $800 salary, $556.64 with which to support himself and family.

4. The increases in salary which accrue during the third, fourth and fifth year of the policeman's first five years of service, do not result in a corresponding increase in income for his support and that of his family, because much of this increase usually goes toward paying the debts contracted during his first and second years of service.

5. The danger of increased indebtedness by reason of possible fines is common.

The system of taking money out of the salaries of delinquent policemen is uniformly condemned by the members of the force. In almost every instance it was the opinion of the policemen that the system of fining was one which resulted in disciplining the family rather than the policeman, in that every dollar taken from him, especially during his first year, meant an added dollar of debt to the family, and consequently an extra trip to the loan shark and more frequently a visit to the pawnshop. In fact, it was the experience of the investigators that the pawnshop furnished in sixteen cases the speedy assistance so necessary in emergencies to the policeman's little family.

In many instances patrolmen were ready to cite examples of what they regarded as gross injustices— the general complaint seemed to be inconsistency in the matter of punishment for the same type of offense. Believing the fine to be an injustice, the policemen do not give their best services to the city during the days on which in reality they are serving the City without compensation. In cases where the fine is heavy, as for example 15 days, the hardship is all the more severe, because the full amount is deducted from the next check.

About half the families run monthly accounts and pay almost entirely on the installment plan. The first of each month finds many collectors at the door of the policeman's home, and at the home where a 15-day fine has been imposed the wife is unprepared to meet the monthly bills. Next month, most of the bills have doubled. From this financial difficulty arises a natural condition of home worry and discouragement which does not add to the usefulness of the policeman to the city.

To emphasize the danger of the fining system, one has only to add the possibility of a doctor's bill, due to a sick baby or a sick wife.

The investigators also found in this connection that the families of policemen were denied treatment at the various dispensaries and hospitals when they made known that the father was a policeman.

6. "Little encouragement but plenty of discouragement," seemed to be the general feeling of the policeman during his first few years of service.

There is a widespread lack of enthusiasm among the men, due to the absence of a merit system which would reward for efficiency. At present the delinquent policeman is punished through his pocketbook, and there is no apparent reward for efficiency except in the case of demonstrations of physical courage. In other words, there is no possible chance, even by the most meritorious kind of police work, for the policeman ever to get the money

which the department has taken away from him during a possible period of delinquency.

7. "No reward for overtime," was another complaint. In only one instance did the policemen urge financial reward. The fact is that in the course of a policeman's work a great many hours of extra service are required, due to strikes, riots, parades, and time spent in court. At present no amount of extra duty brings with it any reward, either in salary, time off, or merits. A great many policemen ventured the opinion that if there were some system of merits or reward for extra duty, especially with regard to presenting cases in court, a greater efficiency in the enforcement of law could be had.

In many instances the policemen did not hesitate to say that the human element entered so strongly into the performance of their duty that they hesitated to make an arrest when this involved spending their day off in the court.

Sources

Abelson, Elaine S. 1989. *When Ladies Go A-Thieving: Middle-Class Shoplifters in the Victorian Department Store*. New York: Oxford University Press.

Ayers, Edward, L. 1986. *Vengeance and Justice: Crime and Punishment in the 19th-Century South*. New York: Oxford University Press.

Barnes, Harry and Negley Teeters. 1943. *New Horizons in Criminology*. New York: Prentice Hall.

Beavan, Colin. 2001. *Fingerprints: The Origins of Crime Detection and the Murder Case That Launched Forensic Science*. New York: Hyperion.

Beisel, Nocola. 1997. *Imperiled Innocents: Anthony Comstock and Family Reproduction in Victorian America*. Princeton, N.J.: Princeton University Press.

Bellesiles, Michael A. 2000. *Arming America: Origins of a National Gun Culture*. New York: Alfred A. Knopf.

Bodenhamer, David J. 1992. *Fair Trial: Rights of the Accused in American History*. New York: Oxford University Press.

Bowers, William J. 1974. *Executions in America*. Lexington, MA: Lexington Books.

Boyer, Paul S. 1968. *Purity in Print: Book Censorship in America*. New York: Charles Scribner's Sons.

Brecher, Jeremy. 1972. *Strike!* San Francisco: Straight Arrow Books.

Bruce, Robert V. 1959. *1877: Year of Violence*. New York: Bobbs-Merrill.

Christianson, Scott. 1998. *With Liberty for Some: 500 Years of Imprisonment in America*. Boston: Northeastern University Press.

Cole, Simon A. 2001. *Suspect Identities: A History of Fingerprinting and Criminal Identification*. Cambridge, Mass.: Harvard University Press.

Cresswell, Stephen. 1991. *Mormons and Cowboys, Moonshiners and Klansmen: Federal Law Enforcement in the South and the West, 1870–1893*. Tuscaloosa: University of Alabama Press.

Friedman, Lawrence M. 1993. *Crime and Punishment in American History*. New York: Basic Books.

Hollon, Eugene. 1974. *Frontier Violence: Another Look*. New York: Oxford University Press.

Jeffers, H. Paul. 1994. *Commissioner Roosevelt: The Story of Theodore Roosevelt and the New York City Police, 1895–1897*. New York: John Wiley & Sons.

Jones, Ann. 1981. *Women Who Kill*. New York: Fawcett Columbine.

Kenny, Kevin. 1998. *Making Sense of the Molly Maguires*. New York: Oxford University Press.

Lane, Roger. 1997. *Murder in America*. Columbus: Ohio State University Press.

Lardner, James, and Thomas Reppetto. 2000. *NYPD: A City and Its Police*. New York: Henry Holt.

Lombroso-Ferrero, Gina. [1911] 1972. *Criminal Man according to the Classification of Cesare Lombroso*. Reprint, Montclair, N.J.: Patterson Smith.

McGrath, Roger. 1984. *Gunfighters, Highwaymen, and Vigilantes: Violence on the Frontier*. Berkeley: University of California Press.

McKanna, Clare V. 1997. *Homicide, Race and Justice in the American West, 1880–1920*. Tucson: University of Arizona Press.

McKelvey, Blake. 1977. *American Prisons: A History of Good Intentions*. Montclair, NJ: Patterson Smith.

Monkkonen, Eric H. 2001. *Murder in New York City*. Berkeley: University of California Press.

Morn, Frank. 1982. *"The Eye That Never Sleeps": A History of the Pinkerton National Detective Agency*. Bloomington: Indiana University Press.

Nisbett, Richard E. and Dov Cohen. 1996. *Culture of Honor: The Psychology of Violence in the South*. New York: Westview Press.

Platt, Anthony M. 1969. *The Child Savers: The Invention of Delinquency*. Chicago: University of Chicago Press.

Prassel, Frank. 1972. *Western Peace Officer*. Norman: University of Oklahoma Press.

Rafter, Nicole Hahn. 1985. *Partial Justice: Women in State Prisons, 1800–1935*. Boston: Northeastern University Press.

———. 1997. *Creating Born Criminals*. Chicago: University of Illinois Press.

Redfield, Horace V. 1880. *Homicide, North and South: Being a Comparative View of Crime against the Person in Several Parts of the United States*. Philadelphia.

Reinders, Robert C. 1977. "Militia and Public Order in 19th Century America," *Journal of American Studies*. Vol. 11, No. 1, pp. 81–101.

Rhodes, Henry T. 1956. *Alphonse Bertillon: Father of Scientific Detection*. London: George Harrap.

Richardson, James F. 1970. *The New York Police: Colonial Times to 1901*. New York: Oxford University Press.

———. 1974. *Urban Police in the United States*. Port Washington, N.Y.: Kennikat Press.

Roe, George M. [1890] 1976. *Our Police: A History of the Cincinnati Police Force, from the Earliest Period until the Present Day*. Reprint, New York: AMS Press.

Rousey, Dennis C. *Policing the Southern City: New Orleans, 1805–1889*. Baton Rouge: Louisiana State University Press.

Royster, Jacqueline Jones, ed. 1997. *Southern Horrors and Other Writings: The Anti-Lynching Campaign of Ida B. Wells, 1892–1900*. Boston: Bedford Books.

Sante, Luc. 1992. *Evidence*. New York: Farrar, Straus & Giroux..

Schuetz, Janice. 1994. *The Logic of Women on Trial: Case Studies of Popular American Trials*. Carbondale: Southern Illinois University Press.

Schwartz, Bernard. 1997. *A Book of Legal Lists: The Best and Worst in American Law*. New York: Oxford University Press.

Smith-Rosenberg, Carroll. 1985. *Disorderly Conduct: Visions of Gender in Victorian America*. New York: Oxford University Press.

Sullivan, Larry E. 1990. *The Prison Reform Movement*. Boston: Twayne Publishing.

Vandal, Gilles. 2000. *Rethinking Southern Violence: Homicides in Post–Civil War Louisiana, 1866–1884*. Columbus: Ohio State University Press.

Vila, Bryan and Cynthia Morris. 1997. *Capital Punishment in America*. Westport, CN: Greenwood Press.

Wolfgang, Marvin E. 1961. "Cesare Lombroso." *Journal of Criminal Law, Criminology and Police Science* 52, no. 4 (November–December):232-291. *Pioneers in Criminology*, edited by Hermann Mannheim, Montclair, pp. 232–294. NJ: Patterson Smith.

Woloch, Nancy. 2000. *Women and the American Experience*. 3rd ed. Boston: McGraw-Hill.

Zedner, Lucia. 1998. "Wayward Sisters: The Prison for Women." In *The Oxford History of the Prison*, edited by Norval Morris and David Rothman, pp. 295–324. New York: Oxford University Press.

CRITICAL THINKING QUESTIONS

1. Discuss the impact of Victorian-era criminal justice on women in America.

2. What upheavals in American society during the Victorian years might explain the assassination of two presidents between 1881 and 1901? What was the impact of these events on federal criminal justice agencies?

3. Contrast the development of police organizations in New York, the South, and the West.

4. What impact did the National Prison Congress have on the correctional system?

5. Discuss and compare the various reform movements of the Victorian era (e.g., juvenile court system, antivice societies, police professionalism, and correctional reform).

6. Examine race relations and the criminal justice system during the post–Civil War era.

7. What are the larger lessons in criminal justice and Victorian America that can be gleaned from the Lizzie Borden trial?

CRIMINAL JUSTICE HISTORY
ON THE INTERNET

There are numerous Web sites devoted to the court decisions of the late nineteenth century. Articles dedicated to *Bradwell v. Illinois* include www.brittanica.com/women/articles/Bradwell_v_Illinois.html and http://usinfo.state.gov/usa/infousa/facts/democrac/ demo. For the story of Myra Bradwell, America's first female lawyer, see momo.essortment.com/myrabradwell_rfxv.htm.

For the *Slaughterhouse* case, see www.pearsoncustom.com/allpages/fourteenthamendment_bot.html and www.civil-liberties.com/ cases/slauterhouse.html.

Plessy v. Ferguson is referenced at http://memory.loc.gov/ammem/today/Jul28.html, www.bowdoin.edu/~sbodurt2/court/cases/plessy.html, http://campus.northpark.edu/history/webchron/usa/PlessyFerguson.html, www.encyclopedia.com/articles/10297.html, and http://lawbooksusa.com/cconlaw/plessyvferguson.htm.

There are excellent sites dealing with Jim Crow laws, including examples in different states and actual newspaper articles, at www.encyclopedia.com/articles/10297.html. More on these laws is available at www.nilevalley.net/history/jim_crow_laws. Links to Jim Crowism and black codes can be found at http://afroamhistory.about.com/homework/ afroamhistory/cs/jimcrowlaws.

For articles devoted to the Molly Maguires and the Pinkerton investigation, see www.columbiapa.org/county/historical/molly_maguires.html. This site offers a ballad, stories from the Pinkerton archives, and an 1894 article from *McClure's* magazine. The Molly Maguire trial speeches can be accessed at www.spartacus.schoolnet.co.uk/USAMolly.htm. More on Mollies can be found at www.providence.edu/polisci/projects/molly_maguires and http://njw.injersey.com/schools/Neptune/History/Curious/Dugas.

The criminal theories of Cesare Lombroso, including references to atavism, the tattooing of criminals, and a debate on his theories, are available at www.tsd.jcu.edu.au/hist/stats/lomb. Other related links are at www.epub.org.br/cm/n01/frenology/lombroso.htm, www.cimm.jcu.edu.au/hist/stats/lomb, and www.cimm.jcu.edu.au/hist/stats/lomb/lombro3.htm.

The New York City Police Department, Tammany Hall, Theodore Roosevelt, and the Lexow hearings on police corruption can be found at the NYPD's home page at www.nyc.gov/html/nypd/html/3100/retro.html. A *Harper's Weekly* cartoon on NYPD corruption (1902) is at http://thetimes.org/learning/general/onthisday/harp/0906.html. Related photographs are at www.midtownmedia.com/ndc/Tammany.html.

A number of links to the development of criminal investigation devoted to fingerprinting can be found at http://onin.com/fphistory.html; kyky.essortment.com/fingerprinthist_rmmv.htm and www.edcampbell.com?PalmD-History.htm. Links to dozens of related sites are at www.clplex.com/Articlesmain.htm. The Bertillon system of bodily measurements, a critique of Francis Galton, and pictures and descriptions are available at www.tld.jcu.edu.au/hist/stats/bert. Excellent photographic examples of Bertillon identification cards can be accessed at www.monroesheriffny.org/archive.htm. A forensic science time line is at www.courttv.com/onair/shows/forensicfiles/timeline2.html. For information on criminal profiling as a career, see www.forensic-science.com/faq_career_cp.html. Hans Gross is covered at www.mindpiece.com/Hans%20Gross.html.

For police photography and photos as evidence, see www.nyu.edu/greyart/exhibits/police/html/mug.html and http://chnm.gmu.edu/aq/photos/essay/bib.htm. A historical time line of investigation is at www.criminology.fsu.edu/faculty/nute/history.html. Articles and exhibits on the New York City Police Department's Thomas Byrnes and his *Professional Criminals of America* is available at www.ama_assn.org/sci-pubs/amnews/pick_01/ prca0924.htm and www.nypress.com/14/35/news&columns/oldsmoke.cfm.

The trial of Lizzie Borden continues as a source of great interest, as demonstrated by a number of Web sites. Teacher resources devoted to the case can be found at http://mwes.neric.org/library/LizzieBorden. Other sites related to the case are www.lawbuzz.com/famous_trials/lizzie_borden/lizzie.htm and www.crimelibrary.com/lizzie/lizzietrial.htm.

An excellent site on the history of probation, including a time line, is at www.henrycty.com/courtservices/history.html; see also www.uscourts.gov/misc/history.pdf. The Illinois Juvenile Court Act of 1899 can be found at www.collegecourse.com/sou/crim/crim36/modiz/sld007.htm; the child savers and the Chicago juvenile court movement are covered at www.ncjrs.org/htm/ojjdp/jjjournal1299/2.html.

The death penalty is well documented on the Internet. For a history of the electric chair, see www.theElectricChair.com/topbannersub. Information on firing squads in Utah can be found at www.media.utah.edu/UHE/c/caPiTolPUN.html. Comparisons between the death penalty and life sentences are available at www.impactpress.com/articles/junju100/death6700.html; see also www.nandotimes.com/special_reports/mcveigh_execution/execution/story/22987p-431460c.html.

For policing, police matrons, and early policewomen, such as Alice Stebbins Wells, see www.losangelesalmanac.com/topics/Crime/cr73b.htm; more related links on the history of women in policing are at www.wpoaca.com/archives and www.sdinsider.com/community/groups/sdpolice/women_of_the_SDPD.html. For the history of the U.S. Secret Service, see http://clinton4.nara.gov/wlt/kids/inside/html/spring98-2.html and www.geocities.com/stu_hill/sspage.htm. The presidential assassination home page has many links to the killing of Presidents Garfield and McKinley at www.netcolony.com/news/presidents/assassinations.html; see also dir.yahoo.com/Arts/Humanities/History/By_Subject/Assassinations.

A historical time line for the International Association of Chiefs of Police can be accessed at www.theiacp.org/about/history/timeline.htm.

Haymarket tragedy photos are available at http://cpl.lib.uic.edu/images/disasters/haymarketanarchist.ipg.

The National Prison Congress of 1870 is chronicled at www.suu.edu/scps/distance/cj2200/lessons_12.htm.

NOTES

1. The Freedmen's Bureau was created by Congress on March 3, 1865. Originally called the Bureau of Refugees, Freedmen, and Abandoned Lands, it was charged with the task of guiding the transition of African Americans into a life of freedom. The bureau operated in all the southern states. Among its most important responsibilities was taking over the administration of justice for freed men and women by establishing court systems responsible for the protection of civil rights. By the early 1870s, the bureau had lost most of its authority as former Confederates returned to leadership.

2. Ayers (1986, p. 151).

3. Rafter (1985, p. 14).

4. Rousey (1991, p. 179).

5. Friedman (1993, p. 127).

6. Friedman (1993, p. 127).

7. Schwartz (1997, p. 78).

8. Quoted in Schwartz (1997, p. 78).

9. Woloch (2000, p. 289).

10. Bodenhamer (1992, p. 80).

11. Ayers (1986, p. 151). These crimes were often vagrancy, rape, arson, and burglary.

12. Ayers (1986, p. 154).

13. Smith-Rosenberg (1985, p. 225).

14. Friedman (1993, p. 134).

15. Woloch (2000, p. 372).

16. Smith-Rosenberg (1985, p. 223).

17. Irish dramatist George Bernard Shaw is credited with inventing the term *Comstockery,* referring to it as "the world's outstanding joke at the expense of the United States."

18. Reinders (1977, p. 92).

19. Roe (1976, p. iii).

20. Richardson (1974, p. 54).

21. Richardson (1974, p. 59).

22. Cresswell (1991, p. 4).

23. Cresswell (1991, pp. 4–5).

24. Lardner and Reppetto (2000, p. 50). The green lights supposedly were inspired by the green lamps carried by the early watchmen.

25. Quoted in Lardner and Reppetto (2000, p. 50).

26. Richardson (1974, p. 63).

27. Morn (1982).

28. Sante (1992, p. 97).

29. Beavan (2001).

30. For a comprehensive history of criminal identification, culminating in the success of fingerprinting over rival identification systems, see Cole (2001).

31. Rousey (1991, p. 135).

32. Rousey (1991, p. 188).

33. McKelvey (1977, p. 49).

34. Christianson (1998, p. 177).

35. Quoted in Christianson (1998, p. 180).

36. Friedman (1993, p. 233).

37. Sullivan (1990, p. 14).

38. Rafter (1985, p. xx).

39. Friedman (1993, p. 233).

40. Zedner (1998, p. 302).

41. Zedner (1998, p. 316).

42. Barnes and Teeters (1943, pp. 373–75).

43. Sullivan (1990, p. 29).

44. Platt (1969, p. 77).

45. Meaning the power of the state to act on behalf of the child and to provide care and protection as a surrogate parent would.

46. For a richly nuanced account of New York City's homicide rates during the nineteenth century, see Monkkonen (2001).

47. Quoted in Wolfgang (1961, p. 287).

48. Bowers (1974).

49. Quoted in Vila and Morris (1997, p. 68).

50. Bellesiles (2000, p. 433).

51. Bellesiles (2000, p. 433).

52. Rousey (1991, p. 175).

53. Quoted in Nisbett and Cohen (1996, p. 1).

54. While Redfield's methodology is considered flawed by most historians, having based most of his research on newspaper accounts, he is still credited with making the most extensive examination of regional homicide rates in the nineteenth century.

55. Nisbett and Cohen (1996, p. 4).

56. Lane (1997, p. 149).

57. For similar conclusions, see Hollon (1974) and Prassel (1972). McGrath (1984) incorporated more statistical rigor in his study of mining towns in Aurora, Nevada, and Bodie, California, where the author found high homicide rates. However, McKanna (1997) finds fault with this examination because it dealt with only a relatively short time period, and at the end of McGrath's study, the author states that "in most ways the towns were not violent or lawless places."

58. McKanna (1997, p. 3).

59. Lane (1997, p. 154).

60. Royster (1997, p. 4).

61. For the best examination of the Molly Maguires, their crimes, trials, and execution as well as the role played by private detectives in the investigation see Kenny (1998).

62. In 1979, one of the executed Mollies was given a full state pardon over a century too late, when it was determined that he was probably framed by detectives.

63. Brecher (1972, p. 47).

64. Schuetz (1994, p. 63).

65. Jones (1981, p. 231).

66. Richardson (1974, p. 53).

9

CRIMINAL JUSTICE IN THE PROGRESSIVE ERA (1898–1928)

TIME LINE

1898	Discovery of heroin in Germany	**1909**	National Association for the Advancement of Colored People (NAACP) formed
1905	Lola Baldwin hired as "operative" by Portland Police Department		
1906	Passage of Pure Food and Drug Act	**1910**	Alice Stebbins Wells becomes first female police officer after being hired by the Los Angeles Police Department
1907	Indiana passes first involuntary sterilization statute		
1908	Creation of a permanent Justice Department investigative bureau	**1910**	*Weems v. United States,* the first interpretation of the Eighth Amendment's "cruel and unusual" punishment clause by the Supreme Court
1909	Justice special agent force renamed Bureau of Investigation	**1910**	Congress passes White Slave Traffic Act (Mann Act)
1909	August Vollmer begins twenty-four-year stint as Berkeley police chief	**1911**	August Vollmer puts Berkeley police on bicycles

1911	Sullivan handgun law	1917	Espionage Act passed by Congress, limiting dissent against war
1911	Triangle Shirtwaist Company fire in New York City exposes unsafe workplace conditions	1918	President Wilson passes Sedition Act
1912	August Vollmer establishes motorcycle patrols	1919	Boston police strike
1913	Vollmer establishes automobile patrols	1919	Chicago race riots
1913	Thomas Mott Osborne spends week in Auburn Prison as "Tom Brown"	1919	*Webb et al. v. United States*
		1919	Passage of the Motor Vehicle Theft Act (Dyer Act)
1914	Osborne appointed warden at Sing Sing Prison and establishes Mutual Welfare League	1919	Eighteenth Amendment ratified (Prohibition)
		1920	Palmer anticommunist raids
1914	Passage of Harrison Narcotic Act	1920	Nineteenth Amendment grants women right to vote
1914	*Weeks v. United States*	1920	Wall Street bombing
1914	First public defender's office opens in Los Angeles	1921	Sacco and Vanzetti trial
		1924	Leopold and Loeb trial
1915	Resurgence of Ku Klux Klan	1924	Immigration legislation limits immigration to 2 percent of 1890 census; sets maximum quota at 150,000
1915	Organization of the International Association of Policewomen		
1917	Congress enacts Espionage Act	1927	Execution of Sacco and Vanzetti
1917	Beginning of Russian Revolution	1928	Supreme Court approves Virginia statute authorizing sterilization of imbeciles
1917	United States enters World War I		

The Progressive era (1890–1920) was a time of tumultuous change as urban America tried to accommodate waves of immigrants from eastern and southern Europe and African Americans fleeing the Jim Crow[1] South. Despite tremendous urban and industrial growth, unprecedented social problems created deep anxieties among many native-born Americans who lent their support to immigration restriction and other exclusionary policies.

Between the 1890s and 1920, a variety of Progressive reform efforts were directed at a nation in political, social, and economic transformation. By the 1920s, women had won the right to vote, and electoral reforms were introduced that included the secret ballot, direct election of senators, and a system for recalling elected officials. Workers saw their lots improve with the passage of the first labor protection laws for women and children as well as the shortening of the workday from almost fourteen hours to only eight.

Progressive reformers worked on many fronts in an era when 1 percent of the country's families owned seven-eighths of the nation's wealth. Meanwhile, four-fifths of the nation's population lived a marginal existence, presenting a remarkable juxtaposition to the opulent lifestyles of the captains of industry, such as Andrew Carnegie, who earned $23 million per year when the average working-man brought home perhaps $500 per year.

For the middle classes, the increase in the cost of living surmounted any advantages that may have come their way as the country's monopolies and trusts flourished despite the passage of the Sherman Act in 1890. It is estimated that almost three-quarters of all trusts in 1904 were created since 1898, leading to decreased competition and a declining faith in America as a land of opportunity.

Most of the problems that came to the public's attention were rooted in the Gilded Age of the late nineteenth century. Although reformers had addressed many of the nation's problems in the previous decades, by the first decades of the new century, reform became a national obsession

as diverse interests lent their voices in a call for social change. Among the most vocal reformers were investigative journalists known as "muckrakers,"[2] who capitalized on the American fascination with evil in a series of exposès published serially in popular magazines. Among the most famous and far reaching were Upton Sinclair's description of the appalling conditions in the meatpacking industry published as *The Jungle* and Lincoln Steffens's *The Shame of the Cities,* which examined the crass urban political scene.

Many of the reformers saw themselves as "progressives," as they endeavored to reform the nation's social problems. They believed that injustice and sin could be dispensed with merely through new legislation. At the same time, they rejected social Darwinist individualism and competition in favor of social cooperation. In the process, a cornucopia of organizations were founded that reflected the diversity of reform activity, including efforts for safer working conditions, abolition of child labor, shorter workweeks and higher wages, old-age pensions, and workmen's compensation.

Chief among the advocates for reform were middle-class women and church-related organizations. They found expression in the creation of the Women's Christian Temperance Union (1898) and the Anti-Saloon League (1893), which waged a war against alcohol abuse. In little more that twenty years, their crusade led to nationwide prohibition with the passage of the Volstead Act in 1920. Urban reformers had long recognized the consequences of alcohol consumption, including social problems, such as accidents, pauperism, and domestic violence.

The legislation of morality grew to include the sexual sphere, as opponents of prostitution found expression in the red-light-abatement movement and the passage of the 1910 White Slavery Act, or Mann Act. While prostitution was seen as a social evil because of its association with the sexual exploitation of women and its links to venereal disease, others linked prostitution and alcohol abuse to rising immigration from eastern and southern Europe.

Progressivism was concerned largely with mounting urbanization and the modernization of America as small-town governments attempted to confront rapid population increases. Formerly reliant on political machines to provide the most needed services, by the turn of the century most of these were on their last legs—corrupt and inefficient. Progressive social reform aimed at control and justice, and the criminal justice system in particular would benefit from Progressive concerns over problems of political patronage. In the process of breaking up the political machines, the informal welfare systems that helped the poor were dismantled. It soon became apparent that the states would have to become more involved in solving the problems of the cities.

One of the major goals of the Progressives was workmen's compensation and better working conditions. No event symbolized this concern to America at large more than New York City's 1911 Triangle Shirtwaist Company fire, in which 147 mostly women employees lost their lives. A subsequent investigation of the Manhattan fire discovered that the women were locked inside to prevent them from leaving early and that many of the fire escape ladders were missing. This tragedy only emphasized the escalating number of industrial accidents. Over the next five years, more than half the states would enact workmen's compensation laws.[3]

Further complicating the development of the criminal justice system in the early twentieth century was the immigration of more than twelve million people to America between 1890 and 1910. In 1910, fully one-seventh of the population was foreign-born. Of the Irish, German, Russian, Polish, Slavic, and Italians who thronged urban America, the Irish were the most politically significant, in part because of their literacy and English-speaking skills. Abandoned by the formal political system, immigrants rapidly fell into poverty and under the influence of corrupt political bosses and their city machines. Immigrants were quickly branded with stereotypes. Jews were scorned as anarchists, while Italians fell under the specter of the Mafia and the Black Hand. Mobs targeted European immigrants as well as African Americans, although the brunt of the violence fell on America's impoverished classes. According to sociologist Mark Colvin, "The Progressive movement, and much of what occurred in the arena of criminal justice between 1900 and 1920, must be understood within [the] context of rival orientations and divergent interests of a native, white, Protestant, urban middle class and an ethnic, non-Protestant, urban working class."[4]

Resentment of the new immigrants translated into immigration-restriction legislation, beginning with America's first federal law to check the immigration of a specific ethnic group in 1882, when the Chinese were excluded for ten years. Nativist and racist violence broke out over immigration, while the Ku Klux Klan reorganized and the Immigrant Restriction League emerged as a powerful voice of nativism. Not everyone who came to America would stay, with anywhere from a fourth to a third returning to their native lands.

THE LAWGIVERS

Progressive reform moved to the national level during the presidency of Theodore Roosevelt (1901–1908). The creation of the Bureau of Investigation as an agency of the Treasury Department in 1908 led the federal government to expand its role in law enforcement, a trend that continued into the 1930s and 1940s. Joining in the spirit of Progressive reform, Congress passed the White Slave Traffic Act in 1910 and the Harrison Narcotic Act in 1914 to attack the "moral evils" of prostitution and narcotics addiction. Influenced by the publication of *The Jungle,* Congress passed the Pure Food and Drug Act and the Meat Inspection Act, both on the same day in 1906.

The passage of congressional legislation in October 1917 signaled the beginning of a new era of persecution in America, leading to the criminalization of certain unpopular political views. In

June 1917, Congress passed the Espionage Act, which authorized postal officials to ban newspapers and magazines from the mails and threatened individuals convicted of obstructing the draft with $10,000 in fines and twenty years in jail. The Sedition Act of 1918 made it a federal offense to use "disloyal, profane, scurrilous, or abusive language" about the Constitution, the government, the American uniform, or the flag. More than 2,100 individuals were prosecuted under these acts as civil rights fell victim to the power of the state.

By 1915, the American divorce rate had become the highest in the world, with one out of seven marriages ending in divorce. In California, the rates were even higher, with one out of five in Los Angeles and one out four in San Francisco. In at attempt to stop this growing trend, a number of state legislatures stepped in, passing laws raising the marital age of consent, prohibiting common-law and interracial marriages and polygamy, and imposing new physical and mental health requirements. Various states established separate family courts to handle cases dealing with desertion, child abuse, juvenile delinquency, and divorce. Some states went as far as to strengthen divorce legislation by requiring longer residence requirements before a divorce could be granted. There is little consensus as to why the American divorce rate increased during the Victorian era. Explanations ranged from a decline in family values and the liberation of women to the chauvinism of men and the pressures of urbanization.

The White Slave Traffic Act

The passage of the White Slave Traffic Act, or the Mann Act, in 1910 was the culmination of Progressive reform efforts to legislate morality at a time when middle- and upper-class Americans felt threatened by waves of new immigrants who were rapidly changing the demographics of urban America. Under the direction of the Department of Justice, between 1910 and 1920, 2,801 individuals were convicted of violating the Mann Act. No case epitomized the Mann era more than the prosecution of the African American world heavyweight

boxing champion Jack Johnson (1878–1946). Born into a large, poor family in Galveston, Texas, Johnson ran away from home at a young age and by his teens had gravitated to boxing. Blessed with natural athletic ability, Johnson honed his fighting skills leading to his entrée into the world of professional boxing. His lavish tastes and flaunting of the color barrier in an age of segregation did not deter his winning the world heavyweight title in 1908. Soon the boxing world was searching for a "great white hope" to dethrone the black champion.

Refusing to accept his place in segregated America, Johnson's unconventional behavior and his well-chronicled involvement with white women generated racial prejudice, and soon federal authorities targeted Johnson for violating the 1910 Mann Act, which prohibited the interstate transportation of women for immoral purposes. In 1912, Johnson was charged with sending money to a white girlfriend to meet him in another state. Apparently irked at Johnson's having married another woman, she claimed that he had taken her across state lines for prostitution and other immoral purposes. However, in this case, historian Lawrence M. Friedman suggested he was arrested for "crossing color lines, not state lines."[5] Nevertheless, in 1913 he was convicted of trafficking in white slavery and was sentenced to one year in prison. While out on bail, Johnson and his wife fled the country for Europe and did not return until 1920. On his return, he surrendered to the authorities and served eight months of a one-year sentence in federal prison.

The Sullivan Law and Handgun Legislation

While firearms came to America with the first European settlers, it was not until the twentieth century that a concern over firearms entered the national consciousness. Progressive-era reformers and muckraking journalists targeted the urban slums, courthouse rings, big business, and local taverns and brothels for their reform campaigns. The champions of laws that barred children from dangerous employment and protected animals from abuse, the reformers of this era showed an understanding of the "dangerous classes," formerly scorned by the proponents of social Darwinism.

A new approach to gun ownership came into conflict with the traditional right to bear arms at the very moment that law enforcement adopted new methods of enforcement and gained new insights into police science and criminology. Legal journals soon were awash in articles examining the Second Amendment and its implications for criminal justice. The avalanche of articles such as "Is the Pistol Responsible for Crime?" coincided with a rising concern over new societal demographics as the complexion of urban America was altered by the influx of immigrants from southern and eastern Europe and African Americans from the Jim Crow South.

In 1910, Manhattan, Brooklyn, and Bronx reported a combined 177 murders by firearms, with less than half the perpetrators arrested.[6] That same year, 912 arrests were made for carrying concealed weapons in the same cities. The following year, handgun legislation was discussed by New York politicians, including senator Timothy Sullivan. Opposition soon came from familiar opponents of gun control—arms manufacturers, hardware dealers, and pawnbrokers. Despite the opposition, criminal court judges and the city's leading newspapers publicly supported gun control measures. After Sullivan delivered a rousing speech to the state legislature, the senate passed a bill that was signed into law by the governor. Similar attempts were made to pass legislation in adjacent states, but all were unsuccessful.

Drug Laws

In 1900, American officials estimated that there were between 250,000 and one million addicts of opium and its derivatives in the country, leading one authority to describe America as "a nation of drug takers."[7] With a total population of seventy-six million, this would be the equivalent of one person out of 400. Unlike today, opiates in this era were unadulterated and would probably kill the average heroin addict of today. Although public concern about drug addiction

peaked in the first two decades of the twentieth century, these years were crucial in shaping future American drug policy.

In 1906, the Pure Food and Drug Act imposed federal standards on the patent-medicine industry. Three years later, Congress restricted the importation of opium except for certified medical purposes. Progressive reformers remained unsatisfied, demanding a codified, nationally applied antidrug law. Their idealized society would not tolerate drug addiction, just like it would not tolerate alcohol abuse and political patronage. Reflecting the concerns of Progressive reformers, on December 17, 1914, President Woodrow Wilson signed into law the Harrison Narcotic Act. In contrast to alcohol prohibition, there was little political debate over the act. Primarily a tax law, the act made it unlawful for any "nonregistered" person to possess heroin, cocaine, opium, morphine, or any of their products. Drug enforcement began the following year, resulting in 106 convictions.

Between 1916 and 1928, the vaguely written Harrison Act was the subject of a number of important Supreme Court decisions. One of the most prominent was the 1919 *Webb et al. v. United States* case. This decision developed out of a case in which a Memphis doctor and a druggist were indicted for conspiring to violate the Harrison Act by prescribing morphine only to addicts so that they could maintain their addiction. The high court examined the question as to whether this was allowable under the act and decided against the complainants. This decision had the long-range effect of ruling that providing drugs to an addict "not as a 'cure' but to keep the user 'comfortable by maintaining his customary use' was a 'perversion' of the meaning of the [Harrison] act."[8]

The climax of a generation of concern about drug addiction, the Harrison Act did not stop drug addiction but did make it a more difficult habit to maintain. Once the new antidrug laws went into effect, drug addicts were forced into treatment. The focus would soon be shifted to alcohol in the 1920s.

Prohibition

Deeply rooted in European social custom, prohibition was a subject of much contention, in stark contrast with antiopiate legislation, which had only a brief history in Western culture. But the crusade for national prohibition was decades in the making. The movement saw its first national victory in 1913 with the passage of the Webb-Kenyon Act, which allowed dry states to interfere with the transportation of alcohol across their state lines. The following year, those concerned with the large amounts of narcotics in patent medicines celebrated the passage of the Harrison Narcotic Act, which required a doctor's prescription for the sale of controlled dangerous substances. In addition, Congress demanded drug manufacturers to register with the government and maintain sales records.

What is often lost on Americans as the 1920s fades into distant history is that private drinking was not against the law during the Prohibition years 1920–1933. According to the Eighteenth Amendment, what was prohibited was the manufacture, sale, or transportation of "intoxicating liquors," defined as any beverage with more than 0.5 percent alcohol. Beer had anywhere from 3 to 8 percent, wine 10 to 20 percent, and spirits 40 percent. Courts typically threw out attempts to make social drinkers guilty of conspiracy, concentrating instead on the suppliers. By 1916, saloons were banned in twenty-one states, but the enforcement of prohibition was never fully financed and supported by the government, and the large breweries continued to make beer unimpeded. According to one prohibition agent, it was easy to find alcoholic beverages in most cites in only half an hour.

The Eugenics Movement

Best known to criminalists for developing the modern science of fingerprinting, Sir Francis Galton is also responsible for founding the eugenics[9] movement in the early twentieth century. Galton's biographer claims that his support for eugenics was rooted in a sense of the superiority of his own family and social class.[10] Building on Cesare Lombroso's biological theories of criminality (see chapter 8), by playing on the fears evoked by the "new dangerous classes," eugenicists were responsible for the forced sterilization of hundreds of thousands of people in America and elsewhere.

In her history of the social history of biological theories of crime, Nicole H. Rafter argued that between 1875 and the 1920s, "born-criminal theories incorporated popular hereditarian explanations of social problems and significantly affected public policy."[11] Coming at a time of intense immigration from eastern and southern Europe, the goal of eugenics was to "improve" the human genetic stock. Many of the assumptions about the quality of the new immigrants were based on test scores that suggested that immigrants scored poorly on IQ tests (usually because their English was limited and they had a poor knowledge of American customs).

In 1907, Indiana became the first state to make sterilization policy official policy, noting that "heredity plays a most important part in the transmission of crime, idiocy and imbecility."[12] Each Indiana institution that housed "unfit" inmates hired two surgeons to its staff. California implemented a law that would "asexualize" prisoners convicted twice for sexual offenses beginning in 1909.

Proponents of eugenics became less prominent in the 1920s, as the Progressive movement ebbed away. In 1921, the Indiana supreme court ruled that forced sterilization denied "due process."[13] Rafter suggested that with "middle class authority once again secure," there was less reason to pursue the goals of eugenics. She further argued that the most important legacy of eugenic criminology "lies in the structuring of social values and assumptions about what is good or bad (for example, our society values intelligence)."[14]

Following Galton's death in 1911, his views about the desirability of eugenics flourished in the United States. By the 1930s, more than half the states had passed forced-sterilization laws aimed at those regarded mentally, physically, or even morally and socially unfit.[15] In 1942, the

Supreme Court finally ruled against sterilizing criminals in the case of *Skinner v. Oklahoma*. According to the Oklahoma Habitual Criminal Sterilization Act, if an individual was convicted three or more times for "felonies involving moral turpitude," the defendant could be sterilized. After Skinner was arrested for the third felony, he was sentenced by the state to undergo a vasectomy. However, the Supreme Court ruled against the statute, stating that it violated "the equal protection clause of the Fourteenth Amendment."[16] According to this line of reasoning, only certain crimes, such as robbery, were punishable by sterilization, while others, such as embezzlement, were not. Despite this ruling, sporadic sterilizations continued into the 1970s.

The Red Scare

America's entrance into World War I in 1917 saw a backlash against the German American community. Teaching the German language was banned in schools. Beethoven and Bach disappeared from symphony programs, and temperance leaders used the fact that most brewers were of German nativity to help push through the Eighteenth Amendment. The passage in quick succession of the Espionage Act (1917), the Sedition Act (1918), and the Alien Deportation Act (1918) elevated pacifism and government criticism to acts of sedition. Beginning in 1917, Bureau of Intelligence agents raided the headquarters of the radical International Workers of the World (IWW) in twenty-four cities, suspecting the union of supporting the enemy war effort. In just Chicago alone, 100 IWW members were put on trial for violating wartime statutes. The IWW would never recover from its attacks during World War I. According to one Justice Department official, its main goal was "to put the IWW out of business."

Although many observers hoped the judicial system would protect dissenters, the court system came down hard on IWW members, better known as "Wobblies." Even Oliver Wendell Holmes, the Supreme Court's leading champion of civil rights, approved attacks on civil liberties

as he upheld the Espionage Act in *Schenck v. United States* in 1919 by comparing the denial of free speech during the war to the prohibition against "a man falsely shouting fire in a theater and causing panic." However, Holmes reversed himself by arguing against the Sedition Act later that year in *Abrams v. United States,* but he was outvoted seven to two.

In the summer of 1919, federal, state, and local government agencies targeted a wide range of radical activists fearful of a Bolshevik-style revolution in the United States. The subsequent "Red Scare" was ignited by the successful Bolshevik revolution in Russia and postwar labor unrest, which included the 1919 Boston police strike and several bombing campaigns. On the night of June 2, 1919, a bomb was exploded in front of the residence of the new attorney general. Attorney General A. Mitchell Palmer and his assistant, future FBI director John Edgar Hoover, would lead the federal attack on radical activists. Wartime legislation allowed the federal government to repress criticism of the war effort. Consequently, hundreds of foreign-born anarchists, socialists, and communists were deported in the summer of 1919.

In August 1919, Attorney General Palmer appointed Hoover to lead the recently organized General Intelligence Division. It was here that Hoover demonstrated his proficiency for collecting data and names of enemies. Setting up a card index system listing every radical leader, organization, and publication in the United States, by 1921 Hoover amassed a file of 450,000 names.[17] It was during this period that Hoover discovered what he thought was a worldwide communist conspiracy as well as justification for the raids.

The following year witnessed nationwide raids on IWW halls and offices sympathetic to the communist cause. Palmer's raids led to thousands of arrests, but his star began to dim because of criticism of his unconstitutional methods, and with it went his presidential ambitions. According to Hoover historian Curt Gentry, "The antiradical crusade had been, from its inception, an antilabor crusade" that played on nativist fears. In the end, Palmer lost the support of big business because the new restrictive immigration quotas threatened to end the supply of cheap foreign labor and the Red Scare "was no longer good for business."[18]

Weeks v. United States (1914)

In 1914, Fremont Weeks was convicted for illegally using the mails. His conviction for promoting an illegal lottery through the mails was based to a great extent on information found in his home by police officers who lacked a search warrant. These papers were turned over to the U.S. marshal, who made another search of his home and found more evidence, again without a warrant. Despite Weeks's petition to have the documents returned to him and his attorney's objections, he was convicted. The Supreme Court subsequently overturned the conviction on the grounds that their seizure violated the Fourth Amendment protection against illegal search and seizure. This ruling established what has become known as the "exclusionary rule," which disallows the use of illegally obtained evidence in a criminal trial.

The *Weeks v. United States* ruling had a profound impact on the admissibility of evidence seized by police in federal trials. Before 1914, violations of the Fourth Amendment's protection against unreasonable search and seizures were perceived as common-law trespassing. In order to keep the seized evidence from being admitted at trial, the defendant only had to petition for the property to be returned and then sue the responsible police officer for damages. In 1914, the Supreme Court held for the first time that a violation of the Fourth Amendment in itself could justify excluding evidence from trial. One of the most vexing judicial obstacles for police officers today, after *Weeks v. United States* only property that was legally owned by the defendant and that the defendant specifically requested to be returned could be excluded from the case.

Although this was a landmark case, its greatest limitation was that it did not apply to the states. However, in a practice known as the "silver platter," if state or local police conducted the search and turned over otherwise illegally obtained evidence to federal officials, the evidence was declared admissible. This exception to the exclusionary rule meant that local prosecutors could use illegally seized evidence in trials under state law (if state laws allowed it).[19]

LAW ENFORCEMENT

During the first decades of the twentieth century, the world of work began to change, thanks to the influence of radical politics and unionization. While police work had more responsibilities than most jobs, it shared many of the concerns of other wage-earning occupations. In the early 1900s, the typical patrolmen worked twelve-hour days and was remunerated with low wages. Between 1910 and 1920, policemen began to take an active role in creating labor unions and police organizations. In 1915, two veteran Pittsburgh police officers were inspired to create an organization for the social welfare of police known as the Fraternal Order of Police (FOP). In order to assure the mayor of their nonradical intentions, they promised that the word *strike* would be omitted from any references to the nascent organization since, as police officers, they were "obligated to protect life and property." With the support of the mayor, within months the FOP had 600 members in Pittsburgh. The growth of the FOP continued over the next several decades as it grew into a national organization. While other police organizations were subsequently created, efforts at unionization lagged behind.

The police crusade for better working conditions reached a crescendo of sorts in 1919, when the Boston police force went on strike. As part of one of the most underpaid and overworked urban police forces, the average Boston policeman worked between seventy-three and ninety-eight hours per week for a yearly salary of less than $1,300. With salaries averaging roughly twenty-five cents per hour, this amounted to half the wage earned by workers in war-related factories. Morale had plummeted to an all-time low by

1919. Precinct houses were in dismal condition, and political patronage ran supreme as politicians continued to promote political cronies over more qualified officers who had demonstrated their proficiency on promotional exams. In addition, police officers were still required to perform tasks unrelated to law enforcement.

In 1919, a Boston police fraternal organization known as the Boston Social Club petitioned the American Federation of Labor for a charter. This led Edwin Curtis, the commissioner of police, to issue a proclamation prohibiting union membership among his rank and file. When the union refused to disband, Curtis fired nineteen officers. In response, 1,117 of Boston's 1,544-member force went on strike. The resulting crime wave and civil disorder led to the creation of a volunteer civilian force that resorted to physical violence to suppress the outbreak of crime. The strike and subsequent disorder lost any public support that the police may have garnered. All the striking police were eventually fired, and a new force was recruited. If anything came of the strike, it was the setting back of the police union movement until the 1960s.

Civilian Police Reformers

Police professionalism developed along two fronts in the early 1900s. While reform-minded police chiefs such as August Vollmer and Richard Sylvester received much of the credit for police reform, civilian police reformers such as Leonhard Fuld, Raymond Fosdick, and Bruce Smith placed their stamps on law enforcement agencies as well. Although Fuld (1883–1965) lacked a police background, this Columbia University–trained lawyer wrote the one of the first comprehensive and readable studies of police administration. His prescient vision for policing forecast many of the Progressive reforms that would characterize policing in the coming years, including a better use of police discretion while performing daily duties, more stringent hiring requirements, and a recognition of the dangers of political patronage. Fuld also recommended better police training in the proper use of deadly force and better systems for scrutinizing police misconduct.

At the urging of John D. Rockefeller Jr., Raymond Fosdick (1883–1972) embarked on a study of European police systems that resulted in the 1915 publication of *European Police Systems.* His study of virtually every major European police force fostered an image of a professional brand of policing that outshone the decentralized and more amateurish American counterparts. Fosdick would publish a complementary volume titled *American Police Systems* in 1920. Following a study of seventy-two urban police forces, the author concluded that American policing was victimized by a lack of professionalism and rife with political corruption. The publication of his work created a backlash from the American police establishment but also led to reform efforts in many cities.

In 1916, Bruce Smith (1892–1955) began his career as a police consultant and criminologist when he was hired by the New York Bureau of Municipal Research and studied the Harrisburg, Pennsylvania, police department. After stints with the National Crime Commission and several other criminal justice associations, Smith devoted the remainder of his life to surveying police departments. Following an extensive study of European police procedures, he was instrumental in creating the *Uniform Crime Reports* in 1930. Over the next twenty-five years, he would become the country's foremost expert on police operations as he helped improve many forces, including those in Chicago, Baltimore, San Francisco, Pittsburgh, and Philadelphia.

Police Professionalism

As the twentieth century approached, urban government increasingly came to grips with the partisan manipulation of police agencies. Following several police scandals and the sensational revelations gleaned from the Lexow hearings, New York City finally abolished the police board in 1901 in favor of a single commissioner, appointed by the mayor for a five-year term.

According to the new system, the police commissioner could be removed from office at any time by the mayor or state governor. During the first two decades of the twentieth century, of the fifty-two cities with populations exceeding 100,000, only fourteen still used police boards.[20] Boston followed the lead of New York in 1906, Cleveland and Cincinnati in 1908, and Buffalo in 1916.

Efforts to replace partisan police boards with professional chiefs of police was an important first step toward police professionalism. During the Progressive era, police reform advocates such as Fosdick and Fuld made a point of comparing the early twentieth-century unprofessional American police administrators with their European counterparts.

Among the new crop of professional police commissioners influenced by Progressive police reform efforts was Arthur Woods (1870–1942). The Harvard-educated Woods joined the New York City detective bureau in 1907. After studying European detective bureaus while pursuing postgraduate work, Woods returned to the United States and became a protégé of Theodore Roosevelt. Woods was appointed deputy police commissioner and then police commissioner of the 10,000-man New York City Police Department in 1914. During his tenure, he vigorously attacked the vice problem but made his greatest contributions in the realm of police training and professionalism. Influenced by Scotland Yard and other European police organizations, Woods introduced a homicide clinic and psychopathic laboratory to train homicide and sex crime investigators and established the first school for patrolmen, a precursor of the city's police academy.

August Vollmer, the police chief of Berkeley, California, became one of the preeminent proponents of police professionalism during the Progressive era. Among his earliest achievements was establishing a department code of ethics that barred the acceptance of gratuities and favors under penalty of dismissal.

Vollmer rose to prominence for his requirement that prospective police officers pursue a college education in an era when a high school education was not even required by most departments. Vollmer set up the first formal training school for policemen in 1908, and over the following decade, departments in New York City, Detroit, and Philadelphia established similar training academies. In 1916, Vollmer was instrumental in creating the first university-level police training school at the University of California, Berkeley.

Vollmer's other innovations included rigorous in-service training and probation for first-time offenders. He was the first police executive to champion the lie detector as an investigative tool and in 1922 implemented a single fingerprint classification system. Vollmer was instrumental in inaugurating a series of innovations during his tenure as police chief, including the first modus operandi system (1906) and the first motorcycle patrol (1911) as well as many others. By 1914, Berkeley's police force was the first in the country to be completely mobile, with all officers patrolling in automobiles. Officers were expected to provide their own cars, but the city paid them for their use, thus saving the city budget a huge outlay at one time. Vollmer's emphasis on scientific policing, education, higher standards, and the centralization of police services influences the role of police in society to this day.

Considered the father of the modern police organization, August Vollmer was born in New Orleans in 1876. After a stint in the military, in which he distinguished himself in combat during the Philippines campaign of the Spanish–American War, he settled in Berkeley, California. In 1905, he was elected city marshal and four years later began a twenty-four-year career as the city's police chief. In 1907, he was elected president of the California Chiefs of Police and in 1922 accepted the presidency of the International Association of Chiefs of Police (IACP). In between teaching at the University of California and running his police department, Vollmer was called on to reorganize a number of police departments, including those in San Diego (1915); Los Angeles (1923–1925); Havana, Cuba (1926); Kansas City (1929); and Minneapolis, Minnesota (1930).

The author and coauthor of numerous books and articles, his best-known work includes *The Police and Modern Society* (1936).

Following in the footsteps of other reform-minded police managers in the Progressive era, Fred Kohler (1869–1933) took over the Cleveland Police Department, a force with a reputation for corruption, in 1903 and placed his stamp of reform on the force. Among the reforms implemented by Kohler was a "sunrise court," which allowed minor offenders to get to work on time through quick processing following a minor violation and therefore keep their jobs.

In 1908, Kohler introduced his "Golden Rule Policy,"[21] which dealt more informally with juvenile offenders. Although he claimed it was his own innovation, this policy was probably the 1907 brainchild of Toledo, Ohio, Mayor Samuel "Golden Rule" Jones and his police chief.[22] By diverting minor offenders out of the formal criminal justice system, courts could concentrate on more serious matters, and the offender would avoid stigmatization. Kohler's strategies were viewed with skepticism from some quarters, but Theodore Roosevelt thought he was the best police chief in America. Kohler's career came to an abrupt ending in 1913, when he was forced to step down after an extramarital affair became public knowledge. His legacy was further tainted when it was revealed that he delivered a plagiarized speech to the IACP in 1912 and when after his death his safe deposit box was found to contain half a million dollars in probably illegal payoffs.

Federal Law Enforcement

Created in 1870, the Justice Department by the Progressive era would also be responsible for investigating antitrust violations, fraudulent land sales, crimes on Indian reservations, the shipment of stolen goods from one state to another, and violations of national banking laws. Without a federal police organization, the Justice Department had to borrow investigators and special agents from other departments, including Customs, the Department of the Interior, and the Treasury Department. With the ascendance of former New York City police commissioner Theodore Roosevelt to the presidency in 1901 after the assassination of President McKinley, America now had a chief executive familiar with criminal justice issues. In 1905, Roosevelt appointed fellow Progressive Charles Bonaparte (grandnephew of the French emperor Napoleon I) as his attorney general.

Among Roosevelt's earliest actions in this arena was requesting funds from Congress to hire a detective force for the Justice Department. Despite the opposition of those who feared that a bureau of investigation would be used for political reasons, the Bureau of Investigation (BOI) was officially inaugurated by the attorney general in 1908, when he appointed a small force of special agents on his own (in the 1930s, Congress would change its name to Federal Bureau of Investigation).

The early activities of the BOI were rather limited since the number of federal crimes was much smaller than in succeeding years. Most investigations focused on banking, naturalization, antitrust, and land fraud. The passage of the Mann Act in 1910 expanded the activities of the BOI when it was made a crime to transport women over state lines for immoral purposes. In 1919, the passage of the National Motor Vehicle Act, better known as the Dyer Act, added the transportation of stolen automobiles over state lines to the BOI's responsibilities.

America's entrance into World War I in 1917 led to an expansion of the BOI, which grew to 600 agents and support staff with field offices in major cities and along the Mexican border. During the war, the BOI assumed additional duties with the passage of the Espionage, Selective Service, and Sabotage Acts. Just three months after America entered the war, an ambitious young attorney named John Edgar Hoover (1895–1972) began working for the Justice Department. Hoover's meteoric rise through the department would lead to a fifty-year career as head of the FBI, beginning in 1924. In the 1920s, the bureau was plagued by problems shared by most civil service agencies. Promotions were based on seniority instead of merit, and investigations were inefficient. When Hoover took over in 1924, he established rigorous rules of conduct and procedure for all agents and investigations and instituted a promotion system based on merit.

U.S. marshals became increasingly involved in law enforcement in the years surrounding World War I. The passage of the Espionage and Sedition Acts in 1917, which set limits on the right of free speech, required marshals to enforce measures aimed at public opposition to the war. Marshals were also expected to arrest violators of the Selective Service laws.

The passage of the Volstead Act in 1919 inaugurated the Prohibition era. Despite the availability of Prohibition agents to enforce the laws, the marshals of the Justice Department would be saddled with conducting arrests and investigations and seizing breweries and other bootlegging equipment.

State Police

The first decades of the twentieth century saw the creation of numerous state police forces. Some, such as the short-lived New Mexico Mounted Police and the Arizona Rangers, were inspired by the Texas Rangers. The Arizona Rangers were inaugurated in 1901 after a consortium of Republican cattlemen, mine owners, and railroad officials convinced the territorial governor that a force modeled on the Texas Rangers was required to dispatch the growing lawlessness in Arizona. Shortly after its creation, Democrats complained to the governor that the Rangers were all Republicans. The patronage issue would creep into any discussion of the Rangers. The demise of the Rangers was the result of several developments. While opposition to the force revolved around its payroll and expenditures, it seemed that the force worked itself out of a job when only two dozen arrests were reported in just more than eight years of existence. In 1909, the Arizona Rangers were

disbanded following an anti-Ranger campaign led by county sheriffs and district attorneys.

The Arizona Ranger legacy suggests that they had much better relations with the Mexican government than with their Texan counterparts. Unlike the relationship between the Texas Rangers and the Mexican Rurales, the Arizona Rangers cooperated with the Mexican government, which permitted them to launch manhunts and extradite criminals to the United States. Ultimately, in 1912 Arizona achieved statehood, and a highway patrol was created in 1931. As with past mounted police forces, the introduction of the automobile, rapid population growth, and political infighting signaled the end of the Arizona Rangers. The New Mexico Mounted Police was established in 1905 "for the protection of the frontier." However, this organization would be dissolved after persistent friction with local law enforcement.

A new era of state policing was launched in 1905 with the creation of the Pennsylvania State Police. Following a half century of rural crime, industrial disorder, and ethnic conflict, widespread labor strikes continued to paralyze the Pennsylvania economy. In the late nineteenth century, immigrants from eastern Europe and Italy were drawn to the mining country once dominated by Irish, English, and Welsh miners. In 1902, Pennsylvania took steps toward creating a state police force based on the Royal Irish Constabulary and Philippines Constabulary military models.

Under the command of Spanish–American War veteran John C. Groome, the 220-man force was selected from the ranks of the armed forces and required to be unmarried and live in barracks. While they were charged with policing the entire state, for the most part the force patrolled the immigrant-dominated mining districts. Mounted on horses and equipped with carbines, pistols, and riot batons, opposition groups compared them to the nefarious Cossacks of Russia.

Supporters saw the force as protecting the country against foreigners, labor agitators, and people of color, as the state police often were embroiled in jurisdictional disputes with local police. As the labor strikes of the 1910s diminished, the state police became more involved in rural crime and traffic problems as well as enforcing Prohibition laws.

After reading about the "heroic" exploits of the Pennsylvania State Police, former New York City police commissioner Theodore Roosevelt lobbied the state legislature to contemplate a state police force on the Pennsylvania model, and in 1917 the New York State Police was established. The New York legislature had considered a state police force for years prior to 1917, in part because of the success of the neighboring state police force as well as the inadequacy of New York's rural police. America's entrance into World War I in 1916 apparently provided the impetus for the force. A large force of 232 men and officers, like its neighbor, it was commanded by a superintendent appointed by the governor. Unlike its neighbor, however, it developed a rapport with organized labor because it was not imbued with the powers to suppress riots in cities without the approval of the governor and was not used for strikebreaking. In addition, it had the power to arrest, without warrant, anyone violating state or federal laws throughout the state.

The emergence of the New Jersey State Police force in 1921 is considered a turning point in the history of American state policing. The impetus for its creation was the ineffectiveness of county law enforcement and a rash of violent industrial disorders between 1910 and 1915. Between 1915 and 1923, twenty-seven states would create some type of state police force. While some states created highway patrols in response to increasing popularity of the automobile, others adhered to the Pennsylvania paramilitary model of policing.

Women and Minorities

The first female police officers were hired in the early twentieth century. While most female participation in law enforcement was limited to serving as matrons in jails in earlier years (since 1845), in 1910 Alice Stebbins Wells became the first full-time paid policewoman in America (according to a recent biography of Lola Baldwin, this claim has been brought into question, but although Baldwin was sworn in as the "nation's first municipally paid policewoman"[23] in 1908, Wells is still widely considered the nation's first policewoman).[24]

A strong advocate for women in modern police work, Wells lobbied Los Angeles social and political leaders before obtaining her appointment. According to her job requirements, she was expected to "enforce laws concerning dance halls, skating rinks, penny arcades, picture shows, and other similar places of recreation; the suppression of unwholesome billboard displays; and maintenance of a general bureau for women seeking advice on matters within the scope of the Police Department."[25] Over the next five years, twenty-five cities appointed policewomen to the forces. Initially, policewomen were expected to repress dance hall vice,[26] help children, and return runaway girls.

One of the early pioneers in female law enforcement, Lola Baldwin was working for the Portland, Oregon, National Traveler's Aid Association in 1905, when she was asked to perform protective work on behalf of women attending the city's Lewis and Clark Exposition that year. She performed her duties with such distinction that when the fair ended, she continued to provide the same services for women visitors to Portland and was eventually given police powers by the Portland police. She focused much of her energies on closing down saloons and brothels. By 1913, she held the rank of captain, and she directed her officers to prohibit young women from working in sordid environments such as pool halls and bowling alleys. During her long career with the organization, she outlasted six police chiefs and five mayors but was never officially referred to as a policewoman. However, her biographer considers her the "first female police agent hired under civil service in the United States." Author Gloria E. Myers claims that many firsts attributed to Alice Stebbins Wells are "easily discredited by Baldwin's ample records."[27]

In 1915, the International Association of Policewomen (IAP) was established, leading the effort to include more women in policing. According to recent research, while this meeting in Baltimore "was the point at which the policewoman movement became self aware," its success was the result of Lola Baldwin's work with women's organizations and social service agencies.

By the end of World War I, 220 cities across the nation employed 300 policewomen, including Georgia Robinson of the Los Angeles Police Department in 1919, the first African American policewoman. In 1920, the IAP was encouraging women police candidates to pursue college educations in order to join police departments, but as late as 1950, according to the U.S. census, women made up only 1 percent of the nation's police force.

African Americans found many obstacles blocking attempts to enter law enforcement. In 1900, police forces were overwhelmingly white, with blacks making up only 3 percent of urban police forces. Those African Americans that were fortunate enough to find employment often faced hostility and were usually placed in black communities. The career of Samuel J. Battle (1883–1966) offers a glimpse at early twentieth-century policing. Battle became the first African American on the New York City police force in 1910 but was given the silent treatment by officers for his first year. It was not until he saved the life of a white officer during a race riot that he won acceptance from his peers. Battle eventually became the first black sergeant on the force and continued to march through the ranks, rising to parole commissioner in 1941. Despite Battle's inspiring story, few African Americans found success on American police forces until after World War 2, with most relegated, like women, to secondary status.

The son of former slaves, Samuel Battle moved north to escape segregation. Early on, he set his sights on becoming a police officer, a rare accomplishment for an African American in turn-of-the-century America. While working grueling twelve-hour days as a porter in New York City, Battle prepared for the civil service exams that were required to join the police force. He passed the exam in 1910; nonetheless, administrators vacillated on whether to hire him.

Battle endured a year of silent treatment and accepted his rejection while flourishing as a police officer consigned to the African American community. Despite passing the sergeant's exam, he was forced to wait seven years before becoming the first black sergeant on the force. Battle would make headlines in 1943, when Mayor Fiorello La Guardia authorized now parole commissioner Battle to quell race riots in Harlem following a police shooting of a black youth. His influence in the black community helped end the disturbance in short order. Retiring in 1951, Battle was honored in a special ceremony in 1964 as "the father of all Negroes in the Police Department."

Private Police

In the years before an effective federal police apparatus and the birth of the FBI, banks, railroads, and other enterprises often avoided local law enforcement by hiring private agents to cross jurisdictions to apprehend wide-ranging criminal gangs, such as the James Gang and the Younger brothers.

A variety of private police services were established during the early twentieth century to compete with the Pinkertons and traditional law enforcement. Among the most prominent was the Burns National Detective Agency, the brainchild of William John Burns (1861–1932), who had served a stint with the U.S. Secret Service in 1889. He left government employ to cofound the Burns and Sheridan Detective Agency, which was operated like the Pinkertons as a quasi-private police force. After buying out his partner and shortening the agency's name to its more familiar title, regional offices were opened across the nation. However, the Burns agency came under heavy criticism for its unpopular support of big-business interests against labor unions. Despite such controversy and Burns's heavy-handed investigation of the 1910 bombing of the *Los Angeles Times* building, the agency prospered, and Burns returned to government service in 1921 to head the fledgling Bureau of Investigation, the precursor to the FBI. Although he would win acclaim for successfully prosecuting the Ku Klux Klan in the 1920s, his mishandling of the Teapot Dome scandal, involving the sale of federal oil leases to private interests for profit, would force Burns to resign in 1924 and return to private life.

Technological Innovations

Although the call box, telephone, and telegraph had made the transition to police stations prior to the 1900s, technological advances in the new century would transform American policing. In the years following the war, the teletypewriter evolved into a "police workhorse" as it was used for printing telegrams. By 1911, police could transmit a facsimile photo of a criminal from one city to another (telephotography). Transportation technology would see police officers make the transition from bicycle "scorcher squads" to the motorcycle and automobile. By the 1920s, many cars would be equipped radios, although the two-way radio would not be installed until the 1930s. The authentication of fake documents, fingerprint classification, and the modern polygraph would round out the new police technology.

CORRECTIONS

Chief among the criminal justice–oriented reform movements of the Progressive era were attempts to transform the prison system. According to historian Larry E. Sullivan, during this period "criminal justice was largely taken out of the hands of judges and prosecutors and given over to bureaucrats, psychiatrists, social workers, and professional penologists."[28] In this new climate, the important correctional innovations of probation, parole, and indeterminate sentencing flourished. Beginning in the 1840s, probation took years to gain widespread acceptance. Only six states had statutes offering this alternative in 1900, but within a decade all the northern states

outside New Hampshire had adopted it. Over the next five years, the majority of western states adopted probation as well.

Explanations for the popularity of probation in these years revolved around the Progressive predilection for community improvement, hence the use of supervised freedom over incarceration. Other explanations suggest that it was cheaper to use probation instead of incarceration.

The beginnings of parole can be traced back to Alexander Maconochie's mark system in the 1840s, in which prisoners had to work through various stages to win release. By 1900, more than half the states offered some form of parole or indeterminate sentencing alternative. Unfortunately, parole boards created to decide each case became increasingly politicized and inefficient. According to one estimate, in 1920s New York, the state board gave only five minutes to each case.[29]

Throughout the first decade of the twentieth century, yearly prison congresses gave rise to a number of new recommendations for prison reform. In 1908, the American Prison Association was created. Here was a forum for experts to debate the evils of the southern lease system and to discuss European developments that revolved around the causes of crime and the fate of discharged inmates. Occasionally, debate would degenerate into acrimony as European criminologists belittled the American efforts at reform that elucidated new theories of crime causation and criminal types. At the same time, England was developing the Borstal system for the care of offenders under twenty-one and applying Elmira-like control.

America's state prisons saw their inmate populations swell by 62 percent between 1870 and 1904. However, this would be only a precursor to the tremendous increase in population over the next three decades. According to the Bureau of the Census, state prisons experienced an unprecedented 162 percent population growth between 1904 and 1935. During this era, ten new prisons based on the Auburn design were built, and one following Jeremy Bentham's Panopticon model was constructed at Stateville, Illinois, in 1925.

The reformatory prison movement peaked in 1910. Although, several prisons were inspired by the Elmira pattern over the next twenty years, the reform movement had reached an impasse. During the first twenty-five years of the new century, American prison policy relied on total control, punishment, and hard labor. With less emphasis on classification, moral instruction, and education, prison practice seemed to have drifted back to a nineteenth-century policy that was custodial, punitive, and financially productive.

Thomas Mott Osborne and the Mutual Welfare League

One of the most controversial prison reformers of the early twentieth century, Thomas Mott Osborne (1859–1926) was the Harvard-educated scion of a wealthy manufacturer. Following graduation from college, Osborne entered local politics in Auburn, New York, where he was elected mayor in 1903. It was natural that he would take an interest in prison reform in one of America's leading prison towns. By 1906, he had developed a keen interest in reform and addressed a meeting of the National Prison Association, where he expounded his notion that "prison must be an institution where every inmate must have the largest practical amount of individual freedom, because it is liberty alone that fits men for liberty."

Osborne was given a chance to put his philosophy to the test in 1913, when he was appointed chairman of the New York State Commission for Prison Reform. To prepare himself for the task, he served as a convict under an alias for a week behind the walls of Auburn Prison. The following year, he published an account of his experience in his book *Within Prison Walls,* which he used to illustrate the weaknesses of a current prison regime that stamped out individuality and destroyed manhood. The erstwhile reformer claimed that while he was behind bars, an inmate offered him a plan for limited self-government. Osborne based his Mutual Welfare League experiment on this advice, and on his appointment as warden of Sing Sing Prison in 1914, he instituted a system of self-government that was fashioned to give inmates a sense of corporate responsibility that, it was hoped, would aid in their subsequent rehabilitation.

Osborne's penchant for criticizing political overseers of the prison system earned him a number of enemies who mounted a campaign against his administration. Although charges of perjury and neglect of duty were never proven, he resigned as warden in 1916. Over the next four years, he continued his efforts at prison reform, leading to the founding of the Welfare League Association, which helped recently discharged prisoners, and the creation of the National Society of Penal Information, a clearinghouse for data on prison conditions.

The Industrial Era

The first quarter of the twentieth-century prison era has been referred to as the industrial period for its concentration on producing a wide range of products for government consumption in prison factories. The military, public, and state government sectors in regions outside the South provided a ready market for prison-made materials.

Paralleling the growth of prison industry was a steady breakdown in the former silent system. American correctional practices made a significant departure from the formerly punitive regime. Emphasis was shifted from strict discipline and negative sanctions, such as corporal punishment as well as religious instruction, education, and trade training, and refocused on promoting parole in return for good behavior.

The Federal Prison System

Prior to the late nineteenth century, prisoners convicted of federal crimes were housed in state prisons. Initially, state prisons were given boarding fees and were allowed to use federal prisoners in the prison labor system, including the leasing system. Between 1885 and 1895, the number of federal prisoners more than doubled. But by 1887, Congress was becoming disenchanted with convict leasing and subsequently outlawed the contracting of federal prisoners. In response, a number of state prisons refused to accept federal prisoners. In 1891, the federal government decided to construct a federal prison at Leavenworth, Kansas. (Construction began 1898.)

The federal prison system diverged from its state counterparts in the early 1900s. The construction of the Atlanta Penitentiary in 1902 introduced several new innovations. It would be among the first prisons to feed prisoners in a dining hall at eight-person tables as opposed to the one-way bench tables of state facilities. Atlanta also implemented an eight-hour workday for guards. In 1910, federal prisoners were afforded the opportunity to earn parole with the passage of the first Federal Parole Law. In less than two decades, problems caused by prison overcrowding and poor record keeping would lead to the creation of the Federal Bureau of Prisons in 1929.

CRIME AND PUNISHMENT

The years before World War I saw Americans becoming increasingly concerned with the rising crime problem. By 1914, New York and Chicago were experiencing more murders than England, Scotland, and Wales combined, and smaller cities, such as Detroit and Cleveland, were witnessing more burglaries than London. Public confidence in American policing had fallen to an all-time low.

More like organized gangs than criminal syndicates, the early twentieth century witnessed a phenomenon known as Black Hand gangs. Although these gangs are often confused with the Mafia or viewed as precursors to modern organized crime, there was nothing monolithic about the Black Hand. Composed of Italian and Sicilian immigrants, their major activity revolved around extorting money from their fellow immigrants. Gangs ranged in size from six to ten members under one leader. The gangs typically extorted money by sending sinister letters threatening injury or death if the victim did not comply with their demands. Letters often featured crude draw-

ings of daggers, skulls, coffins, and black hands in the margins. By Prohibition, most of the Black Handers had either been killed off or gravitated to the more lucrative selling of bootleg liquor.

In the years leading up to World War I, New York City experienced a growing youth gang problem. Nurtured by poverty and discrimination, gangs became part of urban America as Jews and Italians replaced the Irish and German immigrants who preceded them. Future Jewish and Italian gangsters, such as Meyer Lansky, Lucky Luciano, and Bugsy Siegel, entered the criminal world after graduating from juvenile gang activity.

One of the worst calamities for police reform was the implementation of national alcohol prohibition with the passage of the Volstead Act in 1920. Although it was intended to end the social problems associated with alcohol abuse, it would have the opposite effect as wealthy crime syndicates emerged, energized by the enormous financial opportunity associated with illicit alcohol activities. Extensive corruption of politicians, police, and other officials in this era seriously undermined public respect for the law and government.

Capital Punishment

The introduction of the electric chair in 1890 appealed to the efficiency-motivated reformers of the Progressive era. During the first decades of the new century, the technologically efficient electric chair replaced the noose in most states. Meanwhile, studies by social scientists demonstrating the lack of deterrence value of the death penalty convinced nine more states to abolish capital punishment. But this second crusade against the death penalty would end in the aftermath of the Progressive era as concerns shifted to race riots, the Red Scare, and rising crime rates. Four states would in fact reinstate the death penalty in the early 1920s, while others would add new capital offenses. Despite the machinations of death penalty foes during the Progressive era, there was no real diminution of executions, which continued at the rate of two per 100,000 as in the late nineteenth century.[30] Two of the most famous death penalty trials of the century would take place in the 1920s (Sacco and Vanzetti and Leopold and Loeb).

The twentieth century began with a recrudescence of abolitionist activity against the death penalty. Throughout the Progressive era, abolitionists, such as lawyer Clarence Darrow (1857–1938), eloquently attacked capital punishment.

Clarence Darrow was one of America's greatest criminal defense lawyers. With little in the way of a formal legal education, Darrow rose to national prominence while representing radical leaders Eugene V. Debs (1895) and William "Big Bill" Haywood (1907). Over time, Darrow became disenchanted with his labor clients but continued to represent publicly unpopular clients. His participation in the Leopold–Loeb murder case in 1924 marked perhaps his greatest victory. In this case, two wealthy and intellectually gifted young men kidnapped and murdered a small boy, hoping to get away with the perfect murder and demonstrate their intellectual superiority. Both men were caught, and the public clamored for the death penalty.

Hired by Leopold and Loeb's wealthy parents, Darrow decided to forgo a jury trial and plead his case directly to the judge, asking for life in prison. According to most sources, this case was the first one in legal history to introduce the concept of psychopathology as a mitigating circumstance. Arguing that the defendants were unable to comprehend moral right from wrong (not the insanity defense), the attorney was successful in persuading the judge to sentence them to life in prison. Darrow would capture the nation's attention again the following year, when he defended biology teacher John T. Scopes, who was arrested for violating state law by teaching Darwin's theory of evolution.

Criminal Identification

The early 1900s saw criminal identification receive increased attention as the Bertillon system proved too cumbersome and unreliable. New incentive was given to criminal identification when New York City authorities adopted the fingerprint system used by Scotland Yard in 1902. First employed in India in the 1860s and then by Scotland Yard in the 1890s, novelist Mark Twain popularized this identification system in his book *Pudd'nhead Wilson,* and soon police departments and prisons adopted the procedure.

Although the Bertillon system had become widely accepted in the United States in the 1890s, the system faced its greatest challenge in 1903, when a man named Will West was arrested and sentenced to prison at Fort Leavenworth, Kansas. Despite his claims that he had never been arrested before, his photograph seemed to match that of a convicted criminal, and apparently so did his Bertillon measurements. It would turn out that there was another man named Will West incarcerated in the same prison, with the same measurements and bearing an uncanny resemblance to the other Will West. The only evidence that distinguished the two men was their fingerprints. From this time forward, emphasis was placed on fingerprinting combined with photographs. It was not long before the Bertillon system was abandoned.

AMERICAN VIOLENCE

The years surrounding World War I were marked by increased racial tensions and violent crime. Following the war, the media began to sensationalize crimes such as bank robbery, while law enforcement began to concentrate on better firearms training to combat the era's well-armed desperadoes. During the late 1890s, New York City police commissioner Theodore Roosevelt had introduced firearms training after a spate of "firearms-related accidents." But it was not until the 1920s that police firearms training, with the help of the National Rifle Association, began in earnest.

While many Americans assume that the World Trade Center bombing of 1993 was the first attack on the nation's financial district, in reality the Wall Street bombing on September 16, 1920, was the first and, until the Oklahoma City bombing, the "most deadly terrorist attack in American history."[31] Today, scars can still be seen if you look closely enough at the old J. P. Morgan offices on the corner of Wall and Broad streets.

More than seventy people died either immediately or later from injuries sustained in the explosion. Although no one was ever brought to justice for the crime, investigators figured that the explosion was the result of a horse-drawn cart carrying dynamite and sash weights that acted as shrapnel. The blast was so strong that an automobile was thrust twenty feet into the air.

William J. Flynn, chief of the Secret Service, concluded that the bomb was not directed at J. P. Morgan, although one of his firm's clerks was beheaded by the blast; rather, it was directed at the financial heart of American society. Others thought that it was either an accident or the result of a botched robbery or attack on the U.S. Treasury (on that particular day, $900 million in gold bars was being moved next door, which was the epicenter of the blast). A. Mitchell Palmer, the attorney general, suspected that the attack was the work of anarchists or communist workers and as "a precaution" arrested IWW leader William "Big Bill" Haywood. Still others were convinced that it was payback for the execution of Sacco and Vanzetti (see "Notable Trials" later in this chapter). Considering the tensions of the day, there was no lack of potential suspects.

Race Violence

By the twentieth century, African Americans faced disenfranchisement and discrimination throughout the country, as they found themselves excluded by employers and labor unions from white-collar jobs and many of the skilled trades. In the South, Jim Crow laws and tenancy characterized daily life, leading to a significant migration of blacks to the North. Unfortunately, they would be met by the very hostility they sought to flee from. Often, hostility led to violence and riots in cities ranging from New York (1900) and Springfield, Ohio (1904), to Springfield, Illinois (1908), and Greensburg, Indiana (1906).

The birth of the National Association for the Advancement of Colored People (NAACP) sought to eliminate class distinctions and end Jim Crow laws. But during the first quarter of the twentieth century, the federal government failed to pass new legislation to protect black civil rights, and by the 1910s the nation's capital was as segregated as any of the southern states.

Violence continued to be directed at black communities in both the North and the South. In 1917, a riot in East St. Louis claimed the lives of thirty-nine blacks and nine whites. Although its cause is clouded in rumor and innuendo, the consensus was that it resulted from white fears that black migrants would take their jobs. During World War I, African Americans were drafted but were reserved for mostly menial duties. Race relations would continue to deteriorate as black veterans returned home. In 1919 alone, ten black veterans were lynched in the South and fourteen burned at the stake. The Chicago riots of 1919 were the worst of this era. Sociologist Morris Janowitz draws a distinction between the riots prior to the 1960s and more recent unrest, describing the earlier riots as communal in nature, involving "a direct struggle between the residents of white and Negro areas."[32] The riots were rooted in several years of tension between the races in which twenty-seven black dwellings had been targeted by bombers. Other complex issues played a part in the riots. Chicago's black population had more than doubled by 1919, but no new housing or tenements were erected to absorb the new residents. Meanwhile, thousands of black soldiers had returned from World War I determined to find a voice in the "new" America. In Chicago, housing, the psychological effects of war, and the organization of jobs and labor would collide with the racial politics of the early twentieth century. This contributed to a new development in race rioting: African Americans were now fighting back with fists and weapons.

Chicago was one of the northern cities most impacted by black migration in the aftermath of the war. A riot began on a summer afternoon when a young black man swam past an invisible line of segregation at a Chicago public beach and was hit with rocks and drowned. This set off three days of rioting that led to the deaths of twenty African Americans and fourteen whites. More than 100 people were injured, and numerous black properties went up in smoke.

Following the Chicago riots, the Chicago Commission on Race Relations was created in 1922 to investigate the causes of the riots and to seek solutions for preventing future conflagrations. The formation of this commission signaled a new element in criminal justice: commissions to study the reasons for race riots. Such commissions would become familiar to Americans following riots in Los Angeles (1964 and 1992), Newark, Detroit, and Chicago and in the aftermath of Martin Luther King Jr.'s assassination in 1968. The Chicago Commission was comprised of eighty-one leading citizens, both black and white. Members examined the role of the police in the riots, riot control problems, examples of racial discrimination, and the generally poor relations between the races in Chicago.

The Ku Klux Klan

The Ku Klux Klan reorganized in 1915 and within four years was flourishing once again. The second and largest incarnation of the Klan began in Atlanta, Georgia, in 1915. Initially concentrating its animosity against blacks, in 1920 it launched a nationwide membership drive under the slogan "native, white and Protestant." Taking advantage of the temper and fears of the time, the Klan used the nation's anticommunism and rampant xenophobia as a device for rallying members to their repugnant banner. In 1925, Klan membership crested at between four and five million. Not just a southern phenomenon, crosses would burn from coast to coast as the Klan used the whip and the noose to terrorize Jews, Catholics, blacks, evolutionists, bootleggers, Bolshevists, and any others who crossed the moral divide. Between 1921 and 1926, the Klan controlled the election of governors and senators in Alabama, Georgia, Arkansas, Texas, Oklahoma, California, Oregon, Indiana, and Ohio. Although a number of politicians launched their administrations under the Klan aegis, by the late 1920s the second resurgence of the organization was in decline after several well-publicized scandals discredited Klan leaders.

Labor Violence

According to professors Philip Taft and Philip Ross, "The United States has had the bloodiest and most violent labor history of any industrial nation in the world."[33] Industrial violence reached its zenith between 1911 and 1916 with major confrontations occurring in Michigan, West Virginia, and Colorado. Two of the bloodiest episodes occurred in Washington State in 1916, when members of the IWW tried to organize lumber workers. Both incidents led to killings on both side of the picket lines and subsequent prison terms for IWW members.

Between 1916 and 1920, labor union membership almost doubled to close to five million members, heightening tensions between workers and management. In one of the worst episodes of labor violence, a fifteen-hour battle between strikers and militiamen at Ludlow, Colorado, in 1914 led to the suffocation deaths of two mothers and eleven children during a fire in the strikers' tent city. Over the next ten days, miners took part in a violent episode of "class warfare" in southern Colorado. The culmination of thirty years of sporadic conflict in the region, the events at Ludlow shocked the nation.

NOTABLE TRIALS

Sacco–Vanzetti Trial (1921)

Nicola Sacco and Bartolomeo Vanzetti were Italian-born anarchists who immigrated to America and became involved in the radical politics of the World War I era. They settled into an Italian community in eastern Massachusetts but in 1917 moved to Mexico for a brief time to avoid military conscription, an act that would further stigmatize them as "draft dodgers" during their subsequent murder trial.

On April 15, 1920, a paymaster and a guard were gunned down during a payroll robbery in South Braintree, Massachusetts. The two gunmen made away with more than $15,000 and were seen getting into a car with several others while making their getaway. Witnesses identified the suspects as Italian in appearance. Police were already investigating a similar holdup by Italians in a nearby town and were soon focusing on a suspect's car waiting for repairs at a garage.

On May 5, Sacco and Vanzetti, along with two friends, went to pick up the car at the garage and were arrested as they returned home on a streetcar. At the time of their arrest, both were carrying handguns. During questioning at the police station, both gave evasive answers and reportedly acted "suspiciously." While the prosecution would use this to suggest guilt, defense attorneys emphasized that they did not even know what the charges were at this point (they were not told the charges until four months later, when they were arraigned by the grand jury) and thought they were being held because of their radical views. Nonetheless, both were charged in the earlier holdup attempt and the double murder during the payroll robbery.

Despite other possible suspects, police concentrated solely on gathering evidence on the two anarchists. This should not be surprising when gauging the current political climate. It is impossible to separate the Sacco–Vanzetti case from the events of 1918 and 1919, when the U.S. government in effect waged war against subversive political groups.

During the trial for the earlier robbery, Sacco had a solid alibi since he could prove he was at work at a shoe-making factory at the time. However, Vanzetti, who worked as a fish peddler, claimed he was selling fish that evening. But witnesses identified him as one of the robbers, and he was sentenced to twelve to fifteen years in prison. Both men would be forced to face trial for the Braintree murders when it was found that Sacco had taken the day off from work.

Anarchist supporters organized a fund drive and hired radical labor lawyer Fred H. Moore to defend the two men. In the opening proceedings of the trial, it was found that both anarchists lied about their guns and that Vanzetti's weapon was identical to that of the murdered guard's, which happened to be missing at the scene of the crime.

Next, the prosecution made Sacco try on a cap found at the scene that was similar to one he regularly wore. Foreshadowing the famous O. J. Simpson trial faux pas when the prosecution had him try on gloves that did not fit, the prosecution had Sacco try on the cap, which was much too big, and as the defendant drew it down over his ears for effect, the courtroom burst into laughter, a rare instance of levity in the proceedings. Lawyers for the state then introduced a cap that was the same size as that found in Sacco's home. When it proved to be oversized as well, it seemed that the joke was on the defense.

During then ensuing proceedings, both Sacco and Vanzetti admitted lying about their reasons for visiting the garage because they feared deportation for radical charges if they told authorities they went to get the car to deliver radical literature. On July 14, 1920, the jury returned a guilty verdict on both murder charges, unleashing a wave of violent protest around the world Embassies from Europe to South America were bombarded by letters of protest. Ten thousand police protected the American embassy in Paris against thousands of protesters.

During the next six years, numerous motions for a new trial were denied. In 1927, the Massachusetts governor reviewed the entire case while considering an appeal for clemency. Despite a whirlwind of protest, the governor concluded that the initial findings were fair and that Sacco and Vanzetti were guilty. On August 23, 1927, both men were executed in the electric chair. Concluding that much of the evidence was questionable and that the judge and jury were prejudiced against the defendants because they were aliens and anarchists, fifty years later Massachusetts Governor Michael Dukakis signed a special proclamation admitting the unfairness of the trial.

To many critics, this case symbolized the failure of the criminal justice system as well as the inequity of capitalism. Over the past seventy years, debate over the case has continued as revisionists examined court transcripts and interviewed surviving participants. In the 1960s and 1980s, ballistics tests on Sacco's rusting forty-year-old gun seemed to determine that it did indeed fire a fatal round during the payroll robbery, calling into question the innocence of at least one of the "martyrs."

Summing up the impact of the case on American criminal justice, historian Vincenza Scarpaci stated, "Perhaps the greatest legacy of the Sacco-Vanzetti case concerns state-authorized violence: the methods used to bring criminals and terrorists to justice and efforts to ensure fair trial continue to place the political and judicial system in a delicate balancing act, attempting to protect the rights of the accused while also ensuring the public right to safety."[34]

To this day, there are still more questions than answers about the case: Who were the other three bandits in the car? What happened to the $15,000? How and when did Sacco and Vanzetti plan the perfectly executed robbery? Even noted Harvard law professor Felix Frankfurter penned a critique of the American justice system in the 1920s in which he noted the prejudices, errors, and absurdities of the prosecution's case. Perhaps the most enduring legacy of this "crime of the century" are the twenty-three gouaches by artist Ben Shahn and a number of poems, plays short stories, and novels that commemorate the case for posterity. Although opinion is still split as to whether Sacco and Vanzetti were guilty, we can never know with certainty whether they took part in the murders. However, a survey of the physical evidence suggests that Sacco was probably guilty (he shouted "Long live anarchy" as he was put to death) and that Vanzetti was innocent (declaring his innocence to his death).

CONCLUSIONS

According to criminal justice historian Samuel Walker, during the Progressive era, "virtually every state completed the modern criminal justice system, establishing probation, parole, and the juvenile court."[35] But the Progressive reformers left behind a mixed legacy. An era in which it was believed that progress could be leg-

islated saw a plethora of reform legislation, most of which was disappointing and rarely worked. Some urban reforms led to more efficient and noncorrupt civic government; however, the criminal opportunities of the Prohibition era that followed would nullify many of the Progressive reforms. In the end, most attempts to legislate morality led to profitability at the hands of organized crime groups. Most important, the criminalizing of once-noncriminal offenses, such as alcohol consumption and prostitution, fostered a widespread disrespect for law and its enforcement that would last for decades.

In the years following World War I, the abolition of the death penalty became a low priority, as tremendous changes in demographics focused the attention of reformers on poverty, civil rights, and political reform. In contrast to the idealistic prognostications of the reformers, the era actually deepened ethnic tensions and threatened civil liberties, dashing the hopes of the Progressive reformers. The war years intensified the old fears of native Americans who saw their vision of a strong, isolated country inhabited by white middle-class Protestants changing before their eyes. In response, they lashed out at those who had contributed to the transformation: immigrants, socialists, anarchists, communists, and radical labor organizers.

However, prison reformers are credited with breaking down the former punitive penal regime and by the 1930s could cite such victories as the end of striped uniforms, lockstep marching, silence, and draconian punishments outside the southern states. The onset of Prohibition in 1920 began the most disastrous period in twentieth-century law enforcement. Prohibition not only required the police to enforce laws that were almost impossible to enforce but also triggered widespread corruption in police departments throughout the nation.

As criminal justice historian Roger Lane has noted in his history of murder in America, "Progressive reforms had begun, and were always strongest at the local level, with attacks on municipal waste and corruption."[36] Local attempts at crime control and regulating morality stimulated the federal response to Progressive-era social problems that found expression in broadly worded federal laws against drugs and prostitution as well as the creation of the Bureau of Investigation.

Point–Counterpoint

Cossacks or Constabulary: The Pennsylvania State Police (1911)

The state of Pennsylvania had been beset by widespread rural crime, industrial disorder, and ethnic conflict since the 1850s. In 1905 the Pennsylvania State Police was created and charged with policing the entire state. However, for the most part they patrolled the immigrant dominated mining districts, to their opposition they were the Cossacks and top their supporters the Black Hussars. In the following passages state police advocate Katherine Mayo (1867–1940) describes a 100 percent American state police protecting the nation from foreigners, labor agitators, and people of color. In grim contrast the Pennsylvania State Federation of Labor collected a number of letters and abstracts testifying to the brutality and xenophobia of the new force.

The period immediately following the enlistment of the command, laconically as it was summarized by Captain Groome, was a period long to be remembered by the men of the four Troops. Assembled in their four quarters of the State they now faced each other practically for the first time. A few of them had served in the regular army together, here and there about the world, but for the most part they were as strange one to another as to the questions that they had to solve.

"Now, you are the State Police Force," they heard. And the Superintendent, interviewing them severally and apart, had said, in a way that none of them will ever forget:

"Your duty is to make the Pennsylvania State Police Force the finest thing in the world."

The Superintendent, in those memorable private interviews, had probed their minds as to their own conception of the work, giving them therewith certain illuminating flashes of his own purpose. He had indicated, also, a cardinal point or two, as:

Source: Katherine Mayo, *Justice to All: The Story of the Pennsylvania State Police,* Boston, 1929, pp. 24–25, 31–34; Pennsylvania State Federation of Labor, *The American Cossack,* pp. 17, 18, 20–22.

"It is possible for a man to be a gentleman as well as a policeman."

"I expect you to treat elderly persons, women, and children at all times with the greatest consideration."

"When once you start after a man *you must get him.*"

"In making an arrest you may use no force beyond the minimum necessary."

"One State Policeman should be able to handle one hundred foreigners."

The general locations of the four Troop stations had been determined by two considerations: First, that the entire command should be so distributed as to reach as far as might be over the State; and, second but not less, that the regions of greatest criminality should be under the closest observation. A glance at the map shows that the posts are placed in the northern and southern halves of the eastern and western sections. These sections, by year-round criminal record, produced more murder, more manslaughter, more robbery, more rape, more burglary and thieving, more lawlessness and disorder of every sort, by far, than were shown by the records of the other parts of the Commonwealth. The central section of the State was and is mainly a farming region, with an old, homogeneous population, by no means free from trouble but not yet as ceaselessly troubled as the regions to the east and west.

The reason of this condition was obvious. In the eastern and western sections lie the great coal fields, with other allied industries. The coal fields, ever since their opening, have attracted an unending stream of foreign immigration. This immigration, at first largely tainted with lawlessness and turbulence, constantly undergoes a process of assimilation and improvement and is as constantly reflooded below by crude material of the roughest type.

In the beginning the major part of the mine laborers came from Ireland and from the Scandinavian peninsula. Out of the former of these two elements sprang that unspeakable society of murderers, the "Molly McGuires." After successfully maintaining a reign of nightmare for some years, these monstrosities were wiped out of existence by heroic methods, while the Irish in general, like the Scandinavians, are now but little found in their earlier walks, having graduated to more desirable employ. The Welsh passed quickly through the transition stage and beyond it. Then came the Slavs and the Italians, who practically filled the field at the period in hand.

Peoples totally unused in their countries of origin to any form of self-government, but accustomed on the contrary to see the sword of the king always bared before their eyes, Slavs and Italians alike here looked in vain for outward evidence of authority and law. Peoples used to the narrowest means, they here found themselves suddenly possessed of greater earnings than they had ever dreamed of before. Peoples used to free drinking, in climates where the effect of alcohol is less marked than here, they still continued that free drinking, and in strange raw mixtures of peculiar virulence. Liberty that they knew not how to use, money that they knew neither how to spend nor how to save, meant license, greed, drunkenness— and through drunkenness all brutalities let loose.

The State Police has no purpose save to execute the laws of the State.

The State Police, therefore, was properly placed in the centres of greatest offense to the people. Its sole concern was to protect the people in their peace. At no time could it check in the slightest degree the movements of any person not breaking the law. A "strike" is a perfectly lawful proceeding, and the State's Police could have no cognizance of a "strike" other than of a picnic or a county fair. Called in by the proper authorities with convincing proof of need, the State Police would see to it, at picnic, strike, or country fair, alike, that general order was maintained by all present without fear, favor, or respect to persons. And therein lies the whole story.

The first activities of the four Troops now entering the field were of a general and various nature. Here they picked up a country store robber; there a stabber of a night watchman; again, a molester of women; a carrier of concealed weapons; a farm thief; a setter of forest fires; and always a little harvest of killers of song-birds, greatly to the derision of the imperfectly endowed. Meantime they were dealing constantly with the unassimilated foreign element, teaching it by small but repeated object-lessons that a new gospel was abroad in the land.

At feasts, christenings, balls, and the like, these alien people were given to heavy and prolonged drinking bouts, which ended often in wild and murderous disorder.
New Alexandria, Pa., Feb. 21, 1911.
Gentlemen:
State Police came to New Alexandria July 31, 1910, Sunday.

The State Constabulary are of no use in this country to farmers and workingmen. They make all efforts to oppress labor.

Six of them were stationed at this town for a period of two months for the benefit of the coal company. Their duty was in and around the works.

At the time they were here there was trouble between them and the miners. There was a camp located within two hundred feet of my house. There were three State Constabulary and two deputy sheriffs went into camp. They rode their horses over men, women and children. They used their riot clubs freely on the miners without cause or provocation.

One of the men had to be sent to the hospital, one received a broken arm, one woman was clubbed until she was laid up for two weeks. At that time she gave birth to a child and remained in bed for four weeks after the birth of her child. They used their clubs on everyone that protested against their conduct and I was an eye-witness to the affair.

There were no lives lost and no one hurt before their arrival.

The majority of citizens are not in favor of the Constabulary.

I cannot see that anyone but the coal company is benefitted by the Constabulary.

Yours truly,
S. P. Bridge,
New Alexandria, Westmoreland County, Pa.
Latrobe, Pa., Feb. 13, 1911.

Report of Investigating Committee, Local No. 405, U. M. W. of A., as follows:

Question No. 1. The first arrival of the State Constabulary was at Bradenville, morning of April 22, 1910. On their arrival at Bradenville on said morning, they acted more like heathens than human-beings. They drove their horses up on the sidewalks and knocked people in all directions, ordering people away from their own homes. They arrested one man for hollering "bah," drove others from the public highway and away from the street car station, regardless of who they were.

Question No. 2. The conditions before their arrival were good, no trouble having occurred whatever.

Question No. 3. No lives were lost prior to their arrival, and no property had been destroyed.

Question No. 4. There were four lives taken, namely: Mike Cheken, Mike Mizrak, one colored man and one deputy sheriff. After the arrival of the

Constabulary the property loss was— three double houses at Superior No. 2, private property damaged by explosion, one small child lost its life, which occurred at 12 P. M. There was also damage done to the property of Mike Godula at Peanut Works, blowing down his bake-oven and fence, on the morning of July 4, 1910. There was dynamite found in the yard next morning.

Mary Riech lost her life at Superior No. 2, in an explosion which occurred on Jan, 27, 1911.

Two were blown up in Superior No. 2, between the 27th and 28th. The explosion damaged the houses and all the things in them. About ten minutes after there was about eighteen to thirty rifle shots fired at the house. Some went into the bed but no one was hit. After the explosion, the man came out on his porch and all of the company employees told him to go into the house.

There were people who saw them placing some dynamite against the house.

Signed by the citizens of Superior No. 2.
Noah Panizza,
Emrico Balarmene,
Tonie Debaco,
Mary Perodi.
Irwin, Pa., Feb. 21, 1911.

To the Legislature of Pennsylvania:

This is to certify that the following evidence is true, as given by different members of our Local Union, No. 2088:

1. The State Police came to Irwin about the 15th of June.

2. The condition of the town of Irwin was peaceable before the arrival of the police, no lives being lost or property damaged before they arrived, and the town being quiet until the arrival of the State Police.

3. I, Frank Nameska, was going home peaceably from the election board at the hour of 5.30 and was stopped by two State Police and compelled to be searched.

The second time I was going to Irwin, with three other men and was stopped and asked where we were going. We said, "None of your business." One man jumped from his horse and said, you better go back. Then they pushed us about, trying to start a fight because we were out on strike, but we managed to get to Irwin after them pushing us about, during which I received a crack on the jaw.

4. I, Frank Fletcher, was going to Irwin and was arrested by two State Police, taken to burgess' office after being taken from jail for being drunk and disorderly, and forced to pay the sum of $6.75.

5. I, William Colliner, was at Rilton; when I came back to Irwin, I was arrested by the State Police and taken to Greensburg. After I was put in jail, I was released the next day.

6. I, David Thomas, was arrested and abused by the State Police on the 16th day of December. The State Police were taking a few men to the mines. I just asked the men if they knew that there was a strike going on. One of the State Police turned and hit me with a black-jack, bursting my head and I was taken to jail, then to 'Squire Davis. He put the case to Greensburg, where I was fined $14.14 for witness fees and $41.32 costs, for assault and battery and resisting an officer. The State Police were dressed in citizens' clothes, not having any badge.

7. I, David Thomas, Jr., was coming down street and saw my father all over blood. I asked him what was the matter. He then told me of being hit by a man. I asked where the man was then. I was shown. I asked the man why he hit my father. I, not knowing that he was a State Police, asked him again what was the matter. The State Police said, "He is under arrest." Then I said, "Well, if he is under arrest, don't knock his brains out." Then the other State Police yelled out, "You are under arrest." I was then taken with my father to jail, but was let free.

The State Police acknowledged, at court, that they arrested the men without showing any badge or having on their uniforms.

8. The conduct of the State Police toward citizens not interested in the strike was favorable.

9. The names of the men abused are Mike Klemans, Frank Fletcher, Tony Fletcher, Frank Nameska, David Thomas, Jr., David Thomas, Sr., William Colliner, John Clark.

10. The conduct towards the strikers is very severe and on all occasions they tried to raise trouble on the slighest provocation, beating men, women and even children.

11. About 85 per cent, of the people of Irwin signed petition against the State Police.

12. Their conduct is very bad. Known to sit back of Brunswick Hotel and drink.

13. The presence of the State Police is favorable to the coal companies.

14. The farmers are not being benefitted at all by the State Police.

SOURCES

Appier, Janis. 1998. *Policing Women: The Sexual Politics of Law Enforcement and the LAPD*. Philadelphia: Temple University Press.

Asinof, Eliot. 1990. *1919: America's Loss of Innocence*. New York: Donald I. Fine.

Avrich, Paul. 1991. *Sacco and Vanzetti: The Anarchist Background*. Princeton, N.J.: Princeton University Press.

Bennet, Lerone, Jr. 1984. *Before the Mayflower: A History of Black America*. New York: Penguin Books.

Brown, Richard Maxwell, ed. 1970. *American Violence*. Englewood Cliffs, N.J.: Prentice Hall.

Caesar, Gene. 1968. *Incredible Detective: The Biography of William J. Burns*. Englewood Cliffs, N.J.: Prentice Hall.

Carte, Gene E., and Elaine H. Carte. 1975. *Police Reform in the United States: The Era of August Vollmer* Berkeley, CA.: University of California Press.

Colvin, Mark. 1997. *Penitentiaries, Reformatories, and Chain Gangs: Social Theory and the History of Punishment in Nineteenth-Century America*. New York: St. Martin's Press.

Ellis, Edward Robb. 1975. *Echoes of Distant Thunder: Life in the United States 1914–1918*. New York: Coward, McCann and Geoghegan.

Fried, Albert. 1980. *The Rise and Fall of the Jewish Gangster in America*. New York: Holt, Rinehart and Winston.

Friedman, Lawrence M. 1993. *Crime and Punishment in American History*. New York: Basic Books.

Gentry, Curt. 1991. *J. Edgar Hoover: The Man and His Secrets*. New York: W. W. Norton.

Gillham, Nicholas Wright. 2001. *A Life of Sir Francis Galton: From African Exploration to the Birth of Eugenics*. New York: Oxford University Press.

Graham, Hugh Davis, and Ted Robert Gurr. 1969. *The History of Violence in America*. New York: Bantam Books.

Grant, Robert, and Joseph Katz. 1998. *The Great Trials of the Twenties: The Watershed Decade in America's Courtrooms*. Rockville Centre, N.Y.: Sarpedon.

Kennett, Lee, and James LaVerne Anderson. 1975. *The Gun in America: The Origins of a National Dilemma*. Westport, Conn.: Greenwood Press.

Keve, Paul W. 1991. *Prisons and the American Conscience: A History of U.S. Federal Corrections*. Carbondale: Southern Illinois University Press.

King, Joseph. 1999. "Police Strikes of 1918 and 1919 in the United Kingdom and Boston and Their Effects." Doctoral diss., City University of New York.

Lane, Roger. 1999. "Capital Punishment." In *Violence in America*, vol. 1, ed. Ronald Gottesman, pp. 198–203. New York: Charles Scribner's Sons.

Lane, Roger. 1997. *Murder in America*. Columbus: Ohio State University Press.

LeBrun, George P. (as told to Edward D. Radin). 1962. *It's Time to Tell*. New York: William Morrow.

Morgan, H. Wayne. 1974. *Yesterday's Addicts: American Society and Drug Abuse, 1865–1920*. Norman: University of Oklahoma Press.

Morris, Norval, and David J. Rothman, eds. 1995. *The Oxford History of the Prison: The Practice of Punishment in Western Society*. New York: Oxford University Press.

Myers, Gloria E. 1995. *A Municipal Mother: Portland's Lola Greene Baldwin, America's First Policewoman*. Corvallis: Oregon State University Press.

Rafter, Nicole H. 1997. *Creating Born Criminals*. Urbana: University of Illinois Press.

Richardson, James F. 1974. *Urban Police in the United States*. Port Washington, NY.: Kennikat Press.

Roberts, Randy. 1983. *Papa Jack: Jack Johnson and the Era of White Hopes*. New York: Free Press.

Rosen, Ruth. 1982. *The Lost Sisterhood: Prostitution in America, 1900–1918*. Baltimore: Johns Hopkins University Press.

Russell, Francis. 1975. *A City in Terror: 1919, The Boston Police Strike*. New York: Viking.

———. 1986. *Sacco and Vanzetti: The Case Resolved*. New York: Harper & Row.

Sandburg, Carl. [1919] 1969. *The Chicago Race Riots, July, 1919*. Reprint, New York: Harcourt, Brace and World.

Scarpaci, Vincenza. 1999. "Sacco-Vanzetti." In *Violence in America: An Encyclopedia*, vol. 3, ed. Ronald Gottesman, pp. 75–78. New York: Charles Scribner's Sons.

Sjoquist, Arthur W. 1984. *Los Angeles Police Department Commemorative Book: 1869–1984*. Los Angeles: Los Angeles Police Revolver and Athletic Club.

Stein, Leon. 1962. *The Triangle Fire*. New York: Carroll & Graf Publishers.

Sullivan, Larry E.. 1990. *The Prison Reform Movement: Forlorn Hope*. Boston: Twayne Publishing.

Taft, Philip, and Philip Ross. 1969. "American Labor Violence: Its Causes, Character, and Outcome." In *The History of Violence in America*, ed. Hugh Davis

Graham and Ted Robert Gurr, pp. 281–395. New York: Bantam Books.

Tuttle, William M. 1980. *Race Riot: Chicago in the Red Summer of 1919.* New York: Atheneum.

Walker, Samuel. 1998. *Popular Justice.* New York: Oxford University Press.

Ward, Nathan. 2001. "The Fire Last Time: When Terrorists First Struck New York's Financial District." *American Heritage,* December, pp. 46–49.

Wilder, Harris Hawthorne, and Bert Wentworth. 1918. *Personal Identification.* Boston: Richard G. Badger.

CRITICAL THINKING QUESTIONS

1. What criminal justice issues were Progressive reformers most concerned with?

2. Why were laws passed controlling so-called victimless crimes, such as prostitution and narcotics addiction? Discuss the transition from legality to prohibition of these vices.

3. Who were the "new dangerous classes?" What was their impact on the development of the "science" of eugenics?

4. Discuss the impact of the years 1919 and 1920 on the criminal justice system.

5. How did civilian police reformers such as Leonhard Fuld, Bruce Smith, and Raymond Fosdick impact police professionalism? Contrast their contributions with traditional police reformers such as August Vollmer and Fred Kohler.

6. Trace the development of state police forces in the early twentieth century.

7. Discuss the evolution of parole from indeterminate sentencing.

8. Discuss the following statement: Progressive reformers left behind a mixed legacy.

9. How did the criminal justice system change between 1895 and 1925?

CRIMINAL JUSTICE HISTORY
ON THE INTERNET

There are a number of Web sites devoted to the White Slave Traffic Act, better known as the Mann Act. The actual Mann Act can found at www.law.du.edu/sterling/Content/ALH/mann.pdf. Three documents showing the changing views of female sexuality after the turn of the century are available at womhist.binghamton.edu/aoc/doc22.htm. Two of the more famous convictions under this act involved actors Charles Chaplin and Errol Flynn. Their FBI files can be found at www.fadetoblack.com/foi/charliechaplin/filehints.html and foia.fbi.gov/flynn.htm. For more on this controversial act, see www.straightdope.com/classics/a990115.html, www.lexisnexis.com/academic/guides/immigration/ins/insa5.htm, and web.grinnell.edu/individuals/kramerj/collpaps/CasePrep.html.

A biography of August Vollmer can be found at www.prospector-utah.com/vollmer.htm and photos and a biography at http://history.sandiego.edu/gen/classes/social/prison-vollmer.html.

For Lola Baldwin and the policewomen's movement, see www.orst.ed/dept/press/motherIntro.html, mcel.pacificu.edu/history/herrick/Bios.html, and pythia.uoregon.edu/~cyberj/historyside.html. The life of Alice Stebbins Wells can be accessed at www.wpoaca.com/archives/wells.html and www.losangelesalmanac.com/topics/Crime/cr73b.htm.

There are a variety of sites devoted to the sensational crimes and trials of the century. For Leopold and Loeb, see www.law.umkc.edu/faculty/projects/ftrials/leoploeb/leopold.htm; the trial transcript is at www.leopoldandloeb.com. The Scopes trial is featured at www.law.umkc.edu/faculty/projects/ftrials/scopes/scopes.htm and www.msu.edu/course/mc/112/1920s/Scopes. The Sacco and Vanzetti case is examined from a number of perspectives at www.english.upenn.edu/~afilreis/88/sacvan.html, www.crimelibrary.com/saccomain.htm, www.theatlantic.com/unbound/flashbks/oj/frankff.htm, www.courttv.com/greatesttrials/sacco.vanzetti, www.msu.edu/course/mc/112/1920s/Sacco-Vanzetti, and www.law.umkc.edu/faculty/projects/ftrials/SaccoV/SaccoV.htm.

The full text of the Harrison Narcotic Act is at www.druglibrary.org/schaffer/history/e1910/harrisonact.htm. For the Pure Food and Drug Act, see http://coursesa.matrix.msu.edu/~hst203/documents/ pure.html, www.commomlink.com/users/carl-oslen/DPF/whitebread03.html, and www.druglibrary.org/scahffer/Library/szasz.1htm.

The year 1919 witnessed a number of important episodes crucial to understanding the development of the criminal justice system. The Boston police strike is at www.iboston.org/mcp.php?pid=policeStrike&laf=hope andwww.law.umkc.edu/faculty/projects/ftrials/SaccoV/redscare.html. The Chicago race riots are given ample coverage at www.suba.com/~scottn/explore/scrapbks/raceriot/raceriot.htm, including photographs and period newspaper accounts. An examination of Chicago gangs and the riot is at www.uic.edu/orgs/kbc/ganghistory/Industrial%20Era/Riotbegins.html.

The Palmer raids and the Red Scare can be examined at http://chnm.gmu.edu/courses/hist409/red.html, www.vdare.com/fulford/palmer.htm, and www.lewrockwell.com/orig/felkins10.html. A 1920 essay by communist nemesis Attorney General A. Mitchell Palmer, namesake of raids, is at http://chnm.gmu.edu/courses/hist409/palmer.html.

For tragedies delving into criminal justice issues, students can find documents and photos of the Triangle Shirtwaist Factory fire at www.ilr.cornell.edu/trianglefire and www.historybuff.com/library/refshirtwaist.html. See other photo galleries at http://newdeal.feri.org/library/ac44.htm and www.csun.edu/ghy7463/mw2.html. For the 1920 Wall Street bombing, visit www.acessatlanta.com/ajc/opinion/1201/1920bomb/1216bombing.html, www.newamerica.net/articles/article.cfm?publD=552&T2=Article, and www.spectrum.ieee.org/INST/dec01/history.html.

For court cases and the court system, see http://abcnews.go.com/onair/2020_000322_eugenics_feature.html. For the U.S. Supreme Court and forced sterilization, see www.eugenicsarchive.org/html/eugenics/essay8text.html. The Nineteenth Amendment is covered in a 1919 newspaper article at www.fordham.edu/halsall/mod/1920womensvote.html. The text of *Weeks v. United States* can be found at www.greatsource.com/

amgov/almanac/documents/supreme/1914_wvu_1.html, *Webb et al. v. United States* at www.druglibrary.org/schaffer/History/webb.html, and *Weems v. United States* at http://caselaw.lp.findlaw.com/scripts/getcase.pl?navby=case&court=us&vol=217&invol=349.

The Sullivan handgun law is covered at http://infoweb.magi.com/~freddo/whitemanslaw.html. The Scopes trial is at www.msu.edu/course/mc/112/1920s/Scopes/index.html. For World War I legislation, see the U.S. Sedition Act at www.lib.byu.edu/ ~rdh/wwi/1918/usspy.html. Read a contemporary statement against this act by union leader Eugene Debs at www.wfu.edu/~zulick/341/Debs1918.htm. For the Espionage Act, see www.ku.edu/carrie/docs/texts/esp1918.htm and www.staff.uiuc.edu/~rcunning/espact.htm.

For prison reformer Thomas Mott Osborne and his work at Sing Sing and Auburn prisons, see photos and text at www.co.cayuga.ny.us/history/cayugahistory/prison.html and www.geocities.com/MotorCity/Downs/3548/facility/singsing.html. For correctional education, see www.ceanational.org/history.htm.

The return of the Ku Klux Klan and immigration restriction is examined at www.history.ohio-state.edu/projects/clash/Imm_KKK%20pages/KKK-page1.htm. See also www.tsha.utexas.edu/handbook/online/articles/print/KK/vek2.html.

NOTES

1. "Jim Crow" referred to the de facto segregation that characterized the South. The name of Jim Crow was tied to a white actor in blackface who worked as a song-and-dance man in the 1830s. According to historian Lerone Bennet Jr., by 1838 the term was being used as a "synonym for Negro," enforcing the image of the African American as a "comic, jumping, stupid rag doll of a man."

2. Some of the critics of the journalists compared them to a character in John Bunyan's *The Pilgrim's Progress*, who was too engrossed in raking muck to look up and accept a celestial crown, hence the moniker "muckraker."

3. For an excellent account of this tragedy, see Stein (1962).

4. Colvin (1997, p. 174).

5. Friedman (1993, p. 328).

6. LeBrun, (1962, p. 105).

7. Morgan (1974, p. 8).

8. Quoted in Friedman (1993, p. 355). See also *Webb et al. v. United States, U.S. Reports 96*, March 3, 1919.

9. The term *eugenics* was first coined in 1883 by Galton but did not enter the American lexicon until the turn of the century.

10. Gillham (2001).

11. Rafter (1997, p. 6).

12. Quoted in Friedman (1993, p. 335).

13. Indiana passed new laws that incorporated new sterilization procedures in 1927 and 1931.

14. Rafter (1997, p. 212).

15. Galton biographer Nicholas W. Gillham (2001) noted that eugenic experiments in America "were followed with interest by German race hygienists" (p. 355).

16. Friedman (1993, pp. 338–39).

17. Gentry (1991, p. 79).

18. Gentry (1991, p. 103).

19. In 1961, *Mapp v. Ohio* would apply the exclusionary principle to all federal and state criminal trials.

20. Richardson (1974, p. 69).

21. According to police historian James Richardson (1974, p. 79), Kohler borrowed this idea from the mayor and police chief of Toledo, Ohio, but "characteristically claimed it was his original idea."

22. Richardson (1974, p. 79).

23. Myers (1995, p. 22).

24. Although Wells is generally regarded as the first woman given the title of police officer as well as the powers of arrest, in 1893 the Chicago Police Department gave police widow Marie Owens the title of police officer, albeit without any arrest powers.

25. Quoted in Sjoquist (1984, p. 148).

26. The dance halls were one of the most popular entertainment spots for young men and women at the turn of the century. Here, for as little as a nickel, men and women could come and escape the tedium of the twelve-hour workday. According to historian Albert Fried, by 1900 New York City had one or two on every block. Reformers would naturally target the immorality of the dance halls during the Progressive era.

27. Myers (1995, p. 171).

28. Sullivan (1990, p. 27).

29. Sullivan (1990, p. 31).

30. Lane (1999, p. 201).

31. Ward (2001, p. 46).

32. Quoted in Brown (1970, p. 126).

33. Taft and Ross (1969, p. 281).

34. Scarpaci (1999, p. 77).

35. Walker (1998, p. 112).

36. Lane (1997, p. 211).

10

CRIMINAL JUSTICE IN THE CRISIS DECADES (1919–1938)

TIME LINE

1919	Congress ratifies Eighteenth Amendment
1919	Passage of National Motor Vehicle Theft Act
1921	Tulsa race riot
1921	J. Edgar Hoover transferred to the Bureau of Investigation
1921–1941	Fifteen state police forces created
1924	Congress approves transfer of fingerprint records to FBI
1924	Nevada introduces nation's first gas chamber
1924	Teapot Dome scandal
1924	John Edgar Hoover appointed director of Bureau of Investigation
1924	Publication of Edwin Sutherland's *Criminology*
1925	*Carroll et al. v. United States* establishes right of the police to search a vehicle without a warrant if sufficient probable cause of illegal activity exists
1928	O. W. Wilson professionalizes the Wichita, Kansas, police
1929	Stock market crash and beginning of the Great Depression
1929	St. Valentine's Day Massacre
1929	Passage of Hawes-Cooper Bill

1930	*Uniform Crime Reports* comes under management of Justice Department's Bureau of Identification	1934	Congress empowers Bureau of Investigation agents to make arrests and carry firearms
1930	Seabury Investigation	1934	Bank robber John Dillinger killed in Chicago
1930	Bureau of Narcotics created	1934	Bonnie and Clyde ambushed and killed in rural Louisiana
1931	Arrest of Scottsboro Boys		
1931	Al Capone convicted of tax evasion after IRS investigation	1935	Bureau of Investigation renamed Federal Bureau of Investigation
1931	Wickersham Commission issues *Report on Police*	1935	FBI establishes National Police Academy
1931	San Jose State College opens first complete police major program	1935	Ashurst-Summers Act
		1936	Bruno Hauptmann executed
1931	282 reported kidnappings	1936	Movie *Reefer Madness* released
1932	In wake of Lindbergh case, Congress makes kidnapping a federal crime when victim is transported across state lines	1937	First Gallup Poll on death penalty finds overwhelming support
		1937	Marijuana Tax Act
1932	*Powell v. Alabama*	1937	*Norris v. Alabama*
1933	Kansas City Massacre	1938	*Johnson v. Zerbst*
1933	Prohibition ends		

The passage of the Eighteenth Amendment and the onset of Prohibition in 1920 led to what many observers have referred to as the "lawless decade." Others have described the 1920s and 1930s as "the crime control decades."[1] Prohibition would cast a pall over the presidencies of Woodrow Wilson, Warren G. Harding, Calvin Coolidge, and Herbert Hoover before being brought to an end in 1933 under the Roosevelt administration.

Following the Wall Street crash in 1929, America and the Western world seemed to be standing on the brink of an abyss. As America's farmers saw their dreams turn to dust, by 1932 between one-quarter and one-third of America's workers stood in unemployment lines as the country's national output was pared in half.

During the 1920s and 1930s, crime emerged as one of the nation's greatest political and social issues as popular attention was focused on the exploits of bootleggers, gangsters, public enemies, and crime waves, both real and imaginary. One historian of the social bandit tradition noted that although the 1930s saw a sustained drop in serious crimes, the "concentration of famous fugitives and their infamous crimes [between 1933 and 1935] has no equal in the nation's history."[2] By the 1930s, law enforcement became a national obsession thanks to the publicity-minded genius of FBI director J. Edgar Hoover, who consciously projected the onset of a fearful crime wave. In response, Congress would broaden the mandate of federal law enforcement to include policing prostitution, drugs, and the sale of alcohol.

Until recently, many chroniclers of the 1920s and 1930s have persuasively perpetuated an image of a lawless land of tommy-gun-toting killers, when in actuality the 1930s was a safer era than the 1980s. The numbers spewed out by the publicity machine have long overshadowed a reality that would suggest that the numbers of violent and serious property offenses actually fell in the 1930s. America's homicide rate had doubled between 1900 and 1919, but in the 1920s there was little increase and perhaps a slight decline. What had increased by the 1920s and 1930s was an awareness and fear of crime thanks in part to the omnipresent news media. Highly publicized "crimes of the century," such as the Lindbergh kidnapping, the St. Valentine's Day Massacre, and the Leopold and Loeb case, transfixed the country. Forecasting the modern era, newspaper and radio station owners had figured out that crime news sells. As prohibition criminalized once-acceptable behavior, it just added to America's fixation on rising crime rates.

The years between World War I and World War II saw the federal government become increasingly involved in crime fighting. In 1929, President Herbert Hoover authorized the Wickersham Commission to direct the first "comprehensive survey of American criminal justice at the national level."[3] That same year, Hoover appointed Sanford Bates to lead the new U.S. Bureau of Prisons. During the next five decades, the federal correctional system would set the standards for state prisons.

On the national level, President Franklin D. Roosevelt exploited political and economic crises to maneuver through Congress a series of laws to promote economic recovery and reduce social and economic misery. The creation of the New Deal ran counter to the prevailing policy of laissez-faire, which placed limits on the federal government's power to set standards governing prices, pensions, wages, and labor relations. The New Deal empowered the federal government to assume more social welfare responsibilities at the expense of states' rights. Coinciding with the sharp rise in crime, New Deal principles would be applied to criminal justice as well, leading to a revolution in law enforcement. Paralleling the growth of most federal agencies during this era was the expansion of the FBI in the 1930s and a burgeoning federal war against crime. During the early New Deal years, federal control over crime was expanded to include kidnapping (1932), crossing state lines to avoid prosecution (1933), interstate transportation of stolen goods (1934), and marijuana prohibition (1937).

THE LAWGIVERS

In the first half of the twentieth century, the court system saw a major shift in emphasis from property to personal rights. The Bill of Rights had little practical impact on government powers until the 1920s and 1930s, when the first amendments were given practical meaning by the law. It should not be surprising that this was the case since the Bill of Rights was aimed at the federal government and its policies. The federal government had little concern for individual rights until the Progressive era. Even the interpretation of the post–Civil War amendments was usually confined to economic issues (e.g., the Fourteenth Amendment and the *Slaughterhouse* cases). Historian David Bodenhamer, one of the foremost authorities on the rights of the accused, suggested that "the nationalization of the Bill of Rights travelled an uncertain course because the justices lacked a sure theoretical foundation for their decisions." He concluded that "there was no consensus on principles to guide interpretation of the amendments, in part because of the novelty of the idea that defendants' rights needed protection against state misconduct."[4]

Beginning in the 1920s, the Supreme Court held that states were bound by certain guaranties of the Bill of Rights. In 1923, the Court for the first time reversed a state criminal conviction on the grounds that the trial had departed from due process. Two years later, the Court issued two decisions that held that certain guaranties of the Bill of Rights were so fundamental as to be included in due process. Both decisions involved rights protected by the First Amendment.

Among the most significant challenges to search-and-seizure laws during the 1920s was the 1925 *Carroll et al. v. United States* Supreme Court ruling. In this case, a bootlegger by the name of George Carroll and some of his associates were arrested and convicted of violating prohibition statutes after law enforcement officers seized sixty-eight bottles of whiskey and gin from his car during a search of his car without a warrant. The defendants charged that this search violated their Fourth Amendment rights and that the liquor found in the car should have been inadmissible as evidence in court. However, the Supreme Court upheld the convictions despite the absence of a warrant, citing the fact that the search of a moving vehicle is not the same as searching a home because crucial evidence can be moved quickly in moving vehicles and thus lost forever. Therefore, if there is probable cause of illegal activity, under what has become known as the "Carroll Doctrine," police can conduct a search of a vehicle, such as a car or a boat, without a warrant.

The campaigns against narcotics and alcohol shared many similarities in part because "both were first directed against the evils of large-scale use and only later against all use."[5] However, where the two efforts differed was in the realm of public opinion. Few Americans argued with the antinarcotics crusade, while temperance was a matter of vitriolic public debate for decades.

Drug Enforcement

Harry Anslinger (1892–1975) rose to national prominence as the first commissioner of the Bureau of Narcotics of the U.S. Treasury Department in the 1930s. During the 1920s, the association of the Narcotics Division with the Prohibition Bureau led to public disenchantment with the bureau in part because of the unpopularity of Prohibition as well as the ineptitude of its enforcement. In 1930, Congress removed drug enforcement from the Prohibition Bureau and created a separate agency in the Treasury Department. Initially, the powers of the Bureau of Narcotics were limited to the enforcement of registration and record-keeping laws.

Born in Altoona, Pennsylvania, after graduating from law school, Harry Anslinger entered public service with the War Department before moving to the Treasury Department in 1926. During the early Prohibition years, he attended seminars on international drug and alcohol smuggling, which would lead to his appointment as commissioner of Prohibition in 1929. Following his appointment as commissioner of the Bureau of Narcotics, he embarked on a get-tough policy against drug abusers. During the 1930s, he led the crusade against marijuana, which culminated in the passage of the Marijuana Tax Act of 1937. During World War II, Anslinger made the unsubstantiated claim that the Japanese were using an "opium offensive" as part of a strategy to enslave conquered countries through drug trafficking. The U.S. government was sufficiently alarmed to grant him access to the Coast Guard, the U.S. Customs Service, and the Internal Revenue Service in his battle against the narcotics trade.

Few states had any drug control statutes by 1930, but with the establishment of the new federal bureau, the states were encouraged to enact their own antidrug legislation. The following year, every state had introduced laws to restrict the sale of cocaine, and most also restricted the sales of opiates. However, drug enforcement was hampered by the lack of uniformity in state statutes and the weakness of enforcement strategies. By the late 1930s, thirty-five states had embraced the Uniform Narcotic Act, which regulated or prohibited cocaine and opium and their derivatives. Despite opposition to including marijuana on the list, most of the states had already enacted marijuana statutes.

There was little fear over marijuana use throughout the 1920s, although the federal government was expressing increased concern. By the 1930s, sixteen states, most with relatively large Mexican populations, enacted antimarijuana legislation. Thanks in part to hysterical films such as *Reefer Madness* (1936) and recommendations by drug commissioner Harry Anslinger, a growing concern among the public and legislators led Congress to pass the Marijuana Tax Act in 1937. Although it made the recreational use of marijuana illegal, it did not become much of an issue until the 1960s. In fact, the Bureau of Narcotics opposed publicity campaigns by private organizations that portrayed the marijuana problem as out of hand and discouraged the creators of the "killer drug marijuana" posters from selling their materials.[6]

Prohibition

In December 1919, Congress approved the Eighteenth Amendment, which was ratified by the states the following year. Under the new law, it became illegal to manufacture, import, distribute, or sell alcoholic beverages in the United States. However, it created a major paradox in that the amendment did not prohibit the purchase and consumption of alcoholic beverages.

Although Prohibition has been branded an unmitigated disaster for providing the opportunity for organized crime to thrive, it was not the total failure as popularly depicted. During Prohibition, public drunkenness all but vanished, and deaths and diseases from alcohol, such as cirrhosis of the liver, declined. Looming large in the face of historians who would suggest that Prohibition had more beneficial effects than negative ones, the increased fatalities from the deadly concoction of rubbing alcohol–based consumption of

"bathtub gin" and the hundreds of killings associated with the rise of organized crime must be taken into consideration.

The consumption of alcohol would not return to pre-Prohibition levels until the 1970s. In the early 1920s, public sentiment favored enforcement, but with the growing corruption and crime, public opinion changed, and in 1930 a poll of five million people found only 10.5 percent in favor of enforcement.

The Wickersham Commission (1929–1931)

In 1929, former U.S. Attorney General George Wickersham (1858–1936) was selected to chair the National Commission on Law Observance and Enforcement. His dominant presence ensured that his name would become synonymous with police reform after the commission became better known as the Wickersham Commission. Although derided by some as "a monument to equivocation"[7] for its failure to reach any conclusions about crime and Prohibition, it is considered the first national commission to consider issues of crime and law enforcement in a serious manner as well as to make recommendations. Under President Herbert Hoover, the commission was given the task of proposing methods for the enforcement of the Eighteenth Amendment. In addition, the commission was charged with surveying the entire federal criminal justice system and examining the administration of justice in relation to the amendment. The Wickersham Commission recommended not repealing the Eighteenth Amendment but urged better methods of enforcing it.

Between 1929 and 1931, the commission produced a fourteen-volume report. Its most important findings related to policing were published in two volumes, *Report on Lawlessness in Law Enforcement* (No. 11) and *Report on Police* (No. 14). According to No. 11, the use of the third degree[8] was a violation of constitutional privileges. The commission recommended eleven solutions for eradicating procedures that often denied fundamental rights to suspects and defendants.

Report No. 14 was a critique of police administration and bore the stamp of August Vollmer, who was credited with directing the report and writing several of the chapters himself. The conclusions of this survey inveighed against the corrupting influence of politics on police organizations. Despite the noble intentions of the Wickersham Commission, most of its suggestions went unheeded. Its main legacy was informing the public that the criminal justice system needed to be reevaluated and improved. Among its harshest critics were police executives who found that many of the conclusions were hastily drawn.

The Seabury Investigation (1930)

The 1930 Seabury Investigation began as a probe of the New York Magistrate's Court after several judges were linked to mobster Arnold Rothstein and other organized crime figures. Judge Samuel Seabury concluded that not much had changed since the Lexow Committee investigation of the 1890s and that the New York City Police Department was riddled with corruption. Seabury had started his legal career as a champion of the poor and the labor unions before serving terms on the state supreme court and the court of pleas. His findings led to the dismissal of twenty members of the vice squad and the exposure of rampant political bribery and corruption among city leaders, including police commissioners and the mayor.[9]

Other scandals involving corrupt judges led to the adoption of a plan for selecting judges that had been proposed almost twenty years earlier. According to the plan endorsed by the American Bar Association and the American Judicature Society, judges would be selected by a merit plan that allowed voters some choice in the selection of judges through nonpartisan elections. Judges would in this way run on their records. In 1940, several cities in Missouri adopted a plan that allowed an impartial committee of lawyers and laypeople to compile a list of qualified candidates when there was a vacancy and submit the list to the governor for selection.

LAW ENFORCEMENT

Perhaps the greatest development in policing in the 1920s and 1930s was the growing involvement of the federal government in law enforcement. While the expansion of the FBI is well documented, other federal agencies saw their duties change because of the exigencies of Prohibition- and Depression-related crime. Between 1920 and 1933, the Bureau of Alcohol, Tobacco and Firearms, which traces its origins back to 1862 (Alcohol, Tobacco, Tax Unit), saw considerable action disposing of illegal whiskey and arresting bootleggers. Meanwhile, the Customs Service was kept busy trying to stem the flow of illegal liquor into America by boat. The Internal Revenue Service (IRS) enjoyed one of its brightest moments in the 1930s with the conviction of Al Capone on income tax evasion. And in 1940, the Immigration and Naturalization Service became part of the Department of Justice.

Also reflecting the influence of the police professionalism movement was the emphasis placed on professional police training programs at various levels of government. State police forces led the way in implementing professional training programs in the 1930s. As early as 1931, San Jose State College boasted the first complete police major program, and in 1935 the FBI introduced an academy for training local police officers.

Federal Law Enforcement

The Bureau of Investigation grew gradually during its first decades. The Mann Act (1910), World War I, and the Russian Revolution saw the expansion of the bureau's role in federal law enforcement. In these years, the bureau investigated white slavery, espionage, sabotage, and draft violations. In 1919, the force was empowered to investigate interstate motor vehicle theft with the passage of the National Motor Vehicle Theft Act. The bureau underwent growing pains in the 1920s, and to lead the organization into the new era, John Edgar Hoover was selected as director in 1924. Hoover brought professionalism to the agency, establishing rigid codes of conduct and replacing the seniority-based system of promotion with one based on merit. Under his direction, special agents were required to be college educated, with degrees in law or accounting.

Born in Washington, D.C., John Edgar Hoover (1895–1972) graduated from law school in 1917 and joined the U.S. Department of Justice, where he would devote the next fifty-five years of his life, forty-eight of them as head of the FBI. Hoover rose to prominence as head of the Justice Department's Intelligence Division under Attorney General Mitchell Palmer. During his first years under Palmer, Hoover oversaw a campaign of persecution of foreigners who had been identified as communist sympathizers. Mass arrests and the trampling of constitutional protections resulted in hundreds of deportations and illegal searches and seizures. It was in this period that Hoover developed a predilection for maintaining secret files on individuals under investigation, a practice that would haunt civil libertarians for the next half century. In 1921, he was transferred to the Bureau of Investigation, where he served as assistant director. Following a series of scandals, bureau director William Burns retired in 1924, and Hoover took the reins, inaugurating a new era in professionalism that introduced the latest scientific methods of detection, expanded the fingerprinting bureau, and began the hiring of better-educated agents.

Throughout the 1930s, Hoover concentrated his war on crime on bank robbers and high-profile crimes, targeting such "public enemies" as Pretty Boy Floyd, John Dillinger, and Baby Face Nelson. A genius at public relations, Hoover convinced Hollywood to produce a series of films promoting the traditional image of the FBI agent as incorruptible and professional. In 1935 alone, more that sixty films fostered this portrait, including the James Cagney vehicle *G-Men*.

In 1924, Congress approved the transfer of fingerprint records at Leavenworth Federal Prison and the criminal records maintained by the International Association of Chiefs of Police to the FBI. The collection of over 810,000 records became the nucleus of the FBI Identification Division, created in 1924. In 1932, an FBI laboratory was established to aid federal and local investigations through the scientific analysis of blood, hair, firearms, handwriting, and other types of evidence.

In 1930, the power of the FBI was enhanced by a congressional act that required police agencies to compile crime statistics that would be disseminated through the FBI *Uniform Crime Reports*. This proved a major coup for Hoover's FBI. Although these reports have come under fire as being flawed because of their reliance on only crimes known to police, these yearly reports represent America's first national crime records system.

Hoover proved a master at promoting the FBI by enhancing the federal role in law enforcement. Rising crime and repercussions from the 1933 Kansas City Massacre (see the section "American Violence" later in this chapter) led Congress to enact a wave of legislation in 1934 that increased the power and prestige of the FBI. Agents were henceforth given full arrest powers and the authority to carry firearms, and new laws significantly expanded the number of federal crimes as well as the FBI's jurisdiction. Subsequently, it became a federal crime to cross state lines to avoid prosecution, to extort money with telephones or other federally regulated methods, to rob a federal bank, or to transport stolen property valued at over $5,000 across state lines.

During the Prohibition and Depression years, the FBI focused much of its attention and energies on the pursuit of "public enemies," such as John Dillinger, the Barker gang, Pretty Boy Floyd, Machine Gun Kelly and other media sensations.[10] Although Kelly was credited with introducing the G-men (government-men) moniker in reference to the FBI, its origins can be traced to earlier sources. All the bureau's functions were consolidated and transferred to the Division of Investigation in 1933, and on March 22, 1935, it was renamed the Federal Bureau of Investigation.[11]

Despite the best efforts of the FBI and the Chicago Police Department, Al Capone (1899–1947), America's public enemy number one and the architect of perhaps 300 unsolved murders, was finally brought to justice by agents of the IRS in 1931. Long pursued by Prohibition agent Eliot Ness and his "Untouchables," it was not until IRS agent Frank Wilson convinced a Capone employee to testify to Capone's illicit income that the crime boss was brought to justice. Thanks to a 1927 Supreme Court case that ruled that income from illegal transactions was taxable, the IRS used its agents to demonstrate that Capone had cheated the IRS, and on October 24, 1931, he was sentenced to eleven years in prison, effectively ending his reign as Chicago crime boss.

One of the unanticipated results of the growth of the FBI was the diminution in importance of the U.S. marshals, America's first federal crime fighters. As Prohibition ended in 1933, the bureau had reached national prominence. Under Hoover's direction, the FBI became increasingly specialized and professionalized. Unable to keep pace with these developments, the U.S. marshals were forced to make the transition to little more than process servers and court policemen.

Prior to America's entry into World War II, the FBI was authorized to gather information regarding potential espionage activity. With more than one million aliens from Axis countries residing in America, the FBI soon focused its attentions once more on spying on American residents. Between 1933 and 1937, the FBI investigated an average of thirty-five espionage cases per year. But as the war heated up, so did FBI investigations, reporting almost 20,000 cases of suspected espionage during the war years.

Hoover took one of his most controversial steps when President Roosevelt removed the information-gathering limitation on the FBI, allowing the bureau to investigate individuals for their beliefs rather than actual deeds. However, their pursuit of Nazi agents during the war would lead to some spectacular successes, including the 1941 destruction of one of the largest spy rings to operate in the United States.

State Policing

The proliferation of the automobile in the 1920s led many states to establish police agencies to handle traffic problems. Maryland created the first of these in 1916 and was followed by six more states in 1921. These highway patrol units were typically small, unarmed, and restricted to enforcing state

highway laws.[12] The state police movement lost momentum between 1923 and 1928, with only seven states establishing such units, most of which were of the highway patrol variety.

The onset of the Depression stimulated the state police movement, leading to the creation of fifteen state forces between 1929 and 1941. Of these, twelve were along the highway patrol model. A new pattern also developed in which earlier state forces were reorganized into larger forces. Some states formed highway patrols or state police forces to replace more specialized units, while other opted to increase existing manpower or to ease limits on police powers.

The evolution of the Texas Rangers offers an excellent example of the need for police departments to reorganize to meet a changing social climate. Between 1919 and 1935, the Rangers were faced with new social problems, including labor strikes, Mexican border raids, Prohibition violations, and surging Ku Klux Klan activities, as Texas made the transition from the frontier era. By the 1930s, the Texas Ranger tradition was in dire need of updating. Traditionally undermanned, their numbers were cut back and were in danger of obsolescence because of urbanization and modern science. With the introduction of the automobile and the train, the Rangers' days as an effective mounted police unit became a nostalgic memory, and in 1935 they were consolidated into the Texas Department of Public Safety.

As 1941 came to an end, each state had developed some type of police force based on either the state police or the highway patrol model. Managing to stay above the political fray and maintaining good relations with the public, according to historian David R. Johnson, "until the 1940s, at least, the state police were America's elite lawmen."[13]

Drug Enforcement

The forerunner of today's Drug Enforcement Administration (1973), the Bureau of Narcotics was established in 1930 under the direct control of the Treasury Department. Most studies trace the inception of federal drug enforcement to the 1914

Harrison Narcotic Act. Drug enforcement began the following year, and by the 1920s federal agents were homing in on Chinese opium smugglers. At the time of the Volstead Act and the inauguration of Prohibition in 1920, the Narcotics Division of the Prohibition Unit of the Revenue Bureau consisted of 170 agents and seventeen offices. In 1922, the drug agents saw their power expanded with the passage of the Narcotic Drugs Import and Export Act. Following a scandal in which drug agents were arrested for accepting payoffs from drug dealers, Congress established the Bureau of Narcotics in 1930 and removed drug enforcement from the Bureau of Prohibition.

Prohibition Enforcement

Once Prohibition was legislated into reality, it dawned on most observers that was virtually unenforceable. Unpopular with both the public and organized crime, Prohibition agents were drawn from a relatively weak pool of applicants. The qualifications and pay were so lackluster that many agents accepted bribes and kickbacks. One agent was reportedly offered $300,000 per week. In an era characterized by corruption, it should not be surprising that many agents were attracted by the lucrative prospects for graft. The Treasury Department fired more than 700 agents for corruption between 1920 and 1928. The following year, the Department of Justice took over the enforcement of Prohibition. In Chicago, Eliot Ness reportedly had to go outside the Windy City to find enough agents to fill the ranks of the Untouchables.

The two most famous Prohibition agents were New Yorkers Izzy Einstein and Moe Smith, better known as Izzy and Moe, although others referred to them as "Tweedledum" and "Tweedledee." The pair were credited with making a total of 5,000 arrests.

Isadore "Izzy" Einstein and Moe Smith were two of the most successful and honest Prohibition agents at a time when 706 agents were dismissed for corruption and incompetence. Both weighed well over 200 pounds, leading to their monikers "Tweedledum" and "Tweedledee." Izzy and Moe made great newspaper copy during a time when there was little good news to report. Disguised as rabbis, bootleggers, or football players, they were credited with confiscating five million bottles of contraband liquor and making thousands of arrests. In order to successfully prosecute liquor scofflaws, it was necessary to produce samples of evidence in court. The pair's modus operandi began with gaining entry to a speakeasy. After ordering a drink, they would pour the illegal beverage into a funnel connected by a tube to a flask hidden in one of the agent's back pockets. They were so successful that other cities soon coveted the duo. They set the record for the quickest bust in New Orleans, where they made their first arrest thirty-five seconds after arriving. In the end, their careers were short-circuited because of their penchant for publicity, and they resigned in 1925.

Criminology and Police Professionalism

Shortly after the turn of the twentieth century, the more theoretical field of criminology emerged, with its emphasis on the behavioral and social aspects of criminal activity and the accompanying explanations for its causes. In the 1920s, the earliest criminology textbooks were written by sociologists such as Edwin H. Sutherland (1924), John Lewis Gillin (1926), and Talcott Parsons (1926). Between 1930 and 1950, criminology continued to develop as an academic discipline but was confined to university sociology programs.

During the early 1900s, the first hesitant steps were taken toward developing schools for training law enforcement officers. As previously mentioned, August Vollmer initiated the first college-level training programs for police in 1908, when he established America's first formal training for police officers with his Berkeley Police School, a forerunner of in-service and academic programs in California. The Great Depression, however, halted the further development of police and criminological studies program at the University of California at Berkeley.

As Vollmer became increasingly identified with academe in the 1930s, he began to lose some of his credibility among leading police figures. His efforts to establish a professional school of criminology at Berkeley were obstructed both by economic hard times and by the intransigence of police leaders who felt that he was concerned more with publicity than with police training. His goal of creating a professional police school where police personnel could be trained at the higher administrative levels eluded him at Berkeley throughout the 1930s. However, his former students carried his work into the 1940s. In 1939, Vollmer's position at Berkeley was filled by his protégé Orlando Wilson. Formerly a police officer in Berkeley, Wilson studied engineering before returning to policing in 1928. Following Vollmer's example, he advocated the use of higher-education facilities for police training whenever possible. Between 1928 and 1939, Wilson professionalized the Wichita, Kansas, Police Department and then returned to academic work. In 1936, during his tenure at Wichita, he persuaded the political science department at the Municipal University of Wichita to integrate courses such as criminal law, patrol practices, traffic control, police administration, and identification procedures into the existing curriculum.

In 1939, a Bureau of Criminology was organized within the Department of Political Science at the University of California at Berkeley, although eleven years would pass before a separate School of Criminology offered degrees. Wilson was appointed a professor of police administration in 1939 and in 1950 was promoted to dean of the School of Criminology. The Berkeley Police Program spurred other schools into action. By the end of the 1930s, the University of Chicago, Indiana University, Michigan State University, San Jose State University, and the University of Washington had established criminal justice programs. Although they adhered in part to Vollmer's program, they emphasized the practitioner and training components of the curriculum.

CORRECTIONS

Throughout American history, African Americans have been disproportionately represented in the prison system. As more blacks left the South, northern prison statistics reported that blacks were imprisoned at a higher rate than whites for the same crimes. One historian suggests that because World War I drastically reduced immigration, northern industrialists turned to the South for unskilled labor, leading to a new migration of blacks to the North.[14] Trading one region's racism for another, many of the migrants were victimized by the discrimination practiced by social and legal agencies in the North. This in turn would be reflected by the increase of blacks in northern prisons in the postwar years. According to the U.S. Bureau of the Census, in 1926 African Americans made up 9.3 percent of the adult population but 31.3 percent of the prison population.[15] Meanwhile, the South persisted with the highest rates of execution and overall imprisonment. Conversely, the South had the highest regional rate of crime and violence.

As the nation's economy plunged into the depths of depression, the country's rate of imprisonment rose from 79 to 137 per 100,000 in the years between 1925 and 1939. According to national surveys, the United States contained almost 4,300 penal institutions by 1933. Out of a total prison population of 233,632, there were 137,721 housed in state penal institutions.[16]

While prison camps and leasing continued to dominate southern penology in the 1920s, the 1920s and 1930s saw the introduction of the "new penology" in many northern states with the implementation of the concepts of diagnosis and classification. Specialized personnel, such as psychologists and psychiatrists, were introduced to the prison environment as well. By 1926, 112 prisons employed either a psychologist or a psychiatrist. The dark side of these figures is that the professional-to-inmate ratio was too small to make much of an impact. The same was true with classification. Although the intention of classifying prisoners by psychological types was commendable, again, because of the dearth of qualified therapists on prison staffs, there was little hope of effective treatment.

Reform efforts directed at classification, education, vocational training, and discipline made little headway in the interwar years, leading noted prison educator Austin McCormick to report in 1929 "that prison education was a failure."[17] While most of the vestiges of the Auburn system, including lockstep marching, striped uniforms, and silence, were eliminated, many prisons continued to use solitary confinement in the "pit" or "hole" during the 1920s and 1930s. Although new prison routine allowed for more freedom, including communication between inmates, athletics, and exercise, as late as 1926, prisoners in Ohio and Illinois were punished in solitary confinement in small cages, nourished on a starvation diet of bread and water.

The late 1920s saw the development of the "big house" prisons, which could hold more than 2,500 inmates. The huge capacity of prisons such as Stateville, Illinois, and San Quentin, California, saw the development of more diverse populations, often leading to complicated social divisions among the inmates. Managed by a new generation of penal professionals instead of political appointees, prisons such as San Quentin and Sing Sing went to great lengths to root out abusive punishment and prison labor. At the same time, these institutions attempted to integrate mass production into the practice of incarceration.

The Federal Prison System

As Congress became increasingly uncomfortable with the prisoner leasing systems and state prisons began refusing federal prisoners, the federal government decided to join the prison business in the 1890s. One of the most important developments in prison reform was the organization of the United States Bureau of Prisons in the late 1920s. With an increase in the number of federal offenses, including violations of prohibition laws, the three existing federal prisons were overcrowded, prompting the federal government to step in and assume some of the responsibilities.

To deal with the burgeoning number of federal prisoners during Prohibition, the Bureau of Prisons converted Alcatraz Island to "a prison of last resort." Prisoners who ended up here were considered the worst of the worst with little hope for rehabilitation. With no privileges and little opportunity for contact with the outside world, prisoners were not even allowed to receive original copies of their mail. To prevent secret messages, prison employees transcribed the letters before passing them on to the prisoner. To counter the punitive nature of confinement at Alcatraz, inmates were afforded better food and library facilities than most prisons. Alcatraz's thirty years of serving federal prison castoffs came to a tumultuous end in 1963, when the federal penitentiary at Marion took its place. Despite its reputation, few inmates actually served time at Alcatraz, with its highest population at 302 in 1937.[18]

Taking the lead in prison reform in the 1930s, the Federal Bureau of Prisons under Sanford Bates not only improved training for corrections officers but also enhanced a number of educational and vocational programs within the prisons. Other innovations followed, including a new type of prison design known as the "telephone pattern," which is credited with placing cell blocks and buildings in order to maximize the segregation of offenders by type. Bates also supported a classification program to place inmates in maximum-, medium-, and minimum-security prisons. The federal government has also been acknowledged for reorganizing the parole system by centralizing its administration in 1930.

Prison Industries

Since the early nineteenth century, prison industries flourished in America, with many prisons showing a healthy profit. Perhaps the biggest change in prisons during the interwar era was the rapid decline in the number of inmates employed in prison industries. According to prison historian Blake McKelvey, between 1895 and 1923, antilabor legislation saw a drop in employment from 72 to 62 percent. Leading the opposition against prison labor was organized labor, which recognized the unfair business competition that prisoners posed to free paid workers.[19] Between 1932 and 1940, the proportion of productively employed prisoners in state and federal institutions fell from 52 to 44 percent. Paralleling this development was the value of goods produced, which dropped by 25 percent.

In 1929, Congress passed the Hawes-Cooper Act, which allowed any state to ban the sale of any goods made in another state's prison within its borders. Although it did not become effective until 1934, most states had already passed legislation placing limits on the sale and shipping of prison products. The passage of the Ashurst-Summers Act in 1935 would strengthen Hawes-Cooper by prohibiting transportation companies from accepting prison products for transportation into any state in violation of the laws of the state and provided for the labeling of all prison products shipped in interstate commerce. Despite the intentions of these statutes, the death knell of prison industries would sound with the 1929–1933 Depression, when state legislatures responded to the needs of unemployed free workers. Twenty-nine states passed laws restricting the sale of prison goods to government use only. The passage of these laws in effect eliminated the "industrial prison" as it made the transition back to its original functions as a custodial and punishment facility.

One of the unforeseen results in the decline of prison contracting and leasing and the victory of free labor was that prisons saw their budgets precipitously decline. Without any feasible alternatives to profitable labor, by the 1930s convicts languished in interminable idleness.

The only form of labor supported by labor was the state-use system, which saw labor involvement rise from 33 to 65 percent between 1915 and 1930. Support for the state-use system led to the diminished influence of independent industrial managers and contractors on prison administrators. According to the state-use system, prison-manufactured goods could be produced if they did not compete with free manufacturers. By 1940, state purchase of furniture, stationary, and other state-used goods had become mandatory in twenty-two states. Despite the best intentions to constructively occupy the prisoners with work, one estimate in the mid-1930s suggests that 60 percent of the prisoners nationwide remained idle.[20] Steps were slowly taken to introduce a modicum of vocational and educational training programs.

Prisoner Classification

Prisons had dabbled in inmate classification since the Progressive era. However, without effective rehabilitation programs, there was little to do with prisoners once they were classified other than to let them mix with other convicts. The movement for prisoner classification began in earnest in the years leading up to World War I. At that moment, prison administrators began to apply some of the findings of the rapidly developing field of the social sciences. In the process of putting theory into practice, prison administrators set up clinics to screen and separate certain types of prisoners, including the mentally ill and retarded.

In the aftermath of the 1930 Ohio State Prison fire, in which 322 prisoners died, efforts were directed toward finding better ways to house and employ inmates as well as better systems of classifying inmates. In the 1930s, classification "advocated greater institutionalization diversification for reform goals, along with segregation of types of prisoners."[21] Using various methods, institutions classified prisoners on the basis of their medical, psychiatric, psychological, educational, religious, and disciplinary backgrounds. In addition, attention was paid toward classifying inmates for treatment according to their crimes, personalities, and special needs. It was hoped that classification would lead to attempts to separate hard-core offenders from those who could be rehabilitated, that narcotics addicts would be placed on penal farms, and that minor offenders could be directed to minimum-security settings.

I Was a Fugitive from a Georgia Chain Gang

Dramatizing the deplorable conditions of southern prisons was the 1930s release of the book and motion picture *I Was a Fugitive from a Georgia Chain Gang*. The true story of Robert Elliott Burns, a World War I veteran who was sentenced to six to ten years on a Georgia chain gang for a $5.80 grocery store robbery, touched a chord with many Americans and was in part responsible for the exposure (and eventually the end) of the punitive Georgia chain gangs. Burns escaped from the prison gang in 1922 and remained free until 1930. By that time, he had worked his way up the management ladder at a Chicago newspaper. On his own volition, he returned to Georgia on the condition that he would be given a pardon. However, he was sent back to the chain gang. He then became the first person to escape a chain gang for the second time. Assuming a new identity in New Jersey, he began publicizing the barbaric conditions in Georgia in a series of magazine articles. These became the basis for a book and then a movie starring Paul Muni.

Georgia officials were offended and demanded his extradition. Hearings over this matter turned into an examination of the Georgia penal system. Through his attorney, Clarence Darrow, Burns described the "sweat box" and other punishments endured by chain gang prisoners, and ultimately the New Jersey governor refused the request for extradition. In 1945, Georgia repealed the chain gang system and soon after commuted Burns's sentence to time served.

CRIME AND PUNISHMENT

The 1920s and 1930s were marked by rampant lawlessness. Exacerbating rising crime fears were a combination of factors, including the onset of Prohibition and the Depression. This era proved one of the deadliest for peace officers, with an average of 169 killed in the 1920s and 165 per year in the 1930s. Police deaths on duty would not surpass these figures until the 1970s.

The lawlessness and sporadic violence that gripped the nation during the crisis years led Baltimore journalist Henry L. Mencken to conclude that it was safer to kill a man in America "than in any other civilized society." According to one 1932 crime survey of 130 cities in the United States, the total homicide rate had reached one per 10,000. During the same period, the combined murder rate for Wales, England, and Scotland was one per 200,000.

Although studies of individual cities exist demonstrating the characteristic waxing and waning of crime rates, prior to the 1930s there are no comprehensive crime figures for the entire nation. Most evidence suggests that the crime rate rose after World War I and the 1920s and that crime rates dropped as the nation sank into the Depression and continued to decline into the 1940s.

Despite the run on the banks that inaugurated the Depression, between 1929 and 1934, two banks were robbed every day (twenty-five per day are robbed today). Faced with growing demands from the government to crack down on bank robbers and public enemies, J. Edgar Hoover began a crusade to change public attitudes about criminals—attitudes that had formerly elevated desperadoes such as John Dillinger to hero status.

The Roaring Twenties began with a peculiar tolerance of crime due in part to Prohibition, which is credited with criminalizing the behavior of otherwise law-abiding citizens. Stigmatized for breaking Prohibition laws, many of these citizens developed sympathy for other lawbreakers. However, the Kansas City Massacre and the murderous crime sprees of Bonnie and Clyde and other Depression-era bandit gangs led to a public backlash against lawbreakers. Concern with the random brutality led to support for expanding the role of the federal government in law enforcement. The deaths of Bonnie and Clyde, John Dillinger, Pretty Boy Floyd, and others during the 1930s ended the American tradition of the social bandit that began with the James brothers and Billy the Kid in the years following the Civil War.

The Teapot Dome Scandal (1924)

No scandal overshadowed the 1920s as much as the Teapot Dome scandal, which, according to one source, "proved to be a major watershed in U.S. political history."[22] Named after an oddly shaped geological feature near its location in Wyoming, Teapot Dome was a naval oil reserve that had been set aside by the government for emergency use in 1915. But in 1920, Congress passed legislation to establish private leasing of public mineral lands. Soon contracts for Teapot Dome and other oil reserves were given to various bidders with the support of Secretary of the Interior Albert Fall (1861–1944). Ironically, in the months before his death (1923) and the Teapot Dome scandal, President Warren G. Harding had remarked that "if Albert Fall isn't an honest man, I'm not fit to be president of the United States."

By 1922, the Interior Department was leasing the emergency oil reserves. As it turned out, Fall had begun leasing the oil reserves to close friends without allowing competitive bidding on the property. In return, they secretly compensated Fall with almost $400,000. A subsequent senatorial inquiry uncovered the scandal, and the government canceled the leases with the support of a Supreme Court decision. In 1929, Fall was found guilty of bribery and sentenced to one year in prison. It was the first time a cabinet officer had been jailed for crimes committed in office. Teapot Dome entered the American lexicon as a synonym for government graft and a lingering reminder of the corruption-plagued Harding administration.

Prohibition and Organized Crime

One of the greatest ironies of the Prohibition era is that while it was intended to impose virtue on ethnic Americans through repression, it actually made them the beneficiaries of the very laws intended to limit their cultural influence. In a short time, second-generation Italians, Jews, and Poles would control a $2 billion-per-year illegal industry. No criminal enterprise is more shrouded in myth than the development of organized crime

and the growth of "Mafia"-inspired crime syndicates in the United States. As historian David Johnson succinctly noted, while some Italian gangsters "borrowed some terms and concepts from the Sicilian Mafia," their "basic rationale and structure were purely American."[23]

Modern organized crime was given its greatest opportunity to flourish thanks to the convergence of two events: Prohibition and the rise of Benito Mussolini to the dictatorship in Italy. On his ascendance to power in the early 1920s, Mussolini was determined to wipe out the Mafia and any other groups not under his control. While some Mafia chiefs converted to fascism, others were either imprisoned or fled to America, following the exodus of Italian immigrants that had begun in the 1880s. But the repressive measures of the fascist regime were only partially responsible for the temporary collapse of the Mafia in Italy. When the fascists abolished elections, they hit the real source of Mafia power, namely, its partnership with and control of political candidates and leaders, so when it lost control of the political apparatus, its demise was assured. Not until the death of Mussolini and the end of World War II did the Mafia regain its political influence.

Envisioned by its supporters as a cure for America's social ills, Prohibition instead created new ills and in the process gave birth to modern organized crime. Seduced by the lure of beer money, peace officers were bribed like never before. While organized gangs had operated in urban America since the 1830s, they functioned with the support of political machines. With the onset of various Progressive reform efforts and the changing face of urban America, by 1914 most of the gangs were in disarray. With red-light abatement in full sway, vice centers from New Orleans' Storyville to San Diego's Stingaree were closed down. It seemed that the era of the gangs had ended by the end of World War I.

However, the birth of Prohibition resuscitated organized gangs. With tens of thousands of speakeasies flourishing throughout the country, bootleggers had to replenish the illegal liquor supply either by smuggling across borders or by making their own illegal potions. It was not long before alcohol became an underground cottage industry with entire neighborhoods besieged by the foul odors of bootleg brew.

In New York, Bugsy Siegel, Frank Costello, Lucky Luciano, Meyer Lansky, and other future mob luminaries collaborated to make $12 million a year from booze alone. In Chicago, Al Capone and his mentor John Torrio made tens of millions of dollars. Capone was the best-known American of his era, and although his career as Chicago crime boss was rather ephemeral, in 1930 alone he made $100 million.

One of the more perplexing questions left unanswered from this era is why J. Edgar Hoover refused to recognize the rise of criminal syndicates in big cities from coast to coast. While the Bureau of Narcotics, big-city police forces, and crusading journalists recognized the growth of organized crime, the FBI seemed to ignore this phenomenon until the 1950s. As late as 1959, Hoover employed 400 agents in the New York City office investigating communists and only four concentrating on organized crime. Although several unsubstantiated reasons for Hoover's inaction have been cited, including the blackmail of his personal life and horse-betting debts to the mob, others have offered more convincing explanations. Obsessed with maintaining the bureau's reputation for high conviction rates, Hoover set his sights on kidnappers and bank robbers, who were much easier to catch than complicated cases of organized criminal activity. With access to the best lawyers that money could buy, mob figures often were acquitted. Hoover also feared that his agents could be corrupted in the process of taking on the mob.

Racket Busters

Prohibition introduced modern organized crime to urban America. In response, cities such as New York responded with special prosecutors such as Thomas Dewey to round up the denizens of organized crime ranging from bookmakers and loan sharks to mob leaders, including Charles "Lucky" Luciano.

 Born in Michigan, Thomas Dewey (1902–1971) practiced law after earning his law degree from Columbia Law School in just two years. In 1935, he was appointed by the New York governor to investigate statewide organized crime. Over the next two years, he successfully attacked police corruption and organized crime figures. Not only was he credited with restoring integrity to the New York Police Department, but he engineered the demise of criminals Lucky Luciano and Dutch Schultz. Dewey became a national hero and revered racket buster in his time, survived death threats from Dutch Schultz, and served as New York governor three times. As New York's crusading district attorney, Dewey is considered the quintessential law-and-order prosecutor.

No crime fighter captured the public's imagination during the Prohibition years more than Eliot Ness (1902–1957), who rose to prominence as head of Chicago's "Untouchables" during the heyday of nemesis Al Capone. After being selected to lead a special Prohibition unit, Ness personally selected members of his unit. But despite the credit accorded the Ness legend, the Untouchables, as with most Prohibition-oriented law enforcement units, was rather ineffective in its war against Capone's bootleg empire. Following Capone's conviction by the IRS, Ness turned to Capone subordinates such as Frank Nitti and later to moonshine operations in America's heartland.

Ness and his Untouchables made great newspaper copy but were rather underwhelming in the war against alcohol. Ness would survive three assassination attempts by Capone's henchmen, including a drive-by, a car bomb, and a runover. He would have more success as public safety director in Cleveland, Ohio. Following the repeal of Prohibition, he moved to Cleveland in 1935 and made short work of a police department riddled with corruption, forcing several hundred policemen to resign and sending at least a dozen officers to state prison.

Kidnapping

Most historians trace the first kidnapping for ransom in America back to the 1874 abduction of "little Charles Ross." This case was never solved and his body never found. No era saw more kidnappings than the 1920s and 1930s. In 1931 alone, there were 282 reported kidnappings. According to ransom expert Ernest Kahlar Alix, two types of ransom cases predominated: the ransom of wealthy (unharmed) businessmen and the ransom slayings of children. The most prominent ransom cases of this era involved the deaths of Bobby Franks by Richard Loeb and Nathan Leopold (1924) and Charles A. Lindbergh Jr. by Bruno Hauptmann (1932).

While organized criminals were often kidnapped by other members of the underworld and Black Hand members targeted Italian immigrants, in the 1930s organized kidnap rings began to victimize private citizens. The 1933 kidnappings of William A. Hamm Jr. by Alvin "Kreepy" Karpis and that of Charles F. Urschel by the George "Machine Gun" Kelly gang ended with the payments of ransoms of $100,000 and $200,000, respectively, and the safe release of both victims. By this time, the public was clamoring for the suppression of this crime.

No criminal case of this era garnered more publicity than the kidnapping of the twenty-month-old son of America's aviation hero Charles Lindbergh, the first person to fly solo across the Atlantic Ocean. At this time, kidnapping was not a federal offense, and the FBI had no jurisdiction in the case. However, once the baby's body was discovered, President Herbert Hoover ordered all federal agencies to participate in the subsequent investigation. The arrest and trial of Bruno Hauptmann became one of the most sensational murder trials of the century. Although the evidence seemed overwhelming—Hauptmann had the ransom money, and experts testified that he made the ladder from wood in his attic and that he had written the ransom note—questions linger to this day as to Hauptmann's culpability. Nonetheless, he was electrocuted in 1936.

The Lindbergh case foreshadowed the sensationalism that would plague news reporting over the next century. What made this possible was the "emergence of modern media technology," which made this trial an even "more compelling national drama than the Lizzie Borden case" four decades earlier.[24] As Walter L. Hixson makes clear in his examination of sensational crime trials, with the emergence of the radio and movie newsreels in the 1920s, America became linked in a "single media culture."[25]

By most accounts, the Lindbergh kidnapping case had major ramifications for law enforcement when Congress passed the "Lindbergh Law" in June 1932, giving the FBI jurisdiction in kidnapping cases where the victim had been taken across state lines. Kidnapping was also elevated to a capital offense. However, at least one authority argued that it is historically false to attribute the passage of this legislation to the Lindbergh kidnapping. Sociologist Ernest Kahlar Alix suggests that "the Lindbergh case initiated neither the noncapital nor the capital federal legislation, despite the fact that the legislation came to be known as the Lindbergh Law." To support his case, Alix notes that the 1932 federal ransom legislation was introduced four months earlier than the Lindbergh kidnapping and had nothing to do with the "ransoming or ransom slaying of any child."[26]

Capital Punishment

Between 1918 and 1959, more than 5,000 Americans were executed, with few generating much publicity. Except for high-profile capital cases, such as those of Sacco and Vanzetti and Bruno Hauptmann, most executions were followed with little fanfare. In 1937, the first Gallup Poll on the death penalty found that a vast majority of Americans supported the death penalty. For the next twenty years, support would remain strong for capital punishment.

During the 1930s, America used the death penalty more than any previous decade in American history. According to one study, 1,676 executions took place in this decade, compared to an average of 1,148 per decade between 1880 and 1920. However, this spate of executions coincided with a rising population and murder rate.[27] In the never-ending quest for more humane methods of execution, death by lethal gas was introduced by Nevada in 1924. During the 1930s, seven states adopted this method.

The Kansas City Massacre (1933)

On June 17, 1933, four law enforcement officers, including an FBI agent, were reportedly ambushed and killed by machine-gun fire in what has become know as the Kansas City Massacre. Three other FBI agents were wounded. This being 1933, they were not yet authorized to carry weapons, but all this would change following the carnage. Although recent research conflicts with the accepted account of events,[28] FBI director J. Edgar Hoover used its tragic consequences to launch a high-profile campaign to hunt down public enemies in the nation's heartland. In 1934, President Franklin Roosevelt signed into law nine anticrime bills that enlarged the crime-fighting powers and jurisdiction of the FBI. Following the passage of these measures, FBI agents would be responsible for suppressing federal bank robberies, the transportation of stolen property across state lines, and other crimes and would be allowed to carry and use firearms.

AMERICAN VIOLENCE

America witnessed every variety of violence in the crisis decades. Labor violence, race riots, mob warfare over the liquor trade, and police brutality contributed to a climate of fear and social disorder as the country entered the 1920s. In the 1930s, industrial violence resulted in dozens of killings as police and army troops battled strikers during a national cotton textile strike and several steel strikes. One of the last memorable labor confrontations resulted in the Memorial Day massacre of ten strikers during the 1937 Republic Steel strike. Killings also resulted from assaults by strikers against strikebreakers, as was the case in 1922, when union workers savagely murdered nineteen scabs at the Herrin massacre in Illinois.

Perhaps the worst race riot of the interwar years, the 1921 Tulsa, Oklahoma, riot was ignited after a black resident was accused of rape and arrested. When rumors of a lynching reached the black community, a group of armed blacks hurried to the jail to protect the potential victim. After gunfire broke out, the overwhelming force of whites chased the blacks back into their neighborhood. In the ensuing violence, at least sixty blacks were killed, although the director of gravediggers later reported burying 150 victims. By the time martial law was declared, virtually the entire one-mile-square black district had been burned to the ground.

In February 2001, nearly eighty years after whites laid waste to Tulsa's black community in the Tulsa race riot, a state panel investigating the violence agreed that reparations should be paid to survivors. The result of a four-year effort to uncover the truth of one of the nation's deadliest race riots, the Tulsa Race Riot Commission recommended that the 118 survivors and descendants be compensated for their losses, adding that the death toll was probably as high as 300.

One of the turning points in racial violence came in 1935 during the Harlem riot. Here the racial pattern of rioting diverged from tradition. Formerly, whites initiated race riots, leading to violence between the races. But the Harlem riot featured not fighting between the races but rather mostly black rioters attacking white property and the police. While few deaths resulted, property damage reached more than $2 million. The subsequent commission impaneled to look into the causes, following an example set by the 1919 Chicago riot, blamed the outbreak of violence on police brutality, discrimination, and unemployment.

If there was one positive development in race relations during the crisis years, it was the decline in lynchings. According to the National Association for the Advancement of Colored People, between 1882 and 1927, almost 5,000 mostly African American victims perished at the hands of lynch mobs. Lynchings substantially declined in the early 1900s, with an average of sixty-two a year between 1910 and 1919. By the late 1930s and 1940s, lynchings became a much rarer event.

The St. Valentine's Day Massacre (1929)

No event signified the brutality of the bootlegging wars and the brazenness of the 1920s more than the St. Valentine's Day Massacre, the biggest gangland murder of the era. This event was the culmination of a long-term war in Chicago between the Capone gang and the North Side gang led by Dion O'Banion. By 1929, O'Banion and numerous allies had been killed, leaving George "Bugs" Moran as Capone's last obstacle to taking over the bootlegging empire.

In an attempt to lure Moran into his own demise, Capone arranged for a gangster to offer Moran a load of hijacked liquor that would be delivered to the gang's garage headquarters. Several Capone henchmen, dressed in police uniforms, drove up to the garage and lined up the seven occupants against the wall, a group that included a gang groupie and local optometrist. Figuring that it was just a routine police roust, the gangsters offered no resistance and meekly stood face first against a wall. All seven were cut to ribbons with submachine fire. However, Bugs Moran was not among them, having overslept that day. Moran arrived shortly after the massacre, and when he was queried as to the perpetrators, he responded, "Only Capone kills like that." Initially, there was a split opinion as to the killers. The police were held in such low esteem to many that it seemed altogether possible that they were the perpetrators. But public opinion soon turned against Capone.

Any question as to the killers was put to rest when ballistics expert Calvin H. Goddard (1891–1955) tested the bullets and reported that they did not come from any machine gun owned by the Chicago Police Department. In 1930, machine guns and bullets found in the home of Fred Burke, a known killer for hire, matched the St. Valentine's Day bullets. Chicago authorities were so impressed with his acumen that they decided to establish a special institute under the leadership of Goddard. The forensic expert would spend three months in Europe visiting police laboratories before returning to set up the Scientific Crime Detection Laboratory in Evanston, Illinois. The facility would eventually become part of Northwestern University Law School, and as a professor, Goddard would teach the world's first courses in police science.

Murder Incorporated

For most of its existence, Murder Incorporated, a group of hired killers composed of a combination of second-generation Jews and Italians, worked behind the scenes in anonymity. During Prohibition, ethnic mobs had discovered the advantages of working together, and by 1930 rules of cooperative behavior had been laid down and territories mapped out by a national board of directors, which reportedly included Lucky Luciano, Frank Costello, Meyer Lansky, and other notables. As the days of Prohibition came to a close, organized crime diverted its attention to other lucrative businesses, ranging from loan-sharking, gambling, and narcotics to prostitution and labor racketeering.

Organized crime turned to Brooklyn-based Murder Incorporated for "muscle" and for the hiring of hit men. The group was led by Albert "Lord High Executioner" Anastasia and Louis "Lepke" Buchalter as the enforcement arm of the mob. Each contract murder had to be approved by the national board. The killing of peace officers and journalists was prohibited, and the killers were not available to civilians. During the 1930s, the killers are suspected of at least 300 murders in New York alone. They also introduced the terms *contracts* and *hits* into the popular underworld lexicon.

One enduring slogan and principle credited to the gang was the notion that "we only kill each other." In 1935, this ethic was tested when crime lord Dutch Schultz demanded that Murder Incorporated kill Thomas Dewey in violation of organization protocol. When his request was voted down, Schultz vowed to do the job himself. In response, Schultz was given the death penalty by his mob associates, and a contract on his life was approved. Arthur Flegenheimer (a.k.a. Dutch Schultz) was killed shortly thereafter as he ate dinner at a Newark chophouse.

In 1940, Murder Incorporated came to the attention of law enforcement when killer Abe Reles turned state's evidence following his implication in several murders. His testimony stunned the New York district attorney as Reles laid out the existence of a national crime syndicate that had probably committed more than 1,000 murders across the country. As to the moniker Murder Incorporated, most sources credit it to a New York police reporter named Harry Feeney. Reles's testimony would lead to the end of the gang and would send several killers to the electric chair, including Louis "Lepke" Buchalter (1897–1944), one of the highest-ranking mob bosses to ever be executed. Reles met his ignominious end when he either committed suicide or was pushed out a window.

NOTABLE TRIALS

The Scottsboro Trials (1931–1937)

On March 25, 1931, nine black youths aged thirteen to twenty were arrested at Paint Rock, Alabama, accused of raping two white girls as they traveled as hoboes on a freight train headed south from Chattanooga through Alabama. The subsequent trial and sentencing of the so-called Scottsboro Boys focused international attention on the segregated Jim Crow South and "exercised a profound influence on the way that criminal justice came to be administered in the United States forever after."[29]

Rape was still a capital crime in Alabama, and the rape of two white women at the hands of African Americans in this era was considered acceptable grounds for lynching. Despite the suspects' claims that they did not rape the girls or ever see them prior to their arrests, armed farmers waited for the delivery of the prisoners at the Jackson County seat. It was not long before the nine men were confined in a cage in a small Jim Crow jail fearing for their lives. The National

Guard was called out for protection, and the prisoners were moved to another jail for safekeeping.

The nine men were indicted by an all-white jury in Scottsboro, and the following week the capital case began. The accused were not offered lawyers or any contact with each other, typical of such trials in the Deep South in this era. Although physicians testified that after examining the two women they could find no evidence of a rape, this had little influence on the racially charged atmosphere. In the words of Haywood Patterson, who later published his own account of the trial, "Color [was] more important than evidence down there."[30]

The subsequent evidence presented against the accused consisted primarily of the allegations presented by the two women. Since the defendants could not afford counsel, the local judge appointed the entire bar of Scottsboro, which included six men, to defend the Scottsboro boys. Of these, only one agreed to comply, and then only on the morning of the trial. With little preparation or time to investigate, the final reckoning was a forgone conclusion, and all eight defendants were sentenced to death by the all-white jury. Less than four months after the trial began, eight of the nine men were sentenced to the electric chair. The ninth was a fourteen-year-old who was given life imprisonment because of his small stature and youthful appearance. Haywood Patterson proved one of the most visible of the nine and soon began to learn to read and write while he awaited his death. The widespread publicity accorded the case won the young men support from around the world, including contributions from Albert Einstein and writers Thomas Mann and Maxim Gorky.

On November 8, 1932, the Supreme Court reversed its convictions in *Powell v. Alabama,* citing the fact that the defendants had been denied their right to adequate counsel. This was a landmark decision in that for the first time the Supreme Court took steps to guarantee that almost all criminal defendants would actually have counsel. It did this by requiring the government to appoint and pay for a lawyer if a defendant could not do so. The Court based its decision to reverse the original convictions on the protection guaranteed by the Fourteenth Amendment, which prohibits states from depriving any person of life, liberty, or property without due process of law. However, many issues were still unsettled, and the case left unresolved "whether appointed counsel would be required in noncapital cases."[31] Although the Court's decision was based on the specifics of the Scottsboro case, the ruling came to be viewed as requiring appointment of counsel for young, inexperienced, illiterate, and indigent defendants in capital cases.

In 1935, the Supreme Court ruled unanimously in *Norris v. Alabama,* after the retrial of defendant Clarence Norris, that his conviction violated his right to equal protection of the laws under the Fourteenth Amendment. Chief Justice Charles Evans Hughes noted in the ruling that no black had served on a county jury within the memory of any living person and found the evidence sufficient to reverse Norris's conviction. *Powell v. Alabama* (1932) and *Norris v. Alabama* (1935) became collectively known as the Scottsboro cases.

In their subsequent, second trial, four of the nine were convicted. One was sentenced to death and the other three to seventy-five to ninety-nine years in prison. The rape indictments were dismissed against the other five defendants. Despite the severity of the sentences, in some quarters the result was seen as a victory during this era of rising racial violence and lynchings.

Lawyers continued the appeals process until 1937 as Patterson and his fellow defendants languished in jail. Tired of waiting in jail for a crime he did not commit, Patterson made an escape attempt in 1948 and was arrested two years later in Detroit, but the Michigan governor refused to sign extradition papers. The three other defendants were released on parole between 1943 and 1950.

In 1938, the Supreme Court ruled in *Johnson v. Zerbst* that according to the Sixth Amendment, the government is required to pay for a lawyer if a defendant could not afford one. But this applied only to federal criminal trials. Since almost 90 percent of criminal prosecutions were tried in state courts, this ruling had little impact. In 1942, the Court refused to extend the *Johnson* decision to state trials. Until *Gideon v. Wainwright* in 1963 (see chapter 12), "states remained free" to "prosecute and convict indigent defendants in one-sided proceedings in which the state was represented by a lawyer and the defendant was left to fend for himself."

The Scottsboro case captured international attention at a time when African American defendants rarely made it so far through the court and appeals process. For police historian Samuel Walker, the legacy of this case and the subsequent *Powell* decision was that it was the "first organized attack on race discrimination in the southern criminal justice system."[32]

CONCLUSIONS

By the 1920s, prison reformers were once again grappling with the horrendous state of prison affairs. In the wake of a series of prison riots in Illinois, Colorado, Kansas, and New York, the National Commission on Law Observance and Enforcement issued a report detailing the deplorable state of the nation's prisons. Following in the footsteps of Progressive reformers, the authors of what became known as the *Wickersham Report* linked the current climate of lawlessness in America with the failure of the prisons to rehabilitate inmates. Noting the impact of immigration and unemployment on crime rates as well as the concomitant costs of crime, the report placed the blame for failure of the prison system squarely on the backs of prison administrators who promulgated arbitrary rules and punishments.

Prison populations dramatically increased, as did some crime rates, in the 1920s. With the growth in interstate regulatory laws and Prohibition, the number of state and federal prisoners increased as well. In response, the federal government created the Federal Bureau of Prisons.

With the jobless rate spiraling out of control, thirty-three states passed laws in the 1930s that prohibited the sale of prison-made commodities on the free market.

After 100 years of success, with the impetus of the Depression and rising unemployment, the 1930s saw federal and state legislation eliminate the sale of prison products on the open market as prisons returned to the more punitive and custodial roots of an earlier era. Despite advances in classification and efforts at reform, America's prisons became overcrowded, leading to tension and prison riots.

The 1920s and 1930s had fanned the flames of a burgeoning civil rights struggle that would culminate with the civil rights crusade of the 1960s. Changes in national attitudes and public opinion toward race indicated that Jim Crow and *Plessy v. Ferguson* were losing support. No juxtaposition of images makes this more clear than the 1925 Ku Klux Klan march through the streets of Washington, D.C., and the 1939 concert honoring black singer Marian Anderson in front of the Lincoln Memorial. The concert drew more than 75,000 people after Anderson was barred from singing in Constitutional Hall by the Daughters of the American Revolution.

Prohibition and the Depression, like other pivotal events of this era, ultimately contributed to making the federal government even stronger. No single episode in the early twentieth century conspired to increase the mandate of the criminal justice system than did Prohibition. According to criminal justice historian Lawrence M. Friedman, "Prohibition filled the federal jails; it jammed the federal courts," and "under prohibition, the idea of a national police force became no longer unthinkable."[33] Not the final word but a warning of what was to come, historian Claire Bond Potter noted that "the legacy of the transformation of federal policing during the New Deal has been a continuing war on crime, one that is fully integrated into daily political and civic life in the United States."[34]

In 1933, following the repeal of Prohibition, a news publication revealed that the final cost of Prohibition was more than one-third greater than the national debt of $22 billion and $10 billion more than the cost of America's participation in World War I, which was $26.361 trillion. A tabulation of Prohibition killings totaled 1,170 citizen and 512 agent deaths between 1920 and 1932.[35]

On the other hand, with criminal syndicates deeply embedded in American society by the end of Prohibition, they were organized well enough to successfully turn their attention to traditional vices, such as gambling, drugs, and prostitution. By the 1930s, American policing was dismal if not ineffective. While the hiring of more police officers has proved a panacea for contemporary policing, a 1926 report noted that the New York City police hired 3,522 officers in 1926 and 1927 but saw only a 4 percent drop in crime. Even the 1931 Wickersham Commission concluded that many police departments were corrupt, untrained, and poorly administered. Police professionals such as J. Edgar Hoover, August Vollmer, O. W. Wilson, and others would help guide the transformation and professionalization movement that would lead to tremendous improvements in American policing by the 1950s. The end of Prohibition and the Depression would usher in an era of police professionalism. With the diminished influence of political machines on police departments, efforts at reform could be directed at raising salaries and improving hiring practices, training, technology, and investigative procedures.

Point–Counterpoint
National Prohibition: Legislating Morals (1930)

Between 1920 and 1933 the government of the United States prohibited the manufacture and sale of alcoholic beverages. Following his election to the presidency in 1928, Herbert Hoover felt that more knowledge of prohibition enforcement was needed. In 1929 he created the National

Source: *National Commission on Law Observance and Enforcement,* Report on the Enforcement of the Prohibition Laws of the United States, 71st Congress, third session, House Document 722, 1931, pp. 44–56; Charles W. Eliot, *A Late Harvest,* Boston, 1924, pp, 261–267.

Commission on Law Observance and Enforcement, chaired by former Attorney General George Wickersham. There was little consensus among commission members about prohibition enforcement practices. When the Commission's final report was released in 1931, its pessimistic approach to Prohibition added more ammunition to the wets who supported repeal. In the following passage from the report the authors assess the difficulties of enforcing Prohibition. The second excerpt is from an address given at Harvard University in support of Prohibition. The author, Charles W. Eliot, president of Harvard University from 1869 to 1909, notes an association between alcoholism, venereal disease, and threats to "white civilization."

A number of causes of resentment or irritation at the law or at features of its enforcement raise difficulties for national prohibition. A considerable part of the public were irritated at a constitutional "don't" in a matter where they saw no moral question. The statutory definition of "intoxicating" at a point clearly much below what is intoxicating in truth and fact, even if maintainable as a matter of legal power, was widely felt to be arbitrary and unnecessary. While there was general agreement that saloons were wisely eliminated, there was no general agreement on the universal regime of enforced total abstinence. In consequence many of the best citizens in every community, on whom we rely habitually for the upholding of law and order, are at most lukewarm as to the National Prohibition Act. Many who are normally law-abiding are led to an attitude hostile to the statute by a feeling that repression and interference with private conduct are carried too far. This is aggravated in many of the larger cities by a feeling that other parts of the land are seeking to impose ideas of conduct upon them and to mold city life to what are considered to be their provincial conceptions.

Other sources of resentment and irritation grow out of incidents of enforcement. In the nature of things it is easier to shut up the open drinking places and stop the sale of beer, which was drunk chiefly by working men, than to prevent the wealthy from having and using liquor in their homes and in their clubs. Naturally when the industrial benefits of prohibition are pointed out, laboring men resent the insistence of employers who drink that their employees be kept from temptation. It is easier to detect and apprehend small offenders than to reach the well organized larger operators. It is much easier

to padlock a speakeasy than to close up a large hotel where important and influential and financial interests are involved. Thus the law may be made to appear as aimed at and enforced against the insignificant while the wealthy enjoy immunity. This feeling is reinforced when it is seen that the wealthy are generally able to procure pure liquors, where those with less means may run the risk of poisoning through the working over of denatured alcohol, or, at best, must put up with cheap, crude, and even deleterious products. Moreover, searches of homes, especially under state laws, have necessarily seemed to bear more upon people of moderate means than upon those of wealth or influence. Resentment at crude methods of enforcement, unavoidable with the class of persons employed in the past and still often employed in state enforcement, disgust with informers, snoopers, and under-cover men unavoidably made use of if a universal total abstinence' is to be brought about by law, and irritation at the inequalities of penalties, even in adjoining districts in the same locality and as between state and federal tribunals—something to be expected with respect to a law as to which opinions differ so widely—add to the burden under which enforcement must be conducted.

Resentment is aroused also by the government's collecting income tax from bootleggers and illicit manufacturers and distributors upon the proceeds of their unlawful business. This has been a convenient and effective way of striking at large operators who have not returned their true incomes. But it impresses many citizens as a legal recognition and even licensing of the business, and many who pay income taxes upon the proceeds of their legitimate activities feel strongly that illegitimate activities should be treated by the government as upon a different basis.

Lawyers everywhere deplore, as one of the most serious effects of prohibition, the change in the general attitude toward the federal courts. Formerly these tribunals were of exceptional dignity, and the efficiency and dispatch of their criminal business commanded wholesome fear and respect. The professional criminal, who sometimes had scanty respect for the state tribunals, was careful so to conduct himself as not to come within the jurisdiction of the federal courts. The effect of the huge volume of liquor prosecutions, which has come to these courts under prohibition, has injured their dignity, impaired their efficiency, and endangered the wholesome respect for them which once obtained. Instead of being impressive tribunals of superior jurisdiction, they have had to do the work of police courts and that work has been chiefly in the public eye. These deplorable conditions have been aggravated by the constant presence in and about these courts of professional criminal lawyers and bail-bond agents, whose unethical and mercenary practices have detracted from these valued institutions.

. . . I remember well that, twenty years ago or thereabouts, I was entertained by the Harvard Club of Louisiana at a large dinner in the city of New Orleans, where I sat next to a gentleman who was generally recognized in New Orleans as the leader of their Bar. I noticed the moment we sat down that there was an extraordinary variety of things to drink on the table; and I also noticed that my neighbor took everything that was passed and in large quantity, so much so that I began to be a little anxious about his condition later. But suddenly he turned to me and said, "Mr. President, do you know that the New Orleans Bar, and I as its leader, are going in for complete prohibition in the State of Louisiana?" I could not help expressing surprise that *he* was going in for that. Whereupon he said, "Well, you don't suppose that we, the members of the Bar, expect to have the law applied to us, do you?" *(Laughter)* He was positively a vigorous advocate of complete prohibition for Louisiana, but all the time had not the slightest notion that a prohibitory law could be applied to him or any of his friends, or would be.

That opened my eyes somewhat in regard to the expectation with which the sudden, unanimous support of prohibition came to pass in the Southern States. It was nearly unanimous, you remember, and remains so to this day. The Southern States are the strongest supporters in this country of prohibitory legislation.

Then, some time later, I found myself attending a Harvard Club dinner in the State of Missouri. There were many things to drink at that dinner also. I was informed that some of the leading citizens of Missouri, engaged in manufacturing operations, were going to move their plants over into the State of Kansas. I observed later that a large number of Missouri manufacturers did move their plants over into the State of Kansas, and learned, on inquiry, that those manufacturers had made up their minds that they could conduct their businesses much better in a State where a prohibitory law existed than they could in a State where the law did not exist.

I have had the delight of passing my summers for more than forty years—yes, it is fifty-two years since I first began to go to Mount Desert in summer—in the State of Maine. There I observed that the prohibitory law in Maine was not observed at all excepting in communities where, as one guest has said to-night, the great majority of the population was in favor of prohibition. There alone was the distribution of alcoholic drinks restrained. I lived there fifty summers, observing the fact that the prohibitory law in Maine was not generally enforced; observing that the summer residents of the State of Maine, who, as you know, live all along the shore and in several of the beautiful lake regions, paid no attention to the prohibitory law.

What inference did I draw from that experience? Simply that unless the strong majority of any government unit in the States where prohibitory laws exist was in favor of prohibition, the law would, as a matter of fact, not be enforced.

But further: It was obvious that no single State could possibly enforce prohibition, because it had no power to prevent the manufacture of alcoholic drinks outside the State or their importation into it. You must have national prohibition to make prohibition effective. It must be nation-wide, or it simply cannot be enforced.

So I supported for many years in Massachusetts, not prohibition, but local option; but then I learned that the sale of distilled liquors in saloons licensed to sell light wines and beer cannot be prevented. Nobody should advocate the repeal of the Volstead Act except those who believe in the unrestricted sale of alcoholic beverages. I ought perhaps to say that I took wine or beer when I was in the society of people who were using them. I never had any habit of drinking them at home; but I always took them when I was in the company of men or women who were using them. I had no feeling that alcohol was bad for everybody, or bad for me. I never knew alcohol to do me any harm; but then I never drank distilled liquors at all. When the United States in the spring of 1917 went to war, you remember that with the support of all the best civilian authorities and of the officers in the Army and Navy, our Government enacted a prohibitory law for the regions surrounding the camps and barracks where the National Army was being assembled. The Act proved to be effective and highly beneficent.

Then I said to myself, "If that is the action of my Government to protect our soldiers and sailors preparing to go to war, I think it is time for me to abstain from alcoholic drinks altogether." It is only since 1917 that I have been a total abstainer; but that is now six years ago, and I want to testify here, now, that by adopting total abstinence, after having had the opposite habit for over seventy years, one loses no joys that are worth having, and there is no joy-killing about it. On the contrary, I enjoy social life and working life more since I ceased to take any alcohol than I did before.

That talk, gentlemen, about joy-killing and pleasure-losing, and so forth, is absolute nonsense for a man who has any sense himself. . . .

We all know that our Puritan ancestors and our Pilgrim ancestors were not persons who cultivated the finer joys of life. They left behind them the great architecture of England, and its parks and its music. The Pilgrims came over from Holland, having lived there for ten or fifteen years in sight of all the glorious Dutch paintings, sculpture, and architecture. They abandoned all those things, and settled in the wilderness, where there was little possibility of cultivating the love of beauty and little power, too, of resisting the theological dogmas they had imbibed, which taught that human nature was utterly depraved, and that most of the human race were bound for a fiery hell.

Those are the people from whom the leading thinkers and doers of America sprang; and it is naturally inevitable that we, their descendants, should lack the love of beauty in nature and in art, and even in music. We do lack it. The Pilgrims and the Puritans lacked it to an extraordinary degree.

Where did they find their pleasures? Largely in drink. They drank hard at weddings, funerals, and all public festivals. We have that inheritance, but can we not resist and overcome it? Can we not grow up into a love of beauty in nature and in art? Can we not cultivate in ourselves the delight in music—in singing and in playing instruments? We are not hopeless in those respects; and those are the things we have got to learn to love, in order to escape from this wretched evil of alcoholism.

But how shall we do it? We must cultivate in ourselves the finer inspirations, the purer delights, and the greater joys in art and in work. But, more than that, we have got to practise resistance to acknowledged manifest evils in our common life.

That has always been my way of living, from day to day, in the practice of my profession. From the beginning, that was the way I lived. I attacked what seemed to me a plain, acknowledged, manifest evil, and advocated the best remedy I knew for that evil. That is just what we have got to do to-day, gentlemen, about this abominable evil of alcoholism associated with venereal disease; because that evil will kill us unless we kill it. By "us" I mean the white race, and particularly the American stock. Must we not accept the proposition that we must either destroy alcoholism and venereal disease, or those evils will destroy us? I believe that to be the plain truth; and I want to call on every lover of his kindred and of his country, hourly, daily, year after year, to contend against these evils, alcoholism and venereal disease, until they are obliterated from the world. Finally, may we not reasonably distrust the legal view that has been repeatedly presented here this evening, namely, that the rights and privileges of decent and vigorous people should not be abridged for the sake of indecent or weak people who abuse their privileges?

Charles W. Eliot, address before The Economic Club of Boston, March 6, 1923, in *A Late Harvest* (Boston, Atlantic Monthly Press, 1924), 261-267 *passim*. Copyright by Charles W. Eliot; reprinted by permission.

SOURCES

Alix, Ernest Kahlar. 1978. *Ransom Kidnapping in America, 1874–1974: The Creation of a Capital Crime.* Carbondale: Southern Illinois University Press.

Bechtel, H. Kenneth. 1995. *State Police in the United States: A Socio-Historical Analysis.* Westport, Conn.: Greenwood Press.

Bodenhamer, David. 1992. *Fair Trial: The Rights of the Accused in American History.* New York: Oxford University Press.

Bonnie, Richard J. and Charles H. Whitebread. 1970. "The Forbidden Fruit and the Tree of Knowledge: An Inquiry into the Legal History of American Marijuana Prohibition." *Virginia Law Review.* Vol. 56, no. 6, pp. 971–1970.

Carter, Dan T. 1969. *Scottsboro: A Tragedy of the American South.* Baton Rouge: Louisiana State University Press.

Cashman, Sean David. 1981. *Prohibition: The Lie of the Land.* New York: Free Press.

Christianson, Scott. 1998. *With Liberty for Some: 500 Years of Imprisonment in America.* Boston: Northeastern University Press.

Cole, David. 1999. *No Equal Justice: Race and Crime in the American Criminal Justice System.* New York: New Press.

Friedman, Lawrence 1973. *A History of American Law.* New York: Simon and Schuster.

Geis, Gilbert, and Leigh B. Beinen. 1998. *Crimes of the Century: From Leopold and Loeb to O. J. Simpson.* Boston: Northeastern University Press.

Hall, Kermit L. 1989. *The Magic Mirror: Law in American History.* New York: Oxford University Press.

Helmer, William, with Rick Mattix. 1998. *Public Enemies: America's Criminal Past, 1919–1940.* New York: Checkmark Books.

Hixson, Walter L. 2001. *Murder, Culture, and Injustice: Four Sensational Cases in American History.* Akron, Ohio: University of Akron Press.

Johnson, David R. 1981. *American Law Enforcement: A History.* Wheeling, Ill.: Forum Press.

Kennedy, Randall. 1997. *Race, Crime, and the Law.* New York: Pantheon Books.

Kobler, John. 1974. *Ardent Spirits: The Rise and Fall of Prohibition.* London: Michael Joseph.

Lane, Roger. 1997. *Murder in America: A History.* Columbus: Ohio State University Press.

Lender, Mark Edward, and James Kirby Martin. 1987. *Drinking in America: A History.* New York: Free Press.

McKelvey, Blake. 1977. *American Prisons: A History of Good Intentions.* Montclair, N.J.: Patterson Smith.

Mitgang, Herbert. 2000. *Once upon a Time in New York: Jimmy Walker, Franklin Roosevelt, and the Last Great Battle of the Jazz Age.* New York: Free Press.

Musto, David F. 1987. *The American Disease: Origins of Narcotic Control.* New York: Oxford University Press.

Patterson, Haywood, and Earl Conrad. 1951. *Scottsboro Boy.* Garden City, NY.: Doubleday.

Potter, Claire Bond. 1998. *War on Crime: Bandits, G-Men, and the Politics of Mass Culture.* New Brunswick, N.J.: Rutgers University Press.

Powers, Richard Gid. 1983. *G-Men: Hoover's FBI in American Popular Culture.* Carbondale: Southern Illinois University Press.

Prassel, Frank Richard. 1993. *The Great American Outlaw: A Legacy of Fact and Fiction.* Norman: University of Oklahoma Press.

Ross, Shelley. 1988. *Fall from Grace: Sex, Scandal, and Corruption in American Politics from 1702 to the Present.* New York: Ballantine Books.

Rotman, Edgardo. 1998. "The Failure of Reform: United States, 1865–1965." In *The Oxford History of the Prison,* ed. Norval Morris and David J. Rothman, pp. 151–177. New York: Oxford University Press.

Ruth, David E. 1996. *Inventing the Public Enemy: The Gangster in American Culture, 1918–1934.* Chicago: University of Chicago Press.

Schneider, Victoria, and John Ortiz Smykla. 1991. "A Summary Analysis of Executions in the United States, 1608–1987: The Espy File." In *The Death Penalty in America: Current Research,* ed. Robert M. Bohm, pp. 1–19, Cincinnati: Anderson Publishing.

Sloman, Larry. 1979. *Reefer Madness: The History of Marijuana in America.* New York: Bobbs-Merrill.

Sullivan, Lawrence E. 1990. Boston: Twayne Publishers.

Unger, Robert. 1997. *The Union Station Massacre: The Original Sin of J. Edgar Hoover's FBI.* Kansas City: Andrews McMeel Publishers.

Walker, Samuel. 1998. *Popular Justice: A History of American Criminal Justice.* New York: Oxford University Press.

CRITICAL THINKING QUESTIONS

1. How did the passage of the Eighteenth Amendment affect patterns of criminality and the American criminal justice system?

2. What is meant by the phrase "police professionalism?"

3. How did the nation's prison systems respond to the 1920s and 1930s?

4. What role did the media play in creating an image of lawlessness during this era? How did law enforcement exploit the rise of sensationalism in the press?

5. How did the crisis decades affect American opinion on the death penalty?

6. Discuss the growth of organized criminal activity in this era.

7. What impact did the civil rights movement have on the criminal justice system?

8. Compare and contrast regional differences in crime and criminal justice in the crisis era.

9. What was J. Edgar Hoover's impact on federal law enforcement?

10. How did the New Deal years affect the growth and development of the criminal justice system?

CRIMINAL JUSTICE HISTORY ON THE INTERNET

The events leading to the Great Depression are well chronicled on the Internet. For Black Thursday, see *New York Times* headlines at http://sac.uky.edu/~misunde00/hon202/p4/nyt.html. The causes and government reaction to the 1929 stock market crash are available at www.arts.unimelb.edu.au/amu/ucr/student/1997/Yee/1929.htm. The crash is remembered in contemporary songs and more at http://mypage.direct.ca/r/rsavill/Thecrash.html.

More than 100,000 photos from the Library of Congress are devoted to the Depression at http://memory.loc.gov/ammem/fsowhome.html. At outline of the era can be found at http://econ161.berkeley.edu/TCHEH/Slouch_Crash14.html. Reminiscences of the Depression are stored at www.sos.state.mi.us/history/museum/ techstuf/depression/teacup.html. Lyrics and songs of the Depression are at www.library.csi.cuny.edu/dept/history/lavender/cherries.html. An Internet sourcebook on American life histories in this period is at www.fordham.edu/hallsall/mod/modsbook41.html.

The Senate minutes of the Teapot Dome scandal can be found at www.senate.gov/learning/min_5c_html; a 1924 cartoon of the scandal is at www.wwnorton.com/college/history/tindall/timelinf/teapot.htm. An in-depth investigation and the presidential appointment of a special counsel is examined at www.brook.edu/gs/ic/teapotdome.htm.

The complete *Carroll et al. v. United States* proceedings are at http://laws.findlaw.com/us/267/132.html.

The 1931–1937 trials of the "Scottsboro Boys" are well documented at www.law.umkc.edu/faculty/projects/FTrials/scottsboro/scottsb.; photographs and biographies of the defendants are at www.law.umkc.edu/faculty/projects/FTrials/Scottsboro/SB_bSBs.html. Excerpts from the trials, letters, chronology of events, and photos can be accessed through www.law.umkc.edu.

For the Lindbergh kidnapping and subsequent events, see www.lindberghtrial.com, www.lindberghtrial.com/html/front.shtml, and www.crimelibrary.com/lindbergh/lindmain.htm. More information and documents can be found at http://members.aol.com/lindytruth.

Significant criminals of the 1930s are overrepresented on the Internet. Some of the more informative and insightful include the Kansas City Massacre and Pretty Boy Floyd at www.fbi.gov/fbinbrief/historic/famcases/floyd/floyd.htm, http://foia.fbi.gov/floydsum.htm, and http://kansascity.fbi.gov/contact/fo/kc/massacre.htm. Several articles on John Dillinger are at www.oklahombres.org and on Bonnie and Clyde at http://foia.fbi.gov/bonclyd.htm. Links to others can be found at the FBI Famous Cases home page at www.fbi.gov/fbinbrief/historic/famcases and www.crimelibrary.com/revclas/6.htm.

A description of records related to the Wickersham Commission is at www.edwardhumes.com/wickersham.htm. Conclusions on alcohol prohibition are at www.druglibrary.org/schaffer/Library/studies/wick/wick10.html.

Prohibition and prohibition agents are examined at www.cohums.ohio-state.edu/history/projects/prohibition. An interesting 1932 article is at www.cato.org/pubs/pas/pa-157.html. A more contemporary article is at www.nytimes.com/books/98/09/27/specials/lindbergh-federal.html. The history of alcohol prohibition is at www.druglibrary.org/schaffer/LIBRARY/studies/nc/nc2a.htm, and music related to the Prohibition era is at www.legacyrecordings.com/prohibition. A number of links devoted to the Eighteenth and Twenty-First Amendments are available at http://dir.yahoo.com/Arts/Humanities/History/U_S__History/By_Time_Period/20th_Century/1920s/Prohibition.

Historical research on drugs and drug policy in the 1920s is at www.druglibrary.org/schaffer/History/1920.htm. For information on the career of Harry Anslinger and the creation of the Bureau of Narcotics (precursor of the Drug Enforcement Administration), see www.lycaeum.org/graphics/people/anslinger. Letters by Anslinger can be accessed at www.druglibrary.org/schaffer/hemp/taxact/anslett.html, www.cannabis.net/prohib, and www.1930reefermadness.com/anslingerlie.htm. A 1937 "Assassin of Youth" article on the dangers of marijuana can be found at www.reefermadness.org/propaganda/kidax.html and www.bright.net/~fixit/anslinger.htm. A related time line is at www.pbs.org/wgbh/ pages/frontline/shows/dope/etc/cron.html.

Links related to the history of the FBI can be accessed through www.fbi.gov/fbinbrief/historic/history/newdeal.htm. More than 1,500 pages on J. Edgar Hoover and the FBI can be found on the FBI Freedom of Information Act home page at http://foia.fbi.gov/hoover.htm. More on this subject is at www.crimelibrary.com/hoover/hooverfiles.htm.

The history of uniform crime reporting is covered at http://ucr.psp.state.pa.us/UCR/News/AboutUCRHistory.htm. Prison labor, the Hawes-Cooper Act, and related issues are covered at www.ncpa.org/studies/s206/s206rw.html and http://laws.findlaw.com/getcase/US/299/334.html.

Informative coverage of the Chicago Police Department in this era is at www.sos.state.il.us/departments/archives/massacre.html and www.hollywood.com/movies/detail/movie/164796. Sites related to Al Capone, the St. Valentine's Day Massacre, and other Chicago organized crime figures are at http://foia.fbi.govmassacre.htm, www.btinternet.com/~dreklind/threetwo/valentine.htm, www.crimelibrary.com/capone/caponesaint.htm, and www.apbonline.com/crimesofthecentury/stories/stvalentines.html.

NOTES

1. Hall (1989, p. 253).

2. Prassel (1993, p. 271).

3. Walker (1998, p. 173).

4. Bodenhamer (1992, p. 94).

5. Bonnie and Whitebread (1970, p. 976).

6. Musto (1987, p. 228).

7. Helmer and Mattix (1998, p. 61).

8. The phrase "third degree" refers to police-sanctioned brutality, which was more prevalent during the pre-Miranda rights era. In the 1930s, parlance ranging from "shallacking" and "massaging" to "breaking the news" and "giving him the works" was synonymous with giving a criminal suspect the third degree. Many police departments condoned the beating of suspects to extract confessions. Methods of third-degree interrogation included the water cure (which involved forcing water down the nostrils of supine victims), beatings with a rubber hose, and drilling into the nerves of the teeth.

9. For a detailed account of Seabury and his crusade against corruption, see Mitgang (2000).

10. The concept of "public enemies" has been usually credited to the FBI when in reality it was the brainchild of the Chicago Crime Commission, a watchdog group formed in 1919 to investigate crime in Chicago. The commission issued its first public enemies list in 1930; it was headed by none other than "Public Enemy Number One" Al Capone. The FBI later capitalized on the "public enemies" idea and released a "Ten Most Wanted List."

11. The bureau had actually been renamed the United States Bureau of Investigation in 1932. However, confusion ran supreme when the Department of Justice began a two-year experiment with a Division of Investigation that also included a Bureau of Prohibition. The public soon could not differentiate between Bureau of Investigation special agents and Bureau of Prohibition agents, leading to the permanent name change to Federal Bureau of Investigation in 1935.

12. Bechtel (1995, pp. 40–41).

13. Johnson (1981, p. 164).

14. McKelvey (1977, p. 293).

15. Quoted in Christianson (1998, p. 228).

16. Christianson (1998, p. 238).

17. Rotman (1998, p. 164).

18. Rotman (1998, p. 168).

19. Convict wages had little if any impact on the popularity of prison labor since only a small percentage of prisons paid any wages. In 1940, Auburn was paying its agricultural workers five cents per day and shop employees twenty cents per day.

20. Sullivan (1990, p. 40).

21. Sullivan (1990, p. 40).

22. Ross (1988, p. 159).

23. Johnson (1981, p. 147).

24. Hixson (2001, p. 75).

25. Hixson (2001, p. 75).

26. Alix (1978, p. 186).

27. Schneider and Smylka (1991, pp. 6–7).

28. Unger (1997) claims that none of the official accounts was true. After an exhaustive search through

the eighty-nine-volume FBI case file, he concluded that most of the victims were killed by friendly fire because of the proximity of the individuals to one another and one agent's unfamiliarity with his shotgun.

29. Geis and Bienen (1998, p. 75).

30. Patterson and Conrad (1951, p. 299).

31. Cole (1999, p. 68).

32. Walker (1998, p. 156).

33. Friedman (1973, p. 568).

34. Bond (1998, p. 196).

35. Quoted in Helmer and Mattix (1998, p. 65).

11

CRIMINAL JUSTICE AT MIDCENTURY (1941–1959)

TIME LINE

1941	America enters World War II after attack on Pearl Harbor
1942	Relocation of Japanese Americans
1943	Zoot-Suit Riot
1943	Race riots in Detroit and Harlem
1944	IACP argues against police unionism
1946	Sodium pentothal used for first time in William Heirens case
1947	House Un-American Activities Committee hearings
1947	*Patton v. Mississippi*
1947	The Flamingo Hotel and Casino opens in Las Vegas
1947	Bugsy Siegel murdered in Los Angeles
1948	Caryl Chessman trial
1949	Psychologist William H. Sheldon inaugurates discipline of "constitutional psychology"
1949	Howard Unruh commits first rampage killing of modern era
1950	Beginning of Korean War
1950	Publication of O. W. Wilson's *Police Administration*
1950	William Henry Parker appointed Los Angeles police chief

1950	National execution statistics to *National Prisoner Statistics Series*	1955	Murder of Emmett Till
1950	Beginning of the Kefauver hearings	1957	Publication of *Parker on Police*
1950	FBI introduces "Ten Most Wanted" program	1957	Apalachin Conference alerts nation to existence of organized crime
1950	Brink's robbery	1957	Publication of Marvin Wolfgang's *Patterns of Criminal Homicide*
1952	Riot at State Prison of Southern Michigan	1958	J. Edgar Hoover details his strategy for defeating communism at home in *Masters of Deceit: The Story of Communism in America and How to Fight It*
1953	Execution of the Rosenbergs		
1953	Earl Warren appointed chief justice of U.S. Supreme Court		
1954	Sam Sheppard convicted of wife's murder	1959	Murder of Clutter family inspires Truman Capote to write *In Cold Blood*
1954	*Brown v. Board of Education*		
1954	Army-McCarthy hearings		

World War II transformed American society more than any other war in its history. During the 1940s, the federal government became much more centralized and united the population as never before. Wartime industry not only ended the Great Depression but also began several decades of unrivaled prosperity. But old fears still lingered. Fear of communist subversion at home and rising juvenile crime and the battle for civil rights presented the criminal justice system with new challenges in the 1940s and 1950s.

Fortunately, the end of World War II did not end on a somber note like World War I, which saw America reeling from race riots, labor strife, police strikes, and attacks on civil liberties. In sharp contrast, the postwar years were marked by great advances in civility, with race relations improving in different regions and murder rates declining. Rather than slipping into the post–World War I violent morass surrounding Prohibition, the 1940s and 1950s seemed mighty tame in comparison.

However, there was a darker side, a harbinger of sorts that would find resonance in the 1990s. Sensational rampage killings periodically dominated the headlines in the 1940s and 1950s. When Howard Unruh stepped out on a busy Camden, New Jersey, street in 1949, mowing down twelve of his neighbors in thirteen minutes, few could have imagined the school-yard and workplace shootings that would punctuate the 1990s.

Returning home from the world war, servicemen were confronted with a changing home front. Many returned with different cultural values than the ones they went off to war with. In the years following the war, outlaw motorcycle gangs were organized by "groups of young men, many newly-returned soldiers, who formed motorcycle clubs and rejected normal civilian lifestyles. In the next several years their behavior became not so boisterous as surly, less rebellious than openly criminal."[1] In the aftermath of a motorcycle riot in Hollister, California, in 1946 the phrase "outlaw motorcycle" was reportedly used for the first time, referring to the actions of a gang that evolved into the notorious Hell's Angels.

Others challenged the status quo on a less bellicose level but would still disrupt the social fabric and arouse fear among conservatives. On May 21, 1957, a San Francisco police officer arrested bookstore owner Lawrence Ferlinghetti for selling "obscene literature" shortly after purchasing a copy of poet Allen Ginsberg's *Howl and Other Poems* from his establishment. In the 1950s, "beats" or "beatniks," such as Allen Ginsberg and Jack Kerouac, captured media attention with their writings as they tapped into a reservoir of discontent among the younger generation.

While informal networks of gambling halls operated in various parts of the country prior to the war, no one could have imagined the development of the American gambling scene beginning in the 1940s or how widespread gambling would become by the end of the twentieth century. In the months before Pearl Harbor, several gambling clubs and fledgling casinos were operating in Las Vegas, where gambling was legalized in 1931. However, most visitors still came to marvel at Hoover Dam or perhaps to take advantage of the easy divorce laws.

THE LAWGIVERS

While cultural tensions seemed to have diminished in America since the 1920s, they were still a source of social conflict. In December 1941, just weeks after the attack on Pearl Harbor, President Franklin D. Roosevelt issued an executive order suspending naturalization proceedings for immigrants from enemy nations (Italy, Germany, and Japan). The new legislation required these immigrants to register, restricted their movements, and prohibited them from owning items that could be utilized for sabotage, such as cameras and shortwave radios. In reality, not all enemy aliens were treated the same. German and Italian aliens would receive more compassionate treatment compared to the Japanese.

The Japanese had been barred from immigrating to the United States by the Immigration Act of 1924, and by 1924 only 110,000 lived on the mainland, mostly in California (another 150,000 lived in Hawaii). The outbreak of World War II ignited simmering racial tensions on the West Coast, where many Japanese Americans had lived for generations. An amalgamation of factors, including racism, nativism, and wartime security concerns, led President Roosevelt to issue Executive Order 9066 on February 19, 1942. Less than six months after America's entry into the war, the president signed into law the order that relocated more than 100,000 Japanese Americans, most of whom were American citizens, from the West Coast to ten relocation camps in remote locations, including Jerome, Arkansas, and Heart Mountain, Wyoming. There, American citizens who had committed no crimes were locked behind barbed wire and crowded into accommodations resembling minimum-security prisons.

Most constitutional historians consider this one of the greatest violations of individual rights in the history of the country. Almost overnight, thousands of Japanese Americans, without trial or hearings, were forced to dispose of their homes, personal property, and businesses, leading to tragic consequences for many families. However, almost 18,000 Japanese American men effected their release from the camps and served gallantly in combat.

Throughout the war years, Japanese Americans protested their treatment, claiming that their civil rights had been violated. However, in 1944 the Supreme Court supported the federal government by a vote of six to three in *Korematsu v. United States,* citing current national security concerns. It was not until the waning months of the war that the federal government ended a shameful chapter in American legal history by taking steps to close down the camps. However, many were still held prisoner until mid–1946, almost one year after the ending of hostilities.

Joseph McCarthy and Communist Hysteria

Fear of communism in America had existed since the Bolshevik revolution in 1917. However, with the birth of the atomic age and Russian nuclear power, tensions over the Soviet threat were heightened. Soon, politicians such as Richard M. Nixon and Joseph McCarthy would use communist bashing as a strategy for political advancement.

As early as 1947, President Harry S. Truman was pressured to inaugurate the communist "witch hunts" by creating loyalty boards to check on reports of communist sympathizers in the federal government. Thousands were investigated as innuendo superseded evidence in the hunt for communist spies. Out of this venomous cloud of hysteria emerged Wisconsin Senator Joseph McCarthy. During the 1950s, paranoia over communist subversion swept America. No politician is more associated with the excesses of this era than McCarthy, who took advantage of the political climate of the time to further his own career by destroying the working lives of hundreds of individuals.

Beginning with the 1798 Alien and Sedition Acts, there have been several attempts to limit civil liberties at the expense of the Constitution. One of the more notable twentieth-century examples involved the 1947 House Un-American Activities Committee (HUAC), which attempted to outlaw the Communist Party. The HUAC had been created in the 1930s and had become increasingly oppressive in its dedication to stifling dissent and liberty of thought. In 1947, the HUAC targeted Hollywood and in the process destroyed the livelihoods of the "Hollywood Ten" (writers, directors, and producers). Their hearings proved a travesty of justice. The committee refused to allow nine of the witnesses to make prefatory statements on their civil rights privileges. When the ten refused to give yes-or-no answers to the questions "Are you now or have you ever been a member of the Communist Party of the United States?" and "Are you a member of the Screenwriters' Guild?" they were found guilty of contempt, jailed for a year, and illegally blacklisted by Hollywood. The so-called American Inquisition contributed to the climate of fear that would allow Senator McCarthy to ride roughshod over the Constitution and the Fifth Amendment in the 1950s.

As chair of the Senate Committee on Government Operations, McCarthy accused the military of harboring communist infiltrators. In response, the army demanded that he support his allegations, and on April 22, 1954, an estimated twenty million viewers watched the televised Army-McCarthy hearings.

Deviating little from his aggressive no-holds-barred style of examining witnesses, McCarthy seemed at the outset of the hearings to overmatch his sixty-three-year-old opponent and attorney for the army, Joseph Welch. But he had taken up a battle that would turn against him when he challenged the U.S. Army to purge supposed communists from the Pentagon. Welch proved more than a match for his antagonist. After McCarthy launched into his usual relentless attacks, Welch asked the senator to support his accusations. After a withering barrage of cross-examination, McCarthy accused Welch's own Boston firm of harboring a communist. Welch responded in a calm dignified manner. His response is considered a high point of civility in an era dominated by baseless attacks on persons and civil liberties. Welch ended his rebuke of McCarthy with the familiar "Have you no decency left at all?"—a question that by that point must have resonated with many of the millions of viewers. Although the hearings continued for five more days, McCarthy's inquisition had been brought to a stunning climax, and two months later he was censured by the Senate.

"Tail-gunner Joe" would die in 1957 from the effects of alcoholism (Welch would enjoy a scintilla of celebrity as a lecturer and as an actor, playing a judge in the 1959 James Stewart vehicle *Anatomy of a Murder*).

Brown v. Board of Education of Topeka

Since the Supreme Court's *Plessy v. Ferguson* (1896) ruling, everything from maternity wards to morgues, even prisons and polling places, were either segregated or for whites only. While white schools were well staffed and maintained, black schools, particularly in the South, were typically single-room shacks without toilets or heat. It should be little wonder, then, that illiteracy among America's largest racial minority was commonplace. Among the most important spokesmen in the battle to end the injustice of "separate but equal" educational systems was Thurgood Marshall. As the head of the Legal Defense and Educational Fund of the National Association for the Advancement of Colored People (NAACP), Marshall represented the plaintiffs in what would become known as *Brown v. Board of Education*.[2]

When eleven-year-old Linda Brown decided that she did not want to make the long ride to school from her home in Topeka, Kansas, when there was a school just blocks away, she sued the Board of Education. The board ruled that since she was African American, she must attend an African American school despite its distance from her home. The Topeka court responded that the "buildings, transportation, curricula, and educational qualifications of the teachers" at her black school were equal to those provided to white students as mandated in the *Plessy v. Ferguson* decision.

When several other African American children in other parts of the country sued to switch from segregated schools as well, the Supreme Court agreed to hear the case. Represented by a legal team headed by Thurgood Marshall, between 1952 and 1954 the nation's highest court listened to testimony before taking six months to conclude by a unanimous vote that separate educational facilities were not equal in the arena of public education.

In 1954, the Supreme Court struck down the principle of "separate but equal," which had buttressed legally sanctioned segregation as unconstitutional. The Court's decision called on states to move "with all deliberate speed" to desegregate, but most ignored the order. During a painfully slow process, the NAACP would lead the civil rights struggle by challenging specific segregationist systems through a series of individual lawsuits.

In 1957, the NAACP won a court order that allowed nine black students to enroll in an all-white Little Rock, Arkansas, high school. In response, the segregationist governor ordered the Arkansas National Guard to surround the school to prevent the students from entering. Following a riot by white citizens, President Dwight D. Eisenhower federalized the National Guard and sent in 1,000 members of the 101st Airborne to protect the nine teenagers, the first time since Reconstruction that U.S. troops were ordered to the South to protect the rights of black citizens. While some question Eisenhower's intentions, to many it was clear that he was concerned more with enforcing federal law than with protecting the students.

The U.S. Supreme Court

President Roosevelt placed his stamp on the Supreme Court with his nomination of former law professor William O. Douglas (1898–1980) in 1936. During a thirty-six-year tenure, longer than any other justice in history, Douglas often shocked America with his opinions. His best-known work was associated with civil liberties, opposing censorship and the death penalty, and even granting the Rosenbergs a stay of execution in 1953 (leading to a call for his impeachment). A staunch supporter of the Bill of Rights, his steadfast support of the First Amendment angered many, particularly in the 1960s, because he refused to impose any restrictions on the publication of "obscene" material.

One of the most influential chief justices in American history, Earl Warren (1891–1974) was nominated to the Supreme Court by President Eisenhower in 1953 after becoming the first three-time elected governor of California. Over the next two decades, Warren placed his indelible liberal stamp on the Court, leading Eisenhower to declare that his nomination was one of the worst mistakes of his presidential administration. It is often deceptive to identify the Supreme Court by the name of its chief justice, but in rare instances (in the nineteenth century, John Marshall and Roger B. Taney had similar influence), the chief justice can influence the direction of the court in such a way that the court is overshadowed by the chief justice. A testament to Earl Warren, his court is one of the few in American history to be so identified (as in "Warren Court"). According to one study of the legal profession, "Chief Justice Earl Warren changed the legal landscape of America more than any other judge except Chief Justice John Marshall."[3] His tenure was marked by a judicial activism that made the Court an active participant in the campaign for social change and civil rights.

Among the Warren Court's most significant rulings was *Brown v. Board of Education of Topeka, Kansas* (1954), which overturned the earlier decision of *Plessy v. Ferguson,* which established the doctrine of "separate but equal" public facilities for whites and African Americans. Warren's court held that separate but equal facilities were intrinsically unequal, taking the first major strides toward ending segregation not only in education but also in all other facets of American life as well. In 1966, the Court profoundly altered law enforcement with the *Miranda v. Arizona* decision, which ruled that defendants must be made aware of their rights to counsel and that anything they say can be used against them in a trial (see chapter 12 for more on this decision).

The grandson of slaves, Thurgood Marshall (1908–1993) was born in Baltimore, Maryland, and educated at several universities before graduating first in his class at the Howard University Law School in 1933. Shortly after graduation, Marshall was hired by the National Association for the Advancement of Colored People. Between 1940 and 1960, he served as the director of the organization's Legal Defense and Education Fund.

Marshall rose to national prominence in the civil rights struggle of the 1950s. In 1954, he helped convince the Supreme Court to declare segregation unconstitutional in the *Brown v. Board of Education* decision. President John F. Kennedy appointed Marshall as a federal district judge in 1961, and four years later President Lyndon Johnson made him the nation's first black solicitor general. In 1967, Marshall became the first African American Supreme Court justice. Over the next twenty-four years, Marshall would stamp his enduring imprint on civil rights law in the United States.

LAW ENFORCEMENT

The 1940s and 1950s witnessed police departments across the nation continue the trend toward professionalization. Following trails blazed by Bruce Smith and Raymond Fosdick, police administrators began to upgrade standards for new officers while casting off the yoke of political interference and manipulation of police forces by political bosses and ward leaders. By the 1930s, it had become clear that the only way to gain the public's trust and respect was to reduce the influence of politicians, train and educate police officers, and promote an image of professionalism in the eyes of the public.

Police reformers such as William H. Parker and Orlando W. Wilson personified the model of professional, impartial law enforcement. Both eschewed political involvement in professional decision making, and both would write new chapters in their careers as they took office in Los Angeles and Chicago, respectively, in the wake of police scandals.

It had been more than twenty years since the Boston Police Department's unsuccessful attempt to unionize. Similar to the union movement of the post–World War I era, police union activities in the 1940s were stimulated by wartime inflation. Despite the support of AFL-CIO affiliates, the International Association of Chiefs of Police (IACP) vehemently opposed unionization, arguing in 1944 that police unions were "contrary to the basic nature of police duties." Ultimately, the police union movement was stopped dead in its tracks by a combination of IACP opposition and the banning of police unions by police authorities in Los Angeles, St. Louis, Detroit, Chicago, and other cities. Those officers who refused to cooperate were fired.[4]

Orlando W. Wilson

Orlando "O. W." Wilson (1900–1972) succeeded his mentor August Vollmer on the faculty at the University of California after winning a national reputation for cleaning up the Wichita, Kansas, police department. When the IACP adopted a "Law Enforcement Code of Ethics" in 1957 as a standard for ethical police conduct, it borrowed in part from Wilson's "Square Deal Code," which he developed in 1928 as chief of police in Wichita. Wilson taught police administration at Berkeley for several years before leaving to fight in World War II. He returned to the university in 1950 as dean of the School of Criminology, and despite attempts to diminish the academic standing of the criminology program, over the next decade he elevated the program to one of the best in the country. Sensitive to criticism that he lacked a PhD and was a poor lecturer, Wilson was most comfortable when visiting police departments, where his real acumen was appreciated.

Wilson resigned his position at Berkeley to become commissioner of the Chicago Police Department in 1960 after Mayor Daley promised him there would not be any political meddling. Wilson reorganized the number of police districts to eradicate remnants of the patronage system and established the Internal Investigative Division to root out police corruption. By hiring hundreds of new employees, 1,000 police officers were released from clerical duties to pursue criminals on the streets.

 Wilson watchers had learned to expect the unexpected. In 1966, he invited police critic and civil rights leader Martin Luther King Jr. to police headquarters to discuss how to improve interactions between the police and African Americans. King was quick to draw comparisons between his treatment by southern police officers and Wilson's respectful approach. Wilson retired from the force in 1967. Of his books and articles, his most influential was *Police Administration* (1963).

William H. Parker and the Los Angeles Police Department

The Los Angeles Police Department (LAPD) is one of the most storied and controversial police agencies in American history. During the Prohibition era, corruption reached into the highest levels of the department, and despite attempts by its chief, August Vollmer (1923–1924), to reform the force, Depression- and Prohibition-related corruption pervaded city politics unabated. To Vollmer's credit, he reorganized the department and implemented drastic changes that led to more efficient administration and scientific investigation.

Although the 1930s saw the introduction of police radios, improved communications, a border patrol, and a new police academy, the tumultuous years following Vollmer's stint as police chief continued to be characterized by political patronage and corruption. In the late 1920s, police chief James Edgar Davis resigned after a major bootlegger testified that he had paid the chief $100,000 per year for police protection.

In 1939, many corrupt high-ranking officers were purged from the ranks, ushering in an era of reform and professionalism. In 1950, William Henry Parker (1902–1966) was appointed police chief, a position he would hold for the next sixteen years.

 Born in Lead, South Dakota, William H. Parker moved to California in the 1920s and joined the Los Angeles Police Department (LAPD) in 1927. At night he studied law, earning his degree in three years. His rise through the ranks was meteoric before leaving the force to fight in World War II. Following the war, he helped organize new police systems in Munich and Frankfurt, Germany. Returning to the LAPD, he was tabbed as police chief in 1950.

As police chief, Parker implemented higher standards for police officers and encouraged his recruits to pursue additional academic training. An advocate of professionalism, Parker introduced the Internal Affairs Division; coauthored the board of rights procedure, which guaranteed the separation of police discipline from municipal politics; and founded the Bureau of Administration.

Almost as skilled as FBI director J. Edgar Hoover in the arena of public relations, the radio and then television show *Dragnet* promoted Parker and the LAPD, which became a nationally recognized police department in the 1950s. The 1952 Kefauver crime investigation commended Parker's department for its crime-fighting prowess. The 1957 publication of *Parker on Police*, edited by O. W. Wilson, did much to enhance Parker's impact on the professionalization of American policing. Parker's tenure as police chief was tarnished by racial conflict in Los Angeles, culminating in the 1965 Watts riots. Parker regarded the growing liberal shift of the 1960s with some suspicion, and in 1962 he was accused of racial bigotry and discrimination by a group of Los Angeles religious leaders. Despite a public outcry for his resignation, he refused to step down. Parker died of heart failure in 1966.

Federal Law Enforcement

The outbreak of World War II saw the mandate of the FBI change course from chasing gangsters to more sophisticated cases involving spies, espionage, and intelligence gathering. During the war, Hoover shifted the focus of the FBI toward fighting the activities of the communists and fascists, and in 1939 President Roosevelt placed Hoover in charge of domestic counterintelligence, a role that suited him well. The years surrounding World War II saw the rapid expansion of the FBI, with the number of agents increasing from 896 in 1940 to 4,370 in 1945 and appropriations rising from $8.8 million to $44.2 million.[5]

Hoover solidified public support by collaborating on books and films such as *The FBI in Peace and War* (1943) and *The House on 92nd Street* (1945). He took credit for the capture of nine German saboteurs (six would be executed) off Long Island in 1942, although recent research indicates that one of the Germans gave up his comrades in order to save his own life.

In the 1950s, FBI director Hoover continued his hunt for subversives, making the transition from hunting "Hot War" Nazi saboteurs to Cold War communists and spies. Although Hoover's FBI performed admirably in the war years, during the post-1945 Cold War years, Hoover once again reverted to Red-baiting tactics as the FBI's war against the Communist Party led to his veneration among conservatives and loathing and fear among liberals. During the 1950s, the FBI gathered evidence that uncovered the Klaus Fuchs atomic spy ring and led to the execution of Julius and Ethel Rosenberg for espionage activities. Hoover allied his organization with his close friend Senator Joseph McCarthy during the communist "witch hunt" of the 1950s and wrote the book *Masters of Deceit: The Story of Communism in American and How to Fight It* (1958), which detailed his strategies for defeating communism and contributed to the growing hysteria over Soviet expansion. Hoover continued his masterful manipulation of popular entertainment with the release of the hagiographic *The FBI Story* (1959). Also published was Don Whitehead's best-selling book by the same name.

In 1950, the FBI introduced its list of "Ten Most Wanted" fugitives. The first number one on the list was a convicted train robber and murderer named Thomas J. Holden. Director Hoover loved publicity, and with this new strategy he found a perfect tool for trumpeting the FBI's war against the underworld. What is less known is that Hoover probably borrowed the idea from a newspaper reporter who wrote a popular story based on names and descriptions of the ten fugitives the FBI would most like to apprehend. According to the bureau, the list was created to publicize certain fugitives. As testimony to its success rate, more than one-quarter of those captured since its inception were located through the assistance of citizens familiar with the list.

The names of fugitives placed on the list are submitted by the fifty-six FBI field offices and then reviewed by the agency's Criminal Investigative Division and the Office of Public and Congressional Affairs. Criminals who are selected for the list must either have lengthy records or pose a serious threat to the public. If a criminal is already notorious, it is doubtful he or she will make the list. The changing nature of America's crime problem can be documented by each decade's most wanted lists. In the 1950s, it was dominated by bank robbers, car thieves, and burglars, whereas in the 1960s it was dominated by radicals wanted for the destruction of government property and kidnapping. Most recently, terrorists and organized crime figures have predominated, along with serial killers and drug kingpins.

CORRECTIONS

The American declaration of war on Japan, following on the heels of the attack on Pearl Harbor, brought out strong expressions of patriotism from the most unlikely of places: America's prisons. Prisoners not only volunteered blood to the Red Cross but also purchased war bonds. According to a new Selective Service Act, all convicts were required to register for the draft. Many who were allowed to enlist did so. As prisons and prisoners lent their hand to the war effort, the number of inmates declined for the first time in more than a decade, dipping from 190,000 in 1940 to less than 120,000 in 1943.[6]

America's entry into World War II led to a temporary correctional philosophy that found expression in vocational training in support of the war effort. Soon prison assembly lines were turning out twine, model planes for pilot training schools, army mattresses, shoes, assault boats, and even aircraft engines. Institutions made the transformation to factories, churning out a wide range of products, with perhaps 98 percent of all convicts engaged in the work.[7]

Paralleling the war effort was the willingness of qualified teachers, counselors, and psychologists to help staff prison administrations. By the time the war ended in 1945, the American prison system had made the transition from a warden-dominated authoritarian system to one that embraced the developing social sciences and that increasingly relied on professional treatment in dealing with criminals.

One of the foremost American penologists of his era, Joseph Edward Ragen (1896–1971) rose to prominence as the reform-minded warden of the Illinois State Penitentiary at Joliet in the 1940s and 1950s. During his tenure at Joliet, Ragen eliminated the barnboss system, which created a hierarchy of power among the inmates, worked on beautifying the prison grounds, and introduced a policy for allowing prisoners to volunteer for medical research experiments. He would receive a special award for his prison's contribution to research on hepatitis and malaria. As a penologist reformer, he was credited with introducing progressive programs of rehabilitation, vocational training, and educational programs, including college-accredited courses, while at the same time maintaining strict discipline among his charges. During his twenty-five years at Joliet-Stateville, his strict control transformed the institution into a "paramilitary institution." However, in an era when many facilities were plagued by escape and riots, Joliet-Stateville did not report any riots or escapes.[8]

While the prison population increased slightly between 1930 and 1940 from 121 to 132 per 100,000, by 1950 America's inmate population had declined to 110 per 100,000. As the soldiers returned from the war, prison populations began to increase once more. By 1950, African Americans represented 7 percent of the population of Michigan but made up 40 percent of the prison population. As foreign-born white immigrants became a rare presence in correctional facilities (in 1946 only 3.2 percent of American prisoners), their places were filled by Hispanics, blacks, and Native Americans. One explanation for the rising number of inmates was the increasingly punitive nature of drug penalties in the postwar years.[9] By the mid-1950s, Louisiana enacted mandatory prison sentences from between five and ninety-nine years for minor narcotics violations.

Introduced in 1932, by the 1950s the "telephone pole" plan of penitentiary flourished from California (Soledad, Tracy, and Vacaville) and Texas (Eastham and Ferguson units) to Massachusetts and Connecticut. In this plan, cell blocks, dining halls, chapels, shops, and administrative offices diverged from a central corridor. This design better accommodated new treatment programs, maintained security, and offered inmates a new openness with the introduction of floor-to-ceiling security windows.

Despite advances in treatment and the decreasing emphasis on punitive methods, the 1950s were plagued by numerous prison riots, with one of the largest occurring in 1952 at the State Prison of Southern Michigan (resulting in the death of only one inmate). A subsequent investigation by the American Correctional Association concluded that the riot was caused by poor sentencing and parole practices, overcrowding, lack of professionalism at all levels, enforced idleness, inadequate funding, and the political domination of management. Between 1950 and 1955, more than forty-seven riots broke out in American prisons.

Although several outbreaks of prison violence took place in the South, the major prison riots occurred in northern and western prisons. One of the explanations for the dearth of southern prison riots was the fact that large penal farms were the dominant form of incarceration in the South. Therefore, it was more difficult to foment a riot in these conditions than in the fortresslike settings of the northern penitentiaries.

While most southern states had at least a centrally located penitentiary, the majority of prisoners languished in the plantation-like settings of the immense prison farms. With little opportunity for rioting or other mass expressions of resistance, to express their contempt for the punitive system, prisoners resorted to self-mutilation or escape. One of the more shocking examples of protest took place on the Louisiana prison farm at Angola, when thirty-seven prisoners slashed their heel tendons with razor blades in 1951 to remonstrate against the intolerable conditions at what was characterized as "America's worst prison."[10]

Several commissions were convened to study prison conditions in the 1950s. In 1953, the American Prison Association identified the causes of riots as relating to official indifference, substandard personnel, lack of professional leadership and professional programs, excessive size and overcrowding of institutions, and unwise sentencing and parole practices. Much of the criticism was leveled at the "big house" design of the 1940s, but few if any remedies to the situation were offered.

The prosperity and declining crime rates of the 1950s gave rise to a rehabilitative optimism and led to more input by behavioral scientists. Working on the assumption that most inmates were psychologically disturbed, a therapeutic orientation gained increased support among correctional administrators. Borrowing a page from the inmate classification systems of the earlier twentieth century, in the years following the war, teams of professional psychologists, sociologists, vocational counselors, caseworkers, and other specialists worked together to create a case history for each inmate. Prisoners could then be assigned to the appropriate prison for treatment and rehabilitation.

CRIME AND PUNISHMENT

The 1940s and 1950s were punctuated by a number of sensational crimes. The 1950s were inaugurated on January 17, 1950, with the Brinks robbery, the biggest heist in American history up to that time. While the FBI would unravel the case, none of the more than $1.2 million was ever recovered. In an event that eerily resembles the rampage killings of the 1990s, war veteran

Howard Unruh stepped out on a Camden, New Jersey, street in 1949 and for no apparent reason killed twelve of his neighbors in less than fifteen minutes. In 1957, James Dean wannabe Charles Starkweather, with girlfriend in tow, embarked on a murderous spree in rural Nebraska. On the surface, they seemed like typical teenagers except for one important difference: their youthful rebellion included murdering eleven persons during an eight-day rampage through two states. Further demonstrating that crime was no longer the bailiwick of the big city, novelist Truman Capote would chronicle the 1959 murder of a close-knit farm family in rural Kansas in his groundbreaking book *In Cold Blood* (1965).

Providing the inspiration for the television series *The Fugitive,* on July 4, 1954, Dr. Sam Sheppard described a "bushy-haired intruder" who bludgeoned to death his pregnant wife and knocked him out. The public was fascinated by the case, which became one of the most notorious murder trials of the 1950s. In the moralistic atmosphere of the mid-1950s, the case featured a well-to-do handsome doctor, a pregnant wife, a secret lover, and a mysterious killer, all feeding the public's curiosity and creating a media sensation. Sheppard was found guilty of second-degree murder in 1954, and his conviction would be overturned twelve years into a life sentence because the judge in the original case "did not fulfill his duty to protect Sheppard from inherently prejudicial publicity which saturated the country."[11]

During the 1990s, an ongoing investigation by Sam Sheppard's son, Sam Reese Sheppard, and private investigators uncovered evidence that has led some authorities to link the murder of Marilyn Sheppard to the family window washer, who was currently serving time for another homicide. Sam Sheppard Jr. believed that there was sufficient evidence to warrant a civil suit, charging the State of Ohio with wrongful imprisonment. The subsequent three civil trials proved to be three more media sensations. Facing a judgment that could have cost the state millions of dollars, the state mounted a spirited defense. After a brief deliberation, a jury on April 12, 2000, ruled unanimously in favor of the state. This case, like other controversial cases that seem to linger in the American consciousness, demonstrates the continuing advances in DNA and other investigative technologies. It also demonstrates how history is an ongoing process, particularly in the arena of modern crime and punishment.[12]

The Specter of Organized Crime

During the 1930s and 1940s, Hoover's FBI had carte blanche to chase Nazi saboteurs, Russian spies, and black marketeers, ignoring the more threatening criminal threat of organized crime syndicates. By the 1950s, it was impossible to deny the existence of organized crime on the national level. In 1950, Senator Estes Kefauver convened a committee to investigate racketeering. The Senate Special Committee to Investigate Crime in Interstate Commerce, better known as the Kefauver Committee, would subsequently hold hearings in fourteen cities and listen to testimony from over 600 witnesses, many of whom testified to the existence of a sinister nationwide criminal conspiracy known as the "Mafia."

Thanks to the introduction of the television, Americans were treated to the Kefauver Committee hearings, the longest-running television series of 1950–1951 and the first significant investigation of organized crime in America. Numerous crime figures and politicians were introduced to a national audience as the hearings were convened in city after city. The hearings reintroduced the public to the Bill of Rights as the phrase "taking the Fifth" became part of the American lexicon. Following the denouement of the hearings, the committee recommended tightening up the law against the Mafia, corrupt politicians, and other racketeers.

Apalachin Conference

The 1957 Apalachin Conference of organized crime kingpins in rural upstate New York is generally considered a turning point in the war on organized crime. Prior to this episode, J. Edgar

Hoover had denied the existence of organized crime syndicates for almost thirty years. However, when a New York State police officer stumbled on the clandestine meeting of some sixty mobsters at the home of Joseph Barbara Sr., Hoover could demur no longer. Soon the FBI was forced into the fray, beginning a campaign of wiretapping and electronic eavesdropping that would see few triumphs before the 1980s. Part of the problem was that having denied the existence of the Mafia or any monolithic crime organizations for decades, the FBI was forced into a game of catchup. This was most noticeable in the agency's early attempts to interpret surveillance, when they could not recognize much of the wise-guy vernacular. Hearing the Mafia phrase "cosa nostra," meaning "our thing," agents concluded that this "new" criminal organization they had uncovered was called "La Cosa Nostra," hence another chapter in the Mafia legend.

When authorities rounded up the underworld leaders, they discovered that nineteen were from upstate New York, twenty-three from New York City, three from the mountain West, two from the South, eight from the Midwest, two from Cuba, and one from Italy. These demographics were used by the media to bring pressure on Hoover to admit the existence of a national organized crime syndicate. In the process, not only was Hoover embarrassed, but the revelations had a damaging effect on the FBI's image and reputation for professionalism.

While Hoover would only privately concede the existence of an organized crime syndicate, publicly he established the Top Hoodlum program, an initiative against organized crime by which each FBI field office was required to identify ten major mob members in its geographic area and then closely watch their activities.

Capital Punishment

American executions substantially decreased between the late 1940s and early 1950s. In fact, the number of capital crimes had been steadily reduced since the eighteenth century. By the beginning of the 1950s, there were capital crimes for which no one had been executed in years, including kidnapping, treason, and bombing. Since the 1930s, the only capital crime that had regularly received the death penalty was murder. Although public opinion continued to support the death penalty, fewer executions were taking place. Between 1950 and 1954, an average of eighty-three executions were conducted, compared to 155 per year between 1930 and 1934.[13]

A watershed of sorts for the study of American executions was the commencement of collecting and publishing national statistics on executions. Before the 1930s, most figures concerning execution were unofficial, but beginning in 1930, the Bureau of the Census began including execution as one of the causes of death in the *Vital Statistics of the United States*.

National execution statistics were disseminated to a wider audience beginning in 1950, thanks to the inclusion of these figures in the Federal Bureau of Prisons' *National Prisoner Statistics Series*. A survey of the execution data "unequivocally documented the fact that for the preceding twenty years, the black man had been the principal victim of the death penalty in America, and almost the exclusive victim of executions for rape."[14] Further research demonstrated that blacks on death row were less likely to receive commutations than their white counterparts.

In the postwar years, several Supreme Court decisions addressed the unequal application of the death penalty. In 1947, an African American man named Eddie Patton was sentenced to death by an all-white jury for killing a white man. Citing the exclusion of blacks from the juries that indicted him and then convicted him, Patton argued that he had been denied equal protection under the law as guaranteed by the Fourteenth Amendment. Patton claimed that it had been a long-established tradition in his county to exclude blacks from jury lists, jury boxes, and jury service. In the 1947 decision *Patton v. Mississippi*, the Supreme Court reversed the decision of the state court. By ordering a new trial, the Court established a new precedent for the prohibition of racial discrimination in jury selection.

◈ Among the capital murder cases that led many to begin questioning the wisdom of the death penalty was the case of Caryl Chessman (1921–1960), California's infamous "Red Light Bandit." By the time he was sixteen, Chessman, a veteran of California's juvenile criminal system, had learned how to expertly manipulate the legal system. Beginning in early 1948, however, he made the transition from committing petty crimes to capital ones. He was suspected of using a flashing red light to stop cars by creating the impression that he was somehow connected to law enforcement. He robbed several victims at gunpoint in two cases and in a third incident ordered a woman to undress and perform oral sex on him. Two more robberies followed, including one in which he forced a woman into his car and attempted to rape her.

It was not long before Chessman was arrested on suspicion of armed robbery. When police found tools that seemed to connect him with the Red Light Bandit case, he was arraigned on eighteen charges. In the subsequent trial, Chessman was convicted of kidnapping (for moving a woman from her car into his) and committing "unnatural sexual acts." Sentenced to death for violating the so-called Little Lindbergh Law by kidnapping with intent to commit robbery, the Chessman case was the harshest sentence handed down in California to a criminal who had not actually killed anyone. Between 1948 and 1960, his execution was repeatedly postponed as it went through the appellate process. During those twelve years, he became a well-known, articulate opponent of the death penalty. He wrote three books, including *Cell 2455, Death Row*, selling hundreds of thousands of copies. But after eight stays of execution, he was finally confronted with the gas chamber on May 2, 1960.

Like many controversial American executions, this one resonated throughout the world, leading to demonstrations and attacks on U.S. embassies in Europe and South America. Governor Edmund "Pat" Brown of California, who had been widely criticized for his vacillation over the fate of Chessman, would later write that he believed he "should have found a way to spare Chessman's life."[15] Over the next few years, unfavorable public opinion would lead to an informal moratorium on the death penalty beginning in 1965.

The 1950s and 1960s saw the NAACP and the American Civil Liberties Union come to the aid of a number of individuals sentenced to death, leading to the reversal of several convictions. During the 1960s, five states abolished the death penalty, and still more demonstrated a reluctance to schedule and perform executions. Judges and juries also became increasingly disinclined to impose death sentences.

Sensational Crimes

There were a number of high-profile crimes that accented the war years. None was stranger than that of the teenage killer and burglar William Heirens. An alarming case that presaged the sex criminals and serial killers of the modern era, Heirens was arrested for burglary in 1946. A subsequent fingerprint check connected him to a number of unsolved crimes, including the murders of two women and of a six-year-old child who had been dismembered. Heirens was then questioned under the influence of the highly promoted truth serum sodium pentothal. Originally used to treat shell-shock victims during the war, its use in the Heirens case was its first in a criminal case. Despite warnings from a director of a psychiatric institute that the drug was not reliable and that any revelations uncovered could not be used in court, the state's attorney went ahead with the procedure.

Under the influence of the drug, Heirens revealed the existence of what proved an imaginary companion whom he blamed for the murders. The American Civil Liberties Union soon protested the use of sodium pentothal, citing it as a violation of the defendant's civil rights. In later years, Heirens claimed to have been taking the drug for months prior to the questioning so that he could manipulate his inquisitors. The seventeen-year-old Heirens eventually reached a plea agreement and confessed to three murders. In one of the murders, Heirens wrote with lipstick on a living room wall "For Heaven's sake catch me before I kill more. I cannot control myself," probably one of the most memorable quotes in the annals of American homicide. Despite the potential of sodium pentothal as a truth serum, the business of lie detecting would remain the bailiwick of the polygraph machine, pioneered by the Berkeley Police Department years earlier.

Juvenile Delinquency

In the 1950s, America was confronted with a new wave of hysteria: rising juvenile delinquency. During hearings on the problem chaired by Estes Kefauver, a now familiar refrain was heard: "blame it on the mass media." However, one needs to go back only to the 1920s and 1930s to discover similar concerns about the impact of mass culture on America's youth. Historian James Gilbert suggests that "the 1950s' dispute over mass culture was protracted and perhaps more universal and intense than at earlier periods."[16] Gilbert explained that while the 1950s was a decade of "declining civil liberties," it was also an era of "remarkable liberalization," citing the civil rights movement and class mobility stimulated by the G.I. Bill of Rights, which offered educational opportunities to more people.

As America reaped the economic benefits of the postwar boom, the mass-media industry enjoyed greater independence from censorship and control. As juvenile delinquency rose, so did the furor over violent comic books, rock-and-roll music, clothing styles, and hot-rodders. However, what escaped many of the era's critics was that delinquency had been on the rise since 1940. Criminal justice authorities cited a variety of explanations, including broken families, mothers away from home working for the war effort in factories, and family mobility, all of which were slowly creating a nation of strangers.

In 1949, following in the discredited steps of Lombroso, who had concluded that one could recognize "born criminals" by studying body measurements and physical traits, William Sheldon collected the physical measurements of 200 boys at a Boston reform school. Whereas Lombroso argued for atavism—that born criminals were biological throwbacks to an earlier stage of evolution—Sheldon determined that basic body structures were linked to delinquency. He found that the more athletic and aggressive mesomorphs were more inclined to delinquency over the more lethargic endomorphs and taller and intellectually inclined ectomorphs. However, unlike Lombroso, Sheldon argued that mesomorphy did not result in delinquency but rather predisposed delinquents to delinquency.

In subsequent years, Sheldon's findings came under increasing scrutiny and have been roundly criticized for lacking empirical rigor. In 1956, Sheldon and Eleanor Glueck tested Sheldon's hypothesis by comparing 500 identified delinquents with 500 nondelinquents in a controlled experiment. What they found was that body type in itself did not incline individuals to delinquent behavior but was one of many factors that led to delinquency.

Sheldon and Eleanor Glueck were two Harvard-based criminologists who collaborated on a number of works investigating issues ranging from juvenile delinquency and recidivism to criminality and rehabilitation. In one their best-known publications, *Predicting Delinquency and Crime,* published in 1959, the Gluecks developed a "social prediction table" that was designed to gauge criminal potential in young children. Although this was considered innovative in its time, many criminologists have questioned the validity of the Gluecks' findings, citing their failure to examine the role of ethnicity since their study included many Italian immigrants.

AMERICAN VIOLENCE

The nation's prospects for peace and order following World War II stood out in sharp contrast to the denouement of World War I, which was followed by racial and economic turmoil. Thanks in part to a long duration of full industrial employment in the war years, the late 1940s and 1950s saw homicide rates plummet to an all-time low of less than five per 100,000. According to historian Roger Lane, a new pattern of homicide emerged in which murders were "domesticated," explaining that "compared to earlier eras, proportionately more of them [murders] involved fights with family, friends, and acquaintances, rather than strangers or robbers."[17]

As Lane and others have demonstrated, America's urban homicide rate declined in the 1940s and 1950s. A pioneering study by criminologist Marvin Wolfgang, *Patterns of Criminal Homicide* (1957), analyzed homicides in Philadelphia between 1948 and 1952. His findings are considered the era's most accurate academic study of homicide and demonstrate the long-term impact of the "ongoing urban industrial revolution."[18]

However, while homicide rates had declined, racial tensions and violence persisted throughout the country. The war years saw an African American migration to cities in the Northeast (New York and Philadelphia), the Midwest (Chicago and Detroit), and the West (Los Angeles and Portland), particularly as bars to black employment were lifted in industrial centers. While most tensions were held in check by the ongoing war and patriotic fervor on the home front, the end of the war brought lingering animosities to the surface.

An unforeseen result of the war years was the labor shortage that imperiled America's war industries as the country slowly rebounded from the Great Depression. Both Puerto Rican and Mexican immigration flourished. Most Puerto Ricans ended up in the New York City area, while Mexicans recruited for agricultural labor settled in the Southwest. Although racial tensions were exacerbated by these migrations, with the most serious riots breaking out in Detroit in 1942 and 1943, it was not until the end of the war that a wave of violence engulfed cities in every region of the country.

An examination of the 1943 Detroit riot offers an excellent microcosm from which to view similar race riots in the 1940s. While the armed forces were still segregated as America went to war, steps were taken against segregation and discrimination on other fronts. In one campaign, black organizations promoted the "double V" as a symbol for victory at home and overseas. Blacks had traditionally been barred from the automobile unions, and the UAW-CIO sought to remedy the situation at Ford plants in 1941. Subsequently, the strike succeeded, and they were accepted into the union by the thousands.

Whites, however, felt threatened by such advances. Egged on by right-wing demagogues such as Father Charles Coughlin and the almost-fascist Black Legion, a violent campaign of terror was initiated against Detroit's black population, culminating in a June riot. According to one study by Dominic Capeci, white rioters in Detroit were often young, single, and employed men who went to great lengths to reach the riot, where they could confront black rioters, who were typically "older, married, and employed" but had a stake in a community that seemed to unfairly deny them advancement in the building trades.[19] Fueled by racism and rumor, Detroit's blacks fought back against white agitators, looting and burning stores. Whites responded with iron pipes, knives, and clubs. Police gunfire raked the rioters as well. When the riot finally ended, thirty-four people were dead, including twenty-five blacks.

In Birmingham, Alabama, a city that was 43 percent black, several homes were dynamited in 1949 as the resurgent southern Klan returned to threatening black citizens. Far from an isolated incident, between 1950 and 1951 racially motivated bombings were reported in Nashville, Miami, Dallas, and other cities. As segregation came under attack throughout the 1950s, individual instances of bombings, arson, and violence were directed at black communities from California to Florida.

The *Brown v. Board of Education* decision led to racial violence in most southern states. With little opposition from state law enforcement, more than 500 reprisals against African Americans were reported between 1955 and 1958. As the leader of the school integration movement, the NAACP was often targeted by segregationists. In an attempt to block the integrationists, Virginia passed sedition laws, South Carolina barred public employment of NAACP members, and Texas and Alabama initiated injunctions against association branches.

The notorious murder of fifteen-year-old Emmett Till further reinforced black fears of racially motivated violence in the South. In August 1955, Till, who was raised in Chicago, was spending a summer vacation with relatives in rural Tallahatchie County, Mississippi, when he mistakenly broke the conventions of southern etiquette. Unfamiliar with a culture that expected black men to answer whites with "yes sir" or "no sir," Till responded in several confrontations with the less conventional "yeah" and "naw." Compounding his "flaunting" of southern racial etiquette, Till kept a photograph of his white girlfriend back home in his wallet. Till sealed his fate when, on a dare by local friends, he whistled at a young, married white woman and even went so far as asking her for a date. It was not long before he disappeared. Till's badly decomposed body was soon found in the Tallahatchie River. Suspicion focused on the white woman's husband and another man, who were identified as having visited the cabin where Till had been staying to inquire about his whereabouts. Both men were arrested and indicted for the murder. After a trial in front of an all-white jury (despite blacks making up 63 percent of county residents) and deliberating for little more than one hour, both defendants were acquitted. According to one of the jurors, "If we hadn't stopped to drink pop, it wouldn't have taken that long."[20] Despite an international uproar, the case had little impact on race relations and the criminal justice system in the South.[21]

The Zoot-Suit Riot

The racial tensions that exploded in Los Angeles in the 1940s "were a precursor of the searing racial turbulence that would mark America's cities in the decades to follow."[22] During the war years, Los Angeles was teeming with young men—black, Mexican American, and white. In the

racially charged atmosphere of the period, there was little interference from the Los Angeles Police Department (LAPD) if whites sometimes lashed out at defiant African Americans seeking jobs in wartime industries or stylish Mexican "zoot-suiters" (the term referred to the gaudy clothing preferred by some Mexican youths) flaunting their individuality. By 1943, the racial demographics of Los Angeles were clearly changing. In 1940, its African American population stood at 62,000. However, more than 200,000 blacks would arrive in the city in the mid-1940s to fill the demand for workers in the aviation, shipbuilding, and other wartime industries.

Although the LAPD employed black officers as early as the nineteenth century, segregation became the hallmark of the early LAPD. Black and white officers were forbidden to work together. If blacks were promoted, it was only to the plainclothes division. There was an unspoken rule against blacks wearing stripes, which would allow them to supervise white officers. With the introduction of the police car in the 1920s and 1930s, black officers were consigned to the midnight shift (apparently so that whites would not see them in a patrol car) and were still segregated and restricted to black neighborhoods. Reflecting the rampant discrimination of the era, similar conditions existed for Mexican Americans on the force, with little opportunity for advancement, except as detectives, in which case bilingualism was necessary.

In the same summer that witnessed the Detroit race riot, tension resulting from the assault of several sailors by a group of Mexican youths resulted in violence between Mexicans and whites on the streets of Los Angeles. Between June 3 and June 13, 1943, mobs attacked Mexican and black youths in Los Angeles. Those attired in zoot-suit garb were most often singled out. On June 7 alone, over 1,000 soldiers, sailors, and civilians dragged mostly Mexican youths from movie theaters, streetcars, and homes and into the streets, where they were summarily stripped and beaten. Police stood by, either helpless or reluctant to intervene. What was probably most remarkable about this riot was that no one was killed or seriously injured, and there was little property damage.

Following the Zoot-Suit Riot, Governor and future Supreme Court Justice Earl Warren ordered an investigation into its causes. The resulting Citizen's Committee Report was a classic in understatement, concluding that racial prejudice was a factor in the outbreak. Demonstrating the long-standing animosity between Mexicans and Anglos in southern California, the Hearst papers headlined every episode that reflected negatively on Mexicans. Despite attempts by the Office of War Information to end this practice, following the riot one Los Angeles County supervisor proclaimed to the media that "all that is needed to end lawlessness is more of the same action as is being exercised by the servicemen."[23]

After the June riots, the Los Angeles City Council made wearing this form of attire a misdemeanor, foreshadowing the uproar over gang paraphernalia in schools today. According to James Gilbert, the Zoot-Suit Riot also "pushed delinquency to the forefront of national concern."[24]

NOTABLE TRIALS

The Trial of Julius and Ethel Rosenberg (1951)

Julius and Ethel Rosenberg were arrested in 1950 for what J. Edgar Hoover labeled the "crime of the century": allegedly passing the secret of the atomic bomb to the Soviets five years earlier, only three months before America dropped the atomic bomb on Hiroshima. The Rosenbergs were taken into custody after a Russian espionage ring in the United States began to unravel. Along with associate Morton Sobell, the three were charged and tried in 1951 for "conspiracy to commit espionage." What makes this case stand out was that while it was probably the most publicized capital case

of its era, it concerned espionage rather than homicide.

The Rosenbergs pleaded innocence at their trial and took the Fifth Amendment when queried as to whether they were communists. Their trial was conducted in a climate of fear and conspiracy while American forces were in the midst of the Korean conflict. Following the trial, the Rosenbergs were found guilty and sentenced to death, and Sobell was sentenced to thirty years in prison. Julius and Ethel Rosenberg spent the next two years at New York's Sing Sing Prison as their lawyer filed numerous appeals on their behalf. Despite international pressure to spare the parents of two children and the persistent claims of innocence by the Rosenbergs, both went to the electric chair in June 1953.

Harking back to past history when treason was always treated as the worst secular offense, the Rosenbergs were the first and last Americans executed for treason against the United States (John Brown had been executed for treason against the State of Virginia). What is most noteworthy about the case, which was the endgame of a complicated series of Cold War spy cases, was that the Rosenbergs had not given information to an enemy during wartime but rather to America's wartime ally, an act that technically would not be considered an act of treason. Gripped in the postwar anticommunist hysteria of the McCarthy era, America no longer held a monopoly on the atomic bomb. Prosecutors and the public alike were eager to find a scapegoat. The testimony of fellow spies Harry Gold and Ethel Rosenberg's brother David Greenglass, both of whom cooperated with the authorities, made a compelling case for their guilt. In 1995, decoded wartime cables from the Soviet consulate in New York to the KGB in Moscow were made public, revealing the complicity of Julius Rosenberg beyond a reasonable doubt (but there was little evidence against Ethel). None of these intercepts were made public in the 1951 trial because the United States did not want the Soviets to know that their "unbreakable code" had been broken.

CONCLUSIONS

The Cold War and "Hot War" tensions of the 1940s and 1950s transformed criminal justice institutions, but many American tensions remained unchanged. The 1955 murders of Emmett Till and Reverend George Lee[25] demonstrated that white murderers who killed blacks in southern white communities had little to fear from the criminal justice system.

In the climate of the postwar era, security at home and abroad dominated American concerns. Many civil libertarians were alarmed by the government's attempt to protect national security at the expense of certain constitutional liberties. For the first time since the Alien and Sedition Acts of 1798, people were imprisoned for peacetime sedition, beginning with the Smith Act of 1940. By the late 1940s, leaders of the American Communist Party were prosecuted because of the postwar standoff with the Soviet Union. The Cold War concern for national security would give rise to another series of witch hunts against dissenters, this time finding expression in the House Un-American Activities Committee hearings and the McCarthy hearings.

While the trial of the Rosenbergs and Caryl Chessman garnered domestic headlines, trials in Nuremberg and Tokyo unveiled an underworld of criminal excess unsurpassed in criminal justice history. More than twelve million Jews, Gypsies, Russians, and homosexuals were murdered in the Nazi holocaust. Millions more perished in Russia during Stalin's reign. Forty percent of Americans held by the Japanese perished in death marches and from disease. Sixty percent of Soviet prisoners held by the Germans died in captivity.

As America's crime rates declined into the 1950s, so too did the nation begin to abandon capital punishment. According to death penalty authority William J. Bowers, the decline initially coincided with the decline in the homicide rate, but by 1950 "there were definite indications that the nation was becoming more reluctant to execute."[26] As the 1960s approached, research by the social scientist Thorsten Sellin (1896–1982) suggested that capital homicide was not an effec-

tive deterrent and that it had little impact on homicide rates.

The impact of the 1940s and 1950s on Americans varied from group to group. The war had a great impact on population demographics, as people flocked from the countryside to the cities. New opportunities opened for women and minorities, yet sexual and racial barriers persisted. With the birth of the civil rights movement in the late 1950s, remnants of the Ku Klux Klan that had remained active in the South through the war years returned with a fury in the early 1960s.

Point–Counterpoint
Separate But Equal? (Mississippi 1948–1954)

By the 1890s, Jim Crow laws had spread through the South, leading some African Americans to turn to the courts to defend the rights they felt had been granted them under the Fourteenth Amendment. In Plessy v. Ferguson (1896) the Court ruled that "separate but equal" accommodations did not violate the Equal Protection Clause. Midway through the next century not much had changed with most southern states enforcing the separation of blacks and whites at schools, train stations, and even having separate schools for blind children of both races. In 1948 Southern whites launched a third-party presidential campaign with a platform based on segregation. The first reading is a set of passages from Mississippi's legal code in the late 1940s. In 1954 Plessy was overturned when the Supreme Court concluded that "separate educational facilities are inherently unequal." The second passage is an excerpt from Brown v. Board of Education of Topeka (1954). The struggle against segregation still had a long way to go.

In the first cases in this Court construing the Fourteenth Amendment, decided shortly after its adoption, the Court interpreted it as proscribing all state-imposed discriminations against the Negro race. The doctrine of "separate but equal" did not make its appearance in this Court until 1896 in the case of *Plessy v. Ferguson* . . . involving not education but transportation. American courts have since labored with the doctrine for over half a century. In this

Source: Mississippi State Criminal Code, 6927, 6973, 6974, 2339, 7848, 2351, 7784, 7785, 7786, 7787; *Brown v. Education*, 347 U.S. 483 (1954).

Court, there have been six cases involving the "separate but equal" doctrine in the field of public education. . . . In more recent cases, all on the graduate school level, inequality was found in that specific benefits enjoyed by white students were denied to Negro students of the same educational qualifications. . .. In none of these cases was it necessary to re-examine the doctrine to grant relief to the Negro plaintiff. . . .

In the instant cases, the question is directly presented. Here . . . there are findings below that the Negro and white schools involved have been equalized, or are being equalized, with respect to buildings, curricula, qualifications and salaries of teachers. . . . Our decision, therefore, cannot turn on merely the comparison of these tangible factors in the Negro and white schools involved in each of the cases. We must look instead to the effect of segregation itself on public education.

In approaching this problem, we cannot turn the clock back to 1868 when the Amendment was adopted, or even to 1896 when *Plessy v. Ferguson* was written. We must consider public education in the light of its full development and its present place in American life throughout the Nation. Only in this way can it be determined if segregation in public schools deprives these plaintiffs of the equal protection of the laws.

Today, education is perhaps the most important function of state and local governments. Compulsory school attendance laws and the great expenditures for education both demonstrate our recognition of the importance of education to our democratic society. It is required in the performance of our most basic public responsibilities, even service in the armed forces. It is the very foundation of good citizenship. Today it is a principal instrument in awakening the child to cultural values, in preparing him for later professional training, and in helping him to adjust normally to his environment. . . .

We come then to the question presented: Does segregation of children in public schools solely on the basis of race, even though the physical facilities and other "tangible" factors may be equal, deprive the children of the minority group of equal educational opportunities? We believe that it does. . . .

To separate them from others of similar age and qualifications solely because of their race generates a feeling of inferiority as to their status in the community that may affect their hearts and minds in a way unlikely ever to be undone. The effect of this separation on their educational opportunities was well stated by a finding in the Kansas case by a court which nevertheless felt compelled to rule against the Negro plaintiffs:

"Segregation of white and colored children in public schools has a detrimental effect upon the colored children. The impact is greater when it has the sanction of the law; for the policy of separating the races is usually interpreted as denoting the inferiority of the Negro group. A sense of inferiority affects the motivation of a child to learn. Segregation with the sanction of law, therefore, has a tendency to retard the education and mental development of Negro children and to deprive them of some of the benefits they would receive in a racially integrated school system." Whatever may have been the extent of psychological knowledge at the time of *Plessy v. Ferguson,* this finding is amply supported by modern authority. Any language in *Plessy v. Ferguson* contrary to this finding is rejected.

We conclude that in the field of public education the doctrine of "separate but equal" has no place. Separate educational facilities are inherently unequal. Therefore, we hold that the plaintiffs and others similarly situated for whom the actions have been brought are, by reason of the segregation complained of, deprived of the equal protection of the laws guaranteed by the Fourteenth Amendment. . . .

State Charity Hospitals

Mississippi State Charity Hospital

§6927. Races to be separated.—The white and colored races shall be kept separately in said hospital and suitable provisions made for their care and comfort by the board of trustees. [Codes, Hemingway's 1917, §3949; 1930, §4594; Laws, 1910, ch. 115.]

§6973. Separate entrances for races.—There shall be maintained by the governing authorities of every hospital maintained by the state for treatment of white and colored patients separate entrances for white and colored patients and visitors, and such entrances shall be used by the races only for which they are prepared. [Codes, 1930, §4618; Laws, 1928, Ex. Ch. 95.]

Source: 347 U.S. 483 (1954).

§6974. Separate nurses for different races.—In all such institutions it shall be the duty of the superintendent and others in authority to furnish a sufficient number of colored nurses to attend colored patients, such colored nurses to be under the supervision of such white supervisors as the head of the institution may determine. A failure to comply with this and the next preceding section shall authorize the governor to remove the person in authority responsible for such violation. [Codes, 1930, §4619; Laws, 1928, Ex. ch. 95.]

Social Equality

§2339. Races—social equality, marriages between—advocacy of punished.—Any person, firm or corporation who shall be guilty of printing, publishing or circulating printed, typewritten or written matter urging or presenting for public acceptance or general information, arguments or suggestions in favor of social equality or of intermarriage between whites and negroes, shall be guilty of a misdemeanor and subject to a fine not exceeding five hundred [$500.00] dollars or imprisonment not exceeding six [6] months or both fine and imprisonment in the discretion of the court. [Codes, Hemingway's 1921 Supp.§ 1142e; 1930, §1103; Laws, 1920, ch. 214.]

Transportation

Depots

§7848. Regulations for passenger depots.— [Requires passenger depots in cities of 3,000 or more inhabitants to maintain in connection with reception room for whites, two closets labeled respectively "Closet, white; females only," "Closet, white; males only," and similarly in the waiting room for Negroes, closets labelled respectively substituting the word "colored" for "white".] [Codes, 1892, §4303; 1906, §4855; Hemingway's 1917, §7640; 1930, §7072.]

Railroads

§2351. Railroads—not providing separate cars.— If any person or corporation operating a railroad shall fail to provide two or more passenger cars for each passenger train, or to divide the passenger cars by a partition, to secure separate accommodations for the white and colored races, as provided by law, or if any railroad passenger conductor shall fail to assign each passenger to the car or compartment of the car used for the race to which the passenger belongs, he or it shall be guilty of a misdemeanor, and, on conviction shall be fined not less than twenty [$20.00] dollars nor more than five hundred [$500.00] dollars. [Codes,

1892, §1276; 1906, §1351; Hemingway's 1917, §1085; 1930, §1115.]

[Note: This provision applies to sleeping cars. See *Alabama & V. R. Co. v. Morris*, (1912) 103 Miss. 511, 60 So. 11, Ann. Cas. 1915B 613.]

§7784. Equal but separate accommodations for the races.—Every railroad carrying passengers in this state shall provide equal but separate accommodations for the white and colored races by providing two or more passenger cars for each passenger train, or by dividing the passenger cars by a partition to secure separate accommodations; and the conductor of such passenger train shall have power, and is required, to assign each passenger to the car, or the compartment of a car, used for the race to which such passenger belongs; and should any passenger refuse to occupy the car to which he or she is assigned by the conductor, the conductor shall have power to refuse to carry such passenger on the train, and for such refusal neither he nor the railroad company shall be liable for damages in any court. [Codes, 1892, §3562; 1906, §4059; Hemingway's 1917, §6687; 1930, §6132; Laws, 1904, ch. 99.]

Street Railways and Busses

§7785. [1948 Cum. Supp.] — Separate accommodaitons for races in street cars and busses— common carriers by motor vehicle.—All persons or corporations operating street railways and street or municipal buses, carrying passengers in this state, and every common carrier by motor vehicle of passengers in this state as defined by section 3 (e) of Chapter 142 of the laws of 1938 [§7634, Code of 1942] shall provide equal, but separate, accommodations for the white and colored races.

Every common carrier by motor vehicle of passengers in this state, as defined by section 3 (e) of Chapter 142 of the laws of 1938 [§7634, Code of 1942], by buses or street cars operated entirely within the corporate limits of a municipality, or within a radius of 5 miles thereof, shall divide its passengers by the use of an appropriate sign 4 x 9 inches, for the purpose of, and in a manner that will suitably provide for, a separation of the races, and all other buses and motor vehicles carrying passengers for hire in the state of Mississippi shall use a latticed movable partition extending from the top of the seat to the ceiling of the vehicle, said partition not to obstruct the view of the driver of the vehicle to secure such separate accommodations; provided, however, that this act shall not apply to buses operated exclusively for the carrying of military personnel, and the operators of such passenger buses shall have power, and are required, to assign each passenger to the compartment of the bus used for the race to which such passenger belongs; and in no case shall any passenger be permitted to stand in the aisle of the compartment in which he does not belong and is not so assigned; and should any passenger refuse to occupy the compartment to which he or she belongs and is assigned, the operator shall have power to refuse to carry such passenger on the bus; or should either compartment become so loaded in transit as not to permit the taking on of any further passengers for that compartment, then the bus operator shall not be required and shall refuse to take on any further passengers in violation of this act. Even though such additional passengers may have purchased and may hold tickets for transportation on the said bus, the only remedy said passengers shall have for failure or refusal to carry them under such circumstances is the right to a refund of the cost of his ticket, and for said refusal in either case neither the operator nor the common carrier shall be liable for damages in any court. Such partition may be made movable so as to allow adjustment of the space in the bus to suit the requirements of traffic. [Amends §7785, Code of 1942.] [Codes, 1906, §4060; Hemingway's, 1917, §7558; 1930, §6133; 1942, §7785; Laws 1904; ch. 99; 1940, ch. 169; 1944, ch. 267, 1.]

[Note: §7634, Code of 1942, Subsection (e): The term "common carrier by motor vehicle" means any person who or which undertakes, whether directly or by a lease or by any other arrangement, to transport passengers or property for the general public by motor vehicle for compensation, over regular routes, including such motor vehicle operation of carriers by rail or water, and of express or forwarding companies under this Act. [Laws 1938, ch. 142]]

§7786. [1948 Cum. Supp.]—Passengers required to occupy compartments to which they are assigned.— The operators of such street cars and street buses and motor vehicles, as defined by Chapter 142 of the laws of 1938 [§7632 – 7687, Code of 1942] shall have the power and are required to assign each passenger to the space or compartment used for the race to which such passenger belongs. Any passenger undertaking or attempting to go into the space or compartment to which by race he or she does not belong shall be guilty of a misdemeanor, and, upon conviction, shall be liable to a fine of twenty-five dollars ($25.00) or, in lieu

thereof, by imprisonment for a period of not more than thirty (30) days in the county jail; and any operator of any street car or street bus or motor vehicle as herein defined, assigning or placing a passenger to the space or compartment other than the one set aside for the race to which said passenger belongs shall be guilty of a misdemeanor and, upon conviction, shall be liable to a fine of twenty-five dollars ($25.00) or, in lieu thereof, to imprisonment for a period of not more than thirty (30) days in the county jail. [Amends §7786, Code of 1942.] [Codes 1906, §4061; Hemingway's 1917, §7559; 1930, §6134; 1942, §7786; Laws, 1904, ch. 99; 1940, ch. 169; 1944, ch. 267, §1.]

§7786-01. [1948 Cum. Supp.]—Penalty for Violation.—Every person or corporation operating street railways and street or municipal buses carrying passengers in this state, and every common carrier of passengers in this state by motor vehicle, as defined by section 3 (e) of Chapter 142 of the laws of 1938 [§7634, Code of 1942], guilty of wilful and continued failure to observe or comply with the provisions of this act shall be liable to a fine of twenty-five dollars ($25.00) for each offense, and each day's violation of the provision hereof shall constitute a separate violation of this act; provided, however, that in the case of persons or corporations operating street railways and street or municipal buses, the fine shall be ten dollars ($10.00) instead of twenty-five dollars ($25.00). [Laws 1944, ch. 267, §2.]

§7787. Penalty for refusal of street railway officers and employees to comply with this provision.— [Officers and directors who neglect or refuse to comply with §§7785, 7786, 7787, Code of 1942 are punishable by fine of not less than $100 or 60 days to 6 months in prison in the county jail. Conductors and other employees who have charge of vehicles to which this section applies are punishable by fine of not less than $25.00 or imprisonment of 10 to 30 days for each and every offense; *provided,* however, chapter is not to apply to nurses attending children of the other race.] [Codes, 1906, §4062; Hemingway's 1917, §7560; 1930, §w6135; Laws 1904, ch. 99.]

SOURCES

Allen, William. 1976. *Starkweather: The Story of a Mass Murderer.* Boston: Houghton Mifflin.

Appier, Janis. 1998. *Policing Women: The Sexual Politics of Law Enforcement and the LAPD.* Philadelphia: Temple University Press.

Bopp, William J. 1977. *O. W. Wilson and the Search for a Police Profession.* Port Washington, N.Y.: Kennikat Press.

Bowers, William J, and Glenn L. Pierce, and John F. McDevitt. 1984. *Legal Homicide: Death as Punishment in America, 1864–1982.* Boston: Northeastern University Press.

Brown, Edmund. 1989. *Public Justice, Private Mercy: A Governor's Education on Death Row.* New York: Weidenfeld and Nicolson, 1989.

Capeci, Dominic J., Jr., and Martha Wilkerson. 1991. *Layered Violence: The Detroit Rioters of 1943.* Jackson: University Press of Mississippi.

Christianson, Scott. 1998. *With Liberty for Some.* Boston: Northeastern University Press.

Cooper, Cynthia L., and Sam Reese Sheppard. 1995. *Mockery and Justice: The True Story of the Sheppard Murder Case.* Boston: Northeastern University Press.

Domanick, Joe. 1994. *To Protect and to Serve: The LAPD's Century of War in the City of Dreams.* New York: Pocket Books.

Fogelson, Robert M. 1977. *Big-City Police.* Cambridge, Mass.: Harvard University Press.

Gilbert, James. 1986. *A Cycle of Outrage: America's Reaction to the Juvenile Delinquent in the 1950s.* New York: Oxford University Press.

Hixson, Walter. 2001. *Murder, Culture, and Injustice: Four Sensational Cases in American History.* Akron, Ohio: University of Akron Press.

Hofstadter, Richard, and Michael Wallace, eds. 1971. *American Violence: A Documentary History.* New York: Vintage Books.

Kennedy, Randall. 1997. *Race, Crime, and the Law.* New York: Pantheon Books.

Kluger, Richard. 1976. *Simple Justice: The History of* Brown v. Board of Education *and Black America's Struggle for Equality.* New York: Alfred A. Knopf.

Knappman, Edward W. 1995. *American Trials of the 20th Century.* Detroit: Visible Ink Press.

Lane, Roger. 1997. *Murder in America: A History.* Columbus: Ohio State University Press.

———. 1999. "Capital Punishment." In *Violence in America,* ed. V. I. Ronald Gottesman, pp. 198–203. New York: Charles Scribner's Sons.

McWhirter, Darien A. 1998. *The Legal 100: A Ranking of the Individuals Who Have Influenced the Law.* Secaucus, N.J.: Citadel Press.

President's Commission on Organized Crime. 1986. *The Impact: Organized Crime Today.* Washington, D.C.: U.S. Government Printing Office.

Richardson, James F. 1974. *Urban Police in the United States.* Port Washington, N.Y.: Kennikat Press.

Sabljak, Mark, and Martin H. Greenberg. 1990. *Most Wanted: A History of the FBI's Most Wanted List.* New York: Bonanza Books.

Schrecker, Ellen. 1994. *The Age of McCarthyism: A Brief History with Documents.* New York: St. Martin's Press.

Sullivan, Larry E. 1990. *The Prison Reform Movement.* Boston: Twayne Publishers.

Theoharis, Athan G. ed. 2000. *The FBI: A Comprehensive Reference Guide.* New York: Checkmark Books.

Whitfield, Stephen J. 1988. *A Death in the Delta: The Story of Emmett Till.* Baltimore: Johns Hopkins Press.

CRITICAL THINKING QUESTIONS

1. Discuss the postwar impact of World War II on the American criminal justice system.

2. What impact did the McCarthy "witch hunts" have on civil liberties?

3. How did the growth of the civil rights movement impact criminal justice institutions and the legal system?

4. How did police reformers William H. Parker and Orlando W. Wilson personify police professionalism? What innovations can be attributed to them? What did their critics think?

5. How did the war years affect the mandate and role of law enforcement? The corrections system?

6. What were some of the explanations for prison violence in this era?

7. What was the impact of the Apalachin Conference on American perceptions of organized crime?

8. Discuss race relations, riots, and the criminal justice system in the war years.

9. What lessons do the Zoot-Suit Riot offer the student of justice in America?

10. Why were the Rosenbergs executed? Should they have been? Why are similar crimes not punished the same way today?

CRIMINAL JUSTICE HISTORY
ON THE INTERNET

The growth of legalized gambling in Las Vegas and the concomitant involvement of organized crime is chronicled at www.crimelibrary.com/gangsters/ bugsy/bugsymain.htm, dmla.clan.lib.nv.us/docs/ thiswas/thiswas50.htm, www.lasvegassun.com/ sunbin/stories/sun/1996/dec/20/505410502.html, and www.ipsn.org/siegel.html. The Kefauver Committee hearings on organized crime and other investigations of organized crime in the 1950s can be found at http://organizedcrime.about.com/ cs/lawenforcement, wwwehit.flinders.edu.au/ screen/SCRN_3001_lectures/Lecture_3/kefauver. htm, www.murderinc.com/feds/Kefauver.html; www.senate.gov/learning/min_6cxyc.html, and www.americanmafia.com/ Feature_Articles_171.html.

The career of William Henry Parker and the history of the Los Angeles Police Department is online at www.lapdonline.org/ general_information/history_of_the_lapd/ gen_history_main.htm. Another informative police history site for this era is at http:// faculty.ncws.edu/toconnor/205/205elect04.htm.

For information on the FBI's Most Wanted program, see www.fbi.gov/mostwanted.htm. For current Most Wanted lists, see www.fbi.gov/ mostwant/fugitive/fpphome.htm.

Excellent sources for the McCarthy-era hearings and "witch hunts" are available at www.historictrials.freeservers.com/mccarthy/ trialinfo.htm and www.c-span.org/special/ mccarthy.asphuac.tripod.com.

Famous murder cases are widely covered on the Internet. For this era, the William Heirens case and identification procedures and sodium pentothal use are covered at www.crimelibrary.com/serial4/ heirens. The mass-murder case of Howard Unruh is examined at www.courierpostonline.com/ 125anniversary/unruh.html.

Relations and violence between the Anglo and Hispanic communities of southern California (with particular focus on the Zoot-Suit Riot) are available at www.ethnomusic.ucla.edu/student/ csharp/zootriot.html, http://dir.yahoo.com/Arts/ Humanities/History/U_S__History/By_Time _Period/20th_Century/ 1940s/Zoot_Suit_Riots, www.losangelesalmanac.com/topics/History/ hi07t.htm, www.gangsorus.com/identifiers/ ideahistory/.html, and www.iso.gmu.edu/~/ smithc/zoot.html.

Sites devoted to *Brown v. Board of Education* and the early civil rights movement are numerous, including www.digisys.net/users/hootie/brown/ brownvboard.org, www.pbs.org/jefferson/enlight/brown.htm, www.nara.gov/education/cc/brown.html, and www.nationalcenter.org/brown.html.

Controversial issues involving the federal government and the criminal justice system are many. For Japanese relocation during World War II, see an actual relocation pamphlet at www.lib.washington.edu/exhibits/harmony/ Documents/wrapam.html; photos and documents related to relocation are available at www.nara.gov/education/cc/relocate. Other links are at www.geocities.com/Athens/ 8420/main.html.

The Rosenberg trial and subsequent execution are covered at www.crimelibrary.com/ rosen/rosenpil.htm, www.studyworld.com/ Rosenberg_Espionage_Case.htm, and www.epals.com/20thcentury/52rosenbergs.html. For poignant letters between Julius and Ethel on the evening before the execution, see www.law .umkc.edu/faculty/projects/ftrials/rosenb/ ROS_STOR.HTM. A time line related to this case can be found at www.law.umkc.edu/faculty/ projects/ftrials/rosenb/ROS_TIME.HTM.

NOTES

1. President's Commission on Organized Crime (1986, p. 58).

2. Although this case included suits from four different states, the Supreme Court's majority opinions in all four became known as the *Brown* decision because that name was first alphabetically among the plaintiffs.

3. McWhirter (1998, p. 69).

4. Fogelson (1977, pp. 195–96).

5. Theoharis (2000, p. 58).

6. Christianson (1998, p. 244).

7. Christianson (1998, p. 244).

8. Sullivan (1990, pp. 58–59).

9. Christianson (1998, p. 250).

10. Sullivan (1990, p. 48).

11. Quoted in Knappman (1995, p. 250).

12. For more on this case, see Cooper and Sheppard (1995) and Hixson (2001).

13. Bowers (1984, pp. 25–26).

14. Bowers (1984, p. 18).

15. Brown (1989, p. 52).

16. Gilbert (1986, p. 5).

17. Lane (1999, p. 201).

18. Lane (1997, p. 255).

19. Capeci (1991).

20. Quoted in Kennedy (1997, p. 62).

21. For a comprehensive examination of this case, see Whitfield (1988).

22. Dominick (1994, p. 137).

23. Hofstadter and Wallace (1971, p. 336).

24. Gilbert (1986, p. 32).

25. Lee was shot to death while driving his car, although the coroner reported that he died from a heart attack and that the buckshot that riddled his face was probably just "dental fillings."

26. Bowers (1984 p. 29).

12

NATIONALIZATION OF CRIMINAL JUSTICE (1960–1977)

TIME LINE

1960	National murder rate stands at 4.7 per 100,000	1967	Publication of *The Challenge of Crime in a Free Society*
1961	*Mapp v. Ohio*	1967	*In re Gault*
1963	President John F. Kennedy assassinated	1967	Riots take place in 127 cities
		1967	*Katz v. United States*
1963	*Gideon v. Wainwright*	1968	*Terry v. Ohio*
1964	*Escobedo v. Illinois*	1968	Congress passes Omnibus Crime Control and Safe Streets Act
1965	Los Angeles Watts riots leave thirty-four dead		
		1968	LEAA established
1966	*Miranda v. Arizona*	1968	Kerner Commission on civil disorder issues report
1966	Richard Speck murders eight nurses in Chicago		
		1968	Assassination of Martin Luther King Jr. in Memphis, Tennessee, is followed by rioting in 168 cities
1966	Charles Whitman's mass murder at the University of Texas		

1968	Robert F. Kennedy assassinated	**1972**	Death of J. Edgar Hoover
1970	Organized Crime Control Act	**1972**	Watergate break-in
1970	National Guardsmen kill four Kent State University students	**1973**	*Roe et al. v. Wade* decision makes abortion widely available
1970	Police shooting at Jackson State College	**1976**	*Gregg v. Georgia* upholds new death penalty statutes
1971	Attica Prison riot	**1977**	Execution of Gary Gilmore by firing squad
1972	*Furman v. Georgia* leads to commutation of all death row prisoners' sentences		

In 1960, the national murder rate stood at 4.7 per 100,000, the lowest for any census year. As America made the transition from the 1950s to the decade of President John F. Kennedy's "New Frontier," the crime rate was so low that sociologist Daniel Bell commented that "there is probably less crime today in the United States than existed a hundred, or fifty, or even twenty-five years ago."[1] He had reasons for such optimism, as America enjoyed a decrease in murder from 6.9 per 100,000 in 1946 to 4.5 per 100,000 by 1962.[2] Other crimes fell as well.

But the assassination of John F. Kennedy in 1963 and America's participation in the Vietnam War would touch off a decade of national turmoil that did not diminish until well into the 1970s. One of the most tumultuous eras in American history, the 1960s and 1970s were marked by civil rights and war protests, boycotts and sit-ins, race rioting, and domestic terrorism. Criminal justice historian Samuel Walker has described this period as "the most turbulent in all of American criminal justice history."[3]

The criminal justice system was challenged on many fronts in this era. In an attempt to understand rising crime rates and to create strategies for suppressing crime in the 1960s, the federal government launched a variety of official inquiries. Among the most significant was the 1965 President's Commission on Law Enforcement and Administration of Justice (LEAA), which concluded that police officers had become increasingly isolated from the communities they served. Its report, *The Challenge of Crime in a Free Society,* published in 1967, found that city officials had given police chiefs too much latitude in running their departments. In an era of rising concerns over the role of police in contemporary society, the extensive report suggested more than 200 recommendations concerning criminal justice reform, including raising educational requirements and improving training programs for police officers.[4] A number of other crime commissions were created to study a criminal justice system in crisis during the 1970s, most focusing on the changing nature of policing. Many of these investigations were not limited to policing, focusing attention on organized crime, corrections, drug abuse, and juvenile delinquency.

Politicians saw the potential of using the civil disorder to their advantage. Senator Barry Goldwater in 1964 and presidential candidate Richard Nixon in 1968 began to link street crime to the civil disobedience that accompanied the civil rights movement. In the process, law and order emerged as an important campaign issue that found an audience with conservative and mostly white Americans.

THE LAWGIVERS

The social unrest of the 1960s prodded the federal government to establish a number of inquiries into the causes and prevention of crime. In 1968, Congress passed the Omnibus Crime Control and Safe Streets Act, creating the Law Enforcement Assistance Administration (LEAA) as its centerpiece in a "national war on crime." By design, the LEAA was supposed to support state and local crime control efforts by carrying out a broad program of aid to state and local authorities for crime control, targeting street crime, riots, and organized crime. Starting with $60 million in seed money in 1968, by 1982 the agency had spent more than $7 billion on updating law enforcement departments around the country.[5]

The Omnibus Crime Control and Safe Streets Act impacted the criminal justice system in a number of ways. Building on *Katz v. United States,* the 1967 Supreme Court decision that limited the use of electronic eavesdropping because of concerns about invasions of privacy, the Omnibus Crime Control Act in 1968 prohibited lawful interceptions except by warrant or with consent. Other features of the crime control legislation focused on the regulation of firearms sales, the establishment of the Bureau of Justice Statistics, and the awarding of grants for the construction and renovation of courtrooms, correctional facilities, treatment centers, and other criminal justice related structures.

In 1967, the Supreme Court applied the Fourth Amendment to police wiretapping, maintaining that evidence collected by listening to private conversations by a defendant using a public telephone booth violated the constitutional protection of personal privacy. The following year under the Omnibus Crime Control and Safe Streets Act, Congress authorized certain forms of electronic surveillance as long as officers had obtained a lawful court order first. Over the ensuing years, a number of states implemented electronic eavesdropping laws inspired by the federal act.

No region in the nation's criminal justice system was transformed more than the southern states. The onset of the civil rights movement of the 1950s and 1960s has sometimes been referred to as a "Second Reconstruction," particularly in the South.[6] Beginning with the civil rights laws of 1957 and subsequent legislation, such as the Voting Rights Act of 1964, millions of black voters regained the franchise after several generations of racial confrontation over the ballot box.

The South proved one of the most challenging fronts for law enforcement during this period as white segregationists brutally attacked nonviolent civil rights protesters, while police officers targeted peaceful black marchers with high-pressure hoses and attack dogs. The early 1960s witnessed a number of well-publicized murder cases in the South, including the murder of Medgar Evers, organizer of the National Association for the Advancement of Colored People (NAACP) and the bombing deaths of four young black girls in a Birmingham, Alabama, church.

In order to win southern congressional support, President John F. Kennedy did little to placate civil rights activists in his first two years in office. Influenced by daily television coverage demonstrating the repugnant brutality in the South and partly at the behest of his brother, Attorney General Robert F. Kennedy, in 1963 Kennedy changed his position on civil rights. During the Kennedy administration of the early 1960s, Attorney General Kennedy pursued an aggressive agenda of crime control, shifting the federal government's attention to civil rights and suppressing organized crime. Publicly proclaiming that the time for "the nation to fulfill its promise" had arrived, President Kennedy did not live to fulfill his pledge, gunned down by an assassin's bullet in November 1963.

Lyndon Johnson's ascendance to the presidency in 1963 coincided with some of the most significant civil rights legislation since the post–Civil War period. Events in Birmingham, Alabama, roused the national conscience and stimulated a formerly reluctant administration into becoming a stalwart supporter of potent civil rights legislation. Intended to protect the right to equality in public accommodations, the right to have federal funds spent in a nondiscriminatory manner, and the right to racial and sexual equality in employment, the passage of the 1964 Civil Rights Act enacted the strongest civil rights measures since the Reconstruction era. Considered the most far-reaching statute enacted by Congress, the Voting Rights Act of 1965 provided for the replacement of state election machinery by federal law and ad hoc federal officials when it was found necessary to eliminate a pattern of Fifteenth Amendment violations of voting rights.

For many other Americans, the 1964 civil rights legislation had little if any impact. Generations of government neglect had left the country's Native American population demoralized with attendant high rates of disease and infant mortality rates, unemployment, illiteracy, malnutrition, and alcoholism. In response to these conditions and the continued plight of the first Americans, Native American activists Dennis Banks and Clyde Bellecourt organized the American Indian Movement (AIM) in 1968. Although they championed earlier reform efforts, their goals and tactics were guided by a more militant approach than past efforts. Borrowing a page from the black militants of the era, they used guns in their takeovers and effected a sinister image to threaten those who opposed them. AIM members used these new tactics to occupy the abandoned prison island of Alcatraz in 1969 and take over the main offices of the Indian Bureau in Washington, D.C., in 1972. Their most significant protest took place at Wounded Knee, South Dakota, in 1973, where several hundred Sioux had been massacred by the army in 1890. During the subsequent seventy-one-day protest, AIM leaders held firm to their demands

for the restoration of treaty lands. Several gunfights ensued between Indians and FBI agents and National Guardsmen, leaving two dead. While 300 protesters were eventually arrested, most were acquitted on legal technicalities. Over the rest of the 1970s, Native Americans across the nation launched lawsuits to recover their treaty lands and rights.

The Supreme Court

In the 1960s, the Supreme Court played a crucial role in promoting a climate of political liberalism during the Kennedy and Johnson presidencies. Beginning with the *Brown v. Board of Education* decision in 1954, the Court demonstrated remarkable courage in erasing the distinctions that had supported a racially segregated society and, through a series of decisions, diminished Jim Crowism. While discrimination and poverty persisted in black communities, so too did the goals for equality set forth by the chief justices. In their crusade for equal rights, African Americans became increasingly politicized during the 1960s.

Sweeping decisions on the electoral process, political representation, school desegregation, public support of religion, obscenity, and free speech were accompanied by widespread debate and vitriol. But according to legal historian David Bodenhamer, "No judicial reforms were as bold or ignited more protest as the landmark cases involving criminal process."[7] Diverging from preceding courts, the Warren Court applied the federal procedural guarantees of the Bill of Rights to the application of state criminal justice. In the process of "nationalizing" the Bill of Rights, the Supreme Court reshaped the nature of federalism by applying the same standards to both state and federal criminal proceedings. The high court rejected the application of the entire Bill of Rights, rather emphasizing those amendments that apply to "due process" as defined by the Fourteenth Amendment.

The 1960s and 1970s provided a stage for some of the Supreme Court's most important decisions, leading some commentators to suggest that the Court "made more changes in criminal procedure" during this period "than had been made by the Court in the previous 175 years of its existence."[8]

In 1961, the Supreme Court greatly increased the ability of criminal defendants to defend themselves in the landmark case of *Mapp v. Ohio* by ruling that evidence secured by the police through unreasonable searches must be excluded from trial. This decision was shortly followed by the *Escobedo v. Illinois* (1964) and the *Miranda v. Arizona* (1966) decisions by the Warren Court, both of which are credited with significantly changing the way law enforcement officers carried out interrogations and at the same time guaranteed the rights of the accused.

In the *Mapp* case, Cleveland police officers arrived at the home of Ms. Dollree Mapp to search for a suspect in a recent bombing case. After forcing their way into the residence, the officers searched the house without a warrant and found obscene material unrelated to their initial search. Mapp was subsequently convicted for possessing the obscene materials. Building an appeal based on the 1914 *Weeks* decision, which held that the Fourteenth Amendment barred the use of evidence secured through an illegal search and seizure, Mapp's conviction was overturned by the Supreme Court in 1961. In the process, the exclusionary rule was extended to the states.

Two years before Miranda, Daniel Escobedo was arrested for killing his brother-in-law in Chicago. After two rounds of intense police interrogation, Escobedo confessed and was then convicted in court. According to the narrow five-to-four Supreme Court decision, without an attorney present during his police interrogation, it was ruled that his confession had been illegally obtained under the Sixth Amendment, which guarantees the right to legal counsel during police questioning.

The landmark *Miranda* decision stemmed from the arrest of Ernest Miranda (1940–1976) for rape and kidnapping on March 12, 1963. Miranda would claim that police officers coerced him into confessing to the crime during a grueling two-hour interrogation and was not allowed to consult an attorney. Despite objections from his attorney, who protested that Miranda had not been informed of his rights or given legal counsel to apprise him of his protection against self-incrimination under the Fifth Amendment, Miranda was convicted.

In 1966, *Miranda v. Arizona* reached the Supreme Court, where Miranda's conviction was overturned. The landmark case substantially altered American police practices in the interviewing of suspects. According to the Warren Court's majority decision, all individuals must be notified of their constitutional rights, including the right to have an attorney present during questioning. Lauded by civil libertarians, the "Miranda decision" has been roundly criticized by law enforcement and was later modified under the more police-friendly Warren Burger Court in the 1980s. Miranda was retried and reconvicted. Released from prison in 1972, Miranda was stabbed to death in a barroom fight four years later. Not lost on most historians was the irony of Miranda's killer being read his Miranda rights in Spanish while Ernest Miranda was succumbing to his stab wounds.

These Supreme Court rulings have come under fire in recent years, with peace officers arguing that the decisions have placed unreasonable burdens on them. What is often forgotten is that the decisions regarding Miranda, Escobedo, and Mapp had little effect on their ultimate fates since all were eventually sentenced to prison on various other charges. Although the fundamental rights guaranteed by these decisions will never be taken away from defendants, many legal experts believe that the decisions will be modified. One major Supreme Court decision from the late 1960s did just that. In the 1968 *Terry v. Ohio* ruling, the Court validated an officer's right to stop, question, and even search a person who acted suspiciously as long as the officer had reasonable grounds for doing so. During a decade that was notable for placing restrictions on police powers, *Terry v. Ohio* clearly augured a new climate that was more favorable for enhancing them.

Following on the heels of the 1963 Supreme Court decision *Gideon v. Wainwright* (see the "Notable Trials" section later in this chapter), in 1967 the Court extended the *Gideon* ruling to juvenile delinquency proceedings in *In re Gault*, giving children many of procedural rights guaranteed to adults. Five years later, the decision was extended to adult misdemeanor cases if imprisonment was sanctioned in the *Argersinger v. Hamlin* decision.

The due process clause contained in the Fourteenth Amendment guaranteed certain protections to "persons." But until 1967, the word *person* did not apply to the nation's children, which made up one-third of the population. In that year, the Supreme Court ruled for the first time that many of the procedural protections extended to adults charged with crimes should also apply to juveniles.

The events leading up to this landmark decision began in June 1964, when fifteen-year-old Gerald F. Gault and a friend were picked up by the Gila County, Arizona, sheriff. According to a neighbor, the boys had made an obscene phone call to her. The boys were then picked up and held for several days at a detention center. Gault was already on probation for petty theft when he was picked up, and the juvenile officer had enough reason to hold him.

Gault appeared before the juvenile court judge and, when questioned, admitted to placing the obscene call. The judge then gave Gault's family the impression that there would be little repercussions despite his probationary status. However, they were soon asked to appear before the judge for a second hearing. Following the usual juvenile court practices of the time, no records of the previous hearing had been kept. Disagreement over what Gerald admitted in the first hearing suddenly became important after finding out that a report had been made charging him for having made lewd and obscene remarks in the presence of a woman. Following the usual protocol, no copy of this report had been made available to the youth's family, nor were they allowed to confront their accusers. After another period of questioning and some discussion over what took place during the first hearing, the judge sentenced the teenager to the state reform school until he reached the age of twenty-one.

If Gault had been an adult and was convicted of similar charges, he would have been fined between $5 and $50 or faced a prison term of not more than two months. As a youth, he faced six years in prison. At the time, the Gaults had little recourse since the state did not provide for appealing juvenile cases to a higher court.

While Gerald was in the state reformatory, his parents filed a writ of habeas corpus (a petition for a hearing on the legality of confinement). The writ asserted that Gerald was being confined illegally. This was the only way they could appeal the case. The family argued for the writ on the grounds that he had been denied due process of law, claiming the son had been denied his basic constitutional rights during the juvenile court proceedings. After being denied by the state supreme court, the ruling was appealed to the U.S. Supreme Court, making it only the second time in American history that the court reviewed a juvenile proceeding. After listening to arguments from both sides, almost three years after the initial obscene phone call, the Court ruled that due process of law as guaranteed by the Fourteenth Amendment applies to juvenile proceedings when a child is charged with being delinquent. As a result, the juvenile court hearings became more equitable by granting standards of due process to juveniles.

When Richard M. Nixon was elected president in 1968, he promised to alter the balance between the rights of criminal defendants and society's rights, choosing Warren Burger (1907–1995), a moderate conservative, to replace the retiring Earl Warren as chief justice. Considered a "law and order" judge with little approval for the recent due process revolution, the Burger Court disappointed many conservatives by continuing to support laws governing the rights of defendants while attempting to limit the role of the Court.

Roe v. Wade (1973), which gave women a qualified constitutional right to abortion, was one of the most controversial Supreme Court decisions of the twentieth century, setting off a legal debate that continues to resonate today. This highly charged case reached the high court in two cases brought by women under pseudonyms.

In *Roe v. Wade,* a Texas woman challenged the state law that forbade abortion except to save a pregnant woman's life. Georgia's *Doe v. Bolton* case confronted provisions in the state's law that dictated that abortions could be performed only in an accredited hospital and required several other points of procedure, including an examination of the woman by two other doctors besides her own physician. By a vote of seven to two, the Supreme Court upheld the challenges, citing an individual's constitutional right to privacy. However, the right to abortion was limited to include government regulation "at some point in the pregnancy" to ensure the state's "important interests in safeguarding health, maintaining medical standards, and protecting potential life." This landmark court case was the first to confirm that a woman, rather than her physician, might be the party harmed by a state's criminalization of abortion.

LAW ENFORCEMENT

The turbulence and social conflict that shook America in the 1960s also had important consequences for law enforcement. Police organizations were tested on a number of fronts. The 1960s saw a convergence of a variety of large-scale protests involving civil rights and antiwar demonstrators. Meanwhile, a revolution in U.S. civil rights law championed by the Supreme Court placed limitations on police work. Supreme Court decisions challenged long-standing police customs and practices, including search and seizure, brutality, and in-custody investigations.

In 1964, the Philadelphia Police Department established its 100-member Special Weapons and Tactics Squad, considered by many to be the precursor to modern SWAT teams. Designed to respond quickly and decisively to bank robberies in progress, it was soon also used to resolve other types of incidents involving heavily armed criminals. Its media popularity and successful field implementation led other police forces to develop similar units, most notably the Los Angeles Police Department (LAPD). During the late 1960s, the LAPD created Special Weapons and Tactics (SWAT) teams in response to new trends in criminal violence that included skyjackings, shoot-outs, and hostage taking. The 1974 gun battle with the Symbionese Liberation Army catapulted SWAT teams to national prominence.

In 1967, the LEAA reported that "the quality of police service will not significantly improve until higher educational requirements are established for its personnel."[9] August Vollmer had created a police school at Berkeley as early as 1916, and by the 1960s criminal justice programs flourished. In 1968, a survey by the International Association of Chiefs of Police found that sixty-four colleges and universities offered classes in criminal justice education. Many of the programs had been established in response to the large numbers of Korean War veterans taking advantage of the GI Bill and returning to school to follow programs related to criminal justice in the 1950s and 1960s. Within thirty years, more than 1,000 programs were offered throughout the country.

Beginning in the early 1970s, research in several cities, including Kansas City, demonstrated that increasing neither the number of police officers on random motor patrol nor the speed of their response had little effect on crime reduction. The 1973 Kansas City study was one of the best-known and most controversial studies of police patrol efficiency in this era.

The Kansas City Preventive Patrol Experiment

Since the inception of the London "bobbies" and New York City "cops" in the first half of the nineteenth century, routine police patrol has been considered a hallmark of modern preventive policing. The notion that crime could be prevented or at least suppressed by a highly regular and visible police presence has been a long held belief. Beginning in 1972, a one-year study was conducted in Kansas City to test this conviction. The release of *The Kansas City Preventive Patrol Experiment* report in 1974 found that police patrols, whether stepped up or diminished, had no significant impact on crime, police response time, public fears of crime, or their attitudes toward police in the area. Led by George L. Kelling and supported by the Police Foundation, Kelling described this experiment as "unique in that never before had there been such an attempt to determine through such extensive scientific evaluation the value of visible police patrol."[10] With traditional methods of policing under scrutiny, new concerns about the role of police in American society sent police experts back to the drawing board for answers.

Policewomen

The 2,610 total policewomen in the United States in 1950 represented just 1 percent of the national total. But as the women's movement gathered steam in the 1960s, these numbers multiplied. But it took until 1968 for women to be assigned to official police cars, when two women on the Indianapolis Police Department achieved this level of success. The following year, the Washington, D.C., police chief tore down another barrier when he eliminated separate police force applications for men and women.

Although the first documented employment of women with police powers can be traced back to 1910, women made few inroads as crime fighters in the male-dominated profession until the 1960s and 1970s. According to one of the foremost authorities on policewomen, women made significant progress in this direction in the 1950s but did not make the transition "from social workers to crimefighters" until 1968.[11]

The federal government led the way in removing impediments blocking women from the police ranks. The creation of the Equal Opportunity Commission in 1968 provided the impetus for bringing women into policing in more meaningful roles. Another barrier fell

when the federal government amended the 1964 Civil Rights Act in 1972. The passage of the Equal Employment Opportunity Act prohibited discrimination by public and private employers.

A number of court decisions removed many administrative and social barriers, further opening law enforcement to women. But the reality was that while women were joining the "thin blue line" of policing, they were being utilized in a secondary capacity, consigned to gender-based roles from another era. In Catherine Milton's 1972 report on policewomen, she found that women were being used mainly in clerical and juvenile functions, much like their counterparts a half century earlier. Milton also found that women were required to conform to higher-educational standards, regulated by hiring quotas based on gender, and were allowed to compete for positions only in the women's bureau.[12] By 1974, women made up only 2 percent of the country's 166,000 police officers, with few assigned to street duty.[13]

The social ferment of the 1960s led many women to question the limitations imposed on them based on gender. However, in 1968, when Indianapolis policewomen Betty Blankenship and Elizabeth Coffal "donned uniforms, strapped gunbelts to their waists, and got into their marked police car," they left "behind their history as police social workers to assume the role of crimefighters along with their male colleagues."[14]

While women had indeed made the transition to crimefighters, by the 1970s they still represented only a small percentage of the total number of police officers nationwide. According to one authority, female police officers only represented 2.1 percent of sworn officers in 1975. This number grew to 9,000, or 3 percent of all law enforcement personnel, three years later, and by 1980 the number of women in policing had doubled since 1960.[15] However, a trend developed in which larger cities lagged behind smaller cities in the hiring of policewomen.

Federal Law Enforcement

Few critics had dared to publicly challenge J. Edgar Hoover and the FBI prior to the 1960s. But the new era witnessed an increasing chorus of Hoover critics, including journalists, college professors, congressmen, and even ex–FBI agents. In 1969, the *New York Times Magazine* published what became a much-quoted article by the respected journalist Tom Wicker titled "What Have They Done since They Shot Dillinger?"

Disapproval of Hoover and the FBI had been building since the 1950s, when the FBI supplied Senator Joseph McCarthy and the House Committee on Un-American Activities with information on "suspected" communists. With the election of John F. Kennedy as president and the ascendance of his brother Robert to attorney general, it seemed that Hoover's days were numbered as FBI director. It has been speculated that despite rancor between Hoover and the Kennedys, he kept his job because he had secret files on the two brothers. Waving the mandatory retirement age of seventy, Hoover was reappointed by Presidents Lyndon Johnson and Richard Nixon.

In the Johnson years, Hoover expanded his COINTELPRO program from investigating the Communist Party to the Ku Klux Klan, antiwar radical groups, and black activists. Hoover reserved his harshest words for Martin Luther King Jr., whom he once referred to as a "tom cat with obsessive degenerate urges."[16]

Although the popular media has tended to promote FBI agents as heroes in the civil rights movement, it was not until Attorney General Robert Kennedy pressured FBI director Hoover to send a large contingent of agents to investigate the killing of three civil rights workers in 1964 that the FBI became actively involved in the murder case.

As testament to the concern that Hoover had for the civil rights movement and the return of the Ku Klux Klan, the FBI did not even have a field office in Mississippi. The thirteen FBI agents who were responsible for federal law enforcement in the state either worked out of their homes or were housed in federal buildings. Most of their attention was focused on tracking down stolen cars and fugitives. Despite a mounting terror campaign that included the bombing of twenty black churches in Mississippi, at the time of the disappearance of the three civil rights workers, FBI agents claimed they had no authority to act. It was not until Attorney General Kennedy ordered the case to be treated under the Lindbergh kidnapping law that the FBI was called into the case, which became known as MIBURN, or "Mississippi Burning."

An informant's tip would lead agents to the missing workers' burned-out car and eventually their bodies, buried in an earthen dam. However, murder was not a federal crime, so charges against the suspected nineteen Klan perpetrators would have to come from the state. In order to arrest and convict the Klansmen, the FBI turned to federal legislation from the late 1860s. By falling back on Reconstruction-era statutes, the Justice Department brought charges that the Klan members had participated in a conspiracy to deprive the three civil rights workers of their constitutional right to register voters in the state of Mississippi. After several false starts, seven of the nineteen defendants were convicted by an all-white jury, the first time in the state's history that an all-white jury convicted white officials or Klan members for crimes against civil rights workers and African Americans. However, the maximum sentence received by the seven was for ten years. None would serve a full term in prison, and by the mid-1970s most had returned to their homes.

While Martin Luther King Jr. and other civil rights leaders held to a path of peaceful nonviolence, others, such as the Black Panthers and black Muslims, stressed black separatism and militancy. Both Presidents Johnson and Nixon were outraged by the activities and success of the Black Panthers. Johnson was convinced they had a subversive agenda and directed the FBI to begin collecting information on them. Under Nixon, the FBI used surveillance to infiltrate and suppress the organization. In a short span of time, twenty-eight Panthers were killed and many imprisoned on debatable charges.

Having receded into the background as federal peace officers, the social unrest and protests of the 1960s led to a resurgence of the U.S. marshals. Beginning in the early days of the civil rights movement in the mid-1950s, the Justice Department recommended the creation of the Executive Office for U.S. Marshals to supervise the marshals in their new duties. In 1962, U.S. marshals protected black student James Meredith from violent protesters as he broke the color barrier at the all-white University of Mississippi. U.S. marshals were called on during the 1960s to protect government buildings from antiwar demonstrators and to assist peace officers whenever federal laws were violated. In 1969, the Executive Office for U.S. Marshals made the transition into the U.S. Marshals Service. For the first time, the marshals, America's oldest federal law enforcement organization, had a headquarters and a bureaucracy directly under the executive branch of government.

Under President Nixon, their duties were expanded to include suppressing air piracy and civil disturbances, prisoner transportation, and court, personal, and witness security. Early in 1971, following the passage of the Organized Crime Control Act (1970), marshals became responsible for protecting witnesses in the Witness Protection Program.

In 1967, President Johnson took drug enforcement and regulation out of the hands of the Treasury and the Food and Drug Administration, respectively, and created a new agency under the Justice Department called the Bureau of Narcotics and Dangerous Drugs. Coinciding with this reorganization, Johnson asked Congress to "create a "super agency" to strengthen ties between the federal government and local police."[17] In response, Congress authorized the Law Enforcement Assistance Administration, which over the next decade would dispense billions of dollars to improve policing through specialized education and training programs and to

recast the shape of traditional policing with the adoption of new weaponry and communications technology. According to Christian Parenti, "Johnson laid the groundwork for the tremendous combination of police power, surveillance, and incarceration that today so dominates domestic politics."[18]

A growing drug problem led to the creation of the Drug Enforcement Administration (DEA) in 1973, resulting in the merger of several agencies. A branch of the Department of Justice, the DEA was given the single mission of enforcing federal drug statutes and investigating major drug traffickers. While illegal drugs were nothing new to American culture, the explosion of the counterculture in the 1960s led to a vociferous antidrug lobby. The growing drug culture had several dimensions that made it increasingly incomprehensible to the non-drug-taking public in the 1960s and 1970s. The war on drugs continues to be one of the most disappointing criminal justice efforts as America enters the second millennium.

Corruption

Long before a police scandal in the New York Police Department became public, police officer Frank Serpico (b. 1936) made numerous allegations of corruption in the department, all of which were ignored. Serpico felt he had no choice but to go to the press with his story, and in 1970 the *New York Times* printed an exposé of corruption in the department. An independent citizens' commission was subsequently established to investigate the charges. Named after its chairman, Wall Street lawyer Whitman Knapp, the Knapp Commission investigated New York City police corruption for two years before releasing its conclusions in 1973.

According to the Knapp Report, more than half the city's 29,600 police officers had participated in some type of corrupt activity. The Knapp Commission uncovered two types of corrupt officers. "Meat-eaters" were the relatively small contingent of officers who spent their working hours looking for opportunities that they could exploit for financial gain, including gambling and illegal drugs. "Grass-eaters," on the other hand, were the majority of patrolmen who did not necessarily take payoffs but would occasionally accept gratuities from various entrepreneurs. The Knapp investigation led to mass resignations within the department, including that of the city's police commissioner. Serpico, however, had violated the so-called blue curtain of silence, and finding life in the department untenable, he retired in 1974.

CORRECTIONS

During the early 1960s, correctional facilities began to experiment with less formal arrangements. New prison architectural designs were created to accommodate treatment programs while maintaining security. In March 1963, Alcatraz closed after nearly thirty years as America's foremost maximum "prison of last resort." After several highly publicized but unsuccessful escape attempts, the Bureau of Prisons was convinced that the structure had outlived its usefulness. Increasingly seen as unsafe and too expensive to run, its proximity to San Francisco led to its demise. Officials soon sought a replacement somewhere in America's heartland, settling on the Illinois town of Marion.

Although America's prison population enjoyed a short decline in the early 1960s, by 1968 it was on the increase once more, and by 1971 new commitments had risen 35 percent over 1968. The following year saw a trend develop toward longer sentences that would contribute to swelling prison populations. By the end of 1976, the prison population was 42 percent higher than the 1968 low. With 196,000 prisoners by 1970, rising crime rates and longer sentences led to widespread overcrowding. Despite new prison construction, the number of inmates continued to outstrip the number of cells into the 1980s.

The burgeoning civil rights movement also impacted the history of the prison system as inmates familiarized themselves with their consti-

tutional rights. Among the most popular mainstays of the so-called prison lawyer were the writ of habeas corpus and the Civil Rights Act.[19] By means of the writ of habeas corpus, inmates can challenge the legality of their confinement. Other prisoners fastened their hopes to the Reconstruction-era Civil Rights Act, which protected freed slaves from having their new civil rights violated. In any case, some prisoners began to accept litigation as a better alternative to violence.

In 1961, the Supreme Court (inspired by the Civil Rights Act of 1871) ruled in *Monroe v. Pape* that blacks could avoid biased local courts and sue directly in federal court on constitutional matters. This decision laid the foundation for the Court to allow prison inmates to sue state officials in federal court for the first time in *Cooper v. Pate* (1964).[20] These edicts laid the groundwork for the avalanche of litigation that transformed prison conditions in the 1970s.

Until the 1960s, U.S. courts allowed prisons to operate unimpeded by the courts. This "hands-off" policy was dramatically altered, with virtually every aspect of correctional operation coming under court scrutiny by the 1970s as inmates played a vital role in prompting the courts to define the scope of their constitutional rights. Housing, health care, recreation, mail privileges, classification, and diet were targeted by the increasingly litigious prisoners, leading the federal courts to declare nine state correctional systems to be unconstitutional in the 1970s.

During the 1960s, prisoners in several states filed complaints with the federal court, complaining that they were being brutally disciplined. In many prisons, particularly in the South, a "trusty" system had been institutionalized to make up for the shortage of prison guards and to save money. So-called trusties were empowered to help control the other inmates with an iron fist, leading to a number of lawsuits. In one of its more high-profile decisions, the federal district court ruled in *Holt v. Sarver* (1970) that the practices at the Arkansas prison farms at Cummins and Tucker were so atrocious that the entire correctional system was censured. In its condemnation of the

Arkansas prison system, the federal court noted that its management was "so bad as to be shocking to the conscience of reasonably civilized people."[21] This case led to the hiring of a more professional corrections staff and the dismantlement of the trusty system.

One of the earliest forays by the Supreme Court into correctional reform in the 1960s took place in 1962, when it used the Eighth Amendment for the first time to invalidate a state law. By a vote of six to two, the Court held in *Robinson v. California* that it was cruel and unusual punishment to sentence individuals whose only crime was habitual drug use to prison terms.

The prisoner rights movement applied standards of due process to a number of correctional issues that were ultimately arbitrated by the Supreme Court, including prisoner disciplinary hearings. In *Wolff v. McDonnell,* the Court ruled in 1974 that due process rights did apply to inmates since "the state did give some valued things to prisoners that could later be taken away."[22] Due process in front of a prison disciplinary board gave prisoners a chance to hear the charges against them twenty-four hours before the hearing and permitted inmates to call witnesses and present evidence that favored their defense. In addition, substitute counsel would be provided for illiterate prisoners.

Although a series of court decisions ruled the racial segregation of prisoners unconstitutional in the 1960s, as late as the 1970s the practice continued in many prisons, especially in the South, leading one convict to observe, "I thought segregation was dead, but there it was, as vivid as an Alabama lunch counter in the 1950s."[23] Although this policy has been outlawed, research indicates inmates often self-segregate along racial and ethnic lines by choice. The rise and expansion of prison gangs has perpetuated the de jure (or officially sanctioned) segregation that characterized prisons until the 1960s.[24]

One of the consequences of the war on crime was the growing racial disparity among prison populations beginning in the 1960s. In 1960, close to 40 percent of prison inmates were classified as "nonwhite." Less than fifteen years later, this figure grew to 49 percent. Nationwide black incarceration rose from 46.3 to 65.1 per 100,000 between 1973 and 1979, a figure more than nine times higher than for whites.[25]

Mandatory Sentencing

Further exacerbating the prison-overcrowding dilemma was the introduction of mandatory sentencing laws beginning in 1973, when New York State experimented with the Second Felony Offender Law, which required those convicted of selling illegal drugs to serve a minimum prison sentence. Subsequent studies indicated that the law had no impact on recidivism, but this did little to stop the clamor for sentencing reform as conservatives continued to push for stricter punishments.

In 1974, Florida followed New York's example, stipulating three-year minimum prison sentences without parole for any felony involving a firearm. By the mid-1970s, other states implemented mandatory sentencing guidelines, all resulting in prison overcrowding. The trend toward mandatory sentencing filled American prisons beyond capacity by the end of the 1990s, facilitating a prison-building boom and a growing opposition to this type of fixed sentence.

Prison Construction

In 1972, the LEAA required a survey of American prisons in order to decide how to utilize funds granted by the federal government for the construction of state and local prisons. After visiting more than 100 facilities in twenty-six states, a team that included an architect and a psychologist reported they were shocked by the oppressive regimes they found at various prisons, reformatories, jails, and correctional institutions.[26] Instead of recommending any precise reforms, they advocated halting any new prison construction until the existing institutions were better managed. The moratorium on prison construction eventually contributed to more prison over-crowding as the decade wore on.

At the beginning of the 1970s, of the 113 maximum-security state prisons in operation, only six had been built in the previous century. One of the solutions to the traditional over-crowding of prisons in the 1970s was to start building more prisons, a trend that continues into the twenty-first century. Between 1971 and 1978, America's prison population swelled by 64 per-cent, in part because of the return to a punish-ment model of corrections that saw prisoners serving longer periods of time behind bars.

Prison Riots

Reflecting the increasingly tense social relations in the free world, America's prisons seethed with racial tension beginning in the 1960s. Racial segre-gation and the continuing inequities of the prison system may "explain why more than 90 percent of all recorded prison riots, strikes, protests, rebellions, and other disturbances in the United States have occurred since 1960."[27]

The 1960s gave birth to a number of prison gangs as blacks, Chicanos, and white supremacists fought for dominance behind prison walls. New York's Attica uprising in 1971 saw the worst fears of prison administrators come to reality when, on September 9, more than half the prison inmate population of 2,600 went on the ram-page, taking guards hostage, destroying property, and preparing for a showdown with the rapidly assembling force of correctional and police offi-cers and National Guardsmen gathering outside the prison walls.

Following on the heels of the assassinations, urban riots, and war coverage that rocked the 1960s, televised images of the Attica uprising were seared into the national consciousness. Sev-eral days of negotiations followed the outbreak, involving a stellar cast of characters, including radical attorney William Kunstler, Black Panther Bobby Seale, and *New York Times* writer Tom Wicker. But fearing for the safety of the numer-ous hostages, New York Governor Nelson

Rockefeller, who had refused to come to the prison in person to negotiate, ordered prison officials to retake the prison.

On September 13, eight blindfolded hostages were brought to Attica's catwalks, each with an inmate holding a knife to his throat. Rejecting an ultimatum to surrender, the assault team fired tear gas and bullets into the hundreds of inmates huddled in the makeshift village in the yard. In the ensuing confusion, thirty-nine individuals were killed, including ten hostages. Initially, offi-cials claimed that the hostages had their throats slashed by the inmates. However, a medical examiner's report the next day announced that all had been killed by gunfire. According to the New York State Commission Report on Attica, "With the exception of the Indians massacred in the late nineteenth century, the State Police assault which ended the four-day prison uprising was the bloodiest one-day encounter between Americans since the Civil War."[28]

Almost 100 riots convulsed prisons between 1969 and 1970, convincing even the most die-hard progressive reformers that the correctional system was a failure. Confidence in most rehabil-itation programs was waning and support for the treatment model of corrections rapidly eroding. Yet the 1970s and 1980s would be marked by even worse prison revolts and violence.

CRIME AND PUNISHMENT

In a poll taken in February 1968, Americans rated crime as the nation's leading domestic problem for the first time since scientific public opinion polls were introduced in the 1930s.[29] The 1968 killings of Robert F. Kennedy and Martin Luther King Jr. exacerbated these crime concerns. By 1970, murder rates were double those of the previous decade, and violent crime rose from 190 to 298 per 100,000 between 1963 and 1968. A reflection of public opinion and the social ferment of the 1960s, state authorities became more reluctant to utilize capital punish-ment in these years, although the number of death row prisoners grew from 219 in the 1960s to 608 a decade later.[30]

Juvenile crime continued to be a serious national problem. Between 1960 and 1973, juvenile arrests for violent crimes rose by 144 percent. Richard Nixon exploited the crime issue to win the presidency in 1968, but in 1974, during his second term in office, he was forced to resign from office after he was implicated in a "third-rate" burglary at the Democratic headquarters in the Watergate Hotel.

There is no consensus as to why crime became such a problem in the early 1960s. Law-and-order advocates argued that the upsurge in lawlessness was a result of growing social tolerance. However, criminologists have persuasively argued that it was due more to the changing demographics as postwar baby boomers reached their crime-prone years at the same time.

Organized Crime

Finally forced to publicly acknowledge the existence of organized crime after the 1957 Apalachin meeting in upstate New York, the FBI intensified efforts in its war against organized crime through its so-called Top Hoodlum program. But few if any convictions followed. In response, the government, under Attorney General Robert F. Kennedy in 1961, proposed new legislation to intensify the war against the mob, including the use of wiretapping.

Sparking the new initiatives was the testimony of Mafia informer Joseph Valachi during the televised Senate Committee hearings in 1963. The first testimony by an actual Mafia insider captured the nation's and the government's attention as Valachi churned out, in gut-wrenching detail, the national character of organized crime activities. His conspirational description of a monolithic organized crime presence in America became the accepted portrait of organized crime during the 1960s. While Congress did not immediately pass the new legislation promulgated by Attorney General Kennedy, federal efforts against organized crime

did intensify. Legislation legalizing wiretapping was enacted in 1968, and two years later new legislation to facilitate the prosecution of racketeering was signed into law.

During the 1960s and 1970s, a number of government commissions and hearings were convened to investigate organized crime, including investigations by the Task Force on Organized Crime in 1967 and 1976. The 1967 task force was most influenced by the hearings of the 1950s Kefauver Committee and the 1963 McClellan hearings led by Senator John McClellan. During the 1963 hearing, small-time mobster Joseph Valachi testified to the existence of a nationwide, organized conspiracy that he called "La Cosa Nostra." Although his testimony did not directly lead to any arrests, the barely literate mobster became one of the first Mafia members to break the vow of silence. On national television, the gravel-voiced killer captivated television audiences as he described the inner workings of organized crime. In retrospect, his testimony often strains credulity. Recent autobiographies and reminiscences by leading mobsters throw considerable doubt on Valachi's revelations.

Following on the heels of the Omnibus Crime Control and Safe Streets Act, the 1970 Organized Crime Control Act (OCCA) was created "to seek the eradication of organized crime in the United States by strengthening the legal tools in the evidence-gathering process, by establishing new penal prohibitions, and by providing enhanced sanctions and new remedies to deal with the unlawful activities of those engaged in organized crime."[31]

Chief among the crime control provisions of the OCCA was the creation of the Racketeer Influenced Corrupt Organizations (RICO) statute. RICO is considered by many to be the most significant piece of legislation ever enacted against organized crime. Originally designed to keep organized crime from infiltrating legitimate business, it has been used to combat all manner of criminal enterprises.

Despite its success, the RICO Act is not without its critics, who claim that it is too vague and broadly worded and violates many due process standards. Although RICO was enacted in 1970, it was not used until five years later. Since then, it has been used in more than 100 cases each year, mostly against white-collar crime, violent groups, organized crime, and political corruption.

Capital Punishment

Beginning in the 1950s, the NAACP and the American Civil Liberties Union became increasingly involved in the defense of death row inmates, leading to the reversal of numerous sentences. As the court system paid more attention to death row appeals, states became more reluctant to schedule executions. Together with growing death row populations and the declining number of executions, the Supreme Court focused its attention on the constitutionality of the death penalty.

American public opinion had turned against the death penalty by the mid-1960s, leading states to informally stop executions in 1967, with the last ones occurring in Colorado and California. For the next five years, an informal moratorium on the death penalty existed while the Supreme Court evaluated its constitutionality. But executions had been declining since the height of capital punishment in the 1930s, when 218 were executed. In the first half of the 1950s, forty-two inmates were executed. However, only sixteen were put to death between 1955 and 1959 and again between 1960 and 1964.[32]

On September 20, 1968, twenty-six-year-old William Henry Furman was charged in the superior court of Chatham County, Georgia, with murdering a white man while fleeing a burglary. Furman, who was African American, was caught shortly after the crime still holding the murder weapon.

As a poor man, he was given the typical poor-man's trial, defended by a court-appointed lawyer. During a one-day trial, a jury was selected in the morning, the trial heard by 3:30 P.M., and the judge's guilty verdict delivered at 5:00 P.M.

Despite a psychological examination prior to the trial in which Furman was diagnosed as mentally deficient and prone to psychotic episodes, the court denied his insanity plea.

Furman had testified that he accidentally fired the weapon as he was fleeing the crime scene and had not intended to hurt anyone. But according to Georgia's death penalty statute, capital punishment stood for accidental killings as well as intentional ones. In April 1969, Furman's death sentence was affirmed, but his execution was stayed the following month so that he could file a petition with the Supreme Court. Three years later, in 1972, his case reached the high court, where it was argued in the context as to whether the death penalty violated the Eight Amendment. Despite deep divisions among the justices, Furman's conviction was overturned by a five-to-four margin, with the judges voting that the death penalty did indeed constitute cruel and unusual punishment. In one fell swoop, the Supreme Court gave some 600 death row prisoners new life, including Robert F. Kennedy's assassin Sirhan Sirhan and murder cult leader Charles Manson.

Speaking for the majority, after reviewing the history of capital punishment under common law, Justice William O. Douglas (1898–1980) concluded that the death penalty was disproportionately applied to blacks, the poor, and other disadvantaged groups. *Furman v. Georgia* is regarded as a landmark decision protecting marginalized Americans from the death penalty. The decision did not abolish the death penalty but merely placed stricter requirements on death penalty statutes at both the state and the federal level. According to the Court, the death penalty had become "cruel and unusual" punishment because it was being invoked in a capricious and arbitrary manner, violating the constitutional protections guaranteed by the Eighth Amendment.

In 1976, the Supreme Court upheld the death penalty in the case of *Gregg v. Georgia,* and in 1977, the states, under public and political pressure, began revising their capital punishment statutes to fall under the new Supreme Court guidelines. In the *Gregg* decision, the Court ruled that convicted killers in Georgia were protected by a revised statute that required sentencing hearings and other protective procedures. The majority of other death penalty states have revamped their statutes in a similar manner. In addition to making strides to protect the poor, the mentally ill, and minorities, most states have repealed the death penalty for accidental killings and other homicides less serious than premeditated murder.

Despite strict requirements on death penalty statutes, most abolitionists continue to cite the persistent execution of the poor, minorities, and the mentally ill. As late as March 27, 2001, the Supreme Court was reconsidering whether executing mentally retarded killers violates the Constitution's ban on cruel and unusual punishment in the case of a North Carolina death row inmate. The following day, the Court was scheduled to hear the case of Texas death row inmate Johnny Paul Penry. Twelve years earlier, in 1989, the Court had upheld the constitutionality of executing the mentally retarded Texas killer. In this decision, the Court ruled that "there was no national consensus warranting a decision that executing the mentally retarded violated the Eighth Amendment's ban against cruel and unusual punishment."[33]

Ten years after America's last execution, the death penalty returned to American criminal justice. Despite a crescendo of protest from opposition groups, Gary Gilmore was determined to die for his crimes. There was little that could be done when a convicted prisoner was determined not to miss his own execution. Sentenced to die for two robbery/murders in 1976, Gilmore was steadfast in his resolution to see the state execute him. This rather ordinary murder case eventually led to an extraordinary conclusion, as Gilmore would become the first person to be executed in ten years. The case received worldwide attention and inspired famed author Norman Mailer to chronicle Gilmore's plight in the Pulitzer Prize-winning account of his life and death in *The Executioner's Song*. On January 17, 1977, Gilmore's lawyers managed to overturn a restraining order halting

the execution, and Gilmore had his final wish granted when he was shot to death by a firing squad at the Utah State Prison.

AMERICAN VIOLENCE

The civil rights movement of the late 1950s and early 1960s led the dormant Ku Klux Klan to once more raise its pestilent head. Not as large or powerful as the Reconstruction-era Klan, the 1960s incarnation was no less violent. Of the numerous Klan factions, the most violent was in Alabama, where it was responsible for a number of murders, including the 1963 Birmingham church bombing in which four black schoolgirls were killed.

No era in American history was marked by the murder of as many leading public figures as the 1960s. Leaders as diverse as Martin Luther King Jr., John F. Kennedy, Medgar Evers, Robert F. Kennedy, and Malcolm X were silenced by assassin's bullets. In the 1970s, President Gerald Ford narrowly escaped death on two separate occasions. And in 1972, presidential candidate George Wallace was permanently crippled by gunfire while campaigning.

The assassination of President John F. Kennedy (1917–1963) on November 22, 1963, is one of the most chronicled murders in American history. Sworn in as the thirty-fifth president on January 20, 1961, his term was cut short when he was shot and killed by a sniper's bullet while traveling in a motorcade in Dallas, Texas. Lee Harvey Oswald was arrested for the murder, but only two days after his arrest, Oswald was shot and killed by Dallas nightclub owner Jack Ruby.

Assuming the presidency, Vice President Lyndon B. Johnson appointed a commission to investigate the killing. Led by Chief Justice Earl Warren, the Warren Commission ruled in 1964 that Oswald acted alone, firing the fatal shots from a window of the sixth floor of the Texas Book Depository. The assassination has been shrouded ever since in mystery and rumors of conspiracy plots. A number of commissions have investigated various conspiracy theories, but despite many unanswered questions, no evidence of conspiracy has been substantiated.

In 1965, American black nationalist leader Malcolm X was shot to death while addressing a crowd in New York City. In April 1968, the Reverend Martin Luther King Jr. (1929–1968), America's leading civil rights figure, was murdered in Memphis, Tennessee. The recipient of the Nobel Peace Prize in 1964, King had become nationally identified with the civil rights movement in the 1950s while leading boycotts and protests in the segregated South. Murdered by a sniper while standing on the balcony of his hotel, King was in Memphis in support of striking sanitation workers. Black urban neighborhoods erupted in violence following the assassination. James Earl Ray was eventually arrested for murder. Although Ray pled guilty and was sentenced to life imprisonment, questions still persist as to how the uneducated, provincial, and indigent Ray was able to escape to London (unassisted), where he was apprehended.

On the election of his brother as president in 1960, Robert F. Kennedy became the youngest attorney general in U.S. history. Although his earlier career was tarnished by his association with communist hunter Joseph McCarthy in the 1950s, by the 1960s Kennedy had become a leading supporter of the civil rights movement and an implacable foe of organized crime. Three months after announcing his own candidacy for president, on June 5, 1968, Robert Kennedy was slain by Sirhan Sirhan the very night he celebrated his victory in the California primary.

Rioting and Civil Disobedience

During the 1960s, the law enforcement establishment was increasingly tested by a wide variety of mass confrontations. Violent riots have sporadically punctuated urban American life since the colonial era. Despite the deaths of thirty-eight individuals in the 1943 Detroit riot, race riots began to follow a new pattern in which rioters targeted buildings and commercial goods more than people.

The best-known race riot of the 1960s occurred in the Watts area of Los Angeles in 1965. On the evening of August 11, two young African American men were stopped by the California Highway Patrol for reckless driving in the inner-city neighborhood of Watts. Soon after the arrival of members of the Los Angeles Police Department, the scene deteriorated into chaos. The department had a reputation for brutality and bad relations with the city's black community. A rumor spread through the area that police had roughed up a pregnant black woman. Although it proved false, it was enough to ignite one of the nation's worst episodes of civil unrest. Over the following week, more than thirty mostly black residents were killed. Looting and arson damage estimates reached $200 million. President Johnson appointed a commission led by former CIA director John McCone to investigate the riots.

According to the findings of the McCone Commission, black Los Angeles was like a powder keg ready to explode. Black migrants had been drawn to the city during the 1940s to take advantage of wartime employment. However, they were confronted with limited housing opportunities and racial discrimination. Since mass transportation was limited in the city, blacks had to shop locally, where stores were notorious for selling poor goods at high prices. The retail community bore the brunt of most of the property damage during the riot.[34]

The race riots of the 1960s were marked by the destruction of property and communities, shocking citizens of all races. The urban riots of 1966 and 1967 proved particularly destructive. Of the thirty-eight riots that took place in 1967, some of the most serious took place in Chicago, Cleveland, and San Francisco, resulting in seven deaths, more than 400 injuries, 3,000 arrests, and property damage exceeding $5 million. The following year would be even worse. By the end of October, there had been more than 150 outbreaks of civil unrest. Of these, thirty-three necessitated the intervention of the state police and eight the

National Guard. Observing the aftermath of the Detroit riot that left thousands of buildings in ruins, Mayor Jerome Cavanaugh remarked that the city "looks like Berlin in 1945."[35] The forty-three deaths during the Detroit riot surpassed those during the Watts uprising.

In the wake of the assassination of Martin Luther King Jr. in 1968, looting and burning erupted in more than 150 cities, with some of the worst damage occurring in the nation's capital. Of the forty-six deaths during the riots, all but five were black. While this ratio of black to white deaths was a familiar refrain from past rioting, what was new was the amount of power summoned to end the disturbances. In what was probably the largest single deployment of military and paramilitary forces for a civilian purpose since the Civil War, 34,000 National Guardsmen, 21,000 federal troops, and thousands of local police were brought in to quell the "disturbances."

Many black and white residents of the nation's capital had considered the city "riot-proof" in 1968. Unlike other urban centers with large black populations, many blacks were well entrenched in good-paying government jobs. According to one study[36] of the Washington riot, one out of every four federal employees in the area was African American. A black sat on the Supreme Court (Thurgood Marshall) and in the president's cabinet (Housing Secretary Robert C. Weaver). Federal troops had been called to Washington, D.C., on three previous occasions during the past fifty years but only once for racial strife.

However, like most other cities, there was a darker side that tourists and visitors rarely saw. By the 1960s, Washington, D.C., had foundering hospital and school systems and was surpassed only by Mississippi in infant mortality. More than one out of every four families lived below the poverty line. In addition, the city had some of the highest rates of tuberculosis and syphilis in the nation. Large sections of the city were bereft of public transportation, limiting job prospects in the suburbs. Civic leaders began warning of unrest, which was narrowly averted on several occasions. Particular disdain in the black community was reserved for the Washington police force, which they regarded as racist. With blacks representing 67 percent of the population, the highest percentage in any major city, four out of every five police officers were white. Despite urgings from the White House to modernize and become more responsive to the community, the department dragged its feet.[37]

In 1967, President Johnson appointed the National Advisory Commission on Civil Disorders, chaired by Otto Kerner, former Illinois governor. Kerner's committee queried social scientists, police officers, politicians, and civic leaders for solutions to the civil unrest plaguing the nation. According to the commission's findings, better known as the Kerner Commission Report, the torpid initial police response to many riots allowed civil unrest to often flare out of control. The Kerner Commission was reminiscent of the commission created in the wake of the 1919 Chicago riot. Whereas earlier commissions convened to study civil disorder, the Kerner Commission was the "first federally funded, national and Presidential-level examination of race relations in the United States."[38] The *Kerner Report* was published in 1969, selling two million copies.

A survey of the black residents in Detroit following the 1967 riot revealed that three-quarters of them believed that the police acted too slowly to control the disorder.[39] Henceforth, departments would need to adhere to new requirements if they were to be effective in controlling disorder, which meant being able to deploy manpower quickly and efficiently. This would take some doing since the Kerner Commission noted that the average police department had only 13 percent of its patrol force available between the hours of 4:00 P.M. and midnight, the hours when most riots began. There were other concerns that needed to be addressed as well. Few if any departments had any contingency plans for controlling disorder once it began, and most were likely to be short of essential equipment. During one major eruption of civil disorder, the commission found that out of a police force of 5,000, only 192 were on duty for a city of one million.[40] However, the commission reserved its greatest criticism for the lack of police training for riot control, finding that the only riot training was provided in recruit school.[41]

Running on a law-and-order platform in the 1968 presidential campaign, Richard Nixon castigated the Kerner Commission for blaming "everybody for the riots except the perpetrators."[42] After taking office in early 1969, Nixon recommended more funding for the LEAA in order to supply police departments with tanks, armored cars, helicopters, riot control equipment, and a national computerized identification system for fighting crime. A reflection of the new administration's support for law enforcement was its increased funding for LEAA, from $63 million in 1969 to $268 million in 1970 and $700 million just two years later. In order to seem tough on crime, Congress was coerced by the White House to pass questionable bills, such as the "no-knock" provision, which allowed police to break into a house without a search warrant, and preventative detention, which would allow judges to jail suspects for sixty days before trial. In response, Senator Sam Ervin Jr. referred to these provisions as "A Bill to Repeal the Fourth, Fifth, Sixth, and Eighth Amendments to the Constitution."[43]

In the early 1960s, leftist groups, such as Students for a Democratic Society (SDS), participated in freedom rides and voter registration drives in the still-segregated South. By the mid-1960s, their attention was diverted to the antiwar crusade, and in 1968 the organization counted more than 100,000 members. Still thousands more belonged to the Yippies and other radical groups.

One of the most memorable images of 1968 was of thousands of antiwar protesters being beaten by Chicago police during the Chicago Democratic Convention. A subsequent investigative commission later described police tactics as a "police riot."[44] In reality, much of the blame rested with the administration of Chicago Mayor Richard Daley.[45] In the riots following the assassination of Martin Luther King Jr. earlier in the year, the Chicago police had reacted with remarkable leniency. Afterward, the mayor had admonished the force for its timidity in putting down the riot, having ordered them "to shoot to kill arsonists and maim looters."

One of the most egregious episodes of the Vietnam War era, the Kent State shootings on May 4, 1970, demonstrated the growing antipathy between prowar and antiwar factions. President Nixon's order for an American incursion into Cambodia on May 1 ignited strident student protests on many campuses across the country. Protests at Kent State University in Ohio led the mayor to declare a state of civil emergency and to request the National Guard to keep order. With the arrival of the Guard, tensions mounted. As students launched projectiles and profanities at the National Guard, the armed Guardsmen directed tear gas canisters at their adversaries. Shortly after noon, the Guardsmen opened fire on the protesters, wounding nine students and killing four in just thirteen seconds. Following an investigation by the FBI, the Justice Department declared the shootings unwarranted. Following several other investigations, the National Guardsmen were exonerated, leading to many years of civil and criminal suits.

Equally controversial but less well known were the shooting deaths of two black students and the wounding of twelve others by state troopers and city police at Jackson State University (formerly Jackson State College) in Jackson, Mississippi, ten days after the shootings at Kent State. The shootings followed anti–Vietnam War draft protests targeting Mississippi's all-white draft boards. This, combined with the ongoing legacy of racial discrimination, led to the fatal encounter on May 14, 1970. Tensions escalated after a series of confrontations between African American students and white police officers. After one student threw a bottle in their direction, the police unleashed a barrage of gunfire in front of one of the dormitories. As at Kent State, no one was ever indicted for the homicides, adding to the political divide that cleaved the nation. Many attributed the Jackson State shootings to tensions lingering from the "Freedom Summer" of the late 1960s, when civil rights activists targeting the state to register black voters antagonized white police officers.[46] Although the incident provoked nationwide indignation for several days, it soon faded from memory. Many observers suggested that national outrage at the shooting of the African American students would have been greater if they had been white.

Murder

Seemingly new types of homicides captured the nation's and the law enforcement community's attention beginning in the 1960s. The omnipresence of television, together with the newsprint media, would bring the horrors of Vietnam and mass murder to the evening dinner table. There were ample crimes to capture their attention. During the early 1960s, serial killer and rapist "Boston Strangler" Albert DeSalvo killed thirteen women. As the decade moved to a conclusion, the "Zodiac" targeted couples in the hills outside San Francisco, and serial killer Edmund Kemper began a killing spree that would conclude with the murder of his mother in 1973. According to one expert, "serial murder" became much "more frequent since the late 1960s and offenders tend to kill larger number of victims."[47]

James Alan Fox, one of the country's leading authorities on homicide, suggested that "the onset of the age of mass murder" began in 1966.[48] The summer of 1966 would introduce Americans to the horrors of mass murder as Charles Whitman gunned down sixteen people with devastating accuracy from the top of a tower at the University of Texas (like Kennedy assassin Lee Harvey Oswald, Whitman was also a former Marine) and Richard Speck stabbed to death eight student nurses in Chicago.

The rising incidence of mass murder in the 1970s led several states to recognize this crime as a distinct type of homicide. California, for instance, had previously made first-degree murder punishable by seven years' imprisonment followed by parole eligibility. In the aftermath of highly publicized mass shootings in the 1970s, the law was amended to allow the jury to add the additional charge of multiple murder. In these cases, the only applicable sentence was the death penalty or life in prison.[49]

Meanwhile, older, more traditional regional patterns of murder continued to prevail. In the summer of 1964, three civil rights activists, two of them white, were arrested for speeding in Philadelphia, Mississippi. After their arrests, they were then conveniently released into the waiting hands of local white supremacists who brutally murdered them and then hid their bodies in an earthen dam. At the time of the crime, Mississippi was considered the nation's most segregated state. It had the highest percentage of blacks and the lowest percentage of registered black voters, with only 6 percent of its black population of almost one million eligible to vote.

In the summer of 1964, national civil rights leaders called on student volunteers to use their vacation to help register Mississippi's black citizens to vote in what became known as "Freedom Summer." While students were given a "survival course" before leaving for Mississippi, it would do little to prevent the murder of three civil rights workers and the beating of dozens more. More than 150 FBI agents ultimately investigated the murder of the civil rights workers, and an investigation led to the arrest and conviction of seven members of the newly revived Ku Klux Klan.

Klan membership had peaked in the 1920s. However, membership surged upward in response to the growing civil rights movement and then after the election of a Catholic president (Kennedy) in 1960. The Klan was far from monolithic. There was no central headquarters, but regional offices flourished throughout the South. By 1965, the Mississippi Klan boasted 5,000 members.

No murders or crimes symbolized the 1960s more than those committed by the Manson family in California in the late 1960s. After Charles Manson left prison in 1967, he moved to San Francisco, which was in the last stages of the so-called Summer of Love. Manson used his magnetic personality to great advantage, drawing a number of runaways and homeless young girls to his paranoid banner, forming the nucleus of what became known as the "Manson Family." Their many crimes have been well chronicled and reached a crescendo of sorts with the massacre of movie starlet Sharon Tate and four others on the evening of August 9, 1969. The subsequent nine-and-a-half-month trial led to the conviction of four defendants for murder, but their lives would be spared in 1972 when the Supreme Court declared the death penalty unconstitutional, converting all death sentences to life in prison.

NOTABLE TRIALS

Gideon v. Wainwright

Early on a June morning in 1961, a Panama City, Florida, police officer on patrol noticed an open door at a local pool hall well after closing time. On further examination, the officer noted that someone had burglarized a jukebox and a cigarette machine. This was hardly the crime of the century, but nevertheless suspicion quickly settled on an indigent drifter named Clarence Gideon. Few could have imagined the consequences of such a seemingly inconsequential crime.

While federal law had guaranteed the right to counsel at the federal level since the inception of the Republic, as the law stood on the state level, courts did not have to offer court-appointed attorneys to defendants in noncapital trials. Most penniless defendants had no recourse but to defend themselves without the benefit of a court-appointed attorney.[50] Although several states provided felony defendants with counsel, Florida was not among them. Chronicling Gideon's case in *Gideon's Trumpet,* author Anthony Lewis wrote, "Judging from the externals it would be hard to imagine a figure less likely to be the subject of a great case in the Supreme Court" than Clarence Gideon. With little education, Gideon was no match for the prosecuting attorney, particularly after the jury heard the testimony of an individual who

claimed to have observed Gideon pilfering the poolroom vending machines. In a trial that lasted less than one day, Gideon was found guilty of breaking into a poolroom in order to commit a felony and was sentenced to five years in prison.

But the Supreme Court had not counted on the resourcefulness of the intrepid Gideon. After having a writ of habeas corpus denied by the Florida Supreme Court, in which he claimed to have been illegally imprisoned, Gideon wrote a five-page penciled document to the U.S. Supreme Court asking the court to hear his case. With thousands of similar petitions filed each year, the odds were stacked against the Court's considering his case. However, for once in his life, the odds were in his favor, and the Court agreed to hear his case in January 1963.

Shortly before the case was heard, the director of Florida's Division of Corrections was replaced by Louie L. Wainwright, ensuring the new director of his place in legal history. In the initial hearing of *Gideon v. Wainwright,* there was harsh debate among the justices over the need to change the law. But the 1960s had inaugurated a new vantage point from which to discuss the rights of defendants, and on March 18, 1963, the Supreme Court unanimously ruled that all felony defendants were entitled to legal representation no matter what crime had been committed. Overturning Gideon's conviction, Justice Hugo L. Black wrote, "Reason and reflection requires us to recognize that in our adversary system of criminal justice, any person hauled into court, who is too poor to hire a lawyer, cannot be assured a fair trial unless counsel is provided for him."[51]

In August 1963, Gideon returned to court, this time accompanied by an experienced trial lawyer. But angered by adverse publicity, the prosecution made sure a "dream team" of lawyers were on hand to see that the charges stuck this time. However, with the aid of his defense attorney, the witness from the first trial was shown under questioning to have withheld his criminal record from the earlier jury. Subsequently, Gideon was acquitted of all charges. Clarence Gideon died at the age of sixty-one in 1972 but not until he had ensured that the right to counsel under the Sixth Amendment had become absolute and applicable everywhere in all courts of the land.

CONCLUSIONS

As the 1960s spiraled to an end, Americans had become increasingly concerned about the high levels of disorder and violence in the culture. Between 1963 and 1970, the national homicide rate had doubled from 4.6 to 9.2 per 100,000.[52] No place was more deadly than America's urban centers. Americans increasingly feared crime during the 1960s and 1970s. By 1978, 85 percent of Americans believed that the criminal justice system should be more punitive.[53] Public opinion that once favored a moratorium on the death penalty was shifting as well. The 1960s began with a decline in executions and then an informal moratorium that existed from 1967 to 1972. By the 1980s, two out of every three Americans favored the death penalty.[54]

The National Commission on the Causes of and Prevention of Violence recorded 239 urban riots in America between 1963 and 1968. Historian Paul Gilje suggested that there was "a contagion of disorder, just as in the 1760s and 1770s and the 1830s and 1840s spreading across the land."[55] Subsequent commissions blamed the riots on insufficient police response, while others saw the conflagrations as an outgrowth of police and civilian confrontations. Whatever the cause, extensive television coverage reminded Americans that while there was progress in breaking down southern segregation, de facto segregation persisted in much of urban America. Among the commissions to investigate the rioting was the Kerner Commission, which concluded that urban disorder resulted from the unequal treatment of blacks that created two separate societies.

Building on a tradition begun by the 1930 Wickersham Commission Report, communities convened committees to investigate various facets of the criminal justice system during the 1960s and 1970s. According to John Conley, "The establishment of blue ribbon commissions to study complex social problems has been a common element of American political history . . . to study problems related to crime and the administration of justice."[56]

Although the Wickersham Commission was the first national commission on crime, some of the best-known commissions of the 1960s and 1970s were more local in scope. While the Kerner Commission investigated civil disorders nationwide, the Knapp Commission examined corruption in New York City only. There were a number of lesser-known investigations conducted at almost every level of government. Cities, including Philadelphia, Chicago, and Washington, D.C., were examined in great detail. In 1965, President Johnson oversaw the creation of the President's Commission on Crime in the District of Columbia. Assisted by a staff of criminologists, psychologists, social workers, and correctional experts, the commission investigated the causes of crime and delinquency, the adequacy of existing criminal laws, the relationships between the police and the community, and many other related issues. Its mammoth 1,041-page report was published in 1966.[57] Despite many well-thought-out conclusions and recommendations, most went unheeded, and these cities continued to be characterized by criminal activity and economic despair as the 1980s loomed on the horizon.

Demonstrating the cyclical nature of violence in America, in April 2001 an unarmed African American male was gunned down by Cincinnati police, the fifteenth such incident since 1995. Racial tensions quickly erupted into violence after years of confrontations between the police and black residents. Considered the city's worst racial violence since Martin Luther King Jr.'s assassination in 1968, the city established a curfew as helmeted police joined ranks with sheriff's deputies and state highway patrol officers. This outbreak followed a civil suit the previous month brought against the police department by the American Civil Liberties Union and the Cincinnati Black United Front, which accused the department of failing to end thirty years of harassment. While blacks made up 43 percent of the population, they represented only 28 percent of the 1,000-member police force. Many observers consider these developments a wake-up call for other American cities.[58]

Police work changed dramatically in the 1960s and 1970s. The publication of *The Challenge of Crime in A Free Society* in 1968 devoted considerable attention to the changing nature of police work. Among its most controversial conclusions was that it had been unable to discover "the relationship between police patrol and deterrence."[59] Rising crime rates, urban riots, and antiwar violence led police executives and political leaders to examine the role of police as crime fighters. Although a number of police authorities blamed the rising crime problem on the limitations imposed on them by *Miranda, Mapp,* and *Escobedo,* a more convincing explanation perhaps could be found in the number of young males fifteen to twenty-four coming of age in the 1960s and 1970s, an age-group that has traditionally been responsible for most violations of the law.

In its final report on the riots following the killing of Martin Luther King Jr., the Kerner Commission noted, "Our nation is moving toward two societies, one black and one white— separate and unequal." However, the commission's report was not all doom and gloom, suggesting that the "deepening racial division is not inevitable" and could "be reversed."[60]

The death of J. Edgar Hoover in 1972 ended an era in American criminal justice history. His last years as FBI director became increasingly bizarre, and although he is credited with creating the professional FBI, suppressing kidnapping and bank robbery in the 1930s, and containing the espionage menace during World War II, Hoover will probably be remembered for violating constitutional protections and keeping secret files. Unfortunately, future historians will be able to only presume what was in his personal files since his secretary apparently had them destroyed following Hoover's death.

Congressional investigations during the 1970s uncovered numerous flagrant violations of

civil liberties by the FBI. Defying federal laws, FBI agents broke into the homes, tapped the phones, and opened up the mail of American citizens; illegally infiltrated antiwar groups and black radical organizations; and compiled dossiers on thousands of dissidents. Following these investigations, Congress laid down strict guidelines for FBI activities.

The correctional system was rent by political activism and large-scale violence in the 1970s, leading by the end of the decade to the "demise of the treatment model . . . a breakdown in prisoners' unity, and a return to classical notions of punishment."[61] The extensive media coverage of the Attica riot in 1971, still the bloodiest prison riot in American history, "crystallized doubts about the purposes of imprisonment in America" at a time when the criminal justice system was becoming increasingly punitive.[62] Rising prison populations in the next two decades would only intensify doubts about these institutions.

While law enforcement and the machinery of crime fighting were bolstered by hundreds of millions of dollars through the LEAA, little attention was paid to the underlying social and economic problems that led to crime and incarceration. Despite the concerted get-tough war on crime, serious crimes continued to skyrocket into the 1980s.

Point–Counterpoint

On the Pad: The Criminal Justice System and Police Corruption

Corruption is nothing new to metropolitan America. Cities big and small have been plagued by this problem since the inception of modern policing. In 1967 the President's Commission on Law Enforcement and Administration of Justice released its Task Force Report on the Police. The main charge of the task force was to examine the role of the police in modern America. Among its many conclusions was that there was a need to emphasize police integrity and ethical conduct. According to the authors of the report police

Source: Task Force on the Police: *The Police,* Washington, 1967, pp. 212–213; Knapp Commission, *Commission to Investigate Allegations of Police Corruption and the City's Anti-Corruption Procedures,* Dec. 26, 1972, pp. 65–66.

leaders were currently making inroads on stemming police corruption. However, within five years the nation's best known city force was rocked by scandal. The first passage is from the task force report chapter on police integrity. The Knapp Commission investigated police corruption in New York City for more than two years before releasing its report in late 1972. According to the report, more than half of the city's 29,600 police officers had participated in some type of corrupt activity. The Knapp Commission uncovered two types of corrupt officers—"grass-eaters" and meateaters. The passage from the Knapp report describing these types follows.

GRASS-EATERS AND MEAT-EATERS

Corrupt policemen have been informally described as being either "grass-eaters" or "meat-eaters." The overwhelming majority of those who do take payoffs are grass-eaters, who accept gratuities and solicit five- and ten- and twenty-dollar payments from contractors, tow-truck operators, gamblers, and the like, but do not aggressively pursue corruption payments. "Meat-eaters," probably only a small percentage of the force, spend a good deal of their working hours aggressively seeking out situations they can exploit for financial gain, including gambling, narcotics, and other serious offenses which can yield payments of thousands of dollars. Patrolman William Phillips was certainly an example of this latter category.

One strong impetus encouraging grass-eaters to continue to accept relatively petty graft is, ironically, their feeling of loyalty to their fellow officers. Accepting payoff money is one way for an officer to prove that he is one of the boys and that he can be trusted. In the climate which existed in the Department during the Commission's investigation, at least at the precinct level, these numerous but relatively small payoffs were a fact of life, and those officers who made a point of refusing them were not accepted closely into the fellowship of policemen. Corruption among grass-eaters obviously cannot be met by attempting to arrest them all and will probably diminish only if Commissioner Murphy is successful in his efforts to change the rank and file attitude toward corruption.

No change in attitude, however, is likely to affect a meat-eater, whose yearly income in graft amounts to many thousands of dollars and who may take payoffs of $5,000 or even $50,000 in one fell swoop (former Assistant Chief Inspector Sydney Cooper,

who had been active in anti-corruption work for years, recently stated that the largest score of which he had heard—although he was unable to verify it— was a narcotics payoff involving $250,000). Such men are willing to take considerable risks as long as the potential profit remains so large. Probably the only way to deal with them will be to ferret them out individually and get them off the force, and, hopefully, into prisons.

It is the police themselves, in the vast majority of cases, who are ridding their profession of the unethical and the corrupt. An ever-increasing number of law enforcement leaders are realizing that vigilance against such practices is a continuing part of their responsibilities. For over 40 years Director J. Edgar Hoover and his associates throughout the FBI organization have set an outstanding example of integrity within a law enforcement agency. Through the influence of its special agents throughout the country, working in close contact with local police officers, and through its training programs at the FBI National Academy and local training schools, the FBI has encouraged thousands of police officers to emulate its standards.

National, State, and local police associations have also done a great deal to encourage police integrity. The Law Enforcement Code of Ethics has been adopted by all major police associations and agencies throughout the Nation. In California, for example, State law requires that police ethics be taught and that the code be administered as an oath to all police recruits training in the 45 police academies certified by the State Commission on Peace Officers Standards. In 1955, the International Conference of Police Associations developed a lesson plan for the teaching of ethics within police organizations. The California Peace Officers Association and the Peace Officers Research Association maintain highly active committees on police standards and ethics and are responsible for most of the high ethical standards established throughout the State. And the International Association of Chiefs of Police constantly strives to establish and maintain honest police leadership. Other police consulting firms have made similar recommendations. Through numerous surveys of police departments, it has pointed up the need for maintaining police integrity through the establishment of internal investigation units. The Fraternal Order of Police has stressed the need for attracting high caliber police recruits through adequate salaries, sound retirement systems and other benefits.

Such groups should increase their activity in this field. Local police associations especially must be alert to the problem, recognizing the relationship between maintaining integrity and good conduct and improving the public image of the police. This can lead to more adequate pay and equipment, along with improved working conditions. Associations that come to the aid of dishonest officers render an obvious disservice, not only to themselves, but to the entire police profession.

SOURCES

Bell, Daniel. 1960. *The End of Ideology*. New York: Free Press.

Blomberg, Thomas G., and Karol Lucken. 2000. *American Penology: A History of Control*. New York: Aldine de Gruyter.

Bodenhamer, David J. 1992. *Fair Trial: Rights of the Accused in American History*. New York: Oxford University Press.

Brauer, Carl M. 1977. *John F. Kennedy and the Second Reconstruction*. New York: Columbia University Press.

Cohen, Jerry, and William S. Murphy. 1966. *Burn, Baby, Burn!: The Los Angeles Race Riot, 1965*. New York: E. P. Dutton.

Congressional Record. 1970. 116th Congress.

Conley, John, ed. 1994. *The 1967 President's Crime Commission Report: Its Impact 25 Years Later*. Cincinnati: Anderson Publishing.

Cummins, Eric. 1994. *The Rise and Fall of California's Radical Prison Movement*. Stanford, Calif.: Stanford University Press.

Friedman, Lawrence M. 1993. *Crime and Punishment in American History*. New York: Basic Books.

Garrow, David J. 1983. *The FBI and Martin Luther King, Jr.* New York: Penguin Books.

Gilbert, Ben W. 1968. *Ten Blocks from the White House: Anatomy of the Washington Riots of 1968*. New York: Praeger.

Gilje, Paul A. 1996. *Rioting in America*. Bloomington: Indiana University Press.

Hindelang, Michael J., Michael R. Gottfredson, and Timothy J. Flanagan, eds. 1981. *Sourcebook of Criminal Justice Statistics—1980*. Washington, D.C.: U.S. Government Printing Office.

Holli, Melvin G. 1999. *The American Mayor: The Best and the Worst Big-City Leaders*. University Park: Pennsylvania State University Press.

Horne, Gerald. 1995. *Fire This Time: The Watts Uprising and the 1960s*. Charlottesville: University Press of Virginia.

Jenkins, Philip. 1994. *Using Murder: The Social Construction of Serial Homicide*. New York: Aldine de Gruyter.

Jonnes, Jill. 1996. *Hep-Cats, Narcs, and Pipe Dreams: A History of America's Romance with Illegal Drugs*. New York: Scribner.

Kerner Commission. 1968. *Report of the National Advisory Commission on Civil Disorders*. New York: Bantam Books.

Levin, Jack, and James Alan Fox. 1985. *Mass Murder: America's Growing Menace*. New York: Plenum Press.

Lewis, Anthony. 1964. *Gideon's Trumpet*. New York: Random House.

Lord, Leslie Kay. 1995. "Policewomen." In *The Encyclopedia of Police Science*, ed. William G. Bailey, pp. 627–636. New York: Garland.

McKelvey, Blake. 1977. *American Prison: A History of Good Intentions*. Montclair, N.J.: Patterson Smith.

Meltsner, Michael. 1974. *Cruel and Unusual: The Supreme Court and Capital Punishment*. New York: William Morrow.

Milton, Catherine. 1972. *Women in Policing*. Washington, D.C.: Police Foundation.

New York State Special Commission on Attica. 1972. *Attica*. New York: Praeger.

Padover, Saul K. 1969. *The Living U.S. Constitution: Including the Complete Text of the Constitution and 35 Historical Supreme Court Decisions*. New York: World Publishing.

Parenti, Christian. 2001. *Lockdown America: Police and Prisons in the Age of Crisis*. London: Verso.

Platt, Anthony M., ed. 1971. *The Politics of Riot Commissions, 1917–1970*. New York: Macmillan.

Powers, Richard Gid. 1987. *Secrecy and Power: The Life of J. Edgar Hoover*. New York: Free Press.

President's Commission on Law Enforcement and Administration of Justice. 1967. *The Challenge of Crime in a Free Society*. Washington, D.C.: U.S. Government Printing Office.

Reid, Sue Titus. 1987. *Criminal Justice Procedures and Issues*. New York: West Publishing.

Reinert, Patty. 2001. "Court to Revisit Execution of Retarded." *Houston Chronicle*, March 27, pp. 1A, 6A.

Schulz, Dorothy Moses. 1995. *From Social Worker to Crimefighter: Women in United States Municipal Policing*. Westport, Conn.: Praeger.

Shachtman, Tom. 1983. *Decade of Shocks: Dallas to Watergate, 1963–1974*. New York: Poseiden Press.

Smith, Alexander B., and Harriet Pollack. 1980. *Criminal Justice: An Overview*. New York: Holt, Rinehart and Winston.

Spofford, Tim. 1988. *Lynch Street: The May 1970 Slayings at Jackson State College*. Kent, Ohio: Kent State University Press.

Stolberg, Mary M. 1998. *Bridging the River of Hatred: The Pioneering Efforts of Detroit Police Commissioner George Edwards*. Detroit: Wayne State University Press.

Sullivan, Larry E. 1990. *The Prison Reform Movement*. Boston: Twayne Publishing.

Useem, Bert, and Peter Kimball. 1989. *States of Siege: U.S. Prison Riots, 1971–1986*. New York: Oxford University Press.

Wilson, James Q. 1983. *Thinking about Crime*. New York: Basic Books.

Wright, Kevin N. 1985. *The Great American Crime Myth*. Westport, Conn.: Greenwood Press.

CRITICAL THINKING QUESTIONS

1. What does the "Nationalization of Criminal Justice" refer to?

2. Explain why there was so much friction between different segments of the public and law enforcement during the 1960s.

3. Discuss the transition from the 1967 "Summer of Love" to the bloodshed and civil disruptions that marked the 1960s and 1970s.

4. According to Samuel Walker this era was "the most turbulent in all of American criminal justice history." Do you agree or disagree? Explain your reasons.

5. Discuss the changing nature of policing and corrections during this period.

6. Examine American popular opinion concerning the death penalty during the 1970s. How did it impact the legal system?

CRIMINAL JUSTICE HISTORY

ON THE INTERNET

The Internet offers numerous sites for most landmark court decisions. *Mapp v. Ohio* is covered at http://laws.findlaw.com/us/367/643.html and http://lawbooksusa.com/cconlaw/mappvohio.htm. *Miranda v. Arizona* is covered at http://laws.findlaw.com/us/384/436.html, www.lectlaw.com/files/case04.htm, http://supreme.findlaw.com/documents/miranda.html, and www.crimelibrary.com/classics4/miranda. *Escobedo v. Illinois* is discussed at http://lawbooksusa.com/cconlaw/escobedovillinois, http://laws.findlaw.com/us/378/478.html, and http://ncl.chass.ncsu.edu/garson/dye/docs/ escobedo.htm. Interesting commentary on the case is available at www.jus.state.nc.us/NCJA/ mar97.htm. *Gideon v. Wainwright* is covered at http://laws.findlaw.com/us/372/335.html, www.lectlaw.com/files/case17.htm, and www.thisnation.com/library/gideon.html. *Terry v. Ohio* is discussed at http://laws.findlaw.com/us/ 392/1.html and http://lawbooksusa.com/cconlaw/terryvohio.htm. Interesting commentary on the case is at www.jus.state.nc.us/ NCJA/aug97.htm. *Roe v. Wade* is examined at http://laws.findlaw.com/us/410/113.html. *Katz v. United States* is covered at http://students.washington.edu/kcgrogan/cmu300.wiretapping.html.

The death penalty and capital punishment are amply represented on the Internet with a number of sites. Students should be circumspect when viewing these sites since many are managed by pro or con organizations, offering biased coverage. For an examination of the Caryl Chessman case, see www.crimelibrary.com/classics3/chessman, www.gadflyonline.com/10-29-01/ftr-caryl-chessman.html, and www.usc.edu/isd/archives/la/scandals/chessman.html. The execution of Gary Gilmore is chronicled at www.nytimes.com/books/98/05/10/specials/mailer.html, www.lib.latrobe.edu.au/AHR/archive/Issue-March-1997/petch.html, www.pbs.org/wnet/americanmasters/database/mailer_n_timeline, and www.crimelibrary.com/serial10/gilmore/3htm. Much of the coverage is devoted to author Norman Mailer's study of the case published as *The Executioner's Song*.

Pivotal capital punishment cases can be found at a number of sites. *Furman v. Georgia* is discussed at http://laws.findlaw.com/us/408/238.html, http://home.twcny.rr.com/pistolpete/furman.html; www.aclu.org/news/n062797.html, and www.wku.edu/Dept/Academic/AHSS/

Government/furman.htm. *Gregg v. Georgia* is covered at www.amnesty-usa.org/abolish/greggvgeorgia, www.findlaw.com/us/428/153.html, and www.lectlaw.com/files/case26.htm.

There are a number of sites devoted to high-profile mass murders in 1966. For tower sniper Charles Whitman, see www.crimelibrary.com/serial/whitman and www.popculture.com/pop/bio_projects/charles_whitman.html. Links related to Chicago nurse killer Richard Speck are at www.suburbanchicagonews/joliet/prisons/speck, www.crimelibrary.com/serials/speck/speckbib/htm, and www.suntimes.com/century/m1966.html.

Although there many sites devoted to prison history, those focusing on the Attica riot and related links include http://dir.yahoo.com/Society_and_Culture/Crime/Correction_and_Rehabilitation/Prison_History/Attica_Prison_Riot .Prison history and reform are discussed at www.ceclibrary.org/prisres.html. A 1971 editorial on Attica is available at http://past.thenation.com/historic/19710913attica.shtml.

Civil unrest on campuses and urban race riots frequently punctuated this era. For the Kent State shootings, see links at http://homepages.msn.com/cerfst/rikkebj/kentframe.htm. A debate on the killings is found at www.spectacle.org/1996/kentr.html. A chronology of the events related to the incident can be found at http://members.aol.com/nrbooks/chronol.htm. Less well known but equally controversial were the killings at Jackson State University, discussed at www.collegian.psu.edu/archive/1995/06/06-19-95tde/06-19-95dops-column.asp.

The Watergate scandal is well documented at http://vcepolitics.com/wgate.htm and www2.sbbs.se/hp/ramon. Transcripts and other links can be found at www.washingtonpost.com/wp-srv/national/longterm/watergate/front.htm.

Hundreds of sites are devoted to the assassination of John F. Kennedy. The Warren Commission Report can be downloaded at www.informatik.uni-rostock.de/Kennedy/WCR/download.html. The FBI report on the JFK autopsy is at www.thesmokinggun.com/jfk2/bethesda1.shtml. The House Committee on Assassinations interviews by the FBI can be found at www.smokinggun.com/jfk2/oneilll.shtml. The Zapruder film account of the assassination is examined at http://204.233.52.217/cooper/vivo/clip1288vcp.htm. The JFK assassination home page is at www.informatik.uni-rostock.de/Kennedy/body.html.

The Omnibus Crime Control and Safe Streets Act is examined at www.usdoj.gov/crt/split/42usc3789d.htm. The RICO Act can be found at links on http://fedlaw.gsa.gov/legal10.htm and www.ricoact.com. Riot and urban unrest resulting in the Kerner Commission and the McCone Commission are profiled at www_lib.usc.edu/~anthonya/la/reb/causes.htm.

NOTES

1. Bell (1960, p. 151).
2. Wilson (1983, p. 15).
3. Walker (1998, p. 180).
4. President's Commission on Law Enforcement and Administration of Justice (1967).
5. Reid (1987, p. 130).
6. See, for example, Brauer (1977).
7. Bodenhamer (1992, p. 113).
8. Smith and Pollack (1980, p. 199).
9. President's Commission on Law Enforcement and Administration of Justice, (1967, p. 126).
10. Kelling et al. (1974, p. iii).
11. Schulz (1995, p. 115).
12. Milton (1972).
13. Lord (1995, p. 629).
14. Schulz (1995, p. 131).
15. Schulz (1995, p. 135).
16. Powers (1987, p. 417).
17. Parenti (2001, p. 6).
18. Parenti (2001, p. 6).
19. Rotman (1995, p. 172).
20. Sullivan (1990, p. 92).
21. Quoted in Friedman (1993, p. 313).
22. Blomberg and Lucken (2000, p. 144).
23. Quoted in Parenti (2001, p. 195).
24. Cummins (1994, chap. 4).
25. Christianson (1998, p. 280).
26. McKelvey (1977, p. 380).
27. Christianson (1998, p. 268).

28. New York State Special Commission on Attica (1972, p. xi).

29. Christianson (1998, p. 276).

30. Bowers (1974, p. 12).

31. *Congressional Record* (1970, p. 602).

32. *National Prisoner Statistics* (1971, table 3).

33. Reinert (2001, p. A1).

34. Horne (1995).

35. Quoted in Patterson (1996, p. 663).

36. Gilbert (1968, p. 1)

37. Gilbert (1968, pp. 1–12).

38. Platt (1971, p. 341).

39. Richardson (pp. 190–91).

40. Kerner Commission (1968, p. 485).

41. Kerner Commission (1968, pp. 484–93).

42. Shachtman (1983, p. 79).

43. Shachtman (1983, p. 267).

44. Walker Report (1968, pp. 255–65).

45. In Holli (1999), Daley is ranked as one of the best mayors in American history between 1820 and 1993.

46. Spofford (1988).

47. Jenkins (1994, p. 41).

48. Quoted in Jenkins (1994, p. 41).

49. Levin and Fox (1985, pp. 219–20).

50. Under the 1942 Supreme Court decision *Betts v. Brady,* only defendants facing capital charges were entitled to a court-appointed attorney at the state level.

51. Padover (1969, p. 345).

52. *New York Times,* October 23, 1994.

53. Hindelang et al. (1981, pp. 196–97).

54. Hindelang et al. (1981, pp. 200–201).

55. Gilje (1996, p. 158).

56. Conley (1994, p. ix).

57. Author (1966).

58. Author (2001, p. 8A).

59. President's Commission on Law Enforcement and Administration of Justice (1967, p. XXX).

60. Kerner Commission (1968, p. 1).

61. Sullivan (1990, p. 114).

62. Useem and Kimball (1989, p. 11).

13

CONTEMPORARY CRIMINAL JUSTICE (1980–1999)

TIME LINE

1980	New Mexico State Prison riot
1981	Sandra Day O'Connor becomes first woman Supreme Court justice
1982	Lethal injection used for first time
1982	Publication of Kelling and Wilson article "Broken Windows"
1982	*Eddings v. Oklahoma* rules that courts must take into account youthfulness of juvenile offenders during capital sentencing
1982	LEAA abolished
1983	President Reagan survives assassination attempt

1984	Comprehensive Crime Control Act
1987	*McCleskey v. Kemp*
1987	DNA first used in a criminal case
1988	Omnibus Drug Law
1988	*Thompson v. Oklahoma*
1990	Congress passes Omnibus Crime Control Act
1991	Beating of black motorist Rodney King by LAPD officers captured on videotape
1991	Christopher Commission recommends that LAPD abandon professional model of policing in favor of community policing approach

1991	George Hennard murders twenty-three in Killeen, Texas, coffee shop	1993	Passage of Brady handgun Violence Prevention Act
1991	Arrest of serial killer Jeffrey Dahmer in Milwaukee	1994	New Jersey passes "Megan's law"
1992	Riots break out in Los Angeles after officers cleared in Rodney King beating	1995	O. J. Simpson murder trial ends in acquittal
1992	Ruby Ridge–FBI confrontation	1995	Bombing of Alfred P. Murrah Federal Building in Oklahoma City
1993	Four federal agents killed at Koresh compound in Waco, Texas	1995	Alabama reintroduces the chain gang
1993	Bombing of World Trade Center in Manhattan	1999	New York City police shoot an unarmed Amadou Diallo
1993	Washington State hangs child killer Westley Allan Dodd, the first hanging since the 1960s	1999	Columbine school-yard shootings

By the time the federal Law Enforcement Assistance Administration was abolished in 1982 (it became the National Institute of Justice, which still sponsors criminal research projects), hundreds of millions of dollars had been directed at improving the criminal justice system. So much focus on crime and criminal justice (and so much federal money available) led many colleges and universities to establish criminal justice programs. Additional funding for more police officers, prosecutors, courts, and prisons led to more reported crimes and arrests and convictions, leading to more prisoners for an overcrowded prison system. Not surprisingly, between 1970 and 1983, the number of criminal justice employees rose from 701,767 to 1,270,342.[1] But despite better-trained and better-equipped law enforcement personnel, crime rates and prison populations continued to escalate.

The ascendance of Ronald Reagan to the presidency in 1980 signaled a new era in criminal justice policy. With the support of the New Right, fundamentalist Christians, and a loose coalition of conservative idealists, the 1980s would witness the reversal of many liberal social, political, and economic forces, as a conservative backlash targeted the increasing availability of abortion, the spread of pornography, and illegal drug use.

The economy was deep in recession in the late 1970s and early 1980s. Since the 1960s, wages had been consistently on the rise, and union wages remained high. But beginning in 1980, union workers faced pay freezes and cuts for the first time in the modern era, and unemployment reached 10 percent. "Reaganomics" was blamed by many critics for exacerbating class and race tensions, the deterioration of the inner cities, declining public education, and increased homelessness. By 1987, several million desperate and poor Americans were homeless.

The Reagan and Bush administrations of the 1980s and early 1990s responded to the drug crisis by boosting spending for law enforcement. Preparing for a new blitzkrieg in the so-called drug war, the Reagan administration doubled the FBI's funding, and the U.S. Bureau of Prisons was the benefactor of a 30 percent increase in spending. Legal restraints were loosened on police investigators as well, with federal wiretaps increasing by more than 20 percent between 1981 and 1982.

The get-tough policies of the 1980s led to the hiring of more than 1,000 new DEA agents, 200 more district attorneys, and an unprecedented reallocation of funds from drug treatment, research, and prevention to law enforcement. By the late 1980s, the Reagan administration had announced a "zero-tolerance" policy, leading to a record number of drug seizures, indictments, arrests, convictions, and asset forfeitures.

Spurred on by fears of a crack cocaine epidemic in the 1980s, the criminal justice system became increasingly more punitive. During the late 1990s, construction of a new jail or prison was completed almost every week. Crack cocaine poisoned many communities as dealers waged war against each other over markets, leading to an upsurge in homicides. However, within a decade, the worst fears of urban America had failed to materialize as the crack trade began to diminish. But the so-called crack wars have made a lasting imprint on American criminal justice, prompting the country to rewrite its drug laws, shift money from schools to prisons, and lock up a record number of people. Yet the new harsh laws have not reduced overall drug use in America.

According to a National Household Survey on Drug Abuse conducted by the Department of Health and Human Services, despite the limited appeal of crack cocaine, a high percentage of prisoners serving time for drug offenses are incarcerated for crack cocaine. Yet it is estimated that in 1997, eleven million Americans smoked

marijuana, 1.5 million used powder cocaine, and 0.6 million used crack. However, incarceration rates tell another story. More than 40 percent of drug offenders are in state prisons for crack cocaine (26.6 in federal prisons), 33.4 for powder cocaine (42.1 in federal prisons), and 12.9 for marijuana violations (18.9 in federal prisons).[2]

The rising crime concerns of the 1980s led to a change in sentencing laws throughout the country. In 1984, Congress passed the Comprehensive Crime Control Act, which created the United States Sentencing Commission. Two years later, the commission announced that "the rehabilitation of a criminal was of secondary importance to protecting the public and that sentences should reflect the seriousness of the crime committed."[3] This reflected a major transition from a rehabilitative model to a punitive one, where there was little to confuse the purpose of prison: punishment not rehabilitation.

Recent research indicates that only one national drug policy saw success over the past quarter century. According to journalist Michael Massing in his book *The Fix,* the Nixon administration's program for treating heroin addicts led to a reduced demand for drugs in the Nixon years. Faced with a heroin epidemic in the 1970s, Nixon responded by allocating hundreds of millions of dollars to set up a nationwide network of methadone clinics and other drug treatment facilities. However, most of this program has been dismantled by succeeding administrations. The reallocation of money from treatment to law enforcement, together with the cutting of the federal drug treatment budget in the Reagan years, perhaps explains why the crack epidemic was worse than it had to be.

Public concern over crime and criminal justice issues continues to dominate the national agendas of politicians and pundits. Some observers suggest that "media coverage of crime stories explains much of the public's interest in criminal justice, as well as the limited extent of their knowledge of the criminal justice system."[4] For most Americans, the perception of crime often conflicts with the reality of crime statistics.

During the past thirty years, crime has surfaced as a concern of the public, but not until the mid-1990s did it register as the major concern of the public. With the concomitant merging of news and entertainment in the 1990s, an excellent opportunity was created to manipulate and sensationalize crime concerns.

THE LAWGIVERS

During the 1980s, President Reagan took advantage of his opportunity as chief executive to appoint conservative-minded justices to the Supreme Court. While the new court leadership did not abandon the advances of the due process revolution, the Court became "more tolerant of police behavior and less receptive to further expansion of rights for criminal defendants."[5] Compared to the 1960s, subsequent rulings would lean toward the prosecution.

In 1983, the Supreme Court ruled in *Gates v. Illinois* that police could obtain a search warrant on the basis of an anonymous tip rather than going through an extensive investigation to corroborate by independent sources the reliability of the tip (as in *Aguilar v. Texas,* 1964). Another important decision reflecting the new conservative bias of the Court was *United States v. Leon,* which held that the exclusionary rule did not apply to evidence obtained by law enforcement who seized the evidence using a warrant that was unsupported by probable cause. In effect this allowed the police to use warrants that contained factual errors and inadequate probable cause. According to one critic, this decision "gave police a 'good faith' exception to the 'exclusionary rule' which requires that courts suppress or disregard illegally obtained evidence."[6]

In 1981, Sandra Day O'Connor became the first woman to be appointed to the Supreme Court.

Born in El Paso, Texas, in 1930, Sandra Day graduated from the Stanford University Law School in 1950 (along with William H. Rehnquist). Rebuffed in her attempts to join major law firms in San Francisco, Day married and raised three sons before opening her own law office in Arizona. She would serve in the Arizona state senate between 1969 and 1974, when she was elected Superior Court judge. Appointed by President Ronald Reagan to the Supreme Court in 1981, during the 1980s and 1990s O'Connor is credited with writing some of the most significant decisions in the area of constitutional law. Among her most important decisions was the case of *Planned Parenthood v. Casey,* in which she upheld *Roe v. Wade,* which made a woman's right to have an abortion a constitutionally protected right in 1973. Resisting pressure from her more conservative colleagues, she convinced two of her more moderate colleagues to join her in upholding the right to choose abortion.

Crime control measures entered the political debate in presidential elections during the 1960s. Republican presidential candidate Barry Goldwater ran on a platform that claimed that rising crime rates were the product of misguided Democratic policies and that by electing Republican candidates voters could reduce the rising tide of violence and lawlessness. Republican candidates for president continued to exploit the crime problem through the candidacies of Richard Nixon, Ronald Reagan, and George H. Bush. During his successful run for president in 1988, many observers credit this campaign issue with helping Vice President Bush defeat Massachusetts Governor Michael Dukakis after convicted felon Willie Horton, out on a weekend furlough from a Massachusetts prison, raped a woman and stabbed her fiancé.

The Insanity Defense

The insanity defense was prominent in several high-profile murder cases in the late 1970s and early 1980s. After former policeman Dan White killed San Francisco Mayor George Moscone and city supervisor and gay rights activist Harvey Milk in 1978, White claimed that his mental capacity was impaired by eating too much "junk food," thereby introducing the "Twinkies defense" to the modern legal lexicon.

White's trial attracted wide media attention not only for the novelty of the defense but also for its volatile mix of politics, revenge, and homosexual intolerance. White's insanity defense led to two verdicts of voluntary manslaughter, and after only five years in prison, White was released in 1984. The following year, he committed suicide. For homosexuals, the trial became a battle cry in that it seemed to them that the jury sanctioned gay murder. Most felt that if White had killed only the mayor, he would still be in jail.

In 1982, a celebrated crime once more challenged the foundations of the insanity defense. On March 30, 1981, John Hinckley Jr. fired six shots at President Ronald Reagan and members of his staff as they entered the Washington Hilton Hotel. Several people were hit, including the president, Press Secretary James Brady, a police officer, and a Secret Service agent. Hinckley was quickly arrested and charged with attempted murder.

Testimony during the 1982 trial escalated into a battle between medical opinions. Almost immediately, the defense team entered a plea of not guilty by reason of insanity. What would soon shift the outcome of the trial toward the defendant was the judge's decision to hear the case under federal procedural rules, which meant that the prosecution would bear the burden of proving Hinckley's sanity beyond a reasonable doubt. If the case had been tried under local rule, the defense attorneys would have borne the pressure of having to prove their client insane. In June 1982, after listening to hours of confusing and contradictory testimony, the jurors brought back a verdict of not guilty by reason of insanity. Although Hinckley was committed to a mental institution, the verdict stimulated a vociferous debate over the insanity defense.

Mandatory Sentencing

Congress implemented more than twenty new mandatory sentencing laws between 1985 and 1991. By 1994, virtually every state had adopted at least some form of mandatory sentencing legislation. These laws typically applied to serious offenses, such as murder, rape, and handgun crimes, but also applied to drunk driving and drug offenses.[7] Mandatory minimum drug sentences have come under increasing scrutiny by critics because they take sentencing discretion from the hands of the judges who in times past could consider an offender's life history, potential for rehabilitation, job status, and family responsibilities before delivering sentence. As a result of this facet of the war on drugs, the proportion of incarcerated drug offenders has increased, while that of violent offenders has decreased. Most alarming is the overrepresentation of minorities due to disparities in drug sentencing.

In 1993, the refrain "Three strikes and you're out" became the rallying cry for get-tough politicians. This phrase was coined in Washington State after voters approved a ballot measure requiring life sentences without the possibility of parole for third-time serious felony offenders. Over the next few years, more than a dozen states introduced similar provisions. California introduced three-strikes legislation that sentenced any adult convicted of a third serious felony to prison from twenty-five years to life. Although the intent of this legislation is to remove vicious predators from the streets, these laws are somewhat misleading to a public enamored by get-tough legislation. The current federal three-strikes law does not even distinguish between violent and nonviolent felons.

The three-strikes sentencing policy originated in California after the abduction and murder of Polly Klaas in the early 1980s by a career criminal who had been in and out of prison for most of his life. This high-profile case led to harsher sentences for violent offenders for their second offense and life without parole for their third offense.

The murder of Polly Klaas resonated throughout the country. A young girl was snatched from her own bedroom and brutally killed. This crime, according to legal historian Lawrence M. Friedman, "was a powerful stimulus to some draconian pieces of legislation."[8] Unfortunately, as Friedman and others have noted, never have television and the news media influenced criminal justice policy as they do today.

Although California's statute remained the most austere, other states followed its example in subsequent years. In 1994, New Jersey passed "Megan's law" after young Megan Kanka was raped and murdered by a neighbor. Area residents had no idea that the perpetrator who lived among them had two prior convictions for sex offenses. Under the new law, on release from prison, sex offenders were required to register with the police. By 2000, at least twenty-two states even listed sex offender registries on the Internet.

Despite the good intentions of three-strikes legislation, defendants are less likely to plea bargain (plead guilty) if they already have two felonies. One of the unforeseen results has been an increase in the amount of defendants going to trial. As a result, an already overburdened criminal justice system is faced with a growing number of nonviolent criminals facing their third strike in court. In previous years, close to 90 percent of similar cases were handled with plea bargains, saving the expense and time of a trial. Unwilling to plead guilty, these defendants wait in jail pending trials, further contributing to overcrowded correctional facilities.

The Brady Handgun Bill

Between 1987 and 1993, gun control advocates campaigned for an enactment of a waiting period for handgun purchases. The notion of having a waiting period for gun buyers can be traced back to at least the 1930s, when the District of Columbia enacted a forty-eight-hour waiting period for gun buyers. Gun control proponents argued that a waiting period for gun purchases was necessary to provide authorities time to conduct a background check on the purchaser and to void gun purchases by felons and the mentally incompetent. Although the idea of a waiting period seems moderate, it has touched off a rancorous debate between supporters and opponents.

The Brady bill was named after James Brady, Reagan's former press secretary, who was seriously injured in the assassination attempt on the president in 1981. The bill was first introduced in

Congress in 1987 but was quickly challenged by the National Rifle Association (NRA), which argued that any handgun legislation would lead only to more strict gun control. NRA spokespersons claimed that the proposed law would not prevent criminals from getting guns but merely inconvenience legitimate purchasers.

After several unsuccessful attempts, the Brady bill, imposing a seven-day waiting period, was finally approved by Congress in 1991. Although then President George H. Bush opposed the bill, he agreed to sign the measure if it included a five-business-day waiting period in 1993. The Brady Handgun Violence Prevention Act of 1993 emerged after a lengthy debate in Congress. According to the law, handgun purchases were to be rejected if the applicant had been convicted of a crime that carries a sentence of at least one year (not including misdemeanors). Others prohibited included anyone with a violence-based restraining order pending, persons convicted of domestic abuse, those arrested for using or selling drugs, fugitives from justice, anyone certified as mentally unstable, and illegal aliens. In 1998, the five-day waiting period was replaced by instant background checks conducted by the FBI's National Instant Criminal Background Check System. The jury is still out as to whether this measure has had much impact on gun crime, but between 1993 and 2000 almost 600,000 handgun sales were blocked as a result of the law.

LAW ENFORCEMENT

Women and minorities continued to make inroads on police forces in ever-increasing numbers. By the early 1980s, women would make up more than 5.5 percent of sworn officers nationwide.[9] Over the next decade, the portrait of the typical police officer had changed substantially. Most studies credit "the women's movement and laws barring employment discrimination based on sex" for a quadrupling of the number of female sworn officers between 1972 and 1986.[10] The number of racial minority peace officers increased as well. By the end of the 1980s, major American cities boasted African American police chiefs, including New York City, Atlanta, Chicago, and Houston.

During the 1980s, police forces made concerted efforts to improve their tarnished image and relations with the communities they served. Among the public relations strategies toward this end were crime prevention programs that instructed communities how to protect themselves and initiating identification programs so that residents could mark their possessions for future identification. Many communities also established "neighborhood watch" programs that encouraged citizen cooperation with the police.

Attempts at improving the often rancorous relationships between police departments and the communities they served were widely heralded in the 1980s. Better police–community relations were given a high priority by most departments, particularly after the publication of George Kelling and James Q. Wilson's widely read *Atlantic Monthly* article in 1982, "Broken Windows: The Police and Neighborhood Safety," in which the authors articulated a vision for improving police relations in the community, using what the two justice policy experts called the "broken-windows model."

According to the broken-windows model of policing, neighborhood disorder creates fear, and neighborhoods give out crime-promoting signals, such as broken windows and deteriorated housing. An increase in the physical deterioration of a neighborhood then leads to increased concern for personal safety among local residents. Offenders often target these neighborhoods because they see certain signs that translate to vulnerability. Police, then, need the cooperation of citizens if they intend to reduce fear and successfully fight crime in these environments.

The endorsement of "broken windows" by many police administrators represented a major step toward enlisting communities in the war against crime by theoretically reverting back to an earlier historical model of policing. Since the Progressive era, August Vollmer, and the intro-

duction of the police car, proponents of "broken windows" claim that the patrol officer has been increasingly removed from the mainstream of the community. Rather than encouraging citizen confidence and cooperation, generally the reverse was occurring. While police cars maintained a presence, ensured rapid response to a crime scene, and covered a wider area, they also alienated many community members who might otherwise help the police.

In the 1980s, some urban police departments returned to an earlier style when police walked a beat or foot patrol and maintained intimate contact with the area they served. The implementation of community policing took officers out of patrol cars and put them on a walking beat to strengthen ties to the community. Although early studies indicated that foot patrols did not decrease the crime rate, residents who lived in these areas reported they were less afraid of crime and felt safer.

However, some observers believed that community policing was anything but new. Police and criminal justice historian Samuel Walker has suggested that the authors of the "broken-windows" thesis "have misinterpreted police history in several important respects," while former San Jose Police Chief Joseph McNamara added that "the good old days [of policing] weren't all that good."[11] Walker, McNamara, and others argued that although modern police departments and officials claimed to be returning to an earlier "watchman style of policing," this style was "inefficient and corrupt" and did "not involve any conscious purpose to serve neighborhood needs." According to Walker, "There is no older tradition worthy of restoration."[12] Reaching back in time using a historical analysis, historians such as Walker have been able to demonstrate that "depersonalization" of policing has been "greatly exaggerated." The introduction of the squad car may have isolated police to a certain extent, but other technological advances, such as the telephone, allowed more private contact between residents and police who were called in to mediate personal disputes more than ever.

A reflection of the conservative mood of the country, the New York City Police Department under Mayor Rudolph Giuliani embarked on a campaign to take illegal handguns off the streets in the mid-1990s. Although civil liberties groups claimed that the police targeted minority group members with "street justice tactics," new police strategies were credited with helping to reduce violent crime in New York City in the 1990s.

Targeting certain precincts where gun violence was high, the police department saturated the area with plainclothes officers and detectives using what was referred to as "flood and frisk tactics." They would be followed by uniformed officers into the anointed "hot zone." Looking for any legal excuse to stop and question suspected drug dealers or suspicious drivers, officers frisked individuals, hoping to find illegal guns or contraband. While only a few guns were taken off the streets, the aggressive police presence convinced many to keep their guns at home and off the streets.

Many police departments retooled for the 1990s, including New York City, which added thousands of police officers to the force. At the end of 1996, 37,871 police officers served New York City's 7.3 million residents, a ratio of one for every 193 citizens.[13]

Although there is little evidence that having officers live where they work makes any difference in the quality of policing, in the late 1990s police residency requirements became an issue. According to figures released in early 1999, only 54 percent of New York City's police force lived in the city (down from 60 percent the previous decade). Following the botched shooting of Amadou Diallo, an unarmed West African street vendor, community advocates intensified calls for a residency requirement after it was revealed that two of the four officers did not live in the city. Mr. Diallo was the target of forty-one bullets as he stood in the vestibule of his Bronx apartment. While community leaders and civil libertarians are quick to suggest that residency requirements would familiarize officers with the environment they serve, others argue there is no empirical evidence to back up this contention. Neverthe-less, police and city officials quickly embarked on a hiring campaign to lure more New Yorkers to the force in hopes that it would lead to more racial diversity.

Residency requirements for city workers originated in the nineteenth century. According to the Justice Department, close to 25 percent of America's municipal police departments with more than 100 officers require them to live within city limits. Forty percent of departments require officers to live within a certain radius of the city they serve. In New York City, where police are currently exempt from residency restrictions, less than 43 percent of the white officers lived in the city, while more than 70 percent of black, Hispanic, and Asian American officers lived in the city's five boroughs. Compared to New York City, in 1994 more than 80 percent of the Los Angeles Police Department lived outside the city.

Federal Law Enforcement

During the 1980s and 1990s, the FBI turned its focus to a number of new militant antigovernment groups. Domestic in origin, militia groups popped up throughout America's heartland. It was not until 1985 that the FBI targeted specific groups, when the white supremacist group known as The Order committed a string of violent bank robberies to finance future activities. During the 1990s, the FBI came under heavy criticism for its handling of several major standoffs.

The confrontation between federal agents and the Randy Weaver family in Ruby Ridge, Idaho, in 1992 led to public condemnation and debate over the abuse of federal power. What is lost in much of the controversy was the connection between this incident and the ongoing federal campaign against The Order in its stronghold in the Northwest. Randy Weaver came to the attention of federal agents of the Bureau of Alcohol, Tobacco, and Firearms (ATF) when he sold illegal sawed-off shotguns to an ATF informant. In January 1991, Weaver was arrested on gun charges in Idaho. Posting bond, Weaver retreated to his mountain cabin, where he held out with his wife and three children, ignoring a failure to appear warrant.

Fearing impending arrest and the possibility of losing their home, the Weavers became increasingly militant during the eighteen-month standoff. In August 1992, a U.S. marshal was killed during an exchange of gunfire, signaling an escalation of the tension. The following day, an FBI sniper killed Weaver's wife and wounded a houseguest. Soon after, Randy Weaver was persuaded to surrender. The siege at Ruby Ridge had major ramifications for federal law enforcement fighting domestic terrorism in the twentieth century. According to one writer, "The distinguishable features of the American right were becoming blurred," and "in time it would allow anti-government sentiment to become nationalized, thus gaining a larger and more moderate constituency."[14]

A young cult leader named David Koresh tested federal agents in Waco, Texas, the following year. The handling of the initial raid on the Branch Davidian compound by the FBI led once more to questions about the judgment of the FBI. The FBI took over after the efforts by the ATF failed, leading to one of the longest standoffs in law enforcement history. After trying for fifty-one days to convince Branch Davidian members to peacefully withdraw from their sanctuary, the FBI stormed the compound with the aid of tanks and tear gas. The entire facility was almost immediately consumed by fire, leading to the deaths of eighty-five men, women, and children.

Subsequent congressional hearings in 1995 witnessed FBI director Louis J. Freeh admitting to "serious deficiencies in the FBI's performance during the crisis." Further investigation found the operation to be flawed and a violation of FBI policy and the Constitution. Following this episode, the FBI director promised to revise the agency's deadly-force policy and to limit the use of the rules of engagement. With the lessons gleaned from Ruby Ridge and Waco, the FBI peacefully negotiated a lengthy standoff with a "patriot group" called the Freemen in 1996.

Fifty years ago, the FBI introduced its Ten Most Wanted List. Long considered a publicity gimmick rather than a measure of criminal menace, the list does chronicle the changing nature of American crime over the past half century. In the past, bank robbers, serial killers, and campus radicals dominated the list in various time periods. The current list reflects contemporary concerns over the globalization of crime, the drug wars, and domestic terrorism. In 1999, Osama bin Laden, suspected of masterminding two deadly embassy bombings the previous year, was added to the list, where he joined Eric Rudolph, implicated in several bombings that included an Alabama abortion clinic and the 1996 Atlanta Olympics. Of the 458 men and women who have graced FBI Most Wanted Lists over the past fifty years, 429 have been apprehended, 134 of them with the help of private citizens. Where formerly the radio and newspapers primed the FBI's publicity machine, citizens can now find twenty-four-hour descriptions of wanted fugitives on the Internet, which sometimes includes home movies of the fugitives showing undisguisable mannerisms, accents, and idiosyncrasies.

Rodney King and the Los Angeles Police Department

Following a three-mile high-speed car chase in the early hours of March 3, 1991, Rodney King was ordered to get out of his car by several Los Angeles police officers. According to officers, King was noncompliant and scuffled with the officers, who were forced to resort to batons and stun guns to subdue the hulking King.[15] Unknown to the police was the fact that someone had tape-recorded much of the incident. The eighty-one-second tape of police officers beating and kicking a supine King while other officers stood and watched resonated in African American and other minority neighborhoods of Los Angeles, where tension with police continued to fester since the 1960s Watts riot. According to a *Los Angeles Times* poll taken two weeks after the beating, 87 percent of the African American and 80 percent of the Hispanic respondents reported incidents of brutality at the hands of the Los Angeles Police Department (LAPD) as either "very common" or "fairly common."[16]

Following the beating of King, a commission was convened by Mayor Tom Bradley to investigate the LAPD. The so-called Christopher Commission, chaired by future U.S. secretary of state Warren Christopher, published its findings and recommendations in July 1991. The ten-member commission was comprised of six lawyers, two professors, a college president, and a corporation chairman. The findings of the Christopher Commission report called for reform in the department, demanding the end of excessive force and racism by the police force. Its report would ultimately lead to the resignation of LAPD chief Daryl Gates.

Widespread anger over the taped beating led to grand jury indictments against four of the officers for assault (twenty-three were actually present at the assault) and the use of excessive force. The defense would successfully have the trial moved to the mostly white community of Simi Valley on the grounds that it would be impossible to get a fair verdict in the city of Los Angeles. With the eyewitness testimony of the videotape, conviction of the officers seemed a forgone conclusion. But on April 29, 1992, the jurors acquitted the four officers, sparking some of the worst race riots in American history.

Within minutes of the verdict, black and Hispanic Los Angeles exploded in violence. Whites were dragged from their cars and beaten as Korean merchants engaged in gunfights with gangs of looters. Fifty-eight deaths were reported during the riots. After several days of violence, the National Guard, together with federal troops, helped quell the riots. Their trial, acquittal, and the subsequent riots in 1992 made the second trial of the officers in 1993 one of the highest-profile cases in American legal history.

CORRECTIONS

Between 1970 and 1980, the population of America's prisons doubled. By the time they doubled once more between 1981 and 1995, American prisons and jails held 1.75 million inmates. With a rate of imprisonment of 426 per 100,000 in 1991, America had one of the highest rates of incarceration in the world and the highest in its brief history.[17] Unlike the 1970s, which saw a marked increase in crime rates, the 1980s and 1990s saw only periodic increases in crime (1985–1990), never reaching the heights of the previous decade. But prison populations continued to soar at record levels. Rates of incarceration continued to vary by region, with the South imprisoning more people per capita than any other region.

While blacks made up only 12 percent of the nation's population, they represented more than 44 percent of the total local, state, and federal prison population. According to one authority, America's black incarceration rate was "more than 4.2 [times] higher than South Africa's before the fall of Apartheid."[18] By the middle of 1994, the number of black inmates exceeded whites for the first time, with almost 7 percent of all black men in prison or jail compared to less than 1 percent of the white male population.[19]

When considering the racial disparity of America's prisons, there are other implications to consider. A substantial number of African Americans are disenfranchised since many states prohibit convicted felons from voting. Together with the fact that the imprisoned are universally prevented from voting, this is a large voting bloc that has effectively lost its political voice.

By the 1990s, the federal prison had kept pace with rising crime rates and the expanding state prison systems. In previous eras, federal criminal law targeted violators of the Mann Act, bootleggers, and the interstate transportation of stolen motor vehicles. In the 1990s, more than 60 percent of federal prisoners were convicted for drug offenses.

Except for the "dot-com" explosion at the end of the twentieth century, no business flourished to the extent of the prison business. In former days, prison construction was a tough sell to communities. With a downward turn in the economy in the 1980s, communities were less reluctant to host such enterprises. By the middle of the 1990s, more than 5,000 correctional facilities dotted the landscape, including more than 3,000 local jails. In rural America, towns even competed for prison construction. There was no greater job security than working for a prison. Unlike General Motors or a military base, there was no threat of closure or moving south of the border.

Since the 1970s, correction officers have followed their police counterparts who in the 1960s formed labor unions. The unionization of corrections has coincided with the unprecedented expansion of the prison system. Other segments of the working force have benefited from prison expansion, including legions of building contractors, architects, hardware and electronics companies, and security firms.

By the end of the 1990s, California was operating the nation's largest prison system with a budget of almost $4 billion a year. The state added twenty-one prisons between 1984 and 1999. But many politicians worry that this building boom was at the expense of other budget items, such as higher education. While salaries remained stagnant in the state's university system (average pay for a first-year professor was $41,000), prison guards were making $51,000 per year.

By the 1980s, it became clear to most correctional authorities that the rehabilitative model of corrections was a failure, citing high rates of recidivism. Thus, a new policy of warehousing serious offenders to protect society gained increasing popularity as deinstitutionalization initiatives soon fell by the wayside. As a consequence of the new "lock-'em-up" strategy, American prisons became seriously overcrowded. Between 1980 and 1999, the state and federal prison populations tripled in size from 329,000 to more than 1.2 million inmates.[20] Beginning in 1990, a major program of prison expansion was implemented that helped reduce some of the overcrowding by the end of the

1990s. Among the biggest administrative difficulties caused by warehousing of prisoners is the extreme expense and the unmanageability of prison populations.

Prison Privatization

The 1980s witnessed an increase in both prison populations and prison labor. In order to reduce some of the costs of warehousing inmates, prisons increasingly turned to the private sector. Between 1985 and 1995, private prisons increased at a 500 percent clip. By the mid-1990s, at least thirty states were contracting out prison labor to private companies. Returning to developments of a previous century, there was a movement to deregulate prison industry so that prison-made items could be sold on the free market.

With "the growth of privatization and anti-government and anti-union sentiments" in the 1990s, "the appeal of prison as a source of cheap labor"[21] led to a variety of privatization models. In some cases, private companies built and operated prisons and jails on behalf of various branches of the government, while others leased prisons to the government to be run by the department of corrections. Often paid less than the minimum wage, inmates performed a multitude of tasks, including packing golf balls for Spalding, sorting inventory for Toys R Us, and manufacturing uniforms for McDonald's. While unions and civil rights organizations have lobbied against the privatization of prisons, few critics of human rights violations overseas have made the connection with the use of American prison labor at home.[22]

At the conclusion of the 1990s, the debate over prison labor became a topic of conversation once more. Recalling the prison labor movement of the late nineteenth century, when prisoners worked for private employers without pay, prison laborers now work under better conditions. In 1979, Congress authorized the hiring of prisoners by private employers after years of prohibiting this arrangement.

With unemployment at a record low and with more Americans than ever behind bars, the number of prisoners working in the private sector has doubled since 1995. In sharp contrast with traditional prison labor, such as making license plates and painting school buses, the 1990s saw prisoners working in telemarketing and the computer industry. By the end of the first quarter of 2000, more than 80,000 inmates were employed at traditional jobs, working for companies and government at anywhere from twenty-five cents to seven dollars per hour.[23]

While criminal justice officials see these programs as a path to reform and employers appreciate the cheap labor, there are others who would insist that prison labor is a human rights abuse and a potential economic threat to free-world workers. According to one California lawsuit, since prisoners have no bargaining power, they can be easily exploited. The verdict is still out on prison labor programs, but most law enforcement authorities and small businessmen see it as a panacea for the current labor shortage and the swelling prison populations, which reached two million in 2000.

Supermax Prisons

One trend that continued to draw support was the construction of super-maximum security, or "supermax," prisons in the 1990s. Although the federal government opened its first maximum-security prison at Alcatraz in 1934, it was not until 1994 that the Federal Bureau of Prisons opened its first supermax prison at Florence, Colorado. It has housed criminal luminaries ranging from Oklahoma City bomber Timothy McVeigh and "Unabomber" Theodore Kaczynski to World Trade Center bomber Ramzi Yousef (all in the same wing). It is estimated that one-fourth of the 387 inmates have killed or attempted to kill a prisoner.

Prison rights advocates have criticized these solitary confinement prisons as inhumane, much in the way Charles Dickens attacked Eastern State Penitentiary in the 1840s. At supermax prisons, inmates spend almost twenty-three hours per day confined in seven-by-twelve-foot cells. One critic

suggests that there was barely room to hold a sports-utility vehicle in one of these cells. Every cell contained a stool, a writing desk, and a mattress pedestal made of concrete (to prevent weapon making). At least thirty-six states operate such institutions, where prisoners can squint through a four-foot-by-four-inch vertical window at the exercise yard below or at a sky crisscrossed by steel beams and helicopter-resistant wires. Some prisons prohibit cigarettes and television.

Much in the vein of the "mark system," bad behavior "gets you in," and good behavior "will get you out." Good behavior can win a "program out" to a traditional penitentiary in three years as prisoners advance through various stages where they are rewarded with more time out of the cell and other perks.

Crack Cocaine and Sentencing Disparity

According to one Justice Department study, one out of every twenty Americans born in 1999 will serve time in prison. An African American male had a one in four chance compared with 0.8 for white males. Statistics indicate that these odds were more even at one time. However, the get-tough sentencing of the 1980s and the criminal justice system's special treatment of crack cocaine has dramatically altered the balance. America, unlike any other country, makes no distinction between the properties of crack and powder cocaine. Under federal law, five grams of crack (which is cocaine processed to be smoked) is recognized as the equal to 500 grams of cocaine, a 1-to-100 ratio. The possession of five grams of crack by statute is a felony, while five grams of the drug in powder form is a misdemeanor, with rarely any jail time. The disparity is glaring.

CRIME AND PUNISHMENT

The 1980s and early 1990s were characterized by an overwhelming fear of crime. While serial killers, mass murderers, and drug crime continued to dominate the nightly television news blitz, new crime fears beckoned on the horizon featuring school-yard shootings and domestic terrorism.

In 1999, the "deadly tower" on Austin's University of Texas campus was reopened. It had been closed following the murderous sniper shootings by Charles Whitman in 1966. Demonstrating the continuing threat of mass murder in American society, Whitman's body count of sixteen dead and thirty-one wounded would be exceeded several times in the 1980s and 1990s, most notably by George Hennard, who killed twenty-three and wounded twenty-three at a Killeen, Texas, restaurant in 1991. In 1984, James O. Huberty murdered twenty-one and wounded nineteen at a California McDonald's restaurant. Two years later, a disgruntled postal worker killed fourteen and wounded six, giving credence to the expression of "going postal."

The increased concerns over crime victimization in the 1980s led many Americans to carry concealed weapons. No case illustrated the potential ramifications of carrying concealed weapons better than the Bernard Goetz trial. In December 1984, a thirty-six-year-old electrical engineer named Bernard Goetz was approached by four black youths while riding a New York City subway. Having been injured in an assault just three years earlier, Goetz took to carrying a concealed handgun whenever he went out. When one of the youths asked him for five dollars, Goetz went for his revolver and shot at the men. Two were critically wounded, including one that Goetz shot in the spinal cord after he fell down while trying to escape. Goetz turned himself in to the police nine days later and was charged with a number of offenses, including attempted murder and criminal possession of a gun.

During the subsequent trial two years later, Goetz was turned into the victim of the case by his defense team, noting the criminal backgrounds of the actual victims. The trial would challenge the criminal justice system on several fronts, addressing the question of a citizen's right to defend oneself. In June 1987, the jury returned a verdict of not guilty on twelve counts and guilty on one charge of criminal possession

of a weapon in the third degree. Three months later, Goetz was sentenced to six months in prison (two years later, on review, his sentence was doubled to one year).

Other Crime Trends

Between 1980 and 1997, property crimes in the United States declined by almost 50 percent. The drop in property crimes, such as burglary, larceny, and auto thefts, did not receive the same attention as more dramatic crimes of violence. However, explanations for the decline of both types of crimes received similar explanations. Many law enforcement administrators and criminologists suggested that the drop in property crime was the result of improved police tactics, a decline in the teenage population, and greater community involvement and that longer prison sentences were responsible for the drop in violence in crime. Others explained that the drop in property crime was the result of the enhanced use of alarm systems. However, criminologist Scott Decker dissents, noting that most burglaries take place in poor neighborhoods that lack alarm systems, not the more affluent suburbs. Decker argues that the decline has more to do with crack addicts giving up "burglary because it required too much planning and involved the uncertainty of whether a resident might be home, perhaps with a gun." In need of a quick high, crack addicts made the transition to robbery, which was considered a faster and safer strategy for providing quick cash.[24]

Although the drop in property crime has been felt in most major cities, none has seen the numbers drop as great as San Diego, California. As of 1997, San Diego witnessed a 68 percent drop in burglary between 1980 and 1996. Police also claimed that larceny crimes, such as petty theft, shoplifting, pickpocketing, and motor vehicle break-ins, declined by 37 percent. In addition, auto thefts plummeted 61 percent.[25] Unlike New York City's former police commissioner William Bratton, who credited his city's crime decline to an increased police presence,

San Diego's police chief Jerry Sanders gives credit to new types of community-oriented policing.

San Diego has a 2,036-member police force that is augmented by 8,000 volunteers. Many of these volunteers patrol their neighborhoods during the weekends or help fill out excess paperwork at the police stations. With only 1.7 police officers per 1,000 residents (compared to New York's 5.2 and Washington, D.C.'s, 6.84), community-oriented policing is crucial to San Diego, which has the lowest ratio of officers per capita in the country.[26]

Beginning in the early 1990s, American crime rates continued to drop, although homicides by juveniles were on the rise. According to criminologist James Alan Fox, the rate of homicide by juveniles fourteen to seventeen years old rose from 8.5 per 100,000 in 1984 to 30.2 per 100,000 in 1993 before declining to 16.5 per 100,000 in 1997, still almost double that of 1984 levels.[27]

Several high-profile juvenile slayings led prosecutors and legislators to try more juveniles as adults. Traditionally, eighteen has been the age most commonly used to define adulthood in the United States. However, state, federal, and local laws now set a variety of thresholds for young people's responsibilities. While in times past lawbreakers under eighteen were consigned to the juvenile courts where their names were kept private and sentence structured to maximize the chance for rehabilitation, over the past decade more and more juveniles are ending up in adult courts.

On November 17, 1999, thirteen-year-old Nathaniel Abraham was convicted for the fatal shooting of a stranger two years earlier. This case once more fueled the national debate over the juvenile justice system. Abraham was the youngest child to be charged with murder in Michigan and the first to be tried under the state's 1996 juvenile justice law, roundly considered one of the most severe in the nation. Similarly, in Florida, fourteen-year-old Nathaniel Braziel faced trial as an adult for killing an English teacher at his middle school.

In 1998, a series of school shootings in Pennsylvania, Arkansas, and Oregon raised more concerns about juvenile access to firearms. In 1999, the worst of these shootings took place at Columbine High School in Littleton, Colorado, where two teenage students killed thirteen before committing suicide (see the "American Violence" section later in this chapter).

Decline of Traditional Organized Crime?

The 1980s finally saw law enforcement make inroads on organized crime. Mob expert James B. Jacobs credits the Racketeer Influenced and Corrupt Organizations (RICO) statutes and the government's campaign with winning convictions against twenty-three major mob bosses and their associates since 1981. While Jacobs suggests that it is too early to write the obituary for America's mob families, new crime-fighting strategies demonstrate the sudden vulnerability of mobsters confronted by effective law enforcement.[28]

Since the 1920s and 1930s, the federal government has attempted a variety of methods to destroy if not cripple America's entrenched Mafia groups. However, until 1970 these groups were virtually immune from prosecution. The FBI was indifferent to organized crime for much of this period, and local policing was often inept or corrupt.

The turning point in the war against Italian American organized crime was 1970, when Congress passed the Organized Crime Control Act, the first legislation designed specifically to strike at organized crime activity. This act created a witness protection program and established a formal system to encourage informers to testify by giving them new identities and financial aid and relocating them and their families far from the danger of reprisals. The most significant part of the new legislation was the RICO sections, under which mob bosses and their subordinates could be implicated if prosecutors prove they were linked to a criminal group or enterprise. Except for New York and Chicago, the American Mafia's major families have been largely destroyed or diminished in power.

Besides the utilization of RICO, generational changes have also conspired against the Mafia and have undermined Mob discipline and weakened the code of silence. By the end of the 1980s, organized crime leaders were agreeing to cooperate with the government in return for leniency and admission into the Witness Security Program. In the 1992 trial of Gambino family crime boss John Gotti, the government used the testimony of his underboss Sammy "the Bull" Gravano (Gotti's second in command) to strengthen its case. It would be unthinkable in years past that someone of Gravano's stature would break the code of silence. But times had changed. Gotti had been acquitted in three previous trials, but this time he was found guilty on all counts and was sentenced to life in prison without parole.

Capital Punishment

In 1999, 3,555 men and women sat on death rows across the nation. Although most Americans continue to support the death penalty, only about 2 percent of death row inmates are actually executed. Between 1976 and May 31, 1999, there were 546 executions, with Texas leading the way with 170, including a record forty in 1999. Never of one mind about the death penalty in America, twelve states and the District of Columbia do not use the death penalty, while several others imposed moratoriums on its use (Illinois and Maryland). Having legally shelved the death penalty in 1972, in 1977, following a nine-year moratorium (there were none between 1968 and 1972), it returned with a vengeance, beginning with the firing squad execution of Gary Gilmore in Utah in 1978.

In January 1993, Washington State conducted the nation's first hanging in twenty-eight years when Westley Allan Dodd was hanged for raping and murdering several children. Although by law Dodd was allowed to choose between hanging and lethal injection, he selected hanging since, as he explained, that was the method he used to dispatch his young victims.

Since the eighteenth-century Enlightenment, criminal justice reformers have continued to seek more humane methods of execution. For many, 1982 would represent a watershed of sorts when Texas inmate Charles Brooks became the first person to be executed by lethal injection. With no sparks, blood, or the wafting odor of burning flesh, reformers were convinced that they had hit on a scientific method of execution that would be amenable to the modern era. However, law-and-order advocates opposed it on the basis that the criminal should suffer like the victim.

Between 1977 and 1989, the number of death row prisoners increased from 423 to 2,250. Death row stays of execution continued to keep pace as well, thanks in part to the frequency of habeas challenges and abolitionist strategies ranging from petitions for grants of clemency and public demonstrations to legislative lobbying. Between 1977 and 1989, average time between sentencing and execution increased from fifty-one months to ninety-five months.[29]

Rising public support for capital punishment in the 1970s and 1980s accompanied the growing crime rates. A 1985 Gallup Poll study found that seven out of ten Americans favored the death penalty, the highest level of support since the poll began querying support for the death penalty in 1936. Often lost in any discussion of the death penalty is the drop in support for it when the alternative of life without parole is offered as well.

In 1987, the death penalty was once more called into question in the case of *McCleskey v. Kemp*. Charged with armed robbery and the murder of a white police officer during a robbery in Georgia, Warren McCleskey, who was black, was quickly arrested, convicted, and sentenced to death. McCleskey appealed his sentence on the grounds that it had been imposed in a racially discriminatory manner. His attorneys presented evidence from the results of a statistical study profiling 2,000 Georgia murder cases from the 1970s that demonstrated that black defendants were more likely than other defendants to be sentenced to death. Investigators concluded that black defendants who killed white victims were much more likely to receive the death sentence than any other racial combination. Ultimately, the Supreme Court denied McCleskey's appeal on the grounds that the statistical study presented as evidence was insufficient to prove racial discrimination in his case. The Court also held that his treatment did not violate the Eighth Amendment's prohibition of cruel and unusual punishment.

In the 1980s, several Supreme Court cases took up the constitutionality of executing juveniles. In *Thompson v. Oklahoma,* the Court overturned the death sentence of Monty Lee Edwards, who was fifteen when he participated in a murder in 1982. The defense argued that the sentencing judge failed to consider the defendant's age and abusive childhood. In 1988, the Court ruled that executing an individual who committed a crime before the age of sixteen violated the Eighth Amendment's prohibition against cruel and unusual punishment, thereby establishing sixteen as the minimum age for the death penalty at the time of offense (eighteen states had already set this age as minimum for death penalty).

By 1990, thirty states had adopted life without parole as an alternative to the death penalty while 2,400 prisoners awaited execution on death rows from coast to coast. In 1994, the Gallup Poll continued to demonstrate overwhelming support for the death penalty, registering an all-time high of 80 percent.

America is the only country in the world that uses the electric chair and the gas chamber for executions. Utah, Oklahoma, and Idaho still use firing squads, and every few years Delaware, Washington, or New Hampshire resort to hanging. An ABC News Poll in early 2000 found that support for the death penalty decreased from 64 to 48 percent when there was an option of life without parole. Other surveys captured similar results. With recent accounts of wrongfully convicted death row inmates having their sentences overturned because of DNA evidence, a growing number of citizens favor alternatives to capital

punishment. A 2000 Gallup Poll examined why Americans support state-sanctioned killings, or executions. According to the survey, the most frequently cited reason was "a life for a life," retribution so reminiscent of earlier and less sophisticated civilizations.[30]

Cruel and Unusual?

Originally used as a form of punishment in the South, the rattle of the chain gang returned to America in 1995, when Alabama reintroduced this measure as a cheaper and more effective way to manage exploding prison populations. Chained in five-man groups eight feet apart, prisoners worked twelve-hour days cutting and trimming roadsides and cleaning up litter. In the 1960s, Georgia became the last state to abolish the chain gang. According to one prison commissioner, the return of chain gangs should be considered a deterrence measure "that would leave a lasting impression on young people."[31]

Not confined to the South, the chain gang was revived in Arizona and Wisconsin as well. Reverting to criminal justice strategies of a previous era, the Wisconsin chain gang also borrowed a page from the future when it became the first state to equip its prisoners with stun belts. Capable of delivering an eight-second burst of 50,000 volts of electricity, the belt would be triggered by a guard at a control panel in the event of an escape attempt. Despite the concerns of Amnesty International, according to Wisconsin prison officials, prisoners were eager for any outside activity.[32]

AMERICAN VIOLENCE

Historian Roger Lane chronicled the history of American murder patterns in *Murder in America.* Published in 1997, his work came at a curious moment in American history, at a time when the nation was transfixed by the O. J. Simpson murder trial, unsurpassed incidents of domestic terror, and a series of school-yard shootings and rampage killings, leaving most Americans under the impression that the nation was under siege by violent crime. Lane, however, concludes that if one were to compare 1990s homicide rates with times past, except for intermittent ups and downs, "not much had changed."[33]

What gave Americans their bleak impression of current murder rates was the saturation coverage given to certain high-profile crimes. Some of these crimes were unprecedented in scope. Among the most notorious crimes of the era was the eighteen-year murderous bombing spree of "Unabomber" Theodore Kaczynski between 1978 and 1996. The math professor turned Luddite targeted university professors and a cornucopia of other representatives of what Kaczynski saw as the "Industrial Society." After killing three and wounding more than a dozen with carefully constructed mail bombs, Kaczynski blackmailed several newspapers to publish his manifesto "Industrial Society and Its Future." Despite the intense manhunt, it was his own brother who identified him after recognizing the jargon of the Unabomber as phrases and philosophy often espoused by his brother.

Historian Paul Gilje has suggested that one of the legacies of the 1960s "was the ghetto riot."[34] Unlike the 1960s, which saw each hot summer explode into urban orgies of looting and arson after seemingly ordinary confrontations with police officers, race riots occurred only sporadically in the 1980s and 1990s but could be just as combustible and violent as in previous years. In May 1980, the Miami area was hit hard by rioting after an all-white Tampa jury acquitted four policemen charged with shooting a young black man. This disturbance, even by earlier standards of ferocity, was particularly violent. Three whites were beaten to death by blacks, but police officers would kill eleven blacks, and the riot would not conclude until the National Guard was called in.

Rioting was not to be confined to traditional patterns of black–white conflict as the century moved to a conclusion. Rioting would occur in Overtown, Florida, after a Hispanic police officer was acquitted after shooting a black youth in 1984 and again in 1989. Dominican Americans rioted in New York City after a similar incident, and in 1991 Hasidic Jews were targeted by blacks in New York City after a Jewish man ran over and killed a young black girl. Reaching back to the patterns of race riots past, in 1986 whites in Howard Beach, Queens, chased a black youth onto a highway where he was struck and killed by an automobile. As the racial and ethnic makeup of America became more diverse during the 1990s, so too would the characteristics of rioters. Whether involving Vietnamese or Korean American, black or white, virtually all riots took place in urban America, where opportunities were scarce for America's newest underclasses.

There is no consensus as to why violent crime dropped in the 1990s. Surely, there were many factors at work. In urban America, the decline of the crack market and police efforts to seize handguns from criminals and juveniles get much of the credit.[35] Between 1991 and 1998, homicide and robbery rates declined more sharply than any other serious crimes. According to criminologists, these two offenses were most often linked to the crack epidemic and were most associated with handguns. In 1995, the 30 percent drop in murders and shootings in New York City was considered the result of police frisking efforts that drove illegal guns off the street. Gang members and drug dealers reportedly began to leave their guns at home rather than risk losing them to a police search. Despite criticism from civil libertarians, few would argue that police assertiveness in this arena did not at least contribute to the crime decline.[36] Others suggest that the decline in violent crime was attributable to the aging of the population and the growing number of police officers on the street.

Other explanations focused on the demographics of age. During the late 1980s and early 1990s, the explosion of homicides coincided with the rise in killings perpetrated by persons under twenty-four years of age. The drop in such crimes in the 1990s, then, can be associated with a downturn in youthful involvement in the crack trade.

Not every region experienced a dramatic decrease in violent crime in the 1990s. There were few places more violent in America than the Indian reservations of the American West. In 1995, New Orleans had one of the highest murder rates in the country, at one per 1,259 residents. The Fort Peck Reservation in sparsely populated Montana had a murder rate of one per 675 residents, twice as high as New Orleans. The results were similar on other Indian reservations. While residents remained frustrated over the ongoing crime wave, it has proven almost impossible to stem the violence because of the lack of police officers and lack of equipment.[37]

Rampage Killings

Although rampage killing is not a new phenomenon, the 1990s witnessed a dramatic rise in such killings, in which one or two individuals went on killing sprees that would not end until they ran out of bullets or were killed or taken prisoner. A recent *New York Times* study identified 100 rampage killings between 1950 and 2000. Of these, only ten occurred before 1980, with seventy-three taking place in the 1990s. This phenomenon took 425 lives and injured 510 in half a century. Rampage killings occur in all cultures; in fact, the phrase "running amok," meaning "frenzied or indiscriminate killing," was first introduced in Malaysia.

Among the most overlooked issues concerning the perpetrators is that at least half had shown serious mental health problems prior to their crime sprees. While politicians have targeted a violent popular culture that includes video games, movies, and television, there is little evidence that these forms of entertainment predispose individuals to mass murder. The 1990s saw a drop in most types of murder but an increase in rampage killings. Although rampage killings represent less than 1 percent of all homicides, the sheer number of deaths often leads to rash judgments on behalf of the mass media and its poorly informed constituency.

In the wake of heavily publicized school-yard shootings that culminated but did not end with the 1999 Columbine shootings, there has been an increased call for better law enforcement and greater security at American schools and workplaces. But according to the *New York Times,* closer scrutiny of each offender suggests that "these cases have more to do with society's lack of knowledge of mental health issues, rather than lack of security." In virtually every case teachers, family members, and mental health professionals overlooked signs of mental instability.

An examination of rampage killers indicates that these were "anything but random or sudden," with perpetrators often giving either verbal or behavioral warning signs. The most common precipitator for rampage killings was the loss of a job or romantic problems. What sets these crimes apart from typical murders is that the average murderer tries to get away with the crime. Of the more than 100 rampage killers in the *New York Times* survey, not one escaped apprehension. Eighty-nine never even left the scene of the crime.

Rampage killers differed from the typical profile of a murderer in that they were usually older, better educated, mostly white, and more likely to kill a stranger. Moreover, few of the demographic patterns of race and poverty usually associated with crime applied to rampage killers. As the *New York Times* report made clear, mental illness played a huge role in these killings, and since mental illness does not vary from race to race, a racial profile of the perpetrators reflects the actual diversity of America—the killers were mostly white, almost 18 percent black, and 7 percent Asian.

Explanations for the surge in these type of killings in the 1990s included the increasing availability of more lethal weapons with larger ammunition magazines and faster reloading. Although rampage killings increased in the 1990s, other types of multiple killings declined or remained static. Multiple killings of relatives and killings of three or more persons to cover up a felony declined in the 1990s. As the domestication of murder continued to decline, the workplace and school yard become more dangerous than the home when it came to these type of killings. Some experts blame the news media for the saturation of crime coverage leading perhaps to "copycat" killings. At least fourteen of the rampage killers in the survey expressed knowledge of earlier killing sprees.

NOTABLE TRIALS

People v. O. J. Simpson (1995)

Few "trials of the century" could top the public spectacle and intrigue of the 1995 trial of former football hero and movie star turned car rental pitchman O. J Simpson for the murder of his ex-wife Nicole Brown Simpson and Ron Goldman, a male friend. The Simpsons had divorced in 1992 but had continued to keep in contact and had even considered reuniting at one point even though Nicole reported to police dispatchers that O. J. had threatened to kill her during an assault as early as 1985.

According to the most irrefutable facts of the case, during the early morning hours of June 13, 1994, a lone intruder knifed to death Simpson and Goldman in the narrow entrance to Nicole's apartment. Forensic evidence indicates that the woman was attacked first. Twenty-five-year-old Ron Goldman apparently had the misfortune of stopping by to drop off a pair of sunglasses that Nicole had left at the restaurant where he worked earlier that evening. More than three hours after the murders, their savagely mutilated bodies were found.

Almost immediately, attention was focused on Nicole's former husband, Orenthal James (O. J.) Simpson. Reports filtered out of the Los Angeles Police Department that blood had been found matching that of O. J. outside his wife's residence. The news media would quickly report that a bloody glove was found behind Simpson's house that supposedly matched one at the crime scene. O. J.'s hastily assembled attorneys proclaimed his innocence.

After reneging on his promise to turn himself in on June 17, Simpson was spotted on Interstate 5 in the back of a Ford Bronco driven by his friend

A. C. Cowlings. What ensued was perhaps one of the most bizarre live television events of all time. Before ninety-five million viewers, a legion of law enforcement officers slowly followed the white Bronco on the interstate past hundreds of cheering spectators who lined the roads leading to Simpson's upscale Brentwood home. Arriving home, Simpson was arrested, and the following month he pled "100 percent not guilty." In the process, he became one of the most famous murder defendants in the annals of American criminal justice. Simpson was denied bail and would languish in the Los Angeles County Jail during his almost two-year trial.

Without such unprecedented media coverage, the Simpson trial would have been rather mundane. The trial itself is well chronicled by now. Dozens of books were published after and during the trial. Friends and family of the victims, a houseguest of O. J.'s, O. J.'s friends, prosecutors, and defense members all published quickly forgotten books. While there were several that stood out, most were eminently forgettable and quickly were consigned to remainder tables.

The particulars of the case are all too familiar by now. The night of the murder, O. J. flew to Chicago for a business appointment. Returning to Los Angeles the next day, he was interrogated by the police, who focused attention on a deep cut on his right hand. Stating that he did not remember the cut, Simpson offered a number of explanations for the cut—then the sixty-mile car chase on the Los Angeles freeway, which, according to the media, was "the most famous ride on American shores since Paul Revere."[38]

The escape attempt and other crucial evidence should have made the case a slam dunk for the prosecution. But from the start, the prosecution was characterized by ineptitude and miscalculation. First of all, the district attorney's office allowed the trial to be held in downtown Los Angeles instead of Santa Monica, where the crime occurred. Having the trial in Santa Monica would have conformed to protocol since its court would have jurisdiction over crimes committed in the vicinity. Various explanations were given for the change of venue. Most convincing was the explanation that it was an attempt to avoid the sort of rioting and unrest that accompanied the initial acquittal of the police officers in the Rodney King case. What was clear was that the district attorney's office wished to avoid the implication that the jury would be stacked against Simpson.

The prosecution also gave up another strategic advantage by not seeking the death penalty. It is common knowledge in the legal field that "death-case-qualified" jurors tend to convict a defendant more readily than panels that are more reticent to inflict the death penalty.

Public opinion concerning Simpson's guilt became a national litmus test regarding race relations in America. According to attorney David Cole, the division in public opinion in this case reflected "an even deeper divide on the fairness and legitimacy of American criminal justice."[39] One finding that the news media focused on during the trial was the existence of a racial divide concerning the ex-football star's guilt or innocence. In poll after poll, it was reported that most white Americans believed the prosecution, while almost "three-quarters of black citizens" were inclined to side with the defense.[40] Some observers saw these polls as a statement on the racial inequities of the criminal justice system.

Joining civil rights activists and others in the growing media circus were women activists who used the case to campaign against domestic violence. Pointing out that the death of Nicole Brown Simpson was the result of systematic domestic abuse that led to murder, activists noted that almost one-third of all female homicide victims were killed by a husband or boyfriend. While O. J. would be acquitted, the activists were successful in drawing attention to the problem of domestic violence. Following their campaign during the trial, battered-women's shelters reported more calls, and judges began to hand down stiffer sentences in domestic violence cases. In Los Angeles alone, reports of domestic abuse to police increased by 60 percent.

As Gilbert Geis and Leigh Bienen make clear in their book *Crimes of the Century*, for the student of criminal justice the Simpson case was remarkable for the number of challenges it posed to the criminal justice system. Should television be permitted in the courtroom? Should juries be sequestered? Should unanimous verdicts be required in order to convict in a criminal trial?[41] While the trial contributed little to the development of constitutional principle, it did demonstrate a number of interesting applications of existing legal principles. Among these were the right to confront accusers, which in California meant extending the right to the pretrial stages of a case. According to one legal authority, "The constitutional right most visibly on display was Simpson's Fifth Amendment privilege against self-incrimination."[42]

For almost two years, the world was transfixed by the O. J. Simpson trial played live on television. One could only wonder what Chief Justice Earl Warren would have thought about such a high-profile trial televised in the courtroom, having stated in 1965 that if television was allowed in the courtroom, "we can turn back the clock and make everyone in the courtroom an actor before untold millions of people." In the process, it would "make the determination of guilt or innocence a public spectacle and a source of entertainment for the idle and curious."[43]

The O. J. Simpson trial was one of the most expensive in America history. It is estimated that the defense team cost their client some $6 million, while the state spent $9 million on the prosecution, one-third of it going toward housing, feeding, and sequestering the jury.

Simpson was an atypical black defendant—famous, wealthy, and well represented. While in times past he would have faced an all-white jury, Simpson was judged by nine blacks, two whites, and one Hispanic. Attempting to place the case in a historical perspective, author David Cole, an African American attorney, suggested that for a brief moment, "for many black citizens, the acquittal was a sign of hope," noting that "for much of our history, the mere allegation that a black man had murdered two white people would have been sufficient grounds for lynching. . . . To many blacks, the jury's not guilty verdict demonstrated that the system is not always rigged against the black defendant, and that was worth cheering."[44] Ultimately, Simpson's acquittal, similarly to Lizzie Borden's a century earlier, hinged on one of the most prominent aspects of common law, namely, that a conviction requires proof beyond a reasonable doubt.

CONCLUSIONS

A harbinger of the intelligence failure leading up to the terrorist attacks of September 11, 2001, as late as December 1997 criminologists began focusing on one of the least discussed problems of the criminal justice system: the archaic state of record keeping in the criminal justice system. As late as May 2002, columnist Robert D. Novak claimed that when the new FBI director Robert Mueller took over on September 4, 2001, "the Bureau's computer system was so obsolete that he asked the CIA for help."[45] According to one 1994 Justice Department report, only 18 percent of the nation's felony records were complete and computerized. Without adequate records, police and prosecutors face obstacles in recognizing the dangerous offender from the nondangerous, judges face obstacles hampering the recognition of multiple and repeat offenders, and prison officials cannot determine whether an inmate merits maximum security.

Although the FBI collects names of people who have been arrested, it does not reveal whether individuals have been convicted or acquitted (as of 1997). In its own defense, FBI officials explain that it is difficult to gather this information from the thousands of local agencies that vary in record-keeping practices.

Throughout much of the Western world, countries have adopted a "harm-reduction" approach to illegal drug use. Proponents of the continuing drug war have learned little since the fourteen-year experiment with alcohol prohibition. According to Ethan Nadleman, director of a New York drug policy research institute, "Drugs are here to stay . . . we have no choice but to learn how to live with them so that they cause the least possible harm."

The United States spent $4 billion on drug control in 1980. This figure now stands at more than $32 billion per year, just twenty years later. The number of people incarcerated on drug charges has also increased by eight times, from 50,000 to more than 400,000. Because of mandatory sentencing, many thousands of otherwise law-abiding citizens are serving long sentences for first-time nonviolent offenses. Some critics of the drug war would argue that it has damaged our constitutional protections against abusive law enforcement without an appreciable impact in ending the drug trade.

The law enforcement community has been quick to take credit for the reduction of violent crime in the 1990s. New police strategies and the increase of police officers on the streets certainly share some of the credit for the decline in crime in this time period, but other factors have also contributed to this phenomenon, including declining unemployment rates, demographic changes, and the decline in the crack cocaine market.

Between 1977 and 1994, Americans were executed by firing squad, hanging, electrocution, the gas chamber, and lethal injection.[46] Twenty-six states used the electric chair at its peak, but over the past half a century, most of the thirty-eight death penalty states have switched to lethal injection. In 2000, only Nebraska and Alabama continued to use electrocution as the primary form of execution after Georgia and Florida agreed to switch to lethal injection. Florida switched only after a series of grisly executions led state legislators to brand electrocutions as unconstitutional as "cruel and unusual" punishment.

With close to two million prison inmates by the end of the 1990s, America incarcerates a greater percentage of its people than any industrialized country except Russia. Nationally, one of every 113 adult males was behind bars. Since 1990, the nation's state prison population increased 65 percent compared to 106 percent in the federal prisons. While there had indeed been a decline in serious crime, more people are going to prison under harsher sentencing laws. Critics of drug enforcement policies blamed the growing racial disparities of American prisons on sentencing disparities that saw crack cocaine (minorities were more likely to be convicted for crack-related offenses) offenses carry penalties that were 100 times greater than powdered cocaine (favored by middle-class white consumers).

Point–Counterpoint

The Aftermath of Waco: Changes in Federal Law Enforcement

In July of 1995, hearings were held to examine the activities of federal law enforcement agencies during the siege of the Branch Davidian compound in Waco, Texas in 1993. The sequence of events began with the killing of four law enforcement officers on February 28, 1993 and concluded with the deaths of more than 80 at the Branch Davidian compound, including 22 children. Subsequent Congressional hearings investigated the facts surrounding the entire operation and 51-day stand-off between the two incidents. In the first passage Larry Potts, former Assistant Director for the FBI's Criminal Investigation Division explains the FBI's strategy for resolving the Waco standoff. The second excerpt contains some conclusions by the committee chairman on how these types of episodes can be better handled.

The FBI's strategy for resolving the situation in Waco was twofold: (1) to verbally negotiate a peaceful surrender of Koresh and his followers; and, (2) to gradually increase the pressure on those inside the compound by tightening the perimeter around the compound and denying the Davidians certain comforts. In formulating this strategy and throughout the events in Waco, the FBI utilized its Behavioral Science Unit, the National Center for the Analysis of Violent Crime, and a host of outside experts in such specialties as religion and theology, psycholinguistics, cults, medicine, threat assessment, negotiation techniques, psychology and psychiatry. The experts provided a wide range of information on Koresh's state of mind and behavior, as well as information on an array of issues the FBI faced. The FBI also

Source: Committee on the Judiciary, U.S. Senate, 104th Cong., *Activities of Federal Law Enforcement Agencies Toward the Branch Davidians*, Part 2, July 25–27, 1995, pp. 591–593, 604–605; *The Aftermath of Waco: Changes in Federal Law Enforcement*, Oct. 31 and Nov. 1, 1995, pp. 216–217.

received hundreds of unsolicited telephone calls from individuals offering advice on how best to resolve the standoff with the Branch Davidians. As part of its exhaustive efforts to gather as much information as possible, the FBI followed up on most of these telephone calls which appeared legitimate. Not all of the expert opinions were consistent on all issues but the FBI considered the information it received and made the best judgment it could towards achieving a peaceful resolution to the standoff.

Despite these efforts and all of the outside expert advice, the FBI was unable to convince the compound's occupants either as a group or individually to surrender peacefully. The response of Koresh was always to consistently promise to come out at certain times and to consistently break his promise and fail to do so. Eventually, he advised that the Davidians would emerge only when God gave such an instruction to him.

Based on the developments on-site and the advice of experts, the FBI concluded that permitting the standoff to continue would never lead to the peaceful surrender of Koresh, but instead would continue to elevate the risk to the innocent children inside the compound, as well as to the law enforcement officers at the scene. As a result, a strategic plan was then developed to deliver non-lethal tear gas into the compound in hopes of causing the evacuation of the occupants. For nearly two weeks, the FBI wrestled internally with the details of the plan, before presenting it to the Attorney General for approval, to best ensure a safe and satisfactory end to the standoff. In developing its plan to release tear gas into the compound, the FBI thoroughly considered and examined numerous strategic and tactical issues, including the possibility of a hostile reaction from the Davidians; the night vision capability of the Davidians; the strategic firing point that the compound's tower provided the Davidians; the risk of harm to the children inside the compound; the possible harmful effects, if any, of tear gas; and, of course, the massive amount of weapons and ammunition in the compound and the dangerous people who had already killed four federal agents.

As a result of its extensive analyses of these issues, the FBI developed a non-combative plan to release tear gas incrementally into the compound over a two-day period, gradually causing certain portions of the compound to become uninhabitable. The plan provided for increasing the release of gas only to the degree needed to accomplish evacuation of the compound. The plan also included notifying the Davidians that the gas was going to be inserted into specific portions of the compound and providing them the time and means to exit the building safely. Extensive medical support, to include 12 physicians and 13 paramedics, would be standing by and loudspeakers and signs would be used to guide the people out of the compound. In the event that the Davidians opened fire on the FBI agents, the plan provided for the agents to return fire and to escalate the delivery of the tear gas into the entire compound to suppress the gunfire.

Since 1986, the FBI has been involved in the DOJ's quest for alternatives to the use of deadly force. This technology search has evolved into the current "Less Than Lethal Weapons" (LTLW) Program. The SWAT Training Unit, now a component of CIRG, has participated in a number of research efforts during the past two years and has created a working LTLW Committee to review various avenues of research and development of LTLW technology. The LTLW Committee is keeping abreast of both classified and unclassified research and development in this area through liaison with the military, national laboratories, federal law enforcement, private industry, and other involved entities. Research encompasses the full spectrum of relevant technologies including mechanical/impact, electrical, chemical, and biomedical, all designed to safely subdue dangerous subjects without resorting to the application of traditional weapons.

In addition to the above changes in jurisdiction, operations, and research, the Attorney General, the FBI Director, a large number of SACs, all FBI profilers, and an FBI Agent from every field office are all receiving or have received crisis management training, including behavioral science expert training, to become familiar with CIRG, its components, capabilities and procedures.

These and other changes have improved our crisis response capabilities and have maximized the likelihood that the FBI will be better prepared to resolve future crisis situations successfully.

The CHAIRMAN. Let me just thank all of our witnesses and the public at large for their close attention during these hearings. In conclusion, I want to reiterate the message that I began with yesterday. Throughout my years of service in Washington, I have been a very strong supporter of Federal law enforcement. I have the utmost respect for both agencies and the individual agents who put their lives on the line every day for us. It is the quality and heroism of these people that guarantees that, as a whole, Federal law enforcement is a success across the Nation.

As a result, none of us should overlook the fact that for every Waco or Ruby Ridge, there are thousands of safe, successful, and uneventful law enforcement actions carried out each year. It is because of my interest in and respect for law enforcement, though, that these hearings have become necessary.

During the past 3 years, I have become particularly aware of a number of growing problems in law enforcement. These problems include the increased militarization of law enforcement agencies, the inability of agencies to gather and assimilate gathered intelligence and act on it, the public's loss of confidence in law enforcement, the lack of organization between negotiations and tactical wings of law enforcement, and the reckless and overly aggressive attacks of field commanders. Both in Ruby Ridge and Waco, law enforcement actions failed as a direct result of these problems, and I therefore decided to convene these hearings with the intention of correcting these problems.

I am encouraged by the progress we have made during the past few days. We have learned that ATF and FBI have recognized the problems that exist in law enforcement. We have also learned of the various steps that both ATF and FBI are taking to correct the errors that occurred at both Ruby Ridge and Waco. Some of these steps include the placement of a greater emphasis on negotiations, the creation of the Critical Incident Response Group, the CIRG, and the development of better lines of communication between the various law enforcement teams.

Unfortunately, not all of the problems discussed have been addressed. More needs to be done to bolster the role of behavioralists and negotiations generally in barricade and hostage situations. We need to have greater data processing and computerization in our behavioral group of people down there at Quantico. That costs money, and it is Congress' fault that we are not putting enough money into these matters so that we are more skilled and better than we currently are.

But more needs to be done to rid law enforcement of its current militaristic mentality. We have got to bolster the role of behavioralists and negotiations generally, especially in these barricade and hostage situations.

Finally, more needs to be done to restore the confidence of the American people in law enforcement. This last issue becomes especially poignant in light of the tragedy at Oklahoma City. If law enforcement can work to accomplish these goals, my aims in convening these hearings and those of the other members of this committee, of course, are realized. If law enforcement fails, our Nation is going to suffer.

One thing is certain: In the future, this committee is going to redouble its efforts in diligently overseeing the use of force by law enforcement agencies. Misuses of power by law enforcement will be carefully investigated. As long as I am chairman of this committee, I will see to it that law enforcement in this country is held to the highest standards. I don't think you gentlemen mind that. I think you want to be held to the highest standards because that is what has always characterized the FBI and ATF through the years.

So, in summary, I believe that the best way to restore the public's confidence in law enforcement is for us to put Waco and Ruby Ridge behind us. Law enforcement has to move away from paramilitary operations and recommit itself to high-quality crime prevention. Additionally, I look forward to hearing from the administration as to how they further intend to ensure that tragedies like those at Ruby Ridge and Waco are never repeated.

SOURCES

Beck, Allen J., and Christopher J. Mumola. 1999. *Prisoners in 1998.* Washington, D.C.: Bureau of Justice Statistics.

Beckett, Katherine, and Theodore Sasson. 2000. *The Politics of Injustice: Crime and Punishment in America.* Thousand Oaks, Calif.: Pine Forge Press.

Bessler, John D. 1997. *Death in the Dark: Midnight Executions in America.* Boston: Northeastern University Press.

Blomberg, Thomas G., and Karen Lucken. 2000. *American Penology: A History of Control.* New York: Aldine de Gruyter.

Blumstein, Alfred, and Joel Wallman, eds. 2000. *The Crime Drop in America.* Cambridge: Cambridge University Press.

Bobit, Bonnie. 1999. *Death Row: Meet the Men and Women of Death Row.* 9th ed. Torrance, Calif.: Bobit Publishing.

Bodenhamer, David. 1992. *Fair Trial.* New York: Oxford University Press.

Bragg, Rick. 1995. "Chain Gangs to Return to Roads of Alabama." *New York Times,* March 26.

Butterfield, Fox. 1994. "Homicide Data Defy a Basic Crime Tenet." *Houston Chronicle,* October 23.

———. 1997. "Plunge in Rate of Property Crimes Catches Cities' Officials by Surprise." *New York Times,* October 12.

———. 1998. "Drop in Crack Use, Crackdown on Guns May Be behind Plunge in Violent Crime." *Houston Chronicle,* December 28.

Christianson, Scott. 1998. *With Liberty for Some.* Boston: Northeastern University Press.

Cole, David. 1999. *No Justice: Race and Class in the American Criminal Justice System.* New York: New Press.

Conley, John A. 1994. *The 1967 President's Crime Commission Report: Its Impact 25 Years Later.* Cincinnati: Anderson Publishing.

Currie, Elliott. 1998. *Crime and Punishment in America.* New York: Metropolitan Books.

Dershowitz, Alan M. 1997. *Reasonable Doubts: The Criminal Justice System and the O. J. Simpson Case.* New York: Simon and Schuster.

Eldredge, Dirk Chase. 1998. *Ending the War on Drugs: A Solution for America.* Bridgehampton, N.Y.: Bridge Works Publishing.

Friedman, Lawrence M. 2002. *American Law in the 20th Century.* New Haven, Conn.: Yale University Press.

Geis, Gilbert, and Leigh B. Bienen. 1998. *Crimes of the Century: From Leopold and Loeb to O. J. Simpson.* Boston: Northeastern University Press.

Gilje, Paul A. 1996. *Rioting in America.* Bloomington, IN: Indiana University Press.

Hamm, Mark. 1999. "Ruby Ridge." *Violence in America,* vol. 3, edited by Ronald Gottesman, New York: Scribners, pp. 69–71.

Harcourt, Bernard E. 2001. *Illusion of Order: The False Promise of Broken Windows Policing.* Cambridge, Mass.: Harvard University Press.

Hays, XXX. 1997. "New York Celebrating Murder Toll for 1996." *Houston Chronicle,* January 1.

Hixson, Walter L. 2001. *Murder, Culture, and Injustice: Four Sensational Cases in American History.* Akron, Ohio: University of Akron Press.

Jacobs, James B., with Christopher Panarella and Jay Worthington. 1994. *Busting the Mob: United States v. Costa Nostra.* New York: New York University Press.

Jacobs, James B., with Coleen Friel and Robert Radick. 1999. *Gotham Unbound: How New York City Was Liberated from the Grip of Organized Crime.* New York: New York University Press.

Jones, Richard P. 1997. "Stun Belts for Prisoners Controversial." *Houston Chronicle,* June 15.

Jonnes, Jill. 1996. *Hep-Cats, Narcs, and Pipe Dreams: A History of America's Romance with Illegal Drugs.* New York: Scribner.

Karmen, Andrew. 2000. *New York Murder Mystery: The True Story behind the Crime Crash of the 1990s.* New York: New York University Press.

Kelling, George, and Catherine M. Coles. 1996. *Fixing Broken Windows: Restoring Order and Reducing Crime in Our Communities.* New York: Free Press.

Knight, Alfred H. 1996. *The Life of the Law: The People and Cases That Have Shaped Our Society from King Alfred to Rodney King.* New York: Crown Publishers.

Krauss, Clifford. 1995. "Shootings Plummet in New York as Police Frisking Drives Illegal Guns off the Streets." *New York Times,* July 30.

Lane, Roger. 1997. *Murder in America: A History.* Columbus: Ohio State University Press.

Leonhardt, David. 2000. "As Prison Labor Grows, So Does the Debate." *New York Times,* March 19.

Levy, Harlan. 1996. *And the Blood Cried Out: A Prosecutor's Account of the Power of DNA.* New York: Basic Books.

Lifton, Robert J., and Greg Mitchell. 2000. *Who Owns Death?: Capital Punishment, the American Conscience, and the End of Executions.* New York: HarperCollins.

Marion, Nancy E. 1994. *A History of Federal Crime Control Initiatives, 1960–1993.* Westport, Conn.: Praeger.

Massing, Michael. 1998. *The Fix.* New York: Simon and Schuster.

McArdle, Andrea, and Tanya Erzen, eds. 2001. *Zero Tolerance: Quality of Life and the New Police Brutality in New York City.* New York: New York University Press.

Miller, Jerome G. 1996. *Search and Destroy: African-American Males in the Criminal Justice System.* Cambridge: Cambridge University Press.

Monkkonen, Eric H. 2001. *Murder in New York City.* Berkeley: University of California Press.

Novak, Robert D. 2002. "But FBI Intelligence Also Let Us Down." *Houston Chronicle,* May 21.

"On Indian Reservations in the West, Violent Crime Soars." 1998. *New York Times,* August 16.

Parenti, Christian. 2001. *Lockdown America: Police and Prisons in the Age of Crisis.* London: Verso.

Roberts, Julian, and Loretta J. Stalans. 1997. *Public Opinion, Crime, and Criminal Justice.* Boulder, Colo.: Westview Press.

Schwartz, Bernard. 1997. *A Book of Legal Lists.* New York: Oxford University Press.

Schulz, Dorothy Moses. 1995. *From Social Worker to Crimefighter.* Westport, Conn.: Praeger.

Sourcebook of Criminal Justice Statistics, 1973. 1974. Washington, D.C.: U.S. Government Printing Office.

Sullivan, Larry E. 1990. *The Prison Reform Movement.* Boston: Twayne Publishers.

Vila, Bryan, and Cynthia Morris. 1997. *Capital Punishment in the United States: A Documentary History.* Westport, Conn.: Greenwood Press.

Walker, Samuel. 1985. "Broken Windows and Fractured History: The Use and Misuse of History in Recent Police Patrol Analysis." *Justice Quarterly* 1 (March): 77–90.

Walker, Samuel. 1992. *The Police in America: An Introduction.* New York: McGraw-Hill.

Williams, Willie L. with Bruce B. Henderson. 1996. *Taking Back our Streets: Fighting Crime in America.* New York: Scribners.

Wright, Richard and Scott Decker. 1997. *Armed Robbers in Action: Stickups and Street Culture.* Boston: Northeastern University Press.

CRITICAL THINKING QUESTIONS

1. What events led to the decreased prestige of the FBI in the 1980s and 1990s?

2. Contrast the tenor of criminal justice in America during the 1980s to that of the 1960s. What changes in law enforcement, court rulings, and corrections come to mind?

3. What led to the introduction of lethal injection? Contrast this innovation with the general pattern execution in American history.

4. Discuss how mandatory sentencing impacted the corrections and the court systems.

5. Since 1919, riot commissions have convened in the aftermath to discuss the reasons for the violence. What did the Christopher Commission's findings have in common with earlier reports?

6. What impact did the article "Broken Windows" have on policing (read the article; it can be found on the Internet [see the next section]). Discuss the various opinions regarding the efficacy of this philosophy.

7. What are the various explanation for the decline in homicide during the 1990s?

CRIMINAL JUSTICE HISTORY
ON THE INTERNET

The Constitutional Rights Foundation offers dozens of criminal justice–related links (by chapter) at www.crf-usa.org/links/cja/cja_links.html. For example, chapter 15 offers links to the Federal Bureau of Prisons, supermax prisons, private prisons, and prison revolts, such as Attica and New Mexico State. Chapter 7 offers links to police corruption, the Serpico case, Los Angeles police scandals, Rodney King, the Abner Louima torture case, and the shooting of Amadou Diallo. Chapter 11 has connections to the O. J. Simpson trial transcripts, jury instructions for the actual Simpson jury members, and Court TV's famous cases. Chapter 23 offers a Gallup Poll on crime, a "Crime and Punishment in America" report from 1999, and information on school violence. Chapter 22 focuses on gun control and laws (such as the Brady bill), militias and the Second Amendment, race and the criminal justice system, and the *McCleskey v. Kemp* decision.

Students can read the complete 1982 *Atlantic Monthly* article "Broken Windows" by Wilson and Kelling at www.theatlantic.com/politics/crime/windows.htm. For a critique of "Broken Windows" or to join an online debate on this issue, see "Poking Holes in the Theory of Broken Windows" by D. W. Miller at http://chronicle.com/free/v47/i22/22a01401.htm. An analysis of San Francisco's alternative crime policies is at www.cjc.org/pi/windows.html. For a history

of uniform crime reporting and community policing, see www.cj.msu.edu/~people/cp/uniform.html.

The complexities of the prosecution resulting from Ruby Ridge fiasco can be located at http://121.org/SuptDocs/Waco/rrprosecu.htm; the Justice Department report can be found at www.byington.org/Carl/Ruby.htm and www.foxinternet.net/web/amerika/ruby001.htm. For links to articles related to the FBI at Ruby Ridge, see www.spokesmanreview.com/NewsTrak/newstracks.asp?Direc=lists&Direc=ID=L32.

Court files, documents, and court transcripts for Oklahoma City bombing suspect Timothy McVeigh are available at www.courttv.com/casefiles/oklahoma. More on McVeigh and trial coverage can be found at www.time.com/time/2001/mcveigh and www.crimelibrary.com/serial9/mcveigh. For conspiracy links and theories related to the case, see http://members.aol.com/bcrimdb/mcveigh.html.

For the Louima New York City police assault pleas, see www.the smokinggun.com/archive/louimasent1.shtml. Important questions on the drug war are answered at www.mapinc.org/17ques.htm. A great source for crime news is at www.apbnews.com. The Internet Crime Archives, at www.mayhem.net/Crime/archives.html, is an excellent source for information on serial and mass killers, including Ted Bundy, Jeffrey Dahmer, the Unabomber, George Hennard, and other miscreants.

Supreme Court decisions from 1990 to the present are available at http://supctlaw.cornell.edu/supct. Earlier Supreme Court decisions can be found at www.findlaw.com/casecode/supreme.html. Links to the Department of State, the U.S. Government Printing Office, the Treasury Department, and the Department of Justice, including the FBI, the Federal Bureau of Prisons, and the Drug Enforcement Administration, can be accessed at www.albany.edu/scj/links.html. Community-oriented policing services are discussed at www.usdoj.gov/cops/home.htm.

Links to the most famous trials in American and world history can be found at www.law.umkc.edu/faculty/projects/ftrials.htm.

A forensic science time line is located at www.forensicdna.com/Timeline.htm. For the history of DNA use in crime solving (including many links to profilers), see www.karisable.com/crdna.htm. For case information on *Eddings v. Oklahoma* and the juvenile death penalty, see www.againstdp.org/eddings.html, http://ojjdp.ncjrs.org/pubs/juvoff/death.html, and www.pbs.org/wgbh/pages/frontline/angel/procon/deathissue.html.

For an illustrated article on how lethal injection works, see www.howstuffworks.com/lethal-injection.htm. For more on lethal injection, see www.cdc.state.ca.us/issues/capital/capital4.htm and www.geocities.com/Capitol Hill/6142/ijection.html. For other methods of execution, see www.derechos.net/amnesty/dp/methods.html and www.courttv.com/national/death_penalty/history_dpenalty.html. For a complete history of the death penalty, see www.pbs.org/wgbh/pages/frontline/shows/execution/readings/history.html.

NOTES

1. According to pp. 58–59, In 1970, 146,273 of the employees were in corrections and 507,877 in policing. By 1980, corrections employed 298,722, and another 723,923 were in policing (*Sourcebook of Criminal Justice Statistics, 1973* [1974, pp. 58–59]).

2. Bureau of Justice Statistics (1998).

3. Sullivan (1990, p. 125).

4. Roberts and Stalans (1997, p. 3).

5. Bodenhamer (1992, p. 130).

6. Parenti (2001, p. 48).

7. Beckett and Sasson (2000, p. 176).

8. Friedman (2002, p. 591).

9. Schulz (1995, p. 145).

10. Walker (1992, p. 26).

11. Walker (1984, p. 76).

12. Walker (1984, p. 88).

13. Hays (1997).

14. Hamm (1999, p. 71).

15. Besides a number of stitches, King sustained fractures to the skull, cheekbone, and ankle from the beating. Blood and urine tests taken five hours after the incident indicated that he was legally drunk under California law and had recently smoked marijuana.

16. Williams (1996, p. 17).

17. Christianson (1998, p. 283).

18. Christianson (1998, p. 283).

19. Department of Justice annual survey quoted in Christianson (1998, p. 281).

20. Beck and Mumola (1999).

21. Christianson (1998, p. 291).

22. Christianson (1998, p. 291).

23. Leonhardt (2000, p. 22).

24. Leonhardt (2000, p. 22). See also Wright (1997).

25. Butterfield (1997).

26. Butterfield (1997).

27. Butterfield (1998).

28. Jacobs (1994).

29. Vila and Morris (1997, p. 170).

30. Lifton and Mitchell (2000, pp. 218–19).

31. Bragg (1995, p. 9).

32. Jones (1997).

33. Lane (1997, p. 306).

34. Gilje (1996, p. 172).

35. Butterfield (1998).

36. Krauss (1995).

37. "On Indian Reservation in the West, Violent Crime Soars" (1998).

38. Geis and Bienen (1998, p. 174).

39. Cole (1999, p. 1).

40. Cole (1999, p. 1).

41. Geis and Bienen (1998, p. 171).

42. Knight (1996, p. 263).

43. Quoted in Schwartz (1997, p. 257).

44. Cole (1999, pp. 1–2).

45. Novak (2002, p. A22).

46. Bobit (1999). Between 1978 and January 1, 1999, of the 500 inmates executed, 142 were executed by electrocution, 2 by firing squad, 10 by gas chamber, 3 by hanging and 343 by lethal injection.

14

CRIMINAL JUSTICE IN THE NEW MILLENNIUM (2000–2002)

TIME LINE

1993	*Daubert v. Merrell Dow*
1999	First challenges to Daubert guidelines for fingerprinting
2000	Supreme Court reviews electrocution for the first time since its inception in 1890
2000	Illinois announces moratorium on the death penalty
2001	Supreme Court considers execution of mentally retarded
2001	Mississippi votes to retain Confederate symbol on state flag
2001	Suspects go on trial for 1963 Birmingham bombing
2001	*Shafer v. South Carolina*

2001	Arrest of suspected antiabortion sniper James Charles Kopp in France
2001	Delegates from twenty-six countries celebrate centennial of Scotland Yard's fingerprint bureau
2001	Timothy McVeigh executed for bombing of Alfred P. Murrah Federal Building in Oklahoma City
2001	FBI director Louis Freeh steps down in June
2001	Terrorist attack on America leaves more than 3,000 dead
2001	FBI puts counterterrorism at top of Most Wanted List

2001	New York City settles $8.75 million suit with police torture victim Abner Louima	2002	More than $1 billion authorized to fight bioterrorism
2001	President Bush signs USA Patriot Act into law	2002	Justice Department challenges reliability of fingerprint evidence
2002	100th prisoner freed because of DNA testing		

On September 11, 2001, a concerted attack on America by nineteen Arab airplane hijackers on four planes left more than 3,000 dead.[1] It was the second-bloodiest day in American history (next to the Civil War battle of Antietam in 1982). In the aftermath of the attacks, the criminal justice system faced reorganization and challenges unparalleled in its 200-plus-year history. Attorney General John Ashcroft said that he expected the Justice Department and federal law enforcement to undergo a "wartime reorganization" to prevent future terrorist attacks. Ashcroft recommended shifting many law enforcement responsibilities from the FBI to state and local authorities. The FBI was expected to make the dramatic and historic conversion from apprehending bank robbers and drug dealers to placing more emphasis on antiterrorism efforts.

Among the most controversial antiterrorism measures was the detaining of hundreds of mostly Middle Eastern men. Other measures to fight terrorism include the convening of military tribunals to try foreign suspects, expanded wiretapping, and the monitoring of conversations between lawyers and detainees. Although polls suggest that Americans support these measures, civil liberties groups and some lawmakers have complained that the new tactics undermine a number of civil rights principles, comparing the roundup to the Justice Department's Palmer raids in 1920.

Despite the controversy over the new tactics, the majority of Americans in a survey conducted by the *National Law Journal* in October 2001 favored the increased wiretap and surveillance powers and pointed to a general pro–law enforcement shift among potential jurors in criminal matters. This was a dramatic shift in opinion from earlier polls that reflected an antipolice bias after highly charged police brutality cases in New York City and corruption cases in Los Angeles. More than half the respondents also indicated that racial profiling is acceptable under certain circumstances. Nonetheless, the polls indicate that the public is rather inconsistent on its opinions in criminal justice matters, as September 11 caused many to reverse course in their thinking about racial profiling, the death penalty, and civil liberties protections.

It would seem as America entered the twenty-first century that its increasing racial and ethnic diversity would have paved a more peaceful path to the future. Many of the country's old problems that have laid dormant for the past decades have been rekindled for familiar reasons. Many scholars point to urban rioting as one of the stimuli that led to the creation of modern policing. With the first police riot training occurring in the aftermath of the 1849 Astor police riot in New York City, riot training has been given short shrift on departments except for the civil rights and antiwar years of the 1960s and 1970s. The Los Angeles riots of 1993 proved once again how unprepared city police are for dealing with widespread civil unrest. In April 2001, the Cincinnati police faced three nights of rioting over the killing of an unarmed black man by police, the fifteenth such

episode in the past six years. Pulling a page from criminal justice past, the city mayor implemented a dusk-to-dawn curfew. Police finally brought the riot under control with help from local residents and religious leaders.

Several factors as old as policing help explain the outbreak of violence in Cincinnati, including the economic decline of inner-city communities, police harassment and brutality, racial profiling, and a disproportionate number of white police on the force, a force that did not reflect the demographics of the community it serves. Considering complaints by citizen board members who lament that police do not communicate with them and that they are not given the authority to properly investigate complaints against the police, from a historical vantage point the imperious styles of the Los Angeles Police Department under William Parker and the pre-Roosevelt New York Police Department instantly come to mind.

THE LAWGIVERS

The backlash against violent youth crime that saw zero-tolerance strategies applied to public schools began to soften in 2001. These strategies came to prominence when the federal government mandated that any school that received federal funds was required to expel any student who brought a firearm onto campus. California widened the net to require expulsion for any student caught selling drugs. The spate of highly publicized school-yard shootings in the late 1990s led school boards to take these policies further, calling for expulsion of students who possessed any item that could be construed as a weapon, including toy guns and nail files. Others added home remedies, such as aspirin and Tylenol, to the list of banned substances.

Leading the resistance against the draconian policies were educators and other teachers who felt that suspensions for relatively minor alcohol and weapons infractions were too punitive a response. The rush to judgment that had been zero

tolerance led to expulsions of Boy Scouts for mistakenly bringing scout knives to school as well as a ten-year-old girl who turned over her mother's kitchen knife to authorities when she realized she had brought it with her to school by mistake. But despite well-publicized exceptions, many school administrators credit these policies with reducing campus violence and deterring substance abuse. In the spirit of compromise, some campuses are implementing lighter sentences, attempting to make the punishment fit the offense.[2]

Medical Marijuana

One of the more contentious debates in the long-simmering controversy over medical marijuana put the states on the front line of the federal drug war when the Supreme Court considered a California referendum that legalized the cultivation and possession of marijuana for medical use in 1996. In March 2001, the Court made its first foray into the medical marijuana debate when the federal government sought to close down several California marijuana distributors. At stake for backers of the current legislation is whether their suppliers can claim "medical necessity" to protect them from federal drug charges. A decision was not expected until the summer of 2001. Nine other states[3] have passed laws similar to California's, so the decision will have far-reaching consequences.

Advocates for the drug war argue that state laws easing marijuana restrictions are based on bad science and will go a long way toward undermining the war against drug traffickers. Many see the medical marijuana issue as a smoke screen by which supporters hope to eventually legalize the drug for recreational use. Patients and some doctors, however, have embraced the drug as a panacea for the debilitating effects of chemotherapy, touting its aid in stimulating the appetite in cancer and AIDS patients and its benefits in treating glaucoma.

Marijuana was classified under the 1970 Federal Controlled Substances Act as a drug in the highest category of potential for abuse. But despite studies that convinced the Drug Enforcement Administration's chief administrative-law judge to proclaim in 1988 that marijuana is "one of the safest therapeutically active substances known," federal prosecutors refuse to budge in their prohibition approach.[4]

September 11 and Its Impact on the Courts

The terrorist attacks of September 11 had a tremendous impact on America's criminal justice system. Taking a page from the historical record (such as martial law during the Civil War and Japanese internment during World War II), following September 11 many civil liberties long taken for granted have taken "a back seat to safety." Some scholars suggest that American civil liberties had already "grown to an extent that the Founding Fathers probably never imagined."[5] Historian Eric Foner argued that the acceptance of civil liberties as being "very ingrained in our culture" is a fairly recent phenomenon. Foner asserted that "for most of our history, the Bill of Rights was pretty irrelevant," citing examples of violations during the Red Scare of the 1920s and the detention of Japanese Americans during World War II.[6] An examination of the development of civil liberties in America suggests that rather than being "fixed and immutable," civil liberties have often "expanded and contracted" throughout American history, particularly during periods of social upheaval and war.

In the months following September 11, the federal government gave law enforcement permission to tap telephones and read electronic mail and created an environment that endorsed self-censorship of free speech. On October 26, 2001, President George W. Bush signed the USA Patriot Act into law, which expanded the government's power to monitor private conversations and e-mail and allowed police to obtain search warrants and enter a citizen's home without their knowledge. The new law also made it easier to deport noncitizens suspected of being security threats. Foreigners, in most cases of Middle Eastern background, have been targeted by investigators

and suspicious citizens, following an era in which noncitizens had been enjoying their greatest freedom in American history because of a number of Supreme Court decisions.

In the summer of 2001, one Supreme Court decision upheld that once immigrants entered the country, they were protected by the Constitution, "whether their presence here is lawful, unlawful, temporary, or permanent." This policy came under scrutiny following the terrorist strikes on September 11, when Attorney General John Ashcroft ordered the detention of more than 1,000 foreigners suspected of posing a security threat or of perhaps holding information about the attacks. Little information about the detainees was forthcoming initially, with many having been barred from meeting with family and lawyers. As late as March 2002, more than 100 were still held on criminal charges (none related to September 11).

While many supporters of the new security proposals claim that "extraordinary times call for extraordinary measures," civil libertarians have expressed outrage at some of the new measures, particularly plans to permit suspected foreign terrorists to be tried by military tribunals. Military tribunals have rarely been used outside military circles and are regarded as rather sinister by liberals and civil libertarians. Recalling the sessions of the Star Chamber in Tudor England (fifteenth century), military tribunals are held in secret and afford defendants less rights than regular courts do. In these trials, a panel of military judges has the latitude to decide guilt or innocence without a unanimous vote and can even impose the death penalty. Once defendants are sentenced, they have little recourse, being barred from appealing to a higher court. A verdict of a military tribunal can be overturned only by the president or the secretary of defense.

"Civil Death" Laws

For more than two centuries, many states have denied ex-felons the right to vote and to rejoin the democratic process.[7] This tradition was highlighted during the closely contested presidential election of 2000. According to one columnist, Florida's civil death law "kept so many African-Americans away from the polls" that the state and subsequently the presidency was "delivered to George W. Bush."[8] According to the estimates of the Washington-based Sentencing Project, 400,000 black Floridians, making up 31 percent of the state's black men, were disenfranchised because of past felony convictions. In another study, criminologists at the University of Minnesota and Northwestern University found that 13.8 of all Florida blacks were excluded from voting. By all accounts, the civil death penalty, together with the tremendous increase of incarceration, has disenfranchised a large bloc of voters nationwide. This phenomenon is rapidly becoming a cogent civil rights issue. Columnist Neil Peirce has pointed out that "hundreds of thousands of black youth" incarcerated in the drug wars "are being disenfranchised before they have a chance to cast a single ballot."[9]

LAW ENFORCEMENT

As crime becomes increasingly globalized, American law enforcement has responded by assigning more personnel to foreign nations. In 1999, there were 1,649 U.S. law enforcement personnel permanently assigned overseas for intelligence, training, and crime-fighting purposes. Following the bombing of the American embassy in Tanzania in 1998, FBI agents were sent to investigate. According to one estimate, there will be almost 100 FBI agents assigned to thirty-seven overseas offices by 2000.[10] By the end of the 1990s, terrorism had become such a concern that the FBI had even decreased the number of tours through its Washington headquarters.

In March 2002, Attorney General Ashcroft announced plans to shift federal funding from state and local police budgets to programs designed to pursue terrorists and protect against new attacks. According to the new budget, $1.9 billion was allocated for new counterterrorism measures, which include a new immigration

tracking system and better aircraft with new surveillance features.

The Community Oriented Policing Services (COPS) program spent $385 million in 2001 to hire new police officers and was widely heralded as a success. But despite its success, Ashcroft argued that budget cuts were necessary as "the world awakened [on September 11] to a new threat from an old evil." In response to criticism of the budget cuts, the Bush administration has offered to create an $800 million grant program for state and local police for spending projects that would not be decided by Congress.

Technological advances in police weaponry are poised to take policing into the twenty-first century. Law enforcement has emerged as one of the fastest-growing markets for high-tech gadgets, particularly in the realm of "less-than-lethal" weapons and tools. Already on the drawing board for the new century are such weapons as the snare net, the smart gun, strobe goggles, rear-seat air bags to control arrestees, millimeter wave cameras to detect concealed weapons, and backscatter X-ray scanners for detecting drug shipments.[11]

During the past decade, a revolution in less-than-lethal technologies has taken place. Besides the need to find less dangerous methods of controlling criminals, efforts have been devoted toward such goals in order to stem the number of lawsuits for wrongful death filed against police departments as well as accusations of excessive force in making arrests and controlling crowds.

In the late 1990s, police brutality was seldom off the front pages, particularly in New York City, where the beating of Abner Louima and the death of Amadou Diallo, who was shot at forty-one times while standing unarmed at the entrance of his apartment, became national news stories. Louima was sodomized with a broken broomstick in the bathroom of a police precinct house, suffering internal injuries. Two police officers were convicted for the assault, and four others were found guilty of obstructing justice during an attempted cover-up. Almost four years after being tortured by police at a Brooklyn police station, Abner Louima agreed to settle his lawsuit with the city and its main police union for $8.75 million and promises of several reforms in police practices. It was reportedly the most money the city has ever had to pay in a police brutality case. It was also the first time that the Policemen's Benevolent Association has ever paid money to settle a claim against it. Among the departmental policy reforms were changes in the "forty-eight-hour rule," which allowed officers suspected of infractions to wait two days before answering questions from supervisors.

Community Policing in the Twenty-First Century

By 2001, most major police departments had adopted the "community-based" policing philosophy, demonstrating "a fundamental shift from traditional reactive policing" to a more proactive approach. Between 1997 and 1999, the percentage of police departments using routine foot patrols increased from twenty-eight to thirty-four, according to a 2000 Department of Justice report. In 1999, more than two-thirds of departments across the country had some type of community-based police program compared to just 34 percent in 1997. The number of officers designated as community police climbed from more than 20,000 in 1997 to 113,000 in 1999. This crime-fighting philosophy, which came to prominence in the 1980s, typically utilizes foot and bicycle patrols as it attempts to involve local communities in making their neighborhoods more secure.

Except for anecdotal evidence, experts caution that it is difficult to measure how effective community-based policing has been. By the beginning of 2001, almost 12,000 law enforcement agencies across the nation had applied for federal grants to implement some form of community-oriented policing.

According to Katherine Beckett and Theodore Sasson, several new developments in policing, including proactive problem-oriented policing and zero-tolerance strategies, may "further reduce the potential democratizing impact of community policing."[12] Despite a movement from reactive to proactive policing, there is little evidence that the new policy is responsible for suppressing criminal activity.

Civil libertarians and police critics cite the emergence of paramilitary SWAT teams in police departments across the nation as an alarming departure from the community policing model. Supported by federal grants and asset forfeiture laws, these units were initially aimed at the drug trade.

Challenging "Broken Windows"

No police strategy was more influential in the 1980s and 1990s than the "broken-windows" thesis espoused by James Q. Wilson and George L. Kelling. Following a significant drop in serious crimes in many American cities during the 1990s, a number of scholars have begun to reexamine and challenge the crime reduction phenomenon in cities such as New York as a result of the broken-windows thesis.

New York City has been used as the "poster child" by broken-windows advocates. Few could argue that the crime decline in the city was almost unprecedented over the past decade; however, there is little consensus as to why it occurred. Under the leadership of William Bratton, New York City police chief, police activities were directed at "order maintenance," an often-aggressive crusade against a legion of minor offenders such as panhandlers, squeegee men, and jaywalkers. But skeptics argue that the crime drop was the result of a more complicated set of circumstances.

In the early 1990s, criminologist George Kelling convinced Bratton to apply the broken-windows concept to New York's massive transit system. Following the high-profile murder of a Utah tourist in the New York subway, the Transit Police was given $40 million to improve its performance. In his autobiography, Bratton credited this killing with providing the catalyst for causing a turnaround in the crime rate in New York City. While chief of the transit police, Bratton applied the thesis to fighting crime in the subways. Bratton redesigned transit uniforms, renovated and upgraded the Transit Police Academy, introduced better weapons and communications equipment, and improved morale on the force. After identifying fare evasion as the most widespread problem, Bratton stationed police at strategic points to capture turnstile jumpers. Many of those arrested carried concealed illegal weapons, so in the process of arresting minor offenders, they might have been preventing more serious offenses by confiscating weapons. Many erstwhile criminals probably began leaving their weapons at home. In any case, subway crime plummeted.

Selected as police commissioner in 1993, Bratton took credit for reducing felonies by almost 30 percent by combining the computerized tracking of crime hot spots with a "quality-of-life initiative" that targeted disorderly behavior, street prostitution, panhandling, and other unsolicited behaviors. Another crime control initiative involved determining the origin of every gun used in a crime, whereby every handgun suspect was interviewed by a detective. Teaming with his executive assistant, Jack Maple, Bratton took the handcuffs off police officers and used civil law and the broken-windows strategy to enforce regulations against harassment, assault, disorderly conduct, and vandalism.

Bratton, Maple, and his dream team created the Compstat system, a combination of computer statistics analysis and an unrelenting demand for accountability. As Bratton's chief strategist, Jack Maple introduced a groundbreaking computerized map system that was given the moniker Compstat, short for "computer statistics." Maple demanded that every precinct map out shootings, gun arrests, and narcotics violations in order to more accurately deploy police officers. As New York City enjoyed its historic crime drop, other large cities adopted Maple's strategies, which hinged on accurate and timely intelligence, rapid deployment, effective tactics, and relentless follow-up and assessment.

As academics reconsider "broken windows," a growing number of authorities are questioning its most crucial assumptions. One political scientist even argues that the "zero-tolerance" panacea in New York City has "clogged up municipal courts and sapped judicial resources."[13] Still others would suggest that it is too simple to blame all crime on urban decay when there is "rather a constellation of only loosely connected, somewhat separate problems that may require somewhat unique policy responses."[14]

At the same time that New York was enjoying its success, other cities enjoyed similar crime drops using alternative strategies. According to Eli B. Silverman, in cities such as San Diego, the real turnaround is credited to "more intelligent policing."[15] Although there are still critics of "broken-windows policing," most polls indicate that New Yorkers strongly supported the enforcement of quality-of-life laws. According to a July 2001 poll by the Citizens Crime Commission, a nonprofit research organization, support varied little between African Americans, Hispanics, Asian Americans, and whites.

Federal Law Enforcement

The retirement of FBI director Louis Freeh in June 2001 (his term would have expired in 2003) concluded one of the most controversial administrations in the history of the agency. Despite the number of controversies during the past eight years, Freeh could also point to a number of accomplishments during his administration. Under his leadership, the FBI hired thousands of new agents, enjoyed better cooperation with the Central Intelligence Agency, more than doubled the FBI's presence in other countries, and secured a $3.44 billion crime-fighting budget, a 58 percent increase over his first year in office. Freeh made great strides in increasing the diversity of the bureau, adding more women and minorities.

 Born in Jersey City, New Jersey, in 1950, Louis Freeh joined the FBI in 1974 after graduating from law school. During the next six years, he was involved mainly in organized crime investigation. He is credited with having made great strides in moderating racketeering in the longshoreman's union and prosecuting the Sicilian Mafia in the "Pizza Connection" case. Following the resignation of William S. Sessions in 1993, President Bill Clinton appointed Freeh as director of the FBI. His tenure as chief was mired in controversy. High-profile embarrassments that marred his administration included the botched interview with falsely accused Olympic bombing suspect Richard Jewell; the investigation of the Pan-Am plane crash; a series of domestic bombing cases; inefficiency in the FBI crime lab; the Waco, Texas, and Ruby Ridge, Idaho, shootouts; and security lapses in the atomic weapons labs. Many critics blamed Freeh's problems on his previous lack of high-level managerial experience in Washington.

In March 2002, two senators called for sweeping changes in the FBI. Following the arrest of FBI spy Robert Hanssen and other scandals within the agency, the FBI implemented several modifications beginning in July 2001, when the Justice Department's inspector general was given permission to begin investigations of the bureau without needing the previously required permission of the attorney general. In addition, a program was set up to give periodic polygraphs to agents with access to sensitive materials. These changes followed a number of high-profile embarrassments for the FBI, including the loss of weapons and computers, the failure to provide thousands of documents to lawyers for Oklahoma City bomber Timothy McVeigh, the discovery of the spy Hanssen, the Branch Davidian and Ruby Ridge incidents, and the bungled investigation of former nuclear scientist Wen Ho Lee. However, the new legislation proposed by Senators Charles Grassley (R-Iowa) and Patrick Leahy (D-Vt.) goes even further. Besides making it clear that the Justice Department's inspector general has jurisdiction over the FBI, their bill includes provisions for the inclusion of FBI employees under the Federal Whistleblower Act, the creation of an FBI internal security division, and other reporting requirements to Congress.

The Future of Forensic Science

Forensic science technology has become increasingly reliable over the past two decades. While the best-known identification techniques include DNA and fingerprint analysis, new methods exist that allow investigators to use retinal scanning, voiceprinting, and chromatography (the analysis of certain chemicals contained an individual's saliva). The use of computers has greatly enhanced the ability of investigators to sort and process mountains of evidence that would be inaccessible without computer databases.

Recent suggestions for improving criminal identification systems include recommendations to require individuals accused of telephone offenses involving threats, ransom demands, and nuisance calls to have their voiceprints recorded at the same time they are fingerprinted. As part of standard posttrial processing, some states already require criminals to give blood or saliva samples for possible DNA profiling. No matter what identification innovations crime investigators introduce to crime fighting, there is a strong public fear that these techniques could threaten civil liberties or implicate innocent individuals because of errors in taking samples or record keeping.

In April 2000, Texas, with perhaps 3,500 unsolved cases of serial murder, began experimenting with new computer software that targeted serial killers. Similar to psychological profiling in which details of crime scenes are used by experts to make predictions about the emotional and intellectual characteristics of offenders, the new geographic profiling uses computer software programs to disseminate the particulars of crimes and pinpoint the most likely residence or workplace of perpetrators.[16]

Brain "fingerprinting" is one of the latest tools being tested by law enforcement. One of the latest advances in computer-based technology, it allows investigators to identify or acquit subjects on the basis of measuring brain-wave responses to crime-related pictures or words presented on a computer screen. Invented by Dr. Larry Farwell, this innovation is grounded in the pretext that the brain permanently records information, including information related to criminal activity. Through accurate training and technology, brain fingerprinting can retrieve memories stored in the brain. Unlike a polygraph, brain fingerprinting does not look for the distinction between truth and lies but only indicates whether an individual has information related to a specific crime. In one of the first tests of this technology, the FBI and then the U.S. Navy found a 100 percent accuracy rate in its employment.[17]

Fingerprinting

In the summer of 2001, more than 400 delegates from twenty-six countries gathered in London to celebrate the centennial of Scotland Yard's fingerprint bureau. Officials claimed that they solved 10,000 cases the previous year using fingerprint evidence. Although Argentina opened the first such branch in 1892, Scotland Yard was more influential in sparking the adoption of fingerprinting in English-speaking countries.

Beginning in 1911, when American courts first allowed fingerprint evidence, for most of the twentieth century fingerprinting remained one of the standard methods of criminal identification. At the turn of the century, some authorities were speculating that in the next few decades its use will be superseded by DNA identification.

Fingerprint evidence has been facing more and more court challenges in recent years. Beginning with the 1993 Supreme Court decision of *Daubert v. Merrell Dow,* judges were required to take a more active role in determining what scientific evidence is admissible in court. According to the "Daubert" guidelines, new questions would be answered before fingerprints could be entered into evidence. By this decision, the Court introduced five criteria that had to be met before evidence could be considered scientific: (1) peer review and sound methodology, (2) a known error rate, (3) testable hypotheses, (4) application outside of legal proceedings, and (5) general acceptance.[18]

As one forensic scientist noted at the recent London conference, "Twins have the same DNA, but different fingerprints." But one of the main challenges to fingerprinting lies in the fact that there is a lack of universal standards for comparing prints. This has led to several mismatches of partial fingerprints. Regardless of the continuing controversy, the science of fingerprinting has held up to scrutiny. But as one expert has suggested, "The relevant question isn't whether fingerprints could ever be exactly alike—it's whether they are ever similar enough to fool a fingerprint examiner. And the answer is yes."[19] What worries police and prosecutors is that recent challenges to fingerprinting could also undermine ballistics and handwriting tests and other evidence. Law professor Michael Saks of Arizona State University probably sums up the dilemma of forensic scientists best, commenting that "courts are forcing forensic science to become science—to actually test its claims, determine its error rates, and not overstate conclusions."[20]

CORRECTIONS

At the close of the twentieth century, the number of adults either incarcerated, on parole, or on probation reached a record high of 6.49 million, or one in thirty-two American adults. While this was the bad news, the good news was that the percentage increase from 1999 to 2000 was only half the annual average rate since 1990. According to government figures, 30 percent of the adults were in jail in the corrections system.

Following on the heels of three decades of prison building and tougher sentencing laws, at the beginning of 2002 a number of states were forced by budget deficits to close some prisons, lay off guards, or even shorten prison sentences. In January alone, the states of Ohio, Michigan, and Illinois closed prisons. Washington was among the states experimenting with shortening sentences for nonviolent crimes in order to relieve the overburdened correctional system.

One of the leaders of the prison-building boom was California. However, the state was a victim of its own policies and was forced to shut down five small privately operated minimum-security prisons and to consider amending the state's three-strikes sentencing law in order to relieve congestion.

Close to 2.5 million people were released on probation or parole in 2000. In 1990, half of all parolees successfully completed the terms of their release. Ten years later, only 43 percent completed parole and stayed out through the end of the year. As of late 2001, Georgia (6.8 percent) and Texas (5 percent) were the states with the largest percentage of their adult population in the corrections system.[21]

In the aftermath of September 11, a Justice Department lawyer urged the Supreme Court to rule that when an individual chooses probation over prison time, he can be forced to open his home anytime to police searches.[22] Many of the justices were sympathetic to the argument that when an individual agreed to probation rather than a prison term, the individual should be required to submit to searches of home and self. But a number of civil libertarians and members of the criminal justice system feared police encroachment on civil liberties and an increasing pattern of linking probation to the surrender of other liberties.

Juvenile Corrections

By the end of the 1990s, the treatment of juvenile offenders by the correctional system signaled a backlash against the century-old notion of viewing children and adolescents as less censurable and more redeemable through rehabilitation than adults. A harsher view of child criminals has emerged in which they are barely distinguishable from their more adult counterparts. Over the past nine years, forty-five states have passed legislation making it easier to prosecute juveniles as adults. Motivated by high-profile crimes committed by juvenile offenders, such as recent school-yard massacres, fifteen states now allow prosecutors to transfer juveniles from the juvenile system into adult courts for certain categories of crime, most often violent offenses. There is no consensus as to what constitutes adulthood today. Children as young as ten can be prosecuted as adults in Vermont and Kansas, while most other states have set the bar at fourteen and older. Between 1985 and 1997, the number of youths under the age of eighteen in adult prisons more than doubled.

According to a 2001 American Bar Association (ABA) study, young girls were being arrested and jailed in record numbers, and the current juvenile justice system is unable to handle the special needs of young girls. While juvenile crime has fallen overall, the fastest-growing segment of the juvenile justice population are girls under the age of eighteen. Between 1988 and 1997, delinquency cases involving white girls rose 74 percent compared to a 106 percent increase for African American girls. In the wake of its findings, the ABA has recommended that communities develop alternatives to detention and incarceration for minor offenses. The ABA report suggests that girls are detained for less serious offenses than boys and are more likely to be detained for minor offenses, such as public disorder, traffic offenses, and probation violations. Other explanations for this trend target get-tough mandatory sentencing, changes in police practice for domestic violence, and relabeling family conflicts as violent offenses.

Corrections in the Twenty-First Century

There is a strong sentiment among many critics of the criminal justice system that "despite its pretensions, modern criminal justice is no more about crime control that it is about rehabilitation."[23] In the current punitive climate of inmate warehousing, the emphasis of corrections has turned from slogans heralding rehabilitation to more businesslike expressions, such as "managerial efficiency."

In order to save costs, some California prisons have installed lethal electrified fences around prison perimeters. One administrator argued that this was also a security measure, noting that "the fence doesn't get distracted, it doesn't look away for a moment and it doesn't get tired."[24] At the same time, there is a neoconservative impulse supporting anticrime measures, including corporal punishment, chain gangs, and even applying the death penalty to preteen children.

With crime having leveled off over the past decade and where the economy might be on the downswing, a number of states are confronted with having to cut spending in order to balance the budget. Without the political pressure that pushed for the locking up of a record number of prisoners, prisons are now competing for scarce budget resources.

Since the events of September 11, identification technology has become increasingly important. Correctional officials are devoting more attention to identifying who leaves and enters prisons more than ever. Hand geometry and iris recognition are two new forms of identification being used in corrections. After a number of incidents in which prisoners were mistakenly released, the shift to new technology represents an effort "to take the human element out of future releases and make sure the body coming in is the body going out."[25] These same identification technologies are also being used to identify staff to avoid security breaches, particularly in the light of September 11.

The use of DNA is also making a major imprint on corrections. Inmates on death row have been exonerated from crimes ten and even twenty years after being wrongfully convicted. DNA is being used to solve cold crimes as well. Most states now have policies that allow DNA testing for certain classes of offenders, usually sex offenders. This allows authorities to test DNA samples for cold hits (on old cases). Support is increasing to expand these tests to other violent felons as well.

In June 2001, the Michigan Department of Corrections passed a new law that required the testing of all inmates regardless of criminal status. However, the testing of almost 50,000 inmates has required modification in traditional DNA testing procedures by shifting from a blood draw to an oral swab test (which is less expensive). States such as Virginia have been accused by the American Civil Liberties Union of testing inmates not to solve past crimes but to create a database for future criminal activity. Although there is no consensus on how best to use DNA in the correctional system, if testing is done in the early stages of the criminal justice system, advocates argue that fewer postconviction tests will need to be done in the corrections system.

CRIME AND PUNISHMENT

Modern criminal threats to American security have new generations of law enforcement officials preparing for unprecedented criminal acts. Among the most feared are chemical, biological, and computer-based instruments of mass destruction. What is so threatening is that they can be easily constructed, transported, and used cheaply and efficiently. One need look no further than the bombing of the Alfred P. Murrah Federal Building and the World Trade Center, each accomplished with one motor vehicle and one bomb. However, few predicted that the worst fears of criminal justice and security experts would become reality on September 11, 2001.

The end of the Cold War has made it easier to gain access to deadly weapons. In its current state, Russia offers huge arsenals of weapons that are reportedly available for the right offer. The spread of the computer economy offers scenarios in which terrorists attack air traffic control systems, causing jetliners to collide. Since the 1990s, intelligence experts have warned of the growing danger of germ and chemical devastation.

America's greatest strength is its freedom and openness. For the domestic terrorist, it is also America's greatest weakness. With loosely controlled borders, people and goods legally and illegally flow back and forth across these borders. Every year, more than 400 million people enter the United States. Every year, there are

800,000 aircraft arrivals, and every year some nine million cargo containers arrive at U.S. ports. Customs officials report that they can inspect only 2 to 3 percent of these.

Citing the danger of biological, chemical, and nuclear weapons, FBI director Louis Freeh has conceded that "these weapons of mass destruction represent perhaps the most serious potential threat facing the United States." Shadow economies and illegal aliens exist side by side with an illegal drug business that grows each year. If America cannot stop the flow of illegal drugs across its borders (let alone its prisons), it would not be much of a hedge to bet that weapons of mass destruction could be just as easily smuggled.

The advent of the worldwide Internet and other communications innovations has not only created more opportunities for criminals but also changed the way some crimes are defined. For example, a New Jersey man was convicted of aggravated sexual assault even though his only contact with his preteen victim was by telephone, leading writer Wendy Kaminer to suggest that "his case may change the way we think of rape."[26] The question such a case provokes is whether this is overzealous policing playing catch-up with technological crime. In this case, the perpetrator never physically made contact with the victim but simply made obscene phone calls to twelve young girls ages eight to fourteen. According to Kaminer, the precedent set by this case "points to the limits of a therapeutic approach to justice."

Over the past several years, the FBI has been aggressively policing the Internet through its Innocent Images National Initiative, which was begun in 1995. Agents pose as teenagers in order to ferret out pornographers and pedophiles who prowl the Internet. Despite charges of entrapment, individuals arrested under this program have increased 1,264 percent from 1996 to 2000.[27]

Congress has also gotten into the act with several attempts to impose special restrictions on Internet speech to protect children. The Supreme Court has overturned several pieces of this legislation and is currently reviewing the constitutionality of the 1996 Child Pornography Prevention Act, which criminalizes virtual child pornography.

Organized Crime

American organized crime was dominated by Italian syndicates for much of the twentieth century. The changing immigration patterns of the late twentieth century have transformed the face of organized crime in the United States. Not since the turn of the century have so many immigrants flooded into the country. Between 1982 and 1989, some 685,000 legal immigrants settled in New York City alone. While there has been a backlash in some parts of the country, immigration has revitalized many older cities, such as Boston, Chicago, and New York, all of which had been losing residents for years.

The incredible diversity of America has always been reflected in the tapestry of organized crime. Jewish, Irish, and Italian immigrants predominated during the peak years of their respective migrations. However, the diversity and violence of this earlier era pales in comparison to the current-day version. Gangland violence has sporadically marked the assimilation of some Dominicans, Russians, Colombians, Jamaicans, Vietnamese, Laotians, and Chinese immigrants who have been drawn to certain criminal enterprises as they pursue their version of the American dream.

According to journalist William Kleinknecht, "As long as there is an underclass" and "as long as there are American cities," there will be opportunities for organized criminal activities.[28] Whatever the future of organized crime, drugs will surely continue to be a staple commodity as crime groups form stronger international links. International criminal conspiracies, such as the Sicilian and Russian Mafias, Colombian cartels, and Chinese triads, increasingly cooperate in a variety of illegal drug enterprises. In response, international law enforcement agencies have seemed to overcome the traditional reluctance to cooperate and have joined forces to fight organized crime on a number of fronts.

The Return of Shaming

For a country searching for alternative criminal justice strategies, it is surprising how rare it is for policymakers to draw lessons from the past. However, several judges have experimented with forms of exhibitory punishment that are reminiscent of the Puritan New England colonies. Several cases in Texas have made national news. In Houston, Judge Ted Poe wrote legislation in 1999 that allowed state judges in probation cases to order public notice of the crime where it was committed. Poe himself has issued close to 300 "public notice" sentences. In one case, a man who was convicted of domestic violence was required to publicly apologize to his wife on the steps of city hall. In another, a drunken driver was ordered to pace in front of a bar with the sign reading "I killed two people while driving drunk." Inspired by Nathaniel Hawthorne's *The Scarlet Letter,* the judge explained that "if we are held up to public ridicule, we don't like it and things will happen. We will change our conduct and our attitudes."[29]

The recrudescence of shaming led to opposition from critics who viewed it as an attempt to preach morality through the courts. Many of the concerns were based on the separation between church and state. Citing cases where judges ordered offenders to attend church in Texas and Louisiana in lieu of serving jail time or paying fines, the American Civil Liberties Union and other groups were worried that the move to shame-based punishment reflected a broader attempt by religious conservatives to impose their values on the political and legal systems.

Although there is no empirical evidence that shaming affects criminal behavior, it has become a popular alternative of justice. In one New Mexico town, bad-check writers are advertised on a large marquee; in Arizona, prisoners are taped at bookings at the Maricopa County Jail and posted for viewing on the Internet; and one of the more popular programs in Kansas City, Missouri, is shame-based "John TV," which offers photographs of individuals arrested for crimes involving prostitution.

Despite occasional criticisms, there have been few challenges to shame-based sentences. In many instances, shaming is directed at sexual offenders, with some judges requiring offenders to identify themselves. Because shame-based sentences are usually alternatives to prison sentences, there is little objection from the public since these sentences save the taxpayer money while publicizing the local threat of certain sex offenders. According to Marc Klaas, whose daughter Polly's murder in 1993 inspired the so-called Megan's laws (after a seven-year-old New Jersey girl was killed in her own neighborhood), "We all came to realize it is anonymity that breeds crime."

Capital Punishment

Since the return of the death penalty in 1976, 705 men and six women have been executed (as of May 2001). An analysis of this group would find that most of them were poor, usually white (56 percent), and typically high school dropouts. Most were from the South, and most had never killed before. Of the 711 executions, 579 were carried out in the South, with Texas leading the way with 246.[30] Although most nations in the world that use the death penalty bar the execution of juvenile offenders, seventeen of those executed since 1976 committed their crimes before they turned eighteen. Of the thirty-eight states that authorize the death penalty today, eighteen have established sixteen as the minimum age at the time of the crime, five have set it at seventeen, and fifteen have set it at eighteen.

By 2001, support for the death penalty was eroding, although the majority of Americans still favored it. In an October 2001 Gallup Poll, 68 percent of the American public favored the death penalty. Reasons cited for opposition included that it was administered unfairly and that it disproportionately targeted minorities. Others changed their minds after thirteen prisoners on death row in Illinois were discovered to be innocent, an admission that led Governor George Ryan of Illinois to declare a statewide moratorium on the death penalty in 2000. According to Austin Sarat, author of the book *When the State Kills,* the moratorium should be considered the turning point in the national dialogue about the death penalty.

In May 2000, the Supreme Court reviewed electrocution for the first time since its inception in 1890. By 2001, most states had abandoned electrocution in favor of lethal injection. Since its inception in 1890, more than 4,300 people in twenty-six states were executed in the electric chair. In 2000, only Nebraska and Alabama used this method as its primary mode of execution. According to this case, the court was to consider whether Nebraska's particular method constituted cruel and unusual punishment since it entailed four separate jolts of electricity. In November of the same year, the Georgia Supreme Court rejected a challenge to the electric chair, claiming that the condemned prisoner raised his electrocution challenge too late in his appeal, barring it on procedural grounds. No inmate had been electrocuted since Virginia executed Michael Clagett in July 2000.

Having set a one-year record of forty executions in 2000, Texas joined other states by considering the alternative of life without parole as a sentencing option to the death penalty in 2001.[31] As the nation's leading executioner, Texas offers juries the choice of sentencing a capital murderer to either death or life in prison, which carries the potential for parole after forty years. Most opinion polls suggest that if life without parole were an option, few juries would recommend the death penalty. If Texas chooses to offer this option, it will join forty-five states that currently provide the alternative. Opponents of this option in Texas argue that if this passes, it will be one more step toward abolition of the death penalty and will necessitate the construction of more prisons.

One of the foundations of American federalism is that law enforcement should be a state matter. For more than 200 years, the death penalty was authorized for only a small group of crimes, including espionage, murder on federal property, murder during the commission of a bank robbery, and, following the Lindbergh kidnapping, interstate kidnapping. The assassination of a president did not become a federal crime until the killing of John F. Kennedy in 1963. In the throes of the drug war, in 1988 Congress made some drug-related murders capital offenses. As part of an omnibus crime bill in 1994, Congress added more than forty crimes for which federal prosecutors could seek the death penalty, including carjacking that resulted in deaths.

One recent case has catapulted the debate over the federal death penalty to national prominence. In this case, the Justice Department is seeking the federal death penalty for several men charged in the execution-style murders of two college students in Rhode Island. The crime took place during the commission of a carjacking, but Rhode Island does not have the death penalty. However, under the new federal guidelines and with prodding from the victims' families, federal prosecutors are pursuing the federal death penalty. Between 1995 and 2000, Attorney General Janet Reno authorized seeking the death penalty against 285 defendants (only seventeen were from the twelve states without the death penalty). Under Attorney General John Ashcroft, the guidelines have changed so that the absence of the death penalty in a state may now be considered a factor in deciding whether the federal government will become involved.

For death penalty opponents, it is difficult to fathom that almost thirty years after the *Furman* decision, the Supreme Court is still considering whether to execute mentally retarded killers. In March 2001, justices heard the appeal of a North Carolina death row inmate whose execution was interrupted earlier in the month. It had been twelve years since the Court upheld the constitutionality of executing the mentally retarded in the case of Texas killer Johnny Paul Penry. Justice had initially overturned Penry's conviction in 1989 on the grounds that his trial failed to consider his mental retardation as a possible mitigating factor. Penry was later retried, convicted, and sentenced to death for his crime.[32]

At the time of the *Penry* decision, only Maryland and Georgia barred executing mentally retarded murderers. But this practice has become increasingly viewed as a human rights violation. Today, eighteen of the thirty-eight death penalty states and the federal government ban the execution of the mentally retarded.[33]

In March 2001, the Supreme Court ruled that jurors must be told the full truth when they are deciding whether to sentence a killer to death or life in prison. In the case of *Shafer v. South Carolina*, the Court reversed the death penalty for a South Carolina man who was condemned by jurors who were confused about the meaning of the phrase "life imprisonment." In this particular case, eighteen-year-old Wesley Aarin Shafer went to trial for the killing of a convenience store clerk during a robbery. Recent state law offered the possibility of either death or life in prison without the possibility of parole. The judge advised the jurors that they could decide on either "life imprisonment or death." When asked for clarification, the judge refused to respond to the jurors, leading to the death sentence. Over the past decade, all but five states have approved laws that imprison convicted murderers for the rest of their natural lives with no parole option. Of the thirty-eight states with capital punishment, only four have not adopted no-parole laws.

Although there was little controversy over the execution of Oklahoma City bomber Timothy McVeigh on federal charges, recent cases resulting from the September 11 terrorist attacks have brought the federal death penalty into question. Most recently, in an unprecedented move, government prosecutors are seeking the federal death penalty against the alleged twentieth hijacker, Zacarias Moussaoui, for conspiracy charges only. This would be the first time in modern history that state or federal prosecutors sought the death penalty in a case in which the defendant is charged merely with conspiring to commit murder rather than actually carrying it out.

Authorities charge that the four hijacked airplanes were skyjacked by only nineteen men instead of twenty because Moussaoui was in jail on immigration charges, forcing one group of hijackers to act with only four men rather than five like the others. It is likely that if Moussaoui is convicted and sentenced to death, the case will wind up in the Supreme Court. Legal critics have argued that this could set a precedent for a variety of defendants and establish a precedent by which political motivation trumps the rule of law.

AMERICAN VIOLENCE

As America enters the twenty-first century, it continues to exhibit certain tendencies that distinguish the nation from other industrialized nations, such as Germany, Japan, France, and the United Kingdom. Despite a decline in murder over the past decade, America continues to lead the industrialized world in this category. An examination of American violence suggests that national violence patterns are rooted in the past. Nowhere is this more true than in America's love affair with guns. More than half the country's murders are committed with handguns.

The reported decline of the American handgun industry offers perhaps a glimmer of hope for the reduction of future handgun violence. The decline follows a thirty-year period of growth fueled in part by the threat of crime, civil unrest, and the violent crack cocaine epidemic of the 1980s. In 1998, handgun production plummeted to its lowest figure in more than three decades. According to a 2001 report, "The American handgun market has dropped off so steeply that some industry experts worry it may never recover."[34] Among the reasons cited for this trend are tougher rules for purchasing them, an already saturated market, and a backlash from recent highly publicized school-yard and workplace murders.

The passage of the Handgun Violence Prevention Act of 1993 (the so-called Brady bill) may have dissuaded potential gun buyers from purchasing weapons because of its requirement of background checks. Others point out that many people buy guns for security reasons and that, with the recent drop in crime to a thirty-three-year low, they are less inclined to go gun shopping.

Another explanation for the drop in handgun sales is the changing strategy of the gun control lobby. Formerly, advocates of gun control focused on lobbying politicians to pass stricter legislation. A hot potato in any election, most politicians were reluctant to join the fray. Thus, in the late 1990s, champions of gun control set their sights on a new target by suing various gun manufacturers.

Over the past three years, more than thirty suits have been filed against gun makers and sellers by cities and government committees nationwide. The lawsuits charged gun makers with negligence for producing dangerous weapons that resulted in serious consequences in the hands of children and criminals. As part of their strategy, gun control proponents sought to hit the gun manufacturers where it hurt most, in the pocket, by seeking reimbursement for the high cost of preventing gun violence and the enormous costs of treating gunshot casualties in local trauma wards. While some lawsuits have already been dismissed, the potential for financial ruin still threatens the future of most manufacturers. Focusing its historic trade on a military and police market, the venerable Colt Manufacturing has chosen to end its retail handgun sales in 1999, largely because of potential lawsuits. In 2000, Smith & Wesson agreed to include safety locks on all guns and to make significant changes in its marketing campaign.[35]

According to a recent study by the *New York Times*, almost every ten days "a mass, random, public shooting occurs in the United States." No type of shooting receives more news coverage than school shootings, particularly when the victims are white. School-yard killings represent only a fraction of American homicides. Of the 150,000 Americans murdered over the past decade, no more than 150 were killed in or around a school. Critics of selective media reporting of such events cite the discriminatory coverage that all but ignores shootings involving African American and other minority victims, the most likely target of school-yard violence. According to Mike Males of the Justice Policy Institute in Washington, D.C., "White and black youths [are] less menaced by school violence now than a quarter-century ago."[36]

Federal figures show that suicide is the eighth-leading cause of death, killing 30,000 people each year. One-third as many die in homicides. In May 2001, the federal government announced a national strategy for suicide prevention. Among the recommendations strategies are adding more suicide prevention programs in schools, jails, and the workplace and encouraging members of the medical community to ask at-risk patients about the presence of firearms, drugs, and other lethal weapons in their homes.

In the 1990s, antiabortion violence escalated from picketing, verbal harassment, arson, and bombings to the outright assassination of physicians and clinic employees. By the late 1990s, antiabortion snipers began targeting doctors in their very homes, using high-powered rifles. One of the most prominent of these killings was the murder of Dr. Barnett Slepian near Buffalo, New York, killed by a gunshot through the window as he stood in his kitchen. His assailant was identified as James Kopp. In March 2001, Kopp was apprehended in France following an international manhunt. Aided by e-mail traffic and wiretapped conversations with friends, French police aided the FBI in the arrest. Kopp had been on the FBI's Ten Most Wanted Fugitives List since June 1999, and throughout his escape he was helped along the way by antiabortion supporters.

Less publicized than the school-yard shootings and mass murders that sporadically inundate the nightly news was the news in April 2002 that the rate of violent crime against Hispanics fell 56 percent over a seven-year period in the 1990s and is now similar to that against whites. This decrease coincided with drops in violence against other minority groups as well. Except for robbery, rates of victimization for Native Americans were the highest in every category. A spokeswoman for the National Council of La Raza credited the efforts of the nation's police departments to improve relations with Hispanics.

CONCLUSIONS

No matter what technological advances appear in the twenty-first century, the criminal justice system remains adamantly reliant on the time-tested traditions of the past. Witness the return of horse-mounted patrols in shopping mall parking lots and in urban centers and the return of shaming in the courtroom. Since the advent of law enforcement, it has been obvious that an officer on horseback has advantages over a purely bipedal counterpart, particularly when it came to controlling crowds. First introduced by King Charles in 1629, horse-mounted police branches are clearly on the increase. Almost forced out of existence by the automobile, over the past twenty years mounted patrols have once again become a familiar presence in most large cities and are considered advantageous for riot control, community relations, and their high visibility. Also demonstrating the cyclical nature of innovation in criminal justice is the reinvigorated emphasis on community-oriented policing, which has taken the police officer from behind the wheel of an automobile and back to foot patrol in American communities.

Recent polls indicate shrinking support for capital punishment after a decade of almost unshakable support. The debate over the death penalty came into sharp focus after a confluence of several events in 2001, including the execution of Oklahoma City bomber Timothy McVeigh, protests during President Bush's European visit that focused on America's death penalty policy as a violation of human rights, the decision by a New York jury not to sentence one of the African embassy bombers to death, and the execution of a murderer in Ohio who claimed he was schizophrenic. Although a majority of Americans still were in favor of the death penalty, the size of that majority had diminished.

At the conclusion of 2001, a dramatic decline in the use of the death penalty in America saw sixty-six people put to death that year compared to eighty-five the year before. Texas, which executed forty in 2000, witnessed seventeen in 2001 and lost the lead to Oklahoma, which executed eighteen convicts in 2001. In addition, a combination of declining crime rates and a wave of DNA exonerations have made the courts and the public more skeptical about death sentences. While the decline in executions has encouraged the opponents of capital punishment, many are disturbed as the federal government began executing people again for the first time in decades.

America's state prison population increased by 500 percent over the past thirty years. Even while crime rates dropped in the 1990s, prisons remained the fastest-growing item in state budgets. By 2002, more than two million inmates were incarcerated in state, federal, and local correctional facilities at a cost of more than $30 billion a year. Nationwide, guards account for 80 percent of prison costs. In order to slash budgets, some states are laying off guards and supervisory positions. Others are cutting back on educational programs and food services to save money.

In April 2002, the Justice Department announced that the number of people in prison grew by only 1 percent over the previous year, the slowest rate in thirty years (as June 30, 2001, one of every 145 residents was behind bars). Most U.S. prisoners were held in state prisons, where the population rose 0.4 percent. The federal prison population showed the most growth at 7.2 percent. However, this was due in part to the U.S. government's continuing to assume responsibility for District of Columbia prisoners (this transfer ended in 2001). Racial disparities in prison populations continued to haunt critics of the criminal justice system. The Justice Department released figures that showed that 13.4 percent of black males ages twenty-five to twenty-nine were incarcerated, compared with 4.1 percent of Hispanic men and 1.8 percent of white males.

Being contentious issues throughout American history, racial violence and inequality, handgun crime, police brutality, prison overcrowding, concerns about civil liberties, illegal drugs, and the death penalty continue to plague America into the third millennium. Other new and more sinister threats, including nuclear and chemical terrorism, challenge the criminal justice system.

Why Study the History of Criminal Justice?

While recent opinion polls suggest that a majority of Americans believe that the U.S. Constitution is important to them, most evidence suggests that "Americans have an appalling lack of knowledge" about one of the nation's greatest documents.[37] Poll results released by the National Constitution Center in 1997 indicated that more than half the respondents did not know there are 100 U.S. senators. One-quarter could not even name one of the rights guaranteed by the First Amendment. More than one-third were under the impression that the Constitution mandated English as the nation's official language. One out of six "understood" that the Constitution established America as a Christian nation. What is even more frustrating to historians and other educators was how confused Americans were between the Declaration of Independence and the U.S. Constitution, with 84 percent reporting that the latter document states that "all men are created equal."

In 1997, a Vietnamese immigrant responding to a citizenship question on the U.S. Constitution that asked for the year in which the Constitution was signed responded with utmost confidence, "1787." When he received back his exam, it was marked incorrect, much to his chagrin. However, he was correct, and, probably knowing more about the Constitution than most native-born Americans, he was awarded his citizenship.

In mid-April 2001, two seemingly historical anachronisms took center stage in national news reports. While these stories are abstractions to many young students, they demonstrate the short history of America. The late great Hollywood Renaissance man Orson Welles once claimed that he was only several handshakes removed from Napoleon (meaning that he shook the hand of someone who shook the hand of a contemporary of Napoleon). If this is so, the Civil War and the civil rights movement are at least one or two handshakes closer yet still seem distant.

In 2001, the Southern Poverty Law Center, which campaigns against racism and hate crimes, announced that eighteen civil rights–era killings had been reopened in Alabama, Florida, Louisiana, and Mississippi. On April 16, 2001, jury selection began in Birmingham, Alabama, in the trial of Thomas E. Blanton Jr., age sixty-two, and Frank Cherry, age seventy-one, both facing four counts of murder for the fatal bombing of the Birmingham 16th Street Baptist Church almost forty years earlier. While Cherry's case was postponed because of questions about his mental competency, it took the jury less than two and a half hours on May 2, 2001, to convict Blanton of the church bombing and sentence him to life in prison.[38]

Residents of Birmingham (a city once labeled by Martin Luther King Jr. as "the most segregated big city in the nation") wished the trial would go away. Ironically, the case was made against the two men thanks to FBI wiretaps and the testimony of an informant who broke the Klan code of silence after being shown crime scene photos of the four dead youths.

The very same week that two men went on trial for what seemed an ancient transgression, Mississippi was conducting a referendum on whether to choose a new state flag. Georgia, Florida, South Carolina, and Alabama had put the issue to rest by artful compromise, but Mississippi was not expected to follow suit. Long at the center of conflict between blacks who wished to move beyond the Old South and whites who claimed some profound and emotional attachment to a heritage, Mississippi today remains the poorest and least urban state of the Deep South. It is also the most obsessed about its past. To no one's surprise, the citizens voted nearly three to one to keep the flag bearing the Confederate battle emblem.

At the same time that Mississippians were hailing their good fortune of having kept their links to the past, another no-less-serious link to the past, the handgun industry, was given its death knell by some industry experts who worried that it would never recover because of a number of lawsuits and bad publicity.[39] However, it is probably too soon to estimate the potential impact of a declining handgun market on crime in America since the nation is already saturated with handguns.

Because of changes in technology and politics across the country, coupled with rigorous police work, unsolved criminal cases from the civil rights era are now being solved, closing the chapter on twentieth-century criminal justice and giving currency to novelist William Faulkner's often-quoted remark from *As I Lay Dying:* "The past is never dead. It's not even past." As criminal justice historian John Conley so perceptively noted in 1993, the study of history "provides a context for issues and institutions" and "offers a broad foundation for evaluation through comparing and contrasting current issues with past experiences."[40] The criminal justice system is changing more quickly than ever before. What was once a slow evolution based on experimentation and innovation has turned into a dynamic and proactive attempt to contain and suppress criminal behavior that was almost unthinkable in years past. No one can forecast what the next chapter in this saga will hold.

SOURCES

Bardwell, S. K. 2000. "Police to Look at Software That Targets Serial Killers." *Houston Chronicle,* April 21.

Barker, Jeff. 2000. "Tiny Delaware Boasts Highest Per-Capita Execution Rate in U.S." *Houston Chronicle,* December 25.

Beckett, Katherine and Theodore Sasson. 2000. *Politics of Injustice.* Thousand Oaks, CA.: Pine Forge Press.

Biskupic, Joan. 2001a. "Feds Seek Right to Search in Probation Cases." *USA Today,* November 7.

———. 2001b. "Terror Attacks May Have Lasting Effects on Courts." *USA Today,* November 7.

Blomberg, Thomas G., and Karol Lucken. 2000. *American Penology: A History of Control.* New York: Aldine de Gruyter.

Bratton, William J., with Peter Knobler. 1998. *Turnaround: How America's Top Cop Reversed the Crime Epidemic.* New York: Random House.

Burke, Tod W. 1999. "Brain 'Fingerprinting.'" *Law and Order,* June, pp. 28–31.

Carry, David. 2001. "Death Sentence Predicted for Electric Chair's Future." *Houston Chronicle,* August 9.

Cole, Simon A. 2001a. "The Myth of Fingerprints." *New York Times Magazine,* May 13, pp. 13–14.

———. 2001b. *Suspect Identities: A History of Fingerprinting and Criminal Identification.* Cambridge, Mass.: Harvard University Press.

Conley, John A. 1993. "Historical Perspective and Criminal Justice." *Journal of Criminal Justice Education* 4 (fall): 901–12.

"Corrections Population Tops Record." 2001. *Houston Chronicle,* August 27.

Donn, Jeff. 2001. "Plunging U.S. Handgun Market Unlikely to Recover, Experts Say." *Houston Chronicle,* April 14.

Garrison, Jessica. 2001. "Some Public Schools Drop Zero Tolerance." *Houston Chronicle,* February 25.

Goldstein, Steve. 1997. "Poll: Most Americans 'Appallingly' Ignorant about U.S. Constitution." *Houston Chronicle,* September 16.

Grudowski, Mike. 1995. "Not-So-Lethal-Weapons." *New York Times Magazine,* August 13, pp. 40–41.

Harcourt, Bernard E. 2001. *Illusion of Order: The False Promise of Broken Windows Policing.* Cambridge, Mass.: Harvard University Press.

Johnson, Kevin. 1999. "FBI Takes on Expanding Role." *USA Today,* June 8.

Kaminer, Wendy. 2001. "Virtual Rape." *New York Times Magazine,* November 25, pp. 70–73.

Karmen, Andrew. 2001. *New York Murder Mystery: The True Story behind the Crime Crash of the 1990s.* New York: New York University Press.

Kleinknecht, William. 1996. *The New Ethnic Mobs: The Changing Face of Organized Crime in America.* New York: Free Press.

Lake, Anthony. 2000. *6 Nightmares: Real Threats in a Dangerous World and How America Can Meet Them.* Boston: Little, Brown.

Males, Mike. 2001. "Real story behind school shootings going untold." *Houston Chronicle,* March 13, www.houstonchronicle.com.

Maple, Jack, with Chris Mitchell. 1999. *The Crime Fighter: Putting the Bad Guys Out of Business.* New York: Doubleday.

Martin, Keith. 2002. "Utilizing Identification Technology in Corrections." *Corrections Connection News Center,* March 19, database.corrections.co,/news/results2.asp?ID=1944.

McArdle, Andrea, and Tanya Erzen, eds. 2001. *Zero Tolerance: Quality of Life and the New Police Brutality in New York City*. New York: New York University Press.

Miller, D. W. 2001. "Poking Holes in the Theory of 'Broken Windows.' " *Chronicle of Higher Education*, February 9, pp. A14–A16.

Miller, Jerome G. 1996. *Search and Destroy: African-American Males in the Criminal Justice System*. Cambridge: Cambridge University Press.

Murphy, Dean E. 2001. "Justice as a Morality Play That Ends with Shame." *New York Times*, June 3.

"Okla. Governor Says Profiling Has Role against Terror." *Houston Chronicle*, February 3.

Peirce, Neal. 2000. "Civil Death of Felons Is a New Civil Rights Issue." *Houston Chronicle*, December 24.

Reinert, Patty. 2001a. "Supreme Court Weighs Drug Law." *Houston Chronicle*, March 25.

————. 2001b. "Court to Revisit Execution of Retarded." *Houston Chronicle*, March 27.

Remnick, David. 1997. "The Crime Buster." *The New Yorker*, February 24 and March 3, pp. 94–109.

Sarat, Austin. 2001. *When the State Kills: Capital Punishment and the American Condition*. Princeton, N.J.: Princeton University Press.

Silverman, Eli B. 1999. *NYPD Battles Crime: Innovative Strategies in Policing*. Boston: Northeastern University Press.

Stern, Seth. 2002. "A Harder Day in Court for Fingerprint, Writing Experts." http://csmonitor.com, January 31.

Taylor, Ralph. 2001. *Breaking Away from Broken Windows*. Boulder, Colo.: Westview Press.

"Trial Will Revisit '63 Bombing." 2001. *Houston Chronicle*, April 16.

Weinstein, Henry, Darren Briscoe, and Mitchell Landsberg. 2002. "Civil Liberties Take Back Seat to Safety." *Los Angeles Times*, March 10.

CRITICAL THINKING QUESTIONS

1. What criteria would you use to come with a contemporary Ten Most Wanted List? Look back to the 1920s, 1930s, and other decades and determine what would be the Ten Most Wanted Lists for these eras (remember that the concept was not formally introduced until 1950).

2. What impact did the terrorist attacks of September 11, 2001, have on the various segments of the criminal justice system?

3. Is the death penalty declining in popularity? If so, why? If not, is it increasing or staying the same?

4. Has the role of the federal criminal justice system changed over the past several years? Discuss.

5. Following several high-profile police brutality cases in New York City, the New York Police Department was vilified by the public and civil libertarians. Since September 11, public opinion has changed. Discuss.

6. Discuss the impact of new sciences and technology on the criminal justice.

7. Contrast the government response to Timothy McVeigh and Osama bin Laden.

8. What would America's earliest police and corrections reformers think about the state of the modern American criminal justice system?

NOTES

1. Among the dead at the World Trade Center were 494 foreigners representing ninety-one countries, 17 percent of those killed.

2. Garrison (2001, p. A2).

3. These states include Oregon, Alaska, Washington, Maine, Arizona, Nevada, Colorado, Arkansas, Hawaii, and Washington, D.C.

4. Reinert (2001b, p. A23).

5. Weinstein et al. (2002, p. A1).

6. Quoted in Weinstein et al. (2002, p. A28).

7. Today, nine states have lifetime prohibitions on felons voting. These states include Alabama, Florida, Iowa, Kentucky, Mississippi, Nevada, New Mexico, Virginia, and Wyoming, Arizona, Maryland, Tennessee, and Washington have more limited versions of the civil death ban.

8. Peirce (2000, p. C3).

9. Peirce (2000, p. C3).

10. Johnson (1999).

11. Grudowski (1995, pp. 40–41).

12. Beckett and Sasson 2000, p. 208).

13. Miller (2001, p. A15).

14. Quoted in Miller (2001, p. A15).

15. Silverman (1999).

16. Bardwell (2000, p. A36).

17. Burke (1999, p. 29).

18. Cole (2001b, p. 284).

19. Cole (2001a, pp. 13–14). Cole offers the results of a recent proficiency test that found that as many as one out of five fingerprint examiners misidentified fingerprint samples.

20. Quoted in Stern (2002, p. 1).

21. "Corrections Population Tops Record" (2001, p. A3).

22. Biskupic (2001a).

23. Miller (1996, p. 217).

24. Quoted in Miller (1996, p. 222).

25. Quoted in Martin (2002, p. 3).

26. Kaminer (2001, p. 70).

27. Kaminer (2001, p. 72).

28. Kleinknecht (1996, p. 294).

29. Murphy (2001, p. 5).

30. Of the remaining 132 executions, fifty-six took place in the West, seventy-three in the Midwest, and three in the Northeast.

31. Surprisingly, the state of Delaware actually has the highest per capita rate of executions in America. At the end of 2000, with a population twenty-five times that of Delaware, Texas had executed 193 people since 1991, compared to eleven in Delaware. The Texas state rate of execution stood at 0.106 per 10,000 residents compared to 0.137 in Delaware. See Barker (2000).

32. Penry's case is back before the Supreme Court as his lawyers try to save his life on the grounds that his history as an abused child was not considered during the second trial and the jury instructions on mitigation were fumbled.

33. States currently banning this practice include Arizona, Arkansas, Colorado, Connecticut, Florida, Georgia, Indiana, Kansas, Kentucky, Maryland, Missouri, Nebraska, New Mexico, New York, North Carolina, South Dakota, Tennessee, and Washington.

34. Donn (2001, p. A15).

35. Founded in 1852, Smith & Wesson has turned to manufacturing a wide range of products to supplement its ailing gun business. In Smith & Wesson Outlet Stores, shoppers can now buy gym bags, Western-style leatherware, and jewelry, all with the familiar logo.

36. Males (2001, p. A27).

37. Goldstein (1997).

38. The same week that former Klansman Thomas Blanton Jr. was convicted for the 1963 Alabama bombing, Mississippi prosecutors began motions to reopen the 1964 murders of three civil rights workers, referred to as the most "infamous unresolved civil rights–era case," since no one was tried in state court for the killings. However, there is little optimism among investigators for resolving this case. Other civil rights prosecutions were pressured by strong middle-class black communities. Neshoba County in Mississippi remains a rural enclave with little community support for reopening the case.

39. Donn (2001).

40. Conley (1993, p. 904).

Glossary

Abjuration   Process by which a fugitive takes exile from country.

Abolitionists   Zealous opponents of slavery prior to emancipation.

Adultery   Refers to sexual relations between a married person and someone other than his or her lawful spouse.

Alcatraz Prison   Prison of last resort; considered the original supermax prison until its closure in 1963.

Alien and Sedition Acts   Early international scandal in 1797–1798 that led to legislation that led to debate on constitutional freedoms.

American Indian Movement (AIM)   Radical Native American organization founded in 1968 by Dennis Banks and Clyde Bellecourt.

American Prison Congress   In 1870, 130 delegates from around the world convened in Cincinnati to discuss principles of prison reform. The National Prison Congress provided the nucleus for what would become the American Correctional Association.

Anarchists   Individuals who sought to promote violence or revolt against established law, rule, or custom.

Angles   A West German people who migrated to Britain in the fifth century.

Antebellum period   Years of sectional tension leading up to the Civil War (1861–1865).

Apalachin Conference   When authorities stumbled on a meeting of organized crime figures in upstate New York in 1957, federal law enforcement was forced to concede its existence and make it a high priority in the war on crime.

Approvers   Criminal informants in Middle Ages.

Army disease   Refers to morphine addiction that often plagued ex-soldiers when they returned home after the Civil War.

Ashurst–Summers Act   In 1935, this legislation strengthened prohibitions on prison industries first implemented under the Hawes-Cooper Act in 1929.

Assize of Arms   In 1181, freemen in England were encouraged to own arms and armor according to their station and means.

Assize of Clarendon   Established trial by grand jury in 1166.

Assize of Northhampton   Divided England into six circuits traveled periodically by the king's judges. These judges superseded local courts.

Attica Prison   The bloodiest prison riot in American history took place at this New York State prison in 1971.

Auburn prison system   New York prison system that relied on the silent system and allowed convicts to work in a congregate setting at day but at night were kept in solitary cells.

Bailiff   Created by the Statute of Winchester, initially responsible for tracking strangers in medieval towns after dark.

Barathron   A prominent place of execution in ancient Athens.

Barons   Highest level of Norman lords.

Benefit of Clergy   Members of the clergy were given an exemption from secular punishments during the Middle Ages.

Bertillon system   In the 1890s this identification system using a complicated system of measurements was created in France to identify recidivist offenders. It was eventually replaced by fingerprint identification.

Bestiality   Sexual relations between a person and an animal.

Bier rite   A Germanic ordeal in which the suspect was ordered to touch an alleged victim of a homicide. If the corpse bled or frothed at the mouth, the suspect was pronounced guilty.

Bigamy   The crime of marrying while one has a husband or wife living and where no valid divorce has been effected.

Big-house prisons   In the 1920s, huge-capacity prisons were constructed that led to social divisions among inmates at such prisons as San Quentin, California, and Stateville, Illinois.

Black codes   Southern states instituted laws to replace the old slave codes following the Civil War.

Black Death   One of the worst pandemics in world history.

Black Hand gangs   Gangs of Sicilian extortionists who preyed on fellow immigrants.

Blasphemy   Irreverent behavior toward anything held sacred, such as cursing or reviling God.

Bobbies   In respect to Sir Robert Peel, refers to policemen on the London Metropolitan Police.

Body of Liberties (1641)   Early Massachusetts colony law code inspired by Mosaic law.

Bounty jumping   An early organized crime racket. During the Civil War, individuals would collect bounties from individuals seeking to escape the draft. Once the bounty was collected, the individual would desert and repeat this sequence elsewhere.

Bow Street Runners   A specially formed group of constables created by Henry Fielding who were expected to run to the aid of crime victims and pursue criminals.

Bradwell v. Illinois   This 1873 Supreme Court decision temporarily ruled that the equal protection clause of the Fourteenth Amendment protected only men.

Branch Davidians   Cult led by David Koresh in Waco, Texas. The deaths of more than eighty members during a federal raid led to congressional hearings in 1995.

Bridewells   Hoses of corrections, forerunner of modern prison.

Brinks robbery   This 1950 heist was the biggest robbery in American history up to that time.

Broken-windows model   According to this theory, neighborhood disorder gives out crime-promoting signals, such as broken windows. If police target these environments and gain the cooperation of citizens, they can more effectively fight crime.

Bulla   Charm worn by Roman boys to ward off evil spirits.

Canon law   Church law, with the pope as the supreme legislator; originally superseded the law of England.

Carroll Doctrine   In 1925, the Supreme Court ruled in *Carroll et al. v. United States* that police can conduct a search of moving vehicles without a warrant.

Celtic   An ancient people now represented by the people of Ireland, Wales, Scotland, and Britain.

Cherry Hill Prison   Better known as Pennsylvania's Eastern State Penitentiary.

Child Savers   Politically active women at the turn of the twentieth century who tried to protect children from lives of crime.

COINTELPRO   A clandestine FBI program established along the lines of a "department of misinformation" in order to create a climate of confusion among left-wing organizations in the 1960s. The Black Panther Party was a special target.

Coldbath riots   In 1833, the London Metropolitan Police gained the support of the public by suppressing a riot with few serious injuries.

College cops   As police chief of Berkeley, California, August Vollmer insisted that his officers attend college in the early 1900s.

Community policing   Beginning in the 1980s, this philosophy demonstrated a transition to a more proactive approach in policing.

Compurgation   Method of determining guilt or innocence under the Anglo-Saxons.

Comstock Law   Passed by Congress in 1873, it prohibited the transmission of obscene materials through the mail.

Coneymen   Early American counterfeiters.

Constable   Formerly the "head of the stables," this position became identifiable with peacekeeping after the Norman Conquest.

Constantinople   Formerly Byzantium and now Istanbul, Turkey, Emperor Constantine established this city as the new capital of the eastern Roman Empire following its decline in the West.

Convict hulks   Often called "floating hells" or "hell holds," the British used these broken-down warships anchored in rivers and bays as floating prisons.

Cop or copper   Pejorative term for police officer. There is no consensus as to the origin of either word.

COPS program   Community Oriented Policing Services program.

Coroner   Position originated in England in 1194 to investigate suspicious deaths.

Corpus juris civilis   Continental legal system that developed out of Roman law.

Court of Areopagus   Established by Greek lawgiver Draco for trying murder cases and other serious offenses.

Credit Mobilier scandal (1872)   One of the greatest congressional scandals of the nineteenth century.

Crimes Act of 1790   Federal crime act that defined seventeen crimes and prescribed death by hanging for six crimes.

Criminology   The study of crime and criminals.

Curfew   Traditionally used by the upper class to limit movements of the lower classes. Normans ruled that fires had to be out by eight o'clock to keep subversive Anglo-Saxons from congregating.

Dale's Laws   Martial law code in colonial Virginia.

Danelaw   Region of England controlled by the Danes stretching from the Thames River to Liverpool.

Decemvirs   Group of ten men who wrote Roman law at its earliest stages.

Declaration of Principles   Their adoption at the 1870 National Prison Congress represented a great stride toward progressive prison reform.

De jure   Officially sanctioned.

Demon rum   Early temperance groups targeted the popularity of rum as the main cause of social disorder in the Jacksonian era.

Desmoterium   Ancient Athenian prison, or "place of chains."

District attorney   This county attorney or prosecutor was an important colonial modification of the English criminal justice system.

Domesday Book   A comprehensive survey or census of the English land tenure system.

Dooms   Earliest written Anglo-Saxon laws.

Draconian   In homage to the ancient Greek legislator Draco; synonymous with "harsh."

Drug Enforcement Administration   Created in 1973 to enforce federal drug statutes and investigate major drug traffickers.

Dyer Act   In 1919, the National Motor Vehicle Act, or Dyer Act, made the transportation of stolen automobiles across state lines a federal crime.

Eastern State Penitentiary   When it was completed in 1829, it was the largest public building in America and a showplace for prison reform.

Ecclesiastical courts   Church courts presided over by the clergy.

Eighteenth Amendment   Congress approved the Volstead Act in 1919, and it was ratified in 1920, making it illegal to manufacture, import, distribute, or sell alcoholic beverages in the United States.

Eighth Amendment   Prohibits cruel and unusual punishments.

Elmira Reformatory   Originally set up in New York State in 1876 for youths aged sixteen to thirty serving their first prison terms. Emphasis was on trade training and academic education.

Enlightenment   A philosophical movement of the seventeenth and eighteenth centuries characterized by a belief in the power of human reason. This movement had great impact on the development of criminal justice, particularly in the birth of the penitentiary.

Ergastulum   Ancient Roman prison cells.

Espionage Act of 1917   Criminalized certain unpopular political views.

Eugenics   Pseudoscience that attempted to "improve" human genetic stock through such controversial methods as forced sterilization.

Ex parte Milligan   Supreme Court ruled in 1866 that only the legislative branch had the power to suspend the writ of habeas corpus.

Federal Bureau of Narcotics   Established in 1930.

Federal Bureau of Prisons   Created in 1929.

Felony   Since the Norman Conquest in 1066, this has referred to serious crimes.

Female Prison and Reformatory Institution for Girls and Women   In 1874 Indianapolis, Indiana, opened the first separate prison devoted solely to women.

Feudalism   Class system of mutual obligation brought to England by Normans.

Fifth Amendment   Guarantees that no person shall be compelled to testify against himself and ensures due process in capital cases.

Fingerprinting   The adoption of fingerprinting in the late 1890s gave crime investigators the first reliable proof of an individual's presence at a crime scene.

First Amendment   Affirmed rights of freedom of religion, freedom of speech, and freedom of the press and the right to assemble peacefully and to petition the government for a redress of grievances.

Five Points   New York City district where five streets intersected; known as a breeding ground for crime in the early nineteenth century.

Flagrante delicto   While the crime or act is being committed.

Fornication   Voluntary sexual relations between two unmarried persons or two persons not married to each other.

Fourteenth Amendment   Gave blacks citizenship and equal protection under the law in 1868.

Fourth Amendment   Prohibits arbitrary search and seizure.

Fourth Lateran Council   In 1215, this meeting of church officials diminished the importance of trial by ordeal.

Frame of Government (1682)   William Penn's "Great Law," the first criminal code of Pennsylvania.

Freedom Summer   In the late 1960s, civil rights activists went South to register black voters.

Fugitive Slave Act of 1850   By prohibiting alleged runaway slaves from testifying in court, this escalated sectional tensions leading to Civil War.

Furman v. Georgia   In 1972, the Supreme Court voted that the death penalty constituted cruel and unusual punishment.

Gaol fever   A form of typhus often prevalent among early prisoners, particularly on convict hulks.

Gideon v. Wainwright   In 1963, the Supreme Court ruled that all felony defendants were entitled to legal representation.

G-men   Government men; used as moniker for FBI agents beginning in the 1930s.

Golden Rule policy   Advocated dealing more informally with juvenile offenders through diversion programs in order to avoid stigmatization.

Great Depression   Economic crisis that began with 1929 stock market crash and continued through the 1930s.

Gregg v. Georgia   This case upheld the death penalty, leading to a return of capital punishment in 1976.

Habeas Corpus Act of 1679   Prohibited the secret confinement of prisoners and required that an individual accused of a crime be present in court at time of trial.

Harrison Narcotic Act   In 1914, the federal government passed its first antidrug legislation by requiring a doctor's prescription for the sale of controlled dangerous substances.

Hawes–Cooper Act   In 1929, Congress allowed states to ban the sale of goods made in another state's prison within its borders.

Hemlock   This poison was sometimes used as a form of execution in ancient Greece.

Heresy   Opinion or doctrine at variation with accepted church doctrine; once considered the worst religious crime.

House Un-American Activities Committee (HUAC)   Created in the 1930s, its activities were most prominent in the 1940s and 1950s during Senator Joseph McCarthy's "American Inquisition" of American Communist Party members.

Hue and cry   A call for help in apprehending an offender in the Anglo-Saxon era.

Hundreds   Shires were divided into these territorial subdivisions.

Indentured servant   A person who came to America and was placed under contract to work for another person for a specific period of time (usually seven years).

Indeterminate sentencing   Sentencing reform in which convicts could earn marks for good behavior leading to earlier release from prison; precursor to parole.

Infanticide   The act of killing an infant.

Inns of Court   London guilds for lawyers learning the common law.

In re Gault   In 1967, the Supreme Court extended the *Gideon* ruling to juvenile delinquency proceedings.

Inquisition   Special tribunals or official investigations, often political or religious in nature, established in the thirteenth century; originally engaged in combating and punishing heresy.

Institutes   Law textbook published under the reign of Justinian in 533 making the Twelve Tables obsolete.

International Association of Chiefs of Police (IACP)   National police association that since the 1890s has been influential in one form or another in implementing various police reforms.

International Association of Policewomen (IAP) Established in 1915 in an effort to include more women in policing.

Jacksonian America This era coincided with the so-called Age of the Common Man and the presidency of Andrew Jackson, which lasted from 1828 to 1836. Many historians suggest that it was also the period when Americans first perceived crime as a threat to the security of the Republic, extending the era from 1820 to 1850.

Jim Crow A practice or policy of segregating African Americans in public places, employment, and so on.

Judiciary Act of 1789 Created the federal courts system, including the Supreme Court, and the positions of U.S. marshal and attorney general.

Justice of the peace Beginning in 1361, this unpaid peacekeeping position became the cornerstone of British law and order.

Jutes Germanic tribe that invaded Britain in the fifth century.

Kansas City Massacre After four law enforcement officers were killed in ambush in 1933, anticrime legislation enlarged the crime-fighting powers and jurisdiction of the FBI.

Kansas City Preventive Patrol Experiment Reported in 1974 that police patrols, whether absent or present, had no significant impact on crime.

Katz v. United States In 1967, the Supreme Court limited the use of electronic eavesdropping because of concerns about invasion of privacy.

Kerner Report This 1969 report was the first federally funded examination of race relations in the United States.

Kinship groups A form of extended family.

Knapp Commission Independent citizens' commission established to investigate New York City police corruption in the early 1970s.

Know-Nothing Party Nativist and anti-Catholic political party in the 1850s.

Ku Klux Klan White supremacist group created by ex-Confederate soldiers in Tennessee in 1866.

Law Enforcement Assistance Administration (LEAA) Created in 1968 by Congress as its centerpiece in a "national war on crime."

Law of the Goring Ox Early Mosaic law pertaining to the law of liability.

Lawes, Divine, Morall and Martiall Also known as "Dale's Laws," a harsh law code used to keep order in the Virginia Colony. It instituted capital punishment for a wide range of offenses.

Leasing The convict leasing system was used as an alternative to imprisonment after the Civil War. During the 1870s and 1880s, the leasing of convicts under contract to private contractors dominated southern penology.

Leatherheads Slang for 1820s New York City night watchmen who wore leather helmets.

Leavenworth Prison America's first federal prison; opened its doors in Kansas in 1897.

Lethal injection The latest trend in sanitizing executions.

Levellers Outspoken reformers who argued for a simplification of the legal system, a bill of rights, and prohibition of debt imprisonment.

Lexow Committee This 1894 investigation revealed widespread corruption on the New York City Police Department.

Lindbergh Law The kidnapping and murder of aviator Charles Lindbergh's son led Congress to pass legislation in 1932 that elevated kidnapping to a capital offenses and earlier FBI involvement in cases where the victim was taken across state lines.

Liveried lackeys Early police officers opposed wearing uniforms because it would make them resemble uniformed servants.

Lynchings This term evolved from its colonial-era meaning as punishment not sanctioned by law, but not necessarily fatal, to the unlawful execution of persons of color in the 1890s.

Magna Carta The Great Charter of 1215 had a great impact of on subsequent developments in constitutional law and political freedom.

Mandatory sentencing Fixed sentences that take sentencing discretion out of the hands of judges.

Manor Landholdings of Norman barons.

Manslaughter In early sixteenth century, murder without premeditation became distinct from murder with malice aforethought.

Mapp v. Ohio The Supreme Court ruled in 1961 that evidence secured by the police through unreasonable searches must be excluded from trial.

Marijuana Tax Act In 1937, the recreational use of marijuana was made illegal.

Mark system A method of earning early release from prison; considered a precursor to parole.

Mayflower Compact Drawn up by the Pilgrims, this document is considered the first charter of laws ever framed by English common people.

McCleskey v. Kemp The Supreme Court case that tested the constitutionality of the death penalty. In its decision, the Court ruled that an inmate's treatment did not violate the Eighth Amendment.

Medieval Refers to the Middle Ages; originated in sixteenth century as a way to designate the era between early Christianity and the Protestant Reformation as well as the period between classical antiquity and the Renaissance.

MIBURN In 1964, the FBI launched "Mississippi Burning," or MIBURN, following the abduction and murder of three civil rights workers in Mississippi.

Militia groups Militant antigovernment groups that sprouted up in America's heartland in the 1980s and 1990s.

Miranda v. Arizona The 1966 Supreme Court decision that ruled that defendants must be made aware of their right to counsel and that anything they say can be used against them in a trial.

Molly Maguires Predominantly Irish-Catholic secret organization that waged a campaign of terror against mine owners in northeastern Pennsylvania in the 1860s and 1870s.

Monotheism Belief in only one God.

Mount Pleasant Female Prison In 1835, New York established this institution run exclusively by female prison matrons for women.

Muckrakers Investigative journalists who chronicled the social abuses of the Progressive era.

Murdrum Murder fine introduced by Normans; the word *murder* might have been derived from this term.

Mutual Welfare League Prison reform experiment initiated at Sing Sing Prison by Thomas Mott Osborne in 1914.

Nativism The policy of protecting the interests of the native-born inhabitants against those of immigrants.

Neck verse During the Middle Ages, if one could successfully read Psalm 51, a defendant could be saved from hanging. This test became more obsolete when reading became more widespread.

Newgate Prison Opened in New York in 1797, it was the first prison modeled on the Pennsylvania model.

New Penology In the 1920s and 1930s, many northern states implemented concepts of diagnosis and classification and added specialized personnel in psychology to the prison environment.

New York City draft riot This 1863 antidraft riot is regarded as one the worst urban riots in American history.

Night watch Prior to the advent of modern policing, amateur night watchmen patrolled the streets in a peacekeeping capacity.

Normans Inhabitants of northern France who were descended from the Northmen, better known as Vikings.

Nullification Controversy In 1833, South Carolina's John Calhoun proclaimed the right of his state to nullify any federal legislation that it disapproved of.

On Crimes and Punishment **(1764)** Beccaria's celebrated indictment of the eighteenth-century criminal justice system.

Ordeals A primitive method of determining guilt or innocence by subjecting the accused to fire, water, or other serious dangers; the result was regarded as a divine judgment.

Outlawry Beginning in the 800s, individuals could be placed outside the protection of the law if they refused to attend court or tried to evade justice.

Oyer and Terminer, Court of Specialized courts in colonial America convened to handle serious complaints involving slaves.

Parliament Originally designated a meeting of shire knights to discuss new taxes. By 1295, its representative nature had been established.

Parricide The killing of a parent by a child.

Patricians Members of the Roman aristocracy.

Patronage system The distribution of jobs and favors on a political basis.

Peine forte et dure Pressing to death with an accumulation of weights.

Peelers Nickname for Robert Peel's London Metropolitan police officers.

Penny presses Cheap newspapers in the 1830s and 1840s considered precursor to today's tabloids, using sensational and lurid crime stories to sell newspapers.

Pentateuch From the Greek meaning "five books," as in the first five books of the Bible, which contain the Ten Commandments.

Perjury The willful utterance of a false statement under oath during a legal inquiry.

Peterloo Massacre In 1819, British troops fired into a crowd while trying to end civil unrest, killing eleven and wounding hundreds.

Petty treason The killing of a master by a servant.

Pilgrims Religious separatists that refused to conform to the Church of England and eventually arrived in America on the *Mayflower* in 1620.

Pinkertons America's most prominent private detective/police organization in the nineteenth century.

Plan for Preventing Robberies within Twenty Miles of London John Fielding's 1755 pamphlet detailing his strategy for suppressing highway robbery.

Plebeians Refers to the common people of Rome.

Plessy v. Ferguson   In 1896, this Supreme Court decision essentially condoned racial segregation by approving the "separate but equal" doctrine, which held sway until 1954.

Posse comitatus   Power of the county.

Praetorian Guard   Elite soldiers used for law enforcement by Augustus Caesar.

Precipitation   Ancient Athenian execution practice in which individuals were thrown from high cliffs to their deaths.

Probation   Considered the oldest form of noninstitutional corrections, its development in the United States is credited to the efforts of John Augustus in Boston in the 1840s.

Progressive era   Era characterized by reform, urbanization, industrialization, and immigration between 1890 and 1920.

Prohibition era   Inaugurated by the ratification of the 18th Amendment, it lasted from 1920 to 1933.

Punitive   Concerned with inflicting punishment

Pure Food and Drug Act   Imposed federal standards on the patent-medicine industry.

Puritans   A religious movement that sought to purify the Church of England.

Quakers   A radical religious sect that emerged in seventeenth-century England. They would play an important role in various criminal justice reform efforts in America beginning in colonial Pennsylvania.

Rattle watch   Early Dutch peace officer in New Amsterdam.

Reconstruction era   Refers to the years 1866–1877.

Red Hannah   Delaware's whipping device.

Red Scare   Following the Bolshevik revolution in Russia and post–World War I labor unrest in 1919, the Justice Department embarked on a campaign to suppress radical views in America.

Reeve   Anglo-Saxon official who was forerunner of the sheriff.

Reformatory movement   An experiment in prison reform in the late 1860s that emphasized education, indeterminate sentencing, trade training, and parole.

Regulators   America's first vigilante organization appeared in South Carolina in 1767.

Renaissance   Era in European history between the fourteenth and the seventeenth century marking the transition from the medieval world to the modern one.

Report on the Prisons and Reformatories of the United States and Canada   This 1867 publication by Enoch

Wines and Louis Dwight led the movement for the central control of state prisons.

Republic   A state in which the supreme power rests in the body of citizens entitled to vote and is exercised by representatives who are chosen.

RICO Act   The Racketeer Influenced Corrupt Organizations (RICO) statute was created under the 1970 Omnibus Crime Control and Safe Streets Act. It is considered the most significant piece of legislation targeting organized crime.

Roaring Twenties   The era of the 1920s.

Robber barons   Nineteenth-century industrialists reputed to have become wealthy by exploiting natural resources, corrupting lawmakers, and other unethical actions.

Ruby Ridge, Idaho   Scene of an eighteen-month standoff between the Weaver family and federal peace officers in 1990–1991.

Sacrilege   The violation of anything held sacred.

St. Valentine's Day Massacre   The biggest gangland murder of the Prohibition era.

Salem witchcraft trial   Notable 1692 trial in Salem, Massachusetts.

San Francisco Committee of Vigilance   Forced to contend with a growing crime problem and lack of professional policing in San Francisco during the gold rush years, citizens organized vigilance committees in the 1850s to maintain order.

Sanctuary   Fugitives could be protected in churches under certain circumstances in the Anglo-Saxon era.

Saxons   They migrated to England from what is now northern Germany after the Romans left in the fifth century.

Schout   Early Dutch peacekeeper in New Amsterdam.

Scold   A woman who is constantly scolding, usually in loud, abusive language.

Scorcher squads   Bicycle-mounted police initiated by New York City police commissioner Theodore Roosevelt in the 1890s.

Scotland Yard   Original headquarters of the London Metropolitan Police.

Scottsboro trials   Between 1931 and 1937, despite spurious charges, nine black youths fought for their lives in a series of Alabama court battles.

Second Amendment   Protects the right of states to form militias and is currently at the center of the debate on gun control.

Sedition   Any action promoting discontent or rebellion.

Sedition Act of 1918   Made it a federal offense to criticize the U.S. Constitution, the U.S. government, the American uniform, or the American flag.

Shaming   An ancient form of exhibitory punishment that can include letter wearing or public humiliation. Several judges have used this as an alternative to prison sentences.

Shire   Somewhat equivalent to a county, England in the Anglo-Saxon period was subdivided into these.

Simsbury Prison   Connecticut prison opened in an abandoned copper mine in 1773.

Sing Sing Prison   Infamous New York state prison opened in 1825.

Sixth Amendment   Promises an impartial jury in all criminal prosecutions.

Skinner v. Oklahoma   The Supreme Court ruled in 1942 against sterilizing criminals.

Social Darwinism   Theory that individuals should depend on individualism and competition to get ahead rather than depend on social cooperation and reform.

Society for the Prevention of Pauperism   In 1817, this New York group became the first to call attention to neglected children.

Sophists   Professional philosophers, such as Socrates, in ancient Athens.

Speakeasy   Place where alcoholic beverages are illegally sold.

Special Weapons and Tactics (SWAT)   During the 1960s, Philadelphia and Los Angeles police forces created special units in response to new trends in criminal violence.

Spoils system   Practice in which public offices are at the disposal of the victorious party for its own purposes.

Stamp Act   This 1765 tax was the first direct or internal tax that Parliament ever imposed on American colonies.

Star Chamber, Court of   Introduced in fifteenth century to punish wealthy supporters of criminal activity. Since there was no jury, this court was prohibited from imposing capital punishment or other serious punishments.

Star Police   Refers to first New York City police officers who wore copper badges to identify themselves as officers prior to the acceptance of uniforms.

State of the Prisons   John Howard's 1777 report on the abuses of European prisons and suggestions for reform.

States' rights   Rights belonging to the various states. Using a very strict interpretation of the U.S. Constitution, all rights not delegated by the Constitution to the federal government belong to the states.

Statute of Winchester   One of the most important pieces of criminal justice legislation to come out of the Middle Ages. Established watch and ward system of day and night watch.

Sumptuary laws   Laws that restricted certain fashions among the Puritan colonists.

Supermax prisons   Supermaximum prisons. The first was opened at Alcatraz in 1934. The trend of building these escalated in the 1980s.

Surete   Highly professional French detectives; originated in the 1830s.

Sythian   Captured warriors from the North, the Athenians employed them as town guards.

Taboo   A prohibition of something; a system or practice whereby things are set apart as sacred or forbidden under threat of being ostracized.

Tammany Hall   One of the most powerful urban political machines in American history. It dominated Democratic politics in New York City from 1855 to the 1930s.

Tarpein Rock   High cliff used for precipitation by the Romans.

Teapot Dome scandal   In 1924, this scandal led to the first imprisonment of a cabinet officer (1929) and entered the American lexicon as a synonym for government graft.

Telephone pole design   In the 1950s, this penitentiary design flourished. This design better accommodated treatment programs, maintained security, and offered a new openness to inmates.

Temperance groups   Moral reformers dedicated to the prohibition of alcohol sale, manufacture, and consumption.

Teutonic   Pertaining to people of northern European ancestry, including Germanic, Scandinavian, and British peoples.

Texas Rangers   The first statewide law enforcement agency, created in 1823 (but not officially called Texas Rangers until 1874).

Thief takers   Early bounty hunters.

Things   Local assemblies or courts convened by the Danes. Some consider this a precursor to the English jury system because twelve freemen swore an oath not to convict an innocent man.

Thirteenth Amendment   Abolished slavery in 1865.

Thompson v. Oklahoma   In 1988, the Supreme Court ruled that executing an individual who committed a crime before the age of sixteen violated the Eighth Amendment.

Three-strikes policy   This sentencing policy originated in California after the abduction and murder of Polly Klaas in the 1980s. The rallying cry "Three strikes and you're out" became a slogan for get-tough politicians.

Tithings   Anglo-Saxon self-policing in which ten men belonged, each responsible for the other's behavior.

Trailbaston   Commissions convened beginning in 1304 to counter the escalation of organized criminal activities.

Transportation   England used this method to banish convicts to its colonies in America and later Australia.

Treatise on the Police of the Metropolis   Patrick Colquhoun's 1797 concepts on police reform.

Trial by battle   Judicial duels used to determine guilt or innocence.

Trusties   Until the 1970s, most prisons empowered trusties to help control the inmates.

Twelve Tables   Considered the first written laws of Rome.

Twinkies defense   Insanity defense successfully used by Dan White in 1978.

Uniform Crime Reports (UCR)   Crime statistics disseminated by the FBI beginning in 1930.

United States Secret Service   Originally established in 1865 to handle the counterfeiting problem.

Untouchables   Prohibition agents led by Eliot Ness.

Urban Cohort   Daytime peacekeepers in Rome under Augustus Caesar.

Usury   Practice of lending money at an exorbitant rate of interest.

Vigiles   Composed mostly of freed slaves, they patrolled Roman streets and fought fires at night under Augustus Caesar.

Volstead Act   Its passage inaugurated the Prohibition era in 1919.

Walnut Street Jail   Opened in Philadelphia in 1790, it was considered the "cradle" of the American penitentiary.

Wayward Sisters   Refers to female criminals in late nineteenth century.

Weeks v. United States   Landmark case that established the exclusionary rule.

Wergild   Form of compensation designed to replace the blood feud among Germanic tribes.

White Slave Traffic Act   Better known as the Mann Act, this 1910 legislation was the culmination of Progressive reform efforts to legislate morality.

Wickersham Commission   Between 1929 and 1931, the national Commission on Law Observance and Enforcement, chaired by George Wickersham, examined criminal justice in America. Its conclusions were published in two volumes and recommended a number of procedures for improving due process and eliminating corruption.

Wilkerson v. Utah   This 1879 Supreme Court decision upheld the constitutionality of execution by firing squad.

Witan   Considered by some a precursor to Parliament; an assembly of major landlords in Anglo-Saxon England.

Wobblies   Members of the International Workers of the World (IWW) labor union, often targeted by the government for subversive activities.

Xenophobia   An unreasonable hatred or fear of foreigners.

Zero-tolerance policy   Draconian rules that take discretion out of the hands of administrators and other officials. Following several school shootings, these policies were aimed at schools, calling for the expulsion of students who carried anything that could be construed as a weapon.

Zoot-Suit riots   Anti-Hispanic riots in 1940s Los Angeles.

Who's Who in Criminal Justice History

Adams, John (1735–1826) American lawyer, patriot, and future president who defended the British soldiers accused of the Boston Massacre, demonstrating his belief that the accused has the right to a vigorous defense.

Aethelbert of Kent (ca. 552–616) Responsible for the first extant Anglo-Saxon laws drawn up after the example of the Romans.

Anslinger, Harry (1892–1975) During his tenure as commissioner of the Bureau of Narcotics, he waged an unrelenting war against illegal drug use.

Ashcroft, John (b. 1942) Attorney general in the administration of President George W. Bush.

Augustus, John (1785–1859) Boston cobbler who became a leading proponent of probation.

Augustus Caesar (63 B.C.–A.D. 14) Introduced three separate organizations for policing Rome and its provincial towns.

Austin, Stephen (1793–1836) In 1823, Austin created what would later become known as the Texas Rangers.

Baldwin, Lola (prominent in early 1900s) Hired by the Portland, Oregon, Police Department, she was an early pioneer in women's law enforcement.

Barrow, Clyde (1909–1934) Partner with Bonnie Parker in a series of robberies and murders during the late 1920s.

Bates, Sanford (1884–1972) While leading the Federal Bureau of Prisons in the 1930s, Bates improved officer training, enhanced prison education programs, and adopted the "telephone pattern" for prison construction.

Battle, Samuel J. (1883–1966) As the first African American on the New York City police force in 1910, he was subjected to a year of silent treatment by fellow officers.

Beccaria, Cesare de (1738–1794) His theories laid the foundation for the reform of the European criminal justice system.

Bentham, Jeremy (1748–1832) Advocate of legal reform and founder of the philosophy of utilitarianism, which argued that law must be used for the "greatest good of the greatest number" of people.

Bertillon, Alphonse (1835–1914) While employed by the Paris police, he created Bertillon identification system, leading to his reputation as the "father of modern detection."

Bonnie and Clyde *See* Barrow, Clyde, and Parker, Bonnie.

Borden, Lizzie (1860–1927) The alleged perpetrator of one of the most famous American murder cases. She was eventually acquitted of killing her father and stepmother.

Bradwell, Myra (1831–1894) Prominent in the women's suffrage movement, her efforts at legal reform eventually led Illinois to become the first state to pass a law allowing women to practice any profession.

Brady, James (b. 1936) Brady was wounded in 1981 during the assassination attempt on President Ronald Reagan. Subsequently, he has become a leading advocate for gun control.

Bratton, William (b. 1947) While serving as New York City police commissioner beginning in 1994, his crime control strategies were given much of the credit for the city's dramatic drop in crime in the 1990s.

Brockway, Zebulon (1827–1920) Prison reformer who came to national prominence after his participation in the Prison Congress of 1870. Later appointed superintendent of the Elmira Reformatory.

Brooks, Charles (1942–1982) Texas death row inmate who became first person executed by lethal injection. He was also the first African American executed after the death penalty was reinstated in 1976.

Brown, John (1800–1859) Violent abolitionist and insurrectionist who was executed following his capture of the armory at Harper's Ferry.

Burns, Robert Elliott (1890–1965) World War I veteran who escaped from a Georgia chain gang in 1922. During his years of freedom, he publicized the barbaric conditions on the Georgia chain gangs.

Burns, William John (1861–1932) Established Burns Detective Agency before being selected to head the Bureau of Investigation in 1921.

Burr, Aaron (1756–1836) Killed Alexander Hamilton in an 1804 duel and three years later was tried for treason for plotting to create his own empire west of the Appalachian Mountains.

Byrnes, Thomas F. (1842–1910) Chief of the New York City Detective Bureau in the 1880s, he rose to prominence for his photographic "rogues' gallery."

Calhoun, John C. (1782–1850) Tested the rights of states during the 1833 Nullification Controversy in South Carolina.

Capone, Al (1899–1947) Public enemy number one during the 1920s, he was finally brought to justice by the Internal Revenue Service.

Charles I (1600–1649) Best known for suspending Parliament for eleven years and for his execution in 1649. The reliance on the antiquated watch system during his reign inspired the sobriquet "Charleys" for watchmen.

Charles II (1630–1685) King of Great Britain, 1660–1685.

Chessman, Caryl (1921–1960) California's infamous "Red Light Bandit." During his twelve years on death row before his execution, he became an articulate opponent of the death penalty.

Colquhoun, Patrick (1745–1820) Created the Thames River Police and was a campaigner for police reform in London prior to the creation of the London Metropolitan Police.

Comstock, Anthony (1844–1915) Led crusade against obscenity and vice.

Constantine I (ca. 288–337) Roman emperor who converted to Christianity and legally sanctioned the practice of the religion.

Crofton, Walter (1815–1897) Applied Machonochie's parole ideas to the Irish prison system.

Curtis, Edwin (1861–1922) Boston police commissioner who provoked a police strike in 1919.

Cutpurse, Moll (real name Mary Frith) (ca. 1584–1659) She was an English highway robber and fence.

Darrow, Clarence (1857–1938) One of America's greatest criminal defense lawyers and staunch opponent of the death penalty. Among his most prominent cases were those of Sacco and Vanzetti and Leopold and Loeb, both in the 1920s.

Darwin, Charles (1809–1882) English naturalist, best known for his theory that the origin of species is the result of natural selection of those best adapted to survive in the struggle for existence.

Davis, Katherine Bement (1860–1935) Progressive-era penologist and social worker.

Dewey, Thomas E. (1902–1971) Special prosecutor in New York City in 1930s.

Dickens, Charles (1812–1870) Novelist who wrote a critique of the solitary prison system after visiting Eastern State Penitentiary in 1842.

Dillinger, John (1903–1934) Midwestern bank robber and public enemy number one during the Great Depression.

Dix, Dorothea (1802–1887) Early prison reformer who championed the rights of mentally ill prisoners.

Dorr, Thomas (1805–1854) Harvard-educated attorney who organized a campaign to abolish voting restrictions.

Douglas, William O. (1898–1980) Served as Supreme Court justice longer than any other (thirty-six years). Remembered as a steadfast supporter of civil rights.

Draco (ca. 60 B.C.–0) First to put Athenian laws into writing. He introduced laws dealing with homicide and other offenses. He is remembered for the severity of his code of laws.

Dwight, Louis (1793–1854) A supporter of the Auburn prison system, he organized the Prison Discipline Society of Boston in 1825.

Eddy, Thomas (1758–1827) Quaker prison reformer regarded as the "Father of New York State prison" and a leading advocate of the separate-cell system.

Edward the Confessor (ca. 1002–1066) Last Anglo-Saxon king of Britain.

Fall, Albert (1861–1944) Secretary of the Interior and central figure in the Teapot Dome scandal of 1924. He became the first cabinet officer jailed for crimes committed in office.

Faulds, Henry (1843–1930) Pioneer in fingerprint identification.

Fawkes, Guy (1570–1606) English conspirator executed for attempting to blow up Parliament and King James I.

Fielding, Henry (1707–1754) Introduced the Bow Street Runners and was an early advocate for professional, full-time police in London.

Fielding, John (1721–1780) Half brother of Henry, despite being blind from birth, the "Blind Beak" could reportedly identify hundreds of criminals by voice alone.

Forsyth, Robert (d. 1794) First law enforcement officer killed in America following the birth of the Republic.

Fosdick, Raymond (1883–1972) His studies of police systems in Europe and America led to reform in American policing prior to World War I.

Fouche, Joseph (1759–1820) He created a centralized police force in France and served as its director under Emperor Napoleon.

Freeh, Louis (b. 1950) Led the FBI through some of its most controversial years, including the debacles at Waco and Ruby Ridge.

Fuld, Leonhard (1883–1965) Author of *Police Administration,* the first comprehensive study of American police administration.

Galton, Francis (1822–1911) Author of *Fingerprints* and founder of the eugenics movement in early twentieth century.

Garrison, William Lloyd (1805–1879) Massachusetts abolitionist.

Gates, Daryl (b. 1926) Los Angeles police chief from 1978 to 1991 and proponent of the SWAT team concept.

Gilmore, Gary (1940–1977) Utah murderer who became the first American executed after the return of capital punishment in 1976.

Glueck, Sheldon (1898–1972), and Eleanor (1896–1980) Criminologists and pioneers in modern research criminology who collaborated on a number of juvenile delinquency studies.

Goddard, Calvin H. (1891–1955) Forensic expert and pioneer in ballistics testing.

Grant, Ulysses S. (1822–1885) President who declared martial law in parts of the South during the 1870s.

Hammurabi (ca. 1792–1750 B.C.) Best remembered for his great law code detailed in cuneiform (pictographic) writings on a stone slab.

Hauptmann, Bruno Richard (1899–1936) German-born kidnapper executed for death of aviator Charles Lindbergh's infant son.

Hays, Jacob (1772–1850) He served a half century as New York City's first high constable and is credited with introducing the police tactic of patrolling in pairs.

Heirens, William (b. 1929) Suspected of several unsolved murders, as a teenager he became the first person questioned under the "truth serum" sodium pentothal.

Henry, Edward Richard (1850–1931) A career civil servant, he perfected the fingerprinting system in 1896 by developing a more practical method of filing prints. The so-called Henry system was implemented in the United States and Europe.

Henry, Patrick (1736–1799) Politician, lawyer, and revolutionary firebrand who demanded national independence and vigorously opposed the Stamp Act.

Henry II (1133–1189) British law made great strides under his reign between 1154 and 1189. He transformed civil and criminal law as the king's law became national in scope.

Henry VIII (1491–1547) Made the transition from "Defender of the Faith" to cutting all ties with Rome and creating a schism within the Church of England.

Herschel, William J. (1833–1917) Fingerprinting pioneer who discovered the unique "signature" nature of individual fingerprints.

Hinckley, John W. (b. 1955) Attempted to assassinate President Ronald Reagan. Found not guilty by reason of insanity.

Holmes, Oliver Wendell (1841–1935) The Supreme Court's leading champion of civil rights during the Progressive era.

Hoover, John Edgar (1895–1972) Controversial director of the FBI from 1924 to 1972.

Howard, John (1726–1790) Early English prison reformer whose writings led Parliament to pass the first Penitentiary Act in 1779.

Jackson, Andrew (1767–1845) Served as president at a time when Americans began to first perceive crime as a threat to the order and security of the Republic.

John (king of England) (ca. 1167–1216) Son of Henry II and signer of the Magna Carta in 1215.

Johnson, Jack (1878–1946) World heavyweight boxing champion arrested for violating the Mann Act in 1912.

Julius Caesar (ca. 100–44 B.C.) Roman statesman and general.

Justinian (483–565) Under his direction, Roman law was codified.

Kefauver, Estes (1903–1963) Led the Kefauver Committee hearings, the first significant investigation of organized crime in America.

Kemmler, William (d. 1890) New York ax murderer and first person to be executed in the electric chair.

Kennedy, John F. (1917–1963) His assassination is one of the most chronicled murders in American history.

Kennedy, Robert F. (1925–1968) As Attorney General in his brother John's administration, he intensified efforts in the war against organized crime.

Kerner, Otto (1908–1976) Illinois governor who chaired the 1967 National Advisory Commission on Civil Disorders.

King, Martin Luther, Jr. (1929–1968) America's leading civil rights figure assassinated in Memphis, Tennessee, by James Earl Ray.

Kohler, Fred (1869–1933) Cleveland police chief who implemented diversion programs for minor offenses.

Latrobe, Benjamin Henry (1764–1820) Architect of Richmond, Virginia, Penitentiary.

Leopold, Nathan (1906–1971), and Loeb, Richard (1907–1936) Two outstanding university students who were caught after a murder that they thought would be the perfect crime.

Lincoln, Abraham (1809–1865) One of the greatest American presidents, he was criticized for suspending the constitutionally guaranteed writ of habeas corpus during the Civil War.

Locke, John (1632–1704) English philosopher and political theorist, he advocated religious toleration and that government should be based on the consent of the governed.

Lombroso, Cesare (1835–1909) Founder of the positivist school of criminology and "father of modern criminology."

Lovejoy, Elijah (1802–1837) Abolitionist murdered in 1837, he became a martyr for the antislavery crusade.

Luciano, Charles "Lucky" (1897–1962) Prominent New York gangster credited with helping organize the national crime syndicate.

Lynch, Charles (1736–1796) Best remembered for his participation in vigilante activities in colonial Virginia.

Lynch, William L. (1724–1820) Led a 1780 vigilante movement in Virginia.

Lynds, Elam (1784–1855) Credited with establishing Auburn Prison's silent system.

Maconochie, Alexander (1787–1860) Considered the "father of parole" after his experiment with indeterminate sentencing at the English prison colony of Van Diemen's Land.

Marshall, John (1755–1835) Chief justice of the Supreme Court from 1801 to 1835.

Marshall, Thurgood (1908–1993) The grandson of slaves, he rose to national prominence during the civil rights struggle in the 1950s. In 1967, he became the first African American Supreme Court justice.

Mayne, Richard (1796–1868) Served as commissioner of the London Metropolitan Police for almost forty years.

McCarthy, Joseph (d. 1957) Wisconsin senator whose name has become synonymous with anticommunist hysteria during the 1950s.

McCormick, Austin (1893–1979) Noted prison educator and pioneer in correctional reform. When he retired in 1940, he was considered one of the nation's greatest prison executives.

Montesquieu, Charles Louis de (1689–1755) Leading French Enlightenment philosopher and author of *The Spirit of the Laws*.

More, Sir Thomas (1478–1535) One of the earliest to theorize on crime and punishment and to lobby against the death penalty. He was executed for treason under the rule of Henry VIII.

Nast, Thomas (1840–1902) Cartoonist and social commentator.

Ness, Eliot (1902–1957) Rose to prominence as head of Chicago's "Untouchables" during the Prohibition era.

O'Connor, Sandra Day (b. 1930) In 1981, she became the first woman appointed to the Supreme Court.

Osborne, Thomas Mott (1859–1926) Sing Sing Prison warden, prison reformer, and champion of the Mutual Welfare League experiment.

Palmer, A. Mitchell (1872–1936) Attorney general who initiated federal attack on radical activists in 1919.

Parker, Bonnie (1911–1934) Partner of Clyde Barrow in bank robbing and murder spree in early 1930s.

Parker, William H. (1902–1966) An advocate of police professionalism, he served a controversial sixteen years as Los Angeles police chief.

Peel, Robert (1788–1850) As home secretary, he helped pass the Metropolitan Police Act of 1829, creating a uniformed police force along military lines, which included being better disciplined and trained.

Penn, William (1644–1718) Pennsylvania Quaker leader who championed law and criminal justice reform in the early colonial period.

Pinkerton, Allan J. (1819–1884) Founder of what would become Pinkerton's National Detective Agency.

Prosser, Gabriel (ca. 1776–1800) A Virginia slave executed for conspiring to lead a slave insurrection.

Ragen, Joseph Edward (1896–1971) Rose to prominence as a reform-minded warden of the Illinois State Penitentiary at Joliet.

Redfield, Horace (1845–1881) Journalist who publicized the high homicide rate in the South.

Rehnquist, William (b. 1924) Chief justice of the Supreme Court.

Reno, Janet (b. 1938) During the Clinton administration, she became the first female attorney general in America.

Riis, Jacob (1849–1914) New York City social reformer who chronicled the immigrant plight of the late nineteenth century.

Rogers, Mary (1820–1841) Her sensational murder and the subsequent investigation led to reform in the New York City Police Department in the 1840s.

Roosevelt, Franklin D. (1882–1945) During his terms as president, federal crime control went through unprecedented growth.

Roosevelt, Theodore (1859–1919) Prior to his ascendance to the presidency, he served as a reform-minded New York City police commissioner between 1895 and 1897.

Rosenberg, Julius (1918–1953), and Ethel (1915–1953) Executed for espionage during the communist hysteria of the 1950s.

Rousseau, Jean Jacques (1712–1778) French philosopher and social reformer.

Rowan, Charles (1783–1852) Served as co-commissioner of London Metropolitan Police with Richard Mayne until 1850.

Rush, Benjamin (1746–1813) Statesman and penal reformer during the American Revolution era.

Sacco, Nicola (1891–1927), and Vanzetti, Bartolomeo (1888–1927) Italian anarchists executed for double murder during a payroll robbery in Massachusetts.

Schultz, Dutch (real name Arthur Flegenheimer) (1902–1935) New York bootlegger and racketeer who was killed after threatening to kill Thomas Dewey.

Scott, Dred (ca. 1790s–1858) Slave who initiated groundbreaking Supreme Court case after he sued for his freedom in a Missouri state court.

Serpico, Frank (b. 1936) New York City police detective who fought corruption but was shunned by colleagues for violating the "blue curtain" of silence.

Shakespeare, William (1564–1616) English poet and dramatist who introduced early night watchmen and constables as ineffective comic foils.

Sheppard, Sam (1924–1970) Ohio doctor accused of killing wife in a controversial murder case that inspired the television series *The Fugitive*.

Siegel, Benjamin "Bugsy" (1906–1947) American gangster and founder of the Las Vegas Flamingo Hotel and Casino.

Smith, Bruce (1892–1955) Police consultant and criminologist who became the nation's leading expert on police operations.

Smith, John (1580–1631) English colonizer who introduced military discipline and martial law at the Jamestown Colony.

Socrates (ca. 469–399 B.C.) Athenian philosopher and public figure who was a central participant in the city's intellectual debates in late fifth century B.C.

Solon (ca. 638–558 B.C.) Athenian statesman and lawgiver who replaced Draco's harsh laws, except those dealing with homicide.

Surratt, Mary E. (1817–1865) Executed for her role in Lincoln assassination conspiracy. She was the first woman hanged by the federal government.

Sutherland, Edwin H. (1883–1950) Prominent criminologist who coined the term "white-collar crime" and developed concept of differential association.

Taney, Roger (1777–1864) Succeeded John Marshall as chief justice of Supreme Court in 1836.

Till, Emmett (1941–1955) His murder in Mississippi in 1955 reinforced black fears of racially motivated violence in the South.

Torrio, John (1882–1957) Mentor to Al Capone and Chicago crime boss.

Toussaint Louverture, Pierre Dominique (1743–1803) Former Haitian slave who led the first large-scale slave uprising in the Americas in 1791.

Tukey, Francis (b. 1814) Serving in a variety of capacities and with a penchant for the dramatic, Tukey was an unremarkable Boston law enforcement official in the 1840s and 1850s.

Turner, Nat (1800–1831) Led first actual slave revolt in the United States in 1831.

Tweed, William Marcy (1823–1878) New York City Tammany Hall boss who exemplified the corruption of urban America in the 1860s.

Vidocq, Eugene (1775–1857) Former French criminal, often considered the world's first private detective.

Vollmer, August (1876–1955) Police reformer and father of modern professional policing.

Warne, Kate (1833–1868) Became America's first female detective after joining the Pinkertons in 1856.

Warren, Earl (1891–1974) Former governor of California, his tenure as chief justice of the Supreme Court was marked by judicial activism that made the Court an active participant in the crusade for social change.

Wells, Alice Stebbins (prominent in 1910–1920s) Considered by many to be the first full-time policewoman in America.

Wells-Barnett, Ida B. (1862–1931) African American journalist and advocate for racial justice and women's suffrage who led a crusade against lynchings in the 1890s.

West, William (prominent in 1903) Leavenworth Prison authorities were confused when two almost identical men named Will West had the same Bertillon measurements. They were distinguished only by their fingerprints.

Wickersham, George (1858–1936) As chair of the National Commission on Law Observance and Enforcement, his name became synonymous with police reform during the crisis decades.

Wild, Jonathan (1682–1725) Led a posse of thief catchers who got higher prices for stolen goods by returning them to the original owners after they were "found."

William I (1027–1087) Following his victory at the Battle of Hastings, William the Duke of Normandy became the first Norman king of Britain.

Williams, Alexander "Clubber" (1839–1910) A symbol of New York City police corruption during the 1890s.

Wilson, Orlando W. (1900–1972) Author of influential *Police Administration* (1963), as police chief in Wichita, Kansas, and later Chicago, Wilson was an advocate of police professionalism.

Wines, Enoch (1806–1879) Prison reformer who publicized deplorable conditions of several northeastern penitentiaries.

Wolfgang, Marvin (1924–1998) A pioneering criminologist who conducted an early academic study of homicide in Philadelphia.

Wood, Fernando (1812–1881) Regarded as a tool of Tammany Hall, this New York City mayor was reluctant to suppress vice in the 1850s.

Wood, William P. (1819–1903) First chief of the U.S. Secret Service.

Woods, Arthur (1870–1942) As New York City police commissioner, he established the first school for patrol officers.

Zenger, John Peter (1697–1746) American journalist, printer, and publisher whose exoneration in a seditious libel suit became a major step in achieving freedom of the press in the colonies.

Index